The Choice for Europe

A volume in the series

Cornell Studies in Political Economy

EDITED BY PETER J. KATZENSTEIN

The Choice for Europe

Social Purpose and State Power from Messina to Maastricht

Andrew Moravcsik

CORNELL UNIVERSITY PRESS

Ithaca, New York

First published 1998 by Cornell University Press
First printing, Cornell Paperbacks, 1998

Printed in the United States of America

Library of Congress Cataloging-in-Publication Data

Moravcsik, Andrew.
The choice for Europe : social purpose and state
power from Messina to Maastricht / Andrew Moravcsik
p.   cm. — Cornell studies in political economy
Includes index.
ISBN 0-8014-3509-9 (cloth : alk. paper)
— ISBN 0-8014-8509-6 (pbk. : alk. paper)
    1. European federation—History.   2. Europe—Economic integration—History.
I. Title.   II. Series.
JN15.M567   1998
341.242'09—dc21   98-34333

Cornell University Press strives to use environmentally responsible suppliers and materials to the
fullest extent possible in the publishing of its books. Such materials include vegetable-based, low-
VOC inks and acid-free papers that are also recycled, totally chlorine free, or partly composed
of nonwood fibers. For further information, visit our website at www.cornellpress.cornell.edu.

Cloth printing   10   9   8   7   6   5   4   3   2   1
Paperback printing   10   9   8   7   6   5   4   3

To my mother and the memory of my father

Contents

Acknowledgments

This book, perhaps more than most, would have been impossible without the encouragement, assistance, and criticism of many colleagues who offered me the most valuable of all scholarly gifts: serious intellectual engagement. I am grateful to two mentors, Robert Keohane and Stanley Hoffmann, who always encouraged me to follow my scholarly instincts—even when they seemed manifestly to contradict good sense. For comments on individual chapters of the book, I am grateful also to Perry Anderson, Thomas Banchoff, Simon Bulmer, Marc Busch, David Cameron, James Caporaso, Charles Cogan, Thomas Diez, James Fearon, Jeffry Frieden, Geoffrey Garrett, Richard Griffiths, Stephan Haggard, Ernst Haas, Dorothée Heisenberg, Markus Jachtenfuchs, Peter Katzenstein, Stephen Krasner, Beate Kohler-Koch, Margaret Levi, Leon Lindberg, Charles Lipson, Peter Ludlow, Piers Ludlow, Giandomenico Majone, Lisa Martin, Kathleen McNamara, Alan Milward, Kalypso Nicolaïdis, John Peterson, Paul Pierson, Thomas Risse, Alberta Sbragia, Fritz Scharpf, Duncan Snidal, Wolfgang Streeck, Jeffrey Vanke, Daniel Verdier, Helen Wallace, Carolyn Warner, Daniel Wincott, and three anonymous referees. I remain indebted to countless others who were willing to discuss specific issues with me; I can only hope that they recall our intellectual engagement as clearly as I, and will accept this anonymous acknowledgment.

For other exceptional assistance, I thank Elie Cohen, Anne Deighton, Olivier Debouzy, Karl Kaiser, Louise Richardson, George Ross, Patrick Weil, and Joseph Weiler. I recognize the research assistance of Leslie Eden Harris, Brian Portnoy, Alexandra Samuel, Jeffrey Vanke, and especially Kip Wennerlund, who indefatigably checked the footnotes and prepared the index; each provided valuable substantive suggestions as well. And what more could one ask from the editor of a manuscript this long than Roger Haydon's exceptional combination of intelligence and wit?

For organizing and participating in colloquia devoted to my work, I thank (in addition to those above), Ernest May, Yves Mèny, and participants in sessions held at Stanford University, the University of California at Los Angeles and at San Diego, the Mannheimer Zentrum für Europäische Sozialforschung, the European University Institute, Harvard University, Edinburgh University, Copenhagen University, the Conference of Europeanists, and the European Community Studies Association. I am also grateful to the Centre for European Policy Studies in Brussels, the International Institute for Strategic Studies in London, the Centre d'Études et Relations Internationales and the Institut des Sciences Politiques in Paris, and the Deutsche Gesellschaft für Auswärtige Politik and the Atlantik-Brücke in Bonn for logistical support during shorter research visits. I received invaluable outside fellowship support from the German Marshall Fund of the United States, the Institute for the Study of World Politics, and the Morris Abrams Fellowship program.

Three exceptional academic institutions provided me with challenging yet comfortable academic homes for extended periods. The European University Institute—in particular its Robert Schuman Center—provided me numerous opportunities to visit Fiesole, present my work in its singular pan-European environment, and make revisions in a room with a view. At the University of Chicago, the Department of Political Science and the Program on International Politics, Economics, and Security (PIPES) provided extraordinary logistical support and welcomed me as an intermittent member of a unique intellectual community over a four-year period. At Harvard University, the Olin Institute Program on Economics and National Security provided initial support; the Weatherhead Center for International Affairs supported a semester of leave and organized an author's colloquium; and the Minda de Gunzburg Center for European Studies offered research support, supported a study group on European integration, and provided me—as it has so many others—with an unparalleled interdisciplinary environment in which to study modern Europe.

The deepest debts are the most personal and therefore remain understated here. I dedicate this book to my mother, Francesca de Gogorza Moravcsik, and the memory of my father, Michael Julius Moravcsik, who first directed my attention toward Europe and taught me to believe in the power of argument. The extraordinary person by my side throughout the writing of this book, Anne-Marie Slaughter, offered the encouragement, counsel, and criticism—and much more—without which it would never have been completed.

A.M.

Cambridge, Massachusetts

Abbreviations

ABCC	Association of British Chambers of Commerce
BDI	Bundesverband der Deutschen Industrie
BIS	Bank for International Settlements
CAP	Common Agricultural Policy
CBI	Confederation of British Industry
CDU	Christian Democratic Union
CEO	chief executive officer
CET	common external tariff
CFDT	Confederation Française Démocratique du Travail
CFSP	Common Foreign and Security Policy
CNPF	Conseil National du Patronat Français
COREPER	Committee of Permanent Representatives
CSU	Christian Socialist Union
DBV	Deutsche Bauernverband
DGB	Deutsche Gewerkschaftsbund
DGIII	Directorate General 3
DIHT	Deutsche Industrie- und Handelstag
DM	Deutsche mark
EBRD	European Bank for Reconstruction and Development
EC	European Community
ECB	European Central Bank
ECJ	European Court of Justice
ECOFIN	Economic and Finance Committee
ECSC	European Coal and Steel Community
EDC	European Defense Community
EEC	European Economic Community
EFTA	European Free Trade Association
EIB	European Investment Bank
EMF	European Monetary Fund
EMI	European Monetary Institute
EMS	European Monetary System
EMU	Economic and Monetary Union

EP	European Parliament
EPC	European Political Cooperation
EPU	European Payments Union
ERM	exchange rate mechanism
ERT	European Roundtable of Industrialists
ESCB	European System of Central Banks
ESPRIT	European Strategic Program for Research & Development in Information Technology
EU	European Union
FBI	Federation of British Industry
FDI	foreign direct investment
FDP	Free Democratic Party
FNSEA	Fédération Nationale des Syndicats d'Exploitants Agricoles
FO	Foreign Office
FRG	Federal Republic of Germany
FTA	free trade area
GATT	General Agreement on Tariffs and Trade
GDP	gross domestic product
GNP	gross national product
G-7	Group of 7
IGC	intergovernmental conference
IMF	International Monetary Fund
MAC	Mutual Aid Committee
MCA	Monetary Compensation Account
MEP	Member of the European Parliament
MLF	multilateral force
MNC	multinational corporation
MRP	Mouvement Républicain Populaire
NATO	North Atlantic Treaty Organization
NFU	National Farmers' Union
NIC	newly industrializing country
NTB	nontariff barrier
OECD	Organization for Economic Cooperation and Development
OEEC	Organization for European Economic Cooperation
QMV	qualified majority voting
R&D	research and development
SEA	Single European Act
SFIO	Section Française de l'Internationale Ouvrière
SPD	Social Democratic Party of Germany
TUC	Trades Union Congress
UNICE	Union of Industrial and Employers' Confederations of Europe
VAT	value added tax
VSTF	very short-term financing
WEU	West European Union
WTO	World Trade Organization

The Choice for Europe

Introduction

The Choice for Europe

> The study of regional integration should be both included in and subordi-
> nated to the study of changing patterns of interdependence.
>
> —Ernst Haas, *The Obsolescence of Regional Integration Theory*, 1975

The construction of the European Community (EC) ranks among the most
extraordinary achievements in modern world politics, yet there is little agreement about its causes.[1] EC rules influence most aspects of European political
life, from the regulation of the habitat of wild birds to voting within the World
Trade Organization. The EC's complex institutions include a semi-autonomous
legal system, parliament, and bureaucracy as well as detailed norms, principles,
rules, and practices governing direct relations among national governments.
These institutions resemble those of a modern nation-state as much as those of
a conventional international regime. Today the EC is a unique, multileveled,
transnational political system.[2]

THE QUESTION: EXPLAINING MAJOR TURNING POINTS

This book addresses the most fundamental puzzle confronting those who seek
to understand European integration, namely to explain why sovereign governments in Europe have chosen repeatedly to coordinate their core economic
policies and surrender sovereign prerogatives within an international institution.
In the history of the EC, the most important such choices are five treaty-amending sets of agreements that propelled integration forward. Variously termed
constitutive, constitutional, history-making, or grand bargains, they punctuate
EC history at a rate of roughly once per decade. Each grand bargain, three

---

[1] Since the ratification of the Maastricht Treaty, the organization has been referred to as the
European Union (EU). This book deals with major interstate bargains up to and including Maastricht,
so the older term European Community is used throughout.

[2] For theoretical overviews of the EC as a political system, see Helen Wallace and William Wallace,
eds., *Policy-Making in the European Union*, 3d ed. (Oxford, 1996); Robert O. Keohane and Stanley
Hoffmann, eds., *The New European Community: Decision-Making and Institutional Change* (Boulder,
Colo., 1991); Markus Jachtenfuchs and Beate Kohler-Koch, eds., *Europäische Integration* (Opladen,
1996); Fritz Scharpf, *Optionen des Föderalismus in Deutschland und Europa* (Frankfurt, 1994); J. H. H.
Weiler, *The European Constitution* (Oxford, 1997).

aimed at trade liberalization and two at monetary cooperation, set the agenda for a period of consolidation, helping to define the focus and pace of subsequent decision-making.[3] The EC has evolved, as some have said of global economic institutions more generally, as a "sequence of irregular big bangs."[4]

At the core of this book is a series of structured narratives of these decisions or, more properly, bundles of decisions. The account focuses primarily on German, French, and British policies. Chapter 2 analyzes the negotiation in 1957 of the *Treaty of Rome*, which established basic policies and institutions, including a customs union, common agricultural policy, and cooperation on transport, as well as a set of quasi-constitutional institutions and a parallel organization for atomic energy cooperation. Chapter 3 examines *the consolidation of the Common Market* in the 1960s, a set of linked decisions focused around the creation of the Common Agricultural Policy, the implementation of the Common Market, the veto of British membership, and, after France's temporary withdrawal from the EC, the Luxembourg Compromise of 1966 regulating the exercise of national vetoes. Chapter 4 considers the founding of the *European Monetary System* aimed at the stabilization of intra-European exchange rates. Chapter 5 investigates the *Single European Act*, negotiated in the mid-1980s, which expanded the use of qualified majority voting and established the "Europe 1992" agenda for the removal of nontariff trade barriers and the creation of a "single market." Finally, chapter 6 assesses the *Treaty on European Union*, signed at Maastricht in 1991, which set forth a schedule for Economic and Monetary Union (EMU) with a single currency. Together these five decisions have dictated the main lines of European integration over the past forty years.

My aim is neither to duplicate textbook overviews of these decisions nor to recapitulate narrative treatments of their diplomatic history.[5] I aim instead to test alternative explanations of these decisions and, in doing so, to advance a revisionist explanation of my own. This book advances propositions about the underlying causes of integration that are grounded in general social-scientific theories of state preferences, interstate bargaining, and institutional choice. It eschews ad hoc explanation and seeks instead to discover what is generalizable about EC history. The analysis rests, accordingly, on the testing of a series of standardized hypotheses across a structured comparison of all five major decisions in EC history, not an isolated case study. This method, I believe, provides reason to be more confident in the generalizability of the conclusions across EC history and, ultimately, beyond Europe.

[3] Gerald Schneider and Lars-Erik Cederman, "The Change of Tide in Political Cooperation: A Limited Information Model of European Integration," *International Organization* 48 (Autumn 1994), 633–662.

[4] Peter Katzenstein, "International Relations Theory and the Analysis of Change," in Ernst-Otto Czempiel and James N. Rosenau, eds., *Global Changes and Theoretical Challenges* (Lexington, Mass., 1989), 296.

[5] Most informative are Desmond Dinan, *An Ever Closer Union? An Introduction to the European Community* (Boulder, Colo., 1994); Stephen George, *Politics and Policies of the European Union*, 3d ed. (Oxford, 1996); Richard McAllister, *From EC to EU: A Historical and Political Survey* (New York, 1997); Michael O'Neill, *The Politics of European Integration: A Reader* (New York, 1996); Loukas Tsoukalis, *The New European Economy*, 2d ed. (Oxford, 1996); Wallace and Wallace, *Policy-Making*.

THE ARGUMENT: ECONOMIC INTEREST, RELATIVE POWER, CREDIBLE COMMITMENTS

My central claim is that the broad lines of European integration since 1955 reflect three factors: patterns of commercial advantage, the relative bargaining power of important governments, and the incentives to enhance the credibility of interstate commitments. Most fundamental of these was commercial interest. European integration resulted from a series of rational choices made by national leaders who consistently pursued economic interests—primarily the commercial interests of powerful economic producers and secondarily the macroeconomic preferences of ruling governmental coalitions—that evolved slowly in response to structural incentives in the global economy.

When such interests converged, integration advanced. The fact that economic interests did consistently converge reflected fundamental trends in postwar international political economy—in particular, a fifty-year boom in trade and investment among industrialized countries. The resulting expansion of intra-industry trade both predated the EC and induced policy changes regardless of whether the countries in question were EC members. Similarly, rising capital mobility undermined the autonomy of national macroeconomic policies, creating greater pressures for monetary cooperation. At its core, I argue, European integration has been dictated by the need to adapt through policy coordination to these trends in technology and in economic policy.

This explanation of national preferences for integration is grounded in political economy, not economics. Despite the importance of economic benefits, economists themselves were skeptical of, if not outright opposed to, many of the major steps in European integration. Construction of a customs union, a common agricultural policy, monetary union—almost all were, from the perspective of an economist, "second best" policies. Preferences for such policies emerged from a process of domestic political conflict in which specific sectoral interests, adjustment costs and, sometimes, geopolitical concerns played an important role. Consistent with modern theories of foreign economic policy, I argue that the specific conditions under which governments were willing to liberalize trade reflected their international economic competitiveness; the conditions under which they accepted monetary integration reflected prevailing macroeconomic policies and preferences.

Yet the EC was shaped by more than the convergence of national preferences in the face of economic change. There were important distributional conflicts not just within states but among them. These interstate conflicts were resolved only through hard interstate bargaining, in which credible threats to veto proposals, to withhold financial side-payments, and to form alternative alliances excluding recalcitrant governments carried the day. The outcomes reflected the relative power of states—more precisely, patterns of asymmetrical interdependence. Those who gained the most economically from integration compromised the most on the margin to realize it, whereas those who gained the least or for whom the costs of adaptation were highest imposed conditions. To secure the substantive bargains they had made, finally, governments delegated and pooled sovereignty in international institutions for the express purpose of committing one another to cooperate. Where joint gains were large, but each government faced a strong temptation to defect from agreements—as was the case for the Common Agricultural Policy and for Economic and Monetary Union—governments tended to establish qualified majority voting and delegate tasks to supranational institutions.

In short, I argue that a tripartite explanation of integration—economic interest, relative power, credible commitments—accounts for the form, substance, and timing of major steps toward European integration. Chapter 1 of this book elaborates these three theories, introduces their major competitors, and derives hypotheses that permit us to test them in the case of the EC. Chapters 2 through 6 present structured narratives of the five decisions designed to test the competing theories. Chapter 7 concludes.

This explanation of integration breaks with the bulk of existing scholarship on the EC. It rejects the view that integration has been driven primarily—as Jean Monnet and his social-scientific counterparts, the neofunctionalists, long maintained—by a technocratic process reflecting the imperatives of modern economic planning, the unintended consequences of previous decisions, and the entrepreneurship of disinterested supranational experts. The integration process did not supercede or circumvent the political will of national leaders; it *reflected* their will. Nor—as the most prominent critics of neofunctionalism contend—can we account for integration primarily as the result of a coincidental postwar link between the "low politics" of foreign economic policy and geopolitical "high politics." The primary motivation of those who chose to integrate was not to prevent another Franco-German war, bolster global prestige and power, or balance against the superpowers. Nor—as numerous historians, political scientists, and members of the European movement continue to maintain—does integration represent a victory over nationalistic opposition by proponents of a widely shared, idealistic vision of a united Europe, an interpretation known in the classical lexicon as the "federalist" theory of integration. To be sure, technocratic imperatives, geopolitical concerns, and European idealism each played a role at the margin, but none has consistently been the decisive force behind major decisions. Nor, finally—although this book shares much with recent studies of European integration in the 1950s by economic historians such as Alan Milward—was integration primarily an effort to preserve a system of social welfare provision unique to postwar Western Europe or any of its member-states.

All such explanations treat the EC as unique, an exception in world politics that requires a *sui generis* theory.[6] This assumption led the study of regional integration to develop over the past forty years as a discipline apart, one divorced from general studies of international cooperation. The paradoxical result: today no claim appears more radical than the claim that the behavior of EC member

---

[6] This was true of neofunctionalists, whose self-criticism on this ground is reviewed below. It is also true of some critics of neofunctionalism. Milward, for example, argues in favor of a specific "European" theory of integration, as opposed to prevailing "American" theories. Alan S. Milward, *The European Rescue of the Nation-State* (London, 1993).

governments is *normal.* The revisionist quality of the argument in this book lies precisely in its effort to normalize the actions of European governments—to treat them as a subset of general tendencies among democratic states in modern world politics. Governments cooperated when induced or constrained to do so by economic self-interest, relative power, and strategically imposed commitments. Far from demonstrating the triumph of technocracy, the power of idealism, and the impotence or irrelevance of the modern nation-state, European integration exemplifies a distinctly modern form of power politics, peacefully pursued by democratic states for largely economic reasons through the exploitation of asymmetrical interdependence and the manipulation of institutional commitments. If the motivations of postwar European leaders were distinctive, it was because their countries were touched more intensely by economic trends common to all advanced industrial democracies, most notably the rapidly increasing potential for industrial trade among industrialized nations since World War II, disorder in the international monetary system after 1970, and widespread pressures for liberalization and disinflation in recent decades.

Through an analysis of EC history, this book also seeks to advance a distinctive theoretical position in current debates in international relations theory. The explanation of European integration sketched above is formulated as a distinct series of answers to three questions central to modern theories of comparative and international political economy. In a world in which governments are, broadly speaking, rational and instrumental, integration can be seen as a process in which they define a series of underlying objectives or preferences, bargain to substantive agreements concerning cooperation, and finally select appropriate international institutions in which to embed them. Any explanation of rational state choices to coordinate policy through international institutions must therefore address three questions. First, what best explains national preferences, the fundamental motivations underlying support for or opposition to economic integration? Second, given a set of national preferences, what best explains outcomes of interstate bargaining within the EC? Third, given a set of substantive bargains, what best explains state choices to construct European institutions and transfer sovereignty to them? This book suggests a distinct answer to each question. Let us consider each in turn.

Patterns of national preferences, the focus of the first stage, vary greatly over EC history. France, Germany, and Britain promoted and opposed integration in different substantive areas and to different ends. Their respective positions also shifted, if usually only in incremental fashion, over time. In explaining foreign economic policy, international relations theorists concerned with national preference formation have long debated the relative weight of security and political economic motivations.

One theory holds that world politics contains a hierarchy of issues headed by security concerns. Foreign economic policy is driven, therefore, not by its direct economic consequences but by its indirect consequences for national security, termed "security externalities." This is the dominant view in the study of the EC, where diplomatic historians, European foreign policy specialists, and those who

study the role of ideas in foreign policy have long argued that European economic integration has been pursued not primarily for its own sake but to counter
geopolitical threats and realize geopolitical goals. Postwar European leaders who
constructed and extended the EC sought to tie down the Germans, balance the
Russians, establish a third force against the Americans, overcome right-wing and
Communist extremism at home, or suppress nationalism to realize a distinctive
vision of European federalism. Geopolitical interest and ideology explain traditional British semidetachment from Europe, German federalist sympathies, and
French vacillation between the two poles.

I conclude instead in favor of an alternative theory of foreign economic policy that holds that there is no hierarchy of interests; national interests tend instead to reflect direct, issue-specific consequences. National preferences concerning international trade and monetary policy can therefore be understood
as a reflection of the economic incentives generated by patterns of international
economic interdependence—the core of so-called "endogenous" theories of
tariff and exchange-rate policy. The dominant motivations of governments in
the EC decisions studied here reflected not geopolitical threats or ideals but
pressures to coordinate policy responses to rising opportunities for profitable
economic exchange, in particular growing intra-industry trade and capital movements. While more strictly commercial in its focus, this view is consistent with
those of economic historians who have studied EC history. Trade liberalization
followed export opportunities. In monetary policy, preferences for integration
reflected the relative macroeconomic performance and preference of national
governments alongside commercial considerations.[7]

The primacy of economic interests does not relegate geopolitical ideology to
insignificance. Taken by themselves, naked economic preferences would probably have led to a highly institutionalized pan-European free trade area with
flanking policies of regulatory harmonization and monetary stabilization—
somewhat more intensive arrangements than those pursued by the European
Free Trade Area (EFTA) and European Monetary System (EMS). These activities would have been embedded in weaker, less overtly constitutional, but
still autonomous international institutions, such as those found in EFTA, the
World Trade Organization (WTO), and the North American Free Trade Area
(NAFTA). Explaining the emergence and expansion of a geographically more
limited, institutionally more developed, and substantively more diverse institution requires attention to geopolitical ideology.

Yet economic interests remained primary. Pressures from economic interest

---

[7] Unlike neofunctionalist theories of the early 1960s, however, which saw support for economic
integration as a reflection of a broad postwar consensus on the desirability of technocratic planning and state intervention, or more recent works by historians, which attribute them to the emergence of a social welfare state, I argue that it was the existence of a postwar trade boom among all
developed countries, a massive expansion and redirection of trade from colonies to other industrial
nations—a trend focused particularly in Europe—which powered European economic integration.
This explanation, unlike that of the neofunctionalists or economic historians, also explains the striking variation in economic interests across issues and countries, which accord with the position of national producers in international markets.

groups generally imposed tighter constraints on policy than did security concerns and the ideological visions of politicians and public opinion. When one factor had to give way, it tended to be geopolitics. Economic interests, moreover, determined the circumstances under which geopolitical ideology could influence policy. Only where economic interests were weak, diffuse, or indeterminate could national politicians indulge the temptation to consider geopolitical goals. Political economic interests predominated even where we would least expect them to. For example, the vital interest behind General de Gaulle's opposition to British membership in the EC, I argue, was not the pursuit of French *grandeur* but the price of French wheat.

The second question concerns the outcomes of interstate bargaining. Of particular theoretical interest are the extent to which negotiated outcomes are efficient, exploiting all possible joint gains, and the extent to which resolution of distributive conflict over the division of gains in specific cases has favored one or another country. EC bargaining, I argue, is generally Pareto-efficient, but its distributive outcomes vary greatly. Some bargains, such as the one struck over the institutions governing a single currency, favored Germany; others, such as the creation of the Common Agricultural Policy, favored France; and still others, such as the establishment of regional policy, favored Britain. How is this variation best explained?

International relations theorists have long debated the relative importance of various factors for the outcomes of noncoercive interstate bargaining. Theoretical debates divide those who hold that international institutions—in particular, autonomous supranational officials empowered by them—decisively influence interstate bargaining from those who believe that bargaining outcomes reflect the relative power of states.

The first theory, as applied to the EC, focuses on the essential role of "supranational" entrepreneurs in overcoming the high transaction costs of interstate bargaining, which prevent governments from negotiating efficiently. This view, which dominates the study of the EC to this day, follows from neofunctionalist theory, which views the EC as a novel institutionalized realm, but it is also consistent with distinct theoretical approaches to the study of international regimes, negotiation, and law. Many scholars stress the role of international officials, who initiate, mediate, and mobilize societal groups around international agreements. The EC Commission, Court, and Parliament are said to have empowered a particular breed of supranational political entrepreneurs, from Jean Monnet in the 1950s to Jacques Delors in the 1990s. Their interventions, it is argued, have repeatedly increased the efficiency of negotiations and shifted the distributional outcomes in directions favored by international technocrats.

I conclude, by contrast, in favor of a second theory, which maintains that interstate bargaining outcomes are decisively shaped by the relative power of nation-states. This view, termed "intergovernmental" in the EC literature, draws on general theories of bargaining and negotiation to argue that relative power among states is shaped above all by asymmetrical interdependence, which dictates the relative value of agreement to different governments. These distributive results can be predicted to a first approximation through the use of Nash bargaining theory: the governments that benefit most from the core agreement, relative to their best unilateral and coalitional alternatives to agreement, tend to offer greater compromises in order to achieve it. Where the threat to form an alternative coalition is credible, governments have exploited threats to exclude one another. Bargaining tends to be issue-specific with cross-issue linkages restricted to balancing out benefits among governments and generally taking the form of cash payments or institutional concessions.

The entrepreneurship of supranational officials, by contrast, tends to be futile and redundant, even sometimes counterproductive. Governments generally find it easy to act as their own entrepreneurs and to impose distributional bargains through the use of traditional nonmilitary instruments of power politics, including credible unilateral vetoes, threats of exclusion, and financial side-payments. The distributive outcomes of negotiations have reflected not the preferences of supranational actors but the pattern of asymmetrical interdependence among policy preferences. This is not to deny the influence of supranational entrepreneurs altogether, but their influence has been limited to helping improve the efficiency of one of five agreements, namely the Single European Act (SEA) of 1986. This account reverses the focus of recent EC scholarship. While most analysts generalize from a single case, namely the Commission under Jacques Delors in the mid-1980s, and ask why the Commission was so effective, a comparative analysis invites us to pose the opposite puzzle: Why is the SEA the only major EC bargain about which a serious empirical debate about supranational entrepreneurship can be conducted?

The final step is to explain the choices of governments to delegate and pool sovereignty in international institutions. While the formal powers of supranational officials and qualified majority voting do not extend to major treaty-amending negotiations—hence the skepticism about their influence over the bargains studied in this book—the everyday legislative process *within* the Treaty involves pooling of sovereignty in majority voting arrangements and substantial delegation directly to supranational officials. Here there is much variation. In some areas extensive powers of implementation and proposal have been delegated to central authorities. In others, qualified majority voting governs interstate decision-making. In still others, national vetoes and unanimity voting have been retained. How are the varied choices of governments to delegate and pool sovereignty to be explained?

General theories of international relations and institutional delegation suggest three reasons why governments might pool and delegate sovereignty. First is commitment to the ideology of European federalism. Recent writings on international cooperation stress the independent role of ideas in shaping institutional preferences. Numerous historians and social scientists attribute the EC's quasi-constitutional institutions to pressure from federalists, particularly in Germany and the Benelux countries, who favored them for ideological reasons.

Second is the need to economize on the generation and analysis of information by centralizing technocratic functions in an international organization. Some international lawyers, regime theorists, and economists maintain that international institutions are often more efficient than decentralized governments at processing information; the need for centralized economic planning was a central element in the neofunctionalist conception of integration. The historical record suggests that the role of ideological commitment to Europe was limited to cases where little de facto sovereignty was pooled or delegated, or where the substantive implications of doing so remained unclear and relatively modest, such as transfers of agenda-setting power from the Commission to the European Parliament. The role of technocratic information was negligible.

I conclude, therefore, in favor of a third explanation. Choices to pool and delegate sovereignty to international institutions are best explained as efforts by governments to constrain and control one another—in game-theoretical language, by their effort to enhance the credibility of commitments. Governments transfer sovereignty to international institutions where potential joint gains are large, but efforts to secure compliance by foreign governments through decentralized or domestic means are likely to be ineffective. This general explanation lies at the heart of functional theories of international regimes, the central strand of which views international institutions as devices to manipulate information in order to promote compliance with common rules. Significant pooling and delegation tend to occur, I find, not where ideological conceptions of Europe converge or where governments agree on the need to centralize policymaking in the hands of technocratic planners, but where governments seek to compel compliance by foreign governments (or, in some cases, future domestic governments) with a strong temptation to defect. It was in fact often the countries least committed in principle to supranational institutions, such as Gaullist France, that imposed them on purportedly federalist governments.

Viewed, then, from the perspective of modern theories of international political economy, this explanation of integration is distinctive in two ways. First, rather than assess competing unicausal explanations or present an amalgam of factors as necessary conditions, this explanation distinguishes clearly between theories that are complements and theories that are substitutes—thereby grounding a multicausal explanation in an explicit framework consistent with rational state behavior. Such a framework must contain distinct explanations of national preferences, substantive bargaining outcomes, and decisions to delegate and pool sovereignty in international institutions. This framework stresses the priority of state preferences, which define not only the goals states seek but to a very substantial degree—via asymmetries in the intensity of preferences—their relative power.[8] This framework is generalizable to any international negotiation. Second, within this framework, the explanation weighs in on the side of economic interests rather than security externalities as fundamental sources of state preferences, the structure of asymmetrical interdependence rather than the process-level intervention of institutional entrepreneurs as a determinant of bargaining outcomes, and the desire for more credible commitments, rather than ideology or technocratic information management, as a motivation to del-

[8] Andrew Moravcsik, "Taking Preferences Seriously: A Liberal Theory of International Politics," *International Organization* 51 (Autumn 1997), 513–553.

egate and pool sovereignty. In chapter 1, the framework and the theories to be tested are presented in more detail.

THE METHOD: EXPLICIT HYPOTHESES, DISAGGREGATED CASES, PRIMARY SOURCES

Why, the reader might well ask, should we accept a series of assertions about European integration that run counter to the weight of existing scholarship? The primary answer is methodological. A historical revision is only as plausible as the evidence and methods employed to evaluate it. This book is based on methods which, while far from ideal, generate more rigorous, transparent, objective, and replicable tests of competing theoretical claims about European integration than have heretofore been conducted.

The case studies of major decisions in this book adhere to three methodological principles. In each case, a consistent set of competing hypotheses is derived from general theories; the decision is disaggregated to generate sufficient observations to test those hypotheses; and, wherever possible, potentially controversial attributions of motive or strategy are backed by "hard" primary sources (direct evidence of decision-making) rather than "soft" or secondary sources (public statements and journalistic or academic commentary in which authors have less incentive to report motivations accurately). Adherence to these three methodological principles has disadvantages—it accounts for the length of the book, as well as its continuous alternation between narrative and analysis—but the aim is to facilitate more reliable causal inference.

Few existing studies of EC decision-making consistently adhere to these principles.[9] Too often we find evidence selected only to support a single explanation, casual reconstruction of single cases, and citations to secondary sources themselves drawn from journalistic commentary or still other secondary sources. Of the many reasons to be skeptical of such studies, perhaps the most fundamental is that European integration has been a subject of heated public controversy for nearly a half-century, thereby generating an enormous number of conjectures about its underlying causes. Within this secondary material—based largely on official government statements, journalistic accounts, and contemporary specu-

---

[9] Even the best historical work, to which I am deeply indebted, does not always meet these standards. Two examples are Alan Milward's pathbreaking economic interpretation of the Treaty of Rome negotiations, which considers competing theories, gathers primary evidence, and pays some attention to the social foundations of national positions but fails either to formulate consistent hypotheses or to consider a full (or carefully controlled) range of confirming and disconfirming data; and Peter Ludlow's unparalleled study of the founding of the European Monetary System, which assembles a wide range of remarkable primary evidence, including some attention to social foundations, but does not always consider competing theories or consistent hypotheses. Both are also, of course, limited to single decisions. Although this book takes issue with some empirical conclusions of such works, it would be impossible without substantial reliance on them. Milward, *Rescue*; Peter Ludlow, *The Making of the European Monetary System* (London, 1982). Cf. Andrew Moravcsik, "Review of Alan Milward, The Rescue of the European Nation-State," *Journal of Modern History* 67 (March 1995), 126–128.

lation—accurate statements of fact coexist alongside the most casual of observations and the most opportunistically partisan of *ex post* justifications. National decision-makers often express one position in public and the opposite in private, even many years after the events in question.[10] Journalists often repeat the justifications of governments or the prevailing conventional wisdom of the moment without assessing their reliability. The result? One can find abundant support for *any* plausible conjecture about the causes of European integration. Only by deriving competing hypotheses from general theories, multiplying observations, and paying attention to the quality of primary sources can we transcend such indeterminacy and bias. The methodology is presented in more detail in chapter 1.

Methodological arguments notwithstanding, some readers—historians in particular—may object in principle to the notion of using the historical record to test alternative theories of state interest, power, and institutional delegation. Others view such research as parasitic upon prior historical analyses, adding little and perhaps subtracting subtlety. John Lewis Gaddis has criticized this genre of international relations scholarship as a Procrustean attempt to "boil things down to a few simple variables" of concern only to social scientists.[11] This view is widespread, not simply among historians but among political scientists engaged in the study of European integration. Two leading specialists in comparative and international politics working on European integration disparage "tests of alternative explanations" as engendering a "false sense of scientism." "In the end," they conclude, "it is not a matter of which [explanation] is better."[12]

Such criticism would be misplaced here, for four reasons. First, the range of outcomes and explanations I consider in each chapter is contextualized by reference to the work of leading historians and commentators. Theoretical consistency dictates that each chapter test the same hypotheses, yet sometimes important alternatives do not fit the categories neatly. In such cases, I seek to err on the side of comprehensiveness rather than of concision. When counterfactual arguments are prominent in existing accounts of integration or in the perceptions of participants, they are evaluated. Chapter 3, for example, evaluates and disconfirms the widespread claim that the collapse of the British accession negotiations of 1961–63 was due to Macmillan's tactical errors, and chapter 6 does the same for the prominent assertion that central bankers exploited transna-

---

[10] Not only is public misrepresentation of motives an oft-employed political tactic, but many statesmen, concerned about their place in history, are careful to cultivate a specific public impression. This was, for example, Monnet's (substantially correct) interpretation of de Gaulle. Bruno Bottai, "Jean Monnet Visto da Vicino," *LiMes* Summer, 2/1997, 152. Many examples are cited in this book.

[11] John Lewis Gaddis, "History, Science and the Study of International Relations," in Ngaire Woods, ed., *Explaining International Relations since 1945* (Oxford, 1996), 38.

[12] Wayne Sandholtz and John Zysman, "1992: Recasting the European Bargain," *World Politics* 42 (October 1989), 127. For a similar sentiment, see Janne H. Matláry, "Beyond Intergovernmentalism: The Quest for a Comprehensive Framework in the Study of Integration," *Cooperation and Conflict* 28 (1993), 181–210.

tional alliances to impose their preferences on the Maastricht Treaty—neither of which, strictly speaking, belongs to the hypotheses consistently evaluated in this book.

Second, the evaluation of competing theories is not dichotomous. History rarely defeats one theory or fully vindicates another; it does not do so here. The aim is not to prove one theory entirely correct or incorrect, but to assess the relative importance of various factors. A measure of multicausality is built into the case studies, since each distinguishes three stages of negotiations—national preference formation, interstate bargaining, and institutionalization—each explained by a different theory. Within each stage, moreover, where theories are indeed tested against one another, the aim is not to prove one entirely correct or incorrect but to assess their relative power. If, as I argue, the preponderance of reliable evidence consistently confirms the preeminence of commercial interests, relative bargaining power, and credible commitments, this is a conclusion, rather than an assumption, of the empirical analysis.

Third, the major theories tested in this book (though not every conclusion) generally accord not just with the writings of EC historians but also with the subjective concerns of policy-makers who participated in the decisions. Contemporaneous politicians, diplomats, officials, and journalists did not, of course, express themselves in social-scientific language, but they nonetheless posed similar questions about preferences, bargaining, and institutions; weighed similar answers; and often came to similarly unambiguous conclusions. In their retrospective analysis of de Gaulle's veto in 1963, for example, German Foreign Ministry officials sought to assess the relative importance of economic interest and geopolitical ideology in French policy—concluding in favor of the former. In preparing both the Maastricht Treaty and the recent Intergovernmental Conference concluded in mid-1997, Commission officials debated whether active Commission leadership, as in 1985, or member-state leadership without a strong Commission role, as in 1989–91, would be more effective. During public controversy over ratification of the Maastricht Treaty in 1992, French politicians publicly disputed whether delegation of power to a relatively nondemocratic institution was justified by technocratic imperatives, the need for more credible commitments to noninflationary policies, or pro-European ideology.[13] In short, the questions posed in this book, while derived from social-science theory, remain true to the self-understanding of participants.

Fourth, while this book is indebted to studies by historians, who have uncovered many of the sources I cite, I also seek to assemble new types of evidence about EC decision-making, much of it based on primary-source materials. Neither textbooks nor traditional diplomatic histories investigate the range of information available to different governments, the considerations in the minds

---

[13] These events are described in more detail in this book. See Karl Carstens, *Erinnerungen und Erfahrungen* (Boppard am Rhein, 1993), 247–248; Sophie Meunier-Aitsahalia and George Ross, "Democratic Deficit or Democratic Surplus: A Reply to Andrew Moravcsik's Comments on the French Referendum," *French Politics and Society* 11 (Winter 1993), 57–69; interviews with four members of the Commission team preparing the Intergovernmental Conference, August–October 1997.

of national leaders who agreed to delegate authority to supranational institutions, and, above all, the nature of societal support underlying the positions of the three major EC governments—Britain, France, and Germany. Yet information, delegation, and societal pressures are critical to a modern theoretical understanding of interstate cooperation. Though my primary motivation is to test theory, such data are not of concern solely to social scientists. Indeed, measurement of preferences and information is often overlooked in studies of international relations, precisely because it so often requires intensive primary-source analysis. Even prominent historians of European integration today, among them Alan Milward and Peter Ludlow, complain that diplomatic histories have yet to provide a reliable "social history" of European integration. This book seeks to take a first step in that direction.[14]

THE LITERATURE: BEYOND "GRAND THEORY"

Before moving to chapter 1, where the concrete theories and hypotheses are presented, let us take a final moment to consider the relationship of this book to existing theory. In doing so, one turns inevitably to "classical" theories of regional integration, the most influential of which is neofunctionalism.[15] Developed by Ernst Haas and others in the 1950s and 1960s, neofunctionalism remains a touchstone for scholarship on European integration. Neofunctionalists initially maintained that the unintended consequences of integration, once launched, would be self-reinforcing. This, they argued, assures the continuance of integration—though this teleology was later heavily qualified. Such feedback takes two forms. Initial steps toward cooperation bolster a technocratic consensus in favor of further integration by expanding, empowering, and encouraging societal groups supportive of further state intervention in the economy. The establishment of international institutions also centralizes power in the hands of supranational officials whose political entrepreneurship promotes further integration.

This book should not be read as an evaluation of—let alone a wholesale rejection of—neofunctionalism or any other classical theory. To be sure, this book tests (and for the most part disconfirms) some narrower propositions advanced by neofunctionalists—the claims, for example, that national interests are technocratic rather than reflect fundamental domestic conflict, that supranational entrepreneurship decisively alters interstate bargaining outcomes, and that delegation to international institutions reflects the need for centralized, expert

---

[14] Peter Ludlow, "Recasting the European Political System, 1950–1996," *CEPS Review* 1 (Summer 1996), 25–33; Alan S. Milward, "Conclusions: The Value of History," in Milward et al., *The Frontier of National Sovereignty: History and Theory, 1945–1992* (London, 1993), 197–198.

[15] For reviews of neofunctionalism, as well as federalism, functionalism, realism, intergovernmentalism, and other grand theories, see O'Neill, *Politics*, and Charles Pentland, *International Theory and European Integration* (New York, 1973).

planners. In other ways, such as its recognition of the primacy of economic in-terests, the book supports traditional neofunctionalist claims. In still others, such as the extent to which some national preferences for integration may be endo-genous to a path-dependent process of prior integration, it does not directly ad-dress neofunctionalist concerns (though the final chapter does draw some pre-liminary conclusions).

This book is thus not yet another confrontation with neofunctionalism but an acknowledgment and response to criticisms of the style of "grand theory" neo-functionalism represents—criticisms that emerged in large part from the neo-functionalists themselves. By the early 1970s it was evident even to its creators that neofunctionalism required fundamental revision.

At one level the failure of neofunctionalism was empirical. European integra-tion had not expanded steadily but by stops and starts. Significant domestic conflict remained. Integration had focused not on areas of state intervention and planning, such as atomic energy and public transport, but on areas of mar-ket liberalization, such as tariff policy. It had not generated uniformly stronger centralized institutions but a curious hybrid still heavily dependent on unani-mous consensus among governments. And governments did not always privilege regional over global multilateral cooperation. These events seemed to discon-firm early, teleological variants of neofunctionalism.[16]

Yet the most important weakness of neofunctionalism was not empirical but theoretical. For once the simple teleology toward integration was abandoned, neofunctionalism and other grand theories lacked the resources to construct a positive response. Neofunctionalism proved at once too ambitious, too vague, and too incoherent to generate precise predictions suitable for empirical eval-uation. To see why we need only turn to theoretical lessons neofunctionalists themselves drew from these failures. Three stand out.

The neofunctionalists concluded that an explanation of integration must be embedded in a multicausal framework comprised of numerous narrower theo-ries. Scholars came to realize in the 1970s that any single unified theory of American or comparative politics—say, "structural-functionalism"—was too ab-stract and undifferentiated to permit concrete theory testing and development. Most neofunctionalists concluded that no single theory could satisfactorily ac-count for a phenomenon as complex as European integration; more concrete theories were required. However, their response, namely to construct amalgams of variables, failed to overcome, as Haas observed, the "non-additive character of theories [that] coexist on different levels of abstraction."[17] In an influential critique, Donald Puchala invoked the metaphor of the blind men and the ele-

---

[16] Ernst B. Haas, "International Integration: The European and the Universal Process," in *International Political Communities: An Anthology* (New York, 1966), 93–130; Haas, "The Study of Regional Integration: Reflections on the Joy and Anguish of Pretheorizing," in Leon N. Lindberg and Stuart A. Scheingold, eds., *Regional Integration: Theory and Research* (Cambridge, Mass., 1971), 23ff; Haas, "Turbulent Fields and the Theory of Regional Integration," *International Organization* 30 (Spring 1976), 173–212.

[17] Haas, "Study," 23–24, also 26–30.

phant: different theories seemed to explain different aspects of the (elephan-tine) integration process.[18] It follows that any general explanation of integration cannot rest on a single theory, neofunctionalist or otherwise, but must rest on a multicausal framework that orders a series of more narrowly focused theories— a conclusion echoed to the present day.[19]

Variables in the multicausal framework must each be grounded in a general theory of political behavior. Theories that treat regional integration as a *sui generis* phenomenon, Haas argued, could be little better than "pre-theories." They breed theoretical insularity. With the EC as the sole major success, regional integration theory in practice became an ideal-typical summary of factors that appear to have influenced the European case. This focus on a *sui generis* Europe-centered theory cut the study of European integration off from revolutionary theoretical currents in comparative and international political economy over the three decades that followed. Sensing this, Haas proposed that "the study of regional integration should be both included in and subordinated to the study of changing patterns of interdependence." Consistent with this analysis, Stanley Hoffmann, Robert Keohane, Joseph Nye, Henry Nau, and many others drew the conclusion that the EC should be viewed as an international regime designed to manage interdependence.[20]

Finally, each theory should be actor-oriented, that is, it should highlight the purposive choices of states and social actors within constraints rather than the unintended dynamics of broad structural processes. A fundamental weakness of neofunctionalism lay in its aspiration to trace dynamic endogenous effects (incremental feedback, unintended consequences, and the resulting change over time) without a baseline theory of exogenous constraints (state economic interests, political constraints, and delegation) through which dynamic change must take place.[21] For example, neofunctionalists maintained (as I do in this book) that the pursuit of economic interest is the fundamental force underly-

---

[18] Donald Puchala, "Of Blind Men, Elephants, and International Integration," *Journal of Common Market Studies* 10 (March 1972), 267–285. Also Pentland, *International*, 189–194; Carole Webb, "Theoretical Perspectives and Problems," in Helen Wallace, William Wallace, and Webb, eds., *Policy-Making in the European Community*, 2d ed. (Chichester, 1983), 32ff.

[19] Matláry, "Beyond Intergovernmentalism," 181–208; Linda Cornett and James A. Caporaso, "'And it still moves!' State Interests and Social Forces in the European Community," in James N. Rosenau and Ernst-Otto Czempiel, eds., *Governance without Government: Order and Change in World Politics* (Cambridge, 1992), 248; Michael O'Neill, *The Politics of European Integration: A Reader* (New York, 1996), 5.

[20] Haas, "Study," 26; Haas, *The Obsolescence of Regional Integration Theory* (Berkeley, Calif., 1975), 86; Henry R. Nau, "From Integration to Interdependence: Gains, Losses and Continuing Gaps," *International Organization* 33 (Autumn 1979), 119–147; Robert O. Keohane and Joseph S. Nye, "International Interdependence and Integration," in Fred Greenstein and Nelson Polsby, eds., *Handbook of Political Science* (Andover, Mass., 1975), 363–414; Stanley Hoffmann, "Reflections on the Nation-State in Western Europe Today," *Journal of Common Market Studies* 21 (September–December 1982), 21–37.

[21] James Caporaso and John T. S. Keeler, "The European Community and Regional Integration Theory," in Carolyn Rhodes and Sonia Mazey, eds., *The State of the European Union: Building European Unity?* (Boulder, Colo., 1995), 43; Likke Friis, "Challenging a Theoretical Paradox: The Lacuna of Integration Theory," *CORE Working Paper* 2 (Copenhagen, 1995), 2.

ing integration, but they offered only a vague understanding of precisely what those interests are, how conflicts among them are resolved, by what means they are translated into policy, and when they require political integration.[22] This in turn reflected the lack of a generalizable microfoundational basis necessary to support predictions about variation in support for integration across issues, countries, and time.

Without such microfoundations, the predictions of neofunctionalism were indeterminate. Feedback, Haas conceded in his later self-criticism, "*may* transform the system" but need not do so. An entire taxonomy of alternative outcomes consistent with the underlying theory arose: "spillover," "spillback," "spill-around," "encapsulation." Once neofunctionalism dropped the optimistic notion that integration was automatically self-reinforcing and would evolve smoothly to federal union without triggering fundamental distributive or ideological conflicts, it could say "little about *basic causes*" of national demands for integration or interstate agreements to achieve it; so two leading neofunctionalists concluded.[23] More concretely, neofunctionalism lacked explicit theories of interest-group politics, interstate bargaining, and international institutions. With few outcomes theoretically excluded, a rule of thumb emerged in the literature on the European Community: when integration stagnated, scholars criticized neofunctionalism; when integration progressed, they rediscovered it.[24]

By the mid-1970s these three criticisms had inspired a degree of consensus concerning the proper theoretical direction forward. Unintended consequences and feedback, the initial core of neofunctionalism, should take a role secondary to the concrete beliefs, preferences, and strategies of political actors. As Haas said, "all political action is purposively linked with individual and group perception of interest." Greater attention should be focused on purposive behavior and strategic interaction: "the type of demands that are made, the variety of concessions . . . exchanged, and the degree of delegation of authority to new central institutions."[25] Hoffmann, Keohane, and even, if to a lesser degree, Haas himself proposed studying the EC as an international regime constructed through a

---

[22] This lies behind the criticisms of Milward and Ludlow, mentioned above, that a "social history" of integration is required. See note 14. The neofunctionalists did stress the role of economic transactions. Ernst B. Haas and Philippe C. Schmitter, "Economics and Differential Patterns of Political Integration: Projections about Unity in Latin America," *International Organization* 18 (Autumn 1964), 707, 709–710.

[23] Leon N. Lindberg and Stuart A. Scheingold, *Europe's Would-Be Polity: Patterns of Change in the European Community* (Englewood Cliffs, N.J., 1970), 284. Joseph S. Nye, *Peace in Parts: Integration and Conflict in Regional Organization* (Boston, 1971), 64–75; Philippe Schmitter, "A Revised Theory of Regional Integration," in Lindberg and Scheingold, *Regional Integration*, 232–264; Ernst B. Haas, "Technocracy, Pluralism and the New Europe," in Stephen R. Graubard, ed., *A New Europe?* (Boston, 1964), 62–88. Neofunctionalism failed, Haas argued, to capture the real decisions facing governments, for example the choice—repeatedly critical in the evolution of the EC—whether to engage in regional or global cooperation.

[24] Characteristic is Jeppe Tranholm-Mikkelsen, "Neofunctionalism: Obstinate or Obsolete. A Reappraisal in the Light of the New Dynamism of the EC," *Millennium* 20 (Spring 1991); Wayne Sandholtz, *High-Tech Europe: The Politics of International Cooperation* (Berkeley, Calif., 1992); Paul Pierson, "The Path to European Union: An Historical Institutionalist Account," *Comparative Political Studies* 29 (April 1996), 123–164.

[25] Haas, *Beyond the Nation State*, 34–35, 81; Haas, "Turbulent," 173.

series of purposive decisions by governments with varying preferences and power. Hoffmann proposed a synthetic approach that examined first "the domestic priorities and foreign policy goals of the member states, then . . . the impact of the environment [and] finally the institutional interplay between the states and the Community."[26] Keohane and Hoffmann concluded that spillover and unintended consequences required a prior intergovernmental bargain among member-states, thereby refocusing our attention on the exogenous determinants of major decisions.[27]

Yet most scholarship on European integration over the past two decades has ignored these self-criticisms. Few scholars test general theories or employ a multicausal framework. Nearly all continue instead either to structure research around a single variable (e.g., supranational influence, domestic politics, public opinion), often linked to an ideal-typical "grand theory" of integration or IR, or to invoke a theoretically unstructured amalgams of causes.[28] As a result, decades of analysis of the EC have multiplied conjectures about integration but generated few reliable empirical conclusions about the relative importance of forces that have made the EC what it is today. "Confirmed" determinants of integration and "necessary" conditions for its success proliferate unchecked. Some scholars go further, defending this tendency on the ground that integration is the result of an indeterminate, path-dependent process.[29]

The proper measure of our understanding of integration is not the multiplication of intuitively plausible claims; it is the development, evaluation, and ultimately rejection of testable hypotheses. Where hypotheses are rarely discarded, they are rarely confirmed. Thus the basic thrust of this book runs contrary to the current literature on European integration. Rather than employ neofunctionalism and other grand theories as interpretive lenses, it seeks to move beyond them by employing narrower and concrete hypotheses drawn from general theories of economic interest, interstate bargaining, and international regimes to support rigorous testing. The next chapter introduces the multicausal framework, general theories, and concrete hypotheses required for such tests.

---

[26] Hoffmann, "Reflections," 31, 33–34; Ernst B. Haas, *Beyond the Nation State: Functionalism and International Organization* (Stanford, 1964), 23, 30, 32–35, 77. Ultimately Haas moved in a different direction, seeking to reconceptualize "learning" through a process of trial and error and the application of expert knowledge, though he conceded a greater role for learning if integration "enhances the original purposes of the actors."

[27] Robert O. Keohane and Stanley Hoffmann. "Institutional Change in Europe in the 1980s," in Keohane and Hoffmann, *New European Community*, 1–39.

[28] Caporaso and Keeler, "European," 36–42.

[29] It is unclear whether Sandholtz and Zysman mean consistently to adhere to their view that the outcomes of integration are "unknowable, dependent on the timing and dynamics of a long series of contingent decisions," but it is fair to say that disconfirmation of hypotheses is not a focus of their inquiry. Sandholtz and Zysman, "Recasting," 128. For a theoretically more sophisticated and in principle testable formulations of the path-dependent view, see Pierson, "Path to European Union."

CHAPTER ONE

Theorizing European Integration

To succeed, always choose the path of least resistance.

—Jean Monnet (1978)

The central argument of this book is that European integration can best be explained as a series of rational choices made by national leaders. These choices responded to constraints and opportunities stemming from the economic interests of powerful domestic constituents, the relative power of each state in the international system, and the role of international institutions in bolstering the credibility of interstate commitments. I test this account across the five most salient negotiations in the history of the European Community (EC): the negotiation of the Treaty of Rome signed in 1957, the consolidation of the customs union and Common Agricultural Policy (CAP) during the 1960s, the establishment of the European Monetary System (EMS) in 1978–79, the negotiation of the Single European Act (SEA) in 1985–86, and the Maastricht Treaty on European Union signed in 1991.

In this opening chapter, I present the theoretical foundations of my proposed explanation and its most plausible competitors. A theoretical introduction of this kind is necessary because these competing explanations are not simply empirical judgments about the specific case of European integration. Each rests on a general theory commonly employed to explain international economic cooperation. The use of such general theories permits us to formulate more detailed and consistent explanations, to test them more rigorously and in ways that are replicable, and finally to generalize the results to other situations.

In the first section, I present a rationalist framework of international cooperation on which rest all the theories and explanations evaluated in this book. The assumption that states act rationally or instrumentally in pursuit of relatively stable and well-ordered interests at any given point in time implies a division of major EC negotiations into three stages: national preference formation, interstate bargaining, and the choice of international institutions. This rationalist framework is one response to the criticisms of earlier theories of European integration outlined in the introduction.

In the following three sections, I present alternative theories and hypotheses to explain each of the three stages. To explain variation in national preferences, I evaluate theories based on geopolitical and economic interests. To explain the efficiency and distributional outcomes of interstate bargaining, I evaluate theories that stress supranational entrepreneurship and interstate bargaining power. To explain decisions to delegate powers to international institutions, I evaluate theories that stress federalist ideology, the greater efficiency of centralizing the generation of technocratic information, and the need to increase the credibility of national commitments. In the general language of international political economy, explained more fully below, this book poses three theoretical questions. How much do security externalities and endogenous commercial policy contribute to an explanation of national preferences for international economic policy coordination? How much do political entrepreneurship and asymmetrical interdependence contribute to the efficiency and distributional outcomes of interstate bargaining? How much do national identity, informational economies of scale, and the desire for credible commitments contribute to state decisions to delegate or pool sovereignty in international institutions? To evaluate each potential answer, I derive a series of concrete hypotheses from each theory; all are tested in the empirical chapters that follow.

I conclude with a brief description and defense of the methodology employed here, which, for the first time in the study of the EC, employs three techniques either recommended in recent works on qualitative methods in social science or employed as standard practice among historians. These are the formulation of concrete and falsifiable hypotheses from competing theories, the disaggregation of case studies to multiply observations, and the reliance whenever possible on primary sources.

INTERNATIONAL COOPERATION: A RATIONALIST FRAMEWORK

The study of European integration has long remained the preserve of "grand" or "classical" theories of integration, which seek to explain the EC with reference either to a single overarching factor or to an ideal type constructed from an amalgam of loosely related variables. As a result "EC studies" has evolved as a discipline with its own *sui generis* terminology, theories, and empirical generalizations, developing over the past quarter-century in isolation from remarkable developments in the general theory of international and comparative political economy. My contention is that major integration decisions—and multilateral negotiations over international cooperation more generally—are better explained with more narrowly focused yet more broadly generalizable "midrange" theories of economic interest, bargaining, and institutional choice drawn from the general literature on international cooperation.

To structure an inquiry based on such theories, I employ a "rationalist framework" of international cooperation. The term *framework* (as opposed to *theory* or *model*) is employed here to designate a set of assumptions that permit us to disaggregate a phenomenon we seek to explain—in this case, successive rounds of international negotiations—into elements each of which can be treated separately. More focused theories—each of course consistent with the assumptions of the overall rationalist framework—are employed to explain each element. The elements are then aggregated to create a multicausal explanation of a large complex outcome such as a major multilateral agreement.[1]

By positing in advance a particular relationship among aspects of a negotiation—that is, by disaggregating the process we seek to explain within an explicit analytical framework—and applying different theories to each aspect, we can distinguish more rigorously between those theories that are substitutes (those that compete to explain the same stage of the negotiation) and those that are complements (those that explain different stages of the negotiation). This distinction permits the analyst to move beyond simplistic, unicausal claims about the sources of international cooperation without sacrificing rigor entirely and slipping into an unstructured (and often untestable) amalgam or ideal type of many plausible factors—the fate that befell, we saw in the introduction, neofunctionalist theories of integration. The rationalist structure proposed here constrains the analysis and dictates the relationship between different factors throughout. By explaining less at each stage, we seek to explain more overall.

The rationalist framework proposes that international negotiation be disaggregated into a causal sequence of three stages: national preference formation, interstate bargaining, and institutional choice. Each stage is explained by a different theory. First, governments formulate a consistent set of national preferences regarding potential "states of the world" that could emerge from the negotiations. By *preferences*, I designate not simply a particular set of policy goals but a set of underlying national objectives independent of any particular international negotiation to expand exports, to enhance security vis-à-vis a particular threat, or to realize some ideational goal. In the second stage, states then develop strategies and bargain with one another to reach substantive agreements that realize those national preferences more efficiently than do unilateral actions. Finally, they choose whether to delegate and pool sovereignty in international institutions that secure the substantive agreements they have made. Each stage requires distinctive theoretical tools.

This rationalist framework avoids a temptation that bedevils scholarship on international relations, namely to assume that state preferences are fixed—whether conflictual, convergent, or arrayed so as to create a particular collective action problem. While useful for the limited purpose of elaborating particular theories of strategic interaction, the a priori assumption that preferences are fixed is less satisfactory as a postulate for explaining particularly interesting and varied cases of state behavior. The failure to take variation in state preferences seriously has introduced bias into and undermined the viability of many recent research programs, studies of deterrence, hegemonic influence, alliance formation, international negotiation, economic sanctions, and monetary cooperation as well as European integration. Many scholars are now moving toward what Robert Keohane has termed a "fallback" position of systemic theory, whereby exogenous variation in preferences defines a range of outcomes within which

---

[1] Andrew Moravcsik, "Disciplining Trade Finance: The OECD Export Credit Arrangement," *International Organization* 43:1 (Winter 1989), 173–205.

traditional factors such as relative capabilities and institutions explain particular results.[2] No assumption of conflictual or convergent preferences would capture the subtly varied preferences of governments concerning trade, agriculture, money, and other issue-areas considered in this book. In particular, this tripartite framework avoids the tendency to privilege explanations that treat preferences as fixed, often misleadingly termed "systemic" explanations, and to employ theories of state preferences only to explain anomalies.

The specific tripartite sequence proposed here—national preference formation, interstate bargaining, institutional choice—is the only ordering consistent with the rationalist assumptions that underlie most major international relations theories.[3] It is a foundational premise of conventional theories of power or bargaining that influence cannot be analyzed without first knowing what underlying objectives actors seek to realize. Variation in preferences determines the stakes of strategic interaction on the basis of which any strategic calculation of means must proceed. In the case of monetary integration, for example, we cannot assess or predict the credibility and impact of German threats to veto EMU unless we know how strong a preference Germany (and other countries) have for exchange-rate stability and what sort of stability they favor.[4]

Moving to the next stage, the choice of international institutions is theoretically unintelligible within a rationalist framework unless we first understand the specific set of substantive bargains that governments seek thereby to secure. This is the central insight of modern regime theory: the decision to delegate or pool sovereignty in international regimes is analytically separate from (and subordinate to) bargaining over substantive cooperation.[5] Governments debate in-

---

[2] For examples, see Andrew Moravcsik, "Taking Preferences Seriously: A Liberal Theory of International Politics," *International Organization* 51:4 (Autumn 1997), 538–541; Robert O. Keohane, "Theory of World Politics: Structural Realism and Beyond," in Keohane, ed., *Neo-Realism and Its Critics* (New York, 1986), 183.

[3] I leave aside the manifest bias of assuming that any phenomenon explained by a "systemic" theory *cannot* be explained by a corresponding theory based on varying state preferences.

[4] In other words, preferences are by definition independent of strategic calculations, but in many cases, strategies cannot be predicted without extensive knowledge of preferences. Variation in preferences must therefore be explained (or at least controlled for) before testing other theories. To paraphrase Robert Dahl, one cannot know whether "A influenced B" (power) unless they know "what B would otherwise have done" (preferences). Stephen Krasner's well-known metaphor captures this insight in terms of international relations theory: if regime theory helps explain whether governments reach the Pareto-frontier and Realist theories help determine which point on the Pareto-frontier governments select, liberal theories of preferences define the shape of the Pareto-frontier itself. Surely the last task is primary. Accordingly, in previous work I have labeled the approach to European integration employed here "*Liberal* Intergovernmentalist," to distinguish it from regime theoretical or Realist accounts that take preferences as fixed. Moravcsik, "Taking," 513–553. Also Robert O. Keohane, *After Hegemony: Cooperation and Discord in the World Political Economy* (Princeton, N.J., 1984), 6; Stephen D. Krasner, "Global Communications and National Power: Life on the Pareto Frontier," *World Politics* 43:3 (April 1991), 336–366; Lisa Martin, "Interests, Power, and Multilateralism," *International Organization* 46:4 (1992), 765–792; Robert A. Dahl, "The Concept of Power," in Roderick Bell, David V. Edwards, and R. Harrison Wagner, eds., *Political Power: A Reader in Theory and Research* (New York, 1969), 79–93.

[5] Robert O. Keohane, "The Demand for International Regimes," and Stephen D. Krasner, "Structural Causes and Regime Consequences: Regimes as Intervening Variables," both in Krasner, ed., *International Regimes* (Ithaca, 1983), 325–355, 1–23.

stitutions only once they strike a substantive bargain, which tells us the nature of the collective action problem that international cooperation might be meant to solve. It would be quixotic, to return to the monetary example, to analyze the Maastricht negotiations over the autonomy of the European Central Bank without prior understanding of the substantive bargain that governments intend such a bank to secure.

While implicit in most leading theories of international relations and comparative foreign policy, this tripartite framework is not theoretically neutral. It embodies important assumptions that constrain possible explanations. The framework assumes, above all, that the primary political instrument by which individuals and groups in civil society seek to influence international negotiations is the nation-state, which acts externally as a unitary and rational actor on behalf of its constituents. EC history provides much direct evidence, I shall argue, that the assumptions of unitary and rational state action constitute a useful first approximation to the way in which governments have negotiated over the past four decades. These assumptions merit brief elaboration.

The assumption that states are *unitary* maintains that each acts in international negotiations "as if" with a single voice; we can analyze EC governments as pursuing coherent national strategies. I do slightly relax the unitary-actor assumption in a few cases (e.g., at times national executives exploit international negotiations to increase their domestic influence) but such instances are secondary to the core findings of this book. Governments can generally be thought of as pursuing stable interests within a given episode of negotiations.

This is a deceptively simple assumption, about which two potential misunderstandings deserve mention. First, I do not assume states are unitary in their internal politics. National preferences—the underlying "states of the world" that states seek to realize through world politics—are shaped through contention among domestic political groups. The unitary-actor assumption maintains only that once particular objectives arise out of this domestic competition, states strategize as unitary actors *vis-à-vis* other states in an effort to realize them. Second, governments need not necessarily employ a single representative or mechanisms of strict hierarchical control in international negotiations, though in major EC negotiations this is in fact almost always the case. I assume only that political institutions permit governments, even if disaggregated, to act "as if" they were unitary.[6] For example, even if a chief executive and a central bank

---

[6] Some have sought or seek to "test" unitary, rational actor assumptions or "domestic policy" explanations by examining whether domestic divisions exist. Yet formal modeler Christopher Achen persuasively demonstrates that this tactic misrepresents the analytical assumption of unitary rational behavior, which is quite consistent with the observation of domestic divisions. Some constellations of domestic cleavages and institutions generate stable, ordered preferences; others do not. Among those that are consistent with rationalist premises is one, employed here, in which the "national interest" reflects the "power-weighted preferences" of influential domestic actors. One implication of this model, Achen argues, is that many situations in which decisions are attributed to irrationality should be instead attributed to the rational pursuit of varying national preferences. Christopher Achen, "How Can We Tell a Unitary Rational Actor when We See One?" paper presented at the Midwest Political Science Association Convention, April 1995.

have radically different views about proper international monetary policy, are represented separately in international forums, and pursue contradictory goals, the unitary actor assumption may still hold—if divisions do not significantly alter their respective influence on the national negotiating position. We shall see, for example, that Germany, where just such contradictory behavior has been the norm for decades, has pursued a remarkably stable *net* national position in European monetary discussions.

The assumption that unitary states are *rational* maintains that governments make internal decisions "as if" they were efficiently pursuing a weighted, stable set of underlying preferences given a constrained choice of means. Again, this assumption should not be taken too far. It is a weak rationality assumption. State preferences need not necessarily be uniform across issues, countries, or long periods of time. They vary in response to exogenous changes in the economic, ideological, and geopolitical environment within which European integration takes place; the most fundamental task of this book is to explain how and why. Nor need preferences be grounded in material incentives. Some national preferences, we shall see, are grounded in ideas. Rather, the rationality assumption maintains only that within each negotiation, domestic political systems generate a set of stable, weighted objectives concerning particular "states of the world," which governments pursue with the maximum efficiency afforded by available political means. The rationality assumption takes no position on whether states are fully informed, though a framework in which states are assumed to be informed generally performs well.

The resulting tripartite framework of national preference formation, interstate bargaining, and institutional choice structures each of the empirical case studies in this book. It permits us to disaggregate the broad puzzle of what causes each major decision into theoretically more tractable questions. Accordingly, each chapter poses three fundamental questions: What were the fundamental determinants of national preferences? Given those preferences, what factors best explain agreements on substance? Given agreements on substance, what factors best explain choices to construct particular international institutions? The marginal contribution of each stage in the causal sequence (within constraints imposed by previous stages) is explained by a distinct theory or theories. This framework, the one most consistent with the assumption of rational and unitary state action and, therefore, with nearly all major theories of international political economy, is summarized in table 1.

Whether we turn to the testimony of participants, contemporary commentary, retrospective histories, or analyses by social scientists, the plausible answers to each of the three central questions fall into a consistent and limited number of categories. The central task of this book is to weigh the relative importance of these competing answers. Specifically, in explaining national preferences we assess the relative importance of geopolitical interests and economic interests. In explaining interstate bargaining we assess the relative importance of interstate bargaining power and the intervention of supranational entrepreneurs. In explaining choices to delegate sovereignty to international institutions we assess

Table 1.1. International cooperation: A rationalist framework

Stages of Negotiation	National Preference Formation	Interstate Bargaining	Institutional Choice
Alternative independent variables underlying each stage	What is the source of underlying national preferences?	Given national preferences, what explains the efficiency and distributional outcomes of interstate bargaining?	Given substantive agreement, what explains the transfer of sovereignty to international institutions?
	Economic interests or Geopolitical interests?	Asymmetrical interdependence or Supranational entrepreneurship?	Federalist ideology or Centralized technocratic management or More credible commitment?
	↓	↓	↓
Observed outcomes at each stage	Underlying national preferences →	Agreements on substance →	Choice to delegate or pool decision-making in international institutions

the relative importance of federalist ideology, technocratic information management, and the desire for credible commitments. In the remainder of this chapter, these competing theories are elaborated; we begin with those that seek to explain national preferences.

EXPLAINING NATIONAL PREFERENCES

The first stage in explaining the outcome of an international negotiation is to account for national preferences. *National preferences* are defined here as an ordered and weighted set of values placed on future substantive outcomes, often termed "states of the world," that might result from international political interaction. Preferences reflect the objectives of those domestic groups which influence the state apparatus; they are assumed to be stable within each position advanced on each issue by each country in each negotiation, but not necessarily across negotiations, issues, or countries. The term distinguishes such underlying goals—the "tastes" of each state, as it were—from national "strategies," "tactics," and "policies," that is, from the particular transient bargaining positions, negotiating demands, or policy goals that constitute the everyday currency of foreign policy. Preferences, unlike strategies and policies, are exogenous to a specific international political environment. Thus, for example, the phrase

"Country A changed its preferences" in response to an action by Country B misuses the term as it is defined here, implying less than consistently rational behavior.[7]

Of particular analytical importance for understanding international negotiations is the extent to which state preferences are compatible or conflictual—the balance of common gains and distributional trade-offs among countries. Recent scholarship has tended to formulate this question thus: Are state preferences positive-sum or zero-sum? Do states seek absolute and relative gains, efficiency, and distribution?[8] The literature on European integration, in particular, contains numerous discussions of competing "efficiency" and "distributional" explanations of monetary cooperation.[9]

Yet such formulations are widely viewed as inadequate. Particularly important for our purposes here, such dichotomies cannot serve as a foundation for even elementary applications of bargaining theory. To explain bargaining outcomes, we must know the location and shape of the Pareto-frontier, that is, the boundary of the set of agreements that improve welfare for all governments and would therefore secure their voluntary agreement. Accordingly, most fundamental propositions of bargaining theory assume that absolute and relative gains do not just coexist; they *interact*. The relative size of the absolute gains available to each party (its reservation price, win-set, or best alternative to agreement) is the most basic and parsimonious determinant of bargaining power. Accordingly, I assume that the political preferences of states generally contain *both* positive-sum and relative-gains components, which in turn define a bargaining game among governments—the empirical histories leave little doubt that such was perceived to be the case in major EC negotiations. Any explanation of the preferences of European governments should therefore explain not whether preferences are positive- or zero-sum but rather the *mix* of positive- and zero-sum elements in those preferences.[10]

[7] A clear separation between preferences and strategies permits us to distinguish cleanly situations in which a state chooses outcome X over outcome Y because it *prefers* X from situations in which strategic circumstances *compel* or *induce* it to contribute to the realization of X, even though it prefers Y. This gets to the heart of many current controversies: For example, did France accept an autonomous European central bank at Maastricht because it had come to have a *preference* for monetary discipline or because this was the strategic policy concession imposed by Germany for the achievement of other French goals?

[8] Joseph M. Grieco, "Anarchy and the Limits of Cooperation: A Realist Critique of the Newest Liberal Institutionalism," *International Organization* 42:3 (Summer 1988), 485–508; James D. Morrow, "Modeling International Regimes: Distribution versus Information," *International Organization* 48:3 (Summer 1994), 387–423.

[9] E.g., Joseph M. Grieco, "State Interests and Institutional Rule Trajectories: A Neorealist Interpretation of the Maastricht Treaty and European Economic and Monetary Union," *Security Studies* 5:2 (Spring 1996), 261–306.

[10] Fritz Scharpf, *Games Real Actors Play: Actor-Centered Institutionalism in Policy Research* (Boulder, Colo., 1997), chap. 6; Howard Raiffa, *The Art and Science of Negotiation: How to Resolve Conflicts and Get the Best Out of Bargaining* (Cambridge, Mass., 1982), chaps. 1 and 2; Krasner, "Global"; James K. Sebenius, "Challenging Conventional Explanations of International Cooperation: Negotiation Analysis and the Case of Epistemic Communities," *International Organization* 46:1 (Winter 1992), 323–365; Robert D. Putnam, "Diplomacy and Domestic Politics," *International Organization* 42:3 (Summer 1988), 427–461; Moravcsik, "Taking," 538–539; Robert Powell, "Absolute and Relative Gains in International Relations Theory," *American Political Science Review* 85:4 (December 1991),

There is broad agreement among participants, commentators, and scholars that two broad categories of motivation might account for underlying national preferences for and against European integration over the past four decades—and, therefore, for the shape of the Pareto-frontier. These are geopolitical and economic interests. Geopolitical interests reflect perceived threats to national sovereignty or territorial integrity, whether military or ideological; economic interests reflect the imperatives induced by interdependence and, in particular, the large exogenous increase in opportunities for profitable cross-border trade and capital movements in the postwar period. Each serves as the basis for plausible, internally consistent, and widely accepted arguments about the sources of European integration. We can therefore restate the central analytical question about national preferences in major EC negotiations as follows: What is the precise nature and relative weight of geopolitical and economic motivations in the formation of national preferences concerning European integration? [11]

These competing explanations for national preferences are not simply different empirical assessments of motivations for European integration; they rest on distinctive general theories widely employed to explain international cooperation. At the most fundamental level they differ in their views of the relationship among various national preferences. A geopolitical explanation of international economic cooperation assumes that security issues sit atop a hierarchy of foreign policy concerns; hence the indirect security implications ("security externalities") of economic cooperation dominate the direct economic implications. By contrast, an economic explanation assumes that national preferences reflect issue-specific interests. The costs and benefits to powerful domestic economic groups dominate linkages to other concerns, whereas geopolitical interests drive purely politico-military policies. Similar issues are at the core of scholarship seeking to explain phenomena as disparate as British imperialism, the creation of the Bretton Woods economic regime after World War II, and the level of commitment to international human rights regimes.[12]

701–726; Duncan Snidal, "Relative Gains and the Pattern of International Cooperation," *American Political Science Review* 85:3 (September 1991), 701–726.

[11] The distinction may strike some as artificial. True, the two types of preferences are often combined and the goal of this book is thus to determine the *relative* importance of the two factors across an important set of cases, not to isolate a sole motivation for economic cooperation. Some may insist that the two cannot be separated because economic growth is often sought primarily because it enhances national power and prestige. This may be true, but it is extremely difficult to think of observable implications that would permit us to distinguish cleanly whether a statesman (say General de Gaulle) seeks to promote international economic interests for "economic" or for "geopolitical" reasons. In this book I am therefore concerned to distinguish between *imminent* economic and geopolitical motivations: Did governments promote economic objectives (for whatever reason) or did they divert, impede, or suppress the pursuit of such interests in the direction justified by immediate geopolitical interests or ideas? The evidence suggests that this is the distinction that was in the minds of the participants; it is certainly the distinction that has captured the imagination of subsequent commentators, and the question that lies at the heart of current debates in international relations theory.

[12] For cautions concerning potential pitfalls in assuming that pluralist incentives and pressures are translated into outcomes, see Achen, "How"; James E. Alt, Jeffry Frieden, Michael J. Gilligan, Dani Rodrik, and Ronald Rogowski, "The Political Economy of International Trade: Enduring Puzzles and an Agenda for Inquiry," *Comparative Political Studies* 29:6 (December 1996), 689–718; Peter J. Katzenstein, "Conclusion: Domestic Structures and Strategies of Foreign Economic Policy," in

Competing hypotheses are derived concerning five observable implications of each theory. Three concern the pattern of state behavior: variation in state preferences across countries and issues, the timing of policy shifts, and the consistency of EC policy and negotiating demands with broader foreign military and economic policies. Two concern the process of decision-making: the identity of the main domestic actors and cleavages, and the salient considerations mentioned in confidential policy debates. The hypotheses discussed at the close of the section presenting each theory are summarized in table 1.2.

Geopolitical Interest and Ideology: Security Externalities

Most interpretations of national preferences for and against European integration emphasize geopolitical interest or ideology. Analyses of the 1950s stress British Prime Minister Harold Macmillan's visceral antifederalism and his concern to maintain the Anglo-American "special relationship," the desire of German Chancellor Konrad Adenauer to integrate Germany into the West, and the geopolitical lessons drawn by French President Guy Mollet from Suez. Similarly, the 1960s are traditionally portrayed as a clash between two grand ideological alternatives symbolized by Charles de Gaulle and Jean Monnet, one stressing a geopolitical strategy grounded in nationalism, the other a view akin to collective security. European cooperation in the 1970s is generally seen as a by-product of Willy Brandt's *Ostpolitik*, Georges Pompidou's desire to restrain Germany, and later in the decade, Helmut Schmidt and Valéry Giscard d'Estaing's suspicion of Jimmy Carter's foreign policy. The Single European Act of 1986 and the Maastricht Treaty on European Union five years later are often seen as triumphs of the personal federalist commitments of Helmut Kohl and François Mitterrand over the idiosyncratic ideological opposition of Margaret Thatcher. Others point to Maastricht as the result of a concern to lock a newly reunified Germany into Europe.

The essence of geopolitical explanations for national preferences concerning economic cooperation lies in the linkage between economic policies and underlying politico-military goals. The focus is on indirect consequences of economic integration, termed by Joanne Gowa "security externalities."[13] Economic integration is not an end in itself but a means to manipulate "high politics." The goals of high politics may be objective, such as defense against an overt military threat to territorial integrity and political sovereignty, or subjective, as when a threat to territory or sovereignty is perceived as an affront to national identity. Whatever the security externalities, the core of the argument remains the same: governments are more likely to cooperate economically with those states with which they are "allied" in pursuit of a particular geopolitical goal. This theory

---

Katzenstein, ed., *Between Power and Plenty: Foreign Economic Policies of Advanced Industrial States* (Madison, Wisc., 1978), 295–336.

[13] Joanne Gowa, *Allies, Adversaries and International Trade* (Princeton, N.J., 1994); Joseph M. Grieco, *Cooperation among Nations: Europe, America and Non-Tariff Barriers to Trade* (Ithaca, N.Y., 1990). Gowa stresses such dynamics in bipolar systems but similar arguments have been advanced about multipolar Europe

Table 1.2. **National preference formation: Theories and hypotheses**

Dimensions	Geopolitical Ideas and Interests ("Security Externalities")	Economic Interest ("Endogenous Policy Theory")
Variation across issues and countries	Positions vary by country as a function of ideological commitment to federalism or perceived politico-military threat. Foreign policy and defense cooperation are particularly important issues. Generally Germany most favorable to integration, France less so, Britain least so	Endogenous policy theories predict that positions vary by both country and issue. In trade and agriculture, positions vary by producer concerns, with more regionally competitive producers favoring liberalization. In regulatory harmonization, positions vary by competitiveness and also wealth, with richer countries favoring high standards. In monetary policy, positions vary by country, with countries favoring cooperation when consistent with domestic inflation rates. In foreign and defense policy, predictions are the same as those of the geopolitical explanation.
Timing of shifts in preferences	Shifts in preferences and policies follow the onset and precede the resolution of major geopolitical events that reveal new information. Generally we expect over time that concern about the USSR or colonies declines; concern about Germany remains constant; concern about federalism may deepen.	Shifts in preferences and policies follow the onset and precede the resolution of major economic problems. Preferences for integration slowly intensify over time with rising trade flows, capital mobility, and policy convergence.
Policy consistency and negotiating demands	EC policy is consistent with concurrent geopolitical policies in other forums. Major bargaining demands are geopolitical, whereas major concessions may be economic.	EC policy is consistent with concurrent foreign economic policy. Major bargaining demands are economic, whereas major concessions may be geopolitical.
Domestic cleavages	Key actors are foreign and defense ministries, perhaps elite opinion, ruling parties, and chief executives. Major cleavages reflect divergent threat assessments or fundamental ideological beliefs (e.g., nationalist vs. internationalist, Communists vs. centrists).	Key actors are sectoral and factoral interest groups and economic officials, perhaps elite opinion, ruling parties, and chief executives. Major cleavages reflect concerns about competitiveness. Groups interested in regulation may become involved, particularly when well-organized or represented.
Content of domestic deliberations	A clear issue hierarchy leads officials to accord priority to efficient achievement of geopolitical goals. Efficient adaptation to security situation is seen as "necessary."	Lack of a clear hierarchy leads officials to accord priority to achievement of economic goals in economic issue-areas and geopolitical interests and ideas in foreign, defense, and sometimes institutional issue-areas. Adaptation to economic situation is seen as "necessary."

seems plausible because the international system is believed to be an anarchic and potentially dangerous place; hence threats to security and sovereignty remain at the top of a hierarchy of state motives, even when negotiating the price of wheat or the size of truck taillights. Studies of trade liberalization and monetary unions have concluded that geopolitical factors—a common security threat, shared interest in diffusing conflict, a "sense of solidarity"—are often decisive.[14]

The central prediction of this approach is that when economic integration is perceived to generate positive geopolitical externalities, governments tend to favor integration, whereas when integration is perceived to generate negative geopolitical externalities, they are more likely to oppose it. Within this broad approach, there remains considerable disagreement on the precise theoretical relationship between security threats and economic cooperation. Plausible geopolitical explanations of European integration fall into four theoretical categories. Each stresses the need to respond to a perceived geopolitical threat by manipulating the security externalities of economic integration, but the precise nature of the threat and response vary. Such explanations emphasize, respectively, responses to the Soviet threat, perceptions of global prestige and position, collective security *vis-à-vis* Germany, or European federalist ideology.

The first explanation, essentially neo-Realist, stresses the *balance of power*. In this view, integration is a means of strengthening cooperation among alliance partners against a common threat; in Cold War Europe, the preeminent threat stemmed from the Soviet Union and domestic Communist parties allied with it. Scholars have argued that where there is clear bilateral conflict, governments are more likely to consider geopolitical externalities; integration should correlate with the intensity of bilateral conflict. The simplest argument consistent with this view is that each government, particularly those of front-line states, employed economic cooperation to assure the assistance of allies in a crisis and to prevent any unilateral compromise with the adversary. West Germany was worried about abandonment; other European governments were concerned about the possibility that Germany would turn unilateralist or neutralist. A subtler variant, noting that alliances involve the exchange of policy concessions for support against threats, begins from the observation that all postwar German governments, regardless of their varied partisanship and ideologies, were critically dependent on allied support (or, at the very least, the absence of allied opposition) to realize specific goals *vis-à-vis* the USSR. These goals ranged from the restoration of sovereign equality and the defense of Berlin under Adenauer and Erhard to *Ostpolitik* under Kiesinger, Brandt, and Schmidt, and finally to reunification under Kohl and Genscher. Both variants see support for integration as a function of the immediacy of perceived politico-military threats and opportunities. The prediction follows that Germany is likely to be obliged to exchange economic policy concessions for geopolitical support.[15]

[14] Benjamin J. Cohen, "Beyond EMU: The Problem of Sustainability," *Economics and Politics* 5:2 (1993), 187–203; Daniel Verdier, *Democracy and International Trade* (Princeton, N.J., 1994), chap. 1.
[15] Robert J. Art, "Why Western Europe Needs the United States and NATO," *Political Science Quarterly* 111:1 (Spring 1996), 1–39; Timothy Garton Ash, *In Europe's Name: Germany and the Divided Continent* (New York, 1993). For a more general formulation consistent with this position, James D.

A second explanation, which combines Realist and ideational elements, stresses a different superpower balancing strategy. In this view, integration aimed to bolster the power and autonomy of Europe in a world dominated by superpowers—a line of reasoning, as we shall see, that Monnet, Adenauer, de Gaulle, and others often invoked rhetorically. The underlying purpose of integration was to support common foreign and defense policy-making through endeavors like the Fouchet Plan in the 1960s, European Political Cooperation (EPC) in the 1970s, and the Common Foreign and Security Policy in the 1990s. Joseph Grieco has extended this argument, contending that trade among potential adversaries is a zero-sum game. Recent steps toward integration, he maintains, "may in part be explained as an element of a Franco-Italian balancing strategy against Japan . . . and perhaps the United States."[16] Yet Realists concede that in a multipolar world and among middle powers, the choice of balancing strategies may be indeterminate: governments may seek to combine against the superpowers, as Grieco claims France and Italy did against the United States; they may bandwagon with a superpower, as the postwar British sought to do; or they may play both options against each other, as did postwar Germany. The precise outcome may well reflect ideological rather than structural factors.

From a Realist perspective it is therefore unsurprising that most analysts of postwar European foreign policy, most notably Stanley Hoffmann, have argued that the geopolitical interests of individual states must be traced to national values, historical analogies, and "lessons of history" distilled in the minds of leaders, political elites, and the mass public. Critical in such an explanation are historical attachments to former colonies, traditional relations with the superpowers, and salient experiences in World War II. Britain, which had survived the war without defeat and was decolonizing smoothly, sought to preserve "great power" status through maintenance of Commonwealth links and the special relationship with the United States. When this aim failed, British policy came to be driven by the diplomatic imperative of remaining "close to the heart of Europe." France, by contrast, sought to overcome its "historical memories" of wartime defeat and humiliation at Suez by promoting an independent Europe in which France could play a major role and by reinforcing links to the French Union. De Gaulle's repeated vetoes of British membership were designed to block entry of a Trojan horse for Anglo-American geopolitical interests. Germany, lacking an overseas colonial legacy, focused almost exclusively on Europe. German leaders sought to overcome the legacy of repeated German aggression, which encouraged close cooperation with its Western allies, not least the United States.[17]

Morrow, "Alliances and Asymmetry: An Alternative to the Capability Aggregation Model of Alliances," *American Journal of Political Science* 35:4 (November 1991), 904–933.

[16] Grieco, "State," 286, also 291–293; Grieco, "The Maastricht Treaty, Economic and Monetary Union and the Neo-Realist Research Program," *Review of International Studies* 21:1 (January 1995), 21–40; Wayne Sandholtz and John Zysman, "1992: Recasting the European Bargain," *World Politics* 42 (October 1989), 103–106. While Grieco speaks also of economic interest, his underlying theory suggests that "relative gains" ultimately reflect security threats. Grieco, *Cooperation*, 222–223.

[17] Stanley Hoffmann, "De Gaulle, Europe and the Atlantic Alliance," *International Organization* 18:1 (Winter 1964), 1–2, 16–19; Hoffmann, "Obstinate or Obsolete? The Fate of the Nation State and the Case of Western Europe," *Daedalus* 95 (Summer 1966), 892–908. For a more general for-

A third explanation, Institutionalist rather than Realist, treats integration as a regional arrangement—akin to but deeper than a collective security agreement—aimed at preventing conflict among its members. European governments have not balanced against such threats but have sought to engage threatening states and subsume them within a supranational institution. From the activities of wartime resistance groups and the rhetoric of the Schuman Plan to recent statements by Helmut Kohl, integration has been presented to European publics as a way to "anchor" or "bind" an increasingly powerful Germany into western Europe through ties of economic interest and legitimate institutions. Such ties, it was argued, would dampen any German interest in pursuing unilateral aggression or, at the very least, reassure Germany's neighbors. Proximity gave France and the Benelux countries a particularly strong reason to favor integration, but certain domestic groups in Germany may also support efforts to bind themselves to cooperative institutions. A *leitmotif* among German chancellors since Adenauer has been the role of European integration in protecting Germany against itself.[18]

The theoretical underpinnings of this view lie in the belief that integration nurtures shared economic interests, bolsters information flows, generates shared ideological norms, and imposes international institutional control over critical state activities. On this basis leading German scholars have proposed a law of international relations, parallel to the widely accepted claim that democracies do not wage war against one another, that governments embarked on a "process of federal union" do not fight wars.[19] Accordingly, the conviction that integration has been necessary to prevent another Franco-German war is often cited as a factor distinguishing regional integration in Europe from similar, less successful efforts elsewhere in the world. An idiosyncratic variant of this perspective has long enjoyed prominence in Britain: it sees British policy as directed at the disruption of a Franco-German alliance. This view is deeply influenced, the *Economist* recently observed, by the centuries-old "instinctive belief in the need to prevent the rise of a controlling power in Europe."[20]

A fourth and final geopolitical explanation, based on "ideational Liberal" or "Liberal constructivist" theory, stresses the relative strength of "European" and "nationalist" ideologies among elites and populations.[21] In this view, the relative

---

mulation consistent with this position, Dan Reiter, "Learning, Realism, and Alliances: The Weight of the Shadow of the Past," *World Politics* 46 (July 1994), 490–526.

[18] Ash, *Europe's*.

[19] For a debate, see Ernst-Otto Czempiel, "Kants Theorem oder Warum sind die Demokratien (noch immer) nicht friedlich?" and Andrew Moravcsik, "Federalism and Peace: A Structural Liberal Perspective," *Zeitschrift für internationale Beziehungen* 3:1 (Spring 1996), 79–101, 123–132. This assertion suffers from the obvious difficulty that all EC members are already democratic, hence the effect of federalism is redundant. See also Andrei Markovits and Simon Reich, *The German Predicament: Memory and Power in the New Europe* (Ithaca, N.Y., 1995); Altiero Spinelli, "The Growth of the European Movement since World War II," in C. Grove Haines, ed., *European Integration* (Baltimore, 1957), 48–49. Walter Lipgens, "The Major Political Consequences of the Second World War," in Lipgens, *A History of European Integration*, vol 1, *1945–1947* (Oxford 1982), 44ff.

[20] "A Question of Balance," *The Economist*, 3 January 1998, 57.

[21] Kjell Goldmann, "Nationalism and Internationalism in Post-Cold War Europe," *European Journal of International Relations* 3:3 (September 1997), 259–290, especially 269; Peter Katzenstein, "United

legitimacy of nationalist and European federalist thinking varies independently across countries and dictates the willingness of national politicians and publics to accept cooperation within federal European institutions. German, Italian, and Benelux leaders and citizens have traditionally been more favorable. French leaders and citizens have traditionally taken a middle position, exhibiting both strong opposition and strong support for European integration. I include this among geopolitical explanations because it is often impossible to distinguish this view from the second and third views examined just above. Underneath the surface, much ideological support for integration from Jean Monnet to Helmut Kohl rests on the complex, institutionally mediated calculation of its pacific effects. Andrei Markovits and Simon Reich remind us that the historical memory of most modern Europeans remains fixed on the "German problem"; postwar "Germany's actions have a particular immediacy [and its] actions are subject to unusual scrutiny."[22]

Such historical memories may be mediated in other ways. Some argue that the willingness to accept European experience reflects analogies drawn from domestic political traditions: a semisovereign, federal, corporatist, legalistic, militarily dependent country like Germany accepts EC institutions more readily than voluntaristic, centralized, administratively discretionary, and militarily more independent countries like France and Britain. Britain and Scandinavia are often viewed as distinctive by virtue of their strong commitment to parliamentary sovereignty.[23] Other analysts ascribe such cross-national differences to varying wartime experiences and (in parallel with the Realist argument) efforts by Christian Democratic parties to combat domestic communism (or communism within a divided state) by constructing an alternative form of popular internationalism. In this view centrist parties are likely to support integration, whereas parties of the extreme right and left were likely to oppose it. At the opposite extreme from Germany, such claims are commonly advanced with respect to Britain, the "awkward partner" of Europe, where many leaders and, though to a lesser extent, citizens remain skeptical of federalist schemes.[24]

To assess the empirical validity of these four widely accepted geopolitical explanations, it is tempting to reduce each to an objective measure of structural position — proximity to the Soviet Union or Germany, colonial legacy, Christian

---

Germany in an Integrating Europe," in Katzenstein, ed., *Tamed Power: Germany in Europe* (Ithaca, N.Y., 1997), 11–15, 24–29, 41–45. Also Walter Lipgens, *Die Anfänge der europäischen Einigungspolitik* (Stuttgart, 1977), 36; Thomas Risse, "Between the Euro and the Deutsche Mark: German Identity and the European Union," Georgetown Center for German and European Studies *Working Paper Series PS 1.3* (Washington, D.C., 1997); Karl W. Deutsch, "Supranational Organizations in the 1960s," *Journal of Common Market Studies* 1:3 (April 1963), 212–218; Spinelli, "Growth," 44–45.

[22] Markovits and Reich, *German*, 26, also 16–19, 26, 36–37: "Collective memory [is a] social bond among people whose shared experiences and contemporary experiences of the past form a crucial foundation of their community. . . . [It] loves to dwell on the negative. . . . We assert that in the formulation, conceptualization, and implementation of virtually every country's foreign policy, that country's collective memories will play a significant role."

[23] Katzenstein, "United," 33–45; Alberta Sbragia, "Maastricht, Enlargement and the Future of Institutional Change," *Ridgeway Viewpoints no. 93-3* (Pittsburgh, 1993).

[24] For an overview from this perspective, see Stephen George, *An Awkward Partner: Britain in the European Community* (Oxford, 1990).

Democratic influence, wartime military success—and test each in turn.[25] Yet to do so and, in particular, to test geopolitical explanations *against* ideational explanations would lead to the quick disconfirmation of strawmen without doing justice to existing geopolitical interpretations. Leading commentators have long maintained that European governments do not face unambiguous security threats. Instead threats are viewed through filters of ideology and historical memories of salient geopolitical events. Postwar European political ideologies have been so closely linked to objective geopolitical considerations—notably anticommunism, the German Problem, the desire to avoid another pan-European war, and distinctive global roles—as to be near indistinguishable empirically. Detailed historical debates concerning the motivations of leaders such as Adenauer, de Gaulle, and Monnet have failed to separate the two conclusively; a book on European integration is not the optimal place to reopen such debates. The convergence of objective and subjective assessments is consistent with contemporary theories about the role of ideas in foreign policy, which treat ideas as mechanisms for rational adaptation under uncertainty.[26]

I therefore treat the four arguments as variants of a single explanation. Evidence favoring any one counts as support for the role of geopolitics. At first glance, this formulation may appear vague, thereby undermining the validity of the findings. But the reverse is true. It ultimately *strengthens* our confidence in the validity of the causal inferences drawn here, because bundling geopolitical explanations makes it *easier* to find evidence for the importance of geopolitical factors. In short, I deliberately bias the study *against* the idea that commercial interest drives national preferences. The synthesis of these four explanations is facilitated by very substantial convergence of their predictions about the process and outcomes of national preference formation, including the timing of initiatives, the nature of domestic discourse, and the nature of the cleavages. To be sure, within each empirical chapter I note situations in which particularly strong evidence bears on specific explanations—from which, in the last chapter, I draw some tentative conclusions—but for the most part these four explanations are treated as mutually supportive.

From these geopolitical or "security externalities" explanations, predictions about national preferences can be derived across five dimensions of national

---

[25] It should be noted that geopolitical explanations of European integration suffer from two apparent weaknesses. First is a disjuncture between macro- and micro-analyses. Nearly all analyses of everyday decision-making in individual issue-areas—agricultural, environmental, social, monetary, trade policies, for example—stress the primacy of economic and regulatory interests; it is odd that this is not reflected in large decisions. Second is the absence of a plausible explanation for the deepening of European integration over time. All four specifications of geopolitical interests in postwar Europe—except perhaps European ideology, which remains roughly constant for long periods—suggest that the relevant geopolitical threats and distinctive national identities would decline or remain stable over time, whereas integration deepens.

[26] Examples include Wolfram Hanrieder, *Germany, America, Europe* (New Haven, Conn., 1989), 7; Hans-Peter Schwarz, *Adenauer*, 2 vols. (Stuttgart, 1986–1991); François Duchêne, *Jean Monnet: The First Statesman of Interdependence* (New York, 1995), 10. More generally, Reiter, "Learning"; Judith Goldstein and Robert Keohane, eds., *Ideas and Foreign Policy: Beliefs, Institutions, and Political Change* (Ithaca, N.Y., 1993); Yuen Khong, *Analogies at War: Korea, Munich, Dien Bien Phu, and the Vietnam Decisions of 1965* (Princeton, N.J., 1992).

preference formation: the pattern of preferences across countries, across issues, and across time; salient domestic divisions; and domestic discourse.

First, geopolitical explanations predict that governments subordinate specific economic interest to accommodate broad geopolitical goals. We should therefore observe *systematic variation across countries but not across issues.* Variation across countries should follow national politico-military policies. Within each country, support should be consistent across concrete economic issues. At least three of the four geopolitical factors suggest that Germany should be consistently pro-European, France less so, and Britain least. Germany has been a front-line state against the East, lacked a colonial legacy, suffered defeat and delegitimation in World War II, and nurtured a strong indigenous federalist sentiment centered in a powerful Christian Democratic party. Only collective security aimed at Germany is less clearly in the German interest, but the heavy cost of World War II and the overtly pro-Western sympathies of German political elites appear to have led elites to support integration as a form of reassurance. Postwar Britain, by contrast, found itself in the opposite position: comfortably distant from the Iron Curtain and from Germany and possessing an unparalleled colonial legacy, a tradition of parliamentary sovereignty, a weak federalist movement, and neither a Christian Democratic party nor a domestic communist opposition. Structural concerns would position the French in between Britain and Germany. France was nearer geographically to both the Soviet Union and Germany and had a colonial legacy; French governments saw national institutions called into question by wartime defeat and faced a strong domestic communist opposition. On the other hand, France had a tradition of centralization and only a weak Christian Democratic party.

The *timing* of major innovations in EC policy should reflect their role as a response to major geopolitical problems and an instrument of their resolution, while bearing little relation to fundamental economic trends and changes. Major changes in geopolitical situation should trigger shifts in European policy; major shifts in European policy should resolve major problems. The net trend over time is unclear. Colonial considerations decline quickly in the 1950s and 1960s. The Soviet threat also declines, interrupted briefly during the Berlin crises of the early 1960s and perhaps the nuclear missile controversies of the 1980s. Concern about Germany might be expected to rise with increases in German power and in particular the launching of *Ostpolitik* in the early 1970s. Popular support for European integration increases in the 1960s and 1980s; support for the European movement and ambitious federal schemes as ends in themselves declines among political elites over time. Christian Democratic parties play an important role in government in Germany but not in France or Britain.

On the third dimension, *policy consistency and negotiating demands,* the geopolitical explanation predicts that EC policy will be consistent with foreign and military policies, whether unilateral, bilateral, or global multilateral, not with broader foreign economic policy. Major negotiating demands should be geopolitical; major concessions should be, if possible, economic.

34

Turning to *domestic actors and cleavages*, the geopolitical explanation predicts that the chief executive will share primary responsibility for policy with the defense and foreign ministries, as well as elite and public opinion. These actors should advance major initiatives, take major decisions, and impose vetoes. Since defense and broad foreign policy goals are public goods, we should expect to see particularistic economic interest groups organized around them. Domestic cleavages should reflect divergent assessments of geopolitical threats. These may result from divergent technical considerations, from differences in the evaluation of the relationship between foreign and domestic policy (e.g., communists vs. centrists), and from conflicting ideologies of international relations (e.g., nationalists vs. internationalists).

Finally, the geopolitical theory predicts different sets of *salient concerns in domestic policy discourse*. Domestic deliberations should focus on the definition of politico-military objectives and the optimal means of achieving them. This basic position should be particularly evident in confidential deliberations among top decision-makers. Geopolitical accommodation is "inevitable."

Political Economic Interests

Whereas the geopolitical theory of national preferences focuses on the indirect consequences of economic integration, the political economic account stresses its *direct* consequences. Theories of political economy explain international cooperation as an effort to arrange mutually beneficial policy coordination among countries whose domestic policies have an impact on one another. In short, cooperation is a means for governments to restructure the pattern of economic policy externalities—the pattern of uninternalized consequences of national economic activities on foreign countries—to their mutual benefit. In the political economy view, policy externalities are transmitted by international markets. The pattern of externalities reflects not just the particular policies countries choose but also their relative positions in domestic and international markets. Where markets render preferred policies incompatible or permit a unilateral policy to be costlessly adjusted to achieve a particular goal, a zero-sum situation exists with little incentive for cooperation. Where, on the other hand, reciprocal policy adjustment can eliminate negative policy externalities or create positive ones more efficiently than unilateral responses, governments have an incentive to coordinate their activities. High tariffs, detailed regulations, or currency depreciation, for example, damage foreign exporters and so create the potential for cooperation.[27]

---

[27] Richard N. Cooper, "Interdependence and Coordination of Policies," in Cooper, *Economic Policy in an Interdependent World: Essays in World Economics* (Cambridge, Mass., 1986), 292–293; Keohane, *After*, 6, 83. The approach taken here is consistent with Keohane's "institutionalist" argument, though Keohane in fact seeks to explain the emergence of formal institutions, not patterns of cooperation per se. Institutions, Keohane argue, emerge when transaction costs create barriers to decentralized political exchange; the underlying role of policy externalities is assumed.

It is important to note that this is not a purely "economic" explanation. Most economists have viewed most of the major goals pursued by the EC over the years—among them a customs union rather than simple global liberalization, the common agricultural policy, and monetary union—with skepticism if not outright hostility.[28] The political economic explanation differs from a purely economic explanation in that it focuses on the distributional as well as the efficiency consequences of policy coordination. Often domestic conflict over economic policy coordination pits winners and losers from the shift in policy externalities induced by international cooperation against one another. The political power of certain groups, which may or may not reflect aggregate welfare, is an intervening variable between the calculation of economic costs and benefits, on the one hand, and policy outcomes, on the other.

Most important among these winners and losers are producers. The systematic political bias in favor of existing producer groups and against those, notably consumers, taxpayers, third-country producers, and also potential future producers, stems from the former's more intense, certain, and institutionally represented and organized interests. Producers may exert direct, instrumental pressure on politicians or may wield structural power, as when a desire to encourage business investment and growth requires the satisfaction of broad business demands. For the sake of simplicity, I assume throughout that domestic producers influence policy solely through the peak organizations representing three broad economic sectors: industry, agriculture, and services. By focusing on producer pressures, weighted only by their size and the intensity of gains and losses, this explanation remains deliberately simple, abstracting away from complex sectoral splits or "supply side" issues, such as varying levels of collective action, formal institutions, partisan competition, and issue linkage; it is designed to capture only the most fundamental of economic interests.[29]

Yet pressures from producers alone do not explain government policy. Instead, as Gary Becker and Samuel Peltzman have argued, governments promote pro-

---

[28] E.g., Michele Fratianni and Jürgen von Hagen, *The European Monetary System and European Monetary Union* (Boulder, Colo., 1992); Bela Balassa, *The Theory of Economic Integration* (London, 1961).

[29] Charles E. Lindblom, *Politics and Markets: The World's Political-Economic Systems* (New York, 1977). I seek to endogenize some of what are termed in most political economic analyses "supply-side" factors, notably geopolitical concerns of state officials. Both private and public institutions are treated as representative of societal interests. Where societal pressures are intense and powerful, private interests are assumed to be organized and governments narrowly constrained. Existing domestic organization is employed as a proxy: if, for example, wheat, sugar, and beef producers appear to possess disproportionate and stable amounts of political power in French peak agricultural interest groups, this fact is taken as given for French policy and hence for EC politics. "State" actors are treated as proxies for underlying social forces. The independence and anti-inflationary commitment of the Bundesbank, for example, stands in for the broadly accepted anti-inflationary preferences of the German public, which encumber any attempt to revise the bank statute. Similarly, British defense of national prerogatives stands in for elite and popular views about federalism and British sovereignty. Such a simple view of policy-making deliberately downplays collective action problems, log-rolling, and unintended consequences in the process of domestic preference formation. Endogenizing institutional variation would be a logical next step. For a more intensive discussion, see Robert O. Keohane and Helen V. Milner, eds., *Internationalization and Domestic Politics* (Cambridge, 1996); Suzanne Berger and Ronald Dore, eds., *National Diversity and Global Capitalism* (Ithaca, N.Y., 1996).

ducer interests within broad constraints set by general demands for regulatory protection, economic efficiency, and fiscal responsibility.[30] In this view, one objective of foreign economic policy is to maintain and improve the competitiveness of national producers; another is to achieve regulatory objectives and limit government spending. Domestic policies favoring producers, for example subsidies or permissive legislation, are constrained either by the government's fiscal limitations or by conflict with general regulatory objectives. This view suggests a simple explanation of foreign economic policy-making in which governments promote commercial interests until confronted with an intolerable fiscal burden or a conflict with strong regulatory preferences. The decision to cooperate should thus be preceded by pressure from domestic producers and by the overt failure of unilateral policies to achieve domestic regulatory or fiscal objectives. In the political economy view, competitiveness concerns and policy failure combine to catalyze cooperation.

The relative importance of regulatory and fiscal constraints *vis-à-vis* commercial considerations varies across issues. To simplify analysis of the shifting balance between the two, I assume that their relative importance in EC politics parallels their relative importance in domestic politics. Governments committed to a particular balance between, say, economic liberalism and environmental protection at home will pursue the same balance internationally. The strength of commitment to goals such as tariff liberalization, financial liberalization, and monetary discipline at home is employed as a measure of their importance for a government in international negotiations.

The four policies at the core of European economic integration over the past four decades have been agricultural trade liberalization, industrial trade liberalization, the removal of regulatory trade barriers, and exchange-rate stabilization. There is general agreement that in postwar European domestic politics, the direct power of producers *vis-à-vis* fiscal or regulatory concerns has been strongest in agriculture, which has won large, nearly universal subsidies in every country; less strong in industrial trade policy, where subsidies are more modest and uneven; and even less strong both in regulatory policy, such as environmental policy, where independent preferences for regulatory goals play an important role, and in exchange-rate policy, where preferences for high and lower inflation embedded in domestic labor and fiscal practices play an important role in national policy. I assume the same spectrum when governments choose EC policies. In the case of agricultural and some industrial policy, producers tend to be highly mobilized and governments are limited primarily by overall economic efficiency, which is reflected in the fiscal burden of subsidization. In regulatory policy, governments are slightly more constrained by public policy goals, which can be summarized by dividing EC members into rich countries with high

---

[30] In recent years a synthesis has emerged, in which both rent-seeking pressures and efficiency concerns play a role in the rational calculations of policy-makers. Gary S. Becker, "A Theory of Competition among Pressure Groups," *Quarterly Journal of Economics* 98 (1983), 372–399; Samuel Peltzman, "The Economic Theory of Regulation after a Decade of Deregulation," *Brookings Papers on Economic Activity* (1989), 1–41; Giandomenico Majone, *Regulating Europe* (London, 1996), 28–45.

standards and poorer countries with lower standards. Finally, in the case of monetary policy, the many producer preferences are less sharply defined, whereas the constraints imposed by the general macroeconomic preferences and performance of different countries are more important.

The Sources of Preferences concerning Trade Policy Coordination

The political economy perspective suggests that international policy coordination is a means to secure commercial advantages for producer groups, subject to regulatory and budgetary constraints. Modern theories of foreign trade policy suggest that trade liberalization is driven primarily by opportunities for profitable international trade and investment, though constrained by the domestic and international distributional consequences of permitting such transactions. Governments seek multilateral trade liberalization when it is no longer possible to realize producer interests unilaterally. The most important reason is that foreign cooperation is required to open up export markets. Unilateral trade liberalization, while almost universally recommended by economists, is rarely a politically viable policy for any but extremely competitive countries in sectors of greatest competitive advantage. Increased export opportunities offset the political costs and risks of greater imports. International cooperation may also provide "two-level" political legitimation and institutional support for governments in less competitive countries seeking to liberalize.

A simple explanation of trade policy based on these premises can be constructed by assuming that economic investments are specific to particular uses in the short term and that their value is primarily influenced by the scope of the market in which they compete. Producer demands reflect the competitive position of national producers in international markets. Internationally competitive producers favor liberalization; all other things being equal, governments favor the benefits from increased exports. To a first approximation, the greater the exports and export opportunities and the more competitive are domestic export producers, the more intense the pressure for trade liberalization. This rule holds whether we are speaking of "at the border" measures like tariffs and quotas or of regulatory barriers to trade. With the decline of tariffs or quotas, the political economy view predicts the emergence of greater pressure from competitive producers to liberalize or harmonize other types of regulations. More competitive producers, particularly in industries with high economies of scale, will particularly tend to favor the elimination of differentials through harmonization of national regulations.

Such demands are balanced, however, by the difficulty of forcing adjustment on uncompetitive, import-competing producers. The greater the level of potential imports, the lower current profit levels, the higher the levels of surplus capacity, and the more intense the cyclical downturn or long-term decline, the greater will be the domestic pressure for protection and subsidies. In postwar Europe, for example, we should see German industrialists and French farmers, respectively the largest and most competitive potential net export sectors of the two countries' respective national economies, pressing most strongly for liberalization of European trade. Such pressure should be particularly strong during periods of relatively high growth and industrial profits, such as the 1950s, 1960s, and late 1980s.

We expect trade liberalization to generate more support when it creates fewer *net* losers, which occurs when costs and benefits are internalized within individual sectors and firms, thereby avoiding the imposition of large concentrated losses on particular domestic groups. Such patterns of intra-industry trade tend to arise in technologically sophisticated industrial sectors with extensive foreign direct investment, diversification, high growth, and scale economies.[31] Hence, we should expect the acquiescence of import-competing producers to be easier to obtain with regard to industrial trade liberalization than with regard to agricultural liberalization.

Relations with third countries create the same sort of incentives. The greater the competitiveness of third-country producers, the greater the pressure for external protection and regional liberalization, both of which divert trade toward member countries. In industrial sectors, for example, where many postwar European countries were globally competitive, the pressure for trade diversion through external protection is likely to be lower than in agriculture, where many domestic producers are competitive in Europe but uncompetitive globally. Trade diversion places producers in excluded countries at a disadvantage, thereby increasing their incentive to oppose or to join an exclusive regional bloc. The more competitive the producers and the higher the level of trade diversion, the greater the concern. EC discrimination in the 1960s against U.S. and British Commonwealth agricultural commodities, as well as British industrial products, is an important example.[32]

Following conventional theories of collective action, the analysis above assumes that policies are biased in favor of those actors with concentrated, intense, and clearly preexisting interests and against those with more diffuse, uncertain, or unrepresented interests. In the latter category belong consumers, taxpayers, and third-country producers. Liberalization is facilitated when its costs can be offloaded onto such groups. Yet such diffuse groups are not infinitely malleable. If rents for producer groups become extremely high, taxpayers and consumers are more likely to rebel. The interests of nonproducers therefore impose a loose constraint on national trade policies. Under what conditions should such constraints limit policy?[33]

We may simplify the analysis of broad constraints by limiting them to two cases. First, the demands of business groups for protection must give way in the face of an overt failure of unilateral policies to promote competitiveness and sol-

---

[31] Helen V. Milner, *Resisting Protectionism: Global Industry and the Politics of International Trade* (Princeton, N.J., 1988); Elhanan Helpman and Paul Krugman, *Market Structure and Foreign Trade: Increasing Returns, Imperfect Competition and the International Economy* (Cambridge, Mass., 1985); Réal Lavergne, *The Political Economy of US Tariffs: An Empirical Analysis* (New York, 1983), chaps. 5, 7.

[32] Robert Z. Lawrence, *Regionalism, Multilateralism, and Deeper Integration* (Washington, D.C., 1996), 28; Robert A. Mundell, "Tariff Preferences and the Terms of Trade," *Manchester School of Economic and Social Studies* 32 (1964), 1–13. See also chapters 2 and 3 of this book.

[33] James Q. Wilson, "The Politics of Regulation," in Wilson, ed., *The Politics of Regulation* (New York, 1980), 366ff.

vency. In other words, governments will resist pressures for liberalization on behalf of relatively uncompetitive industries unwilling to adjust as long as the cost of the direct subsidies that render such resistance possible remains tolerable. Only when the potential for increasing subsidies to uncompetitive sectors is exhausted will governments consider liberalization.

Second, nonproducers generally impose a tighter constraint on policy coordination if the unilateral policies in question take the form of regulatory standards rather than "at the border" measures such as tariffs and quotas. Such negotiations may mobilize not just producers but organized public interest groups and parties that favor particular environmental, consumer, or heath and safety regulations. Such matters can generate a powerful electoral response. To simplify the analysis, we assume that the height of regulatory protection is a function of the per capita wealth of a country, with more wealthy countries favoring higher levels of domestic protection across the board. Wealthier countries favor international harmonization at higher standards, whereas poorer countries prefer harmonization at lower standards. Such two-dimensional conflicts—with splits between competitive and uncompetitive producers and between high- and low-standard countries—can lead to the formation of complex and curious domestic coalitions, such as so-called Baptist-Bootlegger alliances between protectionists and supporters of high regulatory protection.[34]

There are good prima facie reasons to believe that the incentives described in this simple explanation of trade policy played a significant role in postwar Western Europe, which faced radically shifting commercial opportunities.[35] The most salient trend in post-1945 international political economy has been a vast increase in opportunities for profitable trade among industrialized countries, an increase linked to historically high growth rates. This postwar trade boom in manufactures altered both the geographical direction of trade and the sources of competitive advantage. The focus of the commercial relations of developed countries shifted from peripheral areas to the metropolitan core, with the percentage of world trade among industrialized countries expanding from 46 percent in 1955 to 62 percent in 1990. Half the increase occurred before 1963 within a network of increasing intra-industry trade opportunities focused around Germany. Trade among EC countries would subsequently rise from 38 percent of GDP in 1960 to 57 percent of GDP in 1991, again with the bulk of the shift in the 1950s and early 1960s. It rose again in the late 1980s. Econometric analyses attribute a relatively small percentage of this rise to trade liberalization. The trend begins very early in the postwar period, before significant trade liberalization had occurred, and extends to countries outside regional trading blocs in

---

[34] David Vogel, *Trading Up* (Cambridge, Mass., 1995).

[35] Not only did postwar West European governments face expanding export opportunities; they were also committed, to a much greater extent than previously, to the provision of minimal social welfare for all groups in society. These groups included farmers, whose role in the rise of interwar fascism was considerable, and workers, for whom communism provided an attractive alternative. The relative importance of these two factors cannot be fully assessed here, since it would require comparison with cases in which this commitment did not exist. See Alan S. Milward, *The European Rescue of the Nation-State* (Berkeley, 1992).

Scandinavia and North America, as well as those, like Britain and France, that continued to maintain imperial trading preferences.[36]

The primary gains from trade were found in manufactured goods sectors. Trade in manufactures expanded roughly twice as fast as GDP, rising as a share of world exports from 35 percent in the 1950s to over 60 percent in the mid-1980s. By contrast, agricultural exports declined from 25 to 15 percent, and mineral and energy exports (even with oil price inflation) fell from 40 to 24 percent. In part these changes reflected rapid industrialization, high growth rates, and increasing competitiveness in Latin countries such as France, Italy, and, later, Spain. By 1988 the level of trade in manufactured goods, at 32 percent of GDP, had almost returned to its historic high prior to World War I. This boom was accompanied by increased intra-industry trade, driven by increased product differentiation, economies of scale, and importation of intermediate goods. In Europe intra-industry trade was particularly high, reaching 60 percent by the 1980s, when the tendency was bolstered by a direct investment boom among developed countries.[37]

The political economic approach provides a plausible prima facie explanation of the preferences of postwar European governments for the launching and progressive deepening of the EC. From the 1950s through the 1990s, as trade and investment in Europe expanded, we should expect to see major EC member countries converge slowly toward greater openness in industrial trade. Policies of the major EC countries should converge at different rates, depending on the national percentage of trade with Europe and the competitiveness of local industry. Broadly speaking, we should expect Germany strongly to favor pan-European trade liberalization in industrial goods, with relatively open policies toward third countries, and to oppose agricultural trade liberalization. France and Italy should support agricultural trade liberalization within a protected preferential trading area, preferably at moderate price levels, while accepting industrial trade liberalization with initial caution but accelerating confidence. Britain, with relatively low but rapidly rising levels of exports to Europe, should initially be relatively apathetic about European industrial trade liberalization but rapidly grow more concerned as trading patterns shift. Britain should strongly oppose a high external tariff on agricultural commodities, which would undermine existing Commonwealth relations. Exclusion from a growing industrial trade area should be the worst outcome for each nation.

The Sources of Preferences concerning Exchange-Rate Stabilization

EC monetary cooperation has been directed primarily at the stabilization of nominal exchange rates. It has taken the form of two pegged exchange-rate sys-

---

[36] Michael Chisholm, *Britain on the Edge of Europe* (London, 1995), 14–17; Milward, *European*; Jeffrey A. Frankel, Ernesto Stein, and Shang-Jin Wei, "Regional Trading Arrangements: Natural or Supernatural?" *American Economic Review* 86:2 (May 1996), 52–57.

[37] Commission of the European Communities, "International Trade of the European Community," *European Economy* 39 (1989), 14; United Nations Center on Transnational Corporations, *World Investment Report 1991: The Triad in Foreign Direct Investment* (New York, 1991), pp. 4ff; Jacques Pelkmans,

tems established in the 1970s, the Snake and the EMS, and plans for a single currency set forth in the Maastricht Treaty.

What political economic incentives might lead governments to seek such exchange-rate arrangements? As in the case of trade policy, I shall not present a fully developed model of macroeconomic policy, only the minimal, "first-cut" theory required to generate predictions about the process, timing, and distribution of national preferences concerning exchange-rate stabilization. As in the case of trade policy, my argument is not that there is a compelling macroeconomic or microeconomic justification for exchange-rate stabilization or monetary union but that monetary cooperation helps governments achieve certain political economic goals.[38]

A simple political economy of preferences for (and against) exchange-rate stabilization can be constructed on the basis of three variables: capital mobility, patterns of trade interdependence, and convergence or divergence among expected domestic inflation rates. This outline is consistent with the general political economy approach toward regulatory issues employed in this book, which considers pressures from producers directly influenced by international interdependence, on the one hand, and general regulatory, fiscal, and public goods concerns, on the other. The analysis begins with the same basic intuition as in trade policy, namely that governments seek to promote the most intense preferences held by producers. Yet in exchange-rate politics, as I argued above, specific macroeconomic goals are more important, relative to direct commercial interests, than they are in trade policy. Many accounts focus only on capital mobility and trade interdependence, but it is the convergence and divergence among inflation rates that proves critical. Rising capital mobility, along with high trade, increases the tension between exchange-rate stability and domestic macroeconomic autonomy, as well as eroding the advantages of the latter—not least the capacity of governments to maintain artificially low interest rates. Trade interdependence creates modest incentives to reduce exchange-rate volatility but not necessarily to stabilize exchange rates, which can be costly for exposed sectors of the economy, particularly in weak-currency countries.

With the first two factors—patterns of capital and trade interdependence—indeterminate, the third becomes critical. Given capital mobility and liberal trade, a binding external exchange-rate constraint requires convergent rates of domestic inflation or, at least, a prior commitment to rapid convergence, lest unsustainable costs be imposed on the internationally competitive sectors in economies of countries that would otherwise permit their currency to depreciate. Yet EC governments have often experienced divergent underlying rates of inflation, which are deeply embedded in domestic institutions and expectations

---

Market Integration in the European Community (London, 1984), 64–114; GATT, *International Trade*, various editions (Geneva, 1980–1995), Table A.3.

[38] On skepticism among economists, see Barry Eichengreen and Jeffry Frieden, "The Political Economy of European Monetary Integration: An Analytical Introduction," in Eichengreen and Frieden, eds., *The Political Economy of European Monetary Integration* (Boulder, Colo., 1994), 5; Paul Krugman, "Policy Problems in a Monetary Union," in Paul de Grauwe and Loukas Papademos, eds., *The European Monetary System in the 1990s* (London, 1990), 62.

governing wage-setting, public spending, and monetary policy. Domestic reform to alter inflation rates can be a slow and costly process; until governments commit to, and to a substantial extent succeed in, reducing inflation, there is little reason to believe that binding external monetary constraints are sustainable. Below I consider the impact of the first two factors, capital and trade interdependence, then the impact of macroeconomic convergence.

We begin with the macroeconomic impact of rising capital and trade flows. A government facing a balance-of-payments deficit (or surplus) has three broad policy options: it can impose (relax) trade and capital controls, permit the currency to depreciate (appreciate), or tighten (loosen) domestic fiscal and monetary discipline. To explain the choice among these options, many analyses of European monetary cooperation begin with the insight, drawn from the Mundell-Fleming analysis of exchange-rate policy, that a government cannot target all three of these policy objectives at once. In sum, free flows of capital and trade, nominal exchange-rate stability, and domestic macroeconomic autonomy comprise a so-called inconsistent trio. A government can simultaneously target any two of these goals but not all three.[39]

Until the late 1950s European governments restricted trade and capital flows, permitting European governments to maintain fixed rates and widely divergent macroeconomic policies, along with low interest rates particularly directed at industrial investment—an arrangement that required, however, external subsidies. The European Payments Union, a clearing arrangement among the nonconvertible European currencies of the time, was financed in part by the United States. To maintain equilibrium, weak-currency countries repeatedly imposed trade barriers and capital restrictions.[40]

Over the next two decades, most analysts agree, increases in trade and capital flows rendered restrictions on either progressively more costly and less effective. On balance, as the inconsistent trio predicts, this change appears to have created a steeper trade-off between nominal exchange-rate stability and domestic macroeconomic autonomy.[41] It rendered nominal exchange-rate stability more costly and, therefore, less likely. This, combined with external shocks like high wage settlements, the oil crises, and the collapse of Bretton Woods, led to a period of considerable nominal exchange-rate instability lasting for almost two decades after 1971.

---

[39] Another short-term option is to finance the deficit (or encourage capital exports). For an overview of the trade-offs, see Robert Mundell, "The Monetary Dynamics of International Adjustment under Fixed and Flexible Exchange Rates," *Quarterly Journal of Economics* (1960), 227–257; W. Max Corden, "Monetary Integration," *Princeton Essays in International Finance* 93 (Princeton, N.J., 1972). For an overview and admirably clear explication of the literature, see Kathleen R. McNamara, *The Currency of Ideas: Monetary Politics in the European Union* (Ithaca, N.Y., 1997).

[40] On distinctive national adaptation and change over time, John Zysman, *Governments, Markets and Growth: Financial Systems and the Politics of Industrial Change* (Ithaca, N.Y., 1983); Katzenstein, ed., *Between Power and Plenty*; John Goodman and Louis Pauly, "The Obsolescence of Capital Controls? Economic Management in an Age of Global Markets," *World Politics* 46:1 (October 1993), 50–82.

[41] Goodman and Pauly, "Obsolescence"; Michael C. Webb, "International Economic Structures, Government Interests, and International Coordination of Macroeconomic Adjustment Policies," *International Organization* 45:3 (Spring 1991), 309–342.

Rising trade and capital flows did not simply steepen the trade-off between exchange-rate stability and macroeconomic autonomy; they also progressively degraded the value of macroeconomic autonomy altogether—whether or not exchange rates remained stable.[42] Increasingly costly measures (among them segmented financial markets, draconian controls, rationing, and large domestic subsidies) failed to offset the tendency of international capital markets to equalize covered interest rates. This trend has been attributed to increased transnationalization of production, which permits multinational firms to evade capital controls and trade restrictions. It surely reflected also the more inflationary and disruptive economic environment of the 1970s and 1980s, in the face of which interventionist governments lacked the political will to resist public spending or to compel large firms, particularly nationalized ones, to rationalize—resulting in an unsustainable expansion of state-subsidized industrial finance in France and Italy. The trend may also have been pushed along by financial liberalization radiating outward from the United States.[43]

Whatever its precise causes, the period from the late 1970s onward witnessed a steady movement in nearly all European countries, whether or not they were members of the EC or of common exchange-rate arrangements, toward higher, more market-driven interest rates. Interest rates came increasingly to reflect business cycles and risk premia, not government targets. Except in circumstances where currencies were greatly overvalued, depreciation came increasingly to be linked to *higher* underlying real interest rates—not lower ones, as had previously been the case—because it undermined confidence and led to the imposition of risk premia on international capital markets. By 1986 all but very short-term interest-rate differentials between domestic and offshore markets had disappeared.[44]

According to the Mundell-Fleming framework, a rise in capital mobility does not necessarily generate net macroeconomic incentives for nominal exchange-rate stability. The incentives facing governments are indeterminate. Rising interdependence increases the amount of domestic macroeconomic autonomy that must be sacrificed to stabilize exchange rates, thereby *discouraging* exchange-rate stability, but also reduces the value of macroeconomic autonomy by undermining the influence of policy on domestic interest rates, thereby *encouraging* exchange-rate stabilization. In order to assess the claim empirically, we must specify more precisely the relative values of macroeconomic autonomy and exchange-rate stability.[45]

[42] Jeffry Frieden, "The Impact of Goods and Capital Market Integration on European Monetary Politics," *Comparative Political Studies* 29 (April 1996), 193–222; Robert Mundell, "Capital Mobility and Stabilization Policy under Fixed and Floating Exchange Rates," *Canadian Journal of Economics and Political Science* 29 (1963), 475–485.

[43] Goodman and Pauly, "Obsolesence"; Louis W. Pauly, *Opening Financial Markets: Banking Politics on the Pacific Rim* (Ithaca, N.Y., 1988); Michael Loriaux, *France after Hegemony: International Change and Financial Reform* (Ithaca, N.Y., 1991). Loriaux attributes the external shock to the decline of Bretton Woods, but rising inflation, oil shocks, and lower growth may also explain the shift.

[44] David M. Andrews, "Capital Mobility and Monetary Adjustment in Western Europe, 1973–1991," *Policy Sciences* 27 (1994), 425–445.

[45] Accordingly macroeconomic analyses tend to treat the implications of monetary cooperation as indeterminate or insignificant. See, for example, Alberto Giovannini, "Economic and Monetary

To this end, and still maintaining the basic Mundell-Fleming assumptions, we may consider the microeconomic impact of rising trade interdependence on exchange-rate preferences among specific economic groups. Here indeterminacy is reduced, but the theory predicts that increasing trade interdependence will stimulate net political pressures *against* exchange-rate stabilization. To see why this is so, let us assume an open economy with specific assets (fixed economic investments) and relatively high trade and capital interdependence. Under such conditions, Jeffry Frieden has argued, producer preferences can be predicted from shifts induced by exchange-rate policy in the relative prices of traded and nontraded goods (and services).[46] The greater the magnitude of interdependence, the greater will be the gains or losses and the more intense the demands directed at governments.

Producers have preferences, Frieden argues, across two characteristics of the exchange rate: level and stability. As regards the level of exchange rates, a low value of the domestic currency increases the competitiveness of goods traded internationally. Traded goods producers (exporters and import-competing firms) tend therefore to favor a weak domestic currency to bolster their competitiveness and increase the relative price of traded goods domestically. Producers of goods and services not traded across borders, by contrast, favor a strong currency, which bolsters the relative prices of their goods domestically and internationally. Nontraded goods producers can be thought of as consumers; a strong currency permits them to purchase more traded goods. Investors are said also to support a strong currency, which expands their purchasing power abroad. As regards exchange-rate stability, exporters and foreign investors prefer a stable currency, which reduces their exchange-rate risk and transaction costs. Nontradable and import-competing producers prefer flexible rates, which permit macroeconomic stimulation beneficial to them. Combining concerns about level and stability, exporters prefer low, stable exchange rates; import-competing producers prefer low and flexible rates; producers of nontraded goods and services prefer high and flexible rates; and, finally, international financiers and importers prefer high and stable rates.

Without further assumptions about the relative weight of various groups and the resolution of conflicts among them, the theory does not generate determinate predictions. Increasing exposure to international markets confronts many groups with competing concerns; tradable goods producers in countries in which currencies would otherwise depreciate, for example, will see an advantage in stable but potentially uncompetitive exchange rates *and* in more competitive but less stable ones.

What additional assumptions seem plausible?[47] We might begin by assuming

---

Union: What Happened? Exploring the Political Dimension of Optimum Currency Areas," in Centre for Economic Policy Research, *The Monetary Future of Europe* (London, 1993).

[46] Jeffry A. Frieden, "Invested Interests: The Politics of National Economic Policies in a World of Global Finance," *International Organization* 45:4 (Summer 1991), 425–452; Carsten Hefeker, *Interest Groups and Monetary Integration: The Political Economy of Exchange Regime Choice* (Boulder, Colo., 1996).

[47] Giovannini, "Economic," suggests the problem is inherently indeterminate; McNamara, *Currency*, 56–71, suggests that the role of shifting economic preferences, perhaps grounded in new ideas, is critical. Here I seek to maintain the economic emphasis of the model.

that tradable goods producers are more intensely concerned about the level of the exchange rate (preferably low) than its stability, since significant price effects are likely to outweigh transaction costs for all except risky, long-term, international investments and contracts. Numerous scholars have presented empirical evidence suggesting that welfare gains from the reduction of transaction costs, even in a highly interdependent region such as Western Europe, remain low.[48] Key producer groups in exchange-rate politics, namely tradable goods producers, seek two goals: they seek a *competitive* real exchange rate and, only if that goal is met, a *stable* real exchange rate. We might further assume that the preferences of importers and investor goods producers are less intense than those of tradable goods producers. Using the same logic of collective action we employed in examining trade policy, it is likely that the highly differentiated and diffuse nature of consumers will render them a less cohesive and committed group than producers. For their part, foreign investors tend to have ambivalent preferences concerning the level of exchange rates, because the consequences of exchange-rate shifts depend on the direction and expected duration of the investment, which determines whether they are investing or repatriating funds.

Let us summarize the analysis so far. We may conclude that rising trade and capital interdependence, taken by themselves, do not provide a convincing explanation for the progressive stabilization of exchange rates. Additional assumptions render the explanation slightly more determinate, but insofar as they do, they tend on balance to *undermine* the prediction that as economies become more open, national interests converge toward support for exchange-rate stability. The tendency of "cross-border investors, traders, and exporters of specialized manufactured products . . . to favor exchange-rate stability to reduce risk" is likely to be more than offset by the incentive for traded-goods producers, particular in traditionally weak-currency countries, to seek more competitive exchange rates through greater flexibility.[49] Rising trade interdependence creates modest incentives to reduce exchange-rate volatility but creates incentives to stabilize exchange rates if and only if the gains from reducing volatility overpower the costs to some actors of exchange-rate misalignments.

A political economic explanation of the move to exchange-rate stabilization in Europe must therefore make assumptions about underlying domestic inflation rates and the attitudes of governments toward those rates.[50] Why inflation rates? If nominal parities are fixed—which is what an exchange-rate peg or a single currency is designed to do—the inflation rate relative to other participants in the arrangement determines the appreciation (or depreciation) of the (real) exchange rate, which directly influences the welfare of producers and the value of macroeconomic autonomy. If Germany and Italy, say, fix their exchange rates and the Italian inflation rate is much higher than that of Germany, Italy will

---

[48] Daniel Gros and Niels Thygesen, *European Monetary Integration: From the European Monetary System towards Monetary Union* (London, 1991); McNamara, *Currency*, 37ff.

[49] Frieden, "Impact," 203. Based on such a model, Frieden concludes that rising economic interdependence increases pressure from producers for exchange-rate stabilization.

[50] The strength of a currency is, of course, also influenced by the structure of trade and payments.

grow less competitive externally; the cost of Italian exports in Deutsche marks will increase and the cost of German imports in lire will decrease.[51] In other words, the primary weakness of an analysis based entirely on capital and trade interdependence is that it entirely overlooks the domestic adjustments governments must undertake during the *transition* to exchange-rate stability.

The costs and benefits of nominal exchange-rate stability vary across countries, depending on whether the prevailing domestic inflation rate is above or below that to which they would converge and on the costs of convergence toward that common rate. Governments seek to target particular inflation rates, which vary across countries with the organization of labor, the nature of the central bank, the partisan complexion of the ruling coalition, and public opinion.[52] Domestic alignments will vary accordingly, with the alignments in high-inflation countries being close to the mirror image of those in low-inflation countries.

In countries with relatively low inflation, such as postwar West Germany, exchange-rate stability blocks nominal appreciation, thereby inducing real undervaluation of the currency. Assuming exchange-rate stabilization does not generate higher inflation—an assumption that we shall reconsider below—traded goods producers in low-inflation countries have a clear incentive to support cooperation, which provides them with their ideal outcome, namely a low and stable exchange rate. International investors, primarily interested in stability, will join them. Even producers of nontradable goods would probably benefit from the income effects of a boost to exports and perhaps from lower interest rates. Those who support low inflation will be likely to oppose exchange-rate cooperation, whereas those who support higher inflation will support it.

In countries with relatively high inflation and a weak currency, such as France, Italy, or Britain during most of the 1970s and 1980s, exchange-rate cooperation tends to impede nominal depreciation, thereby inducing real overvaluation of the currency. Exports become more costly, imported goods cheaper. Exporters and import-competing and nontradables producers have an incentive to oppose fixed exchange rates, because higher inflation undermines competitiveness and may perhaps also push interest rates up to the higher levels required to defend the currency against speculation. Only some importers and investors have a clear incentive to demand currency stabilization. The level of opposition is likely to be greatest when there is pressure on both the capital and the current accounts, which has generally occurred in postwar Europe during periods of dollar weakness that undermine Europe's global competitiveness and trigger transnational capital flows out of weak currencies and into stronger ones.[53]

Under conditions of trade and capital interdependence, prior convergence of inflation rates or, at the very least, a willingness to converge rapidly toward

---

[51] This is because import and export prices tend to shift more rapidly than do domestic prices.

[52] Geoffrey Garrett and Peter Lange, "Political Responses to Interdependence: What's "Left" for the Left?" *International Organization* 45:4 (Autumn 1991), 539–564; John T. Wooley, *Monetary Politics: The Federal Reserve and the Politics of Monetary Policy* (Cambridge, 1984).

[53] A more precise analysis depends on price elasticities, as well as the sources of inflation. On the latter, see Giovannini, "Economic."

similar rates, is required to ensure widespread support for an exchange-rate stabilization arrangement that does more than accommodate inflationary differentials. Where countries have widely disparate inflation rates, commercial concerns are unlikely to induce more than modest exchange-rate coordination
aimed at dampening volatility, a secondary goal of exporters and importers. A
partial exception might arise where a government is pursuing a "two-level" strategy to establish greater credibility for efforts to reform macroeconomic institutions and practices aimed either at lowering inflation in high-inflation countries
or at raising it in low-inflation countries; but even in this case, the expectation
that inflation will soon be reduced would be a precondition for cooperation. In
sum, either prior inflationary convergence *or* a combination of concerns about
competitiveness in strong-currency countries combined with efforts to implement fundamental reforms in weak-currency countries is required to explain the
emergence of international support for nominal exchange-rate stabilization.

Taken together, capital mobility, trade flows, and inflationary convergence
provide a prima facie explanation of the progressive shift in national preferences away from, then back toward, exchange-rate cooperation over the two
decades following the collapse of Bretton Woods. This period saw an increase in
economic openness and, beginning in the late 1970s, convergence toward low
inflation. European disinflation was a painful, crisis-ridden process lasting over
a decade, in which a series of policy alternatives had to be shown by trial and error to be ineffective. A comprehensive analysis of the sources of pressures for
disinflation in Europe during the 1970s and 1980s takes us beyond the scope of
this book. Did disinflation reflect a rising consensus among politicians and
producer groups after each oil shock that reductions in government spending,
industrial subsidies, wage settlements, and social welfare burden were preconditions for renewed investment and economic growth? or rising economic interdependence, which generated incentives to maintain external competitiveness while reducing the ability of governments to shield domestic interest rates
from inflation for extended periods of time? or a change in economic ideas and
ideology? For our purposes it is essential only that convergence toward such
norms was an exogenous factor, that is, it occurred whether or not countries
were members of international institutions such as the EC.[54]

From this explanation follow predictions concerning international alliances,
domestic cleavages, and timing of initiatives. Internationally, this explanation
predicts that EC monetary negotiations should induce divisions between high-
and low-inflation countries, with each coalition seeking to shift the burden of
adjustment onto the other. If we assume that each country is committed to
its current inflation rate and adjustment away from it is costly, we should observe higher-inflation countries such as France and Italy seeking to oblige low-
inflation countries such as Germany and the Netherlands to accept higher
inflation or currency appreciation in order to relax the overall constraint on the
value of linked currencies. Low-inflation countries such as Germany should seek
to oblige high-inflation countries such as France and Italy to accept lower infla-

[54] McNamara, *Currency.*

tion. The intensity of such conflicts, which reflects the extent to which inflation rates diverge, may result in demands to exclude governments with extreme macroeconomic preferences or performance from exchange-rate arrangements.

Domestically, the political economy approach predicts that we will observe coalitions among tradable goods producers and governmental authorities responsible for and concerned about macroeconomic policy (whether chief executives, central banks, or political parties). In strong-currency countries, the more governments favor higher government spending and the more competitive pressure tradable goods producers face, the greater their support for exchange-rate stabilization. Central banks and others committed to low inflation and a strong currency should oppose coordination. In weak-currency countries, by contrast, the more governments favor austerity and the less competitive pressure producers face, the more each should favor monetary cooperation. Those committed to high inflation or increased government spending, notably extreme leftist parties and relatively uncompetitive sectors, should oppose exchange-rate stabilization. The most favorable domestic alignment is thus one in which inflation rates are relatively convergent *and* in which the government in a strong-currency country such as Germany seeks a looser macroeconomic policy and the government in a weak-currency country favors a tighter policy, *and* in which there is general competitive pressure, as in situations of dollar depreciation.

If reductions in currency volatility and increased policy credibility for domestic macroeconomic reform are, alongside the level of the currency, primary policy goals, why should a government prefer international monetary cooperation to unilateral policies, such as monetary targeting, fiscal restraint, central bank independence, or a unilateral monetary peg? This question is examined in more detail below, in the section on institutional choice; here I briefly mention a few points consistent with the preference analysis above. One is that international cooperation may reduce volatility by providing reserves and coordinated intervention to governments facing unruly capital markets. Another is that international cooperation may permit a compromise arrangement that facilitates adjustment by both strong- and weak-currency countries. Still another, and most plausible, is that international constraints may appear more credible, politically and economically, than do domestic ones.

Hypotheses Derived from the Political Economy Theory

As compared to the geopolitical or "security externalities" approach, the political economy explanation generates contrasting predictions across the five distinct dimensions of national preference formation: variation in preferences across nations and issues, the timing of preference changes, consistency with broader foreign policy, salient domestic actors and cleavages, and major considerations mentioned in domestic deliberations.

On the first dimension, *cross-issue and cross-national variation*, the political economic approach predicts that national positions will vary by issue and by country, following the nature and intensity of economic incentives. On trade and agriculture, countries will tend to favor liberalization in those areas where they are regionally competitive. On issues of regulatory harmonization and nontariff barrier reduction, commercial incentives are balanced by autonomous preferences for regulatory protection, with richer countries defending higher standards. Monetary policy generates conflict between strong- and weak-currency countries, with concerns about competitiveness and the level of macroeconomic convergence dictating the level of support for cooperation. Only in matters with little or no calculable impact on economic interests, such as parliamentary powers or foreign and defense policy, does political economy theory generate predictions similar to those of the geopolitical theory. Since issue-specific interests prevail, "high politics" concerns will dominate the latter area.

On the second dimension, *timing*, shifts in preferences should follow the onset and precede the resolution of shifts or trends in economic circumstances. Changes in European policy should correlate with major changes in economic circumstances or domestic policy reversals. Over the longer term, rising economic interdependence and new opportunities for profitable cross-border transactions should strengthen incentives to deepen trade liberalization; to the extent these are combined with convergence on macroeconomic performance, the trend should encourage exchange-rate stabilization as well.

On the third dimension, *policy consistency and negotiating demands*, we should expect that governments will pursue a regional EC policy consistent with their unilateral, bilateral, and global multilateral policies rather than one consistent with their geopolitical policies. Negotiating tactics should employ geopolitical concessions to achieve economic ends, not the reverse.

On the fourth dimension, *domestic actors and cleavages*, the political economic theory predicts that economic interest groups and economic officials, along with ruling parties and chief executives, will take the lead in formulating policy. In trade policy, domestic cleavages divide competitive from noncompetitive firms; in regulatory harmonization, cleavages divide those in favor of regulation from those opposed; and in monetary policy, cleavages divide economic sectors (tradable vs. nontradable goods), branches of government (independent financial authorities vs. those concerned with spending), and political parties or factions supportive or opposed to inflation.

On the fifth dimension, *negotiating demands and salient concerns in domestic policy discourse*, the political economic theory predicts confidential policy discourse among top decision-makers about the efficient attainment of economic objectives. Economic accommodation should be viewed as "inevitable"; geopolitical constraints or rhetoric as malleable. We should see geopolitical rhetoric adapted to support economic objectives, not the reverse.

INTERSTATE BARGAINING: EXPLAINING EFFICIENCY AND DISTRIBUTION

Having examined competing explanations of national preferences, the first stage of the rationalist framework of international cooperation, we turn now to the second stage: interstate bargaining. National preferences are often heterogeneous. How, then, can we explain the specific terms of the substantive bargains on which governments agree?

For this purpose we may usefully treat treaty-amending negotiations as bargaining games over the precise terms of mutually beneficial cooperation. Such negotiations tend to be, in game-theoretical language, coordination games with distributional consequences.[55] In such bargaining games, the configuration of (domestically determined) national preferences defines a "bargaining space" of potentially ratifiable agreements—all of which are equilibrium outcomes, that is, all governments prefer them to unilateral or coalitional alternatives. Generally there are numerous such agreements extending out to and along a Pareto frontier of efficient bargains, in which all possible joint gains have been exploited. Since alternative Pareto-improving agreements generally impose differential gains and losses on countries, governments are rarely indifferent among them. Thus they often dispute the precise nature of policy coordination, its speed and scope, and the associated side payments. Interstate negotiation is the process of international collective choice through which potential agreements are identified and one is selected.

Systematic study of bargaining requires a common metric by which to measure the results. Two dimensions of bargaining outcomes are of particular interest: *efficiency* and *the distribution of gains*. Efficiency and distribution lie at the heart of nearly all analyses of international negotiation, whether drawn from international regime theory, negotiation analysis, or abstract bargaining theory. David Lax and James Sebenius distinguish "creating" and "claiming" value, Stephen Krasner movement "toward" and "along" the Pareto frontier, James Morrow "informational" and "distributional" dimensions of international cooperation, Fritz Scharpf "production" and "distributive" dimensions of negotiated agreements, and Richard Walton and Robert McKersie "integrative" and "distributive" bargaining—to name only a few such distinctions.[56]

These efficiency and distributive dimensions correspond to the two types of analytic questions most often asked about international negotiations. The first dimension concerns interstate efficiency: Did governments exploit all potential agreements or were gains "left on the table"? In economic terminology, were interstate negotiations Pareto-efficient?[57] The second dimension concerns interstate distribution: How were the benefits of cooperation divided among the parties? In common language, who "won" and who "lost" the negotiations? To measure distributional outcomes, I employ relative measures: I ask which actor was perceived to benefit most from the "core" bargain (relative to their best uni-

[55] This is the core of modern bargaining and negotiation analysis. See Raiffa, *Art*; James K. Sebenius, "Negotiation Analysis," in Victor A. Kremenyuk, ed., *International Negotiations: Analysis, Approaches, Issues* (San Francisco, 1991), 203–215; Krasner, "Global."

[56] These two elements of negotiation—efficiency and distribution—are often closely related in practice. David A. Lax and James K. Sebenius, *The Manager as Negotiator: Bargaining for Cooperation and Competitive Gain* (New York, 1986), chap. 6; Morrow, "Modeling," 387–423; Scharpf, *Games*, 120–121; Richard E. Walton and Robert B. McKersie, *A Behavioral Theory of Labor Negotiations: An Analysis of a Social Interaction System* (New York, 1965).

[57] On "nondecisions" and measurement issues, see footnote 91 below.

lateral alternative to agreement)—a customs union in the 1950s, agricultural cooperation in the 1960s, pegged exchange rates in the 1970s, nontariff barrier removal in the 1980s, monetary union in the 1990s—and which actors garnered the most important marginal concessions and side-payments outside the core bargain. In each case this determination was relatively uncontroversial among the participants, though there is sometimes subsequent disagreement among analysts.

This book concentrates on two competing theories that explain the efficiency and distributional outcomes of EC negotiations. These theories seek to distill the core of two major informal approaches to explaining negotiations in the European Community and in international regimes more generally. In accordance with common usage, I term one *supranational* bargaining theory, the other *intergovernmental* bargaining theory. Although these labels invoke a language specific to theories of regional integration, the underlying theoretical questions are general: What assumptions should explanations of international economic negotiations make about the distribution of information, the sources of bargaining power, and the resulting influence of political entrepreneurs? The predictions of bargaining theory are notoriously sensitive to shifting assumptions about the information, strategies, and tactics available to actors, as well as their preferences, yet few analyses of EC negotiations render such assumptions explicit.[58] The differences between the two theories are in fact stark.

The supranational theory, drawn from a strand of neofunctionalism that continues to dominate much theoretical writing on European integration, stresses the decisive role of leading supranational officials, among them Jean Monnet and Jacques Delors, in providing the political entrepreneurship needed to overcome inefficient bargaining and to influence distributional outcomes. The supply of information provided by entrepreneurs imposes the binding constraint on the efficiency and distributional outcomes of cooperation. The intergovernmental theory maintains the converse. The underlying demand for cooperation, not the entrepreneurial supply of information, imposes a binding constraint on negotiations. Efficiency is relatively unproblematic because interested governments are able to act as their own political entrepreneurs. Instead negotiators focus primarily on the distribution of benefits, which are decisively shaped by the relative power of national governments, understood in terms of asymmetrical policy interdependence. Patterns of interdependence underlie credible threats to veto, exit, and exclude other governments as well as, though secondarily, linkages between issues and offers of side-payments. In sum, the supranational view assumes that transaction costs are high relative to the gains from agreement for all actors except supranational officials, whereas the intergovernmental view assuming they are low and that therefore the pattern of state pref-

---

[58] For a critique along these lines, Barry Eichengreen and Jeffry Frieden, "The Political Economy of European Monetary Integration: Introduction," *Economics and Politics* 5:2 (1993), 93. More generally, John Harsanyi, *Rational Behavior and Bargaining Equilibrium in Games and Social Situations* (Cambridge, 1977), 6; Scharpf, *Games*, chap. 6.

erences and power—in particular the opportunity costs of foregoing agreement—is the decisive determinant of specific agreements.

Despite the existence of these two strikingly different theories, scholarship on European integration has yet to derive or test falsifiable propositions about treaty-amending bargains from either perspective.[59] Most existing studies of EC bargaining simply observe the tactics of actors said to be influential. Intergovernmental explanations often speak of Germany, France, or Britain as "powerful" or "influential" in negotiations, but such claims are rarely demonstrated by specifying what resources convey "power" or which outcomes demonstrate that one country has been influential. We shall see that this tendency can lead to dubious deductions. In the Maastricht negotiations, for example, most political scientists have concluded—despite the contrary perceptions of participants—that Germany fared poorly in the negotiations. Most such studies, I argue in chapter 6, are misleading because they fail to ground an assessment of gains and losses in a careful, structured analysis of German preferences, and because they generalize from a biased sample of the (relatively few) issues in which Germany did make concessions.

Similarly, many studies conclude that supranational leadership constitutes a "necessary" condition for integration, but nearly all demonstrate only that a supranational entrepreneur attempted to propose initiatives, mediate between governments, and mobilize societal groups, and that some proposals by supranational authorities eventually were accepted. What they do not show is that supranational actors were *essential* actors. Supranational efforts may also be redundant, a coincidental consequence of the EC's institutional structure, with member governments and private groups willing to supply initiatives, mediation, and mobilization whenever supranational actions do not suit them. Or supranational action may be symbolic and pose no binding constraint on common policies. Or supranational actors may "rationally anticipate" member-state opposition, tailoring or revising proposals to fit national preferences—hence their independent influence is nil. For Commissioners and parliamentarians, agreements often constitute an undesirable choice. Monnet himself counseled entrepreneurs always to choose "the path of least resistance."[60]

More rigorous analysis is required. To establish that the privileged access of supranational actors to information actually alters the efficiency or distributional consequences of negotiations, we must pose an explicit counterfactual: What would the outcome have been in the absence of supranational entrepreneurship? Would initiative, mediation, and mobilization nonetheless have been

---

[59] Though the two theories are distinct, the difference between them is dimensional not dichotomous. If transaction costs are moderately high or variable across issues, it is possible for both theories to contribute to an explanation of bargaining outcomes. Two studies that hint at this are Geoffrey Garrett and Barry Weingast, "Ideas, Interests and Institutions: Constructing the European Community's Internal Market," in Goldstein and Keohane, *Ideas*, 173–206; George Ross, *Jacques Delors and European Integration* (Oxford, 1995).

[60] Commission of the European Communities, *Hommage à Émile Noël, Secrétaire général de la Commission européenne* (Luxembourg, 1988), 23.

provided? Existing studies do not address this question explicitly. Thus, however intriguing and plausible their speculations, they offer little firm ground on which to base conclusions.[61] To overcome these weaknesses, this book tests more precise hypotheses about causal processes and mechanisms by which supranational entrepreneurs wield influence. The supranational and intergovernmental bargaining theories generate competing predictions, summarized in Table 1.3. These predictions fall into three dimensions: the availability of information, the process of negotiation, and the pattern of outcomes. Below, drawing on theories of bargaining and negotiation, international regimes, and regional integration, I specify supranational and intergovernmental explanations more precisely and derive these three types of competing hypotheses from them.

Supranational Bargaining Theory: Influence through Persuasive Information and Ideas

From the early work of Ernst Haas to the present, the decisive importance of supranational officials in EC bargaining remains what one analyst has termed "the most common and far-reaching claim" found in scholarship on the EC.[62] The existence of autonomous supranational officials based in the EC Commission—the appointed, Brussels-based executive bureaucracy that oversees EC rules—as well as the Parliament and Court is said to distinguish the EC from other international organizations and to help explain its success. Without the decisive intervention of such officials, major EC negotiations would have remained mired at a lowest common denominator of narrow national and group interests. Supranational entrepreneurship of this kind is particularly essential to the neofunctionalist understanding of integration, which treats integration as a process of self-sustaining and often unintended feedback. Interstate bargains, it is argued, result not from intentional choice on the part of governments but from the unforeseen consequences of large, complex negotiations among linked issues known as "package deals." An organization such as the Commission is necessary to assure that agreement emerges. It is also empowered by those

[61] In this regard it is striking that the results of some of the most sophisticated studies that claim to demonstrate supranational influence, once analyzed with attention to counterfactuals, appear not just inconclusive but in fact to disconfirm the "necessary" role of supranational officials. E.g., Wayne Sandholtz, *High-Tech Europe: The Politics of International Cooperation* (Berkeley, 1992), concl.

[62] Mark Pollack, "The Commission as an Agent," in Neill Nugent, ed., *At the Heart of the Union: Studies of the European Commission* (New York, 1997), 121. There are literally dozens of interpretations of EC as driven by leadership, many of which are cited in the empirical chapters of this book. A representative sample of theoretically explicit works includes Ernst B. Haas, *The Uniting of Europe: Political, Social and Economic Forces, 1950–1957* (Stanford, Calif., 1958); Leon N. Lindberg, *The Political Dynamics of European Economic Integration* (Stanford, Calif., 1963); Wayne Sandholtz, "Institutions and Collective Action: The New Telecommunications in Western Europe," *World Politics* 45:2 (January 1993), 242–270; Neill Nugent, "The Leadership Capacity of the European Commission," *Journal of European Public Policy* 2:4 (December 1995), 603–623; Mark Pollack, "Delegation, Agency and Agenda Setting in the European Community," *International Organization* 51:1 (Winter 1997), 99–134; Ross, *Jacques*; Garrett and Weingast, "Ideas"; Janne Haaland Matláry, "The Commission as Policy-Maker: The Need to Venture beyond State-Centric Integration Theory," CICERO *Working Paper 1995:5* (Oslo, 1995).

Table 1.3. Interstate bargaining: Theories and hypotheses

Dimensions	Supranational Bargaining Theory	Intergovernmental Bargaining Theory
Underlying distribution of information and ideas	Scarcity and asymmetry of technical, political, and legal information and ideas, relative to stakes, leave states less informed than EC officials. EC officials benefit from greater neutrality, political skill, technical expertise, administrative coherence or centrality in transnational networks. National positions should be unstable, due to changes in available information during negotiations.	Low cost relative to stakes means that information and ideas are widely and evenly distributed among national of governments and members of domestic coalitions, with no supranational advantage. Residual asymmetries reflect the relative intensity of preferences concerning the issue in question. National positions are thus stable.
Negotiating process	Scarcity of information and ideas means that national governments cannot provide optimal levels of policy entrepreneurship. We observe too few innovative proposals, insufficient mediation among states, or inadequate mobilization of domestic coalitions. Supranational entrepreneurs exploit their comparative advantage and fill the gap. Negotiations are concerned largely with achieving an efficient outcome.	The most interested national governments and societal groups can act as effective policy entrepreneurs. They initiate, mediate, and mobilize domestic coalitions. Supranational entrepreneurs enjoy no comparative advantage in entrepreneurship. Negotiations focus almost exclusively on the distribution of gains.
Outcomes: Efficiency and distribution	Pareto-efficient agreements require supranational intervention, particularly where innovative proposals, complex linkages ("package deals"), or intense distributional conflict are involved. Agreements are systematically biased toward outcomes preferred by supranational actors. Complex linkages ("package deals) are easily achieved, but only with assistance from supranational officials.	Agreements are efficient even without supranational intervention. Governments that gain the most offer the most significant compromises or side-payments. Concessions on the margin are systematically biased toward outcomes preferred by governments least likely to support the "core" agreement. Where credible for threatening countries and costly to the target governments, threats of exit and exclusion shift the outcome toward the states making the threat. Domestic opposition from losers limits cross-issue linkages ("package deals"). Even within issue-areas, linked concessions are unlikely where the preferences of groups are intense—as with farmers. The more powerful the group, the more likely a linkage will impose costs on unorganized or unrepresented groups, such as consumers, taxpayers, or third-country producers.

agreements that emerge, driving integration further forward through a process of political spillover.[63]

Perhaps unsurprisingly, this view is most widespread among policy-makers themselves. Lord Arthur Cockfield, the active vice president of the Commission under Delors, restates it as a generalization. "If the Commission is ineffective, as tragically it was during the Thorne Presidency, the Community languishes. Where you have a forceful and visionary President, as Jacques Delors has been, backed by a strong and effective Commission, the Community makes progress."[64] More specifically, many assert—this was, for example, Monnet's view—that Commission entrepreneurship is needed to assure that the outcome reflects the general welfare of Europeans rather than particularistic interests.[65] In the 1960s and 1970s such interpretations stressed the intervention of supranational officials such as Monnet, Walter Hallstein, Sicco Mansholt, and Roy Jenkins.

More recently dozens of leading scholars have revived this argument to explain the EC's dynamism in the 1980s, which they attribute to strong Commissioners such as Jacques Delors, Etienne Davignon, and Arthur Cockfield, as well as the European Court of Justice and European Parliament. Of these analysts, Wayne Sandholtz and John Zysman go furthest, asserting that supranational entrepreneurship has been a "necessary" condition for integration; it transformed a "contingent" and "indeterminate" set of structural preconditions into "a common European interest and bargain." They single out entrepreneurship as the only aspect of EC decision-making about which scholars can advance causal arguments. "Without leadership," Sandholtz writes, "the demand for cooperation will remain latent."[66]

Supranational political entrepreneurs can exercise leadership in three ways. From the founding of Jean Monnet's Action Committee in 1956 to Jacques Delors's activism in the 1980s, supranational actors have consistently sought to advance proposals, mediate compromises, and mobilize domestic groups. They may *initiate* negotiations by advancing proposals that call the attention of governments to common problems and potential solutions that may serve as the basis for negotiation. Cockfield's 1985 White Paper, which assembled 287 proposals for single-market liberalization, became the heart of the Europe 1992 initiative. Supranational entrepreneurs *mediate* among governments by working with them to develop compromise proposals. From Commission activism during the negotiation of the CAP, detailed in Leon Lindberg's classic 1963 study, to the Delors Committee on EMU, the Commission is often closely involved in Treaty-amending negotiations. Finally, supranational entrepreneurs *mobilize* domestic politicians, officials, interest groups, and partisan or public opinion in favor of specific policies through the selective dissemination of ideas and information. Many commentators argue that the Commission has repeatedly ex-

---

[63] Ernst B. Haas, "Technocracy, Pluralism and the New Europe," in Stephen R. Graubard, ed., *A New Europe?* (Boston, 1964), 62–88; Haas, *Uniting*, 158ff, 451ff.

[64] Lord Arthur Cockfield, *The European Union: Creating the Single Market* (London, 1994), 23.

[65] For a sophisticated view, see Majone, *Regulating*, 74–79.

[66] Sandholtz, *High-Tech*, 303; Sandholtz and Zysman, "1992," 128.

ploited its central position to foster elite networks of firms and economic interest groups to support proposed reforms.[67] In the 1960s the Commission is said to have made "very full use of its right to direct access to the European Parliament and to the press and other opinion-forming media" to publicize its position, thereby breaking down the monopoly on information held previously by national governments.[68]

The analytic assumptions underlying such claims about supranational entrepreneurship, despite widespread acceptance, are rarely made explicit; to test the theory rigorously, more precision is required. The extensive theoretical literature in negotiation analysis, international regime theory, international law, and American politics devoted to the role of third-party political entrepreneurs as agenda-setters, mediators, and mobilizers in international negotiations suggests that three assumptions underlie such claims.[69]

The first assumption is that bargaining power in international negotiations stems in large part from the generation and manipulation of information and ideas. Since supranational actors lack large financial resources or a credible threat of military intervention (as in, say, superpower involvement in the Middle East) or a formal right of initiative, adjudication, or participation (as in the everyday EC legislative process), the only instrument available to them in Treaty-amending negotiations is the manipulation of information and ideas. As Monnet observed: "I know no other rule except to persuade and be persuaded."[70] The information and ideas that permit supranational entrepreneurs to act as initiators, mediators, and mobilizers can be technical, legal, or political. Technical information and ideas concern the nature of policy problems grounded in scientific analysis or plausible ideas about cause-and-effect relations. Legal information and ideas concern the regulatory and institutional tools, domestic and international, with which policy is made. Political information and ideas concern the nature and manipulation of the preferences, strategies, and influence of national governments or domestic actors.[71]

The second assumption is that information and ideas necessary to reach par-

[67] Ross, *Jacques*; Maria Green Cowles, "The Politics of Big Business in the European Community: Setting the Agenda for a New Europe" (diss., American University, 1994).

[68] Miriam Camps, *What Kind of Europe? The Community since De Gaulle's Veto* (London, 1965), 43.

[69] For a comprehensive overview of this literature and a more detailed elaboration of the theoretical argument concerning entrepreneurship against which this book argues, see Andrew Moravcsik, "Informal Influence: What Can We Learn from the Failures of International Entrepreneurs?" *Weatherhead Center for International Affairs Working Paper Series* (Cambridge, Mass., 1998). For general theoretical work, see Oran Young, "The Politics of International Regime Formation: Managing Natural Resources and the Environment," *International Organization* 43:3 (Summer 1989), 349–376; Abram Chayes and Antonia Handler Chayes, *The New Sovereignty: Compliance with International Regulatory Agreements* (Cambridge, Mass., 1995); L. N. Antrim and James K. Sebenius, "Formal Individual Mediation and the Negotiators' Dilemma: Tommy Koh at the Law of the Sea Conference," in Jacob Bercovitch and Jeffrey Z. Rubin, eds., *Mediation in International Relations: Multiple Approaches to Conflict Management* (New York, 1992), 97–130; Saadia Touval and I. William Zartman, eds., *International Mediation in Theory and Practice*, SAIS Papers in International Affairs, no. 6 (Boulder, Colo., 1985).

[70] Jean Monnet, *Mémoires* (Paris, 1976), 475.

[71] In the absence of force or material resources, successful mediators require information, legitimacy, or expertise. Rubin, "Conclusion: International Mediation in Context," in Bercovitch and Rubin, *Mediation*, 259–269.

ticular negotiated outcomes are costly and scarce for governments and their constituents. The *ex ante* transaction costs of negotiation—the costs of bargaining and contracting efficiently—must be high. Following the Coase Theorem, the centerpiece of modern functional theory of international organization, the influence of supranational entrepreneurs stems from the existence of a "bottleneck" in the generation of the technical, political, or legal information or ideas required to initiate, mediate, and mobilize negotiations. If information and ideas were available at low cost, entrepreneurial initiation, mediation, and mobilization would be necessary but trivial functions. Interested parties, such as national governments and societal groups, would automatically provide optimal levels of leadership—as indeed intergovernmental theorists argue they do. The Coase Theorem reminds us, and empirical studies reconfirm, that where transaction costs are low, negotiations among self-interested actors with clear property rights tend to generate efficient outcomes. In short, any analysis of entrepreneurial activity must begin by specifying the barriers to the resolution of conflict facing the primary stakeholders themselves.[72]

The third assumption is that centralized supranational authorities enjoy privileged access to information and ideas. If supranational actors lack a comparative advantage in generating or manipulating information and ideas, there is no reason to expect them to be more effective than national governments in providing entrepreneurial leadership. If supranational actors can generate information more efficiently (but cannot manipulate its nature or dissemination), we might expect them to increase the efficiency of agreements—to expand the "problem-solving capacity" of the EC, as technocratic language has it. If supranational actors have distinctive preferences and can generate or disseminate information selectively, they may also influence distributive outcomes. Such arguments are central to many analyses of the Commission. Brigid Laffan argues that "knowledge and expertise . . . play a particularly central role in the EU policy process. . . . The Commission uses knowledge in a particularly sophisticated way."[73]

The core of a theory of supranational entrepreneurship must, therefore, be its explanation of why supranational entrepreneurs might enjoy a comparative advantage over states in the generation and dissemination of critical information and ideas. Such arguments fall into three categories, depending on whether they stress creativity, trust, or communication.[74] Arguments stressing creativity see supranational actors as more ingenious, imaginative, flexible, and skillful— a view consistent with Cockfield's assessment. Others attribute greater creativity to culture. George Ross, for example, argues that Delors was effective because

---

[72] Joseph Farrell, "Information and the Coase Theorem," *Journal of Economic Perspectives* 1:2 (Fall 1987), 113–121; Howard Raiffa, *Lectures on Negotiation Analysis* (forthcoming); Keohane, *After*, 85–88; Robert Mnookin and Lee Ross, "Introduction," in Kenneth Arrow, Robert H. Mnookin, Lee Ross, Amos Tversky, and Robert Wilson, eds., *Barriers to Conflict Resolution* (New York, 1995), 3–24.

[73] Cited in Janne Haaland Matláry, "The Role of the Commission: A Theoretical Discussion," in Neill Nugent, ed., *At the Heart of the Union: Studies of the European Commission* (New York, 1997), 275.

[74] For a more thorough treatment, Moravcsik, "Informal Influence."

he and his team came from the unique French political culture of technocratic voluntarism.[75]

Arguments stressing trust maintain that governments and domestic interest groups have strategic incentives to withhold vital information, leaving each without full knowledge about the pattern of preferences and, therefore, about potential compromises. A reputation for or incentive toward neutrality permits supranational officials to act as effective mediators, helping actors to overcome the "preference revelation" problem.[76] For this reason, Monnet himself sought to mobilize only what he viewed as "disinterested" social groups, including European federalists, Socialist parties, and trade unions. Lindberg, following Monnet, asserts that "only . . . institutions representing the 'general interest' are in a position to mediate between the national viewpoints effectively" and "represent the Community interest"—a technocratic perspective common in Brussels.[77] Sebenius generalizes the point to all international bargaining, arguing that there is "an inescapable tension between cooperative moves to create value jointly and competitive moves to gain individual advantage," within which "excessive value-claiming" may lead to inefficient outcomes.[78]

Arguments stressing communication hold that information is costly to coordinate and exchange among a larger number of actors; it can be more efficiently provided by a single, centralized source. Lindberg points to the Commission's "technical competence [that] ensures that its proposals command the serious attention of the member governments." Consistent with Haas's belief that modern industrial economies require centralized, technocratic planning, the Commission's comparative advantage could stem from its position "at the center of an [institutionalized] network of knowledge"—an "epistemic community" of substantive, technical, and legal experts.[79]

If, for whatever combination of reasons, the three core assumptions of the supranational bargaining theory hold—the distribution of information and ideas drives negotiated outcomes, the transaction costs for states of generating and distributing information are high, and supranational actors enjoy a comparative advantage in such generation and distribution—there is good reason to believe that supranational actors may enjoy bargaining power in intergovernmental negotiations. If they do not hold, the supranational model is theoretically inappropriate and empirically disconfirmed. We can observe whether the assumptions hold by observing the process of negotiation.

---

[75] Ross, *Jacques*, 51–77.

[76] Farrell, "Information."

[77] Monnet, *Memoirs*, 406, also 414. Also Lindberg, *Political*, 210; Young, "Politics," 357–359; Antrim and Sebenius, "Formal," 126–128; Keith Middlemas, ed., *Orchestrating Europe: The Informal Politics of the European Union, 1973–1995* (New York, 1995), 238.

[78] James K. Sebenius, "Challenging Conventional Explanations of International Cooperation: Negotiation Analysis and the Case of Epistemic Communities," *International Organization* 46:1 (Winter 1992), 330–331.

[79] Ernst Haas, *Uniting*, 300; Peter Haas, "Introduction: Epistemic Communities and International Policy Coordination," *International Organization* 46:1 (Winter 1992), 1–36. Also Chayes and Chayes, *New Sovereignty*.

Let us summarize the hypotheses above, found also in Table 1.3. On the first dimension, *the availability of information*, supranational bargaining theory predicts that the *ex ante* transaction costs of bargaining—the costs of generating necessary information and ideas for efficient agreement—are high relative to the benefits of agreement. Supranational actors, moreover, enjoy a privileged access to such information and ideas. We should therefore observe that technical, legal, and political information and ideas are distributed asymmetrically, unavailable not to all interested states but only to supranational actors because of the latter's greater expertise, recognized neutrality, or privileged position in transnational networks. Critical ideas and information are introduced into negotiations primarily by supranational actors.

On the second dimension, *bottlenecks and the role of entrepreneurship*, we should observe high transaction costs leading to suboptimal or biased provision of innovative initiatives, compromise proposals, and social mobilization—particularly when connected with a "general" or diffuse interest. The provision of information and ideas by supranational officials helps overcome these biases. Thus governments' negotiating positions change as new information is provided.

On the third dimension, the *pattern of negotiated outcomes*, three predictions follow. First, negotiated agreements tend to be Pareto-suboptimal except when supranational entrepreneurs intervene with new information and ideas. Second, where supranational actors are able to manipulate the available information, outcomes are likely to be systematically biased in favor of their preferences. Third, governments are unlikely to threaten exit or exclusion but are instead committed to current institutions within which they can act to "upgrade the common interest." Supranational bargaining theory makes no specific predictions about linkages, except that they are likely to be mediated by supranational actors—though neofunctionalists do stress the role of linkages and "upgrading the common interest."

Intergovernmental Bargaining Theory: Influence through Asymmetrical Interdependence

The intergovernmental explanation focuses not on the availability of information and the intervention of supranational entrepreneurs but on the issue-specific distribution of bargaining power, which in turn reflects the nature and intensity of state preferences. The literature on European integration often invokes the "power" of one country or another to explain outcomes but rarely specifies such claims in precise terms. I seek to specify interstate bargaining power more precisely by drawing on the basic insight underlying formal theories of bargaining, namely that the pattern of preference intensity or "asymmetrical interdependence" dictates the relative value each state places on an agreement, which in turn dictates its respective willingness to make concessions.

Intergovernmental bargaining theory rests on three assumptions. First, treaty-amending negotiations take place within a noncoercive system of unanimous voting in which governments can and will reject agreements that would leave them worse off than unilateral policies. Like most international treaty changes,

EC treaty amendments require unanimous agreement and subsequent ratification by each member-state. Unlike the EC's everyday legislative process—which can involve formal procedures such as majority voting, unique formal agenda-setting powers for the Commission and Parliament, and regulatory and legal oversight by the EC Commission and Court—treaty amendments are subject to essentially no procedural constraints.[80] Each government can support an agreement, veto it, opt out, or seek to form an alternative coalition with a subset of governments. We assume, moreover, that military coercion, punitive economic sanctions, and noncredible threats of withdrawal are not cost-effective negotiating tactics among European democracies. Since coercion is limited and any rational government would veto any outcome that would leave it worse off, we can assume that negotiations are Pareto-improving as compared to the unilateral or coalitional alternatives. (These joint gains are not measured relative to the *status quo ante*, or to some normative notion of fairness, it should always be remembered, but to the existing alternatives. A government may therefore accept an outcome worse than the *status quo ante* if that outcome improves on the future outcome that would have resulted from unilateral policies.) Since joint gains are presumed to exist—otherwise negotiations would not take place—we can assume that governments are concerned to avoid a potential collapse of negotiations due to exogenous causes, a result that would leave all worse off.

Second, intergovernmental theory assumes that the transaction costs of generating information and ideas are low relative to the benefits of interstate cooperation. The information and ideas required for efficient bargaining are plentiful and cheap. The range of potential agreements, national preferences, and institutional options can thus be assumed to be common knowledge among governments. This assumption is plausible because, at least among modern European democracies, state officials wield large financial and technical resources to generate extensive technical, political, and legal information. Interested national governments (or societal groups), regardless of size, can serve as initiators, mediators, and mobilizers; few "bottlenecks" limit the supply of leadership. EC negotiations are thus likely to be efficient. Given common interests and the absence of military threats, governments have a strong incentive to reveal their preferences in the form of bargaining demands and compromise proposals. Where national preferences make agreement possible, agreement is therefore likely to emerge.[81]

Third, the distribution of benefits reflects relative bargaining power, which is

[80] There is one exception: under the Treaty of Rome a simple majority of governments can vote to call an Intergovernmental Conference to discuss amendments, but any result must still be approved unanimously. For an intriguing effort to model even unanimous voting as de facto qualified majority voting, see Bruce Bueno de Mesquita and Frans N. Stokman, eds., *European Community Decision-Making: Models, Applications and Comparisons* (New Haven, Conn., 1994). One of the negotiations considered here, that surrounding the consolidation of the common market in the 1960s, did not result in treaty amendments, yet voting was unanimous and the Commission did not always enjoy a unique right of proposal.

[81] For a theoretical and empirical critique of the assumption that formal hierarchical institutions necessarily reduce transaction costs, see Donald Chisholm, *Coordination without Hierarchy: Informal Structures in Multiorganizational Systems* (Berkeley, 1989), xii, 17.

shaped in turn by the pattern of policy interdependence. The power of each government is inversely proportional to the relative value that it places on an agreement compared to the outcome of its best alternative policy—its "preference intensity." In the language of international relations, the relationship between preference intensities is what Robert Keohane and Joseph Nye call "asymmetrical interdependence," Albert Hirschman names "influence effect," and Susan Strange terms "structural power." It is closely related to what Robert Putnam labels the relative size of "win-sets."[82] The influence of policy interdependence on noncoercive bargaining under unanimity rules with a small probability of collapse can be formalized through use of the Nash bargaining solution. The Nash solution, it has been formally demonstrated, can be approximated through iterated offers and counteroffers in which marginal concessions are assumed to be made by the government that would have the most to lose by the collapse of negotiations. The assumptions about bargaining made in this book are consistent with this model.[83]

The Nash solution, which lies at the heart of most applied negotiation analysis, dictates that, absent coercive threats, governments would split the utility gains relative to their respective alternatives to agreement. A rational government will reject any agreement that leaves it worse off than the best alternative—often termed the "outside option," "concession limit," or "best alternative to negotiated agreement"—and, having set a floor, participants then split the gains, acting under pressure to avoid the possibility that exogenous events might lead negotiations to collapse, leaving each with nothing. Empirical studies suggest that under conditions of common knowledge—where governments, as the intergovernmental theory assumes, have accurate information about one another's reservation values—the Nash solution generates empirically accurate predictions of bargaining outcomes.[84]

The Nash bargaining model predicts that those countries that most intensely favor a given agreement will make disproportionate concessions on the margin in order to achieve it. A Nash solution tends therefore to reproduce the pre-

[82] Robert O. Keohane and Joseph S. Nye, *Power and Interdependence: World Politics in Transition*, 2d ed. (Boston, 1989), 18; Albert O. Hirschman, *National Power and the Structure of Foreign Trade* (Berkeley, 1945); Susan Strange, *States and Markets* (London, 1988), 23–26; Robert D. Putnam, "Diplomacy and Domestic Politics," *International Organization* 42:3 (Summer 1988), 427–461. In contrast to some of these formulations, bargaining power in this book reflects the marginal values of agreement and nonagreement, not relative concern about the threat of complete closure.

[83] The Nash bargaining solution is not to be confused with the more familiar Nash equilibrium concept. Formal analysis has shown that the outcome of a sequential or extensive noncooperative game of "alternative offers" in which the probability of a breakdown is small approximates the Nash cooperative bargaining solution. Ken Binmore, "Nash Bargaining Theory," in Binmore and Partha Dasgupta, eds., *The Economics of Bargaining* (Oxford, 1987), 1–10; Ariel Rubenstein, "On the Interpretation of Two Theoretical Models of Bargaining," in Arrow et al., *Barriers*, 120–130.

[84] I. William Zartman, "The Structure of Negotiation," in Kremenyuk, ed., *International*, 69ff; Ralph L. Keeney and Howard Raiffa, "Structuring and Analyzing Values for Multiple-Issue Negotiations," in H. Peyton Young, ed., *Negotiation Analysis* (Ann Arbor, Mich., 1991), 131–151; Aveinach Dixit and Barry Nalebuff, *Thinking Strategically: The Competitive Edge in Business, Politics and Everyday Life* (New York, 1991), 290–292; Harsanyi, *Rational*, chap. 8; Scharpf, *Games*, 123; Hirschman, *National*, 45–48; Raiffa, *Art and Science*, 252–255. The precise bargaining outcomes depend on, among other things, the elasticity of demand in both countries.

existing distribution of power and of satisfaction; those most satisfied with current unilateral opportunities tend to benefit most from bargaining. (This may create a subjective sense of having "lost" the negotiations in countries that gain a great deal because their alternatives were worse.) Governments that require unilateral or coalitional policy adjustments by others for the realization of basic domestic policy goals gain more from cooperation. The more intensely a government prefers agreement, the greater its incentive to offer concessions and compromises. Conversely, governments with attractive unilateral and coalitional alternatives value agreement less and are less likely to make concessions or compromises. Hence, for example, the primary European goal of France, I argue, has been preferential access for French agricultural commodities to the German market; to achieve this goal, France was consistently compelled to make concessions to Germany on such issues as agricultural prices, special subsidies, and GATT negotiations.

If the three core assumptions of intergovernmental bargaining theory hold—negotiations take place within a noncoercive, unanimous voting system, transaction costs are low, and asymmetrical interdependence defines relative power—then the negotiated outcome is likely to reflect three specific factors: (1) the value of unilateral policy alternatives relative to the status quo, which underlies credible threats to veto; (2) the value of alternative coalitions, which underlies credible threats to exclude; and (3) the opportunities for issue linkage or side-payments, which underlie "package deals."[85] Let us consider each.

Unilateral Alternatives. We have assumed that a necessary condition for agreement among rational governments is that each prefers cooperation to its best policy alternative. A unilateral threat to veto or exit from an agreement is thus the most fundamental source of bargaining power. Such a threat is credible only if a superior unilateral alternative exists. Leaving aside for the moment alternative coalitions and issue linkages, the "threat of nonagreement" guarantees that the outcomes of rational bargaining must fall within a set of agreements—the "feasible set" or "bargaining space." (Again, this statement does not imply that all governments end up better off than under the *status quo ante*. Unilateral or coalitional policy adjustments by other governments might have an even more negative effect than cooperation on a government, forcing it to accept an agreement less attractive than the status quo but better than the situation that would arise if all adjusted unilaterally.)[86] It follows that governments whose policies have little impact on their neighbors and governments that have poor unilateral alternatives to agreement (in other words, those relatively dependent on foreign governments) find their bargaining power is weak and must make conces-

---

[85] The order of these factors is not arbitrary but suggests an increasingly complex bargaining model: unilateral alternatives assume pure unanimity decision-making over a single issue, alternative coalitions add the option to form a subgroup, and issue linkages multiply the substantive dimensions. Cf. James K. Sebenius, "Negotiation Arithmetic: Adding and Subtracting Issues and Parties," *International Organization* 37:2 (Spring 1983), 281–316.

[86] The most parsimonious way to express this constraint—consistent with standard bargaining theory—is to state that the agreement must be superior to the "best alternative to negotiated agreement."

sions and compromises. By contrast, governments with attractive unilateral alternatives and whose policy shifts are highly valued by other governments (e.g., access to large protected markets or satisfactory macroeconomic performance) are more likely to secure concessions and compromises. In sum, those who more intensely desire the benefits of cooperation will concede more to get them.

Coalitional Alternatives. Where alternative coalitions are possible, a rational government must compare the value of agreement not only to unilateral action but to two other factors: the value of alternative coalitions and the consequences of alternative coalitions that others might join. This becomes important where more than two governments are involved.[87] The existence of attractive opportunities to form alternative coalitions (or deepen existing ones) strengthens the bargaining power of potential coalition members *vis-à-vis* those faced with the possibility of exclusion. In the EC context, such coalitional bargaining power may result either from the threat to cooperate with non-EC countries or, more common today, from cooperation among subgroups—a "multi-speed" or "variable geometry" Europe. Such coalitional dynamics tend to favor large states, whose participation is necessary to more viable coalitions, and states with preferences close to the EC median, who can join more potentially viable coalitions.[88]

The possibility of alternative coalitions broadens the calculus each government faces, because the incentive for a recalcitrant government to compromise must factor in the potential negative policy externalities that the joint policies of an alternative coalition might generate. Coalitional policies are likely to create larger negative policy externalities than are those of a single state. By diverting investment, credit, trade, political influence, or market confidence, for example, exclusion from an alternative coalition may impose significant costs even in the absence of direct military and economic coercion. Hence the credible threat of exclusion is likely to generate an even more powerful pressure on recalcitrant states than does the threat of nonagreement.[89] Credible threats of exclusion can force a rational government to accept an agreement that leaves it worse off in absolute terms than would unilateral policy adjustment—although, of course, it still remains better off than if the feared alternative coalition were to form. This is the situation faced repeatedly in the 1960s by Britain, which opposed the EC but was even more concerned about exclusion; the British government was eventually led to make repeated if reluctant bids for membership.

Alternative coalitions do not always create negative externalities for excluded states, however, so the threat of exclusion does not always create pressure for pol-

---

[87] Raiffa, *Art and Science*, 253. The extension of noncooperative bargaining theory to n-actor cases is problematic. For a review of the issues, see John Sutton, "Non-Cooperative Bargaining Theory: An Introduction," *Review of Economic Studies* 53 (1986), 709–724. Here I extend the Nash cooperative solution as an informal heuristic, explicitly considering the possibilities of exclusion and linkage.

[88] On the dynamics of exclusion, see Andrew Moravcsik, "Negotiating the Single European Act: National Interests and Conventional Statecraft in the European Community," *International Organization* 45:1 (Winter 1991); Kenneth A. Oye, *Economic Discrimination and Political Exchange: World Political Economy in the 1930s and the 1980s* (Princeton, N.J., 1992); Richard Baldwin, "A Domino Theory of Regionalism," CEPR Discussions Papers no. 857 (November 1993).

[89] Binmore and Dasgupta, *Economics*, 9. The consequences for relative bargaining power reflect, moreover, the costs for members of excluding a government, though these can be assumed generally to be modest.

icy concessions or geographical enlargement. Only where exclusion from a co-operative arrangement imposes costs on the excluded—that is, has *negative* ex-ternalities for nonmembers—does the incentive to cooperate increase. Where cooperation has *positive* externalities on nonmembers, governments find them-selves in a prisoner's dilemma—there is an incentive to free ride rather than join, and a contrary dynamic ensues. Where open trade is assured, for example, governments with low social or regulatory standards may face a clear commer-cial incentive to free ride on, rather than to compromise toward, harmonized standards. The distinction between positive and negative externalities provides a means of predicting which policies will be inherently expansive, thus resolving an ambiguity in neofunctionalist thought.

Issue Linkages. Up to now we have assumed that negotiations take place over single and discrete issues. Yet the linkage of issues and side-payments in pack-age deals is a constant theme in the history of EC negotiations. Indeed, many commentators view linkage as the core of the EC's success. To understand link-ages, we can extend the previous analysis of concessions within issue-areas. Linkages occur, simple bargaining theory suggests, when governments have vary-ing preference intensities across different issues, with marginal gains in some issue-areas more important to some than to others.[90] It may thus be to the ad-vantage of both parties to exchange concessions. Political exchanges of this kind increase the benefits of cooperation by helping to overcome one of the major disadvantages of bargaining on the basis of unilateral and coalitional alterna-tives: namely, governments tend to have the least bargaining power on precisely those issues which are most important to them. Where states have identical pref-erences, linkage has no effect on outcomes.

Issue linkage may appear most advantageous where two countries have highly asymmetrical interests on different issues. Yet this does not reflect the logic of preference formation elaborated in the preceding section of this chapter. The major constraint on linkage strategies lies in their domestic distributional im-plications. Linked concessions often create domestic losers as they create net benefits. Since concentrated losers with intense preferences tend to generate more political pressure than winners do, linkage is likely to be domestically vi-able only where adjustment costs are moderate. On this logic, the potential for linkage is far more limited than the potential for concessions within issue-areas.

Thus we should expect to observe linkage in three circumstances: within issue-areas where gains and losses are internalized to the same groups; where benefits are concentrated and costs are imposed only on relatively diffuse, un-organized, or unrepresented groups, such as taxpayers, consumers, and third-country suppliers; and where decisions on the precise details of implementation of a policy are postponed, rendering uncertain the domestic distribution of costs. We should thus be particularly likely to observe linkages taking the form of financial side-payments or symbolic concessions on the design of institu-

---

[90] Frederick Mayer, "Bargains within Bargains: Domestic Politics and International Negotiation (diss., Kennedy School, Harvard University, 1988); Lisa L. Martin, "Institutions and Cooperation: Sanctions during the Falklands Islands Conflict," *International Security* 16:4 (Spring 1992), 143–178; Sebenius, "Negotiation Arithmetic."

tions. In this regard, large, wealthy governments have an advantage in that they can provide diffuse linkages, such as financial support, at a lower perceived per capita cost.

Let us summarize the hypotheses, found also in Table 1.3. On the first dimension, *the availability of information*, intergovernmental bargaining theory predicts low transaction costs and complete information. Persistent informational asymmetries will be rare, with national leaders, ministers, diplomats, and key interest groups sharing similar assessments of data on technical, political, and legal circumstances. Critical information and ideas are introduced into negotiations by the most intensely interested governments or social groups. Supranational actors hold no privileged position.

On the second dimension, the nature of *bottlenecks and available entrepreneurship*, intergovernmental theory predicts that interstate negotiations do not suffer from bottlenecks, because national governments and societal groups, even in the smallest countries, can and do act as effective policy entrepreneurs on their own behalf. Governments remain silent only when supranational actors provide politically optimal proposals. We should observe governments providing a wide and unbiased range of initiatives, compromise proposals, and social mobilization, with particular stress on those that are politically viable because of support from influential and interested governments. National negotiating positions should follow a steady path toward compromise.

On the third dimension, the *pattern of negotiated outcomes*, intergovernmental theory generates contrasting predictions on four issues. First, negotiated agreements tend to be Pareto-efficient even without supranational intervention to provide new information and ideas.[91] Second, distributional bias favors not supranational actors but preference intensities defined by unilateral and coalitional alternatives. Governments gaining the most from core agreement offer the most significant compromises or side-payments in order to achieve it, whereas those for which ratification is difficult are less forthcoming. Third, threats of exit

---

[91] The determination that outcomes were efficient raises the difficult methodological issue of "nondecisions." Superficially, political decisions tend to look efficient in retrospect, since it is often difficult to observe efficient options that were never explicitly considered. To establish that they were in fact efficient, I seek to demonstrate in each case (in addition to examining the nature of information and the range of proposals considered) that no participants complained that the outcomes were suboptimal and no participants or subsequent commentators identified significant gains "left on the table" that a different process might have realized. This measure has two weaknesses. First, it overlooks transaction costs of reaching agreements that were inefficiently high, which may themselves impose a cost on negotiating governments. I assume that in the noncoercive environment of the EC these transaction costs were low relative to the substantive stakes. Where negotiations took a long period, as in the case of the Common Agricultural Policy in the 1960s or nontariff barrier removal in the 1970s, I do search for evidence that an earlier Pareto-improving agreement was possible and find little. Negotiations were sidetracked or delayed because certain governments favored a slowdown. Second, one might argue that the world is complex and there are constantly Pareto-improving bargains of which neither participants nor subsequent commentators are aware. Such an eventuality is not relevant to my theoretical inquiry, however, which focuses on the *relative* influence of third-party entrepreneurs and national governments. If neither is aware of a potential bargain, their relative influence and the determinants of bargaining outcomes remain unchanged. The silence of subsequent commentators suggests that these bargains were comfortably within these bounds. For overviews of the issues, see Bell, Edwards, and Wagner, *Political Power*; Steven Lukes, ed., *Power* (New York, 1986).

and exclusion shape outcomes but are effective only if the threat is credible and exclusion is costly to the targeted country. Fourth, linkages or package deals are limited. The norm remains issue-specific bargaining; linkage is employed to equalize gains rather than balance gains and losses. Where issue-specific preferences are intense (e.g., agriculture), log-rolling dominates; only where it is less intense (e.g., industrial trade) are limited linkages, generally within issue-areas, possible. These linkages are most likely to take the form of policies that impose costs on diffuse constituencies: cash payments, higher taxes, or exclusion of third-country producers.

INSTITUTIONAL CHOICE: POOLING AND DELEGATION OF SOVEREIGNTY

We now turn to the third analytical stage in the rationalist framework of international cooperation: institutional choice. Given substantive agreement, when and why do EC governments delegate or pool decision-making power in authoritative international institutions? Why do they not always retain the prerogative to make future unilateral decisions?

This question, central to modern theories of international cooperation, takes on particular significance in the case of the EC because of the uniquely rich set of institutions it has evolved. The EC comprises four major branches: the Council of Ministers, an intergovernmental decision-making body that routinely legislates by qualified majority vote; the Commission, a powerful technocratic secretariat with formal agenda-setting powers in many areas; the Parliament, a directly elected assembly with more limited powers than any national equivalent but greater influence than any international counterpart; and the Court of Justice, a constitutional court in some ways more powerful than those of many national systems.[92] These institutions transcend the coordinating rules and administrative secretariats found in most international organizations; they manifestly impinge on national sovereignty.

Constraints on sovereignty can be imposed in two ways: pooling or delegation of authoritative decision-making. Sovereignty is *pooled* when governments agree to decide future matters by voting procedures other than unanimity. In the EC legislative process, such decisions occur primarily through qualified majority voting (QMV) in the Council of Ministers, where a supermajority of weighted votes is required for passage. Sovereignty is *delegated* when supranational actors are permitted to take certain autonomous decisions, without an intervening interstate vote or unilateral veto. The Commission enjoys such autonomy in some matters of antitrust enforcement, daily implementation of regulations, and, to a more limited extent, external trade and accession negotiations. Perhaps most important, the Commission has been granted in most areas of economic legislation a unique right to propose legislation and can amend proposals at any time. The Parliament possesses a different sort of pooled sovereignty, in which

---

[92] For an overview of the institutions, see Robert O. Keohane and Stanley Hoffmann, eds., *The New European Community: Decision-Making and Institutional Change* (Boulder, Colo., 1991).

national representatives, generally organized in political parties, can influence the legislative process. For its part, the European Court also enjoys independent powers of judicial scrutiny and enforcement, at least insofar as domestic courts are prepared to implement its decisions.[93] The Maastricht Treaty foresees, in addition, the creation of an autonomous European central bank.

These novel institutional practices, Perry Anderson observes, emerged for the most part not through inattention, emulation, or revolution, as one can argue was the case with national state-building, but through deliberate design "without historical precedent."[94] While this is slightly overstated—the powers of the Court appear to constitute a partial exception—the deliberate quality of the provisions for pooling through QMV is evident from "their selective application to EC policy areas" and the way in which they have been "changed quite differently and discriminately . . . within policy areas" over time.[95] Similar observations apply to pooled sovereignty in the Parliament and delegation to the Commission. A central task of any comprehensive account of major European decisions is thus to understand conditions under which member-states choose to forego ad hoc decision-making under the unanimity rule in order to pool or delegate sovereignty. Why would sovereign governments in an anarchic international system choose to delegate decision-making power rather than make decisions themselves? This question lies at the heart of the modern study of international regimes and of political delegation more generally.

There are three plausible explanations for the delegation and pooling of sovereignty in the context of the EC. These stress, respectively, belief in federalist ideology, the need for centralized technocratic coordination and planning, and the desire for more credible commitments. Each explanation generates a distinctive set of predictions concerning variation along three dimensions of institutional choice: delegation and pooling across issues and countries, domestic cleavages and discourse, and the nature of institutional controls over those to whom power is delegated. The resulting hypotheses are summarized in Table 1.4.

Ideology: Federalism vs. Nationalism?

The willingness of governments to pool or delegate control over policy, one explanation suggests, stems from prevailing ideological beliefs about national

---

[93] Anne-Marie Burley and Walter Mattli, "Europe before the Court: A Political Theory of Legal Integration," *International Organization* 47:1 (Winter 1993), 41–76; Andrew Moravcsik, "Liberal Intergovernmentalism and Integration: A Rejoinder," *Journal of Common Market Studies* 33:4 (December 1996), 611–629. Governments still maintain an element of control through their ability to name Commissioners and ECJ judges and to influence the election of MEPs, often connected by partisan allegiance to domestic parties; through their ability to alter directives or the Treaty; or through noncompliance. Nonetheless, this is much looser and more costly control than that exercised over the diplomats that represent governments in the Council of Ministers. On the resulting principal-agent problems, see Pollack, "Delegation."

[94] Perry Anderson, "Under the Sign of the Interim," *London Review of Books*, 4 January 1996, 17.

[95] Thomas Koenig and Thomas Braeuninger, "The Constitutional Choice of Rules: An Application of the Absolute and Relative Power Concepts to European Legislation," Mannheimer Zentrum für Europäische Sozialforschung AB II/17 (Mannheim, 1997), 14.

Table 1.4. **Institutional choice: Theories and hypotheses**

Dimensions	Federalist Ideology	Technocratic Management	Credible Commitments
Cross-issue and cross-national variation	Support for delegation and pooling varies across countries, not issues. The most important split divides federalist and nationalist governments. The pressures are stronger where issues are ideologically salient—e.g., increases in EC Parliamentary power.	Support for delegation and pooling varies across issues, not across countries. Delegation and perhaps pooling are particularly likely when distributional conflict is low and issues are technically, legally, or politically complex.	Support for delegation and pooling varies across both countries and issues, paralleling national support for substantive cooperation. Institutional delegation and pooling emerge when joint gains, an incentive to defect, and future uncertainty call intertemporal bargains into question. Governments with extreme preferences, at greater risk of being outvoted or overruled, tend to be cautious. Concern about compliance induces delegation: concern about obstruction or log-rolling induces pooling.
Domestic cleavages and discourse	Domestic cleavages pit European federalists against nationalist opponents. Support tends to center in national parliaments, federalist parties and movements, or public opinion Domestic discourse, even behind the scenes, stresses ideology.	Pressure for delegation and pooling comes from experts and officials, with a secondary role for societal elite supporters of a given policy. Domestic discourse stresses optimal technocratic solutions to problems through central planning.	Domestic groups that favor or oppose policy goals take the same view on transfers of sovereignty. Domestic discourse focuses on securing commitments to implementation and compliance. More populist groups remain skeptical.
Institutional form	Institutions empower democratic or otherwise ideologically legitimate decision-makers, spearheaded by domestic and European Parliamentary federalists. Oversight provision reinforce democratic legitimacy and control.	Institutions empower technocratic experts. Minimal democratic, legal, or political oversight required, because there are few conflicting interests in areas of technocratic consensus.	Institutions establish actors and procedures that assure predictable, usually fair, compliance or implementation. National governments carefully limit the scope of mandates, generating an inverse relation between the scope and extent of mandates. To bolster credibility, democratic involvement is limited.

sovereignty. Some national publics, elites, and parties are more federalist; others are more nationalist. National positions concerning institutional form reflect these beliefs rather than the substantive consequences of transferring sovereignty—a view linked to ideological variants of the geopolitical explanation of national preferences explored earlier in this chapter. Such ideas and ideologies may reflect distinctive historical memories of World War II, partisan positions, preferred styles of domestic governance, or broad geopolitical calculations. Whatever the source, we have seen, Germany (along with Benelux and Italy) has traditionally been the most federalist of the three major EC members. France has been less so, balancing nationalism and federalism, with centrist parties generally favoring a more federalist position. Britain is least federalist. The indigenous pro-European movement is weaker than on the Continent, while there is a strong tradition of nationalist appeals at the extremes of both major parties. Three hypotheses follow.

On the first dimension, *delegation and pooling across issues and countries*, the ideological explanation predicts systematic variation across countries rather than across issues. Governments of "federalist" countries and parties should favor consistently delegation and pooling, whereas governments of "nationalist" countries and parties should oppose them—independently of substantive consequences of cooperation.

On the second dimension, *domestic cleavages and discourse*, we should observe domestic divisions along the lines of general public or partisan views about state sovereignty, rather than concrete economic or regulatory interests. "Pro-European" groups will favor delegation and pooling independently of substantive concerns, whereas "nationalist" groups will oppose them. Ideologically motivated leaders, governments, or societal groups, whether favorable or opposed, will focus their attention and rhetoric primarily on the most salient symbolic issues connected with sovereignty transfers, such as the powers of the Parliament *vis-à-vis* national parliaments, majority voting and national vetoes, and the general scope of EC competences *vis-à-vis* those powers reserved to subsidiary levels of national and subnational government. In this regard the ideological approach remains resolutely nonfunctional. Perry Anderson's observation is typical: "A customs union, even equipped with an agricultural fund, did not require a supranational Commission armed with powers of executive direction, a High Court [and] a Parliament. . . . The actual machinery of the Community is inexplicable without . . . the federalist vision of Europe developed above all by Monnet and his circle."[96]

On the third dimension, *the identity of and institutional controls on those holding delegated or pooled powers*, the ideological explanation predicts that EC institutions will be designed to enhance legitimacy by empowering democratically elected officials and neutral judges. Policy processes are therefore transparent and salient and subject to direct democratic oversight. This is the position consistently supported over the years by the "European federalist" movement. Not by chance has this movement been based traditionally in the European Parliament,

---

[96] Anderson, "Under," 14.

whence it voiced strong criticisms of the "democratic deficit" and the central-ization of EC policy-making in the Commission and the Council of Ministers.[97]

Technocratic Governance: The Need for Centralized Expertise and Information?

A second explanation for patterns in the delegation and pooling of sover-eignty focuses on the need for centralized experts to manage complex, modern, transnational economies. In this view, modern economic planning is a highly complex activity requiring considerable technical and legal information. Such information is most efficiently provided by a single centralized authority. This explanation—closely related to elements of the supranational explanation of interstate bargaining considered earlier—assumes that the collective-action problem facing governments is one of coordinating the production of infor-mation. Centralized authorities are best placed to exploit informational econo-mies of scale and overcome coordination problems or national mistrust, thereby generating and disseminating sufficient information required for more efficient decision-making. Around expert proposals—technocratic "focal points"—gov-ernments coordinate their activities.[98]

Like the supranational explanation of substantive bargains, the technocratic explanation of institutional choice is associated with Monnet and Haas, both of whom justified a need for centralized expertise by arguing that modern econo-mies require extensive state intervention and planning by knowledgeable, neu-tral experts. Rational investment decisions, they argued, are best made by cen-tralized technocrats; transfers of sovereignty establish planning capacity. Hence Monnet sought to promote integration in those areas, such as atomic energy, with high levels of technical complexity and state intervention; Haas predicted the success of such efforts. Since a "post-industrial" economy can easily produce enough to satisfy citizens, Haas wrote in 1964, there need be relatively little ide-ological or distributive conflict over economic policy; the central problem is in-stead "upgrading the common interest" through the application of proper tech-nocratic expertise.[99] The Commission's influence is thus often attributed to its technical competence, which, according to Lindberg, "ensures that its propos-als command the serious attention of the member governments."[100] Inter-pretations of the Commission's influence that rely heavily on focal points, tech-nical expertise, and epistemic communities have recently reemerged among scholars who stress the Commission's role.[101]

Whence the advantage of the Commission, Parliament, and Court in provid-ing expert information and analysis? One alternative is to delegate authority to

[97] O'Neill, *Politics*; Altiero Spinelli, *The Eurocrats: Conflict and Crisis in the European Community* (Baltimore, 1966); Spinelli, "Federalism and the EUT," in Juliet Lodge, ed., *European Union: The European Community in Search of a Future* (London, 1986), 174–185.

[98] Majone, *Regulating Europe*, 41ff; Garrett and Weingast, "Ideas." Majone also discusses the credi-bility of commitments.

[99] Haas, "Technocracy," 65ff.

[100] Lindberg, *Political.*

[101] E.g., Laura Cram, *Policy-Making in the EU: Conceptual Lenses and the Integration Process* (London, 1997).

national experts who meet regularly: Why is this not done? Even Council of Ministers committees, Haas argued, were essentially nonideological and non-partisan, consisting of "high civil servants meeting . . . and working out common policies on the basis of their perception of the technical policies inherent in whatever is being discussed."[102] It is hardly obvious that delegated or highly structured decision-making is more efficient than looser arrangements. In a study of "multi-organizational systems"—of which the EC is surely a prime international example—Donald Chisholm has observed, "Where formal organizational arrangements are absent, insufficient or inappropriate for providing the requisite coordination, informal adaptations develop [which] may be quite stable and effective, more so perhaps than formal hierarchical arrangement. Furthermore, because informal organization permits the continued existence of formally autonomous organizations in the face of mutual interdependence, it can achieve other values, such as reliability, flexibility and representativeness, that would otherwise be precluded or substantially diminished under formal arrangements."[103] It is thus unclear, in the technocratic view, why delegation or pooling is required.

One common explanation is that expert information and analysis may require considerable time, money, and expertise to generate yet can be disseminated easily—in short, they are public or club goods within an international organization. They are therefore likely to be underprovided by individual governments, since the costs of provision are relatively high relative to the benefits accruing to any single state. (Governments may also withhold expert information for fear of exploitation if they reveal it.) Yet it is unlikely that the Commission, with a few thousand officials, let alone the Parliament or Court, has more time, money, or expertise at its disposal than a major European government. A more plausible explanation is that Commission officials occupy a privileged position "at the center of an [institutionalized] network of knowledge"—an epistemic community of technical experts committed to political goals and linked through networks of national and international bureaucracies. Scientific and technical elites, it has been argued, are constituted in self-conscious networks within which information, expertise, and shared values are easily disseminated. By manipulating information through such networks, national and supranational officials construct "domestic and international coalitions in support of their policies" and "legitimate package deals." Such actions may generate policies that go beyond the initial intentions of governments—a phenomenon said to be common in international organizations. The EC Court, Parliament, and Commission might also, by virtue of proximity and expertise, be relatively expert in EC legal and administrative procedures, which may give them a comparative advantage in designing original solutions and inventing institutional options—said to be a key skill of successful international entrepreneurs.[104]

---

[102] Haas, "Technocracy," 65ff.

[103] Chisholm, *Coordination*, 17–18.

[104] Emanuel Adler and Peter M. Haas, "Conclusion: Epistemic Communities, World Order and the Creation of a Reflective Research Program," *International Organization* 46:1 (Winter 1992), 381–382; Young, "Politics," 355. Chayes and Chayes (*New*, 271–272, 281–282) argue that "secretariats with [seats], specific locations . . . , identifiable resources and personnel with defined roles"

If the technocratic explanation of pooling and delegation is correct, hypotheses follow along the three dimensions introduced above. On the first, *variation across issues and countries*, the technocratic theory predicts that institutional choices vary more by issue than by country. Delegation is likely where issues are technically complex (e.g., environmental, agricultural, and finance policy). Governments should be largely in agreement concerning the need for such delegation. We should expect delegation where conflict of interest is low and governments are concerned more with the efficiency of policy-making than with the distribution of gains. Given the low level of conflict assumed by the technocratic explanation, however, it is unclear why governments should ever pool, as opposed to delegate, sovereignty.[105] On the second dimension, *domestic cleavages and discourse*, technocratic elites should play a prominent role in domestic debates. Domestic discussions should be concerned more with the efficiency of policy-making than with the distributional outcomes. On the third dimension, *the identity of and institutional controls on those holding delegated or pooled powers*, we should see institutions designed to empower technocratic elites. Little democratic, legal, or political oversight should be required, because of the lack of conflicting interests in areas of expert consensus.

Credible Commitments: Locking in Policy Coordination?

If the federalist explanation for institutional choice is in essence ideological and the technocratic explanation informational, an explanation based on the need for credible commitments is quintessentially political. Pooling and delegation are, in this view, "two-level" strategies designed to precommit governments to a stream of future decisions by removing them from the unilateral control of individual governments. By pooling or delegating the right to propose, legislate, implement, interpret, and enforce agreements, governments restructure future domestic incentives, encouraging future cooperation by raising the cost of nondecision or noncompliance. Governments are likely to accept pooling or delegation as a means to assure that other governments will accept agreed legislation and enforcement, to signal their own credibility, or to lock in future decisions against domestic opposition.

If governments seek credible commitments, why do they pool and delegate sovereignty instead of promulgating precise rules in advance? The answer lies in uncertainty about the future. Pooling and delegation can be viewed as solutions to the problem of "incomplete contracting," which arises when member governments share broad goals but find it too costly or technically impossible to specify all future contingencies involved in legislating or enforcing those goals. Governments therefore require efficient means of precommitting to a series of smaller, uncertain decisions staggered at a series of times in the future, some of which are likely to be inconvenient but which taken as a whole benefit

---

are able to influence policy. "It is no coincidence," they conclude, that more successful regimes "are operated by substantial, well-staffed, and well-functioning international organizations."

[105] Lawrence Susskind and Jeffrey Cruikshank, *Breaking the Impasse: Consensual Approaches to Resolving Public Disputes* (New York, 1987), chaps. 4–5.

each of them. The alternative to delegation and pooling, namely a series of "package deals" linking together various issues explicitly, makes it more difficult to structure intertemporal trade-offs. Issues must be negotiated in large unwieldy bundles. Pooling and delegation may also be used to precommit governments to decisions before the costs and benefits become clear enough to generate opposition—a technique commonly employed in trade negotiations; the equivalent in the United States are "fast track" provisions and GATT norms of reciprocity and nondiscrimination. The lack of precise *ex ante* knowledge about the form, details, and outcome of future decisions precludes more explicit contracts but also helps defuse potential opposition from disadvantaged groups. Majority voting, Commission initiative, or third-party enforcement in the Treaty (like most domestic constitutions) serve as "relational contracts" among member-states—binding agreements that do not specify detailed plans but precommit governments or delegated authorities to common sets of principles, norms, and decision-making and dispute-resolution procedures. Bargaining continues among national governments but under new institutional circumstances designed to assure a particular level of agreement.[106]

In what ways do pooling and delegation bolster the credibility of international commitments? This question hardly arises in domestic settings, where constitutional rules are straightforwardly enforceable, but in the international realm, where there is no state with a monopoly of legitimate force, more subtle mechanisms must suffice. Pooling and delegation may raise the visibility of noncooperation, creating a focal point for mobilization by domestic groups not involved in a particular decision but supportive of subsequent or related decisions. Once sovereignty has been pooled or delegated, any attempt to reestablish unilateral control poses a challenge to the legitimacy of the institution as a whole and may require governments to launch costly and risky renegotiation of the institutions, perhaps involving a suspension of cooperation. International institutions may often enjoy broad ideological support, automatically mobilizing still more groups in favor of any single decision. Such ideological support may also permit national politicians to reduce the political costs of unpopular policies by "scapegoating" international institutions or foreign governments. Finally, international institutions may help establish reputations for member governments, reputations easily damaged by noncompliance in a few areas.[107]

International institutions are particularly likely to be useful for this purpose where no domestic equivalents exist. For example, it is difficult to imagine, absent institutional centralization, Germany credibly committing not to subsidize its farmers or Italy credibly committing to subordinate its monetary policy to those of its neighbors. In monetary policy, the centralization of institutional control over monetary policy in an international institution may increase the credibility of domestic reform. If domestic workers and legislators or international investors and speculators consider targets more credible, it has been ar-

---

[106] Majone, *Regulating Europe*, 44, 70–71; Paul R. Milgrom and John Roberts, *Economics, Organization and Management* (Englewood Cliffs, N.J., 1992), 131.

[107] Keohane, *After*, 105–106; Roland Vaubel, "A Public Choice Approach to International Organizations," *Public Choice* 51:1 (1986), 39–57.

gued, they will not challenge them and the output cost of disinflation will be lower. There is considerable evidence, we shall see in chapters 4 and 6, that governments believed that institutions had precisely these consequences. EC institutions are linked in the public mind to normatively desirable policy outcomes, such as successful trade liberalization and postwar peace. Exclusion from any policy is viewed in some countries with great suspicion. Such ideological linkages permit the EC to be employed as a "scapegoat" in countries where it is a popular organization. Finally, the centralization of future decisions concerning a single currency in a European central bank raises the costs of unilateral behavior, which would require the time-consuming and difficult reconstitution of unilateral decision-making procedures—during which time diplomatic opposition or economic reactions may discourage noncompliance.[108]

The decision to precommit through pooling or delegation marks a willingness to accept an increased political risk of being outvoted or overruled on any individual decision. The specific level of pooling or delegation reflects a reciprocal cost-benefit analysis: governments renounce unilateral options in order to assure that all governments will coordinate their behavior in particular ways. In agreeing to negotiate together in GATT, for example, France and Germany each surrendered unilateral control over tariff negotiations in exchange for greater assurances that they would combine forces, accept common decision-making, and be represented internationally by the Commission. From this perspective, we can think of unanimity voting, pooling, and delegation as striking different balances between the efficiency of common decisions and the desire of individual countries to reduce political risks by retaining a veto. As compared to unanimity voting, which permits recalcitrant governments to demand sidepayments, thus encouraging log-rolling, lowest common denominator bargains, or outright obstruction, QMV and to an even greater extent delegation reduce the bargaining power of potential opponents, encouraging a higher level of compromise.[109]

Three hypotheses follow. On the first dimension, *variation across issues and countries*, the credibility explanation predicts that delegation and pooling will vary by issue and country. Delegation and pooling are most likely to arise in issue-areas where joint gains are high and distributional conflicts are moderate, and where there is uncertainty about future decisions. If there were high conflict, some governments would be likely to reserve their powers. Where decisions are lumpy and risky, with little consensus on desired outcomes or very intense preferences involved, governments are likely to reserve unanimity rights. Where there is little uncertainty and prescribed future behavior involves a clearly defined set of actions aimed at a single goal—for example, the orderly elimination

[108] John Wooley, "Public Credibility and European Monetary Institutions," in Alberta Sbragia, ed., *Europolitics* (Washington, D.C., 1992), 157–190; Gros and Thygesen, *European.*

[109] Majone, *Regulating*, 61–79. This is akin to the problem of designing constitutional protection of minority rights. See James M. Buchanan and Gordon Tullock, *The Calculus of Consent: Logical Foundations of Constitutional Democracy* (Ann Arbor, Mich., 1962); Kenneth Shepsle, "Discretion, Institutions, and the Problem of a Government Commitment," in Pierre Bourdieu and James Coleman, eds., *Social Theory for a Changing Society* (Boulder, Colo., 1991), 254ff. Even unanimity voting with EC legal competence restricts sovereignty by eliminating the alternative to act unilaterally.

of tariffs—states gain little domestically or internationally from pooling and delegation and tend to opt instead for specific binding rules.[110] Pooling and delegation are therefore most likely to be found in limited domains, such as specific issue-areas, implementation, enforcement, and secondary legislation, where a large number of smaller decisions over an extended period, each uncertain, take place within the broader context of a previous decision. Examples include the setting of commodity prices, the steering of monetary policy, and the conduct of competition (antitrust) policy—each of which requires constant adaptation to new economic or political circumstances. The credible commitments explanation predicts no consistent variation by country; national positions vary instead by country and by issue. In those areas where governments favor integration and expect to join a qualified majority coalition (or gain support from supranational actors), they support pooling and delegation. Those that do not favor integration or are not likely to muster a majority oppose grants of sovereignty.[111]

On the second dimension, *domestic cleavages and discourse*, the credibility explanation predicts that the positions taken by domestic groups will mirror their substantive interests. The most intense supporters of delegation will be those that benefit most from future compliance with the common rules. Governments transfer sovereignty to commit other governments to accept policies favored by key domestic constituencies and perhaps also to precommit the government to policies opposed by domestic groups unsupportive of the government. Domestic discourse stresses concern with future compliance.

On the third dimension, *the identity of and institutional controls on those holding delegated or pooled powers*, the credibility explanation predicts an inverse correlation between the scope and the extent of delegation. The idea is to assure future promulgation or implementation of rules despite national opposition, which requires a measure of autonomy and neutrality. We should observe governments limiting political risk by nesting specific decisions inside a set of larger decisions reached by unanimity. To enhance credibility yet maintain control, moreover, arrangements tend to be insulated from direct democratic control but are strictly limited by governmental oversight, resulting in a "democratic deficit."[112]

Unlike the ideological and technocratic explanations, the credibility explanation generates precise predictions concerning the nature of support for pooling and delegation. Where the major institutional objective of those who support cooperation is to facilitate future legislation, pooling is more likely; where the concern is to assure the implementation of and compliance with laws, delegation is more likely. The reason is clear. Legislation is, at least potentially, a more open-ended function, so tighter control is maintained. Adjudication, im-

---

[110] Kalypso Nicolaïdis, "Mutual Recognition among Nations: The European Community and Trade in Services" (diss., Kennedy School, Harvard University, 1993).

[111] We should expect smaller countries to favor more centralized solutions, since equal treatment would increase their influence, but this is of little use in distinguishing British, French, and German policy.

[112] Andrew Moravcsik, "Why the European Community Strengthens the State: International Cooperation and Domestic Politics," *Center for European Studies Working Paper Series* no. 52 (Cambridge, Mass., 1994).

plementation, and enforcement are narrower functions, so governments can afford looser control and greater efficiency.

Are the Findings Reliable?

Before we turn from theory to history, one final question deserves our attention. The massive secondary literature on European integration now comprises tens of thousands of popular, scholarly, and pedagogical books and articles, as well as extensive journalistic reports and commentary. Why, the reader might well ask, should this book be considered more reliable?

This methodological question is rarely addressed explicitly, either in works on European integration or in general studies of international cooperation, whether by political scientists or by historians. At first glance the research design on which this book is based may seem questionable. How much can be deduced from five cases selected primarily for subsequent historical importance rather than their representativeness as an optimal sample on critical variables? It is difficult to draw generalizations from a small set of "successful" cases; the result tends to inflate the number of apparently necessary conditions. To overcome this difficulty, I have adhered to three methodological principles.

The first principle is to test explicit, falsifiable hypotheses drawn from competing, independently derived theories, reporting both confirming and disconfirming evidence.

Testing of alternative hypotheses encourages the analyst to develop clear, defensible standards by which to weigh confirming and disconfirming evidence, with the aim of greater objectivity, reliability, replicability, and precision. Rather than simply demonstrate that some supporting evidence exists for a particular theory—an exceptionally weak standard that almost any plausible conjecture can meet—the analyst must show that this evidence outweighs the evidence favoring competing explanations.[113] The results are more reliable because it is more difficult for the analyst to confirm any particular hypothesis; simultaneous consideration of competing hypotheses also helps us calibrate how much evidence ought to be required to confirm a theory. The use of explicit competing hypotheses specifies openly, in advance, what evidence counts for and against a proposition. Critics can more easily challenge the criteria employed or the interpretation of evidence. By drawing hypotheses from general theories, we also inhibit circular reasoning—the testing of hypotheses against the historical cases from which they were derived. Finally, the procedure obliges the analyst to report disconfirming data. We can assess the relative strength of evidence for competing explanations rather than report confirmation or disconfirmation for one unicausal claim.[114]

---

[113] A similar criticism has been leveled against international political economy more generally, in which the "vast majority" of studies of economic cooperation are said to tell us relatively little about the "*comparative* importance of different factors." Thomas D. Willett and David Andrews, "Financial Interdependence and the State," *International Organization* 51:3 (Spring 1997), 479–511.

[114] Gary King, Robert O. Keohane, and Sidney Verba, *Designing Social Inquiry: Scientific Inference in Qualitative Research* (Princeton, N.J., 1994), 35–38. This principle combines two of King, Keohane,

Despite these clear advantages, explicit hypothesis testing is conspicuously absent from the literature on European integration. Where competing explanations are considered, it is rare to find observable disconfirming implications stated a priori. Without explicit criteria, it is difficult, often impossible, for the reader to judge whether the evidence presented is unbiased, whether evidence for other plausible explanations exists, or whether empirical evidence is sufficient to accept a causal inference. In short, the reader has no way to assess the most important causal claims. Perhaps most troubling, the result, as noted above, has been an unchecked proliferation of supposedly "confirmed" claims. Weaker conjectures are almost never rejected.

This book resists this tendency by testing two or three major competing explanations for each critical aspect of state behavior. Each is drawn from a generalizable theory of political economy, bargaining, or international regimes not yet tested across EC history—though each does correspond to a plausible conjecture about the sources of integration with widespread support among journalists, commentators, and historians, as well as social scientists. From each are drawn explicit, falsifiable, and wherever possible directly competing hypotheses. These are listed in the tables found earlier in this chapter. Wherever possible, the hypotheses generate divergent predictions from the same data, thus increasing the potential decisiveness of the empirical test.

The fundamental goal is not simply to provide narrative reconstructions of events that capture something of their complexity, uncertainty, and subjective impact, but also to assess the importance of causal processes of international cooperation and institution-building which can be applied to a wide range of decisions in the EC and in world politics more generally. Some have coined the term "analytic narratives" for such an analysis—"accounts that respect the specifics of time and place but within a framework that both disciplines the detail and appropriates it for purposes that transcend the particular story."[115]

Finally—albeit at the risk of trying the reader's patience—each chapter reports not just evidence supporting the strongest hypothesis but also evidence that might disconfirm it, supports an alternative explanation, or appears random. Some readers may question how this was done, particularly because some of the conclusions in this book are revisionist—that is, they are extreme views relative to the existing secondary literature. Obviously not all relevant evidence can be reported, but I have sought to weight that which I present in order to give a representative sample of the quantitative and qualitative evidence available for and against any proposition. If this differs from the balance in the secondary

---

and Verba's three basic principles of qualitative inference: specify hypotheses independently of data; report estimates of uncertainty.

[115] Robert Bates, Avner Greif, Margaret Levi, Jean-Laurent Rosenthal, Barry Weingast, "Analytic Narratives: Introduction" (mimeo., University of Washington, n.d.), 4. "Analytic narratives" refers to the use of case studies to test general deductive propositions by seeking to explain previously unexplained variation within the case. On a general method of structuring case studies, the strong point of this mode of analysis is its focus on more rigorous theory even in single case studies, whereas its weaknesses lies in the lexicographical testing of theories and the lack of specific attention to the quality of data, on which points this study employs different methods

literature, it is because—in my judgment—some conclusions in the second-ary literature were not based on the same number or quality of sources. Where some might consider such judgments controversial—as in the claim that Jean Monnet and Jacques Delors were ineffective entrepreneurs, relative to their rep-utation, or in the claim that de Gaulle was motivated by farm interests more than by French *grandeur*—I have sought to provide a more detailed review of the sources.

The second methodological principle is to multiply the number of observa-tions in order to generate variation on critical variables within and across cases.

Numerous observations across a substantial range of theoretically relevant causes and outcomes are a central requirement of social-scientific testing. The absence of such variation, sometimes termed the "n = 1" problem, has tradi-tionally burdened studies of European integration, which deals with the histor-ical evolution of a single, exceptional institution. Comparisons between the EC and other regional integration schemes have proved an unwieldy tool to over-come underdetermination; so much varies across cases that the isolation of criti-cal variables is difficult. Moreover, as one literature review recently concluded, "in the field of Community studies isolated studies . . . have been the rule."[116] Single episodes of integration, viewed in isolation, generally seem to underde-termine the outcome; an infinite number of potential causes seem equally "nec-essary" to generate a single unique result.

This book seeks to structure more reliable tests by multiplying the number of observations. This is done in part simply by examining five "grand bargains" rather than one single decision. This, we shall see in chapter 7, permits some in-ferences impossible to draw when we view each case in isolation. Yet useful vari-ation across the aggregate outcomes of five negotiations remains modest. Each narrative is therefore further disaggregated into hundreds of fine-grained, more precisely measurable, "process-level" observations of decisive relevance to vari-ous hypotheses. This disaggregation generates smaller, more varied observations of potentially important causal variables.[117] I divide each negotiation into the three analytical stages mentioned above—national preference formation, in-terstate bargaining outcomes, and institutional choices. Then each stage is ob-served for a number of substantive issues and, in the case of preference for-mation, three different countries. I further subdivide government positions on specific issues into dozens of theoretically significant process observations em-ployed in the hypotheses summarized earlier, among them the timing of deci-sions, domestic coalitions, the distribution of information among key actors, de-cisive justifications offered in internal deliberations, and specific threats and promises. Each chapter can thus be read either as a narrative history or as a structured set of over one hundred discrete observations.

---

[116] Jeffrey Anderson, "The State of the (European) Union: From the Single Market to Maastricht, from Singular Events to General Theories," *World Politics* 47 (1995), 452. King, Keohane, and Verba point out that absent unit homogeneity, increasing the number of cases beyond a certain point may *undermine* the reliability of causal inference. *Designing*, 119–121.

[117] This procedure fulfills the second of King, Keohane, and Verba's three principles of causal in-ference, to increase the number of observations relative to parameters (*Designing*, 35–38).

Disaggregation not only increases the number of observations but offers other advantages. There is good a priori reason to suspect that smaller, discrete events are more susceptible to causal explanation than are larger, more complex ones. In this case, as we saw earlier in considering Puchala's critique of integration theory, it may well be more appropriate to generalize across and beyond sets of specific national preferences for trade liberalization, concrete outcomes of particular types of interstate bargaining, and acts of institutional delegation than across structural causes of integration in general.[118] Moreover, disaggregation combats bias or indeterminacy resulting from the fact that each of the five cases is centered on a "successful" negotiated outcome. I treat the five cases not simply as five successful decisions but as five open-ended decades and, where appropriate, ask why proposed negotiations concerning other issues were not pursued. (Thus I inquire why the negotiators of the Common Agricultural Policy, the Single European Act, and the Maastricht Treaty did not act earlier—perhaps a decade earlier.)[119] At the disaggregated level, moreover, we observe governments opposing and supporting integration, failing and succeeding to negotiate agreements, and obstructing and promoting the formation of strong institutions. Many of these process-level observations generate new data never before collected.

The third methodological principle, drawn primarily from the practice of historians, is the use, where appropriate and feasible, of reliable evidence, including a representative sample of available "hard" primary sources.

There is always an element of interpretation whenever we seek to describe and explain directly unobservable processes. Among the most problematic tasks are identifying the preferences of actors, their strategic calculations, and the information at their disposal. In a qualitative study, the evaluation of even relatively specific hypotheses requires the interpretation of a complex and potentially contradictory documentary record. In deciding which one of a number of competing interpretations is best supported by the evidence, the quality and representativeness of sources are thus of paramount importance.

Why is it important to be concerned about the quality of sources? For four decades, European integration has been a controversial and ideologically charged public issue. It has generated an enormous secondary literature filled with disparate conjectures about underlying causes, some based on casual ob-

---

[118] Why? Because we can expect greater unit homogeneity and fewer chaotic effects at a more disaggregated level. See King, Keohane, and Verba, *Designing*, 129–130, 134, 217–230; James D. Fearon, "Causes and Counterfactuals in Social Science: Exploring an Analogy between Cellular Automata and Historical Processes," in Philip E. Tetlock and Aaron Belkin, eds., *Counterfactual Thought Experiments in World Politics: Logical, Methodological and Psychological Perspectives* (Princeton, N.J., 1996), 49–54. Two caveats: first, absent a high-n design, it remains difficult to disconfirm the null hypotheses that the outcomes were random. Second, this research design does not address, nor does it deny, the possibility of "path-dependent" causation; earlier cases may have influenced later cases. The determinants of individual decisions are considered in isolation from one another. Nonetheless, a reliable analysis of individual decisions is a precondition for any analysis of the interactions among decisions. This issue is taken up again in chapter 7.

[119] Implications for cases outside the sample remain particularly difficult to draw. Barbara Geddes, "How the Cases You Choose Affect the Answers You Get: Selection Bias in Comparative Politics," *Political Analysis* 8 (1990), 131–133, 148–149.

servation, some on public justifications by interested parties, some on other secondary sources, some on outright speculation. Some secondary analyses are, in addition, partisan or ideological. The resulting literature contains widely divergent, often speculative conclusions on theoretically critical points of interpretation, such as the underlying motivations of groups and leaders, the strategic intent behind various moves, and the power of some actors over others.

The situation is little different at the level of "soft" primary sources. A soft primary source is one in which there is a relatively strong incentive (or a low cost) to distortion or speculation. Soft primary sources include most contemporary newspaper and magazine reports (e.g., unattributed editorials or articles in the *Economist* or *Financial Times*), public statements by government spokesmen and national leaders justifying their actions, and *ex post* justifications in memoirs or interviews by participants who either were not in a position to know the truth or had an evident incentive to inflate (or deny) their own influence.

In the absence of explicit standards of evidence and inference, the relative weight of such interpretations and sources is at best uncertain and at worst questionable, for two reasons.[120] First, falsehood (intentional or inadvertent) costs a politician, journalist, or commentator very little; indeed, speculation or distortion is often politically or professionally profitable. National decision-makers, we shall see, often express one position in public and the opposite in private—even many years after the events in question.[121] Journalists generally repeat the justifications of governments or the conventional wisdom of the moment without providing much with which to judge the nature or reliability of the source. Second and more important, even if soft primary sources were reliable, their sheer number and diversity means that the ability of an analyst to present such evidence tells us little or nothing. Even cursory experience with such sources teaches that one can find extensive evidence for almost any plausible explanation of any major EC decision. Secondary and soft primary sources are useful to identify plausible causal conjectures or hypotheses, but in themselves constitute an unreliable basis on which to test such hypotheses.

Yet nearly all studies of EC policy-making—again excepting the work of professional historians on the 1950s and 1960s (and, in one exceptional case, the 1970s)—rely almost exclusively on evidence drawn from secondary and soft primary sources to support controversial attributions of cause or motivation. Political scientists and policy analysts working on the EC continue to rely on one another's secondary work, government rhetoric, or journalistic commentary. This practice precludes from the start any effort to revise the conventional wisdom. This practice of treating speculation as data has been rightly condemned by professional historians: Paul Schroeder likens it to "brewing tea from already used tea bags."[122] It is particularly questionable if the only evidence reported

---

[120] Ian Lustick, "History, Historiography and Political Science: Multiple Historical Records and the Problem of Selection Bias," *American Political Science Review* 90:3 (September 1996), 605–618.

[121] This was Jean Monnet's reading of Charles de Gaulle. Bruno Bottai, "Jean Monnet Visto da Vicino," *LiMes*, 2/1997, 152.

[122] Paul Schroeder, "History and International Relations Theory: Not Use or Abuse, but Fit or Misfit," *International Security* 22:1 (Summer 1997).

is that supporting a single hypothesis, as is often the case. Few analysts attempt to generate a representative sample of secondary and soft primary sources; and even if such a representative sample existed, it would offer no guarantee against bias. Such sources often include additional inessential explanations and justifications for policies. A lax attitude toward sources renders impossible revision either of government justifications or of existing historiography, except by assertion.[123]

Moving beyond such methodological indeterminacy, as historians quite rightly remind us, requires that we must pay more attention to the quality of evidence. Accordingly this book seeks wherever possible to base controversial attributions of motivation or calculation not on secondary sources, journalistic speculation, or public government statements, but on more reliable sources. The reliability of a source is a function of the extent to which the activity it documents is one in which it is costly to manipulate or misstate the truth.

One more reliable sort of evidence is the pattern of objective facts about the decision-making process. Potentially decisive aspects of the decision-making process include the timing of policy, the nature of related policies, the nature of offers and counteroffers, and patterns of domestic cleavages. Such objective patterns of behavior often provide important insights into the motivations for policy; they are costly, often impossible, to falsify or manipulate. One example must suffice. We can reject the long-standing claim that de Gaulle's decision to veto British entry in January 1963 resulted from his anger at the outcome of the Nassau meeting between the United States and Britain in December 1962; we now know that the French decision was taken some days *before* Nassau.

Such data are useful but are often insufficient. As analysts, we often desire to exploit direct evidence concerning the preferences motivating key decision-makers, their perceptions of external constraints, and what information was available to them. Wherever possible, therefore, I seek to employ "hard" primary sources. As a general rule, the greater the difficulty of manipulating or concealing evidence of what really occurred at the time, the more reliable (the "harder") the source in retrospect. Hard primary sources include internal government reports, contemporary records of confidential deliberations among key decision-makers, verbatim diary entries, corroborated memoirs by participants who appear to lack an ulterior motive for misrepresentation, and lengthy interviews with numerous policy-makers in which the interviewer challenged or sought to corroborate the *ex post* claims of policy-makers. (I drew on archived and published oral histories, as well as conducting over a hundred interviews myself.) The provision of misleading or incomplete public statements is often essentially without cost to governments—indeed it is often advantageous. By contrast, misrepresentation and speculation in hard primary sources—for example, staging a series of phony meetings with close advisers, generating false assessments by government ministries, keeping a phony diary, fashioning the revelations of independent memoirs into a coherent story, or coordinating the independent interview responses of numerous officials to repeated questioning years after the events—is far more costly and difficult. My reliance on hard pri-

[123] King, Keohane, and Verba, *Designing*, 151–168; Lustick, "History."

mary sources is, in comparison to most work on integration by political scientists and policy analysts, an acknowledgment of the more rigorous methods typically employed by historians.

Two caveats are in order. First, it was not always possible, particularly in recent cases, to assemble a comprehensive primary-source record. In cases such as Maastricht, where archives remain closed, politicians remain in office, and the issues remain live, I was often forced to rely more heavily on secondary sources or the objective pattern of decision-making. Second, since the scope of this book precluded comprehensive archival research or personal interviews on all questions of potential interest, it rests on a methodological compromise: I employed as hard sources those sections of secondary sources that themselves report facts based on direct citation of a hard primary source. In citing such passages, I seek to avoid, where possible, citing the *conclusions* and *interpretations* of a secondary author; instead, I cite only the facts drawn from primary sources. Throughout the five case studies, I have sought to offer a representative sample of primary sources found in secondary sources in English, French, and German. Multiple sources are weighed against one another where possible; contrary evidence is reported where relevant.[124] Unless otherwise indicated or obvious from the context, any citation to a secondary source to bolster an assessment of motive, strategy, or knowledge indicates a page on which a primary source appears. Where possible, I collected archival documents, conducted interviews, and consulted existing oral histories to fill holes in the documentary record.

While restricting the analysis to those factual observations drawn in part from secondary sources may not be as reliable as a comprehensive analysis of primary sources alone—I defer to those who have reconstructed the entire documentary record in specific ministries or governments—it marks a methodological improvement on existing work with significant practical implications. On many important questions there is a significant discrepancy between secondary sources and hard primary evidence. Numerous overtly revisionist conclusions in this book were possible *only* by focusing on primary sources.

One example must suffice. Almost without exception, those who analyze postwar French foreign policy treat President Charles de Gaulle as a traditional statesman whose European policies were driven primarily by a distinctive geopolitical ideology—"une certaine idée de la France." A conception of French grandeur incompatible with closer relations with the United Kingdom and United States, it is said, fueled the General's antagonism and drove France's European policy. De Gaulle was a visionary, it is often asserted, who considered it beneath his dignity to concern himself with narrow commercial matters—a view customarily supported by soft primary sources, notably a very selective interpretation of the General's speeches and memoirs, as well as an enormous secondary literature. Here we find an exceptional case in which secondary and soft primary sources have reached something approximating a consensus.[125]

Yet this consensus is not supported by even a small percentage of available

---

[124] A few Italian sources are cited as well.

[125] Of those among the thousands of works on de Gaulle I have consulted, I encountered only two that stress his international economic motivations—and these only as secondary motivations.

hard primary sources—notes taken in Cabinet meetings, the pattern of policy-making, memoirs, and speeches read in context.[126] Instead, the preponderance of concrete evidence, as I demonstrate in chapter 3, suggests that the General's policy toward Europe, not least his veto of U.K. membership and proposal of the Fouchet Plan, was grounded primarily in economic interest, in particular the search for export markets for French farm surpluses. Wheat, not nuclear weapons or French grandeur, was the vital interest that fundamentally moti-vated de Gaulle's European policy. De Gaulle and his associates, moreover, de-liberately manipulated public perceptions in order, in the words of de Gaulle's closest associate, to "seduce" observers into believing that geopolitical factors were decisive. Thirty-five years later, analysts who rely on secondary and soft pri-mary sources remain in the thrall of the General's seduction; only hard primary sources permit us to revise received wisdom.

Though an improvement on prevailing methodological standards in studies of EC decision-making, these three methodological principles—consideration of competing hypotheses drawn from deductive theory, disaggregation of cases into numerous varied observations, and consultation of hard primary sources where possible—fall short of ideals prevailing in history and political science.

Diplomatic or social historians will surely complain that much primary docu-mentation remains classified and many archival sources were not always con-sulted directly. Future revelations may amend or reverse some of the conclu-sions reached here, particularly concerning recent cases. Traditional historians may also be disturbed by continuous interruptions in the narrative to report the results of explicit hypothesis testing. For their part, political scientists may object to the extended use of primary sources alongside more "objective" measures. They may also note that the number and type of cases sometimes remain in-sufficient to permit definitive rejection of null hypotheses—the claim that the outcomes of negotiations were random.

These methodological limitations are regrettable but deliberate. This book seeks not to realize any methodological ideals but to strike a pragmatic bal-ance between problem-oriented and paradigm-oriented research. It is narrow enough to permit detailed research focused on the resolution of concrete his-torical puzzles, yet broad enough to permit the testing and refinement of gen-eral social-science theories. Recent years have witnessed increasing interest in just such a synthesis between historiographical and political science methods. Gordon Craig succinctly summarizes the potential gains, arguing that political scientists would "profit from the fidelity to *milieu et moment*" and greater atten-tion to primary sources, whereas historians might learn from "analytical tech-niques employed by their partners, new questions to ask [and] new ways to test the validity of their hypotheses."[127] The cases are focused enough to facilitate detailed research, yet numerous enough to inform us about their external valid-ity or generalizability.

---

[126] To be sure, the bulk of the primary documents from this period and all later periods remain unavailable.

[127] Gordon Craig, "Presidential Address," *American Historical Review* 88:1 (February 1983). Also Lustick, "History," 605–618; "Symposium [on Diplomatic History and International Relations Theory]," *International Security* 22:1 (Summer 1997).

Cutting across the concerns of political scientists with generalizable hypotheses and of historians with context and reliable sources, however, is one underlying methodological standard. Throughout I have aimed to generate *replicable* results, that is, to render the logic of the argument, the nature of the data, and the empirical inferences that link the two transparent and vulnerable to direct and unambiguous evaluation, criticism, and revision.[128] If I have neglected or misstated plausible causal claims about a given case, misrepresented the quantity and quality of available sources, or drawn biased inferences from the historical record, then my use of explicit hypotheses and claim to provide a representative sample of available evidence greatly simplify the task of would-be critics. Ensuing criticism can focus on concrete hypotheses, evidence, and inferences, not the speculations of political commentators or conjectures of classical integration theory. My aim is not to close the debate over the fundamental causes of European integration but to renew it.

---

[128] King, Keohane, and Verba, *Designing*, 26–27. Only my conduct of confidential interviews creates an impediment to rapid replication, though knowledgeable readers will have little difficulty identifying the category of person, even at times the individual, whom one needs to interview to confirm the claim.

Chapter Two

Finding the Thread:
The Treaties of Rome, 1955–1958

> Our European states are a historical reality; it is psychologically impossible to eradicate them. Their diversity is in fact a blessing. We want neither to equalize nor to level them. But there must be . . . coordination.
>
> —Robert Schuman, former French foreign minister (1964)

The history of the European Economic Community begins with a failure. In the summer of 1954 the defeat of the European Defense Community (EDC) crushed hopes that the European Coal and Steel Community (ECSC), created by France, Germany, Italy, and the Benelux countries a few years previously, would lead automatically to deeper integration. Within a year, however, negotiations had begun that would culminate in the Treaty of Rome establishing the European Economic Community (EEC or EC), a customs union among the six member countries of the ECSC, as well as an atomic energy community called Euratom.[1] The Treaty set a framework to eliminate tariffs and quotas, create a common external tariff, establish common agricultural and transport policies, and coordinate monetary and many relevant regulatory policies. This framework was embedded in a set of quasi-constitutional institutions unique among international organizations, notably the European Commission, a regulatory bureaucracy with powers (often sole powers) of initiative; a Council of Ministers where national governments took decisions by unanimous or qualified majority vote; the European Court of Justice; and a parliamentary assembly.

This "small Europe" customs union, with provisions for agriculture, atomic energy, and supranational institutions, was only one of at least three broad alternatives considered at the time. Another, preferred by many within the German and British governments, was a European industrial free trade area (FTA) without agriculture or supranational institutions, open to a wider Europe—an option that would have preserved each country's third-country tariff autonomy. Yet a third, favored initially by many in the British government and some in France, was the status quo, a haphazard process of multilateral trade and monetary lib-

---

[1] Strictly speaking, these separate documents were the Treaties of Rome, but since the central focus is here on the EEC, we refer to the Treaty of Rome.

eralization through the sixteen-member Organization for European Economic Cooperation (OEEC) in Europe and the General Agreement on Tariffs and Trade (GATT) at the global multilateral level—an option that would have preserved many exceptions and safeguards for individual countries and former colonies, not least British Commonwealth preferences.

Why was the customs union chosen? I start by evaluating alternative explanations for German, French, and British preferences. I then assess alternative explanations for the outcomes negotiated given those preferences. Lastly I consider alternative explanations for the decisions to embed those negotiated outcomes in international institutions that pool or delegate sovereignty. Whereas the bulk of the literature on the Treaty of Rome negotiations suggests that geopolitical considerations, supranational entrepreneurship, and technocratic or ideological motives for institution-building were critical, I hold that the preponderance of hard evidence demonstrates the greater importance of commercial interest, the distribution of relative power, and the desire to establish credible commitments for future elaboration and implementation of policy. Above all, existing scholarship (particularly on Britain) greatly underestimates the extent to which national policies were driven by the desire to promote exports—agricultural exports in France, industrial exports in Britain and Germany. Not only did the centrality of commercial concerns shape the outcomes preferred by each government, but the relative intensity of preferences, themselves a function of export potential, tells us much about bargaining power.

National Preference Formation

German, French, and British preferences varied greatly across issues (see Table 2.1). Leading explanations of national preferences in the negotiations tend to stress the primacy of "high politics," the distinctive geopolitical conceptions prevailing in each government. In this view, varying national preferences reflect varying geopolitical imperatives: distinctive perceptions of threats from one or both superpowers, level of concern with potential German unilateralism, confidence that integration would prevent future wars in Europe, interest in maintaining "great power" status while reconfiguring relations with present and former colonies, European federalist ideology held by German and French leaders, and British nationalism. Events during the mid-1950s demonstrated that the only way to preserve great-power status and peace in Europe was to integrate. Many point to the Suez crisis as a defining event. Indeed, Hanns-Jürgen Küsters goes so far as to call the Treaty a "historical accident" occasioned by the Suez crisis.[2]

This analysis is closer to some more recent analyses, notably that of Alan

---

[2] Hanns Jürgen Küsters, "West Germany's Foreign Policy in Western Europe, 1949–1957: The Art of the Possible," in *Western Europe and Germany: The Beginnings of European Integration, 1945–1960*, edited by Clemens Wurm (Providence, 1995), 69.

Table 2.1. Direction of British, French and German exports, 1958

| Importing Area | Exporting countries | | | | | |
| | % Total exports (value) | | | Exports (%GNP) | | |
	Germany	France	UK	Germany	France	UK
The Six	29	25	13	6	4	3
Other Europe	29	16	13	6	3	3
Colonial/Commonwealth	1	27	52	0	4	12
Other	41	31	22	8	5	5

SOURCE: F. Roy Willis, *France, Germany and the New Europe, 1945–1967* (Stanford, 1968), 265, and F. V. Meyer, *United Kingdom Trade with Europe* (London, 1957), 122. British statistics are from 1954; 1960 GNP statistics are employed. Note that these statistics underestimate the divergence between the interests of the UK and the Six, since the latter statistics count trade with only *five* countries.

Milward, that stress economic factors, in particular national biases in economic policy-making.[3] My analysis follows these writings in deemphasizing supranational entrepreneurship, geopolitical ideology, and interests, yet it diverges from them by focusing consistently on commercial interests rather than general economic concerns. Milward explains national positions in large part by looking to postwar economic reform, the disproportionate influence of finance in British politics, and the concern of French officials with industrial modernization— as well as attributing German policy almost entirely to geopolitical rather than economic concerns. My analysis suggests that narrower commercial concerns— above all, export promotion—were central to the preferences of all three governments. Beginning in the early 1950s, European countries faced a rapid expansion of opportunities for industrial trade, making European trade liberalization seem inevitable in one form or another. This rapid expansion came in the wake of a boom in intra-industry trade in manufactured goods among industrialized countries, driven by reconstruction, increased product differentiation, economies of scale, and importation of intermediate products. Developed countries increasingly imported and exported similar goods, with the percentage of intra-industry trade rising to over 50 percent.

Though the postwar trade boom in manufactures was a general phenomenon among developed countries, differences in export patterns and competitiveness explain varied national preferences concerning the direction and speed of liberalization. In this regard, Britain, France, and Germany occupied different positions in European and global markets. At the end of the 1950s, at least two characteristics clearly distinguished them: the percentage of trade going to colonial and developing markets, and the size and productivity of the agricultural sector. In the 1950s, British industry was relatively competitive but re-

[3] Alan S. Milward, *The European Rescue of the Nation-State* (London, 1993); Frances M. B. Lynch, *France and the International Economy: From Vichy to the Treaty of Rome* (London, 1997).

Table 2.2. The Agricultural sector: Size, income, liberalization, and exports among the Six and the United Kingdom, 1956

Country	%GNP	%Empl	%GNP/ %Empl	%Lib with EC	%Lib with ROW	%Exp
UK	5	5	1.0	68	73	0
Belgium and Luxembourg	8	13	0.62	NA	NA	5
Germany	11	15	0.73	63	22	3
Netherlands	12	15	0.80	92	88	35
France	15	25	0.60	34	0	15
Italy	25	41	0.60	88	1	24

% Empl=Percent of total employment in agriculture.
% Lib with EU=Percent of trade liberalized with Europe OEEC.
% Lib with ROW=Percent of trade liberalized with rest of world.
% Exp=Percent of agricultural products in total exports.
Source: Leon N. Lindberg, *The Political Dynamics of European Economic Integration* (Stanford, 1963), 3.

mained uniquely dependent on preferential access to colonial and Common-wealth markets, which took over 50 percent of U.K. exports, totaling 12 percent of GNP; only 13 percent of U.K. exports went to the six future EC members. Accordingly, Britain favored modest industrial liberalization, preferably within an open FTA, and a continuation of preferential arrangements with the Commonwealth, which took over half of British exports. By contrast, only 27 percent of French exports (4 percent of GNP) and 1 percent of German exports went to such preferential markets; between a quarter and a third of French exports went to the Six. Accordingly, France remained cautious about opening its rapidly developing but still vulnerable industrial sector to free trade. Germany, highly competitive in industry, favored global liberalization of industrial tariffs. At the same time, Germany was highly dependent on developed-country markets outside the Six, reflecting the relative competitiveness of German industry; thus Germany favored multilateral as well as regional trade liberalization (see Table 2.2).

The relative importance of agriculture betrays similar cross-national differences. Farming employed 25 percent of Frenchmen, 15 percent of Germans, and only 5 percent of Britons. Germany and Britain were large net importers but only marginal exporters of agricultural goods, whereas France (along with the Netherlands and Italy) was a large exporter. It was widely agreed, moreover, that the potential for French and Italian agricultural exports would be enormous under any preferential arrangements that maintained relatively high prices relative to the world market, on which no European agricultural producers were competitive. This is evident from the relatively low labor productivity of French (and Italian) agriculture, a fact the French government attributed to low capitalization due to the threat of domestic surpluses.[4] Hence Germany's support for industrial

[4] Lynch, *France*, chap. 2.

Table 2.3. Bilateral trade in agricultural goods among the Six, 1956 (in millions of US $)

Exporting country	Importing country					Total exports	Balance (X-M)
	Netherlands	Italy	France	Belgium and Luxembourg	Germany		
Netherlands	—	37.1	67.0	107.2	262.1	473	+400
Italy	10.8	—	43.5	10.6	142.6	208	+120
France	21.0	22.9	—	36.3	91.7	174	+14
Belgium and Luxembourg	26.5	9.3	29.1	—	31.9	97	−72
Germany	14.3	19.1	19.9	12.8	—	66	−462
Imports from the Six	73	88	160	169	528	1018	

SOURCE: Bundesministerium für Ernährung, Landwirtschaft und Forsten (Bonn 1958), quoted in Fritz Baade, *Die Deutsche Landwirtschaft in gemeinsamen Markt* (Baden-Baden, 1958), 65.

liberalization did not extend to transport, agriculture, or atomic energy production, where it was uncompetitive. France, by contrast, pursued agricultural and atomic energy cooperation but remained cautious concerning industrial trade. Britain supported continued preferential imports of Commonwealth agricultural products at low prices (see Tables 2.3 and 2.4).

Geopolitical ideas and security externalities were not entirely unimportant. Had economic interest been the sole motivation, European governments would probably have converged toward something like an FTA, not a customs union with quasi-constitutional institutions. Yet economic interests were clearly primary, not simply because they constrained governments more tightly but because they determined the conditions under which geopolitics mattered. Where economic interests were uncertain, diffuse, or unrepresented, national leaders (in this case, most notably Konrad Adenauer) were able to realize geopolitical objectives. Where economic interests were entirely concentrated, intense, and well-organized (what Adenauer found in atomic energy policy), national leaders could not prevail. We now examine the links between economic incentives and national preferences in more detail.

Germany: Multilateral Liberalism and European Federalism

The German government favored a customs union with low external tariffs and, if possible, a free trade area but remained skeptical of agricultural, transport, and atomic energy cooperation. It favored a quasi-constitutional structure and the pooling or delegation of sovereignty in industrial trade, as well as competition policy, but not in agriculture, transport, or atomic energy. How might we best explain this set of preferences?

Geopolitical Interest and Ideology: Reassuring and Reinforcing Allies

Adenauer's contemporaries unanimously attribute to him strong support for European integration and a preference, strong even by German standards, for close cooperation with France.[5] In 1945 he proposed the economic integration of France, Germany, Britain, and the Benelux countries, a position he reiterated through 1957. Adenauer maintained a close relationship to Jean Monnet and generally supported his proposals for strong European institutions; like Monnet, he considered the Euratom proposal for sectoral integration in atomic energy more promising than a broader, more diffuse customs union.[6] Finally and most distinctively, Adenauer supported stronger bilateral relations with France—a view that alienated him not only from opposition political figures but from many within his own government.

Some argue backwards from Adenauer's support for integration to the claim that his actions reflected federalist idealism. Altiero Spinelli, himself one of the founding federalist fathers of Europe, has argued that Adenauer, like Schuman in France and De Gasperi in Italy, was "fundamentally conservative, but national sovereignty was not one of the values [he was] anxious to protect."[7] Leaving aside Adenauer's subsequent association with de Gaulle, which calls any deeply federalist commitment into question, a closer examination reveals geopolitical and partisan motivations as well as a hard-nosed attachment to national sovereignty. Adenauer does not appear to have believed strongly in European political union for its own sake, nor that it would follow automatically from economic integration. He remained unwilling, for example, to compromise German demands for sovereign equality or U.S. support in defense matters in order to realize European schemes; hence his consistent caution with regard to defense cooperation. He remained, moreover, relatively uninterested in matters of institutional form, as long as arrangements committed governments to cooperation on equal terms. Adenauer did, however, consistently exploit the domestic and international legitimacy of European integration, as well as the wider array of diplomatic alternatives it created, to promote geopolitical objectives.[8]

From 1948 onward, Adenauer's central geopolitical objective appears to have been to assure Germany's defense, control over West Berlin, and opposition to the Soviet Union. Adenauer's most fundamental strategy to achieve his objectives was to assure the sovereign equality of Germany, including territorial integrity and rearmament for German military forces. By 1956 major issues of sovereignty had been resolved through multilateral or bilateral agreement: Germany was rearming within NATO, was developing an arms industry, and had repatriated the

---

[5] The literature on Adenauer can be divided into that which stresses his personal ideology and that which stresses external threats. Representative of the first category is Hans-Peter Schwarz, "Das aussenpolitische Konzept Konrad Adenauers," in Hans Maier, Rudolf Morsey, Eberhard Pikart, and Hans-Peter Schwarz, eds., *Adenauer-Studien I* (Mainz, 1971). Representative of the second is Wolfram Hanrieder, *West German Foreign Policy, 1949–1963: International Pressure and Domestic Response* (Stanford, 1967).

[6] Franz Knipping, "Firm with the West! Elements of the International Orientation of West Germany in the Mid-1950s," in Ennio di Nolfo, ed., *Power in Europe? Great Britain, France, Germany and Italy and the Origins of the EC, 1952–1957* (Berlin, 1992), 523. Klaus-Jürgen Müller, Power and Awareness of Power in the Federal Republic of Germany 1953–1956/7," in ibid., 483

[7] Altiero Spinelli, "The Growth of the European Involvement since the Second World War," in Michael Hodges, ed., *European Integration: Selected Readings* (Harmandsworth, 1973), 51.

[8] Saki Dockrill, *Britain's Policy for West German Rearmament, 1950–1955* (Cambridge, 1991), 65–73, 91–95.

Table 2.4. Treaty of Rome negotiations, 1955–1958: Preferences and outcomes

Issue area	Germany	France	Britain	Jean Monnet and the Action Committee	Treaty outcome
Industrial trade	Favors customs union among the Six with low external tariffs and competition policy over larger free trade are (FTA).	Rejects FTA and favors customs union with safeguards, veto, preferences for overseas territories, and prior social harmonization in lieu of devaluation. Even this is not expected to be implemented fully without domestic reform	Favors the status quo or a looser and larger FTA with continued access to Commonwealth. Favors membership in a customs union, however, to exclusion from it.	Opposes the customs union. Though ultimately willing to accept any member-state agreement, Monnet repeatedly attempts to dissuade French and German leaders from pursuing the EC.	*Customs union (EEC) with safeguards, veto, preferential arrangements for overseas colonies. Commitment to social harmonization is rhetorical; competition policy is weak.*
Agriculture	Prefers status quo of bilateral arrangements to preferential arrangement unless common price subsidies remain high enough to maintain farm incomes.	Strongly supports regional arrangement to gain preferential access to German (or British) markets for surplus grain, sugar, dairy products, and beef. Seeks to ensure access for tropical products from overseas territories.	Opposes any preferential arrangement in order to protect low domestic prices, high direct subsidies, and grain imports from Commonwealth and world markets.	Opposes customs union.	*Deadlines for elaboration by unanimity vote of a preferential Common Agricultural Policy (CAP) with common prices and external levies. Negotiation of details postponed.*

Atomic energy (Euratom)	Favors only a minimal program.	Favors preferential European market and intensive R&D cooperation. No compromise of French nuclear program.	Favors only a minimal program if any.	Very strongly supports, with clause to ban military use of nuclear materials.	*Euratom is formed but remains minimal, with no preferential purchasing of uranium, modest common research, no ban on military use.*
Transport	Favors minimal nondiscrimination rules but otherwise continued protection.	Favors minimal nondiscrimination rules but otherwise continued protection.	No public position.	Strongly supports interventionist policy, backed by Netherlands.	*Modest and vague provision for common policy subject to elaboration by unanimity vote with no deadline.*
Institutions	Supports qualified majority voting (QMV) and some supranational delegation in industrial trade and commercial policy but not in agriculture, atomic energy, transport, or new policies. Accepts supranational structure.	Favors very limited QMV, little supranational autonomy, continued safeguards and vetoes, but accepts quasi-constitutional structure.	Favors QMV only on FTA. Opposes supranational autonomy and quasi-constitutional structure.	Favors strong delegation and pooling for centralized technocratic planning and management.	*Treaty retains unanimity during the transition. After 4–12 years, QMV and some supranational delegation to be introduced, particularly in external negotiations and competition policy. No QMV on atomic energy, transport, or new policies.*

Saar. Even after sovereign equality had largely been attained, Adenauer sought to commit Germany to a pro-Western alignment as against a resurgence of nationalist or neutralist ideologies of the extreme Right or Left, as well as alternative proposals for *Ostpolitik* from the opposition Social Democratic party. He consistently proclaimed that cooperation with the West would secure strong, reliable allies, thus providing a viable alternative to the SPD proposal for direct discussions with the Soviet Union. In the long run he may have supported eventual reunification on Western terms, but in the late 1950s he eschewed the unilateral, neutralist policies aimed at rapid unification supported by the SPD.[9]

One means of committing a wide range of allied governments to German goals was to embed Germany in common multilateral institutions such as NATO, the West European Union, and, not least, various schemes for European integration. Adenauer and the CDU benefited politically from the success of the Marshall Plan, the economic "miracle" of the 1950s, and Soviet pressure on Berlin. Domestically, European integration had an ideological appeal attractive to many centrist anti-Communist Germans—an appeal that also favored Adenauer's party, the CDU, *vis-à-vis* the SPD opposition. The linking of Germany to Western institutions made an independent, neutralist policy more difficult. Foreign leaders were concerned about German domestic stability: Adenauer often spoke of the need to embed Germany in institutions that would help prevent the revival of totalitarian impulses, as well as temptations to act unilaterally with regard to the Soviet Union. In Adenauer's words, European integration "protects German from itself."[10]

To an extent unique to the chancellor, Adenauer further sought to commit Germany to cooperation with France. While he enjoyed close ties to Britain and the United States, Adenauer also harbored a personal distrust for each. He chaffed under exclusion from proposals for a Anglo-French-American directorate.[11] Above all, intermittent consideration by Britain and the United States of direct negotiation with the USSR over the fate of Berlin, one of his ambassadors reported, "scared him stiff."[12] Through public commitments to continued cooperation, Adenauer sought greater French support for German defense. This policy was consistent with Adenauer's stress on the need for an independent European foreign policy and makes sense of his effort, simultaneous with the Treaty of Rome negotiations, to arrange joint Franco-German development of nuclear weapons—an agreement signed by the French but later repudiated by General de Gaulle. Other Western governments, though skeptical of nuclear

[9] Dockrill, *Britain's*, 55, also 59; Hans-Otto Kleinmann, *Geschichte der CDU 1945–1982* (Stuttgart, 1993), 127–128, 150ff.

[10] Hans-Peter Schwartz, *Adenauer: Der Staatsmann 1952–1967* (Stuttgart, 1991), 288; Küsters, "West Germany's," 62; Dockrill, *Britain's*, 22–23; Konrad Adenauer, *Erinnerungen, 1955–1959* (Stuttgart, 1967), 262, justifies integration as a means of solidifying the commitment of Germany to the West and creating a solid front against the USSR. Note, however, that even his tactful assistant concedes that "Adenauer's memoirs were a new political instrument," Anneliese Poppinga, *Meine Erinnerungen an Konrad Adenauer* (Stuttgart, 1970), 218. Cf. Schwarz, "Aussenpolitische Konzept," 74.

[11] Knipping, "Firm," 527; Pierre-Henri Teitgen, *"Faites entrer le témoin suivant," 1940–1958* (Paris, 1988), 476.

[12] Herbert Blankenhorn, *Verständnis und Verständigung: Blätter eines politischen Tagebuchs 1949 bis 1979* (Frankfurt, 1980), 148–149.

cooperation, generally agreed that deeper Franco-German relations contributed to Western security.[13]

Although few shared Adenauer's pro-French leanings, by the late 1950s neither major party in Germany harbored significant geopolitical objections to European economic cooperation. Though rhetorically pro-European, the SPD had opposed concrete steps toward European integration in the early 1950s. The major reasons were geopolitical: integration, SPD leaders believed, undermined prospects for rapid reunification and promoted the integration of a re-armed Germany into Western military plans, as well as limiting opportunities for state intervention in the economy. Around 1953 that position began to reverse; the reversal was complete by 1956. The most important reason was not a sudden conversion to European ideology, but instead the resolution of outstanding geopolitical concerns: after the failure of Adenauer's 1955 Moscow trip and the Geneva conferences, reunification had been downgraded as an immediate goal. Meanwhile the repatriation of the Saar, collapse of the Paulskirche disarmament movement, entry into NATO and the WEU, and defeat of the EDC had resolved Germany's postwar military and territorial status and disassociated European integration from geopolitical concerns. In addition, the death of Kurt Schumacher, an uncompromising proponent of rapid reunification, marked a generational shift in the SPD, and the *Wirtschaftswunder* and the creation of a social welfare state undermined arguments for state intervention. In addition, the SPD noted that the EC was less supranational than the ECSC and that it contained provisions to accommodate possible future reunification.[14] Less than two years later, this deep trend culminated in the promulgation of the Bad Godesberg program and the selection of Willy Brandt as the party's candidate for chancellor.

Economic Interest: Unilateral Liberalism and Agricultural Protection

Postwar German industry and government pursued a deliberate strategy of export-led growth. World War II truncated German markets, forcing its heavy industry, highly concentrated and disproportionately significant within the German economy, to export in order to realize modern economies of scale. The government accommodated export industrial demands through generous ex-

[13] Dockrill, *Britain's Policy*, 59ff.; lecture by Hans von der Groeben at Tagung des Instituts für europäische Politik, September 1989, 4.

[14] William E. Paterson, *The SPD and European Integration* (Lexington, Mass., 1974), 115–135; Küsters, *Gründung*, 422–427, 444, 450; Rudolf Hrbek, *Die SPD, Deutschland und Europa (1945–1957)* (Bonn, 1972); Mahant, *French*, 59–61, 263ff.; Hrbek, "The German Social Democratic Party, I," in *Socialist Parties and the Question of Europe in the 1950s*, edited by Richard T. Griffiths (Leiden, 1993), 73–75; Jürgen Bellers, "The German Social Democratic Party, II," in Griffiths, *Socialist Parties*, 63–83; Mahant, 264; Juliet Lodge, *The European Policy of the SPD* (Beverly Hills, Calif., 1976), 20–25; Kurt Thomas Schmitz, *Deutsche Einheit und Europäische Integration* (Bonn, 1978), 119–131; Ernst B. Haas, *The Uniting of Europe* (Stanford, 1958), 135–140. Karl Carstens (EC Archives, Fiesole, INT 26/8, 1987), 11, who worked closely with the SPD, calls it "a natural development," that "was occurring over the long-run anyway," though he also stresses the role of Monnet and himself. Von der Groeben argues that it was the SPD parliamentarian responsible for European economic matters who convinced others that the Treaty was simply economic. Interview 29/17 with von der Groeben, 46. While the CDU appeared to enjoy electoral success with European appeals, such appeals played little measurable role in swaying voters.

port financing, export-oriented foreign aid, appropriate border-taxes, currency undervaluation, and a permissive attitude toward industrial concentration.[15] The German peak industrial association, the Bundesverband der deutschen Industrie (BDI), was the most influential economic interest group in postwar Germany. BDI chief Fritz Berg has been described by one historian as "Adenauer's economics minister in everything but name," a relationship underscored by weekly meetings between the two.[16]

The BDI's positions on European integration reflected the commercial interests of its members concerning general and sectoral economic integration. They were not doctrinaire free marketeers. Berg and the BDI, whose internal structure favored large export interests, supported general tariff reductions but split along lines of competitive position over their proper scope. A clear majority of continentally and globally competitive sectors favored a "large Europe" FTA encompassing all OEEC countries. Lacking colonial links and stripped of traditional East European markets, high value-added capital goods industries— machine tools, machinery, transport equipment, and chemicals, together responsible for 88 percent of Germany's manufactured exports and the bulk of its large export surpluses—had rapidly redirected production toward Western Europe and North America. For these firms, low tariffs fueled a virtuous circle of low inflation, increasing competitiveness, and trade surpluses that permitted further tariff cuts. An FTA would avoid a high common tariff, which might disrupt established relations with third countries (e.g., in transport and machine tools) or increase raw materials prices by substituting French colonial raw materials for those from the Western hemisphere (e.g., in metal production). Smaller firms and sectors vulnerable to competition from Scandinavia or Britain, such as textiles, paper, nonferrous metals, and aircraft, totaling only 12 percent of German manufactured exports, favored instead the "small Europe" customs union among the Six. Almost no firms opposed liberalization entirely.[17]

[15] William Wadbrook, *West German Balance of Payments Policy: Prelude to European Monetary Union?* (New York, 1972), 22–29, 79–83; Michael Kreile, "West Germany: The Dynamics of Expansion," in *Between Power and Plenty: Foreign Economic Policies of Advanced Industrial States*, edited by Peter Katzenstein (Madison, Wis., 1978), 191–224; Herbert Giersch, Karl-Heinz Paqué, and Holger Schmiedling, *The Fading Miracle: Four Decades of Market Economy in Germany* (Cambridge, 1992).

[16] Thomas Rhenisch, "Die Deutsche Industrie und die Gründung der Europäischen Wirtschaftsgemeinschaft" (Ph.D. thesis, EUI, 1994), 28; Carl Lankowski, "Germany and the European Communities: Anatomy of a Hegemonial Relation" (Ph.D. thesis, Columbia University, 1982), 136–137; Arnulf Baring, *Aussenpolitik in Adenauers Kanzlerdemokratie* (Munich, 1969), 188–193; Giersch, *Fading*, 112–113, 120–124; Werner Bührer, "German Industry and European Integration in the 1950s," in Wurm, ed., *Western Europe and Germany*, 91–92. For a more nuanced view, see Interview with Hans von der Groeben (EC Archives, Fiesole, INT 26-15), 3–4.

[17] Giersch, *Fading*, 108, 112, 116; Ernst Otto, *Die deutsche Industrie im Gemeinsamen Markt* (Baden-Baden, 1957), 10, 30–34, 38–46; Karl Albrecht, "Gemeinsamer Markt und Freihandelszone im Urteil deutscher Wirtschaftskrise," *Aussenwirtschaft* 12 (1957), 155–162; R. Audouard, "Wirkung der europäischen Wirtschaftsgemeinschaft und der Freihandelszone auf den deutschen Maschinenbau," *Wirtschaftsdienst* 12 (September 1957), 514–518; Rhenisch, *Deutsche*, 28–37, 86ff., 125–127, 205–218; *Die Zeit* (4 July 1957), 10, 17. Even the Deutsche Industrie und Handelstag (DIHT)—the other major business organization, which more strongly represented finance and small, nontradables producers—supported the customs union while complaining even more stridently of its "dirigiste" tendencies. Fritz Berg, *Die westduetsche Wirtschaft in der Bewährung: Ausgewählte Reden aus den Jahren 1950–1965* (Hagen, 1966), 389–402. Erhard's extreme liberalism on issues like DM revaluation,

Despite their preference for an FTA, business and labor groups consistently if somewhat unenthusiastically endorsed Adenauer's efforts to secure a customs union. Berg, backed by Hermann Abs, the powerful president of Germany's largest bank, Deutsche Bank, supported the Spaak Report; neither mobilized business for an FTA nor publicly embraced the skepticism of Ludwig Erhard, Adenauer's minister of economics, his major rival in the CDU, and his successor as chancellor. For industrialists, this endorsement reflected their view that a customs union was better than nothing and that it would probably be followed by the formation of an FTA in any case.

BDI support also reflected, to be sure, big business backing for Adenauer's geopolitical agenda, including German foreign policy autonomy, the suppression of nationalism, and anti-Communism.[18] Yet Berg and the BDI were willing to compromise only a little to achieve geopolitical objectives. They rejected outright Monnet's schemes for sectoral integration. Monnet had been, in their view, a troublesome *dirigiste* who had sought, albeit unsuccessfully, to exploit the ECSC to bust cartels, set prices, and strip protection from coal producers when they were first coming under pressure from imported oil. A 1952 BDI resolution cautioned against the expansion of the ECSC, advocating instead "the resolute pursuit of the liberalization and gradual elimination of customs tariffs."[19] In 1955 Berg described the ECSC as "the typical example of how *not* to do European integration."[20] He welcomed Monnet's resignation and sought unsuccessfully to block the naming of his associate, Pierre Uri, as rapporteur for the Spaak Committee. German business was, in the words of one BDI leader, "realistic" rather than "enthusiastic" about Europe.[21]

Although Euratom was Adenauer's own primary priority, the BDI backed the German atomic industry against the government. The atomic industry's strategy for growth rested on access to uranium subsidized by the United States. German producers feared that Euratom would permit the French to charge monopolistic prices, gain control of German patents, and impose supranational direction. A 1955 public statement of the BDI Presidium rejected Euratom "*completely and decisively.*"[22] Business also criticized proposals for social harmonization, common

---

competition (antitrust) policy, and unilateral tariff reductions sparked their outright opposition. Milward, *Rescue*, 154ff.

[18] Gabriel Almond, "The Politics of German Business," in *West German Leadership and Foreign Policy*, edited by Hans Speier and W. Phillips Davison (Evanston, Ill., 1957), 232–233; Gerhard Braunthal, *The Federation of German Industry in Politics* (Ithaca, 1965), 288; Bührer, "German," 93–95; Albrecht, "Gemeinsamer," 16off.; Berg, *Westdeutsche*, 391; Edelgard Mahant, *French and German Attitudes to the Negotiations about the European Economic Community, 1955–1965* (London, mime, 1969), 275–289, 286–288, 295;

[19] Hans-Jürgen Schröder, "Germany's Economic Revival in the 1950s: The Foreign Policy Perspective," in Nolfo, *Power*, 190.

[20] Rhenisch, *Deutsche*, 72, also 71–73; Mahant, 277–278; Haas, *Uniting*, 168–173.

[21] Mahant, *French*, 231ff. Berg and Abs were apparently also satisfied with the defeat of the EDC, with its supranational implications. Reinisch, *Deutsche*, 68–71, 85; Bührer, "German," 87.

[22] Rhenisch, *Deutsche*, 73, ("mit *aller Entscheidenheit* abgelehnt"). Also, Christian Deubner, *Die Atompolitik der westdeutschen Industrie und die Grundung von Euratom* (Frankfurt, 1977), 2–13; Hanns Jürgen Küsters, "The Federal Republic of Germany and the EC-Treaty," in Enrico Serra, ed., *Il Rilancio dell'Europa e i Trattati di Roma* (Brussels, 1989), 500–501, and von der Groeben quoted at

agricultural and transport policies, and a strong competition policy but supported strict restraints on industrial subsidies.[23]

Business was supported by the Deutsche Gerwerkschaftsbund (DGB), the peak industrial union organization, in which tradable sectors were particularly strongly represented.[24] The DGB, supportive of both the ECSC and the EC and of cooperation with Monnet, pressed the SPD to renounce its economic program of nationalization and subsidized investment toward market-oriented policies, including European integration. SPD criticisms of the early 1950s, namely that the ECSC was a conservative and capitalist federation, were supplanted by views nearly indistinguishable from those of more left-wing members of the CDU. By the time of ratification, SPD economic arguments differed from those of the CDU only in the criticism of agricultural subsidies—a position reversed under electoral pressure in 1960.

German agriculture consistently sought to maintain high support prices behind protective barriers, which led to intense skepticism regarding cooperation with France.[25] Postwar division had left West Germany with relatively small and inefficient farms, except in a few areas of meat production, forcing it to become a massive net importer. German exports totaled less than 5 percent of intra-European commodity trade, while its imports totaled over 50 percent (see Table 1.2.). Led by the Deutsche Bauernverband (DBV), representing over three-quarters of Germany's agricultural sector, farmers were particularly influential in right and center parties. In the early 1950s agricultural interests were represented by about one-fifth of the CDU/CSU deputies in the Bundestag, with particular strength in Bavaria.

During the postwar period of food shortages and high prices, German farm groups embraced European integration as a means of legitimating demands for a permanent system of subsidies. The Franco-German Agricultural Committee advocated a European system of high price subsidies with privileged access for domestic producers through government purchasing. In 1955, however, with production increasing and prices falling, German farmers succeeded in exploiting their electoral and partisan power to secure the Green Law, which provided for price supports higher than in any other country among the Six (though across a limited range of products), linked to a system of external protection. High domestic support prices were necessarily linked to high protective barriers for the products in question. Continuing deficits in overall food production were covered, however, through cheap imports and bilateral quota arrangements

---

189; Deubner, "The Expansion of West Germany Capital and the Founding of Euratom," *International Organization* 33:2 (Spring), 210–215; Bührer, "German," 104–105.

[23] Rhenisch, *Deutsche*, 86ff.; Mahant, *French*, 281–286.

[24] Lankowski, *German*, 136–137; Haas, *Uniting*, 219–225; Giersch, *Fading*, 112, 120; Mahant, *French*, 291–295;

[25] This was not free trade: both groups vehemently opposed Dutch proposals for a European arrangement based on free trade, low subsidies, and low-cost specialization. Elmar Rieger, "Agrarpolitik: Integration durch Gemeinschaftspolitik?" in Beate Kohler-Koch, ed., *Europäische Integration* (Opladen, 1996), 416; Fritz Baade, *Der europäische Longterm-Plan und die amerikanische Politik* (Kiel, 1949), 15–17; Ulrich Kluge, "Du Pool Noir au Pool Vert," in Serra, *Il rilancio*, 239–280; Brusse, *West*, 282–283, 289

with efficient European suppliers, notably Denmark and the Netherlands. This arrangement was stable. With subsidies in place and domestic consumption rising, the displacement of imports would permit 10 percent increases in the production of many commodities for several decades, though more immediate overproduction loomed in rye, pork, and dairy products. Having secured their domestic goals, German farmer groups began to view European agricultural cooperation with greater skepticism. They assumed that common EC prices would be below German rates but above those elsewhere, thereby dampening German production and dramatically increasing production of Italian vegetables, Dutch dairy products, and French grain. German farmers would be exposed to new competition. If European price supports were high, German agriculture would not necessarily suffer, but such an outcome was considered unlikely as it would lead to expensive surpluses across Europe.[26]

Hence the position of farmers toward the Treaty was cautious and ambivalent, but not hostile. The DBV issued public criticisms but did not mobilize against the Treaty. Adenauer's strong electoral position, which was to become an absolute majority in 1957, afforded him autonomy, but his top assistant on the issue nonetheless consulted continuously with Andreas Hermes, head of the Deutsche Raiffeisenverband, the group traditionally responsible for agricultural trade matters. Hermes approved every German negotiating position before it was introduced.[27] Germany was extremely careful in the agricultural area, insisting on unanimity voting, vague rules, and a postponement of decisions concerning the level of price supports—decisions that, as we shall see in chapter 3, generated calculable gains and losses and, therefore, intense mobilization. In 1956–57 the DBV limited itself to advocacy of a lengthy transition period, harmonization of competitive conditions, price increases elsewhere to German levels, and corporatist arrangements in which German farm groups, sure to favor higher prices, could maintain their direct control over policy.

The Domestic Decision:
A "preference for Europe . . . within limits"

What does the process of decision-making in Germany tell us about the relative influence of commercial and geopolitical factors?

In May 1955 top ministers and officials met in Eicherscheid to coordinate the German position for the Messina meeting. The result was open conflict between two factions, one concerned with economic imperatives, the other with geopol-

---

[26] Fritz Baade, *Die Deutsche Landwirtschaft in gemeinsamen Markt* (Baden-Baden, 1958), 12–13, 65; Horst Marmulla and Pierre Brault, *Europäische Integration und Agrarwirtschaft* (Munich, 1958), 170; Mahant, *French*, 304–309; Milward, *Rescue*, 302.

[27] On consultations see Karl Carstens, *Erinnerungen und Erfahrungen* (Boppard am Rhein, 1993), 213; Beate Kohler-Koch, "Beitrag der deutschen Agrarverbände zum Management von internationaler Interdependenz" (paper, Darmstadt, 1984), 8–9. Hermes was a former head of the DBV. The BDV appears, however, to have been quietly skeptical of the Treaty, though afterward they quickly shifted to arguing for high prices. Some argue that German agriculture was too small, weak, and beholden to the CDU to be influential, but this is the same group that had secured the generous Agricultural Law of 1955 and would later force high prices within the CAP.

itics. The first faction was led by economics minister Ludwig Erhard, an economic liberal who favored global free trade.[28] Throughout the 1950s the German government, pressed by business, supported industrial trade liberalization. Erhard favored an FTA in which other policies, including external tariffs, would be subject only to intergovernmental consultation and would be clearly subordinate to existing OEEC and GATT commitments. Thus he opposed a "small Europe" customs union with strong institutions, fearing that such an arrangement would evolve into a closed trading block.

Erhard's position was more extreme than that of German business. The BDI did not support his proposals for *unilateral* trade liberalization. Through the 1950s Erhard had unilaterally driven German tariffs close to the low rates prevailing in the Benelux countries, paying special attention to reduced tariffs on raw materials and intermediate goods from extra-European sources. Business opposition postponed but could not prevent a 20–40 percent reduction in German base tariff rates in 1957—an act of unilateral openness that one commentator termed "a unique event in the history of trade policy." Erhard's extreme free-trade position was backed only by the small Free Democratic Party (FDP) and small minorities in the CDU and SPD, and by a handful of businessmen; few others publicly advocated rejection of the customs union.[29]

The second faction, led by Adenauer, State Secretary Walter Hallstein, and director of West European affairs Carl Ophüls (later replaced by Karl Carstens), represented the Foreign Ministry and Chancellor's Office. Soon after the failure of the EDC, Hallstein had called for a new political initiative for European integration, citing the changing East-West situation, British hesitations, the inadequacy of the OEEC, WEU, and Council of Europe, and the rising enthusiasm for Europe among young Germans. Adenauer and Hallstein agreed that the most promising economic proposal was Monnet's plan for an extension of the ECSC to new sectors, notably atomic energy. Adenauer sought to employ the powers of the Chancellery to secure geopolitical goals. The Foreign Ministry remained under Adenauer's personal control—he served as his own foreign minister until 1955—and was staffed with pro-European officials loyal to him. Most important among them was Hallstein, a former economics professor, who had responsibilities both in the Foreign Ministry and the Chancellor's Office.

The two factions at Eicherscheid hammered out a compromise negotiating position. Its core was support for the customs union. Erhard secured agreement that it was to be fully in accordance with Article 24 of the GATT, thus preclud-

---

[28] For a recent, well-documented treatment representative of an extensive literature, see Sabine Lee, "German Decision-Making Elites and European Integration: German "Europapolitik" during the Years of the EC and Free Trade Area Negotiations," in Anne Deighton, ed., *Building Postwar Europe: National Decision-Makers and European Institutions, 1948–63* (London, 1995), 38ff., esp. 44ff.

[29] Alfred Müller-Armack, *Auf dem Wege nach Europa: Errinerungen und Ausblicke* (Tübingen, 1971), 72. Reductions were achieved by suspending the application of tariff rates, while leaving them on the books as a multilateral bargaining tool. Also Müller-Armack, *Wege*, 93–99, 110–111; *Die Zeit* (4 July 1957), 10; Wendy Asbeek Brusse, *West European Tariff Plans, 1947–1957: From the Study Group to the Common Market* (Florence, 1991), 287–293; Giersch, *Fading*, 108; Küsters, *Gründung*, 116–118; Gabriele Brenke, "Europakonzeptionen im Widerstreit: Die Freihandelszonen-Verhandlungen 1956–1958," *Vierteljahreshefte für Zeitgeschichte*, 42, 4 (October 1994), 598, 625; Mahant, *French*, 243–244; von der Groeben, in Serra, *Il rilancio*, 188–189.

ing any net increase in third-country tariffs. Negotiation of an FTA with other European states was also to follow. Sectoral integration, for example in transport, was rejected, with the exception of atomic cooperation—a quid pro quo for French acceptance of restrictions on external tariffs. Erhard also secured the inclusion of a competition (antitrust) policy. Adenauer achieved his primary goal, namely to support Monnet's plan for an atomic energy community. Yet well before Messina, as we shall see in more detail, the German government accepted that German industry could block such a plan unless it was linked to a customs union. At Eicherscheid it was therefore agreed to link a modest Euratom program to the customs union—a linkage termed the "Junktim." Yet even this proved unsustainable. By February 1957 the German atomic industry had vetoed any arrangement to grant a monopoly on nuclear materials to European producers, gutting the plan.

On institutions, the compromise at Eicherscheid rejected Erhard's demand that Germany should permit no supranational institutions other than a consultative committee under the Council of Ministers but nonetheless retreated from the sort of open-ended authority that had been granted the ECSC High Authority. Major decisions would require the unanimous approval of the EC Council of Ministers, at least initially, with an independent advisory board having power of proposal and a coordinating body of high national officials carrying out daily business. Eventually there would be a transition to QMV, with exceptions for sensitive policies.[30] These proposals bear a remarkable resemblance to current EC institutions.

Throughout the 1950s, Germany had refused to enter into multilateral commitments to liberalize agriculture, including sector-by-sector negotiations in the OEEC, and had blocked the application of unfavorable bilateral agreements, in particular with France and the Netherlands. To be sure, Adenauer himself had been willing to consider the inclusion of agriculture to promote European integration, a concession viewed somewhat skeptically by Erhard. When Dutch agriculture minister Sicco Mansholt had proposed agricultural and industrial liberalization as part of the ill-fated EDC negotiations three years previously, Adenauer, desperate to save the Defense Community, had told the Dutchman that sacrifices in the cause of agricultural integration would be amply compensated by gains from economic integration in other areas. Yet Adenauer's willingness to make agricultural concessions had yet to be translated into policy. At Eicherscheid, the Agriculture and Economics ministries approved the inclusion of agriculture in the German proposal as a means to attract French support, although, with one eye on farming interests, no specific provisions were authorized.[31]

---

[30] On Euratom, see Peter Weilemann, *Die Anfänge der Europäischen Atomgemeinschaft: Zur Gründungsgeschichte von Euratom 1955–1957* (Baden-Baden, 1982). On the long-term German position, see Rita Cardozo, "The Project for a Political Community (1952–54)," in Roy Pryce, ed., *The Dynamics of European Union* (London, 1987), 67–70. Initially, Germany favored a "purely European executive." Adenauer, *Erinnerungen*, 233–235, 252–255; von der Groeben, cited in Serra, *Il rilancio*, 180–181. The Economics Ministry sponsored an official study of economic unions in history, finding that they generally have not withstood economic shocks unless grounded in deeper economic integration.

[31] Kluge, "Pool," 268; Pierre Brault, *Europäische Integration und Agrarwirtschaft* (Munich, 1958), 34–36. Hallstein later observed that the Germans rejected sectoral integration because it was "dis-

The compromise at Eicherscheid remained the basis of the German position until the end of the negotiations. Adenauer repeatedly attempted to extract greater concessions. In January 1956 he went so far as to invoke the Chancellor's constitutional foreign policy powers (*Richtlinienkompetenz*), requesting that agriculture and industry bear "sacrifices" in order to achiéve geopolitical goals, including closer relations with France and European institutions with real autonomy, particularly in the area of nuclear energy. But this move failed to shift the compromise. For his part, Erhard sought to deadlock the Franco-German negotiations on social policy but was overruled by the chancellor, who called a summit meeting with his French counterpart.[32]

In sum, Adenauer succeeded in shifting policy in favor of his geopolitical goals, in particular close relations with France, but only on the margin. As German diplomats told their counterparts, he gave "within the limits of policy, a preference to the European solution rather than to other alternatives."[33] Without geopolitical concerns, which business itself acknowledged, Germany would surely have supported a British-style FTA, and the shift would prove very significant for the outcome of the negotiations. Yet in all other areas Adenauer remained tightly constrained by business pressure. Germany resisted concrete concessions on agriculture and was unforthcoming on atomic energy, Adenauer's most important priority, and transport. Although Adenauer, over Erhard's objections, supported quasi-constitutional institutions, a measure of Commission autonomy, and QMV, he extended none of these to areas in which Germany was immediately vulnerable, such as the creation of transport, agricultural, and atomic energy policies. In addition, Adenauer refused to move forward until outstanding territorial issues—notably the Saar—had been fully resolved.

Negotiation and ratification went smoothly. As in France, the negotiations were coordinated by an interministerial committee that met weekly, though with broader participation. Adenauer's personal prestige, along with the near-majority in the Bundestag held by the CDU/CSU and the support of the SPD, dampened opposition.[34] The government made sure that provisions on questions of reunification, in particular clauses concerning interzonal trade, would gain the support of the SPD. The SPD parliamentary spokesperson justified his party's support for the Treaty by noting that in contrast to the ECSC and EDC,

---

advantageous, possibly harmful" in economic terms. Miriam Camps, *Britain and the European Community, 1955–1963* (Princeton, 1964), 32n. Adenauer had refused bilateral agricultural concessions to Scandinavian countries. Milward attributes support from Agriculture Minister Lübke entirely to his backing of Adenauer's foreign policy, but this is based only on the impression of U.S. observers. Milward, *Rescue*, 310. Carstens's testimony above suggests a different interpretation.

[32] Mahant, *French*, 231, also 58; Küsters, *Gründung*, 117–120, 130, 201, 423; Lee, "German," 50; Adenauer, *Erinnerungen*, 253ff.; von der Groeben, cited in Serra, *Il rilancio*, 179; Baade, *Deutsche*, 17, 23, 25;

[33] Werner Maihofer, *Noi si mura*, selected working papers of the European University Institute (Firenze, 1986), 605; Küsters, *Gründung*, 68ff.

[34] Felix von Eckardt, *Ein unordentliches Leben: Lebenserinnerungen* (Düsseldorf, 1967), 325; Küsters, *Gründung*, 446–448, 481–482, 470–472; Interview with Karl Carstens, EC Archives No. 26/8, 1–3.

the EC did not raise fundamental geopolitical issues, and its social and economic policies were desirable.[35] Among centrist parties, only the FDP and a few scattered SPD members, among them Helmut Schmidt, voted against the Treaty, fearing it would exclude Britain, subsidize agriculture, or impede German reunification. Modest concessions to the SPD on the question of German reunification eliminated all other opposition. In contrast to the ECSC and EDC debates, SPD concerns about rearmament and reunification played little role. For his part, Erhard spoke out critically—in one speech he compared the customs union to an armored car with overdeveloped brakes and an underpowered engine. Then he deferred to the chancellor and loyally supported the Treaty before the Bundestag.[36]

France: Cautious Economic Liberalization

Between 1955 and 1957, under the successive governments of Edgar Faure, Guy Mollet, and Maurice Bourgès-Maunoury, France remained cautiously supportive of a customs union, but its position varied across issues. Exceptionally strong support for a common agricultural policy and atomic energy cooperation coexisted with cautious acceptance of trade liberalization and virulent opposition to any form of pan-European FTA. On institutional commitments, France remained hesitant, consistently seeking to retain institutional safeguards against uncontrolled liberalization. Starting in September 1956 the Mollet government all but dropped atomic energy cooperation and pushed for rapid agreement on a customs union, fearing a political or economic crisis would strip away its electoral mandate. Ratification in the Assembly came in the end by a relatively comfortable margin of 342 to 239, with near-unanimous support from Christian Democrats and Socialists, strong backing from Conservatives and Radicals, split support from Gaullists, and opposition from Communists and extreme-right Poujadists. How best to explain this pattern of preferences?

Most commentators contend that French policy was driven by primarily geopolitical ideas and interests. Like the ECSC, they argue, the EC was a means to tie Germany into Europe and render a future European war impossible. The Suez crisis, many argue, demonstrated to the French that the colonial empire was untenable and that France's primary ally against Germany was untrustworthy. The most detailed study of the period, cited above, calls the Treaty a "historical accident" resulting from Suez. Others point to the pro-European beliefs of politicians like Guy Mollet, a member of Monnet's Action Committee whose government conducted the negotiations.

Yet the preponderance of evidence suggests that French policy was based as much or more on commercial interest as on geopolitical interest or ideas. Key negotiating demands and critical domestic support for ratification reflected economic not geopolitical concerns. In defining the substance of the agreement

---

[35] Bundestag, *Stenographische Berichte* 38:13314ff.
[36] Küsters, *Gründung*, 423, also 450. Also Lodge, *European*, 24.

and securing parliamentary ratification, pressure from farmers was decisive. Farmers had actively promoted cooperation since 1949. Industry was hesitant to liberalize without devaluation and provisions for overseas territories, hence its demands for safeguards and other concessions entered into the government's negotiating position almost verbatim. At most, geopolitical ideology explains the active promotion of the Treaty by insiders within the Mollet government—but even there pragmatists such as Foreign Minister Christian Pineau and Robert Marjolin held the balance. These insiders were concerned as much or more with avoiding economic isolation and only secondarily with securing geopolitical alliances. Most geopolitical arguments—even Mollet's own pro-British instincts— mitigated *against* cooperation with Germany; yet no economic agreement could be reached with Britain. Overall, as compared to the debacle of EDC rejection just a few years before, it was precisely the secondary role of geopolitical interests and ideas that permitted rapid negotiation and ratification. As in Germany, many potential parliamentary opponents—notably Socialists and Gaullists— concluded that little was at stake geopolitically and voted their economic interest.[37] The result was cautious strong support for atomic and agricultural cooperation, cautious support for an industrial customs union, and near-unanimous opposition to a free trade area.

Geopolitical Interest and Ideology: Is France "strong enough for isolation"?

The 1950s was a period of geopolitical ferment in France. The rise of German power, the prospect of decolonization, and the failure of the EDC engendered a fear of diplomatic isolation. The French decision to support the Rome Treaty, one historian observes, focused "less on the conditions of acceptance . . . and more on the costs of non-acceptance . . . [France] would be driven into isolation in both its economic and foreign policies."[38] As Réne Mayer asked during the EDC debate, "If France is not strong enough for a European policy, is it strong enough for isolation?"[39] Underlying this concern to avoid isolation were economic interest and four potential geopolitical motivations: pro-European ideology, the management of the "German problem," the maintenance of France as a great power, and support for the French nuclear program. Each of these considerations was ambiguous, generating both support and opposition to the Treaty. At least until the Suez crisis of November 1956, and perhaps beyond, however, the balance of geopolitical considerations leaned France against European integration.

A first geopolitical consideration, the German problem, played a modest role in domestic debates—a striking contrast to the ECSC and EDC decisions. Maurice Faure, the government's spokesman on Europe, argued before the Assembly that the EC would bind the Federal Republic to the West with "a thousand small linkages," thereby minimizing the possibility of Franco-German conflict or German-Soviet rapprochement. Yet the counterarguments, namely that

[37] For a similar interpretation, see Lynch, *France.*
[38] Lynch, *France,* 178.
[39] Gérard Bossuat, *Le France, l'aide américaine, at la construction européenne, 1944–1954* (Paris, 1992), 2:898.

the Treaty would isolate France from its true ally, Britain, or would facilitate German economic domination of France, were far more widely held. Overall, geopolitical concerns were little discussed, even by Gaullists, the most likely to be concerned about German domination.[40]

A second geopolitical factor, which tended to support the Treaty, was the need to finance the French nuclear weapons program, which had been secretly launched by the Faure and Mollet governments. Civilian cooperation in nuclear energy, a goal of Monnet's, was supported by French government officials as a means of financing military programs. Hence French proposals for atomic energy cooperation (Euratom) involved the establishment of de facto French monopolies in the provision of some basic nuclear materials, which would act to "subsidize" French nuclear development. In the first year of negotiation, until mid-1956, the creation of Euratom was seen as the sole French objective; even Gaullists strongly supported it. But, as we shall see, little came of the Euratom negotiations in the end, which diminishes the potential importance of such considerations.

A third geopolitical factor, which may also have favored the Treaty, was pro-European ideology. To be sure, pro-European ideology did not generate strong support for the EC in French politics as a whole. The European federalist movement in France was modest and faced vehement opponents. Within the Assemblée Nationale, only the small Christian Democratic Mouvement Républicain Populaire (MRP, Monnet's party) had a history of unquestioned support for supranational institutions and federal schemes. Even the MRP was not acting out of purely ideological motives, however. In the late 1940s the party suddenly embraced European federalism, apparently to better pursue the economic interests of its largely rural constituency and to foster anti-Communist internationalism among its considerable labor support.[41] In taking a pro-European position on the Treaty of Rome, the MRP was joined after the EDC by the Socialist Party, within which Mollet had reestablished the pro-European position. Yet Socialist Party rhetoric was more pragmatic than ideological; leading Socialists viewed Europe as economically inevitable more than politically desirable.

These two parties were more than balanced, however, by uncompromising ideological opponents at the extremes of the political spectrum, Poujadists and Communists, completely hostile to the EC for both economic and geopolitical reasons. The underlying partisan distribution in the Assembly was slightly less favorable than that which had voted down the EDC. Gaullists had been replaced by Communists and Poujadists even more strongly opposed to Europe, and the

---

[40] Mahant, *French*, 160; Gerhard Kiersch, *Parlament und Parlamentarier in der Außenpolitik der IV. Republik* (Berlin, 1971), 302; Küsters, *Gründung*, 419–421; Mahant, *French*, 85–97.

[41] Before 1948, MRP leaders had ridiculed the European movement as idealistic. Pierre Guillen, "Le MRP et l'union économique de l'Europe, 1947–1950," Jean-Paul Brunet, "Le MRP et la construction européenne, 1955–1957," and Pierre Letamendia, "La place des problèmes européens dans la vie interne du parti sous la IVe Republique," all in Serge Berstein, Jean-Marie Mayeur, and Pierre Milza, eds., *Le MRP et la construction européenne* (Paris, 1993), 109–110, 131–134, 240. R. E. M. Irving, *Christian Democracy in France* (London, 1973), 179–181, 191ff, argues that the MRP's main reasons for supporting the customs union were economic and social.

MRP had been diminished. Hence the positive outcome in the EC vote, as compared to that for the EDC, stemmed from a shift in the behavior of center-right and center-left parties: whereas the EDC unified the Gaullists in opposition and split the SFIO, Radicals, and Conservatives, the EC unified the SFIO (reorganized by Mollet) in favor, secured strong Conservative support, and split the Gaullists and Radicals. In short, given Socialist support for the government, the balance in the Assembly lay with parties of the center-right—Radicals, Conservatives, and Gaullists. As we shall see, their position reflected economic more than geopolitical concerns.[42]

If pro-European ideology was important, therefore, it was not because of an advantageous split in parliament but because the Faure, Mollet, and Bourgès-Maunoury governments, under which the Treaty was negotiated and ratified, were pro-European. The government of Mendès-France, whose lukewarm support had doomed the EDC, pursued (in his own words) "a policy of balance in Europe, not a European policy." An important shift came when Mendès-France was succeeded by Edgar Faure and then Mollet, perceived at home and abroad as opening a window of opportunity for further integration.

Faure, who entered office in early 1955, was a "pragmatic" European. He had repeatedly proposed and supported trade liberalization plans in the past, but was forced to be cautious due to the presence of four Gaullists among his ministers. In any European intiative he would be generally backed by the pro-European MRP on principle, but the balance in the government was held by moderates—politicians sympathetic to economic integration in general but skeptical, even personally hostile, to federalists such as Monnet, whom Faure called "more a mystic than a pragmatist."[43] Faure named Pinay, an Independent and another pragmatist associated with the Patronat, as foreign minister as a move to conciliate pro-Europeans. He sent Pinay to Messina with instructions to support Euratom, not the Common Market. Olivier Wormser, the Foreign Ministry adviser accompanying Pinay, warned him not to risk another open veto after the EDC debacle. The Messina meeting ended successfully, we shall see, only when Pinay, after a late-night conversation with Spaak, overrode Faure and supported both initiatives.[44]

The resurgence of the Socialist Party in the elections of January 1956, along

---

[42] On the parties, see Mahant, *French*, especially 160–162; and Kiersch, *Parliament*, passim. For a more skeptical view of socioeconomic support, Küsters, *Gründung*, 131. Between signature and ratification of the treaty, Mollet ordered the SFIO to wage "a propaganda battle, a labour of disintoxication and a labour of preparation" to assure ratification: "We shall be attacked, since the employers, craftsmen and farmers will not move at the necessary speed in order to adjust to the new world we are launching ourselves into." Réne Girault, "Decision Makers, Decisions, and French Power," in Nolfo, *Power*, 69ff; Pierre Guillen, "Europe as a Cure for French Impotence?" in Nolfo, *Power*, 516. Also Cardozo, "Project," 57; Mahant, *French*, 85–97, 137, 145ff, 171ff.

[43] Edgar Faure, *Mémoires* (Paris, 1984), 2:212; Gerard Bossuat, *L'Europe des Francais 1943–1959: La IVe Republique aux sources de L'Europe communautaire* (Paris, 1996), 264–266.

[44] François Duchêne, *Jean Monnet: The First Statesman of Interdependence* (New York, 1995), 280–282; interview with Émile Noël (EC Archives, Fiesole, 26–27, 1988), 10. Cf. Interview with Jean Sauvagnargues, then an assistant to Pinay, who sees linking Germany politically to the West as "the fundamental idea" (EC Archives, Fiesole, 26–34, 1987–1988), 6, 11. More generally, Christian Pineau and Maurice Faure in Serra, *Il rilancio*, 281–282, 287; Milward, *Rescue*, 209–211; Cardozo, "Project," 55–57; Wilfried Loth, "The French Socialist Party, 1947–1954," and Denis Lefevre, "The

with the extremist opponents of Europe on the left and right, was initially viewed as a setback for the negotiations. Yet the Mollet government in fact promoted Europe more strongly than its predecessor. Mollet, minister for Europe from 1950 to 1951, president of the Council of Europe from 1954 to 1956, and soon a member of Monnet's Action Committee for Europe, was invited to form a government in large part because he was perceived as "European." His investiture speech took ideas from Monnet—notably support for Euratom. Mollet chose another relatively pro-European, Christian Pineau, as his foreign minister, but not before flirting with the idea of naming the Euroskeptical Mendès-France to the post—though there is no evidence that this was deliberately aimed at influencing European policy. Many top appointed officials, notably Maurice Faure and Robert Marjolin, were sympathetic to Europe, the former largely on political grounds, the latter overwhelmingly for economic ones. From the perspective of some pro-Europeans, Miriam Camps notes, the EC provided an opportunity to "repair the damage to their own prestige and position caused by their rejection of the EDC."[45] Mollet also headed a government containing only dissident Gaullists and no Communists.

A fourth and final geopolitical concern was the influence of European integration on France's great-power status—an argument linked after November 1956 to the Suez crisis. In this period, national decline and the potential for renewal recurred obsessively in the discourse of French political elites. Decolonization and the war in Algeria were by far the most salient foreign policy issues in France during the late 1950s, far overshadowing European integration. In the mid-1950s the two alternatives for renewal looked very similar to those facing Britain: either the reinforcement of Empire, often associated with an Anglo-French alliance, or a move toward European unification. To be sure, some opposed European integration because they saw it as a threat to empire. The view, developed earlier within French officialdom, quickly spread that the military and financial costs of empire were unsustainable for France alone and that an alliance with Britain was little help. The government argued that economic cooperation with Continental European countries was the only remaining way to maintain close relations with present and former colonies at an acceptable financial cost.

The Suez crisis is often invoked in connection with French great-power concerns—it is the most commonly advanced geopolitical argument. The Suez crisis—in which Britain backed out of a joint operation in the face of U.S. pressure without consulting France—seemed to demonstrate midway through the negotiations that French geopolitical strategy had to change. Ideas about a European "third force" began to percolate. We know that the British abandonment of France at Suez weighed heavily on Mollet personally. The crisis was cited in parliamentary debates. Often noted is the striking coincidence of timing: 6 November 1956 saw both a breakthrough in face-to-face discussions with Adenauer

French Socialist Party, 1954–1957," in Griffiths, ed. *Socialist Parties*, 25–56, especially 43–47; Lynch, *France*, 170–172.

[45] Camps, *Britain*, 29. Also Noël Interview, 7–8, 11.

and Anthony Eden's call to inform Mollet of the unilateral British acceptance of the cease-fire. Some supporters also argued that the Treaty would permit France to enhance its dignity and its independence from the superpowers.[46]

Economic Interest: "Any French government was obliged to defend a common agricultural policy"

Beneath the political turbulence of the Fourth Republic, French industry was steadily modernizing. Long-term investment and industrial growth proceeded apace; they were linked to the rapid expansion of manufactured trade with Europe.[47] A doubling of exports to Europe between 1953 and 1957 offset rapidly declining colonial trade. In 1953, 37 percent of French exports went to the Franc Zone and 19 percent to the Six; by 1962 these figures would reverse, a trend evident to French officials and businessmen by the mid-1950s. Big business began to press for lower taxes and social costs, the elimination of price controls, less state intervention in capital markets, and, not least, trade liberalization. "Large-scale business," one observer noted, "now believes that its interests lie in lower prices, expanded output, and wider markets."[48] Yet an overvalued currency and intermittent trade deficits rendered much of French industry uncompetitive. The result was a slow increase in support for liberalization: opposition to the ECSC under pressure from the protectionist elements of the chemical, steel, and metalworking sectors, who mounted a bitter campaign in 1950–51 against the anti-cartel provisions of the ECSC over the objection of firms that consumed these basic industrial materials; failure to reach internal agreement on the Franco-German treaty or the economic provisions of the EDC in 1953–54; then conditional support for the EC in 1956.

Cleavages within business reflected external competitiveness. Support for liberalization was led by exporters and bankers in sectors such as electrical engineering and automobiles, where firms such as Renault planned export drives.[49] Support also came from producers of paper, chemicals, and woodworking, who feared only U.S., U.K., or Scandinavian competition. Yet the bulk of French industry remained skeptical. The textile, steel, and mechanical engineering associations, as well as particularly vocal cotton producers, public utilities, and metal finishers, faced strong competition within the Six. Representatives of small business, a larger sector in France than in the rest of the Six, opposed the customs union. Much of this opposition could be ascribed not to underlying competitiveness but to macroeconomic conditions: French labor costs were relatively high. Observers predicted that "until the French franc has been given a more

---

[46] Küsters, "West Germany's Foreign Policy," 71. More generally, Lynch, *France*, 129–145, 170–178, 180; Mahant, *French*, 97ff, 113ff, 117, 119ff, 136ff. For a more complete discussion, see below.

[47] Philip M. Williams, and Martin Harrison, *Politics and Society in de Gaulle's Republic* (Garden City, N.Y., 1971), 426.

[48] Charles Kindleberger, cited in F. Roy Willis, *France, Germany and the New Europe, 1945–1967* (Stanford, 1968), 395n

[49] By October 1956, large firms in the automobile, television and radio, and cotton sectors had already made major investments on the expectation that the common market would be realized.

realistic value, there is little chance of assuaging fears of foreign competition felt by French industry."[50]

The leading French business association, the Conseil National du Patronat Français (CNPF), headed by George Villiers, moved cautiously toward support for the customs union even before the government formally did so. At an April 1956 meeting with the government, most representatives of private industry opposed the customs union; by July 1956, however, Villiers had moved the CNPF behind the proposal. Thereafter, a CNPF group met biweekly to review the negotiations and comment on government proposals. By the eve of ratification, some sectoral associations still voiced criticisms of specific provisions, but only the textile industry remained openly opposed.[51]

This shift in business strategy was linked primarily to the government's acceptance of a package of six conditions demanded by Villiers. Liberalization, the CNPF insisted, must proceed slowly, with national governments maintaining control through safeguard options, special import and export taxes, escape clauses, and veto rights. Aid for French colonies would benefit less competitive producers. To satisfy competitiveness concerns, prior harmonization of fiscal burdens and social regulations (long a demand of even the strongest supporters of Europe) was seen as a second-best substitute for devaluation. Devaluation was so unpopular domestically, with a Socialist government in power, that business did not advocate it in public.[52]

In contrast to the situation in agriculture, producer support for industrial liberalization should not be thought of as simply reflecting a desire for access to German or Benelux industrial markets. Unilateral German policies already made tariffs low and stable. The willingness of the CNPF to back liberalization also reflected concerns about economic isolation. French producers and government officials sought to protect and to extend preferential trade access to Germany

[50] Carol Levy Balassa, "Organized Industry in France and the European Common Market: Interest Group Attitudes and Behavior" (Ph.D. diss., Johns Hopkins University, 1978), 93–94. On sectoral preferences, see Erling Bjøl, *La France devant l'Europe: La Politique européenne de la IVe République* (Copenhagen, 1966), 264, 387, 40–405, Appendixes; Balassa, "Organized," 83ff, 111, 119; Henri Weber, *Le parti des patrons: Le CNPF (1946–1986)* (Paris, 1986), 100ff. Mahant, *French,* 178ff, 206; cf. Robert Frank, "The French Alternative: Economic Power through the Empire or through Europe? in Nolfo, *Power in Europe?* 160–173. Consistent with economic interests, a proposed Franco-Italian free trade area plan had been opposed by the textile, agriculture, and food processing sectors and supported by the chemical, engineering, and paper industries. Pierre Guillen, "Frankreich und der europäische Wiederaufschwung. Vom Scheitern der EVG zur Ratifizierung der Verträge von Rom," *Vierteljahrshefte für Zeitgeschichte* 28:1 (1980), 16–18. Unions do not seem to have been highly mobilized on the issue. The Socialist Force Ouvrière, largely representing white-collar workers, many public-sector, followed the government; the centrist CFTC and CGC were ambivalent; only the Communist CGT opposed outright. Mahant, *French,* 179–181, 206; interview with Maurice Faure (EC Archives, Fiesole, INT 29/3, 1984), 3; Henry W. Ehrmann, *Organized Business in France* (Princeton, 1957), 403–406, 408, 419; Guillen, "MRP," 142–144.

[51] Bjøl, *France,* Appendix.

[52] No direct evidence appears to support Balassa's claim that business, as in the case of the ECSC, saw no alternative to acceptance, due to the power of the government coalition, and so sought a compromise. The government fulfilled nearly all business demands and it was widely accepted, as we shall see, that even so the Treaty might well not be implemented. Balassa, "Organized," 93–94; Mahant, *French,* 178ff, 195ff.

which had grown under Europe's nonconvertible currency arrangement, the European Payments Union. With other countries, led by Germany or Britain, likely to move to liberalization in the wake of crisis within the EPU, many businessmen believed trade liberalization in some form was inevitable and business should seek the best possible deal.[53] In particular, the customs union was greatly preferable to exclusion from or membership in an Anglo-German FTA. One observer noted that "for the first time in history the CNPF . . . was completely unanimous—in opposing any EFTA."[54] The preferences of big business dovetailed with those of many, though by no means the majority of, French economic officials, who had increasingly come to view economic modernization as possible only through trade liberalization.[55]

With industry no more than cautiously and conditionally supportive, observed Robert Marjolin, former head of the OEEC and the official who handled Mollet's relations with economic interest groups, the strongly positive position of agriculture was decisive.[56] Agriculture accounted for a higher share of employment (25 percent) in France than in any other of the Six except Italy. French farmers were competitive on world markets in capital-intensive commodities—such as high-quality wines and specialty gourmet products—but the bulk of French production was in less competitive, land-intensive agricultural commodities such as grain, sugar, wine, and some dairy and beef products. Subsidies, in the form of price supports, were therefore essential to farmer prosperity. By the mid-1950s, with steady backing from three political parties with broad rural bases—the Christian Democratic MRP, the Conservatives, and the Radical Party (with the exception of the Mendèsist faction)—farm groups imposed a de facto veto over the selection of agriculture ministers and had forced constant increases in agricultural subsidies. The 1952 economic plan aimed at a 40 percent reduction in imported commodities. In 1957, despite the election of a left-wing government and a financial crisis, pressure from farmers led the government to index grain prices. (Milk prices were already indexed.) The Third Modernization Plan (1957–1961) called for 20 percent annual increases in production. Certain basic commodities were favored: wheat and sugar had been subsidized since before the war; milk and meat were added in 1953.[57] Why so? Agricultural interest groups—most importantly the Fédération Nationale des Syndicats d'Exploitants Agricoles (FNSEA)—overrepresented the wealthy, efficient farmers of Northwest France and the Paris Basin and underrepresented poorer farmers in Bri-

[53] Vibeke Sørensen, *The Frontier of National Sovereignty: History and Theory 1945–1992* (London, 1993), 63–64, 84–86; Balassa, *French*, 252.

[54] Robert J. Lieber, *British Politics and European Unity: Parties, Elites and Pressure Groups* (Berkeley, 1970), 75. See also Mahant, *French*, 177–185; Willis, *France*, 251–264; Bjøl, *France*, Annexe. Any preferential tariff area short of an FTA was impossible under GATT rules and would likely have encountered U.S. criticism. P. Gore-Booth, *With Great Truth and Respect* (London, 1974), 253–254; Bossuat, *L'Europe*, 372–374.

[55] Balassa, "Organized," 87–88; Ehrmann, *Organized Business*, 158; Lynch, *France*, 206.

[56] Balassa, "Organized," 450, also Bjøl, *France*, 388; Faure Interview (1988), 3.

[57] Balassa, "Organized," 450; Hanns Peter Muth, *French Agriculture and the Political Integration of Western Europe* (Leyden, 1970), 19–51, 113. More generally, Pierre Barral, *Les Agrariens français de Méline à Pisani* (Paris, 1968), 325–327.

tanny, the Southwest, and the Massif Central, largely producers of wine and vegetables. These priorities were also consistent with government modernization plans at the time, though later governments would unsuccessfully seek to shift production into commodities with higher value-added.[58]

Farmers, in contrast to industry, had consistently pressed for European cooperation since well before the Schuman Plan in 1950. Major farm leaders were open about the structural sources of their preferences:

> Western Europe runs a deficit . . . in precisely those products whose production we could increase. . . . France would thus be assured, in a community which grants a preferential exchange treatment to its member states, that it would be able to increase, without risks, its production in the certainty of seeing it absorbed as a matter of priority.[59]

In 1949 farm groups proposed sectoral liberalization of European agricultural trade, to be pursued simultaneously with efforts to achieve common prices, harmonize the conditions affecting agricultural costs, and promote the circulation of labor and capital. Within Europe, only Britain and Germany imported so much as to have a significant impact on French commodity prices. Initially the focus was on Britain, by far the larger importer, but when British opposition to any agricultural arrangement became clear, the FNSEA reversed position, arguing that Britain should be excluded from any European market. In any case, there could be "no equivocation" in the demand, a FNSEA paper stated in 1952, that a preferential arrangement should protect French producers from world market pressures. This goal required not just an FTA but a customs union.[60]

Pressure for agricultural export markets rose in the late 1950s. As long as France remained a net importer, rising farm prices could be achieved through import substitution, with the cost of price supports born by French consumers and expanded production actually improving the French trade balance. By the mid-1950s, however, agricultural modernization—the co-called *révolution silencieuse*—was creating surpluses, as France's enormous reserve of underutilized land was brought into intensive production. Wheat production increased over 800 percent, sugar and wine over 300 percent each, creating more government-funded stockpiles and subsidized exports. The fiscal burden soon became acute: in 1955 export subsidies totaled 64 percent of the value of French agricultural exports. Faced with a financial crisis, the Mollet government, which did not include the Conservatives, threatened to limit subsidies to agriculture but was unable to do so. (Upon entering office, de Gaulle was to try and fail to do the same.) A domestic crisis loomed, requiring either reductions in agricultural incomes or increases in domestic subsidies.

An arrangement for preferential treatment in German markets was the only way to maintain the system of subsidized farm incomes. Marjolin reported that

---

[58] Mahant, *French*, 219–220; Lynch, *France*, 146–168.
[59] Muth, *French*, 88; Yves Tavernier, *Le Syndicalisme paysan: FNSEA, CJNA* (Paris, 1969), 24.
[60] Muth, *French*, 71n.

farmers were "quite enthusiastic" about the EC, though even they may have required a little encouragement from the government. Cooperation between German and French peak organizations, initiated in 1950, intensified; the two groups continued to consult during the Rome Treaty negotiations.[61] Farm groups were sufficiently influential that, one decision-maker noted, "any French government was obliged to defend a common agricultural policy for the EC." Ratification of any common market proposal without adequate agricultural provisions was considered difficult, perhaps impossible; alone among interest groups, farmers telegraphed all French parliamentarians on the eve of the Treaty vote to ask for their support.[62]

Neither industrialists nor farmers felt any abstract commitment to the European idea or to supranational institutions. Like their German counterparts, they were skeptical of strong supranational institutions. CNPF officials feared a renewal of the cartel-busting, price-setting *dirigisme* associated with Monnet. They frowned on proposals for an investment bank and a European competition policy. Optimal from the CNPF perspective would have been controlled liberalization managed by sectoral business associations; a broader package of safeguards would also be acceptable.[63] A 1952 note from farm groups to the minister of agriculture observed that "function creates the organ. . . . Institutions, to the extent they are necessary, can follow only from the facts."[64] Farmers appear to have favored a long-term, bilateral arrangement with Germany that would assure them a larger share of specific German markets without opening France to stiffer competition from Italy or northern Europe, particularly in fruits and vegetables, cheap wine, and diary products. Alternatively, they proposed a system of sector-by-sector European corporatist institutions in which producers would be directly represented. Like the CNPF in industrial affairs, the FNSEA opposed autonomous supranational institutions patterned on the ECSC High Authority and preferred that unanimity voting be retained until a common policy was in place.[65]

The Domestic Decision:
A "European policy" or a "policy of balance in Europe"?

There were both economic and geopolitical motivations for cautious French support for the Treaty of Rome in 1956. What does the process of preference aggregation in France tell us about their relative weight? The preponderance of evidence, I argue, supports the primacy of economic motivations, as predicted by the economic theory of commercial policy.

The most straightforward evidence in favor of economic interests is simply that the French position was not uniform but highly differentiated across economic sectors precisely in the manner predicted by political economy theory. The most consistent goal of postwar French governments, regardless of their

[61] Muth, *French*, 84, also 71n, 72–78, 88; Mahant, *French*, 224–228, 293ff.
[62] Mahant, *French*, 126ff, 134, 135–153, 168ff; Balassa, "Organized," 104.
[63] Mahant, *French*, 182–192; Bjøl, *France*, Annexe; Balassa, "Organized," 401–402.
[64] Muth, *French*, 85, also 104–105.
[65] Milward, *Rescue*, 312. On the longer-term strategy, 285–293, also reporting that earlier sugar producers had opposed cooperation and throughout dairy producers had opposed supranational institutions, preferring bilateral arrangements.

geopolitical aims, was the development of export markets in France's largest sector of comparative advantage, agriculture. From Minister of Agriculture Pierre Pflimlin's "Green Pool" in 1950 onward, such plans tended to be carefully limited to precisely those commodities—wheat, dairy products, sugar, and wine—in which France produced a substantial exportable surplus. Yet nearly five years of negotiation within the sixteen-nation OEEC, launched on the basis of several French proposals, ended in failure when countries outside the Six, notably Britain and the Scandinavian countries, could not be convinced to cooperate. Negotiations after Messina simply continued an existing French policy, with a redoubled intensity due to the growing fiscal crisis of French agriculture.[66]

French support for industrial tariff liberalization was, as political economy theory predicts, in every way more cautious. Interest in controlled liberalization coexisted with concerns about uncompetitiveness in French policy, whether unilateral, bilateral, regional, or multilateral. In 1950, 1952, and 1954–55 French governments had proposed liberalization only to be blocked at home by balance-of-payments crises and sectoral pressures for protection.[67] Throughout the 1950s, the government and the Ministry of Industry, like the Patronat, remained skeptical about French industrial competitiveness in the face of high imput, labor, and social costs, as well as persistent overvaluation of the franc. Any common market, the French government maintained, would therefore have to be accompanied either by devaluation, considered politically unacceptable, or by safeguards, compensation, and economic policy coordination, as well as arrangements for agriculture, colonial trade, and atomic energy.[68] Only consistent French support for atomic energy and armaments cooperation, while supported by sectoral interests, seem to be of particular geopolitical importance.

Support from big business, the Mollet government quickly concluded, was indispensable. The decisive domestic determinants of parliamentary ratification were, in the view of the Mollet government, the views of economic interest groups, particularly industrialists and farmers. Producers were carefully polled; peak agricultural and industrial groups were constantly consulted. The closeness of consultation reflected relative power: farmers were "almost associated with the negotiations," the Patronat and overseas producers groups somewhat less, and unions, despite close links to governing SFIO, the least.[69]

---

[66] Bossuat, *France*, I/87–189, II/786–794; Milward, *Rescue*, 268, 291–293; Alan S. Milward, *The European Agricultural Community, 1948–1954*, EUI Working Paper no. 86/254 (Florence, 1986), Muth, *French*, 76–90; Barral, *Agrariens*, 325; Lynch, *France*, 129–145, 170–178, 180.

[67] On the immobilism of the IV Republic, Philip Williams, *Crisis and Compromise* (London, 1964), 369, 423, 426.

[68] Lynch, "Restoring," 65–66. Devaluation was viewed as incapable of solving underlying problems of wage inflation and lower productivity, but likely only to lead to stop-go policies, as was beginning to occur in Britain. Socialists viewed it skeptically for political reasons. Cardozo, "Project," 70. This, not geopolitical concerns per se, led the French government to reject supranational institutions and thoroughgoing liberalization embodied in the Beyen Plan of 1953–54, which one Quai d'Orsay report characterized as a plan for the "pastoralization of France, a dominant idea of Nazism." Gérard Bossuat, "The French Administrative Elite and Europe," in *Building Postwar Europe: National Decision-Makers and European Institutions, 1948–63*, edited by Anne Deighton (London, 1995, 27–28.

[69] Faure Interview, 3–4. Even in the 1960s, Europe was an issue of relatively little importance to the French electorate, as compared to the war in Algeria (during the early part of the decade) and the state of the economy (later). Only 4 percent of the French public in 1957 considered interna-

The close relationship between interest groups and the government was not without influence. Mollet himself had initially been skeptical of the French economy's ability to withstand liberalization; more to the point, he doubted the willingness of the Assembly to ratify any Treaty containing a customs union. His view appears to have been changed in part by the support of the CNPF, as well as Marjolin and Pineau, long-time proponents of market liberalization. Support from the CNPF was secured only when the Mollet government wrote CNPF demands essentially verbatim into the French negotiating position. In September 1956 the critical internal government deliberation on the French negotiating position reached the conclusion that six conditions had to be met to secure parliamentary ratification. Five of them were major CNPF proposals: (1) unanimous consent for moving to the second stage; (2) harmonization of social costs; (3) maintenance of export and import taxes until France runs a positive balance of payments; (4) safeguard tariffs for states in balance of payments difficulties; (5) inclusion of overseas territories. Only the suspension of the Treaty in case of a foreign policy crisis, as in Algeria, came from elsewhere.[70] It is striking how consistently such demands, well known to the government from previous negotiations, were pursued, from Pinay's remarks at the Messina meeting to the signing of the Treaty.

The timing is telling. By 1956, with its failure to meet OEEC obligations triggering severe international criticism, a rising prospect of GATT liberalization and an FTA, both Germany and Britain calling for currency convertibility, and French industry enjoying export success despite an overvalued currency, the French government came to see some sort of industrial trade liberalization as inevitable. Many politicians believed that liberalization might increase pressure for industrial modernization and reduce import costs. Between 1948 and 1958, this had been a central objective of the French government, but unilateral structural adjustment policies, such as indicative planning and subsidies, had proved ineffective.[71] Nearly all French leaders involved in the European project during this period—including Edgar Faure, Mollet, Bourgès-Maunoury, Schuman, Pineau, Maurice Faure, and Marjolin—advocated trade liberalization on these grounds; Charles de Gaulle expressed a similar view even more forcefully just a few years later.[72]

Yet this is not to say that the Treaty was an effort by technocrats to impose modernization. The customs union was strongly opposed by ministerial officials, as well as specific disadvantaged economic sectors. A poll of officials at the

---

tional economic issues like the Common Market as the most important problem facing France. Carolyn Warner, *Controlling the Political Costs of European Integration* (mimeo, Arizona State University, Tempe, 1995), 12.

[70] Noël Interview, 25; Guillen, "Europe as a Cure for French Impotence?" in Nolfo, *Power*, 509; Lynch, *France*, 178. In addition, the French government insisted on a long transition period, free circulation of labor, and other proposals strongly advocated by the relevant producer groups.

[71] Lynch, *France*, 210, also 134–143, 211–212.

[72] Noël Interview (1988), 24–30; Journal Officiel, *Debats*, Assemblée 5.7.57, 3299, 3304; 6.7.57 3374; Camps, *Britain*, 80; Francis O'Neill, *The French Radical Party and European Integration* (New York, 1981), 93; Robert Rochefort, *Robert Schumann* (Paris, 1968), 328–329; Milward, *Rescue*, 133, Robert Marjolin, *Architect of European Unity: Memoirs, 1911–1986* (London, 1989), 249–255.

Matignon revealed that 80 percent rejected the Spaak Report. Functional economic ministries strongly opposed both trade liberalization and supranational institutions. In April 1956, representatives of technical ministries rejected the Spaak Report. Typical were the reactions a month later of the Minister for National Economy and Finance, Paul Ramadier, and the Secretary of State for Economic Affairs, Jean Masson. They claimed the custom union reflected a liberal ideology that diverged from the strategy of state intervention and public sector investment pursued since the war and might lead to collapse of entire sectors of the French economy; managed trade with negotiated market shares was preferable.[73] As we have seen, business support was essential.

A secondary concern of the French government, predicted by both the political economy and geopolitical explanations, was to maintain the economic viability of present and former French colonies. The government options aimed at achieving this goal seemingly without consideration for the diplomatic implications—a policy inconsistent with a geopolitical explanation but easily compatible with an economic one. The French government's first choice would have been a bilateral trade agreement with Germany governing agriculture, industrial tariffs, and armaments; it was signed but implementation was obstructed by German officials.[74] Another option that might seem outlandish today, a preferential trading arrangement with the British Commonwealth, was taken seriously. In a daring solo diplomatic foray in September 1956, Mollet traveled to London to explore economic cooperation with Britain. He was rebuffed, not least because the British were aware that France would insist on including agriculture.[75] Another option, construction of a GATT-compatible customs union, was opposed by French agricultural interests and would have done little to provide new investment and trading opportunities for present and foreign colonies. A 1956 French government study concluded that the French Union could be maintained only through European financial assistance, investment, and market opportunities— both major French demands in the Treaty of Rome negotiations. Far from being a threat, trade opportunities and investment capital from other European countries were the only remaining means of supporting it; some accommodation for overseas territories figured prominently among imperial supports, such as the Gaullists.[76] There is no evidence that European integration emerged because it was geopolitically superior to any of these other alternatives; if anything it was less attractive. It emerged because it was feasible and achieved French economic objectives.

While industrial trade liberalization in Europe was increasingly seen as both

[73] Bjøl, *France*, 260; Küsters, *Gründung*, 338–340, 364–368, 436, 476, 508–512; André Siegfried, "Introduction," in Siegfried, Edouard Bonnefous, and Jean-Baptiste Duroselle, eds., *L'Année politique 1957* (Paris, 1958), xviii.

[74] Wormser Papers, MAEF Microfilm, 280/9, 214–219; MAEF 306, 25–26 (EC Archives, Fiesole, 1953–4, 1955); Lynch, *France*, 214–215; Bossuat, *L'Europe*, 274.

[75] Lynch, *France*, 179–180. Mollet explored the possibility of reviving wartime proposals for political union between France and Britain, as well as France and Benelux joining the British Commonwealth. Richard Griffiths, "The Dynamics of Policy Inertia: The UK's Participation in and Withdrawal from the Spaak Negotiations" (Florence, manuscript, 1989), 1; Guillen, "Frankreich," 7, 10–11.

[76] Lynch, *France*, 199–205. Serge Berstein, "The Perception of French Power by the Political Forces," in Nolfo, *Power*, pp. 340–341; Mahant, *French*, 85–97, 165–167.

desirable and inevitable, the numerous reservations of individual ministries, sectoral pressure groups, and individual parliamentarians meant that active government leadership was required. In contrast to the normal decentralized procedures of the Fourth Republic, whereby a weak central executive devolved initiative to individual ministries, Mollet's team tightly controlled information and influence. This small team colluded to dampen the impact of objections from professionals, universities, bureaucrats, and business interests that percolated up through the ministries; Émile Noël, Mollet's *chef du cabinet*, sent back noncommittal responses over Mollet's signature, systematically removing items from the cabinet agenda. Representation in the "conseil économique" was carefully restricted by Marjolin and Faure. Wherever possible, civil servants were consulted only late in the day.[77] The government colluded with the CNPF, deliberately denying detailed information to the majority of sectoral and small business groups, as well as economic ministers, until late 1956, more than a year after negotiations began.[78] While Mollet rarely mentioned the Spaak Committee in meetings with ministers, treating it publicly as a group of experts, not an intergovernmental negotiation, Pineau met quietly with Spaak before each session. Certainly at the Venice meeting in June, Pineau contrived to appear undecided about the Common Market, then agreed quietly to the Spaak Report, while his public speeches stressed French reservations. At this point, however, Mollet had yet to make a firm decision to move forward.[79]

The role of parliament and the public further confirms the primacy of economic interests. The EC was hardly noticed, with all attention on Algeria; the debate was dominated by technical discourse and specialists from interest groups, with whom the government dealt directly.[80] Voting patterns on the EC differed from those on the EDC precisely because geopolitics was now *less* important, the pro-European MRP and the obstructionist Communists and Poujadists aside. The vote united the Socialists, who had split over the EDC on geopolitical grounds; the turning point, several participants recall, was the signing of the London Accords, resolving the German situation. The Treaty won over Conservatives and Radicals largely for economic reasons. Among Conservatives, as well as Gaullists, those parliamentarians with close ties to small business and small farmers remained opposed but were more than balanced by representatives of big business, more prosperous agriculture, and the non-Communist unions.[81] The vote split the Gaullists, the party most likely to oppose on geopolitical grounds, precisely because there was no agreement that any geopolitical issues were at stake. Opponents were motivated primarily by geopolitical concerns and

[77] Marjolin, *Architect*, 297–301; Girault, "Decision," 69; Prate, *Quelle*, 59–61; Bossuat, "French Administrative," 30–31

[78] Balassa, "Organized," 177–180, 263–265; Bjøl, *France*, Appendixes.

[79] Pineau and Rimbaud, *Le Grand pari*, 194–199; Marjolin, *Architect*, 304; Bossuat, *L'Europe*, 320–321.

[80] Faure Interview, 3–8.

[81] Kiersch, *Frankreich*, 903; Noël Interview, 7; Faure Interview, 24. On the evolution of the Socialist Party's commitment, see also Albert du Roy, and Robert Schneider, *Le Roman de la rose: D'Epinay à l'Élysée, l'aventure des Socialistes* (Paris, 1982), 24; Pineau in Serra, *Il rilancio*, 185, 282–283.

a distaste for supranationalism; supporters recognized economic benefits. Despite his virulent antipathy to the EDC and cryptic criticism of Euratom on geopolitical grounds, de Gaulle himself remained silent on the EC from Messina through ratification, supporting his subsequent claim that he would also have negotiated a Treaty of Rome, albeit one that was "somewhat different"—though he was closely informed about the negotiations. After coming to power he quickly stated that France should fulfill its treaty responsibilities. Debré, the Gaullist party spokesman on European issues, initially agreed to support the Common Market if investments were made available for overseas territories and the treaty was not irreversible, but in the end opposed the final text, as he had the ECSC, arguing that majority voting would permit Germany to dominate the proposed structure. Yet the General's silence and the absence of compelling geopolitical arguments permitted a majority to support the Treaty on essentially economic grounds.[82]

Parliamentary rhetoric focused primarily on economic concerns.[83] Faure declared that "the choice for France lay between going on as she had been, accepting that she would always be the feeblest, behind the others, producing at higher prices than anyone else, which was decadence, or accepting economic rehabilitation by Community procedures." He exploited ambiguities in the Treaty to overstate the extent to which French demands had been met in such areas as social harmonization and external tariffs. Farm groups criticized the Treaty for not going far enough but nonetheless telegraphed every Deputy and Senator on the eve of the vote, calling for ratification. Gaining the support of farmers was "our big political success," Noël recalls; it was achieved by Marjolin, who employed economic arguments.[84] As in Britain, the vast majority of prominent references to "German domination" concerned *economic* not geopolitical exclusion: the fear Germany and Britain might form an FTA or liberalize within the GATT.[85] The official arguments of the Socialists were almost entirely economic; the geopolitical arguments weighed on balance against the Treaty. The critique of the Mendèsists, the only centrist partisan group to uniformly oppose the Treaty in the Assembly—for example, "the proposals would reduce France to the status of a province and that she would lose her originality, strength and radiance in the world"—rested not on geopolitical concerns but on fear that free trade would undermine French industry and the balance of payments, thus reducing France to Hitler's dream of a "potato patch [under] the decisive and unilateral influence of Germany."[86]

By contrast, direct evidence of the importance of geopolitical factors is mod-

[82] Bossuat, *L'Europe*; Mahant, *French*, 96–97; Marjolin, *Architect*, 258–259; Edmond Jouve, *Le Général de Gaulle et la construction de l'Europe (1940–1966)* (Paris, 1967), 2:204–205 and on the 1953 Plan Debré, 1:261–316; 2:421–425; Interview with Noël, 18–19.

[83] For an detailed overview of the debate and the positions of the various parties, see Kiersch, *Parliament*, who reaches this conclusion on 292.

[84] Mahant, *French*, 171n; Noël interview, 25.

[85] E.g., Mahant, *French*, 158ff; Kiersch, *Parliament*, passim.

[86] Mahant, *French*, 145, 147; O'Neill, *French*, 93–96, also 79–86; Pineau and Rimbaud, *Grand*, 268ff.; Wilfried Loth, "The French Socialist Party, 1947–1954," and Denis Lefevre, "The French Socialist Party, 1954–1957," in Griffiths, ed., *Socialist Parties* 25–56, especially 43–47.

est. Let us consider below the four most plausible factors, namely the German problem, the impact of Suez on French great-power status, the importance of the French nuclear program, and the pro-European ideology of the government.

Scattered rhetoric aside, little evidence supports an important role for concern about Germany in motivating French support for the Treaty. Most French politicians believed the contrary, namely that the Treaty would isolate France from Britain, its natural anti-German ally, and the resolution of this issue was widely viewed as a demonstration of the primacy of economic over geopolitical interest. Before the cabinet, Marjolin stated that an *FTA* was "politically necessary but economically impossible." The parliamentary committee that considered the FTA in 1957 explicitly recognized that cooperation with Britain was geopolitically preferable but concluded that "concrete objections to a free trade area," including declining French influence over EC economic policy, "outweighed the less well-defined political gains" from cooperation with the British. Even Pineau privately acknowledged that closer relations with Britain were desirable but that FTA was just not in France's economic interest; Faure alone clearly voiced geopolitical support for the EC option.[87] Support for a British alliance was strong in the Quai d'Orsay, where a majority favoring collaboration with Britain split with a smaller group in favor of European integration. Some at the Quai favored Euratom or even the FTA as the "lesser of . . . evils," but even there the loudest voice was that of Olivier Wormser, whose skepticism was generally based on economic objections.[88] During the Treaty of Rome negotiations, France blocked British proposals for an FTA with the promise that they could be negotiated later, but the government had no intention of doing so, as its chief negotiator later recalled. Pineau knew that "one could not find two dozen deputies in France to vote for [the FTA]." The French government proposed to consider the FTA if only agriculture were included. The whole question of relations with Britain was deliberately obfuscated before the Assembly—an act inconsistent with the widespread claim that Suez had created a clear anti-British consensus in France.[89]

The timing of the negotiations also belies a geopolitical explanation. Economic integration followed, rather than preceded, the resolution of outstanding geopolitical issues, such as the formation of NATO and the WEU, the disposition

[87] Balassa, "Organized," 318, also 266–271; Bossuat, *L'Europe*, 371, also 374–377; Prate, *Quelle?* 59–61; Mahant, *French*, 145.

[88] Lynch, *France*, 171, also 129–145, 170–178, 180; Bossuat, *L'Europe*, 267–283, 317–320, 386–389. The Quai d'Orsay also saw the EC as a threat to imperial commitments, an instrument of German political dominance and, probably as a result, questioned the sustainability of trade liberalization. Later Quai d'Orsay criticisms focused on the irrevocable nature of the EC legal commitment and the status of North Africa. Of top civil servants, only the director of Overseas Finances, Jean Sadrin, strongly supported the EC. Küsters, *Gründung*, 338–340, 364–368, 436, 476, 512; Milward, *Rescue*, 208–210; Gérard Bossuat, "The French Administrative Elite and Europe," in Anne Deighton, ed., *Building Postwar Europe: National Decision-Makers and European Institutions, 1948–63* (London, 1995), 26ff.

[89] Lieber, *British*, 75, cites Norman Kipping, head of the main British business federation. Henri Weber, *Le parti des patrons: Le CNPF (1946–1986)* (Paris, 1986), 100ff; Frank, "The French Alternative," 171–173. Cf. Lynch, *France*, 176–177.

of the Saar and Moselle issues, and the launching of the French nuclear program. Thereafter Monnet had to be convinced that the French economy could withstand the pressure; it was Marjolin—hardly a strong pro-European but the individual most strongly favorable to liberalization on economic grounds—who played a decisive role. At this point the French government dropped its emphasis on Euratom, which had been strongly pushed by Monnet, and replaced it with the Common Market.[90]

Direct evidence for the widespread claim that the Suez crisis fundamentally altered French preferences is sparse. The claim rests very heavily on subsequent conjectures by Adenauer's associates, who would have had no way of knowing. More reliable French evidence and, above all, the timing of decisions convincingly refute it. The much-cited coincidence of timing is superficial. It results from the premeditated French decision not to start negotiating seriously until mid-September, after various outstanding geopolitical and territorial issues, not least the Saar, were near resolution. A month *before* Suez, at the latest, Mollet had already decided to seek ratification of the customs union. This decision was taken in February, May, August, or September 1956, depending on how one reads the evidence; serious negotiations began in October, with the French pressing their partners to work quickly. Pineau asserts it had been decided early; his behavior at Venice and Mollet's selection of a staff support it. Hence agreement in early November is hardly surprising. Nearly every oral history rejects a decisive linkage between Suez and Europe. The two leaders appear, moreover, to have agreed before the critical call from Eden came through. The 6 November meeting itself had been scheduled weeks previously with the aim of permitting Mollet and Adenauer to circumvent Erhard's opposition; close associates had been negotiating for days. It was destined to succeed. In any case, would Mollet really make such a momentous decision on a few hours' reflection about the meaning of Suez?[91]

The Suez explanation contains two further contradictions. First, it should have led to increased interest in Euratom. Vulnerability of Middle East oil supplies was "the most portentous argument" advanced by advocates of atomic energy cooperation and the Suez crisis "furnished all the factual evidence they needed." Yet Euratom was all but dropped in favor of the customs union at this point. Second, if Suez were decisive, negotiated agreement should have been reached through a significant softening in the French position. Yet between Suez and the signing of the Treaty the reverse occurred: with the exception of the gutting of Euratom, compromises involved German concessions, notably on agriculture and French overseas territories. In sum, there is little evidence that Suez did

[90] Noël Interview, 24, 30.

[91] In February, Pineau announced to the Assembly that the negotiations on the customs union would move forward beginning in late August. Serious study began in April. Others see a final decision that France could withstand the economic costs under specified conditions as having been taken in August. Noël Interview, 23–24; Von der Groeben Interview; Faure Interview, 4. In French oral history, only Pineau occasionally terms Suez "decisive," though this contradicts his other testimony. See also Bossuat, *L'Europe*, 324–325, 334–337. Cf. Küsters, *Gründung*, 285–304.

more than supply the French government with an extra argument to shift the views of a few wavering parliamentarians.[92]

No doubt the desire to achieve a geopolitical objective, an independent French nuclear weapons program, helps explain French support for Euratom, though economic interests are also consistent with this position. The French military and atomic energy establishments, backed by support from various parliamentary constituencies, had been pressing for an independent nuclear capability since 1954. Though the nuclear program remained secret, Gaullists and Conservatives strongly supported atomic energy cooperation. This was the issue of greatest salience to "Europeans"—it was the only point in a number of prominent statements by the MRP, a party still closely tied to Monnet, and Monnet's Action Committee. Geopolitical concerns meant that no French government was in a position to renounce the military use of nuclear weapons—as the German SPD and Monnet's Action Committee demanded.[93]

Yet Euratom was in the end a sectoral sideshow. Although the French appear to have originally supported negotiations in large part to achieve Euratom, by late 1956 (or earlier, if we are to believe Pineau), it had been relegated to the position of a "smokescreen" for the more controversial customs union—a strategy Pineau claims was discussed only among Mollet, Pineau, and Coty until the Venice meeting. In any case, the French signed the Treaty of Rome although the Germans had all but gutted Euratom, largely due to industrial opposition to France's proposed monopoly on basic nuclear inputs. In the end even a geopolitical goal as fundamental as autonomous nuclear weapons production influenced policy only within a narrow area.[94]

We are thus left with the geopolitical claim that the pro-European position of the Mollet government played an important role in defining the French position. This is surely correct, yet it should be qualified in two ways. First, we have seen that there is at least some reason to suspect that any government, perhaps even one with Gaullist participation, would eventually have promoted similar substantive goals—though perhaps not within the same institutional framework. In the center of the French political spectrum, Mendès-France, not Mollet, was the politician with an exceptional position on Europe. Second, it is important to remember that pro-Europeanism was permitted to prevail in Mollet's own party, and therefore both in his section of ministers and in subsequent ratification votes, not because of the geopolitical implications of the Treaty but because of its *lack* of geopolitical implications.

Here, too, economic interest may well have been more important. Major is-

[92] Jaroslav Polach, *Euratom: Its Background, Issues, and Economic Implications* (Dobbs Ferry, N.Y., 1964), 39.

[93] Bossuat, *L'Europe*, 314, 328–329, 362–363; Serra, *Il rilancio*, 281–282; Mahant, *France*, 66; Jean-Paul Brunet, "Le MRP et la construction européenne, 1955–1957," in Berstein et al., *Le MRP et la construction européenne*, 240; Polach, *Euratom*, 22–23, 63–65; Pierre Guillen, "La France et la négotiation du traité d'Euratom," *Relations internationales* 44 (Winter 1985), 399; Monnet, *Mémoires* (Paris, 1976), 2:620–621.

[94] Pineau and Rimbaud, *Le Grand pari*, 194–199; Marjolin, *Architect*, 304; Bossuat, *L'Europe*, 320–321, 362–363.

sues—French military sovereignty, German rearmament, some territorial issues—had first to be resolved. For the SFIO these were major turning points, after which Mollet could announce support for general economic integration without concern for the geopolitical consequences. Moreover, the increasing tendency to support Europe was not simply Mollet's personal priority: it was consistent with the trend in SFIO policy from 1948 onwards, marking the final victory of moderate pro-European forces inspired by André Philip and Leon Blum, the "two major theoretical influences over the Socialists' European attitude," who had begun in the early 1950s to promote more market-oriented economic policies. One analyst concludes that "if the notion of greater autonomy from the USA influenced the Mollet Government, the belief that economic modernization depended on European integration was of still greater importance." Rather than advance geopolitical arguments, SFIO leaders stressed that the customs union and export-led growth were economic imperatives—though opposition remained from those concerned about France's lack of competitiveness. The two conditions imposed by the Socialist congress of 1956 on the negotiations were in large part economic: social harmonization and the inclusion of overseas territories.[95] Finally, Mollet's continued willingness to consider cooperation with Britain—until the moment when agricultural agreement with Germany was secure—suggests that European ideas were hardly paramount.

One important implication of the government's pro-European stance was acceptance of the generally quasi-constitutional form of the EC. De Gaulle said later that he too would have accepted the customs union, but in a different form; he was apparently referring to EC institutions, the supranational form of which he was to combat for more than a decade. Still, even the Mollet government, like German federalists, pushed for a carefully calculated weakening of supranational institutions as compared to the ECSC High Authority; no serious consideration was given to opposing the pragmatic imposition of a veto of the transition to the second stage and various safeguards. These were pursued to insure France against the dire predictions of economic dislocation. Mollet and Faure remained more comfortable with the confederal Council of Ministers, not a supranational institution like the High Authority.[96]

In sum, the preponderance of evidence—cross-issue variation in positions, timing, domestic cleavages, and political rhetoric—suggests the priority of economic over geopolitical motivations. The geopolitical concerns cited in most accounts (Suez and decolonization, the German problem, atomic energy) played modest roles; on balance these considerations probably mitigated *against* the Treaty. Only pro-European ideology, which was linked to the active role of the Mollet government itself, influenced the French position significantly and even

---

[95] Michael Newman, *Socialism and European Unity—The Dilemma of the Left in Britain and France* (London, 1983), 35. Mahant, *French*, 85–88, 104ff, 155ff, 162, 165; Wilfried Loth, "Der französische Sozialismus in der Vierten und Fünften Republik," *Neue Politische Literatur* 22 (1977), 221–243; Lefebvre, "French Socialist," 46–47; Interview with Noël, 5–6

[96] Bossuat, *L'Europe*, 319; Serra, *Il rilancio*, 281–282, 287; Milward, *Rescue*, 209–211; Faure Interview, 24.

this impact was secondary. Most French demands in the negotiations were economic; they were shared by centrist parties and had been pursued in one form or another for most of the decade. All options for European economic cooperation except a "small European" customs union with a strong agricultural dimension—more rapid cooperation on the Continent, any form of an FTA with Britain, and even, in the medium-term, muddling though—were excluded by economic consideration; at most, geopolitics may help explain why this series of French governments took a proactive stance rather than wait to be forced into some form of cooperation structured by others.

Despite the concessions France received on these points, domestic support remained fragile. Insofar as the French government, acting in part for ideological reasons, exploited domestic procedures and support from the CNPF to promote the Treaty, it remained vulnerable to a backlash in the form of opposition to implementation from threatened industrial sectors. Safeguards and vetoes were poor substitutes for the only policy recognized by business as a solution to its problems: devaluation. As seen earlier in the 1950s, when France repeatedly failed to sustain trade agreements, such opposition could be fatal. Even core members of Mollet's small team of activists doubted France's ability and willingness to implement the Treaty of Rome. Indeed, the last governments of the Fourth Republic soon violated it, first by imposing protectionist measures to cope with a balance of payments crisis, then by announcing that France would disregard the January 1959 deadline for the first EC tariff reductions.[97] Only domestic economic reform, to come under de Gaulle, could consolidate support for the Treaty.

Britain: Between Commonwealth and Continent

Between 1955 and 1961 British policy toward Europe reversed course. What began as a policy of ignoring the customs union proposal and then attempting to subvert it was transformed by 1957 into a search for accommodation and finally for membership. The first two stages in this evolution, apathy and subversion, are analyzed in this chapter; the latter two are considered in chapter 3. What explains Britain's apparent preference for the status quo or an FTA over a customs union? What accounts for the growing realization that some form of accommodation was required?

Most analysts stress ideological hostility of the Eden and Macmillan governments to European federalism and their desire to maintain great-power status, symbolized by close relations with the Commonwealth and the United States. Such analyses often condemn British leaders for "missing the boat" at Messina. The failure of British policies from 1955 through 1957 is often taken as *prima facie* evidence that British policy was ideological, irrational, or ignorant. Anthony Eden, prime minister at the beginning of this episode, and R. A. B. Butler, his chancellor, are often portrayed as old-fashioned statesmen; they themselves later termed their policy "shortsighted."[98] Others point to "the detachment of

---

[97] Balassa, "Organized," 291ff, 320–324, 327–343, 382, 390–391.
[98] Michael Charlton, *The Price of Victory* (London, 1983), 194–195, also 183–184, 186.

[British] elites from the sense of political commitment and open exchange of information that was building up among ECSC governments."[99] Still others cite the British government's instinctive antifederalism and its vague, archaic, but "almost moral obligation to uphold the legacy of British greatness." The most detailed historical account of British policy concludes that "only the psychological underpinnings of British policy can account for the British attitude toward the Messina initiative."[100] On similar grounds, Richard Griffiths calls British policy "irrational."[101]

This analysis challenges such an interpretation, arguing instead that the British policy of apathy and opposition to the customs union was the rational one for a government that traded little with the Continent, had high tariffs in place, and feared competition with German producers. British policy was dictated largely by the rational pursuit of commercial interest, in particular export promotion. This explanation is closer in spirit to the recent interpretation of Alan Milward. Yet even Milward rejects commercial interest per se. He focuses instead on distinctively British macroeconomic ideology related to the strong role of finance, arguing that "what was lacking [in Britain] was links between . . . industrial policies and international commercial policies." This interpretation, however, compels him to add as secondary influences the "long historical tradition [as] a great power . . . ignorance about its closest neighbors, . . . arrogance and myopic conservatism."[102] I argue that if we begin from the assumption that British policy-makers were primarily pursuing commercial objectives, there is no need for recourse to attributions of ignorance or irrationality. The information available to British policy-makers—little different from that available to their Continental counterparts—fully justified the skeptical attitude they took toward Messina. To be sure, British leaders held some old-fashioned views; they were unlucky that the EC proved more successful than they or anyone else expected. Geopolitical ideas (and general economic policy) played a role, but only a secondary one, providing an added reason to be cautious about a commercial venture that even its proponents agreed would probably fail and that ran contrary to British interests. In sum, British policy constituted a rational, remarkably flexible, even far-sighted defense of enduring British economic interests.

Geopolitical Interest and Ideology: "In political terms, quite a stiff price"

Four consistent threads in British geopolitical reasoning about Europe during this period, taken together, justified concern and skepticism about a continental customs union. First was strong British support for the Western alliance and

[99] Christopher Lord, *Absent at the Creation: Britain and the Formation of the European Community, 1950–1952* (Aldershot, 1996), 166, presents this as conjecture. This is also the thesis of Charlton's pathbreaking oral history, *The Price of Victory*. Also Miriam Camps, "Missing the Boat at Messina and Other Times?" in Brian Brivati and Harriet Jones, eds., *From Reconstruction to Integration: Britain and Europe since 1945* (London, 1993), 137. Lieber argues that Macmillan mismanaged accession domestically by underemphasizing geopolitical concerns.

[100] Wolfram Kaiser, *Using Europe, Abusing the Europeans: Britain and European Integration, 1945–63* (London, 1996), 55–56.

[101] Griffiths, "Dynamics," 6–7.

[102] Milward, *Rescue*, 393–395, also 345–434.

the "special relationship" with the United States.[103] An exclusive customs union, it was occasionally argued, might split the Western alliance. Macmillan wrote as late as June 1958 that if the EC formed without some free trade arrangement with Britain "we shall have to reconsider the whole of our political and economic attitude towards Europe. . . . We should certainly put on highly protective tariffs and quotas . . . In other words, we should not allow ourselves to be destroyed little by little. We would fight back with every weapon in our armoury. We would take our troops out of Europe. We would withdraw from NATO. We would adopt a policy of isolationism."[104] This was a concern even though Britain planned to withdraw some troops from Europe anyway.

Second was a concern that the customs union might undermine control over Germany. As Macmillan recalled later, Messina "might be very dangerous to us, [for it] might mean Western Europe dominated in fact by Germany and used as an instrument for the revival of German power through economic means."[105]

Third was the fear that European integration, whether or not Britain joined, would undermine Britain's Commonwealth commitment and the "special relationship" with the United States, widely seen, particularly in the Foreign Office and the Conservative Party, as the foundations of Britain's global prestige and power. This argument appeared in some policy review documents. There exist several strong statements of concern about the transatlantic implications, including a few letters from friends of Macmillan and a 1957 Cabinet meeting in which it was agreed that the purposes of the EC were political and that "our Special Relationship with the United States would be endangered if the United States believed that our influence would be less than that of the EC."[106]

Fourth was the near universal British suspicion of European federalism, symbolized by Winston Churchill's celebrated observation that "We are with them, but not of them."[107] In 1956, to be sure, 65–70 percent of the British public favored the unification of Europe, not strikingly different from 53–67 percent in France, 79–82 percent in Germany, and 55–66 percent in Italy. Yet federalist organizations in Britain were almost nonexistent. Even supporters of membership criticized federalism but maintained that a federalist Europe would not occur for decades, if at all. The great majority simply conceded that Britain would pay, "in political terms, quite a stiff price."[108] No mainstream British politician considered federal institutions acceptable. Eden had said in 1952 that joining a European federation was "something we know, in our bones, that we cannot do"; in secret government memos, he singled out references to federal-

[103] Dockrill, *Britain's Policy*, 102–3.

[104] Cited in Wolfram Kaiser, "Challenge to the Community: The Creation, Crisis, and Consolidation of the European Free Trade Association, 1958–1972," *Journal of European Integration History* 3, no. 1 (1997), 15.

[105] Kaiser, "Challenge," 8.

[106] CAB 128/31, 2 May 1957.

[107] David Butler and Uwe Kiesinger, *The 1975 Referendum* (London, 1976), 5.

[108] Charlton, *Price*, 241. Also Milward, *Rescue*, 432. Harold Macmillan, *Riding the Storm 1956–1959* (London, 1971), 62–63; Anthony Nutting, *Europe Will Not Wait: A Warning and a Way Out* (London, 1960); Alastair Horne, *Harold Macmillan* (New York, 1988), 1:313–317, 2:31.

ism for criticism. His successor Harold Macmillan, the most "European" among major British politicians of his time and the man who spearheaded British association with the ECSC, abhorred federalism and, like Eden, preferred pragmatic, flexible intergovernmental solutions.[109]

Economic Interest: "Open sympathy and frank amazement"

The initial response of British business to the EC was apathy. The president of the Federation of British Industry (FBI), Britain's leading industrial interest group, later conceded that this reaction was based on two miscalculations: underestimation of the prospects for European unification and overestimation of domestic opposition to free trade. Yet, as the British trade press pointed out, trade was shifting away from the Commonwealth and toward the Continent. Intra-industry trade among developed countries was burgeoning. At the same time, a drop in the average imperial preference from 11 percent to 5 percent over two decades, the increase in GATT liberalization, and the creation of a de facto OEEC and EPU trade zone were undermining the "exceptional degree of preference" enjoyed by Britain in the Sterling bloc. Nonetheless, at first neither government nor industry pushed to initiate European trade liberalization. British exports to the Six in 1955, as we saw above, totaled only a quarter of exports to the Commonwealth. British firms focused on "safer" domestic and Commonwealth markets and did not take large risks investing in the sectors (e.g., automobiles) that formed the basis of the West European trade boom.[110]

It was the threat of exclusion that shattered complaisance of both business and government. When the government withdrew from the Spaak negotiations in late 1955, the overseas director of the FBI, concerned primarily about exclusion, immediately expressed "open sympathy with the customs union idea and frank amazement at the UK's decision."[111] A few months later, an FBI committee polled British industry and revealed surprisingly little protectionist sentiment regarding Europe. There remained, however, a split between Commonwealth and Continental export interests. On the one hand, only association with the Common Market could prevent discrimination against British exports. On the other, preferential access to Commonwealth markets linked to reciprocal agricultural imports still benefited many firms. The committee squared the circle by proposing an industrial free trade area (FTA)—an option supported by a large majority of FBI members polled in October 1956 and again a year later. More competitive firms led the supporters, whereas the small group of opponents was disproportionately drawn from smaller, relatively uncompetitive sectors dependent on protected Commonwealth or domestic markets (e.g., paper, timber, cotton, hand tools). Like its counterparts in France and Germany, British business remained suspicious of the "supranational institutions of the ECSC or

---

[109] Peter Morris, "The British Conservative Party," in John Gaffney, ed., *Political Parties and the European Union* (London, 1996), 125. Also Richard Lamb, *The Failure of the Eden Government* (London, 1987), 62–63.

[110] For an overview, Milward, *Rescue*, 396–424.

[111] Griffiths, "Dynamics," 3; Lieber, *Britain*, 58–59.

EC type [and] the 'dirigiste' tendencies that go with them"—a suspicion shared by the Trades Union Congress (TUC).[112]

Britain had been relatively open to commodity imports since the Repeal of the Corn Laws in the mid-nineteenth century, so farming was a less significant occupation in Britain than in France or Germany. By 1957, only 5 percent of the British population still farmed. Although surviving farmers were more efficient on the average than their counterparts elsewhere in the Six, cheap domestic food prices meant that they also received greater per capita subsidies than did farmers in the Six. Under the 1947 and 1957 Agriculture Acts, subsidies were provided not through price supports, as on the Continent, but directly to farmers. Despite its small size, the main agricultural interest group, the National Farmers' Union (NFU), was believed to control more parliamentary constituencies than subsequently appears to have been the case, and thus enjoyed considerable respect among Tory MPs. The NFU voiced public skepticism over plans for European agricultural integration, which threatened existing corporatist relations as well as subsidy arrangements. It also initially opposed a British government proposal for a separate agricultural agreement based on OEEC principles in October 1957 but relented once the government called for a long transition period and safeguards.[113]

The Domestic Decision: "Kill it or let it collapse?"

What does the decision-making process in Britain tell us about the relative importance of economic and geopolitical considerations? Although it is difficult fully to untangle the two motivations, the economic interests appear to have provided, at the very least, sufficient grounds for skeptical opposition.

British skepticism surfaced immediately. Even before Messina, Eden, Butler his Chancellor, and even Foreign Secretary Macmillan, who was to spearhead the British bid for entry five years later, initially rejected participation in a customs union outright. When Anthony Nutting, a young official, "begged Eden" to let him observe the Messina negotiations, the prime minister refused.[114]

Economic considerations were sufficient to explain this negative initial stance, though geopolitical concerns may also have been significant. Economic officials

---

[112] Kipping, *Summing*, 155–157. It was widely believed that membership in the customs union would be difficult for some in heavily protected larger sectors, such as chemicals, textiles, and engineering, and neutral though difficult for the auto industry. Lamb, *Failure*, 74–75; Lieber, *British*, 60–63; Robert L. Pfaltzgraff, Jr., *Britain Faces Europe* (Philadelphia, 1969), 33–34; Miriam Camps, *Britain and the European Community, 1955–1963* (Princeton, 1964), 115; Herbert Schneider, *Großbritanniens Weg nach Europa* (Freiburg/Breisgau, 1968), 115; Macmillan, *Riding the Storm*, 82; Blank, *Federation*, 143–145. In 1956 the FBI conducted a poll: 479 firms with an average of 1,270 employees each were favorable to the FTA, 38 firms with an average of 815 employees each were undecided, and 147 firms with an average of 510 employees each were opposed. Sir Norman Kipping, director-general, noted that responses were correlated with the competitiveness of firms. The TUC initiated consultations with the government in October 1956 and announced its public support for FTA the following month, opposing membership in the customs union but pointing out the serious disadvantages of exclusion. Lieber, *British*, 38–41.

[113] Lieber, *British*, 45–54; 117–134.

[114] Lamb, *Failure*, 68. Charlton, *Price*, 169.

expressed concern earliest and most consistently. Younger Treasury and Board of Trade officials dominated the Mutual Aid Committee (MAC), which was asked to provide a comprehensive assessment of British interests in the negotiations in October 1955. (The Foreign Office initially conceded that the Messina negotiations were essentially an economic matter.) [115] The MAC's analysis focused primarily on commercial considerations, calculating the gains and losses by sector. The long-term interests of Britain, the MAC concluded, clearly lay in closer ties to Europe, with its expanding market for industrial goods, but in the short-term the country faced adjustment costs imposed by eliminating preferences on Commonwealth trade and the lowering of trade barriers with Europe. The MAC report concluded: "(i) membership would weaken the United Kingdom's economic and consequently political relationship with the Commonwealth and the Colonies; (ii) the United Kingdom's economic and political interests were worldwide and a European Common Market would be contrary to the approach of freer trade and payments; (iii) participation would in practice lead gradually to further integration, and ultimately perhaps to political federation, which [would not be] acceptable to public opinion in Britain; and (iv) it would involve the removal of protection for British industry against European competition."

Only the third point (on federalism and public opinion) clearly addresses geopolitics, while the fourth is purely economic and the first two primarily economic. There is no mention of Germany or the Soviet Union. The document closes, however, with the statement: "The establishment of a European Common Market would be bad for the United Kingdom and if possible should be frustrated. But if it came into being without us . . . we should pay an increasing cost commercially. But even this would not outweigh the political objections to joining" at the moment. Frank Lee, also at the Board of Trade and the only official at the time to recommend membership, observed to officials of the FBI: "We could not possibly afford not to be members of a common market of this importance, but we could not see how this could be done without ultimately paying the price of a common currency and considerable merging of political sovereignty." [116]

This skepticism followed from existing British policy, which had consistently supported the GATT system and rejected various forms of economic integration in Europe. Throughout the 1950s, the Treasury had been neutral toward functional integration, and the Foreign Office had been opposed. This skepticism

[115] Griffiths ("Dynamics," 5) notes that even the Foreign Office uncharacteristically stressed economic arguments: "In the early 1950s, the Foreign Office had taken the lead in rejecting supranationalism on political grounds: this argument was now used as a residual factor in supporting other negative considerations." On the continuity of such pressure, Jacqueline Tratt, *The Macmillan Government and Europe: A Study in the Process of Policy Development* (New York, 1996), 16.

[116] Macmillan from Heiser, *British*, 106; Maurice Torelli, *Great Britain and Europe of the Six: The Failure of Negotiations* (Montréal, 1969), 17; Lee from Jock Bruce-Gardyne and Nigel Lawson, *The Power Game: An Examination of Decision-Making in Government* (London, 1976), 41. See also Kaiser, *Using*, 28–32, 35; James R. V. Ellison, "Explaining British Policy toward European Integration in the 1950s" (Canterbury, mime, 1995), 16–17; Young, "British Officials," 95. Of the three major Whitehall centers of power on such issues, the Treasury and "to a lesser extent" the Board of Trade "become predominant" during the 1950s. John W. Young, "British Officials and European Integration, 1944–60," in Deighton, *Building Postwar Europe*, 87ff; cf. Milward, *Rescue*, 393.

stemmed not so much from a belief in "one world" free trade through GATT as from GATT's exceptions for Commonwealth trade and the fear that a European bloc might endanger those relations. For the Conservative party, to an even greater extent than Whitehall, Imperial Preference remained the "Ark of the Covenant." It was simply an article of faith that Commonwealth preferences ruled out participation in a customs union with a common external tariff; in this regard, many Conservative politicians viewed even the GATT with suspicion.[117]

Hence the European negotiations raised a dilemma. As Macmillan stated in December 1956, Britain must "avoid being discriminated against in Europe." It is, he noted during the membership negotiations, "much more appealing to be a simple element in an expanding market than one of the leading factors in a market [the Commonwealth] which is in the process of recession." Yet, as he observed before the Commons shortly thereafter, economic interests constituted a sufficient reason to avoid membership: "We could not expect the countries of the Commonwealth to continue to give preferential treatment to our exports to them if we had to charge them full duty on their exports to us . . . this objection, even if there were no other, would be quite fatal to any proposal that the United Kingdom should seek to take part in a European Common Market . . . so that is out."[118] The customs union was also, one commentator notes, "incompatible with Britain's political relations with the Commonwealth and the United States and, ultimately, detrimental to its position as a world power."[119]

Since the undesirability of customs union and the dangers of economic isolation were understood, disagreements among ministers and officials were limited to tactics. Butler observed in retrospect that "there [was] not the slightest possibility of the Messina 'common market' coming into existence. . . . The only troublesome point was whether we should strive to kill it or let it collapse of its own weight."[120] Macmillan later recalled that "when we decided at the end of 1955 not to take part . . . we were influenced by . . . considerations [which] were to be proved wrong. We thought they wouldn't succeed—or, if they did, that we would work out a satisfactory association."[121] This was not simply the view of a few Foreign Office officials and was hardly myopic (as has often been suggested).

---

[117] Camps, "Missing," 138. This was not support for global free trade; at the Blackpool Party Conference of 1954, liberal Tories were still fighting to persuade the party not to pass resolutions condemning the GATT, which after all *exempted* the Commonwealth. Macmillan, *Riding the Storm*, 65, 77; Interviews in Charlton, *Price*, 171, 178–179, 182, 189; Heiser, *British Policy*, 49–56;

[118] James R. V. Ellison, "Explaining British Policy toward Integration in the 1950s" (Canterbury, mimeo, 1995), 15; Kaiser, "To Join," 144; Griffiths, "Dynamics," 5.

[119] Ellison, "Explaining," 17.

[120] Rab Butler, cited in Charlton, *Price*, 198.

[121] Griffiths, "Dynamics," 6–7. Griffiths interprets this as irrational decision-making, because not all policy options were explicitly considered, but in fact the reasoning was quite consistent and based on the same information available to the European leaders, who were equally pessimistic. Clappier told Bretherton that the French would not join the EC without the British. Ambassador Gladwyn Jebb in Paris did not expect success. Ambassador Christopher Warner in Brussels considered the discussions "woolly and impractical." In early 1956, Spaak doubted a successful outcome to the negotiations and sought British assistance. See interviews in Adolf M. Birke and Kurt Kluxen, eds., *Die europäische Herausforderung: England und Deutschland in Europa* (Munich, Saur), 1987, 134–135, 137–139; Küsters, *Gründung*, 137n, 139–141; Heiser, *British*, 96; Macmillan, *Riding the Storm*, 69.

Paul-Henri Spaak, Monnet, and Bernard Clappier, leading Continential participants, were telling each other as well as the British that the weakness of the
French economy and polity meant that the negotiations would probably collapse—an outcome that would probably lead to the formation of a looser free
trade arrangement, the economic equivalent of the WEU. Hence Eden and
Butler adopted a tone of indifference, making no commitments lest British prestige—and, presumably, its ability to advance independent alternatives—be damaged by association with failed negotiations. In a dinner address before ministers from the Six, Butler dismissed the Messina meeting as an "archeological
excavation." Thirty years later, he described the British position as motivated
primarily by ennui: "Anthony Eden was bored with this. Frankly he was even
more bored than I was."[122]

From the start, however, there were those who favored a more activist policy
of seeking to prevent or destroy the customs union. Sir Gladwyn Jebb, British
ambassador in Paris, summarized the British position when he scribbled in the
margins of a proposal: "Embrace destructively."[123] Younger Tory trade officials
such as Anthony Nutting and Peter Thorneycroft had successfully pressed the
MAC to recommend that Britain participate in the Spaak Committee meetings,
to steer the talks along more sensible lines. The Cabinet agreed to send a "representative"—but on the prior understanding that the decision had already
been made not to participate. Since the Foreign Office had little interest, the
British representative was an undersecretary from the Board of Trade, Russell
Bretherton, who was instructed to appear helpful, to propose an intergovernmental FTA open to the Commonwealth as an alternative, but to make no commitments. He was given, Thorneycroft later recalled, a "completely negative
brief [since] the Cabinet had really decided against the European concept."[124]
Even though Bretherton reported back that the negotiators were placing "little
emphasis on supra-national authority," that the result "looks as if it will be indistinguishable from the OEEC," and that French participation seemed unlikely—in short, that the geopolitical liabilities were minimal—he was recalled
by orders "from the highest levels of government."[125]

The possibility that the negotiations might succeed and the resulting institution exclude Britain instantly transformed Britain's skeptical ennui into virulent
hostility. Beginning in 1953, studies by the Treasury and Board of Trade had
stressed a long-term decline in Commonwealth trade and a corresponding rise
in European exports. Strategy documents consistently argued that if the customs
union succeeded, Britain would again face the dilemma Macmillan had identified: membership was unattractive, because it would compromise Commonwealth relations, but exclusion would be disastrous to British trade in the long
term. The MAC had concluded that the Common Market was unlikely to form,

[122] Charlton, *Price*, 194, 195; also 187–195.
[123] Kaiser, *Using*, 48.
[124] Charlton, *Price*, 182, also 178ff.
[125] Lamb, *Failure*, 73; Bretherton and Uri, cited in Charlton, *Price*, 186–188; Camps, "Missing,"
138; Kaiser, *Using*, 47.

but if it did, "an entirely new situation" would arise. "The disadvantages of ab-
staining would, in the long-run, outweigh the advantages," and Britain "might
be forced to join on their terms."[126] Thorneycroft, director of the Board of Trade,
argued that Britain's major competitor was Germany; the creation of a discriminatory customs union would permit Germany to dominate Continental markets.
Agricultural officials argued that it was necessary to be in on the creation of the
EC to "be sure that it contains fewer embarrassments than it otherwise would."[127]
A prescient Treasury report concluded: "On a longer view the question might
become, not whether we should go into Europe to save Europe, but whether we
should not have to move closer to Europe in order to save ourselves."[128]

Well before the Venice meeting of May 1956, when the success of the negotiations first seemed likely, Macmillan, who replaced Butler at the Exchequer the
preceding December, had became the leader of those who favored a more active response. At his request another committee considered all alternatives in
detail and overwhelmingly recommended a proposal for a pan-European FTA
under OEEC auspices—named "Plan G" within the British government. The
central logic of the committee report was simple and primarily commercial:
membership in the EC, despite its geopolitical advantages in tying Germany to
Europe, was impossible, because it threatened two-thirds of British trade, "particularly that with the Commonwealth."[129] Yet exclusion was costly, Thorneycroft
wrote to Macmillan, because "our businessmen would be ousted from European
markets through discrimination in favor of their German competitors." As Macmillan recorded at the time, "when the Six have ratified they may snap their
fingers at the FTA and leave us in the lurch"; the only alternative to exclusion
was to "redirect the Messina initiative into the orbit of the OEEC."[130] The report
defended a proposal for "some sort of tariff arrangement . . . designed [to] reduce as far as possible the risk of damage to our trade . . . with the Commonwealth."[131] British ministers and officials were not particularly interested either
in pan-European trade liberalization or in encouraging GATT liberalization per
se—the British government had since 1931 resisted deep OEEC tariff cuts—
but in subverting a customs union from which they might be excluded.

When France proved unexpectedly forthcoming at the Venice meeting, the
Cabinet, led now by Macmillan as prime minister, reacted immediately. Two days
later Plan G was adopted; a month later it was publicized as an OEEC proposal.
Domestic support remained firm, since it involved "no real departure from past
policies" pursued through the OEEC.[132] The Commons debate on the subject in
the autumn of 1956 "was remarkable for the absence of controversy and the
unanimity of view on both sides of the House."[133] The internal report on Plan G

[126] Lamb, *Failure*, 74–75, also 80–92; Kaiser, *Using*, 28–32, 35; Young, "British Officials," 96–97.
[127] Eric Roll, cited in Charlton, *Price*, 253.
[128] Kaiser, *Using*, 35.
[129] Lamb, *Failure*, 92–93; Milward, *Rescue*, 428–429; Charlton, *Price*, 182, 187, 190–195.
[130] Macmillan, *Riding*, 435–436.
[131] Milward, *Rescue*, 429, also 428.
[132] Camps, "Missing," 141
[133] Camps, *Britain*, 107–109, also 106–111.

predicted that Continental governments would embrace it because it better served what the British believed to be their dominant geopolitical interest, namely embedding Germany in Europe. To this Macmillan added threats and inducements. Instructions from Macmillan to the Bonn and Washington embassies suggested that an emphasis of destabilization of the Western alliance might soften U.S. and German opposition to an FTA. If the Six "declared economic war on her" by rejecting Plan G, Macmillan threatened to embargo arms shipments to the Netherlands for use in Indonesia and to withdraw from NATO and German defense. Adenauer angrily dismissed the latter threat. To France Macmillan offered nuclear assistance in lieu of Euratom, a U.S.-U.K.-French triumvirate, and closer consultation on Western defense.[134]

When these geopolitical inducements failed, Macmillan tried economic concessions.[135] Initially Plan G excluded foodstuffs, thereby eliminating any concern about Commonwealth trade or British agriculture; when the Six demanded that agricultural trade be harmonized on the basis of common prices, Macmillan took modest steps to accommodate them.[136] Whatever concerns British farmers may have had, "it was clear," Macmillan wrote later, "that the need to maintain Commonwealth free entry was the controlling consideration"—exports to the Commonwealth were 2.5 times greater than British farm production.[137] The failure of Plan G did not become clear until early 1957, whereupon, as we shall see, Macmillan moved even further to accommodate the Six.[138]

Critics often condemn Britain for "missing the boat" at Messina. The skeptical then hostile British policy response from 1955 through 1957 is often taken as prima facie evidence that British policy was ideological, irrational, or ignorant. Even Butler and perhaps Eden were self-critical. Such retrospective criticisms of British policy are misplaced, for two reasons. First, British diplomacy was far-sighted, efficient, and well-informed—close to the ideal rational actor. Macmillan reacted swiftly to new information about Continental developments; the shift to an aggressive response was decided just two days after the Venice meeting, years before domestic pressure forced action. From the start, Whitehall correctly forecast future economic trends, calculating economic consequences sector-by-sector with little bias. It was understood from the start that exclusion

---

[134] Lamb, *Failure*, 96–97, also 84–85. Macmillan hoped to lure the French government, believed to be hesitant to embrace trade liberalism or to face Germany alone, away from the negotiations. Lieber, *British*, 161n; Macmillan, *Riding*, 438–440; Horne, *Macmillan*, 2:429–432, 444–447.

[135] By October 1956, Macmillan was reduced to sending a note to Spaak stating: "I am pleading for a little time before final decisions are made." Lamb, *Failure*, 99.

[136] Macmillan, *Riding*, 439ff.

[137] Macmillan, *Riding*, 434–435.

[138] In Britain, antifederalism, the great-power syndrome, and the resulting overestimation of British influence in Europe may have had one tactical consequence. It led British leaders to the conclusion that their prestige would be strengthened in Britain dropped out of the negotiations early and that they would have little to lose if the negotiations succeeded. When the negotiations succeeded, this led to self-isolation in which the British were trusted by no one; the unforseeable long-term results, once de Gaulle assumed power, turned out to be catastrophic. Spaak claimed later that Britain could have stepped in as the leader of Europe if it were willing to support innovative policies. While incorrect, this was a reasonable judgment at the time. France, too, was unwilling to be placed in the position of vetoing an agreement late in the negotiations.

from a successful customs union would eventually compel an application for membership and that, moreover, it would then be difficult to reform arrangements the British had not had a hand in creating. Yet such an eventuality was some years away and, more important, improbable. British leaders therefore took a calculated risk that the customs union would fail. The risk was fully warranted. Until early 1957 even Continental statesmen expected the negotiations to collapse, and for several years after French leaders doubted that the Treaty would be implemented.[139] In short, critics ascribe to British leaders interests and information they did not possess at the time.[140]

A second reason why retrospective criticisms are misplaced is that most interpretations assume that British policy-makers were pursuing geopolitical goals. So interpreted, British policy does indeed look irrational or short-sighted. If we start instead with the assumption that commercial interests in export promotion were predominant and sufficient motivations for initial British apathy and opposition to the EC, however, no appeal to irrationality is required—nor do we need to shift explanations to account for the subsequent British application for membership. The simple fact that British exports to the Commonwealth were four times larger than exports to Europe explains much about the British strategy; the reciprocal role of agricultural imports explains most of the rest. Commercially, Britain had far less to gain and more to lose from both the agricultural and the industrial aspects of the customs union than did any of the Six. Initial apathy toward industrial liberalization in Europe, concern about long-term industrial exclusion, and strict defense of Commonwealth arrangements are the natural response of a country in Britain's commercial circumstances. Domestic cleavages, both within the government and within business, we have seen, reflected economic interests. In public and in confidential forums, the maintenance of Commonwealth trading patterns and the avoidance of exclusion from European markets were the two most commonly mentioned national interests; they were generally acknowledged to be sufficient long-term justifications for British policy. If we focus on economic interests, British policy toward Europe is rendered consistent with its policy toward the GATT and the Commonwealth.

Geopolitical factors, by contrast, offer a less convincing explanation. They were, to start with, less consistently or coherently invoked. The threat of rising German power, or any other Continental threat, was nearly always treated primarily as an economic rather than a politico-military concern. No evidence sug-

---

[139] Even Kaiser concedes this, "To Join," 54–55. See also Lamb, *Failure*, 76–77. The only clear misperception was tactical: the British government consistently assumed that Continental governments were driven by geopolitical concerns. For this reason, the British did not foresee that, if the CAP was successful, a strong French government would, as we shall see in chapter 3, veto British entry *for economic reasons*. But this was also not foreseen by others.

[140] The underlying economic logic of British policy is sometimes obscured by archaic language (competing effectively with German industrialists is often referred to as "preventing German dominance"), because there was still a need to convince the Foreign Office, and because Macmillan often employed geopolitical arguments to cloak British economic self-interest. This was true in the multilateral arena as well, where Macmillan lectured Kennedy on how a "united free world was more likely to be achieved through joint monetary and economic policies" than military alliances, although British monetary proposals to Kennedy were economically self-interested to the point of irrelevance. Harold James, *International Monetary Cooperation since Bretton Woods* (Oxford, 1996), 165–166.

gests that this was meant in a military sense, though statements are regularly taken out of context in an effort to prove it. Macmillan's oft-cited statement speaks of "a revival of German power *through economic means*." Another, by David Eccles, president of the Board of Trade in 1957 and a man whose writings are often cited in favor of a geopolitical interpretation, notes that "*Although it is not military or hostile in intent*, six countries in Europe have signed a treaty to do exactly what, for hundreds of years, we have always said we could not see done with safety to our country."[141] Even if there were stronger documentary evidence in favor of this view, such a motivation would render British policy incoherent. While its economic advantages were obvious, the FTA was hardly an effective geopolitical means to maximize relative advantage *vis-à-vis* Germany or to restore the Western alliance. The FTA was, after all, the preferred choice among German businessmen. (Nor did France, with even more intense concern about Germany, take such a view.)[142] Finally, as we shall see in chapter 3, geopolitical concerns do not explain why the British would continue to hope for an FTA even *after* the customs union was clearly established.[143]

Macmillan's warnings about the instability of the Western alliance are best understood not as expressions of underlying preferences but as tactical moves and expressions of frustration. The threats make little sense: Macmillan never explains *why* Britain would respond to economic isolation with geopolitical isolation, thereby cutting off its nose to spite its face. We can, to be sure, find only a very few instances where Macmillan's confidential statements can be read as treating the scenario of British withdrawal from NATO and the WEU as realistic; none are unambiguous and none demonstrate that he took them seriously. Certainly many top officials under him did not. Concern about the stability of Western commitments would have been, moreover, inconsistent with British intelligence reports (e.g., from Bretherton) suggesting that EC supranational institutions and geopolitical cooperation were unlikely to emerge, with the absence of British concern about NATO membership on internal lists of major British goals, with British plans to pull some troops back from the Continent in any case, and with the lack of interest Britain appears to have shown toward the militarily more sensitive Euratom negotiations or, previously, with the EDC. For the most part, threats to retreat into self-isolation were employed primarily as a diplomatic tactic to secure support for Britain's FTA proposals from the United States, France, and West Germany. There is no hint that they were meant to be carried out. Thus the celebrated memo calling for NATO withdrawal is best read not as a statement of purpose but as a set of instructions about what "we ought to make . . . quite clear to . . . de Gaulle and Adenauer." After Adenauer angrily dismissed such threats, they disappeared from internal documents—a final piece of evidence that we are dealing with tactics, not fundamental preferences.[144]

---

[141] Cited in Richard Griffiths, "British Policy toward the Common Market, 1955–1960," in George Wilkes, ed., *Britain's Failure to Enter the European Community, 1961–1963* (London, 1997), 39. Emphasis added.

[142] Dockrill, *Britain's*, 7.

[143] Lamb, *Failure*, 88–89.

[144] Kaiser, *Using*, 151–155, concludes this was simply a "bluff."

Political links to the Commonwealth, concern about the special relationship with the United States, and antifederalism are mentioned more often in internal documents. These factors even appear occasionally in early strategy documents as sufficient conditions for avoiding membership, though such documents were based in large part on the expectation that the Messina negotiations would fail. Yet there are reasons to be skeptical.

Of these reasons perhaps the most plausible is concern about global prestige. There is much documentary support for the notion that the Commonwealth political commitment mattered greatly. Yet the relative weight *vis-à-vis* purely economic concerns is difficult to ascertain, since the two predict the same policy response and were often mentioned in the same sentence. What is clear, however, is that British leaders were obsessed with the possibility that commercial exclusion from the dynamic European region would soon outweigh the Commonwealth's importance.

Did Macmillan fear that a united Europe would usurp Britain's global and European prestige as a privileged interlocutor to the United States? For this conjecture there are no more than a handful of references in Cabinet documents, clustered around the year 1957. If the EC's primary purpose was political, it is unclear why an FTA would solve Britain's problem. Nor is it clear why so little attention was paid to Euratom. Finally, this concern about the United States is unable to account for the continuity of British concern about Europe even during periods when—as in late 1955 or in mid-1962—the consensus view was that the EC was evolving into primarily an economic not a political organization.[145]

It is clear that the British opposed federal institutions and that this opposition may have contributed to its initial policy. Yet antifederalism fails to account for the two most salient aspects of the British position: the virulent hostility of British opposition and the choice of the FTA as an alternative. If Britain had been simply antifederalist, it would have quietly abstained, as it did in the case of the EDC and ECSC. Nor was opposition to supranational institutions consistent: Macmillan was, for example, willing to consider majority voting in the FTA if it would convince European governments of British seriousness of purpose.[146] Like the global prestige explanation, a concern with antifederalism does not explain why Britain remained implacably hostile even when it suspected the EC would not become a strong federal institution. In fact, concerns about federal institutions tend to disappear in British documents after 1956 and are replaced with more concrete concerns, which eventually led Britain toward membership.

On balance, rational policy-making and a coherent preference ordering that reflects shifting commercial interests offer the most convincing explanation for British actions, more so than the ascription of geopolitical ideas, let alone irrationality, myopia, or ignorance. Economic factors, moreover, become increasingly important over time. Only they offer a clear explanation why the status quo, with Commonwealth preferences and a slow move to multilateral

---

[145] In addition to Bretherton's reports from the Spaak Committee meetings, see the sections in chapter 3 on the Macmillan–de Gaulle meetings and Charlton, *Price*, 253–254.

[146] Macmillan, *Riding*, 435.

trade liberalization, suited Britain best; hence opposition to the customs union once it had been established was the optimal policy. The FTA proposal, which afforded Britain access to both Europe and the Commonwealth, was second-best. Membership in a customs union was third, followed only by exclusion from a such an arrangement—two options Britain explores in the next chapter. Commercial interests provide the most parsimonious explanation for these preferences; the preponderance of available evidence supports their primacy.

EXPLAINING NATIONAL PREFERENCES: THE PRIMACY, YET INSUFFICIENCY, OF ECONOMIC INTERESTS

The preponderance of evidence presented above confirms the preeminent importance of commercial considerations in forming the national preferences of Germany, France, and Britain. National preferences did not vary across countries, but across specific issues, as the economic explanation predicts. Preferences varied, moreover, as a function of current and, in the case of agriculture, potential exports. Germany favored liberalization for industry inside and outside of Europe, protection for agriculture, and no cooperation in atomic energy. France favored the converse, with particular attention to agriculture and external tariffs. Britain was primarily concerned with access to third countries and avoiding exclusion. Economic actors were active, constituting key veto groups and important policy initiators in all countries. The most important German, French, and British negotiating demands reproduced agricultural and industrial proposals verbatim, among them five of six major negotiating demands advanced by France, Germany's rejection of Adenauer's highest priority (Euratom), and Britain's move from apathy to opposition. Foreign and defense ministries were clearly less important, except in Germany, where they represented the Chancellor's own view and could pursue political goals within broader constraints imposed by economic interest. Intense producer preferences could not be circumvented, even when their demands conflicted with core geopolitical and ideological concerns. This was clearest in the case of Germany, where the atomic industry successfully emasculated Euratom. Economic considerations tended to be more salient than geopolitical factors in key documents and discussions in Britain and France. The major negotiating demands of each government—external openness for the United Kingdom, agriculture and industrial safeguards for France, the elimination of Euratom for Germany—were economic. Economic motivations are more consistent with existing policy in other areas in all three countries: agricultural integration was a goal of all Fourth Republic governments in France, trade liberalization and agricultural protection were goals of Adenauer from the late 1950s, the defense of Commonwealth trade was a key rationale for British support of the GATT. In all three countries, the maintenance of agricultural incomes was politically inescapable.

Timing also strongly confirms the economic view. The EC emerged after, not before, the resolution of major geopolitical issues. The Messina initiative followed a period of East-West thaw and came immediately after an intense period of European diplomacy, culminating in the London Conference of September–October 1954 and the Paris Agreements of May 1955, which resolved the Saar and Moselle issues, terminated the official occupation of Germany, placed controls on German armaments production, established a permanent British military presence on the Continent, quashed any move toward supranational military cooperation in the EDC, and reintegrated Germany into Western defense. Only when these issues were resolved would Adenauer and Mollet negotiate the EC. Their resolution addressed the geopolitical criticisms that the German SPD and French center-right, particularly the Gaullist Party, had directed at the EDC. The focus shifted to the major economic problems—such as the dissolution of the EPU, rising French agricultural surpluses, and the continuing shift from colonial to continental trade—that the EC was meant to address. In every country, potential opponents were mollified not by a conversion to European geopolitical ideas but by the realization that geopolitical issues were no longer at stake.

As a whole, commercial interests offer a sufficient explanation for national positions. This is clearest in the case of Britain, where the EC placed access to Commonwealth and European markets in direct conflict. Many geopolitical factors may have pointed in a similar direction and could explain Britain reticence to join, but few explain the depth of British hostility toward the EC. None offer as consistent an explanation of the process. Geopolitics mattered on the margin in France, giving the Mollet government an added reason to seek liberalization, but only within very narrow conditions imposed by economic interests. Economic interests were weak enough that there was general agreement that, while the Treaty as a whole gained parliamentary support, the industrial provisions could not be implemented without devaluation or, second best, social harmonization. Economic interests appear to have been primary in Germany as well—Germany vetoed atomic energy cooperation and accepted only vague agricultural provisions—but less so. Adenauer could exploit slack in economic interests to move toward a "small European" customs union rather than a pan-European FTA. National positions on smaller issues—competition policy, social harmonization, monetary convertibility, the speed of liberalization—all confirm the importance of economic interest. Finally, the lack of support for Euratom, despite its auspicious start, is a critical test for the geopolitical argument. The core issues of debate—whether to construct a common isotope separator, to limit Euratom to peaceful uses, and to create a European monopoly on nuclear supplies—may seem distinct, but they shared a common root. The basic question was whether "Euratom was to become an instrument not only of atomic and economic, but also of political and military independence from both superpowers."[147] The answer was no.

This is not to say that geopolitics was irrelevant. Although economic currents made the trend toward trade liberalization inevitable, geopolitical ideas helped determine national preferences and negotiated outcomes concerning precise timing, geographical scope, substantive domain, and institutional form. Leading European statesmen in each country understood that trade liberalization

---

[147] Polach, *Euratom*, 61–62, also 128. French rejection of a ban on military use was geopolitically motivated; German rejection of the other two was economically motivated.

was in one form or another inevitable; relative competitiveness determined much of their thinking about preferred geographical scope and substantive domain. Cooperation in atomic energy and transport was doomed from the start, though the former was the major political priority of both French and German leaders. If preferences were primarily reflective of economic interests, these interests still left national leaders with a some variable range of potentially ratifiable agreements—a measure of executive autonomy that could be exploited to achieve geopolitical as well as economic ends.

This autonomy proved particularly significant in Germany, where business preferred either a customs union or an FTA to the status quo, thereby placing the decision in Adenauer's hands. If Erhard had ruled Germany, the likely result would have been an Anglo-German FTA with no agricultural component, and the effects of economic exclusion would eventually have forced France to join. In France, a cautious ideological commitment to Europe bolstered the government's support for the Rome Treaty: There was a rush after July 1956 to complete the Treaty before the governmental coalition in France collapsed. In the longer term, those who supported trade liberalization for economic reasons— Pineau, Marjolin, and apparently also de Gaulle—would surely have prevailed in any case, but the form of liberalization might well have been quite different. Had de Gaulle ruled France in 1956, EC institutions would have been more intergovernmental—a Fouchet Plan before its time—though he would have fought hard to include agriculture. Had a leader like Mendès-France sought to muddle through for five years without a strong European initiative, the result would have been less striking—very likely a series of Franco-German bilateral arrangements, as was emerging in any case, with more decentralized institutions. Bilateral institutions would likely have encountered difficulty in securing German compliance, though they might have been multilateralized at any time. Only the British were truly constrained. Prior to 1958, it is hard to imagine any British government, regardless of the geopolitical arguments employed, challenging the strong economic interests that favored the maintenance of preferential ties with the Commonwealth. There is no reason to believe that either longer participation in the Spaak negotiations or an early commitment to the FTA would have been sufficient to reverse French or German policy.

Interstate Bargaining

We turn now from the formation of national preferences to interstate negotiations. The negotiation of the Treaty unfolded in three stages, each associated with a venerable Italian city. The policy initiation stage culminated in a meeting at Messina in late May 1955, where it was agreed to pursue expert negotiations. A stage of negotiation among experts culminated in a plan for a customs union and an atomic energy community, the Spaak Report, which was approved at Venice in May 1956. Finally, formal intergovernmental negotiations were conducted until March 1957, when a Treaty was signed at Rome. It was ratified shortly thereafter.

The core of the treaty contained strong provisions, including a schedule, for nearly automatic industrial tariff reductions. The treaty also mandated construction of a common external tariff and coordinated conduct of multilateral trade negotiations. A series of safeguards, exceptions, and veto provisions, however, permitted implementation to be delayed or blocked. Access for and assistance to French overseas territories was assured. Provisions for a preferential agricultural trading zone with common support prices, while containing a schedule, remained more vague, provisions for transport liberalization and competition (anti-trust) policy vaguer still, and provisions for atomic energy cooperation, monetary coordination, regulatory harmonization, and any other form of policy coordination essentially symbolic. Majority voting was to be instituted in certain areas once initial policies were in place. There was general agreement that these outcomes were efficient, leaving no potential agreements "on the table." At the core of the arrangement was the customs union, particularly strongly favored by Germany, while most other policies, notably those governing agriculture, overseas territories, and safeguards, favored France.

How is this pattern of bargaining outcomes best explained? The conventional view, consistent with supranational bargaining theory, long held that the efficiency and distributive implications of the negotiations (even ratification of the Treaty itself) reflected the political entrepreneurship of supranational or national European federalists like Paul-Henri Spaak, Pierre Uri, and above all Jean Monnet. Monnet initiated Euratom, mobilized social democratic politicians and labor into the transnational Action Committee for Europe, and sought to coordinate ratification of the Treaty.[148] Such efforts have been much praised; one political scientist likens the Action Committee to a "power elite" of Europe.[149] I hold instead, consistent with intergovernmental theory, that interstate bargaining was dominated by governments, which proved quite capable of providing efficient policy initiatives, mediation, and mobilization. Efficiency was in fact unproblematic. There was no shortage of ideas and information. Governments easily set agendas, mediated compromises, and mobilized social support. Distributional outcomes reflected not the goals of supranational entrepreneurs, whose priorities were all but absent from the Treaty, but the relative intensity of national preferences. Monnet and his Action Committee, by contrast, were strikingly ineffective, sometimes counterproductive—not least because they opposed many of the central elements in the Treaty, including the customs union itself. Outcomes reflected not the availability of third-party political entrepreneurship but the relative ability of governments to make credible threats and promises to veto proposals, exclude other government, or link issues—which in turn tracked underlying patterns of policy interdependence. France was the only country facing potential difficulty in ratification and implementation. To offset its concessions in accepting the customs union, it secured considerable concessions and compromises on the margin. Where this condition did not obtain, as in the

[148] Pascal Fontaine, *Le Comité d'Action pour les Etats-Unis d'Europe de Jean Monnet* (Lausanne, 1974), 207ff.

[149] Walter Yondorf, "Europe of the Six: Dynamics of Integration" (Ph.D. thesis, University of Chicago, 1962), 179.

heart of the Euratom proposal, which was vetoed by German industry, the resulting agreement was weaker and far less favorable to France. Supranational influence, mostly from national groups of federalists, was limited to the EC's institutional form.

Messina: Initiating the Relance

What were the origins of the initiatives for the customs union and atomic energy community agreed at Messina in June 1955? They are often attributed to Monnet, but although he promoted Euratom, proposals for the customs union came from many sources, with Monnet reluctantly and belatedly accepting them after failing to quash them. Trade liberalization had been discussed almost continuously since 1948. During the eighteen months following the defeat of the EDC alone, over a dozen new proposals appeared. Such schemes, Dutch foreign minister Willem Beyen observed in March 1955, were "springing up like mushrooms."[150] The ill-fated atomic energy and transport proposals were more original, but as soon as Monnet advanced them, numerous political entrepreneurs, led by Benelux politicians, stepped in to promote them.

Within twenty-four hours of French Assembly rejection of the EDC in August 1954, the Belgian foreign minister Paul-Henri Spaak, a strong European, was encouraging Monnet to advance a new initiative. Monnet was more opportunistic tactician than long-term strategist. A half-decade earlier, he had believed that integration of coal and steel would automatically spill over into areas of high politics, but the experience of the ECSC and the EDC had led him, like many others, to conclude that a strong political initiative was required. With his close ECSC staff members, he examined more than fifty proposals, including schemes for direct elections to the Assembly and the pooling of European armaments production. In this period Monnet believed that successful political integration was possible only where there was centralized economic planning by strong supranational authority; hence he sought a sector where strong government intervention already existed. He proposed that the "Community method" of sector-by-sector integration be extended to three highly regulated industries: transport, conventional power, and atomic power. He was most enthusiastic about the atomic energy community, a proposal that had originated with a U.S. official seconded to the French government and was championed by Louis Armand, a French technocrat and MRP politician.[151]

[150] Anjo G. Harryvan, "The Netherlands and the Administration of the EC: Early Principles and Practices," in Erik Volkmar Heyen, ed., *Die Anfänge der Verwaltung der europäischen Gemeinschaft* (Baden-Baden, 1992), 141, also 140; Willis, *France*, 232–242. For an overview of dozens of plans, see Wendy Asbeek Brusse, *West European Tariff Plans, 1947–1957: From the Study Group to the Common Market* (Florence, 1991).

[151] Duchêne, *Jean*, 258–308; Interview with Max Kohnstamm, EC Archives 29/2, Fiesole, 34. For a chronology of Monnet's actions, Fontaine, *Le Comité*, 207ff. Also Richard Mayne, "Jean Monnet, Europe and the British: A Witness Account," in Brian Brivati and Harriet Jones, eds., *From Reconstruction to Integration: Britain and Europe since 1945* (London, 1993), 28–29. The idea for nuclear integration appears to have come from Max Eisenberg, an official at the American embassy in Paris, who spoke with Louis Armand, a leading French scientist and government official. Pierre Gerbet in "La 'Relance' européenne jusqu'à la Conférence de Messine," in Serra, *Il Rilancio*, 66–68, also 164,

The domestic political situation in France initially deterred any serious effort to realize such plans. Mendès-France, whose lukewarm attitude toward European integration had helped undermine the EDC, still led the country. The foreign ministers of the Benelux governments—Spaak, Willem Beyen of the Netherlands, and Leo Bech of Luxembourg—decided at a November 1954 summit to delay any new proposals until the political situation in France improved. Monnet, preparing for an extended campaign, resigned from the ECSC High Authority, effective June 1955, intending to form a private committee to promote integration. Yet when Edgar Faure replaced Mendès-France in early 1955, planning immediately resumed. High-level Franco-German negotiations were reinvigorated, focusing on transport, aerospace, conventional power generation, and atomic energy. A Franco-German commercial treaty, completed in August 1955, promoted long-term trade in both industry and agriculture. Spaak, Beyen, and Bech now saw not just an opportunity to relaunch Europe and liberalize trade but a need to obstruct this potentially exclusive Franco-German agreement—Beyen termed it "resurgent bilateralism." Five separate plans for general economic integration emerged from the Benelux governments alone. With the changed situation in France, one British diplomat observed, "everybody [was] bursting with new ideas."[152]

Monnet and Spaak proposed that Monnet chair an international conference to consider extension of the ECSC to transport, conventional energy and atomic power. Spaak blocked plans for a customs union—notably one advanced by another Belgian minister—and instead sent a proposal on transport and energy to the six ECSC members. Germany immediately blocked it. On 6 April, Carl Ophüls, a top German official and a federalist follower of Adenauer, informed Monnet that while the chancellor was sympathetic, German industry rejected sectoral integration as too *dirigiste*; on atomic energy in particular, cooperation with Britain and United States was more profitable. Atomic cooperation would be ratifiable, if at all, only as a quid pro quo for general trade liberalization, strongly favored by industry. (Even this assessment was to prove too optimistic.) Monnet was skeptical and "rather depressed," a close associate recalled, but concluded that "there is nothing else to do." His associate Pierre Uri drafted a memo on this basis, which was circulated on 13 April to the Benelux governments.[153]

Monnet was too late. By then Benelux leaders were moving ahead on their

---

190. In private correspondence of 1952, Monnet portrayed the EDC as a means to avoid the "reconstitution d'une Allemagne souveraine et nationaliste" that would turn to the East and return to past aggressions against the West; it would also permit Europe to act more independently on the world stage. Letter from Jean Monnet to Rène Mayer, 29 December 1952 (Papiers Mayer, 363 AP 28, SD/5).

[152] Harryvan, "Netherlands," 134, also 133–141; Duchêne, *Jean*, 258–283. Various Benelux politicians proposed customs unions, free trade areas, and general economic integration. Meanwhile the French government placed first priority on the ratification of the Paris Agreements, which finally occured on 29 March 1955. Gerbet, "Relance," 73; Faure, *Mémoires*, 2:214; Altiero Spinelli, "The Growth of the European Movement since World War II," in C. Grove Haines, ed., *European Integration* (Baltimore, 1957), 62–63.

[153] Duchêne, *Jean*, 269; Carstens Interview, 16.

own. On 4 April Beyen, a banker by profession and a skeptic of federalism, revived his widely discussed February 1953 proposal for a customs union—itself a descendent of the Dutch "Stikker Plan" of 1950. Beyen's proposal called for institutions stronger than those of the intergovernmental OEEC or the WEU— "fake integration," he termed the latter. Spaak and Beyen agreed to combine their proposals. With France still recovering from the EDC debate, they eschewed the term "supranational," instead referring vaguely to "the establishment of a common authority endowed with the necessary powers." The two leaders then discussed their joint proposal with Monnet and circulated it as an agenda for the ECSC foreign ministers' meeting at Messina, scheduled for 1–2 June 1955. The Six attended, but the British declined to participate.[154]

The Benelux memorandum served as the basis for discussion at Messina, and the final agreement reflected many of its principles. French and German ministers sought to make the most of ambivalent mandates. Monnet did not attend and instead futilely telephoned detailed instructions to his associate Max Kohlstamm, whom the politicians treated, he later recalled, like a "leper." Hallstein spoke favorably of both atomic energy and the customs union, whereas Pinay stressed that his government, too constrained by domestic criticism to accept general economic integration, would consider proposals for atomic energy if the powers of the High Authority were not expanded. The scheduled meeting ended without agreement, but Spaak, Pinay, and perhaps others huddled together between 2:00 and 4:00 A.M. on 3 June to hammer out a final communiqué. When Pinay rejected any conference chaired by Monnet, a sure political liability in France, Spaak proposed the Benelux fall-back position: a committee of experts chaired by a major political figure to study economic integration. Pinay hesitated, but when others underscored that the French alone could not permanently oppose further economic integration, he overrode written instructions from Faure and agreed to meetings of an expert group on the customs union. Spaak reportedly celebrated by standing on his balcony at 4 A.M. and singing "O sole mio" until Pinay silenced him.[155]

The final communiqué, only a few pages long, called on Europe to regain "influence and prestige" in the world and achieve "a continued increase in the standard of living of her people." It noted agreement to focus on sectoral integration in transport, conventional energy, and atomic power, the last of primary interest to France, and to create in stages a customs union, a goal of primary interest to Germany. This was to be complemented by a list of measures, mostly demanded by Pinay, including a common external tariff, fiscal and monetary harmonization, harmonization of social standards (the work week, overtime pay,

---

[154] Harryvan, "Netherlands," 133–135, 144–145; Mahant, *French*, 50–54, 154; Pierre Uri, cited in Serra, *Il Rilancio*, 167. Mayne, "Jean," 285–289; Küsters, *Gründung*, 77–78, 106–109. Uri's claim to have introduced the customs union is unsupported. Pierre Uri, *Penser pour l'action: Un fondateur de l'Europe* (Paris, 1991), 114–115; the Monnet-Uri memorandum did not arrive until 13 April, a week after Beyen had made his proposals.

[155] Duchêne, *Jean*, 280; Noël Interview, 10; René Massigli, *Une comédie des erreurs 1943–1956* (Paris, 1978), 511; Küsters, *Gründung*, 120–122; Mayne, "Jean," 290–293; Harryvan, "Dutch," 155; Rothschild in Serra, *Il Rilancio*, 184.

and vacations), the coordination of social policy, free movement of labor, common regulation of competition, a European investment fund to aid poor regions, and adequate safeguard clauses. The transport provisions foresaw a European network of highways, canals, electric trains, and coordinated airways. A new institution, backed by a common fund, would support common research in atomic energy, facilitate exchanges of expertise, and permit unhampered access to raw materials. A resolution, backed by all six governments, invited the British to join the conference. With domestic criticism in mind, Pinay gained a commitment from the others that the experts would study methods of integration and not negotiate a treaty.[156]

In this phase, as intergovernmental theory predicts, the most interested governments provided the proposals they most wanted: the customs union was proposed by the Netherlands, Belgium, and Germany, agricultural cooperation by France, Italy, and the Netherlands, energy cooperation by France and Belgium, transport cooperation by Belgium. Transaction costs appear to have been low, because of previous experience with similar negotiations and the willingness of many leaders to serve as initiators. In retrospect, nothing viable was left out. Where secrecy was required, interventions in confidential, behind-the-scenes discussions were decisive in shaping the content of proposals, as we see most prominently in the German dismissal of Euratom. By contrast, Monnet's consistent skepticism of the customs union suggests poor information and faulty political judgment. Monnet also lacked any distinctive technical expertise; he and his associates did offer plans, but there was no bottleneck in their provision. Spaak was more active as a mediator, but he was a national official and prided himself on his *lack* of technical expertise—a quality he viewed as contributing to his impartiality and effectiveness.[157] The resulting set of initiatives considered were biased in favor neither of Monnet's nor of Spaak's preferences, but remained comprehensive, ultimately reflecting the willingness of France and Germany to integrate.

From Messina to Venice:
The Spaak Committee and the First Stage of Bargaining

In the fall of 1955 the so-called Spaak Committee convened with experts representing the six governments and Bretherton as the British observer. The committee has been portrayed as an arena in which Spaak exercised considerable autonomy or, alternatively, as a technocratic discussion among autonomous ex-

---

[156] Testimony in Serra, *Il Rilancio*, 176–177, 189; Willis, *France*, 243; Mayne, *Recovery*, 292. Camps (*Britain*, 26–29) conjectures that the French favored British involvement to "shift from their own shoulders the onus of being reluctant 'Europeans.'" Five years previously the French government "had insisted on a prior acceptance of the concept of delegation of power to an independent High Authority as a condition for participation in the drafting of the Coal and Steel Community treaty," but this time the British were issued an invitation to participate on any terms they chose. The invitation to the British was crafted to make the Six seem more open than in fact they were.

[157] Yondorf, *Europe of the Six*, 64, argues that Spaak's position as foreign minister was an "advantage in guiding . . . rank-conscious diplomats" and a guarantee of "easy access to his five ministerial colleagues."

perts. Neither picture is accurate. To be sure, Spaak interpreted his mandate broadly, working quickly to develop a complete blueprint for a common market, transport, conventional energy, nuclear energy, and public works. When the customs union and nuclear energy emerged as the only areas in which either France or Germany had a major interest, transport policy was folded into the customs union and other ideas were dropped. Experts provided technical reports, as was customary in EPU and OEEC negotiations. Yet the experts were selected by and, in most cases, employed by the member states; though some were sometimes given autonomy, their views nonetheless tended to track those of governments. In any case, within a few months discussions among experts stalled and was increasingly supplanted after October 1955 by direct bargaining among national officials. As Spaak observed sarcastically: "Well, *all* that remains for us to do is to choose between the various proposals submitted by the experts"—a process that was to take six months within the Spaak Committee and another year of intergovernmental negotiation. Meanwhile in December Bretherton withdrew after delivering a short speech, approved in London, stressing the futility of further talks and reiterating Britain's refusal to participate in any exclusive customs union.[158]

In February 1956 the foreign ministers approved papers from the experts as the basis for intergovernmental negotiations between national representatives. Each acted on detailed instructions from his government. In the most difficult areas of the Spaak Report, such as agriculture and social policy, text negotiated and written by national officials was incorporated in the report verbatim by France and German representatives. Much of the rest was drafted by Pierre Uri and Hans von der Groeben, the latter a national official. Thus the result of their work, the so-called Spaak Report of April 1956, resembled in its broad outlines the final Treaty of Rome; it recommended a customs union, an agricultural policy, atomic energy union, and supranational institutions much like those that finally emerged. When the foreign ministers met at Venice in May 1956, many expected France to reject the report, but Pineau immediately agreed that the Six should begin intergovernmental negotiations with the aim of creating a common market and an atomic energy arrangement. He stressed, however, the need to associate French overseas territories, to permit military use of nuclear weapons, and to invite other countries to participate. Agriculture also remained vague. These latter elements remained to be negotiated.[159]

From Venice to Rome: The Intergovernmental Conference

When the six governments resumed serious negotiations in October 1956, France was still pitted against the five other governments. With the Saar issue on

---

[158] Willis, *France*, 244; Carlton, *Price*, 186–188; Kaiser, *Using*, 47.

[159] Mahant, *French*, 57–58, 62. Prate and Ophüls both recall initially being given considerable freedom from ministries, since it was assumed that the Treaty would never be signed, but their positions were consistent with those held by their respective governments. Prate, *Quelle*, 54–55; C. F. Ophüls, "La Relance européenne," *Annuaire européen* 4 (La Haye, 1957), 3–20; Interview with Christian Pineau (EC Archive, Interview 10), 6–7.

its way to resolution—French acceptance of the pro-German referendum results, participants recall, was "very, very important . . . in creating trust"[160]—French negotiators signaled their desire to reach agreement quickly, lest economic crisis and political instability endanger ratification. In exchange for accepting an industrial customs union, the French government forwarded the demands of the Patronat—prior harmonization of social regulations concerning the length of paid vacation, gender equality of wages and the workweek, the right to withdraw or veto continuation to the "second stage" after the first 25 percent tariff cut, the right to invoke escape clauses and impose border taxes in the case of balance of payments crisis—plus an agricultural policy.

By late October initial economic concessions, particularly the inclusion of agriculture, had been informally agreed. On this, the most difficult issue to negotiate, the Germans bowed to the French claim, clearly accurate, that the Treaty was unratifiable in France without agriculture. Pineau proposed a compromise on other outstanding issues at a foreign ministers' meeting late in the month: France renounced the right to withdraw unilaterally and conceded that social policy might be harmonized at the beginning of the second stage, but reasserted its positions on safeguards and the veto. Erhard, apparently seeking to block the EC and mobilize German business behind the FTA, rejected the compromises. A visit by Adenauer to Paris, planned for 6 November 1956, was scheduled by French and German participants with the intent to override Erhard and resolve outstanding issues.[161]

Despite inauspicious circumstances, the summit meeting occasioned the first major breakthrough. When 6 November arrived, the Suez crisis was reaching its peak. Adenauer's associates advised him to cancel the visit, lest he associate himself with the Anglo-French operation. He went anyway. Soon after his arrival, the two chief executives detailed their assistants, Robert Marjolin and Karl Carstens, to draft language on social harmonization based on the compromise proposed by Pineau several weeks earlier. Both leaders were so anxious to resolve the issue that, it is said, neither read the final text before signing. Later in the day, when Eden called Mollet to inform him that the British had unilaterally agreed to a ceasefire in the Middle East, which the French had strenuously opposed, Adenauer counseled Mollet to "make Europe your revenge."[162] Further compromises were reached at several ministerial meetings leading up to another summit at the Elysée in February 1957, where Adenauer and Mollet hammered out the final details on agricultural policy and the treatment of French overseas territories. Both required German compromises. In March 1957 the Treaty was signed; within three months all six governments had ratified it.

Most of the negotiators' time was spent on distributive issues. The outcomes

---

[160] Carstens Interview, 9.

[161] Lynch, *France*, 180; Willis, *France*, 248; Lamb, *Failure*, 99–100; Pineau in Griffiths, ed., *Socialist*, 59–60; Interviews with von der Groeben, 6, 11, and Carstens, 16.

[162] As we have seen above, German officials tend to consider Suez and Adenauer's intervention; French officials, with the exception of Pineau's equivocal position, do not. Von der Groeben interview, 6; Carstens, *Erinnerungen*, 205–208; Christian Pineau, *1956/Suez* (Paris, 1976), 176ff; Bossuat, *L'Europe*, 334–337.

were limited by the relative value of unilateral alternatives; those governments who wanted agreement most compromised the most. On trade liberalization Britain and France had little overlap, with Britain preferring the status quo or an FTA to a customs union and France preferring the customs union or the status quo to an FTA. Hence only an Anglo-German or a Franco-German agreement was possible. In Germany either the customs union or the FTA would be supported by domestic economic interest groups, if any agricultural provisions remained vague, and Adenauer's willingness to compromise meant a broad coincidence of interests. The range of alternatives was tightest in France, where the Assembly was unlikely to ratify a customs union without provisions on safeguards, agriculture, and overseas territories. The basic problem, Spaak told the British, was that "France was undergoing serious economic strains" and "certain concessions" must therefore be made.[163] The French government's credible claim that the Assembly would not ratify the Treaty, due to the fears of French industry, combined with Adenauer's flexibility, placed France in a strong bargaining position, which it employed to extract agricultural concessions. Marjolin later recalled that France "set the tone of the proceedings [because] the issues raised by the creation of an economically united Europe had to be settled in Paris, in a series of clashes between the adherents of liberalism, of whom I was one, and those who . . . advocated a France closed to Europe and to the world."[164]

The fates of Euratom and the customs union demonstrate the extent to which mediation by Monnet was redundant, if not counterproductive. Ernst Haas sees 1956 as the year when "Monnet's doctrine of a strong, united Europe . . . resting on a large common market came into its own."[165] The truth was precisely the opposite. Rather than propose issue linkages, as supranational theory predicts, Monnet sought to pick them apart. The first five resolutions of his Action Committee in April 1957 concerned Euratom and did not mention the customs union. Monnet remained so skeptical of the latter than he repeatedly urged Pineau, Mollet, and Adenauer to drop the notion. Adenauer and some of his associates were initially sympathetic, but von der Groeben and other German officials dissuaded him, arguing that sectoral integration lacked domestic support.[166] For most on the Action Committee, the most important resolution was the one limiting atomic technology to peaceful uses. In July 1956, when it had become clear that Mollet (a Committee member) had rejected the Committee's recommendation, the leadership of the German SPD, which had strongly supported Euratom, concluded in a secret memorandum: "Guy Mollet has sacrificed the central core of the Committee's resolution on Euratom. In doing so he endangered the whole *raison d'être* of the committee."[167]

---

[163] Charlton, *Price*, 210.

[164] Marjolin, *Architect*, 281–282; Carstens, *Erinnerungen*, 212;

[165] Haas, *Uniting of Europe*, 299, 317.

[166] Interviews with von der Groeben, 6–7, 21; Küsters, *Gründung*, 309–311. On the Action Committee's poor overall record of achieving its objectives, see Yondorf, *Europe*.

[167] The memo is thus paraphrased in Patterson, *Socialist*, 126. The SPD nonetheless supported a subsequent Action Committee's resolution in favor of Euratom. See contributions by Helmut Schmidt and Andreas Wilkins, at the conference "Jean Monnet et l'Europe" (May 29–30, 1997). Duchêne

At the core of the Treaty stood the basic objective of a customs union, to be implemented through elimination of internal tariffs in predetermined stages. The French initially opposed a fixed schedule, let alone a single date, but agreed to the gradual elimination of tariffs (and most quotas) in three stages of four years each—a strategy Faure described as a "calculated risk." Quotas were to be eliminated according to a formula inherited from existing OEEC but without a precise timetable. Articles 100–102 permitted governments to harmonize regulatory nontariff barriers by unanimity vote. Other wording entered the Treaty more haphazardly: for example, Articles 30–35 banning "measures having equivalent effect" to quotas, later a centerpiece of European jurisprudence, apparently resulted from a query by a mid-level German customs official.[168] On the common external tariff the Six reached a compromise. France and Italy tended to advocate increases in its average value but eventually accepted the German demand that the Common Market comply with the GATT, one implication being that average tariffs could not rise above existing levels. The external tariff was thus to be set at the arithmetic mean of existing French, Italian, Benelux, and German tariffs; governments were permitted to exempt particularly sensitive tariff categories, about 15 percent of imports into the region, by placing them on so-called List G to be negotiated later. Germany insisted that tariffs on imported raw materials be capped at relatively low levels.[169] A common transport policy was added over Franco-German opposition, largely due to Spaak's direct pressure on behalf of Benelux interests. Although the Treaty appeared to grant transport policy the same formal status as agricultural policy, fewer specific measures were outlined and, with the exception of rules against outright price discrimination, any further developments in this area would require unanimous agreement.

Beyond this core agreement, which on balance favored Germany more than France, the number of concessions made to the French seems disproportionate, precisely as intergovernmental bargaining theory predicts. To be sure, some concessions were minor, even symbolic. Safeguards, escape clauses, and border taxes were permitted, but Germany managed to limit them to exceptional, temporary use, subject to oversight, albeit ex post facto, by an independent organization. France was permitted to retain import taxes and export subsidies until external payments were balanced for at least one year—a proxy for a franc devaluation. On social policy, the French settled for a statement of intent by the Six to achieve similar policies. If unequal social legislation disadvantaged French

---

hints that Monnet was decisive because without Euratom, France would not have gotten far enough in the negotiations to reverse its position, drop a serious Euratom initiative, and back the customs union. Even if this somewhat tenuous causal claim is true, surely Monnet did not foresee it. Duchêne, *Jean*, 282–283; Kurt Thomas Schmitz, *Deutsche Einheit und Europäische Integration*, (Bonn, 1978), 130.

[168] Küsters, *Gründung*, 157–179, 240–248; Prate, *Quelle*, 55. The Spaak Report initially proposed a system of negotiated tariff reductions, but it seemed too complicated, and a "semi-linear" system of automatic-percentage tariff reductions was imposed, as favored by the Germans and Dutch.

[169] Küsters, *Gründung*, 164–166, 171–172, 241.

industry, France could delay movement to the second stage or impose sectoral safeguards. France backed away from its initial demand for the right to withdraw from the Common Market, but insisted that the transition to the second stage, scheduled to occur after four years, require a unanimous vote, at least for the first several years.[170]

Other French gains were more concrete. Discussion of the FTA was postponed, and French insistence on an agricultural policy and assistance to overseas territories prevailed. The CAP, Faure told Adenauer during the critical negotiations, would balance out the gains in the Treaty and thereby facilitate parliamentary ratification. Despite the theoretical criticisms of economists, Karl Carstens recalled, this was the "political reality."[171] All governments agreed to keep domestic measures in place until common policies were developed and to encourage long-term contracts at minimum prices, the latter established already in bilateral Franco-German agreement of 1955. Proposals for rapid movement to a liberal regime with low external protection and low or no price support (from the Netherlands and Italy, where agricultural exports were competitive and comprised a high percentage of exports) were rejected. German negotiators remained skeptical of all proposals except discretionary long-term contracts but accepted French proposals for a system of interstate preference, guaranteed prices, and high external protection—with the formally stated purpose of raising the living standard of the rural population. In exchange Germany secured a unanimity rule for any agricultural proposal that reduced the welfare of farmers in any country and a twelve-year transition period during which states could manipulate state purchasing monopolies (akin to bilateral import quotas). Critical also was acceptance of the German demand that the EC competition policy rules governing state subsidies—a central German demand in industrial sectors—not be extended to agriculture. While the Treaty provided the rudiments of an agricultural policy, the most delicate issues, namely the level of prices, the nature of financing, and the extent to which the system would be centralized—would it embody minimal rules on competition, coordination of national policies, or a central European organization?—were postponed.[172]

The French also insisted that the EC provide market access and development aid to French overseas territories, colonies, and associated nations. The Mollet government considered this, like the CAP, a necessary condition for domestic ratification. In exchange the Six were offered commercial access to those colonies. Commodities produced in French colonies, unlike those of Britain, were almost exclusively tropical, hardly competing with European producers, though the resulting increase in the cost of some tropical goods from the dollar zone remained controversial among German consumers and industrialists. (The dispute over quotas on imported bananas, a commodity of great symbolic importance in

[170] Mahant, *French,* 74; Milward, *Rescue,* 220; Bossuat, *L'Europe,* 317; Küsters, *Gründung,* 172–173, 245, 327–333, 337–339, 376.
[171] Carstens, *Erinnerungen,* 212.
[172] Küsters, *Gründung,* 173–174, 242–244, 333–334, 347–359; Mahant, *French,* 67–72; Carstens, *Erinnerungen,* 212–214.

postwar Germany, required the intervention of French and German foreign ministers and chief executives.) Only in February 1957 was the issue of development aid finally resolved. After a futile marathon of official discussions, Adenauer and Mollet went for a stroll in the Park of the Matignon; a Dutch diplomat remarked at the time: "Every minute in that conversation costs Herr Adenauer at least a million." There is no record of the precise length of their conversation, but the Germans agreed to contribute $200 million in aid over five years, in exchange for which France renounced exclusive imperial trading preferences.[173]

Although France came away well from the negotiations, it would be an exaggeration to conclude, as does one leading historian, that "almost everything France wanted out of the treaty it got."[174] The Treaty was a compromise, tilted *on the margin* toward France but still as a whole slightly more difficult for France to ratify than for any other country. The most important failure was Euratom. The German government, facing powerful opposition from Erhard, backed by the politically powerful minister for atomic energy, Franz-Josef Strauss, as well as German industry, obstructed the Euratom talks, imposed an explicit linkage (*Junktim*) with a customs union, then blocked agreement on major clauses of the agreement. In Mollet's view Euratom was stillborn, with the French gaining little more than symbolism.[175]

Three critical issues arose and each was resolved only at the final Franco-German bilateral meeting. The first two—a French proposal for a common European facility for isotope separation, and a Euratom (de facto French) monopoly on the provision of uranium—were rejected by German industry. Just as Ophüls had warned Monnet two years earlier, German industry preferred to deal with Britain and the United States; the Americans had offered European governments cheap supplies of enriched uranium. In these areas France and Germany did little more than reiterate pledges already contained in the Franco-German Treaty of 1955 to perform all (non-weapons related) nuclear research in common. The result was no more than symbolic: a centralized European uranium supply agency was authorized but denied a monopoly. France soon went ahead with its own national isotope separation program. Germany continued to purchase uranium from the United States.[176]

The third and most salient atomic issue was a ban on the development of nuclear weapons. In his Action Committee, Monnet emphasized this above all else, largely to gain the support of German Social Democrats. Mollet himself had signed this Action Committee resolution but privately rejected any ban, since his

[173] "Gemeinsame Markt: Banana für die Affen," *Der Spiegel* (27 February 1957), 14.

[174] Milward, *Rescue*, 220.

[175] Pierre Guillen, "La France et la negotiation du traité d-Euratom," *Relations internationales* 44 (Winter 1985), 411–412, concludes "la montagne accouchait d'une souris," and argues that Mollet understood this. Another analyst notes that "Euratom neither integrates nor has authority over national atomic developments . . . response to Euratom was weak." Polach, *Euratom*, 128.

[176] Germany and the Netherlands immediately concluded bilateral agreements against the spirit of the agreement; existing agreements were also maintained. Polach, *Euratom*, 130–31; Guillen, "France," 408–411; Weilemann, *Anfänge*, 159–161, 167–168.

government was quietly moving ahead with plans launched by the Faure government to develop nuclear weapons. France informed its partners that it would not renounce nuclear weapons. In February 1957 Mollet and Adenauer even began secret planning for joint production of nuclear weapons, with the Germans providing financing and the French technical know-how—and a means of circumventing treaty restrictions on German production. When de Gaulle entered office, he terminated the project.[177]

The other substantive area, in addition to industrial tariffs and Euratom, where Germany succeeded in imposing its view was competition (antitrust) policy. The Spaak Report, at Erhard's insistence, had called for regulation of monopolies and trusts as well as state subsidies. Provisions for action against mergers, monopolies, and dumping (Articles 85–86) were limited, applicable only for mergers and monopolies at the European level. Proposed limitations on state subsidies to firms (Article 93) led to a fundamental philosophical disagreement between the more liberal Germans, backed by the Dutch, and the more *dirigiste* French, backed by the Italians. The former prevailed, and the result was a unique Treaty provision according to which the Commission—once the Council of Ministers had established regulations—could take independent policy decisions to regulate competition. By the 1970s, analysts were considering Germany a modest beneficiary from the competition policy, which promoted a German regulatory vision, even if the provisions were neither effectively enforced nor particularly constraining.[178]

Other agreements directly reflected the extent to which interests converged. Italy sought to export labor and the others, especially Germany, sought to import it, so it was easy to agree in principle on freedom of movement for unskilled labor during the transition period, and for skilled labor thereafter—though many national regulations concerning qualifications, employment, and welfare were retained, thereby providing means to exclude unwanted workers. Although Spaak Committee experts recognized that currency fluctuations might restrict economic activity, the imposition of full convertibility, freedom of capital movements, and monetary union was rejected, largely due to differences in domestic macroeconomic policies. Macroeconomic policy coordination remained only symbolic: central authority was established to make nonbinding fiscal and monetary policy recommendations.[179]

Threats of exclusion and linkage played a subordinate role among the Six but proved decisive for Britain. Threats of exit and exclusion were effective only where credible, namely *vis-à-vis* Britain. Britain was hostile to the customs union, which implied commercial exclusion, but most British leaders—younger economic officials aside—initially felt it was too uncertain a threat to generate an immediate bid for membership. Britain's counterthreat of exit—from NATO—

---

[177] Polach, *Euratom*, 22–23, 63–65; Guillen, "La France," 399; Jean Monnet, *Mémoires* (Paris, 1976), 2:622ff; Henning Köhler, *Adenauer: Eine politische Biographie* (Frankfurt, 1994), 983ff.

[178] Küsters, *Gründung*, 240–241, 245–246, 363–369; Müller-Armack, *Wege*, 114; Bernard May, *Kosten und Nutzen der Deutschen EG-Mitgleidshaft* (Bonn, 1982), 195ff.

[179] Küsters, *Gründung*, 240–241, 245–246.

was not credible, as the British themselves conceded, and was summarily dismissed. Ultimately, we shall see in the next chapter, Britain would be forced to apply for EC membership. French leaders, too, argued for the customs union as a means of avoiding isolation—notably, exclusion from an Anglo-German FTA— and this was one factor pressing for accommodation with Germany. Linkages were secondary, balancing out gains rather than trading off gains and losses. Most trade-offs were within economic sectors, with the costs falling disproportionately on unrepresented or unorganized groups. Germany, for example, compromised on agricultural policy for industrial and geopolitical reasons, but the Treaty remained vague on the issue of prices and would require considerable renegotiation (in Germany's favor) to be viable. The likely losers from any agricultural arrangement—German consumers, taxpayers, and third-country producers— remained unrepresented. France compromised on industrial trade, but even French leaders did not expect full implementation. France gained joint financial assistance for overseas territories, carefully targeted to eliminate parliamentary opposition in France; this outcome benefited German industry but burdened taxpayers. Where linkage did involve intense losses for concentrated constituencies in Germany—in atomic energy cooperation and in social harmonization—concessions remained almost exclusively symbolic.

After Rome: Ratification and Federalist Disillusionment

Net concessions to France reduced opposition to the ideological and geopolitical irreconcilables—the Communists, the Poujadists, some Gaullists. Other French groups cautiously accepted the Treaty. In other countries, as one might expect after concessions to France, there was criticism, but no serious movement to block ratification. Altiero Spinelli, perhaps Europe's leading federalist, charged that the Common Market had betrayed the European ideal in favor of a "Europe of governments" within a treaty that was legalistic rather than participatory, incremental rather than federal, economic rather than political. The Dutch, originators of the customs union and probably its greatest beneficiaries, experienced unexpected controversy because they gained few of their distributive demands, such as low agricultural prices, low external tariffs, British participation, a strong transport policy, equal votes for all countries, and strong supranational institutions. Yet the Dutch, who benefited greatly and thus could not credibly threaten exit, had no choice but to ratify the agreement, though not without parliamentary acrimony. The Treaty, a leading Dutch statesman sadly recalled from the vantage point of 1961, invoking General de Gaulle's phrase, was "a clear triumph for 'Europe des patries.'"[180]

Domestic groups were mobilized or discouraged by governments to assure ratification. In both France and Germany the government colluded with peak

---

[180] Joseph Luns's recollection, circa 1961 in Serra, *Il Rilancio*, 293. The Dutch felt they had suffered more than most. Milward, *Rescue*, 221–222. Opposition within the German government rose as well. Mahant, *French*, 72–73. Also Altiero Spinelli, *The Eurocrats: Conflict and Crisis in the European Community* (Baltimore, 1966).

industrial groups to prevent a broad mobilization of industrial sectors, particularly those opposed to liberalization. In France the government encouraged agricultural groups to mobilize, whereas in Germany the government did the opposite. In Britain peak business groups remained quiet in 1955—which they later viewed as an error—but mobilized within a year and remained active thereafter. Social demands from these groups remained stable throughout the negotiations and, in most cases, had remained unchanged for years.

It has been argued that Monnet, acting through his Action Committee for a United States of Europe, mobilized a transnational elite network to influence domestic debates over ratification. He is said to have coordinated the timing of parliamentary ratification in Germany, as well as convincing German Social Democrats to vote for the Treaty.[181] Neither claim withstands close scrutiny.

With the Action Committee, Monnet's strategy was to find "disinterested groups" and "representatives of the masses" who would support the European ideal. The Action Committee's illustrious members—including Guy Mollet, Maurice Faure, and Kurt Ollenhauer, chairman of the German SPD—were drawn disproportionately from precisely those groups, such as Dutch and French Socialists, already inclined to favor integration. Others, such as union leaders and some Social Democrats, were marginal to domestic decision-making on the Treaty. The Committee included no representation from those interest groups whose support appears to have been decisive in each country, namely industrialists, farmers, and ruling Christian Democratic parties, whom Monnet dismissed as too self-interested and elitist.[182]

Participation in the Assembly of the ECSC, contact with Monnet through the unions, and membership in the Action Committee are said to have convinced certain German SPD leaders to support ratification, in turn giving Adenauer, his majority in the Bundestag temporarily eroded by the defection of the Refugee Party in July 1955 and the Free Democrats in February 1956, more freedom to negotiate. Yet Monnet's role is easily exaggerated.[183] The SPD had supported the negotiations from the beginning—even *before* the founding of Monnet's Action Committee. In June 1955 Herbert Wehner, in the first official party statement on the customs union, endorsed the Messina Resolution before the Common Assembly of the ECSC, reiterating his position a month later before the Bundestag. We cannot dismiss the possibility that earlier participation in ECSC institutions (where Monnet was involved) may have played a role in shifting Social

---

[181] For the most subtle formulation of many, see Duchêne, *Jean*, 287–290, 306–308.
[182] Interview with Max Kohnstamm, Monnet associate (EC Archives Interview 29/2, 1984), 24, 30–31.
[183] Willis, *France*, 271; Arnold J. Zurcher, *The Struggle to Unite Europe, 1940–1958* (New York, 1958), 132–133; Patterson, *Socialist*, 115, 123–129; Richard Mayne, "The Role of Jean Monnet," in *The New Politics of European Integration*, edited by Ghita Ionescu, (London, 1972), 53–55. This skeptical assessment is supported by our general knowledge of the Action Committee. Yondorf (*Europe of the Six*, 176–179) examines all of the Action Committee's resolutions through July 1960. Out of 18 resolutions, 9 were carried out, 6 were not, and 3 were carried out in part. And this is an exceedingly weak test, since these policies and measures, Yondorf notes, might "have been adopted even without the support of the Action Committee."

Democrats, but such experience must be placed in a context of deep structural forces, both domestic and international—in particular pressure from the unions, electoral repositioning, and the resolution of major security issues—that, as we have seen in detail, had been moving the German SPD toward greater acceptance of European integration since the early 1950s. Monnet's activism may have speeded the SPD's evolution slightly, but it hardly seems to have been a necessary condition for it. Finally, since Adenauer controlled a parliamentary majority—after 1957 a single-party majority—SPD support might not have been essential in the longer term.

Monnet is also said to have contributed to rapid French ratification by persuading Maurice Faure to move quickly and by speeding the schedule for German ratification. Yet Faure hardly needed Monnet's encouragement. The French and German governments had been coordinating domestic strategies since October 1956, with Faure constantly reminding the other governments of the need to move quickly; this was universally accepted as the lesson of the EDC debate. Once agreement had been reached, the Mollet and Bourgès-Maunoury governments had deliberately maintained continuity, leaving rapid ratification to Faure and Pineau. The Assembly had in any case approved an unfinished version of the Treaty with even fewer concessions to France just six months previously; the final vote in July 1957 was neither close nor accompanied by heated debate. Nor can any partisan shifts be traced to the Action Committee. Among swing constituencies like the Gaullists and Conservatives, Monnet's involvement may have been, on balance, a liability, as suggested by the French refusal to renominate Monnet as president of the High Authority, involve him in subsequent negotiations, or consider seriously those supranationalist schemes that French business opposed.[184]

Institutionalizing the Common Market

The Treaty set forth a precise and nearly automatic schedule for the reduction of internal tariffs. In all other respects, however, it was a "framework" document, describing institutional procedures through which rules would be elaborated rather than specific rules themselves. Some of these procedures involved the pooling of sovereignty—decision-making by weighted supermajority vote among the member governments—and the delegation of sovereignty to supranational authorities. The member governments agreed upon a list of situations

---

[184] Noël Interview, 28; Willis, *France*, 224–226; Mayne, "Role," 48–49. Cf. Yondorf (*Europe*, 179), who invokes confidential interviews to support the conclusion that "ordinarily a government crisis would have delayed the ratification procedure. But thanks to the pressure exerted by French members of the Action Committee, foremost among them Maurice Faure, the French parliamentary commissions took the unprecedented step of continuing their examination of the Rome treaties during the crisis." Noël hints that Mollet was swayed in 1954–56 away from a pro-British stance toward acceptance of Euratom by discussions with Monnet. Yet Mollet's decisive move appears to have taken place much later; at least as important were economic arguments advanced by Marjolin and others. Noël interview, 5–8. Recall that by this time Monnet opposed the customs union; it was only by moving away from his original support for Monnet's position on Euratom that Mollet found the path to a successful *relance*.

under which QMV, with the Commission enjoying a unique power of proposal, was to be employed after a period from two to fifteen years, depending on the issue. Commission proposals could be amended only by unanimous vote, thereby assuring it agenda-setting power. These issues included authorizing and concluding trade negotiations, small changes in the external tariff, agricultural price setting, and transport policy.[185] In addition, in a number of areas—the daily setting of agricultural prices, competition policy, trade negotiations—where the Commission was granted a measure of autonomy. What combination of European ideology, technocratic management, and enhanced credibility of commitments best explains these decisions?

Analysts have treated sparingly the question why governments decided to pool and delegate sovereignty to European institutions in the Treaty. Most speculate that either the technocratic imperative of regulation by well-informed "experts" or the role of federalist ideology best explains the decision to pool and delegate. Yet the preponderance of evidence suggests instead that governments promoted carefully circumscribed centralization of authority—in particular QMV and delegation to the Commission—when they sought to "lock in" efficient decisions on which governments might later be tempted to cheat, as on questions of implementation and enforcement. While this suggestion explains the major grants of power, federalist ideology is still required to account for the general institutional structure of the EC: its quasi-constitutional form and the modest tendency of more ideologically inclined countries to favor greater transfers of sovereignty.

Preferences concerning QMV varied both across issues and across nations in a way consistent with either ideology or credible commitments, but not with technocratic management. On balance, the evidence strongly disconfirms the technocratic view, both found in neofunctional theory and suggested by regime theory, that economies of scale in production of information make centralized implementation and enforcement more efficient. Economies of scale in information or expertise seem hardly to have existed at all. Governments did not doubt their ability to generate information; technically or politically complex issues—atomic energy and transport as well as agriculture—were not singled out for delegation.

Instead governments pooled or delegated sovereignty where they sought to lock in compliance by other governments at acceptable cost. The two largest countries, France and Germany, rejected simple majority voting with one vote per country (recommended by Italy and the Benelux) in favor of weighted voting, though the smaller countries did gain a provision that support from at least four countries was required for passage. Governments, as predicted by the credible commitments view, did not take unified stands but based policy on an instrumental calculation of substantive costs and benefits in particular issues. Pooling and delegation were both seen as forces for liberalization: lower tariffs, lower agricultural prices, more forthcoming positions in GATT negotiations, lower subsidies, and more competition. The French government carefully calculated

[185] Harryvan, "Netherlands," 246; Küsters, *Gründung*, 346–347.

the risks of each act of delegation or pooling. Mollet, von der Groeben, Beyen, and many others argued that without QMV, the EC would be blocked; an effective organization required it. Marjolin subsequently testified that QMV was required to convince other governments that France was serious about economic integration. He and Pineau argued subsequently, however, that the creators of the Treaty did not believe that, under the rules in place, many policies would be established over the truly determined opposition of one member state—a veto something like what later emerged as the Luxembourg Compromise may have been implicit.[186]

The instrumental purpose of QMV was most clearly evident in the pattern of national positions. Germany and the Netherlands, the two largest beneficiaries from industrial liberalization and the strongest supporters in principle of majority voting as well as the Commission's right of proposal, were as opportunistic as any countries. The primary purpose of these institutions for Germany, according to Hans von der Groeben, who co-drafted the Spaak Committee institutional provisions, was to assure efficient decision-making. Smaller countries were also concerned to protect their rights—a finding consistent across all three explanations. Yet the Dutch also singled out three additional areas where they supported economic liberalism—agricultural policy, competition policy, and the common external tariff—and proposed autonomous Commission decision-making. In general, the Dutch viewed delegation and pooling as substitutes for more legally binding commitments. Despite its federalist principles, Germany opposed QMV on agriculture, atomic energy, and transport; in all three areas it watered down commitments to vague symbolic promises. By contrast, it sought firm commitments or QMV on internal trade liberalization, the common external tariff, and the common competition policy—the last to be managed semi-autonomously by the Commission.[187] This pattern of national demands is consistent only with the desire for credible commitments in areas of support for common policies. Similarly, France sought firm central financing and control in atomic energy, the only way to assure French control of the European nuclear market, and demanded strong commitments on agriculture, yet stopped short of the Dutch proposal for an autonomous Commission role in agriculture and remained cautious about any institutional commitments in tariff, competition, and external trade policies.

---

[186] Noël Interview, 21; Harryvan "Netherlands," 246. Dutch and Italian proposals for equally weighted (simple majority) voting in the Council were rejected. Simple majority was employed only on certain procedural issues—though this was to become important at the Milan summit of 1985. On the institutional history, Uri in Serra, *Il Rilancio*, 310–311; Camps, *British*, 40–45, 61–62; Küsters, *Gründung*, 244, 249–250, 374–375, 394, 401n, 409–410, 437, 513; Serra, *Il Rilancio*, 303–304.

[187] Interview with von der Groeben 26/15, 9–11; Küsters, *Gründung*, 393ff. When Dutch proposals for a binding *traité contrat* were rejected in favor of the French demand for *traité statut*, the Dutch threw their support to the view that supranationality was necessary to make Messina work. Already in 1956 Mansholt was observing that the CAP would become protectionist if the Commission was weak. Harryvan, "Netherlands," 242ff. An intergovernmental agency would be unable to triumph over national interests—especially on agricultural policy.

The credible commitments view explains fine-grained variation in national positions across issues, but we do observe some national variation as well—a finding perhaps more consistent with the ideological view though not entirely inconsistent with commercial interests. The Faure and Mollet governments, concerned that supranational institutions might jeopardize ratification by the Assembly, announced early in the process that they "intended never to accept anything remotely resembling the ECSC."[188] The British government, during its participation, rejected any majority voting—though this stand soon changed in response to French threats to block the FTA. The governments rejected an independent Council bureaucracy, instead formalizing cooperation among national officials, later the COREPER system. Although the British government did not negotiate details of the EC, it voiced opposition to QMV in the customs union but entertained the possibility within the proposed FTA.

The expressed views of participants are also most consistent with the desire for more credible commitments. The German chief negotiator Ophüls asserted at the time that the need for institutions lay most fundamentally in the desire to lock governments into common policies, even more than under the OEEC or the GATT, in light of the inability of governments to foresee all eventualities.[189] The French negotiators, we have seen, argued that QMV and Commission proposal was a means to avoid inefficient international log-rolling. Robert Marjolin admitted, however, that the French would accept QMV only where it was in their interest. The Benelux governments and sometimes Italy, we have seen, defended QMV and Commission autonomy as means to limit collusion among the large governments, which might threaten the integrity of the Treaty and undermine liberalization. In both France and Germany, the OEEC and EPU experience convinced government officials that unanimity voting was disfunctional. At the same time, they recognized that the scope of the EC, greater than that of the ECSC, made a reduction in supranational power desirable. Little attention appears to have been paid to other institutional provisions.[190]

Beyond French Gaullists such as Debré, there was little principled objection to the quasi-constitutional form of the EC. The Court, following previous ECSC and EPC models, was expected to play a marginal role. A strong Court was most strongly promoted by the Germans and the Italians. No country appears to have opposed the basic idea, in part because it was expected to resolve only minor, intra-organizational disputes, as it had in the ECSC. Precise wording was left to a separate group of national judicial experts, which redrafted texts of the Euratom and Common Market groups for legal consistency; all texts were subsequently reviewed and ratified by the political authorities. Even members of the judicial group, though sympathetic to strong European institutions, apparently did not see the Treaty as a constitution, as the ECJ was later to claim, nor do they appear to have comprehended the potential significance that Article 177, which

[188] Mahant, *French*, 75–76; Harryvan, "Netherlands," 242ff.
[189] Ophüls, "Relance," 8–9.
[190] Marjolin, *Architect*, 304.

permitted national courts to submit cases directly to the EC, was later to attain. Of the three versions of Article 177 considered, the weakest was chosen, a version stripped of any explicit reference to the ECJ's sole competence to interpret the Treaty.[191]

Finally, only the credible commitments view accounts for two striking characteristics of EC institutions: the inverse correlation between supranational autonomy and substantive scope of delegation, and the absence of democratic oversight. France and Germany agreed, we have seen, that the Commission should be weaker than the ECSC High Authority—in part because of dissatisfaction with the ECSC but also because the scope of the EC was more open-ended and therefore required greater oversight.[192] Accordingly, QMV and grants of authority to supranational bodies tended to be employed in limited domains, such as implementation, enforcement, and secondary legislation. There was general agreement that unanimity would be required to establish new policies as well as fundamental changes, such as association with foreign countries, accession of new members, the creation of policies not mentioned in the Treaty, and Treaty amendments. At German insistence, the most sensitive areas, such as CAP prices during the transition, were to be negotiated intergovernmentally, without either QMV or Commission participation. QMV was most likely to be employed for measures that implemented specific policies previously approved by unanimity or essential to the industrial common market—and even so, a transition period of between two and fifteen years was envisaged.[193]

The credibility of commitments also required a measure of insulation from domestic pressures. Governments deliberately restricted control over EC policies to national executives, which they saw as consistent with the liberalizing mission of the institution: Robert Marjolin and Pierre Uri, for example, appear to have hoped that the international agreement would permit finance ministries to regain control over agricultural prices. To be sure, some federalists, consistently backed by the Italians and the Dutch, supported more democratic institutions. But even these efforts, for example the Italian proposal for single general European elections, were symbolic. In any case, it was believed that some national parliaments—certainly that of France—would not ratify such an arrangement.[194]

In sum, governments employed international institutions to lock in reciprocal commitments. The slightly greater willingness of Benelux, German, and Italian governments than the French or British governments to consider delegation and pooling—results consistent with both the ideological views—was

---

[191] Pierre Pescatore, "Les travaus du 'Groupe juridique' dans la négociation des Traités de Rome," *Studia Diplomatica* 34, 1–4 (1981), 154ff, 161–177; H. Sperl, *Traité instituant la Communauté Economique Européenne: Travaux préparatoires, Déclarations interprétatives des six Gouvernements, Documents parlementaires* (Luxembourg, 1960), 376–378; Hans von der Groeben, *The European Community: The Formative Years* (Luxembourg, 1987), 176.

[192] This reverses the neofunctionalist assertion that previous experience tends to make governments more willing to accept strong international institutions.

[193] Küsters, *Gründung*, 400–403.

[194] Küsters, *Gründung*, 406, Serra, *Il Rilancio*, 310.

restricted to areas where the substantive consequences of delegation remained unclear.

This account strongly supports the predominant importance of economic interest, relative power, and credible commitments during this period. Commercial opportunities were the basic source of national preferences concerning the nature and speed of integration. In industrial trade, agriculture, transport, and atomic energy, preferences followed commercial export opportunities. Industrial trade liberalization was widely viewed as inevitable; interstate conflict arose over its form and scope. Geopolitical ideology and security externalities played a secondary but significant role where economic interests were weak, divided, or indeterminate. In particular, Adenauer exploited the preference of German business for either an FTA or a "small Europe" customs union to the status quo, to promote closer relations with France. Yet where commercial interests were entirely unsupportive, as in German policy on transport or atomic energy, no national leader could prevail. Agreement on agriculture was possible only by postponing any potentially costly decisions, to be made under unanimity.

Interstate bargaining was dominated by governments, which were quite capable of bargaining efficiently without the assistance of supranational entrepreneurs like Monnet, whose actions were at best redundant and futile. Outcomes reflected the relative ability of governments to make credible threats and promises to veto proposals, exclude other governments, or link issues. The weakness of French support for trade liberalization and the strength of German support led to major concessions to France in other areas.

This arrangement was then embedded in institutions mainly to enhance the credibility of commitments, that is, to "lock in" implementation and enforcement decisions on which governments might later be tempted to cheat. Federalist ideology is still required to account for the general institutional structure of the EC: its quasi-constitutional form, and the modest tendency of more "federalist" countries to favor greater transfers of sovereignty.

The Treaty of Rome was a framework document. It launched a process rather than completed it. From the perspective of economic interests, the Treaty contained "disequilibria"—commitments that could not realistically be implemented by one or more countries without fundamental shifts in market position. These were known to the participants. The French government had overcome substantial industrial opposition in part by employing linkages: support from farmers, overseas producers, and some ideological supporters of Europe as well as safeguards and delays. These linkages did not a provide a stable basis on which to implement the customs union. Even Maurice Faure, France's chief negotiator, did not expect the internal or external tariff provisions to be implemented; with a year the French government had announced it would not reduce tariffs as planned. Similarly, France blocked all efforts to negotiate an FTA.[195] Germany, for its part, had committed itself to an incomplete CAP that, depend-

---

[195] Michel Debré, *Trois républiques pour une France: Agir* (Paris, 1988), 2:248; Bossuat, *L'Europe*, 317.

ing on the price policies chosen, could impose price decreases on its farmers in order to achieve geopolitical and industrial aims. Britain had been excluded, yet since 1955 successive Whitehall assessments of British interests had conceded that if the EC succeeded, Britain would be forced to seek either an FTA or membership. Moreover, governments had accepted an eventual transition to QMV in areas, including agriculture and foreign trade policy, where the prevailing constellation of interests would not sustain it. Finally, to realize the transport policy the Netherlands would have to overcome Franco-German opposition. No matter which new governments assumed power in France, Germany, or Britain, such obstacles would have to be overcome for the EC to function as optimists initially intended. Inevitably it was these areas of compromise and ambiguity in the initial Treaty that would emerge as central points of conflict over the next decade.

CHAPTER THREE

Grain and Grandeur:
Consolidating the Common Market, 1958–1969

> It is clear that nothing gets accomplished without the agreement of all partici-
> pating nations. The success of the Common Market is a daily illustration; the
> failure up to now of political integration is the exception that proves the rule.
>
> —Maurice Couve de Murville, former French foreign minister (1971)

During the 1960s the six member governments of the EC transformed a framework treaty into a fully elaborated system coordinating their trade policies.
Nearly continuous negotiations were punctuated by four overlapping "package
deals." Between 1958 and 1962 agreement was reached on an accelerated removal of internal tariffs and harmonization of external tariff policy. As we have
seen, many negotiators of the Treaty in France had doubted that agreement
could be attained. Between 1960 and 1969 came agreement on the most important deal, namely the creation of the Common Agricultural Policy (CAP)—
a policy only vaguely sketched in the Treaty and left to implementation by unanimity vote. With the partial exception of competition (antitrust) policy, there
was little movement in other economic policies mentioned in the Treaty, notably
transport, social policy, industrial policy, regional policy, and macroeconomic
coordination. Between 1961 and 1971 followed a number of successive discussions and negotiations concerning British membership, the first three fruitless
and the final one successful. Finally, between 1960 and 1966 came discussion of
institutional reform, in part to coordinate foreign policy but mostly to limit the
scope of qualified majority voting (QMV). Such discussions began with the Fouchet Plan and culminated, after French threats to withdraw from the EC (the
"empty chair" crisis of 1965–66), in the Luxembourg Compromise, which informally recognized France's assertion of a unilateral right to veto EC decisions
where "vital interests" were engaged. Taken together, these decisions reshaped
the EC so profoundly that some speak of "a second European constitution."[1]

---

[1] Sabino Cassese and Giacinto della Cananea, "The Commission of the European Economic
Community: The Administrative Ramifications of Its Political Development (1957–1967)," in Erk
Volkmar Heyen, ed., *Die Anfänge der Verwaltung der Europäischen Gemeinschaft* (Baden-Baden, 1992),
86. Also John Lambert, "The Constitutional Crisis, 1965–1966," *Journal of Common Market Studies* 7:3
(May 1966), 195–228.

Most accounts of the EC in the 1960s, whether by contemporary commentators or by recent analysts, are dominated by three claims. First, "high" politics is said to trump "low" politics, at least in the short term. That is, geopolitical interests and ideologies were primary and economic motivations, while perhaps significant, were decidedly secondary. In this view , advanced by Stanley Hoffmann, Miriam Camps, and Ernst Haas, nearly all subsequent historians of the period, statesmen such as Charles de Gaulle, Harold Macmillan, and Konrad Adenauer were old-fashioned thinkers whose major decisions were motivated primarily by distinctive geopolitical ideologies. Even Haas, committed to the technocratic triumph of low politics in the long run, conceded the disruptive effects of "dramatic political" actors, though other neofunctionalists challenged him. Second, EC bargaining was fundamentally influenced by the political entrepreneurship of supranational actors, notably the Commission, which intervened decisively to "upgrade the common interest." Without supranational participation, argue the neofunctionalists, integration would not have been possible. Governments themselves, by contrast, made many tactical errors—a criticism in particular by Robert Lieber and many others since British conduct of the accession negotiations in 1961–63. Third, sovereignty was pooled in qualified majority voting arrangements and delegated to supranational bodies, most notably the Commission, for technocratic reasons. Delegation and pooling provided a technocratically competent means of decision-making on issues on which there was little fundamental conflict; the Commission, many argued, was particular adept at assembling the technical and political information necessary for modern economic planning. In sum, there is a consensus on the importance of geopolitical motivations, supranational entrepreneurship, and technocratic imperatives.

In this chapter I challenge each of these claims. The primary motivations of France, Britain, and Germany, I maintain, were economic; each government sought above all to realize commercial advantages for agriculture and industry. Pressures from producer groups were particularly powerful in agriculture, somewhat less so in industrial tariff policy, and least in other areas. Geopolitical motivations such as de Gaulle's suspicion of supranationalism and the German government's interest in Franco-German relations did matter on the margin, influencing, for example, the willingness of Germany to compromise its free-trade policies, but only after core economic interests were satisfied.

Governments, moreover, were capable of acting as their own policy entrepreneurs, providing policy initiatives, mediating among governments, and mobilizing social groups as needed. Negotiations managed by governments were efficient, whereas interventions by the Commission and other supranational actors were at best redundant and futile; at worst, they were counterproductive, in large part due to the Commission's striking lack of appreciation for fundamental societal and political pressures. This was so although the Commission—unlike in the other four sets of decisions considered in this book—enjoyed some formal powers of agenda-setting and amendment. The distributive outcomes of interstate bargaining reflected asymmetrical interdependence: the greater the gains for each party on core issues, the more the party compromised or conceded to achieve it. Such outcomes continually disappointed the Commission: in particular the high-price, protectionist, and administratively decentralized CAP, often hailed as a triumph of Commission entrepreneurship, was in fact the converse of its initial proposals.

Finally, choices to delegate or pool sovereignty reflected neither technocratic imperatives nor ideological support for European federalism but the need for credible commitments under conditions of uncertainty. Regardless of their ideology or the technical complexity of issues, governments delegated when doing so helped them lock in agreements against defection by foreign governments. Where a government was domestically unable to commit credibly to implement agreed rules—as was the case with Germany in agriculture—its neighbors imposed international commitments upon it.

In sum, commercial interest, relative power, and the desire for more credible commitments explain the main lines of European integration in the 1960s.

NATIONAL PREFERENCE FORMATION

During the 1960s Britain, France, Germany, and the Commission held widely disparate preferences on major matters before the EC. The one area of clear convergence of interest, at least after the French devaluation of 1958, was industrial tariff liberalization within Europe, which was favored by all. Each of the three governments, as well as the Commission, sought more liberal policies, and all sought to avoid exclusion from preferential trading arrangements. German preferences for liberalization, however, were more intense than those of Britain or France. By 1960 Britain strongly favored membership, a position backed by Germany to the extent it did not threaten current EC arrangements. France vetoed proposals for British membership through 1969, when it reversed course, proposing to forsake the veto in exchange for a permanent agricultural financing arrangement. All three also favored global tariff liberalization, though here the differences in intensity were larger between Germany, Britain, and the Commission, on the one hand, and France, on the other.

On agricultural trade the roles were reversed: France most intensely favored liberalization of commodities trade within a preferential European zone with moderate support prices; Germany opposed such liberalization and was unwilling to seriously consider any agreement unless very high common support prices were paid. Britain also remained skeptical of any agricultural policy. The Commission favored a minimal, liberal, but centralized policy that would impose structural adjustment on inefficient farms. France strongly opposed agricultural trade liberalization in the GATT; Germany sought to retain bilateral arrangements and was prepared to make GATT concessions in agriculture that preserved domestic arrangements; Britain favored freer global trade in agricultural commodities to support its traditional policy.

In other areas there was little consensus. Germany and France were skeptical of transport liberalization; there was little support for any other type of economic cooperation, notably in the monetary area. On foreign policy matters

Table 3.1. Consolidation of the Common Market, 1958–1970: Preferences and outcomes

Issues	Germany	France	Britain	Commission	Outcomes
Industrial tariff removal	Strongly prefers accelerated tariff removal.	Prefers accelerated tariff removal.	Strongly prefers to avoid exclusion, accepts tariff removal.	Strongly prefers accelerated tariff removal.	*Slightly accelerated tariff removal: Common Market is completed in 1968 rather than 1970.*
CAP	Strongly prefers delay and status quo of bilateral arrangements, uneven external protection, and national subsidies, unless CAP maintains high German prices.	Intensely prefers rapid creation of CAP with moderate prices, external closure, but mix of centralized and national administration and subsidies.	Opposes CAP in favor of status quo of bilateral arrangements and national policies.	Prefers much more rapid transition to CAP than foreseen in Treaty. Prefers CAP with low prices, modest scope, external openness, no national subsidies, and centralized structural adjustment programs.	*CAP is completed at last possible date in 1970, with very high prices, broad scope, external closure, decentralized administration, and extensive national subsidies.*
External tariff policy	Strongly prefers low industrial and high agricultural protection; favors rapid opening of GATT Kennedy Round.	Increasingly prefers reciprocally lower external industrial tariffs, but strong support for high agricultural protection.	Prefers moderate to low industrial tariffs, low agricultural tariffs, and a cautiously forthcoming position in Kennedy Round. Weakening interest in Commonwealth preferences.	Prefers low external tariffs, accommodation of United States on GATT industrial trade.	*GATT Kennedy Round is delayed but EC is ultimately willing to reduce industrial protection but not agricultural protection.*

British membership	Prefers British entry but will not overrule France nor threaten to leave the EC.	Opposes British entry until 1969, then proposes closer relationship, and membership, in exchange for permanent CAP financing.	Clearly prefers membership to exclusion by 1960 and pursues it aggressively in 1961, 1967, and 1969.	Ambivalent.	*In 1963 and 1967 France, backed by Germany, vetoes British membership. Successful membership negotiations begin in 1969. French support is linked to CAP financing.*
Transport	Strongly opposes liberalization, except minimal non-discrimination rules.	Opposes liberalization, except minimal non-discrimination rules.	No public position.	Strongly prefers any form of centralized liberalization and harmonization.	*Minimal nondiscrimination rules; no liberalization.*
Foreign policy cooperation	Prefers cooperation if NATO obligations not compromised.	Strongly prefers cooperation as an alternative forum to NATO.	Weak preference for cooperation if NATO obligations not compromised.	Weakly prefers cooperation.	*No policy.*
Institutions	Prefers more inter-governmental institutions for creating, running, and implementing CAP, as well as transport policy. Prefers more supranational institutions for foreign trade and competition policy. Appears to tacitly favor Luxembourg Compromise.	Prefers going well beyond the Luxembourg Compromise to limit delegation and pooling. Prefers more intergovernmental cooperation, in particular in external trade policy. Prefers centralized financing and Commission role only in CAP, and weak centralization of trade policy.	Opposes delegation and pooling, though proposes QMV and autonomous oversight in FTA proposals, but eventually accepts *acquis communautaire*.	Prefers centralized delegation and pooling in all areas.	*Outside of CAP financing provisions, institutions become more inter-governmental than the Treaty foresees: COREPER, Special Committee on Agriculture, and 113 Committee are formed. Extreme steps to weaken Commission are blocked.*

Britain and Germany favored a close connection with NATO; Gaullist France was more independent. On institutional matters, lastly, each government tended to favor centralization of authority in Brussels (a practice of course favored by the Commission) in certain areas: France in CAP financing but not price setting; Germany in trade but not agriculture; Britain was skeptical across the board but proposed majority voting for industrial trade within the FTA. To understand the roots of this disparate range of preferences, we must investigate preference formation in Britain, France and Germany in more detail.

Britain: The Experience of Exclusion

The British government, as we saw in chapter 2, had initially assumed the Messina discussions would fail and so adopted an attitude of unconcerned detachment. When the negotiations appeared to be succeeding, it sought to undermine the initiative through Plan G—a proposal for a pan-European industrial free trade area (FTA), which it hoped might supplant or dilute the customs union. With the signing of the Treaty of Rome and de Gaulle's veto of FTA negotiations in December 1958, this effort collapsed. This chapter traces the next two steps. In 1959 the British government sought to bolster support for a free trade area by forming the European Free Trade Association (EFTA) with six other outsider countries, hoping thereby to press the Six to negotiate a bilateral arrangement.[2] Within a year after de Gaulle and Adenauer rejected overtures from EFTA, the British government opened informal discussions with the Six concerning membership. The bid for membership was publicly announced in July 1961. Its failure was followed by a less formal effort in 1967, brief discussions in 1969, and successful negotiations beginning in 1970.

Most analysts see in Macmillan's bid for membership an unexpected and surprising break with well-established British postwar policy motivated by a belated realization of the need to defend Britain's prestige as a great power. With the decline of the Commonwealth, the failure of British efforts to mediate between the superpowers, and the rise of the EC, Britain needed EC membership to maintain its role as interlocutor to the superpowers. Macmillan's hesitance, inspired by his overestimation and old-fashioned vision of world politics and British power, facilitated de Gaulle's extreme opposition.

The preponderance of primary evidence suggests a contrary view. British policy was neither primarily inspired by geopolitical ideas nor myopically conducted. The British membership bid was instead aimed primarily at the advancement of enduring British commercial interests. Business interests consistently supported the effort, despite various political and economic objections. Britain continued to favor an FTA to a customs union, yet the threat of exclusion from a Continental trade bloc, the worst conceivable option from Britain's perspective, and the long foreseen and inexorable shift of British exports away from the Commonwealth

[2] The OEEC disappeared, recast in January 1960 as the OECD, with the United States and Canada as members.

toward Europe, combined to encourage ever greater British concessions. British policy was hardly myopic. A British bid for membership may have been inevitable in the longer run, but British trade with the Commonwealth was not to fall below its trade with Europe until the mid-1960s. Macmillan's move in 1961 was thus well ahead of domestic political economic necessity, which helps explain some of the geopolitical arguments that still needed to be made within British officialdom. He was reticent to compromise too quickly and took care to construct a domestic consensus. In short, Macmillan's membership bid was not a belated geopolitical accommodation to the decline of global prestige but a farsighted effort to maintain British commercial prosperity.

Geopolitical Interest and Ideology: "Britain's position will decline"

As in the period from 1955 to 1957, the British government voiced four geopolitical interests which, on balance, supported membership.

First was *antifederalism*. The prejudices and fears of even pro-European British elites remained unchanged. Prejudice against Europe could reach the level of absurdity, as illustrated by Macmillan's extraordinary remark at a private strategy session in 1959. "There are three elements who want supranationalism and who are playing no small part on the Commission . . . the Jews, the Planners and the old cosmopolitan element" (i.e., Socialists).[3] This was largely an elite concern; public opinion did not oppose integration but instead remained passively favorable.

Second was the *unity of the Western alliance*. To Adenauer, as to de Gaulle and Kennedy, we saw in chapter 2, Macmillan wrote that failure to arrange a free trade area "must lead to . . . the collapse of NATO and the existing system of defense."[4] In Macmillan's personal memo, written over Christmas 1960—the socalled Grand Design document—he stated that "political and economic problems . . . are intermingled" and that the consequences of exclusion from Europe would be "dangerous and perhaps fatal" to the British "overriding aim," namely the "joint struggle against Communism . . . because economic exclusion must in the long run force us into military isolationism and political neutralism."[5] In December 1959, when he first learned from Selwyn Lloyd that an EC-EFTA solution was probably impossible, he responded in a confidential memo: "unless some way can be found of avoiding the economic damage . . . [our] political relationship in Europe will have to be revised."[6] This geopolitical argument figured prominently in Macmillan's initial speech to the House of Commons on British membership and, above all, in discussions with foreign leaders.

Third came a *fear of German domination of Europe*. Parliamentary speakers for both government and opposition highlighted, as one analyst summarized the

---

[3] Cited in Alan S. Milward, *The European Rescue of the Nation-State* (London, 1993), 432, tenses changed.

[4] Harold Macmillan, *Riding the Storm* (London, 1991), 435; Richard Lamb, *The Macmillan Years, 1947–1963: The Emerging Truth* (London, 1995), 106. Telegram from Macmillan to Kennedy, 22 April 1961 (PREM 11/3311); Alistair Horne, *Harold Macmillan* (New York, 1988), 2:113, 256

[5] Memorandum by the Prince Minister, 29 December 1960/3 January 1961, PREM 11/3325, 5–9.

[6] Lamb, *Macmillan*, 64–65.

debates, "the dangers of staying out of a European bloc dominated by our principal competitor, Western Germany."[7] Whether the underlying concern was economic or geopolitical remained unclear.

Fourth and most plausible was *concern about Britain's continued great power role* as a leader of the Commonwealth and European interlocutor for the superpowers. Tory backbenchers were also particularly concerned about the maintenance of the Commonwealth. This was one reason for skepticism about EC membership and concern in the negotiations about access for Commonwealth imports. Macmillan, we have seen, had maintained that "for the first time since the Napoleonic era the continental powers are united in a positive economic grouping, with considerable political aspects, which [may exclude us from] European policy."[8] If Britain did not join and the EC succeeded, one Whitehall committee concluded in 1960, "a new world power will have come on the scene" and Britain's "position vis-à-vis both the United States and Western Europe will . . . decline."[9] After Suez, conflict with the United States over joint nuclear cooperation, the cancellation of Blue Streak in April 1960, South Africa's departure from the Commonwealth, and finally the U-2 crisis, which shattered Macmillan's ambition to establish himself as a privileged mediator between the superpowers at the Paris summit of 1960, EC membership promised to reestablish Britain's global position. The country would emerge, some argued, as spokesman for the European bloc, thereby rejuvenating the special relationship and enhancing Britain's global prestige. Philip de Zulueta, Macmillan's private secretary, points out that Macmillan's final announcement took place fully a year after the EC had rejected negotiations with EFTA, but only a few months after the U-2 crisis— suggesting a link with geopolitical developments.[10]

Macmillan may also have seen domestic political advantages in membership. In addition to strengthening business support, he was aware that Europe split the Labour party more than it did the Conservatives. The Labour left resisted membership, and a strong centrist group, backed by the unions, was favorable. Cleavages within the Labour party and between Labour and the Tories were driven as much by economic as by geopolitical concerns; four of Labour leader Hugh Gaitskell's five conditions for entry were economic. Yet partisan concerns were secondary; entry was not an issue on which either party—or the public— had a strong position. Only in 1962, with negotiations deadlocked, the Conservative party weakening in the polls, and Macmillan exploiting Gaitskell's indecision, did Labour publicly oppose entry—a move subsequently interpreted both

---

[7] Miriam Camps, *Britain and the European Community, 1955–1963* (Princeton, 1964), 110, also 124–125.

[8] Harold Macmillan, *Pointing the Way, 1959–1961* (New York, 1971), 54–55.

[9] John W. Young, "British Officials and European Integration, 1944–60," in Anne Deighton, ed., *Building Postwar Europe: National Decision-Makers and European Institutions, 1948–63,* (London, 1995), 98–99.

[10] Wolfram Kaiser, "To Join or Not to Join? The 'Appeasement' Policy of Britain's First EEC Application," in Brian Brivati and Harriet Jones, eds., *From Reconstruction to Integration: Britain and Europe since 1945* (Leicester, 1993), 152; Robert Pfaltzgraff, *Britain Faces Europe* (Philadelphia, 1969), 76; Jeremy Moon, *European Integration in British Politics, 1950–1963: A Study in Issue Change* (Aldershot, 1985), 36; Lamb, *Macmillan,* 131.

as an opportunistic bid for electoral advantage and as capitulation to rank-and-file pressure. Yet Labour opposition was not consistent enough to force an election, influence by-elections, or pressure Macmillan's negotiating position in any fundamental way; at most it slowed British concessions. The public remained passive.[11]

Economic Interest: Business Is "dangerously in the lead"

The prospect of exclusion from the EC sparked strong pressures for membership. The Federation of British Industry (FBI) and other business groups, we saw in chapter 2, had no difficulty supporting an FTA, which would satisfy both Continental and Commonwealth export constituencies and avoid the construction of invasive supranational institutions. By 1958, however, it became clear that FTA negotiations had failed. As the threat of exclusion and trade diversion loomed, urgency was felt for the first time in British business circles.[12] In February 1959 the FBI launched discussions with their counterparts in six non-EC countries: Austria, Switzerland, Portugal, Sweden, Norway, and Denmark. Though the government approved, one analyst noted that FBI head "Norman Kipping was sometimes dangerously in the lead." Business and government viewed EFTA as a tool to pressure the EC to negotiate a free trade deal, not as an end in itself: U.K. exports to the Six would increase by 55 percent between 1960 and 1962, exports to EFTA by only 32 percent. In May the FBI proved unable to overcome internal distributional disputes, particularly concerning agriculture, and the negotiations were turned over to the government.[13] There was, however, unquestioned support for EFTA-EC negotiation.

EC membership proved far more controversial within the FBI than an FTA, because the promotion of European exports now came at the direct expense of Commonwealth interests. Yet the balance was shifting. Between 1955 and 1965, despite British exclusion, exports to the Commonwealth fell from 50 percent to 25 percent of the British total, while exports to the Six rose from 12 percent to 25 percent—a reflection both of technological developments and, if secondarily, Commonwealth import substitution policies. In Britain sectoral support was, as in the Treaty of Rome discussions, correlated with competitiveness. Support

[11] Michael Newman, "The British Labour Party," in Griffiths, ed., *Socialist Parties,* 168–69; David Butler and Uwe Kitzinger, *The 1975 Referendum* (London, 1976), 10ff. Labour's National Executive Committee document of 29 September 1962 demanded safeguards for Commonwealth and EFTA trade, agriculture and domestic economic planning, while only "freedom to pursue our own foreign policy" referred to geopolitics.

[12] Stephen Blank, *Industry and Government in Britain: The Federation of British Industries in British Politics, 1945–65* (Lexington, Mass., 1973), 145; Robert J. Lieber, *British Politics and European Unity: Parties, Elites and Pressure Groups* (Berkeley, 1970), 67, 158–166; also Douglas Jay, "The Free Trade Alternative to the EC: A Witness Account," in Brivati and Jones, *Reconstruction,* 123–141; Miriam Camps, "Missing the Boat at Messina and Other Times?" in Brivati and Jones, *Reconstruction,* 142; Lamb, *Macmillan,* 109; Michael Charlton, *The Price of Victory* (London, 1983), 235–238; Pfaltzgraff, *Britain.*

[13] Lieber, *British,* 82, also 76–90; P. Gore-Booth, *With Great Truth and Respect* (London, 1974), 254–255; Pfaltzgraff, *Britain,* 36ff, 53, 76; Richard T. Griffiths, "The Importance of Fish in the Creation of EFTA," *EFTA Bulletin* (January 1992), 37–39; Lamb, *Macmillan,* 131. For a chapter-length treatment of the business view, Norman Kipping, *Summing Up* (London: Hutchinson, 1972).

De Gaulle rejects Macmillan yet again.
Cartoon by Michael Cummings. *Daily Express,* 10 August 1962.

for EC membership was concentrated among capital-intensive exporters and foreign investors, with "increasingly outstanding advocates" among Britain's 200 largest firms. Most feared tariff discrimination; others, particularly among financial services and high-economies-of-scale sectors such as petrochemicals, the impact of continued uncertainty on investment plans. The most common justification was exclusion: "We cannot afford to stay out." Smaller firms remained skeptical. The Institute of Directors, which represented major banks and the service sector, justified its support for an accommodation with the Six as a way of defending the preeminent position of the City among European financial centers.[14]

Initially the FBI General Council, a body that overrepresented smaller firms, remained neutral, though top FBI officials lobbied government officials privately in favor of membership. Once the government announced its support for membership, however, large firms and banks favoring entry swiftly assumed control. Combining the FBI's publicity apparatus and their own organizational resources, large firms and banks dominated public debate during the 1961 negotiations—a domination that lasted through the 1975 referendum. The only prominent business criticism came from the Commonwealth Industries Association. This dominance occurred even though the net economic benefits of

[14] Young, "Britain and the EEC, 1956–73: An Overview," in Brivati and Jones, eds., *Reconstruction,* 104; Lamb, *Macmillan,* 137n.; Lieber, *British,* 61–68; Pfalzgraff, *Britain,* 33–34.

membership to consumers (who would face higher food costs) and taxpayers (who would fund net transfers to the EC) remained unclear. Potential opposition groups were also hampered by uncertainty. In a Sunday *Times* poll 25 percent of firms supported entry and 3 percent opposed it; the great majority said their position depended on the negotiated conditions, in particular arrangements for the Commonwealth. Membership was backed also by the Trades Union Conference (TUC), within which export-dependent sectors overcame left-wing opposition.[15]

Over the next decade and a half, big business remained the most prominent backer of membership. By 1964 exports to the Six began to stagnate, a trend attributed to EC discrimination, and reports from the CBI (the FBI's new name) revealed increasing support for membership. Even firms fearing considerable short-term losses, such as many auto makers, recognized the longer-term need to overcome exclusion in order to achieve economies of scale. Higher agricultural prices and the diversion of Commonwealth trade, the CBI argued, would be more than balanced by an end to European tariff discrimination, greater economies of scale, and a rescue from the danger of isolation from the Community. These economic calculations were to remain stable through the 1970s. Big business also continued to dominate domestic debates; in the 1975 referendum, proponents outspent opponents by a factor of ten.[16]

Farmers remained divided. Despite the small size of the farming sector, farmers were viewed as an electoral swing constituency, a position strengthened by a 1959 Tory election pledge not to dilute Britain's distinctive and extremely generous program of direct "deficiency" payments. Uncertainty about EC plans and the negotiated terms of entry, as well as splits among farmers (42 percent, disproportionately the larger and more efficient among them, favored entry, whereas 37 percent, disproportionately smaller and less competitive, opposed it, approximately the same breakdown as among the British public), led the National Farmers' Union (NFU) to remain neutral until 1962, when it came out cautiously in favor of EC membership.[17]

The Domestic Decision:
"Nothing else matters except our export trade"

The process of preference aggregation and strategy formation tells us much about the relative importance of economic interest and geopolitical ideology in

[15] The majority of firms in the iron and steel, automotive parts, machinery, glass, woolen textiles, paper, electronics, rubber, and plastics sectors, as well as many producers of chemicals, drugs, automobiles, and alcoholic beverages, supported membership, while opposition came primarily from less-competitive industries, such as non-woolen textiles, clothing, and shoes. Lieber, *British*, 67-95-134; Pfalzgraff, *Britain*, 33-34, 42ff, 58-59; 80-83; Herbert Schneider, *Großbrittaniens Weg nach Europa* (Freiburg/Breisgau, 1968), 115-116, cf. 112, and passim; Macmillan, *Riding*, 82; Jay, "Free Trade," 125.

[16] Young, "Britain," 107-109; W. G. Jensen, *The Common Market* (London, 1967), 187, 192-202; Butler and Kitzinger, *1975 Referendum*.

[17] The evidence is ambiguous. Christopher Soames, Eric Roll, and R. A. B. Butler in Charlton, *Price*, 242-246, 251-253, Lieber, *British*, 48-54, 116-134, 166-168; Schneider, *Großbrittaniens*, 172.

British policy from 1958 through 1970. Wrongly believing European governments to be motivated primarily by the geopolitical goal of constraining Germany, the British government expected them to embrace Plan G enthusiastically
after the ratification of the Rome Treaty. Despite their antifederalism, British
leaders proposed institutions with supranational elements: automatic tariff reductions, majority voting, an autonomous governing board, limited safeguards,
and the modest inclusion of agriculture. Yet in December 1958 de Gaulle and
Adenauer blocked the FTA negotiations. Efforts to seek foreign allies did not
break the deadlock. In May 1959 the British government assumed control over
negotiations with European countries outside the EC, which had been conducted
by the FBI. By the end of the year an agreement among the EFTA countries had
been forged, including modest side-payments in the form of British concessions
on trade in agricultural commodities, aimed particularly at Denmark. Yet neither business nor leading British decision-makers viewed EFTA as an adequate
substitute for the EC; its "prime purpose," said Edward Heath, was to bring the
EC to negotiation a bilateral agreement.[18]

The sticking point was French opposition. Macmillan's response from the beginning, as we have seen, was to stress geopolitical interests. In particular, he
sought to employ geopolitical threats to wring economic concessions from the
Six. In December 1958 de Zulueta had written to Macmillan: "in the economic
field we do not seem to have any effective cards to play, and the only pressures
we could bring would therefore be political. . . . NATO and our contributions to
the defense of Europe, particularly Germany. . . . Our only course is either to try
and break up the Common Market or watering it down and securing the best
possible terms. . . . Both are disagreeable."[19]

Internal memos termed such tactics "carrots" and "bribes." To Adenauer,
Macmillan threatened to pull troops out of NATO. To de Gaulle he offered to
press the United States for a three-country Western directorate and sharing of
Anglo-American nuclear information, "in return [for which de Gaulle] must give
me the greatest practical accommodation that he can on the economic front."[20]

Aware by late 1959 that prospects for a FTA of any kind were nonetheless
weakening, Macmillan called a meeting with top ministers to reassess British
policy a few months after the Conservative victory in October's general election.
The time had come, he declared, to reappraise British policy toward Europe.
With characteristic deliberation, Macmillan moved to establish a domestic consensus around even closer relations. Two interministerial committees were asked
to assess British interests. The first, based in the Foreign Office, stressed both
geopolitical and economic dangers of exclusion from Europe. The second group,

[18] Reginald Maudling, *Memoirs* (London, 1978), 78.
[19] Lamb, *Macmillan*, 124.
[20] Macmillan, *Pointing the Way*, 112–114; Lamb, *Macmillan*, 151; Kaiser, "To Join or Not to Join."
The threat appears to have been first explicitly made in October 1958. Macmillan sought to reach
a separate accommodation, whereby he would "support de Gaulle on the political front and his
desire to join the ranks of the Great Powers." Memorandum by the Prime Minister, 29 December
1960/3 January 1961, PREM 11/332, 16–26; Memorandum by the Prime Minister, 29 December 1960/3 January 1961, PREM 11/332, 13; Telegram from Macmillan to Adenauer, 5 June 1961
(PREM 11/3775), 2.

widely regarded as more important, was the Economic Steering (Europe) Committee under Sir Frank Lee, known as a long-time supporter of British accession. It embarked on a full-scale review of British policy toward Europe. One analyst has termed the committee's report, issued in April 1960, the "definitive document that was to set Britain on a new course." It concluded that Britain should seek "near identification" with the EC. The commercial effects of exclusion were not yet "disastrous," its report concluded, as only 14 percent of trade went to the Six, but they would become so in the longer term. Membership would be the most advantageous alternative and would become more so over time, despite the weak British bargaining position and the resulting necessity for compromises on agriculture and the Commonwealth. Lee's report is widely credited with transforming Whitehall opinion.[21]

In July 1960, with EFTA-EC negotiations stalled, the Cabinet approved an effort to seek a new relationship with the EC, though a majority remained opposed to an immediate bid for membership. A Cabinet reshuffle a few months later brought pro-European figures to prominent positions: Lord Soames to Agriculture, Edward Heath to the Foreign Office, Duncan Sandys to the Commonwealth Office. "We realized now," Macmillan later wrote, "that it was all-or-nothing, and, if we went ahead, it would be in order to discover what 'all' involved."[22] In November 1960 Britain made unofficial overtures to the Six concerning membership, though Heath, charged with coordinating preparation for membership, warned the Council of Europe that Britain could not join the EC as currently constituted. By July 1961 final efforts to revive EC-EFTA negotiations had collapsed, and Macmillan publicly announced the British intention to seek membership. He secured unanimous support from the Cabinet; only one Conservative MP opposed him in Parliament. Most newspapers were quietly positive; influential pro-Commonwealth spokesmen, such as Lord Beaverbrook, were marginal to the national debate.[23]

Elite and public support for membership was strong and remained so even after de Gaulle's first veto in January 1963. Harold Wilson's move toward membership in 1966 and 1967, blocked by de Gaulle, was supported strongly by the Department of Economic Affairs under George Brown and, after some hesitation, by the Foreign Office, the latter arguing there was now "no alternative" to membership. Business, seeing exports to the Continent stagnant, strongly supported the bid, as did public opinion and the Conservative opposition. When de Gaulle imposed a second veto in 1967, British government officials resolved to wait, exploiting whatever further opportunities arose to enter.[24]

In the first accession attempt under Macmillan, three economic issues—

---

[21] Jacqueline Tratt, *The Macmillan Government and Europe* (New York, 1996), 95, also 85–101; Young, "British Officials," 98–100; Camps, "Missing," 142; Andrew Roth, *Heath and the Heathmen* (London, 1972), 150ff.

[22] Lamb, *Macmillan,* 139–140; Edward Heath, *Travels: People and Places in My Life* (London, 1977), 131–132; Nora Beloff, *The General Says No: Britain's Exclusion from Europe* (Harmondsworth, 1963), 74–75, 114.

[23] Lamb, *Macmillan,* 155–157; A. J. P. Taylor, *Beaverbrook: A Biography* (New York, 1972), 608–609, 614, 647–648.

[24] Young, "Britain," 106–109; Gore-Booth, *Great,* 350–355.

membership for other EFTA countries, satisfactory arrangements for British agriculture, and above all an accommodation for Commonwealth preferences—were the central British demands. Guarantees on EFTA and agriculture soon faded; Commonwealth preferences became the sticking point. Macmillan and the British Cabinet concluded from the start that the key problem was de Gaulle, who might veto any unsatisfactory arrangement. Macmillan dismissed warnings from his ambassadors that de Gaulle would veto regardless.[25]

The consensus view has long been that Macmillan and subsequent prime ministers moved toward membership primarily for geopolitical reasons, with economic interest playing a subsidiary role.[26] Yet the evidence suggests that economic interests were as strong as, if not stronger than, geopolitical ones. Commercial considerations constituted a sufficient long-term reason to seek EC membership.

Among geopolitical concerns, British antifederalism seems to offer the least plausible explanation. It weighed *against* membership and fails to explain Britain's virulent opposition to the EC; if a clash of ideology were all that was at stake, why not simply stay out? Furthermore British negotiating tactics signaled a willingness to compromise antifederalist principle by permitting majority voting and an independent "governing board" in the FTA proposal of 1957. Of this Macmillan wrote to Thorneycroft: "This might well be called a 'supra-national' institution. But does it matter?" One might speculate that British willingness to contemplate membership may reflect the realization that the EC was *not* in fact moving in a federal direction, but this had been known since Bretherton reported back in 1955 and had little effect. Internal discussions reveal little concern about encroaching federalism.

Neither can the desire to balance Germany and Western unity against the Soviet Union, as we saw in chapter 2, make sense of British policy. Concerns about Germany are not prominent in British documents; most refer anyway to economic conflict. Macmillan never explained why Western unity was imperiled, nor why Britain would retreat into isolation if denied membership. Lower British officials, we saw in chapter 2, disbelieved the prime minister. Neither concern explains the major elements of British policy—the fierce attachment to the FTA, the lack of British concern about Euratom, and the long-term desire for the removal of troops from Continental NATO commitments anyway. Most important, an explanation of Macmillan's strategy as an effort to achieve Western unity contains a striking incongruity, namely his willingness to run extraordinary geopolitical risks (threats to withdraw from NATO and embargo arms) in order to secure economic gains—a position strongly criticized by the Foreign Office. It is striking, moreover, that such tactics failed precisely because no other Western country, even those with much more to gain or lose, took such

[25] Wolfram Kaiser, *Using Europe, Abusing the Europeans: Britain and European Integration* (London, 1996); Gladwyn Jebb, *The Memoirs of Lord Gladwyn* (London, 1972), 292–99; Gore-Booth, *Truth*, 247; John Campbell, *Edward Heath: A Biography* (London, 1993), 118–123.

[26] For the best documented, most detailed, and nuanced defense of the conventional position, see Kaiser, *Using*, 120–133, and passim. Charlton concludes: "the British decision was, in essence . . . political. . . . The recovery, maintenance, of a sufficient sovereign power and influence . . . had been judged . . . to lie in membership." Charlton, *Price*, 255.

British fears about the destabilizing implications for Western policy the least bit seriously.[27] All this suggests that Macmillan's concerns represented tactical threats and personal frustration rather than fundamental British preferences. Concerns about Germany and the Soviet Union were aimed at domestic skeptics and, above all, Western allies in an effort to secure economic concessions. Macmillan himself may have believed they were of some importance. Yet neither constitutes a coherent explanation of British policy.[28]

A geopolitical explanation of the British membership bid must therefore rest on the final factor: British desire to maintain its global prestige by protecting its Commonwealth role and retaining its role as European interlocutor *vis-à-vis* the superpowers. This argument finds more consistent support in the documents. In addition to the evidence cited above, Macmillan's Grand Design memo observes that "Sixes and Sevens is not primarily an economic but a political problem."[29] The Lee Report states at one point that economic arguments are balanced, whereas political ones militate in favor of membership. There are intermittent memoranda to and from Macmillan, some cited above, stating that exclusion from Europe might undermine the political position of Britain in the world and, in particular, relations with the United States. To this we may add the testimony of two close associates of Macmillan, Heath and de Zulueta, who in retrospect considered geopolitics the most important factor. Finally, Macmillan himself reminds us of the primacy of the Communist threat in the appropriate chapter of his memoirs.

Yet the conclusiveness of such evidence should not be exaggerated. In nearly all lists of British interests, concerns about economics are just as prominent as geopolitical concerns. The documentary record of internal government deliberations contains more consideration of economic than of geopolitical matters. The most consistent argument voiced in confidential discussions was that closer association was required to prevent discrimination against British goods in the rapidly growing markets of Western Europe. From the start, officials foresaw that commercial exclusion would eventually constitute a sufficient reason to seek membership—between 1955 and 1970 this prediction was never seriously challenged within the government. Agricultural trade consistently appeared as the greatest impediment to successful conclusion of the negotiations.[30]

Both the Lee Report and the Grand Design memo, for example, support an economic explanation more strongly than a geopolitical one. Sometimes the former is mistaken for the latter. The Grand Design memo—not least the cele-

[27] Lamb, *Macmillan*, 128–130; Kaiser, *Using,* 174; Memorandum by the Prime Minister, 29 December 1960/3 January 1961, PREM 11/3325, 16.

[28] Macmillan, *Riding*, 436, also 435–437; Charlton, *Price*, 241, 253–254; Adolf M. Birke and Kurt Kluxen, eds., *Die europäische Herausforderung: England und Deutschland in Europa* (Munich, 1987), 134, 137, 241–242; Roll in Charlton, *Price*, 253.

[29] Quoted in Kaiser, *Using,* 117. Charlton (231), following de Zulueta, argues: "the evidence is that, by itself, the breakdown of the European policy with the collapse of the Free Trade Area was not sufficient to make the Prime Minister contemplate initiating the vital change. . . . Throughout 1958 and 1959 . . . Macmillan was still doing what he could to avoid it."

[30] Lamb, *Macmillan*, 156–157, also 110; Macmillan, *Riding*, 86–87; Camps, *Britain*, 107–108; Lieber, *British*, passim; memo from E.R. to Prime Minister, 21–22 January 1962 (PREM 11/3325). Macmillan in *Hansard* (House of Commons, 26 November 1956).

brated passage that the EEC "is not primarily economic but a political prob-lem"—must be read in context. This was not a discussion of core British inter-ests but of optimal tactics to pressure de Gaulle. The latter included the inflation of threats to Western unity expressed to Kennedy, Adenauer, and de Gaulle—an integral part of the "carrots and bribes" approach described above. The en-tire passage reads: "Exclusion from the strongest economic group in the civi-lized world must injure us. . . . We ought therefore to make a supreme effort to reach a settlement while de Gaulle is in power in France. If he gave the word, all the Wormsers [domestic economic officials] would turn at once. . . . Sixes and Sevens . . . is now not primarily an economic but a political problem and should be dealt with as such." Moreover, the Grand Design memo calls attention to "grave . . . economic consequences to Britain" and recommends that British eco-nomic problems be solved "above all, by *expanding exports.*"[31]

The Lee Report's central argument was that "great economic benefits" would sooner or later drive Britain to seek membership (or its economic equivalent). Sooner was better and a "deliberate act of statesmanship" could swing domestic opinion behind such an effort. The political costs, Lee argued, would be low. Thus geopolitical arguments may well have been employed with intent to offer justification for such leadership.[32] The record of deliberation within the Lee Committee reveals cleavages consistent with an economic interpretation, with opponents stressing economic links with the Commonwealth but Lee himself (with close contacts to business) concluding: "The conclusion is inescapable . . . [Even if political factors are discounted] from an economic standpoint we must maintain our broad objective of having the U.K. form part of a single European market."[33] The view elsewhere in the report, that "economic arguments are bal-anced" (but that political factors tended to favor membership), must thus be read as a statement not about British longer-term interests but about the bal-ance of British exports to the Commonwealth and Continent in 1960, which did not yet compel membership.

Macmillan himself tended to rely on economic arguments in key internal de-bates. Critics such as Robert Lieber have long noted that he employed economic arguments in public, even though geopolitical ones might have been rhetori-cally more effective. This is in part because Macmillan's own view at the time was that the geopolitical case for accession was not particularly strong—a view shared by Lee and others. In public debate, Macmillan was aware that Commonwealth concerns remained strong. He therefore advanced geopolitical arguments—mainly the claim that integration would promote Western unity—only late in the negotiations, under domestic political pressure. In confidential discussions with British officials, he also stressed economics. When his strategy of geopoliti-cal threats was criticized by the British Ambassador to NATO as undermining Western defense, for example, Macmillan remarked to his closest associates:

---

[31] Cited in Kaiser, *Using,* 116–117; Memorandum by the Prime Minister, 29 December 1960/3 January 1961, PREM 11/3325, 5–9. Horne, *Macmillan,* 2:257; Roll, quoted in Charlton, *Price,* 251.

[32] Quoted in Camps, *Britain,* 107, see also 106–111; Moon, *European;* Tratt, *Macmillan,* 85–101, especially 95–96.

[33] Tratt, *Macmillan,* 97.

"[The Ambassador] is still too tempted to play the role of a friend to NATO without regard to other situations. . . . I don't think he realizes that we are a country to whom nothing else matters except our export trade. Our only hope of an agreement on Sixes and Sevens [EEC-EFTA], which is the vital British interest today, is by a political situation arising which brings about the economic solution."[34] This remark was typical of internal debate, particularly after the Lee Report.

Domestic patterns of cleavage and support also offer evidence of economic concerns. From 1955 through 1963 the officials who handled negotiations were primarily drawn from economic ministries; business was closely connected with the negotiations. The arguments that ultimately triumphed—those found in the Lee Report—were already being made by economic officials in 1955. In the EFTA case, business conducted negotiations directly. Internal divisions within business reflected variations in competitiveness. By 1961 sentiment from economic constituencies of the Conservative party in Parliament was running so strongly pro Europe that Macmillan apparently believed it was worth attempting to satisfy those constituent demands even if, as he thought likely, the effort might fail.[35] In internal discussions, geopolitical arguments were advanced primarily by the Foreign Office, which remained skeptical of membership as late as 1967.

British negotiating tactics and the information available to the British government also suggest the primacy of economics rather than geopolitics. From Heath's opening speech, three economic issues—EFTA membership, agriculture, and Commonwealth preferences—were the central British priorities. There was little attention to the EC's political activities. Macmillan realized—at the very latest by mid-1962, as we shall see, but probably much earlier—that the aspirations of federalists and de Gaulle's Fouchet Plan for foreign policy cooperation would not be realized. The EC was not, in fact, becoming a new "superpower." Yet neither Macmillan nor his successors were dissuaded. As we have seen in chapter 2, moreover, economic concerns best explain why Britain preferred various FTA schemes rather than a customs union, though Commonwealth political concerns may have played a role.

In sum, we cannot definitively exclude geopolitical prestige as a motivation for the British membership bid. Yet the decisiveness of geopolitics has surely been exaggerated in existing analyses of the first accession negotiations. The only geopolitical concern with significant documentary support is the British defense of global prestige and relationship to the United States, and this is neither as consistent nor as coherent a motivation as the avoidance of commercial exclusion. The preeminence of economic interest is clearest in the long run. The British government employed a constantly shifting set of geopolitical arguments, many overtly opportunistic, in defense of its policy. Yet from 1955 through 1970 it remained undisputed inside and outside the government that commercial considerations were sufficient to force a British bid for membership *over the long term.* There was uncertainty only about timing. Thus, if geopolitical considerations play a prominent role in internal deliberations between 1958

---

[34] Horne, *Macmillan,* 2:257. Such reliance does not appear, moreover, to have been strategic, since he used such arguments with the Foreign Office as well as with Treasury.

[35] This is a central contention of Kaiser, *Using.*

and 1963, it is because Macmillan was pursuing a far-sighted policy, precisely as recommended by Lee. Before the mid-1960s British exports to Europe had not yet surpassed those to the Commonwealth and thus did not yet constitute an overwhelming case for immediate entry—a view reflected in the FBI's initial indecision and Macmillan's caution in assembling domestic support. With the economic pressure not as yet overwhelming, the wide range of geopolitical considerations cited in internal documents may well have speeded Macmillan's decision or may have served to counter what Macmillan saw as domestic opposition grounded in attachment to the Commonwealth. Much evidence supports an even stronger conclusion, namely that conceptions of geopolitical interests were dragged in the wake of shifting commercial concerns. Yet there is reason to doubt that commercial concerns would soon have forced a British bid, geopolitical considerations aside.

At most, Macmillan's geopolitical concerns hastened a British bid for membership a few years before its time and placed an upper bound on the nuclear concessions he could offer in exchange. Macmillan was indeed no more willing than Adenauer to contemplate a break with NATO. In this light Macmillan's bid appears not the belated acceptance of the postwar power relations by a tradition-bound statesman, as subsequent critics assert, but an extraordinary act of leadership—a far-sighted move taken before the commercial shift from Commonwealth to Continent was complete. Of course Macmillan, like Adenauer, was also concerned about unity against the Soviets and was unwilling to break with the United States on nuclear policy or NATO to satisfy de Gaulle—but this was not the source of British desire for membership. We should resist the temptation to mistake the language of geopolitics for its substance. Metaphors change more slowly than interests. British leaders often employed geopolitical language to describe economic conflict.

The French veto devastated Macmillan. Seeking the best alternative to exclusion, he had led Britain step by step down a relatively stable preference ordering, successively attempting to subvert the EC, to associate with it, and finally to join it. After much expenditure of effort and loss of prestige, Britain had been humiliated by being forced into its least preferred choice: exclusion. Only the form of the failure provided solace; de Gaulle's overt veto permitted Macmillan to blame the failure on the General. Nonetheless, Macmillan's diary entry was despondent: "it is the end . . . to everything for which I have worked for many years. All our policies at home and abroad are in ruins."[36]

France: De Gaulle's Deliberate Deception

Under General Charles de Gaulle and his Gaullist successor Georges Pompidou, the French government promoted agricultural cooperation, preferably with price supports near the moderately high French level; cautiously supported

---

[36] Horne, Macmillan, 2:447, also 430–432, 444–45; Charlton, Price, 229–233, 239–242, 254. Possible Anglo-French misunderstandings at the Rambouillet summit meeting of 15 December and with the United States over Polaris may well have been deliberate on de Gaulle's part.

the industrial customs union; vetoed successive British proposals for association and membership; proposed an alternative intergovernmental structure for the EC focused more on foreign policy cooperation (the Fouchet Plan), and boycotted the EC for six months in 1965–66 (the "empty chair" crisis) in order to force a reduction in Commission powers and a unilateral veto (the Luxembourg Compromise). The most striking aspect of de Gaulle's policy is its consistency. A plan to promote French agriculture, veto British entry, challenge supranational institutions, and exploit Gaullist ideology to mislead foreign and domestic critics—in short, the essence of all French actions through the frontal attack on EC institutions in 1966—was set forth in documents and cabinet meetings in 1960–61 and carried out over the following decade almost to the letter.

Nearly all existing accounts of de Gaulle's European policy—whether by participants, contemporary commentators, political scientists, or the General's myriad biographers and historians—ascribe a predominant influence to his distinctive geopolitical ideology. For such interpreters, de Gaulle personifies nationalist opposition to Monnet's vision of Europe. De Gaulle, it is argued, was the archetype of what neofunctionalists term a "dramatic-political actor," a man driven by archaic ideology rather than by modern technocratic rationality, "high" rather than "low" politics. He promoted European integration in order to foster a European foreign policy independent of the superpowers. In particular, his desire to reinforce French "grandeur" and his suspicion of the United States are said to have inspired his European policy of cooperation with Germany and exclusion of Britain. Particularly galling were U.S. efforts to create a nuclear Multilateral Force (MLF) and Britain's privileged nuclear connection with the United States, symbolized by the Anglo-American Nassau summit of December 1962 at which Macmillan agreed to deploy U.S. Polaris missile technology. This, it is said, triggered his veto of British membership.

I propose to reverse this received view. De Gaulle's European policy, I argue, was aimed primarily at securing commercial advantages for French agriculture and industry, rather than realizing ideological goals. After trying and failing to reform French agriculture domestically, de Gaulle—like his Fourth Republic predecessors—sought to promote its exports through European integration. This implied opposition to British membership and delicate diplomacy with Germany. Among the major elements of de Gaulle's policy only opposition to supranational institutions was motivated primarily by ideology, but this goal was self-consciously compromised to secure the CAP. Much Gaullist rhetoric and many proposals—including the General's alternative view of Europe, delay and veto of negotiations with Britain, and proposal for the Fouchet Plan—were part of an elaborate and deliberate deception designed to maintain the illusion of a positive European vision. The aim, in the words of de Gaulle's closest adviser, was to "seduce" other governments into believing de Gaulle was pro-European long enough to lock in agricultural integration. The imputation of geopolitical motives to de Gaulle, moreover, rests almost entirely on a stylized reading of soft sources—French government statements, contemporary journalism, de Gaulle's memoirs and writings, and secondary speculation. (Though even an unbiased reading of these does not support the primacy of geopolitical concerns.) Hard sources, including records of cabinet meetings, transcripts of diplomatic inter-actions, and government documents, unambiguously support the primacy of commercial concerns.[37]

Geopolitical Interest and Ideology: "Une certaine idée de la France"

Most analyses of de Gaulle's European policy center on his distinctive geo-political ideology—"une certaine idée de la France," as it appears in the cele-brated opening line of his wartime memoir.[38] For our purposes, we begin by noting that the most distinctive element was not de Gaulle's Realist faith in mili-tary force to project national power and influence. To be sure, de Gaulle sup-ported Western cohesion in Cuba and Berlin and believed nuclear weapons would make France a power to be reckoned with, yet his primary policy goal was not a balance of power against either German or Soviet military threats. Nor was the most distinctive element his assessment that German unification was in-evitable in the long term and therefore Germany must be integrated into inter-national organizations, though he appears to have believed this as well. If his pur-pose had simply been to keep the Russians out or the Germans down, he could have done so as easily through NATO, the EDC, or an FTA—all arrangements he strongly opposed. In his view of nuclear weapons and Germany, de Gaulle differed little from his Fourth Republic predecessors.

The most distinctive aspect of de Gaulle's worldview was instead his belief that diverse nation-states were preeminent instruments for the effective and legiti-mate pursuit of historically defined national interests. De Gaulle sought to re-tain France's symbolic heritage and prestige as a great power—its "independence and its grandeur," as he termed it—both to achieve other national interests and

[37] Most French archives for this period, including de Gaulle's personal materials, remain inacces-sible. The analysis in this section rests heavily, therefore, on those memoirs, oral history projects, and leaked documents judged most reliable, as well as on patterns of diplomatic interaction with other governments and the precise sequence of events. Unlike nearly all studies of de Gaulle, it relies spar-ingly on the General's memoirs and public speeches, though for the most part these support the ar-gument here. The first two volumes of Peyrefitte's memoirs are among the critical sources. Alain Peyrefitte, *C'était de Gaulle*, 2 vols. (Paris, 1994). Peyrefitte was de Gaulle's chief minister in this area and one of only two people (the other being the prime minister) permitted to take notes at de Gaulle's cabinet meetings, from which he cites verbatim. Historians Georges Soutou, Charles Cogan, and Gérard Bossuat report that the archival materials they have seen generally support Peyrefitte's account. In addition, his view is corroborated by his strategy document, leaked and reprinted in the mid-1960s, and by his contemporary articles in *Le Monde*. His own sparing interpretations do not contradict my account, except in one passage where he opines that economic, political (NATO), and nuclear questions were "inextricably mixed" (1:303). Supportive on the facts, though sometimes drawing a different conclusion, is Alain Prate, *Les batailles économiques du Général de Gaulle* (Paris, 1978). Overtly speculative and imprecise is Michel Debré, *Entretiens avec le Général de Gaulle, 1961–1969* (Paris, 1993); sketchy is Edgar Pisani, *Le général indivis* (Paris, 1974); solid but cautious is Maurice Couve de Murville, *Une politique étrangère, 1958–1969* (Paris, 1971).

[38] Charles de Gaulle, *Mémoires de Guerre* (Paris, 1959), 1:1. Of the nearly 2,000 books from 45 countries published on de Gaulle, representative selections, from which this summary is consistent, are Phillip H. Gordon, *A Certain Idea of France: French Security Policy and the Gaullist Legacy* (Princeton, 1993), chap. 1; Stanley Hoffmann, *Decline or Renewal? France since the 1930s* (New York, 1974); Jean Lacouture, *De Gaulle*, 3 vols. (Paris, 1974–86); John Newhouse, *De Gaulle and the Anglo-Saxons* (New York, 1970); Michael Harrison, *The Reluctant Ally: France and Atlantic Security* (Baltimore, 1981); Lois Pattison de Ménil, *Who Speaks for Europe? The Vision of Charles de Gaulle* (New York, 1977); Alfred Grosser, *French Foreign Policy under de Gaulle* (Boston, 1967); Charles Cogan, *Charles de Gaulle: A Brief Biography with Documents* (Boston, 1995).

as an end in itself.[39] Often these goals were couched in historical terms: de Gaulle invoked French resentment about being snubbed during World War II or, more spectacularly, "the past 800 years" of European history, in which "our greatest hereditary enemy was not Germany, but England." At other times, they were expressed in terms of a desire for French equality in foreign policy and an opposition to efforts to transform Europe "into a gigantic Atlantic Community . . . dependent on [and] run by America."[40]

The result was extreme skepticism regarding multilateral or bilateral constraints on autonomy. He opposed the EDC and Euratom, canceled secret Franco-German cooperation on nuclear weapons, and criticized postwar U.S. foreign economic policy. He began distancing France from NATO after the Anglo-American rejection of his September 1958 memo proposing a tripartite nuclear directorate—a process that culminated in withdrawal from NATO's integrated military structure in 1966. He interpreted European integration as a conflict between two visions of Europe: the "Commission's supranational claims" and "utopian myths," on the one hand, and a "confederation" in which no sovereign state could be "exposed to the possibility of being overruled on any economic matter . . . and therefore in social and sometimes political matters," on the other. He therefore rejected pooling and delegation; the Treaty of Rome was simply "an improved treaty of commerce." A crisis over supranational institutions, he argued subsequently, was "sooner or later inevitable" because of "certain basic errors and ambiguities in the treaties on economic union of the Six."[41]

Much has been made of the ideological antagonism between France and Britain during this period, but in fact de Gaulle and his associates understood quite clearly that the French and British were natural allies on most geopolitical matters. Both nations were concerned to balance Germany and to maintain independent nuclear forces and ex-colonial commitments. Above all, both opposed supranational institutions; the major internal French strategy document in this period refers to the geopolitical positions of the two countries as "sisters." Discussions between Macmillan and de Gaulle, as we shall see, uncovered more areas of geopolitical agreement than of disagreement.[42] To be sure, the two differed about the United States, but by the mid-1960s, with the Fouchet Plan in ruins and the Franco-German Treaty emasculated by the Bundestag, it is difficult to conclude that Britain was objectively more pro-American than Germany.

Economic Interest: "An Algeria on our own soil"

The most consistent economic pressure for integration continued to come from French agriculture. By de Gaulle's entry into office in 1958, agricultural surpluses had reached the point of crisis. De Gaulle initially tried and failed to

[39] Charles de Gaulle, *Lettres, Notes et Carnets* (Paris, 1980ff), 4:170; Pisani, *Général*, 86–88.

[40] Peyrefitte, *C'était*, 153; Cogan, *Charles*, 140; De Gaulle, *Mémoires*, 3:178–180.

[41] Ménil, *Who*, 15–54; Charles de Gaulle, *Memoirs of Hope: Renewal and Endeavor* (New York, 1971), 182ff.; Macmillan–de Gaulle conversation, 2 June 1962 (PRSM 11/3775); Jacques Leprette, *Une Clef pour l'Europe* (Brussels, 1994), 188.

[42] Edmond Jouve, *Le Général de Gaulle et la construction de l'Europe (1940–1966)* (Paris, 1967), 2:455; also 492–98; Macmillan–de Gaulle conversation, 2 June 1962.

cut agricultural subsidies. Now farmers, an important electoral constituency for Gaullists and other center-right parties, were growing restless; intermittent riots rocked the country during the early 1960s. In ten years, debt among farmers had risen from 20 percent to 50 percent of output. Continued unilateral subsidies were impracticable, de Gaulle concluded; they would "cripple French finances" and burden its balance of payments. At a key cabinet meeting de Gaulle called the stabilization of agriculture through exports the "most important problem" facing France after the Algerian civil war. "If [agriculture] is not resolved," he concluded, "we will have another Algeria on our own soil."[43]

France had commodities largely uncompetitive on the world market yet competitive within Europe, and half the arable land among the Six. The only remaining solution was to dispose of surpluses within a protected European market. To be sure, French agricultural exports to Germany in 1956 were only a quarter the size of French industrial exports, yet the French bilateral surplus in agriculture—even without liberalization—made up for 60 percent of the French bilateral deficit in industrial goods. The only option, de Gaulle noted later, was to create an arrangement with industrial free trade and high common agricultural prices, the latter a sine qua non for Germany, in exchange for access to the German market. A Franco-German deal was viable, he reasoned, because for Germany the maintenance of cheap imports was a secondary concern, whereas for France high prices were secondary. This would serve the purposes of French industry as well, by creating the export opportunities that business demanded, so providing a secondary reason to support the EC. By contrast, Britain strongly opposed any arrangement to import relatively expensive French commodities. In this context (more often than that of geopolitics) de Gaulle noted in cabinet meetings that British entry would create a "completely different Common Market" and that European independence from the United States was an imperative. De Gaulle, like his predecessors, saw no reason to support an FTA, which would increase industrial competition on the Continent and threaten the unity of the Common Market with no offsetting gain in agriculture or for the French Union.[44]

Farmers understood the importance of the EC. Their power was demonstrated by their response to the "empty chair" crisis in 1965–66. The normally nonpartisan peak farmers group, the FNSEA, recommended that its five million members cast votes against de Gaulle in the presidential elections of January 1965, leading to his embarrassing failure to achieve a first-ballot majority. A pro-European but otherwise unremarkable centrist gained over 15 percent of the vote, disproportionately from rural areas, forcing a run-off with the Socialists.

[43] Peyrefitte, C'était, 1:302.

[44] Peyrefitte, C'était, 1:302–303, 67. Also Balassa, Organized, 393; de Gaulle, Mémoires, 158–59; F. Roy Willis, France, Germany and the New Europe, 1945–1967 (Stanford, 1968), 252–253, 287ff.; Jouve, Général, 2:492–498; Debré, Trois, 2:432–34; Lacouture, De Gaulle, 212; Institut Charles de Gaulle, 1958: La Faillite ou le miracle. Le plan de Gaulle–Rueff (Paris, 1986), 126–130, 98–99, 137–38, 126–27; Jouve, Général, 2:195 on Couve; Raymond Poidevin, "De Gaulle et l'Europe en 1958," in Institut, De Gaulle, 5:79–87; Alain Peyrefitte, The Trouble with France (New York, 1981), 39; Alain Prate, Les Batailles économiques du Général de Gaulle (Paris, 1978), 64; Jacques Rueff, De l'aube au crépuscule, Autobiographie (Paris, 1977), 252–56; Rueff, Combats pour l'ordre financier (Paris, 1972), 458–464.

Within a few months of his second-round victory, de Gaulle named Edgar Faure minister of agriculture with "a very precise aim: to bring back to the majority the million and a half rural votes." Faure quickly raised milk and beef prices as well as removing a tax on wheat; de Gaulle returned to the negotiating table in Brussels.[45]

French industry had initially viewed safeguards and escape clauses, social harmonization and unanimity voting, as ways to offset risks stemming from the overvaluation of the franc. As we saw in chapter 2, despite a rapid increase in exports to Europe during the 1950s, even the strongest supporters of the Treaty of Rome doubted that any government could overcome business opposition to strict implementation. In November 1957, facing a balance-of-payments crisis, the Gaillard government violated its OEEC obligations and the spirit of the new EEC by imposing a dual exchange rate system. By May 1958 the government's reserves were exhausted, riots erupted, and the last chief executive of the Fourth Republic, Pierre Pflimlin, announced that France would disregard the January 1959 deadline for the first EEC tariff reductions.

De Gaulle's return to power reversed this situation by giving business what it had wanted all along but thought impossible: a real devaluation of the franc of nearly 20 percent linked to fiscal austerity. The plan (initially proposed by an American expert seconded to Paris) was funneled to de Gaulle through Jacques Rueff, a liberal economist who admired Erhard's policies in Germany and had served in Poincaré's cabinet during the devaluation of 1926. The General's aims of economic reform and trade liberalization did not differ from those of his predecessors, but the power of the Fifth Republic presidency and unified support on the center-right permitted him to achieve them. By 1959 industry was enjoying an export boom and had become an enthusiastic supporter of accelerated tariff and quota removal. Industrial opposition to the British FTA plan softened more slowly. While French business did not become an enthusiastic supporter of GATT negotiations, opposition to multilateral trade liberalization melted away. By mid-decade, French concerns about EC and GATT tariff reductions were limited almost exclusively to their impact on agriculture. The French saw little advantage in liberalization of transport; atomic energy cooperation, still attractive, was moribund. Finally, the French government was encouraging industrial concentration and therefore viewed a strong EC competition (antitrust) policy with some skepticism.[46]

The Domectic Decision: "France is only as European as she is agricultural"

The preponderance of evidence suggests that commercial interests dictated French policy, while geopolitical interests and ideas remained secondary. The public perception of French policy was, moreover, often deliberately manipulated to serve commercial ends. De Gaulle planned years in advance and pursued a consistent policy. As we shall see, each of the major French decisions was part of a strategy, set forth in 1960–61 and executed largely as planned. We can trace

[45] Interview with French official (December 1993). This is also de Gaulle's own gloss. See de Gaulle, *Memoirs*, 217–20.
[46] Willis, *France*, 253ff.

this through four episodes: de Gaulle's acceptance of the customs union and CAP, his promulgation of the Fouchet Plan, his veto of Britain, and his provocation of the Empty Chair boycott over the nature of supranational institutions.

De Gaulle was expected to renounce the Treaty of Rome in 1958, but within a few months he had opted instead to support its swift and full implementation. In addition, he blocked FTA negotiations with the British and pressed for rapid and full implementation of open-ended provisions for the CAP.

There is little direct evidence that either the General's turnaround in 1958 or his subsequent policy was driven by geopolitical interests and ideas; to the contrary, a tension between geopolitical interests and ideas and EC policy arose immediately upon de Gaulle's entry into office in 1958. Debré, de Gaulle's first prime minister, had called for renunciation or renegotiation because it was inconsistent with Gaullist views on federalism. The General himself noted at a confidential session that "if I had negotiated it, I probably would have done it differently"—referring, no doubt, to the existence of supranational institutions as well as the lack of guarantees for agriculture.[47] Nor does de Gaulle appear to have remained in the EC because he sought foreign policy and defense cooperation with Germany to create a European "third force." De Gaulle assured Adenauer and others that he would respect the Treaty of Rome *before* he sent the September 1958 memo to the United States and Britain proposing a nuclear triumvirate or knew of their rejection; the latter events could not have caused the former.[48]

Internal discussions over the Plan Rueff and external liberalization focused instead on commercial implications, just as Fourth Republic discussions over the Treaty had done. On this issue the major difference between de Gaulle and his Fourth Republic predecessors lay not in their underlying motivations but in de Gaulle's stronger domestic position, which permitted him to devalue the franc, at a stroke restoring the competitiveness of French industry. With both industry and agriculture supportive of a customs union—in part to block any free trade area—de Gaulle moved forward swiftly, supporting an acceleration of tariff reductions within the customs union.[49] After the failure of efforts to reduce domestic subsidies and liberalize agriculture, de Gaulle retreated here also to the policy pursued by his predecessors: the establishment of a "small Europe" preferential arrangement for agriculture. Over the next eight years the CAP was de Gaulle's major European priority.

The preponderance of direct evidence concerning de Gaulle's own expression of his motivations confirms the primacy of economic interests. De Gaulle, we have seen, believed agriculture to be the major problem facing France next to

---

[47] Peyrefitte, *Général*, 1:211; de Gaulle, *Memoirs*, 183ff; Jouve, *Général*, 194ff; Jebb, *Memoirs*, 310, reports a January 1957 conversation with de Gaulle in which he opposed Monnet's Europe but accepted economic rationalization; Alessandro Silj, *Europe's Political Puzzle* (Cambridge, Mass., 1967), 114–116; Institute, *1958*, passim.

[48] De Gaulle, *Memoirs*, 177–178; Interview with Baron Snoy et d'Oppuers, July 1987 (Interview 27, 38: EC Archives Fiesole), 14.

[49] For an overview of this decision, Institut, *1958*.

Algeria; his memoirs confirm this position. It was also the EC issue most extensively discussed in de Gaulle's cabinet. Participants in decisions in 1958 report that de Gaulle saw liberalization as part of the Plan Rueff for devaluation of the franc to increase competitiveness, combined with fiscal austerity.[50] Economic concerns punctuate cabinet meetings, whereas there is no record of even a single clear mention of a connection between agriculture and geopolitical goals: The "dominant subject" was "agriculture."[51] Even discussion of the decision in de Gaulle's memoirs mentions only economic concerns, in particular the modernization of French industry and agriculture.[52] The General's closest adviser reports that his "major argument for the CAP was that French industry could not afford to subsidize our agriculture alone."[53] For de Gaulle, another recalls, a preferential arrangement in agriculture, opposed by Germany, was the "primary precondition" for him to accept the customs union.[54]

The only countervailing evidence concerning the source of de Gaulle's attitudes toward the customs union and CAP is indirect. More general discussions of French foreign policy in de Gaulle's memoirs and, though only rarely, in cabinet meetings, stress the need for European political cooperation *vis-à-vis* the superpowers. Yet little identifies these concerns as primary motivations for integration. Whereas de Gaulle did criticize American "hegemony" in various speeches, sometimes mentioning politico-military concerns, nearly all of de Gaulle's recorded references to the potential for Anglo-American influence in the EC in confidential meetings specify U.S. and U.K. *trade* policy, not military policy. In internal deliberations, de Gaulle never so much as hinted at any linkage, nor, as we have seen, is there evidence that he was willing to sacrifice national sovereignty for a European foreign policy. The trade conflict between the U.S. and Europe, he observed after voicing one set of criticisms of U.S.–U.K. influence in Europe, was solely concerned with farm commodities: "It boils down to this, we're both agricultural producers."[55]

The seriousness with which de Gaulle took the CAP is evidenced by the tactical flexibility with which he sought to overcome the major obstacle in its path: German opposition. The predominance of commercial concerns is demonstrated by de Gaulle's willingness to make significant geopolitical concessions and run significant geopolitical risks in order to realize the CAP, including continual threats to exit the EC, a willingness to make geopolitical threats, and a willingness to accept limitations on sovereignty. To induce Germany to open its highly protected domestic agricultural markets and to abrogate bilateral arrange-

[50] De Gaulle, *Memoirs*, 131ff, 159, 178, 182–83; Institut, *1958;* Jouve, *Général,* 195; Pierre Maillard, *De Gaulle et l'Allemagne: Le rêve inachevé* (Paris, 1990), 142; Jebb, *Memoirs,* 310.

[51] Peyrefitte, *C'était,* 2:231–232, also 2:274 and passim.

[52] De Gaulle, *Memoirs,* 135, 159, 171, 173, 174–80.

[53] Peyrefitte, *C'était,* 2:267.

[54] Prate, *Batailles,* 52 and 53ff.

[55] Peyrefitte, *C'était,* 2:265, also 237, 264–266, 271–274. Cf. Miriam Camps, *European Unification in the 1960s: From the Veto to the Crisis* (New York, 1966), 86–87, 91; Stanley Hoffmann, "De Gaulle's Foreign Policy: The Stage and the Play, the Power and the Glory," in Hoffmann, ed., *Decline or Renewal? France since the 1930s* (New York, 1974), 296–97; Hoffmann, "Obstinate or Obsolete? France, European Integration and the Fate of the Nation State," in *Decline,* 388–89.

ments with third countries, de Gaulle linked German approval of CAP to French approval for GATT negotiations. "There will be no Common Market without a CAP," he declared to his cabinet. "France is only as European as she is agricultural." Between 1962 and 1965 de Gaulle and his officials advanced dozens of such threats, both in public and private.[56]

There is no evidence to support the conjecture advanced by Miriam Camps and many others that these "brutal" negotiating tactics resulted from de Gaulle's anger over Kennedy's proposals for the MLF, or from any other geopolitical concern.[57] Instead, we see evidence of the opposite: de Gaulle never threatened to liquidate the EC or compromise on agriculture in order to secure foreign policy or defense cooperation—as geopolitical theory predicts he should. He instead seemed willing to risk geopolitical objectives through a radical reconsideration of French political-military policy, including suspension or denunciation of the Franco-German Treaty of 1963, a shift of alliances away from Germany toward the Soviet Union, withdrawal of French troops from Germany, or abandonment of political cooperation within the EC—all in order to achieve the CAP.[58] Finally, we see de Gaulle and his successor, Georges Pompidou, accepting substantial institutional limitations on French sovereignty to achieve agricultural integration. In the early 1960s it was above all Gaullist France that insisted on moving beyond long-term contracts, initially favored by France as less "supranational," to a more centralized CAP managed and financed in large part by Brussels-based officials. This involved a system of value-added taxation centralized in Brussels, a supranational power of taxation. This delegation of sovereignty served to "lock in" the CAP against persistent efforts by agricultural officials in ostensibly more federalist Germany to frustrate everyday implementation and the efforts of Britain, whose entry was foreseen, to undermine CAP financing. Precisely the converse occurred in external tariff and competition policy, over French objections. After France blocked efforts to develop a flexible negotiating position in the GATT, Germany sought greater Commission autonomy from the 111 and 113 committees.[59]

First proposed in 1961 and often taken as the centerpiece of de Gaulle's alternative geopolitical vision was the Fouchet Plan. The plan called for a new organization, without supranational institutions, to coordinate foreign and economic policy. In its initial form, it was a narrow arrangement limited to foreign policy, which seemed the basis for a modest organization existing alongside the EC. Then in January 1962 the proposal was revised by de Gaulle himself, in a much more intransigent spirit. The General cut acknowledgments of the Atlantic Alliance and the Treaty of Rome, proposed to supplant the EC in economic affairs, removed references to an "indissoluble union," reduced supranational powers, and purged a "revision clause" permitting the institution to be subsumed within the EC. The consequences were obvious; the French negotiator, Jean-

---

[56] Peyrefitte, C'était, 2:222, 265.

[57] Cf. Camps, European, 16, 117.

[58] Peyrefitte, C'était, 2:231–232, 237, 245–246, 249, 251–253, 256, 258, 261; De Gaulle, Memoirs, 182, 188.

[59] Institut Charles de Gaulle, ed. De Gaulle en son siècle: Europe (Paris, 1992), 5:123–24.

Marie Soutou, wrote in his diary: "That's the end of it all." Thereafter he proposed to withdraw some of the new demands but never returned to his initial proposal. The negotiations swiftly collapsed.[60]

De Gaulle's apparently self-defeating tactics have confounded historians. In most negotiations parties begin with extreme positions then compromise toward a median. Here the historical record reveals not a single occasion in which de Gaulle credibly signaled willingness to make even the smallest compromise in order to secure agreement on the Fouchet Plan. If de Gaulle sought an independent European foreign policy, why, for example, did he never link it to elements of economic or political integration of importance to Germany and other member-states—in striking contrast to the far more subtle and flexible French diplomacy on economic issues? Why, in the years following the abandonment of the Fouchet Plan, did he reject proposals from advisers to resurrect it, stating specifically that he was unwilling to concede even a modest quid pro quo in other areas, even elections to the powerless European Parliament, to achieve it?[61]

Historians who treat the Fouchet Plan as the genuine centerpiece of Gaullist European policy have been forced to advance speculative explanations that contradict their own claims that de Gaulle was a skilled diplomatic tactician. Some conjecture that de Gaulle's intransigence reflected pressure from Prime Minister Debré. Yet this would constitute a unique demonstration of ministerial independence by a man with neither significant political support (he was about to be forced to resign) nor a reputation for intellectual creativity.[62] Others speculate that in 1962 de Gaulle suddenly noted details he had previously overlooked or fell prey to a miscommunication within the French bureaucracy. Yet in contrast to the supposed role of de Gaulle in domestic affairs, in which the details were left to the ministers, the realm of foreign policy-making was an extremely centralized "reserved domain" of presidential activity. Records of policy-making in this period leave little doubt that de Gaulle took decisions without prior ministerial consultation and, in important cases like the British veto and the empty chair crisis, without informing his ministers until later. Still others attribute the change to de Gaulle's impetuous personality or his sense of principle.[63]

All these explanations suffer from the same weakness. They assume that de Gaulle placed primary importance on geopolitical goals. It is difficult, perhaps impossible, to maintain simultaneously that de Gaulle was acting rationally with regard to the Fouchet Plan and that achievement of European political cooperation was his major priority. A far simpler explanation of French negotiating tactics is that de Gaulle was primarily concerned not with geopolitical ideas but with French commercial interests, particularly those of agriculture. Though de Gaulle would of course have preferred political relations to be conducted under an intergovernmental arrangement like the Fouchet Plan, he was prepared to give

---

[60] Jean Lacouture, *De Gaulle: The Ruler* (New York, 1991), 349. Silj, *Europe's Political Puzzle*, 15–16; Debré, *Trois*, 440; Jouve, *Général*, 441–448; Georges-Henri Soutou, "Le *Général* de Gaulle et le plan Fouchet," in Institut, *Charles*, 136–137.

[61] Peyrefitte, *C'était*, 2:214–17.

[62] Serge Berstein, *The Republic of de Gaulle, 1958–1969* (Cambridge, 1993), 58–60.

[63] Soutou, "Général," 136ff.

priority to the EC, at least as long as the CAP was not yet complete. De Gaulle had never considered it likely that the others would accept the Fouchet Plan and consistently treated progress toward CAP as a priority. There were reports that de Gaulle was unconcerned by the failure, since the plan would have imposed restrictions on France.[64] In addition to explaining apparently counterproductive French negotiating tactics and the unwillingness to sacrifice economic gains for political union, commercial concern about agriculture accounts for the timing of the French revision. The second revision was drafted at a meeting among de Gaulle and a few of his ministers just four hours after the decisive agriculture compromise of January 1962, which assured that the CAP would move forward. With agriculture secure, de Gaulle was free to set forth a more intransigent position, placing the public onus of the collapse of the negotiations on the rejection of other governments and preserving his "pro-European" image.

The strongest evidence for the primacy of commercial considerations, however, lies in records of strategic planning by de Gaulle and his closest advisers. De Gaulle and the man who became his chief strategist on Europe, Alain Peyrefitte, saw the apparent contradiction between French economic interests in the EC and opposition to supranational institutions as the central tactical problem facing France. It required what Peyrefitte termed—following de Gaulle's language—a "prudently audacious" strategy. The core of this strategy is to be found in a plan drafted by Peyrefitte, soon to be de Gaulle's press spokesperson and then a minister. Peyrefitte's rapid advance within the very small group who helped make Gaullist foreign policy aside, there is direct evidence that de Gaulle immediately read and began to implement the plan. The rest of this extraordinary strategy, which hinted at all the major developments of the EEC from 1960 through 1966, was set forth explicitly in other confidential documents, negotiating instructions, and cabinet discussions during this period.[65]

Peyrefitte argued that the French government must disguise its true goals, agricultural modernization and undermining supranational institutions; France must strive "never to appear negative." To keep negotiations moving and to avoid triggering counterdemands and obstruction from its allies on economic issues, France must avoid conveying any inkling of its desire to destroy EC institutions in pursuit of its true goal: "a British Europe without the British."[66] Any hint of de Gaulle's plan to destroy EC institutions would disadvantage the French or lead the other five to side with the British. France should instead, in Peyrefitte's words, "seduce" the other five governments away from the EC by propos-

---

[64] Pierre Maillard, *De Gaulle et l'Allemagne: Le rêve inachevé* (Paris, 1990), 205.

[65] Jouve, *Général*, 1:72, 2:485–502. Peyrefitte's memoir is corroborated here by documents and by Debré, who recalls that the review of French policy was based not on ideology but on pure national interests: avoiding a free trade area without external tariffs, the role of overseas territories, and the establishment of the CAP. Debré, *Trois*, 2:432ff.

[66] Peyrefitte, *Général*, 1:498, also 489–496. To appreciate the deception, compare Peyrefitte's articles in *Le Monde* (14, 15, 16, and 17 September 1960), which argue that it would be illogical to seek "a British Europe without the British." Jouve, *Général*, 2:439–440. Recall also de Gaulle's characteristically ambiguous advice to Giscard: "Never invoke special interests in public. Talk only about the country's interests and have only its interests at heart." Philippe Alexandre, *The Duel: De Gaulle and Pompidou* (Boston, 1972), 113.

ing positive plans that did not undermine sovereignty, such as the Fouchet Plan. Such plans were needed to create the illusion of a positive French policy toward Europe and thereby to assure forward motion on economic issues and, if possible, to induce other governments to renounce the EC voluntarily. Perhaps, the Peyrefitte memo cynically speculated, this policy might persuade European federalists, who comprised a majority in many national parliaments, that "the President of the Republic had been 'converted' to their principles." For nearly two years, it had precisely this effect on none other than Monnet, who supported de Gaulle's plans for foreign policy coordination until the General's true intentions became clear.[67]

A final added benefit was greater pressure on Britain: the apparent "deepening" of integration, de Gaulle and his associates speculated, might force the British mistakenly to "exclude themselves" from a superficially federalist arrangement.[68] France would of course have to block British entry to achieve the CAP. If the French stalled and made demands, de Gaulle wrongly calculated, British negotiators—too tightly constrained by agricultural and Commonwealth interests in the Conservative party—would be forced either to withdraw or to bargain so intransigently that they would be blamed for a collapse of negotiations. The Fouchet Plan would place even greater pressure on Britain. The apparent "deepening" of integration, de Gaulle and his associates reasoned, might force the British mistakenly to "exclude themselves" from a superficially federalist, but actually more "British" arrangement.[69]

If the Fouchet Plan failed, the British backed off and the CAP was implemented, France would then directly confront its partners, threatening radical action, including withdrawal, if the Treaty were not revised to remove supranational elements. Accordingly, de Gaulle's confidential negotiating guidelines to Michel Debré in September 1960, the month after Peyrefitte's memo, instructed that Debré was not to challenge the EEC overtly. If the Fouchet Plan succeeded, the EEC would wither away; if it failed, France would confront the other five member governments and "deal directly" with supranationalism when the time was right.[70]

Turning from the Fouchet Plan to *Gaullist policy toward Britain*, again only economic interests seem to offer a convincing explanation. From 1958 to early 1969, Gaullist and non-Gaullist governments in France blocked both a free trade area with Britain and British entry into the EC. Curiously, at the end of the decade, the Gaullists suddenly reversed course. De Gaulle held serious discussions on British membership in 1969 and Georges Pompidou, his Gaullist successor, lifted the French veto later that year, leading to British accession.

We have seen that the last governments of the Fourth Republic, de Gaulle's

---

[67] Jouve, *Général*, 2:489–499, esp. 2:498. Also Etienne Burin des Roziers, *Retour aux sources, 1962, l'année décisive* (Paris, 1986), 51–53.

[68] des Roziers, *Retour*, 51–53.

[69] Jouve, *Général*, 2:489–499.

[70] de Gaulle, *Lettres*, 389–390; Soutou, "1961: Le plan Fouchet," *Espoir* 87 (December 1992), 40–55; Susanne J. Bodenheimer, *Political Union: A Microcosm of European Politics* (Leyden, 1967), 77–84; Jouve, *Général*, 2:489–499.

predecessors, opposed any British proposals for an FTA, which might call into question the favorable treatment on agriculture, colonial products, and external tariffs France had won in the Treaty of Rome. In December 1958, after gaining Adenauer's support, de Gaulle vetoed the FTA outright, calling on the British—disingenuously, of course—to join the EEC and accept the same obligations as the other EC partners. Over the next two years EC-EFTA negotiations remained fruitless, largely due to French obstruction.

Little changed when Macmillan announced in mid-1961 the step for which de Gaulle had called, namely a British membership application. De Gaulle simply reversed his rhetoric; he termed the decision "an unpleasant surprise" and encouraged the British to withdraw it. Yet he was initially little concerned, as we have seen, for he expected domestic opposition within Britain to block the economic and political concessions on the Commonwealth and agriculture required for agreement. When French officials finally realized that Macmillan was genuinely willing to make the economic concessions on the Commonwealth, apparently in mid-1962, French demands hardened and pessimistic prognoses were issued in an attempt to force a British withdrawal, thereby transferring the responsibility for the collapse of negotiations onto Britain. A committee was reportedly formed at the Quai d'Orsay to design means of impeding British entry. In an effort to impose a *fait accompli* the French government sought rapid EC agreement on agricultural provisions directly at variance with British proposals, while misleading the British about their intentions. British ambassadors in Paris sensed this, reporting back to London that de Gaulle would probably wait for elections in November 1962, in which support from pro-EC farmers and centrist parties would be useful, then impose a veto. In retrospect, Pierson Dixon, the British ambassador in Paris, viewed this as the "end of the negotiations."[71]

De Gaulle continually reaffirmed to close advisers his absolute rejection of British membership but noted the need to delay. After several rounds of CAP agreements and an unexpectedly successful showing in parliamentary elections, de Gaulle announced the decision to veto at the Cabinet meeting of 17 December 1962, where he ridiculed Macmillan by quoting the famous Edith Piaf song, "Ne pleurez pas Milord" ("Do not cry, my lord")—a quotation that soon leaked. At a press conference on 14 January 1963, the General delivered the coup de grace.[72]

During the final months of de Gaulle's presidency and under his successor, Georges Pompidou, with the CAP almost entirely established, French policy softened. In 1969, de Gaulle—perhaps, some have suggested, disillusioned by a German rejection of French appeals for support in the exchange-rate crisis of November 1968—approached the British government about establishing an intergovernmental substitute for the EEC, which he termed the "European Economic Association." Though the discussions collapsed due to embarrassing

[71] Lamb, *Macmillan*, 175, also 144, 166, 172–175; Peyrefitte, *C'était*, 1:299–304; Wolfram Kaiser, "The Bomb and Europe: Britain, France, and the EEC Entry Negotiations, 1961–1963," *Journal of European Integration History* 1, no. 1 (1995), 85; Horne, *Macmillan*, 2:257; Jebb, *Memoirs*, 292–298; Silj, *Europe's*, 82; Sir Pierson Dixon, *Double Diploma: The Life of Sir Pierson Dixon, Don and Diplomat* (London, 1968), 282–83; Institute, *De Gaulle*, 5:193–196. Recent research suggests that Macmillan may have been pessimistic from the start, expecting a French veto. Kaiser, *Using*.

[72] Maillard, *De Gaulle*, 184–185; Jouve, *Général*, 1:492–98; Peyrefitte, 1:332–337.

British revelations (the "Soames Affair"), Pompidou continued the policy. In his first press conference as president on 10 July, Pompidou noted that France had no objection in principle to British membership, a statement that opened the door to successful negotiations concluded in 1973.[73]

The long dominant view of de Gaulle's motivations in vetoing Britain is geopolitical. Some argue that de Gaulle, already souring on Europe due to the demise of the Fouchet Plan, was concerned that Britain would be a "Trojan Horse" for U.S. geopolitical designs. Others stress de Gaulle's vision of an alternative European confederation based on the Fouchet Plan and his opposition to the Multilateral Force proposed by the United States Charles Cogan speaks for many analysts when he argues that: "De Gaulle's reasoning appears to have been the following. . . . He thought he could establish nuclear hegemony over the rest of the continent of Western Europe by virtue of: (1) the suppression of the Multilateral Force, which would have put nuclear weapons in the hands of continental powers, (2) the exclusion of Great Britain, a nuclear power, from a continental grouping by his veto of British entry into the Common Market."[74] Still others cite de Gaulle's anger at Macmillan's failure to tell him about the Polaris nuclear deal made with the United States at Nassau on 21 December, an impression among pro-Europeans that French officials had every reason to cultivate, since it permitted them to deny culpability for deceiving other governments about their intention to exercise a veto.[75]

Such geopolitical arguments, I contend, are based almost entirely on interpretations of an unrepresentative sample of de Gaulle's writings and statements as well as an unwarranted analogy to his NATO policy. The preponderance of evidence, including most of de Gaulle's own statements, supports instead an economic interpretation. De Gaulle decided against British membership early on, despite common geopolitical interests on many issues—not least shared opposition to supranational institutions and concern about Germany—because Britain was certain to block generous financing for the CAP. This would have negated the principal advantage for France from a customs union.

We begin with the public and private statements of de Gaulle and his ministers. De Gaulle's statements about the unwillingness of Britain to be "truly European," oft-cited by those who see the General as implacably opposed to the Anglo-Saxons, are generally taken out of context. When de Gaulle spoke of weak British commitment to Europe, he generally discussed economic commitments at greater length and in much greater detail than geopolitical ones. In the most important cases, he dwells on economics exclusively. He does this although one might have expected geopolitical concerns to offer a more expedient excuse, the language of "grandeur" and "independence" being popular in France. This

---

[73] Philip Ziegler, *Wilson, the Authorized Biography* (London, 1995), 334; Jay, "Free," 128; Simon Z. Young, *Terms of Entry: Britain's Negotiations with the European Community, 1970–1972* (London, 1973), 4–5.

[74] Charles Cogan, *Oldest Allies, Guarded Friends: The United States and France since 1940* (Westport, Conn., 1994), 128; Jean-Claude Petitfils, *Le gaullisme* (Parity, 1986), 13.

[75] Berstein, *Republic*, 173; Jouve, *Général*, 1:182–85. Others argue that the length of negotiations convinced the French to give up, but French opposition to British membership was consistent from the beginning.

is true even of his memoirs, in which his explanation of opposition to an FTA and British membership never mentions geopolitical or ideational issues but instead repeats that "without the common tariff and agricultural preference, there could be no valid European Community."[76] In the celebrated press conference of 14 January 1963, the most widely cited justification for the veto, de Gaulle devotes almost 1,500 words to what he terms a "clear" explanation of his veto without mentioning any disagreement with Anglo-Saxons over security issues, the Fouchet Plan, political union, or any other geopolitical concerns. De Gaulle dwells instead exclusively on commercial matters, primarily the contradiction between longstanding British trading patterns and future Treaty of Rome commitments in the "essential" area of agriculture. Mention of the United States is restricted to concern about its overwhelming economic influence and its purported desire, along with Britain, to promote European trade liberalization without a preferential arrangement for agriculture.[77]

De Gaulle's statements at closed cabinet sessions and meetings with close advisers during the critical period from 1961 to 1963 further confirm the preeminence of economic considerations—thereby calling into question any claim that de Gaulle was using public statements to curry electoral favor with farmers. The General consistently maintained that agriculture, not geopolitics, accounted for his opposition to British membership. In secret discussions in 1961, he stated that British entry would "overturn everything, [leading to] a completely different Common Market." At a closed meeting at the Elysée in 1962, he asserted that his "principal interest" was the defense of the CAP, which would help French agriculture "take off" as had French industry. The source of the dispute with Britain, he explained, lay in economic structure: the transition from agriculture to industry occurred a hundred years earlier in Britain, while it was still continuing in France—creating different political imperatives. Britain, he noted, would oppose any plans for a CAP, perhaps in alliance with Germany or even Italy and the Netherlands. (This was true; as we saw in chapter 2, one reason for the British membership bid raised in confidential Whitehall discussions was to do just this.) Even if they had been so inclined, the British had no way to provide a credible commitment to permit centralized financing arrangements to be created—decisions that were not taken until the late 1960s. (This accounts, among other things, for de Gaulle's willingness to offer membership to pro-NATO Denmark after the veto of Britain.) At the cabinet meeting of 17 December 1962, where the final decision to veto the British application was taken, the General again stressed agriculture. He emphasized that the one question the British could not answer is why a customs union with the EFTA countries would not simply become an industrial free trade zone. He notes: "The problem is to get the British into the existing Common Market, not to deal with the Commonwealth." He also predicted to Maurice Schumann that Britain would enter not under a Labour government but under Heath thereafter. Hours be-

---

[76] De Gaulle, *Memoirs*, 187, also 187–189, 218–220.

[77] On the press conference, see Jouve, *Général*, 2:283–88. Even in response to a question on the MLF, de Gaulle does not link nuclear issues to the EC. See also other statements on 5 February and 22 April, in Jouve, 2:289, 291; also Peyrefitte, *C'était*, 294.

fore the 14 January 1963 press conference and then again at a cabinet meeting ten days later, he observed to his closest advisers that the British might well be invited to join after the CAP was irreversibly established. Against such evidence, anecdotes about de Gaulle taking revenge for Agincourt and Waterloo carry little weight.[78]

A comprehensive survey of statements by French government officials reveals not a single direct acknowledgment of geopolitical motivations and many of commercial concerns. Just before the veto, Foreign Minister Couve de Murville was clear to the point of tendentiousness that the critical issue was not simply Commonwealth preferences but "financial regulation" of agriculture. In January 1963, when asked to account for the French veto, he responded:

> The answer is simple. The entire history of international cooperation in agricultural matters consists of promises [that] put off future transformations. . . . The keystone [is] the financial provision . . . It is evident that we could not have let a new member enter . . . without having settled in the most precise manner this essential matter.[79]

Both de Gaulle's prime minister and successor, Georges Pompidou, and his agriculture minister, Edgar Pisani, maintained subsequently that the veto forestalled an Anglo-German alliance to undermine CAP financing. "France," Pompidou argues, "is not opposed to British entry into the EC, but it refuses to permit such entry to call into question the CAP. When Britain accepts all the rules, everything will be fine."[80]

De Gaulle and his officials advanced the same arguments to their foreign counterparts, including Macmillan and Adenauer. Around the time of the veto, de Gaulle sometimes mentioned both economic and political concerns regarding Britain, but the economic arguments invariably came first and were treated in more detail. In discussions with German leaders he stressed that an "industrial trade arrangement with England could easily be reached," but not within the EC, because "agriculture is a French vital interest and for France to maintain its agriculture with England as a member, England would have to stop being England." Similarly, a GATT agreement could be reached, but the CAP must be maintained.[81] German diplomats subsequently conducted an extensive review of the diplomatic record and concluded that de Gaulle's primary motivation was

[78] Lacouture, *De Gaulle*, 359; Peyrefitte, *C'était*, 1:303, 332–336, 302–304; 2:224–25; John Campbell, *Edward Heath: A Biography* (London, 1993, 132; Silj, *Europe's*, 87–88; Grosser, *French*, 82–84. To be sure, the British veto would anger other governments, but this was of less concern to de Gaulle than overt British opposition.

[79] Silj, *Europe's*, 89–90. Also Couve de Murville, *Politique*, 335; Roth, *Heath*, 164; Bodenheimer, *Political Union*, 127; Jebb, *Memoirs*, 292ff.; Robert Marjolin, *Architect of European Unity: Memoirs, 1911–1986* (London, 1989), 320, 340, 358, cf. 338–339. There is little reason why these French officials should dissemble; if anything, the last-minute Nassau agreement would absolve him of widespread charges of diplomatic duplicity. See Paul-Henri Spaak, *The Continuing Battle: Memoirs of a European* (London, 1971), 476ff.

[80] Jouve, *Général*, 2:102; Marjolin, *Architect*, 358; Peyrefitte, *C'était*, 1:157.

[81] Hermann Kusterer, *Der Kanzler und der General* (Stuttgart, 1995), 318, 350–352.

to protect the agricultural policy.[82] British officials themselves agreed that it was in the end the issue of agriculture that was the "sticking point" or "Achilles heel" over which France sought to block formation of an Anglo-German coalition. Even Macmillan seems to have accepted this in retrospect. When de Gaulle vetoed Harold Wilson's tentative move toward a membership bid in 1967, Wilson was informed through back channels that it was because Pompidou had raised economic objections.[83]

Perhaps most important (and explored in more detail below), the preeminence of economic interests is strikingly reflected in the transcripts of bilateral summits between de Gaulle and Macmillan, which uncovered more areas of geopolitical agreement than of disagreement. Again, bits and pieces of these summit discussions are sometimes cited to support geopolitical concerns. Taken as a whole, however, these discussions do not support such an interpretation. Each has a similar form: de Gaulle presses Britain on agriculture, while Macmillan resists. Macmillan raises security issues, consistent with the centerpiece of the British strategy, which was from the beginning to offset de Gaulle's fundamental objections with geopolitical concessions. Britain and France consistently find they have more in common in geopolitical matters than in commercial ones— a reading consistent with de Gaulle's own gloss of the meetings.[84]

The timing of the veto further confirms the primacy of economics. We can reject outright a causal link between Nassau and the veto, the event most often invoked to explain the veto's timing. We now know that the General repeatedly hinted that he intended to impose a veto many months in advance and announced the timing at a cabinet meeting on 17 December 1962—some days before the U.S.-U.K. summit at Nassau and a full week before the French government had completed its analysis of it. Neither the summit nor any subsequent sense of "betrayal" by Macmillan could have played a role. An approach more attuned to domestic electoral concerns also provides a superior explanation of

[82] Bundesrepublik Deutschland, *Akten 1963,* contains much evidence. On 5 December 1962, the head of the political department in the German Foreign Ministry, Dr. Jansen, concluded from discussions in Paris that he was "pretty certain" about de Gaulle's intentions; the concern was the conflict between the EC and the Commonwealth, not the United States (Doc. 21). In his first set of face-to-face discussions with Adenauer following the veto, de Gaulle stressed that for him the "critical point" was the lack of British commitment to a "real Common Market," by which he meant that without a "common external tariff" and "common rules . . . particularly in agriculture," a European Community based on "economic interests" would collapse. De Gaulle continued to pursue the agriculture issue until his interlocutor changed the subject (Doc. 43). (De Gaulle's discussions with Macmillan show the same pattern: e.g., Record of Macmillan–de Gaulle meeting, 2 June 1962 [PREM 11/3775], p. 8). In a private meeting with representatives in the National Assembly, de Gaulle observed that Britain was a "Trojan Horse" not for U.S. geopolitical goals but for American efforts to break into the European market. Public speeches by Couve and de Gaulle conveyed the same message (Doc. 94). Italian and German officials agreed that agriculture was "key" (Doc. 24). De Gaulle also mentioned in private the need for a Labour government to make the "necessary changes" on membership—a view consistent with a concern about decolonization (Doc. 32, 39). Both Couve, the French foreign minister, and various German officials who were negotiating directly with the French, stated that economics was predominant (Docs. 60, 77, 94). Only Adenauer himself, in defending de Gaulle's motivations to third governments, stressed geopolitics (Doc. 55).

[83] Campbell, *Heath,* 129–130; Lamb, *Macmillan,* 196–197, 202; Horne, *Macmillan,* 2:428; Ziegler, *Wilson,* 334.

[84] de Gaulle, *Memoirs,* 217–220.

the timing of the veto. Having broken with pro-European parties and survived the parliamentary elections of November 1962 with an unexpectedly strong majority, de Gaulle could now afford the criticism an outright veto was sure to generate—a calculus foreseen by the British ambassador and some French officials some months previously.[85]

Only an economic explanation can account, moreover, for the timing and content of shifts in policy toward Britain during the transitions at the beginning and end of de Gaulle's rule. There was little change during either the transition from the Fourth to the Fifth Republic, or the transition from de Gaulle to Pompidou. The satisfaction of agricultural interests was, as we have seen above, a necessary condition for ratification of the Rome Treaty; the Fourth Republic governments, like de Gaulle, were unwilling to negotiate seriously on an FTA, which enjoyed almost no parliamentary support. De Gaulle simply maintained this policy. Commercial concerns also offer the only plausible explanation of the reversal in Gaullist policy, leading to a lifting of the veto at the end of the 1960s. The straightforward explanation is that with the CAP out of the way and British industrial firms posing a much diminished threat to their French counterparts, Gaullist opposition to British membership had become a liability. This transition began under de Gaulle with the proposals for British membership that led to the Soames Affair. And if any other issue did intervene, it was monetary policy, not geopolitics. Nor is it coincidental that in exchange for finally lifting the French veto de Gaulle's hand-picked successor, Georges Pompidou, demanded a single non-negotiable concession, precisely the one that de Gaulle had predicted just before announcing his 1963 veto: namely, prior agreement on a permanent financing arrangement for the CAP. Britain and France became, as internal French and British documents had predicted all along, natural allies. Explanations stressing commercial interest predict this; those based on geopolitical ideas can make no sense of it.

The road to the final episode, the "empty chair" crisis, began when Commission President Walter Hallstein sought to exploit the need for a permanent financing arrangement for the CAP to attain increased Commission and Parliamentary powers. The General immediately understood the tactic—the Commission, he said, was "like a spider seeking to trap France in its net"—and sought to turn it against the Commission.[86] When the negotiations reached a deadline, the French government did not, as it had happened before, continue the search for a compromise solution; instead it withdrew the French permanent representative from Brussels and boycotted any meetings dealing with new EC policies. Why?

The boycott was not a sudden fit of pique on de Gaulle's part, a negotiating tactic to secure agreement on CAP, or a response to specific institutional proposals of the Commission. On the eve of the crisis, Peyrefitte recalls, the French cabinet concluded that French proposals on CAP were close to acceptance and that the Commission was *already* the "big loser." The Commission had witnessed

[85] Peyrefitte, *C'était*, 1:335; Maillard, *De Gaulle,* 184n.; Lacouture, *De Gaulle,* 356–358.
[86] Peyrefitte, *C'était*, 2:281, 594, 620.

the rejection of its "absurd" proposals by almost all governments (not least the Germans) and had been banished from key discussions. No major government supported the Commission. De Gaulle received and rejected a compromise to implement the CAP proposals and reject those of the Commission. Instead the empty chair crisis reflected enduring national interests—"primordial interests," de Gaulle later called them.[87]

Such moves, as we have seen, had been planned for years, first appearing as the backup to the Fouchet Plan in Peyrefitte's strategy document of 1960–61. With the CAP nearly in place, the British veto behind him, and a weak government in Germany, de Gaulle, still following his "prudently audacious" plan of 1960–61, sought advantageous political terrain on which to provoke a conflict over basic institutional prerogatives. In de Gaulle's words, he sought to "profit from the crisis" in order to get "rid of false conceptions . . . that expose us to the dictates of others" and "replace the Commission with something fundamentally different." In internal discussions, de Gaulle announced that his fundamental goals were to strip the Commission of its unique power of proposal, to block the transition to majority voting, and to fire the current Commission. The conflict had been planned through the first half of 1965.[88]

The preponderance of hard evidence suggests the predominance of economic concerns. There is almost no evidence to support the conjecture that the General, disillusioned by the collapse of the Fouchet Plan, suspicious of U.S. proposals for an MLF, and rebuffed by the Erhard government in Germany, suddenly adopted a more "brutal" style of negotiation, which almost led to the collapse of the EC.[89] A subjective interpretation is more plausible: it is of course not entirely false to assert that de Gaulle's willingness to risk electoral embarrassment and diplomatic isolation during the empty chair crisis of 1965–66 demonstrates the predominance of nationalist ideas in his thinking. Yet this is easily exaggerated. De Gaulle failed to achieve most of his visionary ideals due to limits on the credibility of his threats to withdraw from the EC imposed by domestic opposition from producer groups. Foremost among opponents were farmers, whose interests trumped the General's geopolitical goals.

Two types of evidence do support the view that de Gaulle's opposition to supranationalism stemmed in part from his distinctive geopolitical ideas. One is the ambiguity of French material interests. In January 1965 de Gaulle requested an internal government assessment, which concluded that the transition to QMV was unlikely to undermine any vital French interest. The moribund transport policy posed no threat. While QMV in the CAP and GATT might threaten French gains—a point to which we shall return in a moment—it would also place greater pressure on a consistently recalcitrant Germany to accept lower farm prices, an informal German insistence on an exemption in this area notwithstanding. Finally, the overall impact of majority voting was limited because

[87] Peyrefitte, *C'était*, 2:220, 286–93.

[88] Peyrefitte, *C'était*, 1:66–68, 281–282, 289–292, 296; Altiero Spinelli, *The Eurocrats: Conflict and Crisis in the European Community* (Baltimore, 1966), 210–211.

[89] Berstein, *Republic*, 172–173; Camps, *European*, 104–115.

the Treaty in any case retained unanimity for decisions on new policies, Treaty amendments, harmonization of domestic regulations, fiscal and social policy, new sources of Community funding, association agreements, and accession of new members to the EC.

The second sort of evidence for ideological concerns is the strikingly symbolic nature of some of the General's public and private rhetoric on the subject. He contemptuously dismissed the vision of Hallstein, as one analyst put it, "decked out in the trappings of sovereignty," and consistently criticized the very idea of governance above the nation-state. He lashed out even at Commissioners like Robert Marjolin, who had sided with de Gaulle in recent debates. Occasionally— though this was very rare, as compared to the constant references to farming in- terests—de Gaulle explicitly invoked the *grandeur* of France.[90] He may have felt what Hoffmann has described as a vague "determination to prevent . . . a leap into that supranational nirvana where his chances of directly influencing shared European policies might vanish."[91]

The preponderance of evidence nonetheless supports the primacy of com- mercial considerations. This is clearest from de Gaulle's own utterances on the subject. The General was deeply concerned to retain control over votes on CAP financing, GATT negotiations, and any FTA negotiations, which, he consistently complained, might be exploited to undermine carefully negotiated arrange- ments for net EC financial transfers to French farmers.[92] The logic was simple: even with progress through 1964, the CAP was not yet safe from reversal through the combined efforts of the Danish, British, and Americans, working through the GATT. Under such circumstances, the common market would become a li- ability, stripping protection from French farmers; a free trade area would be preferable. This might, de Gaulle feared, permit the "Americans to inundate the European market with their agricultural commodities."[93] France therefore had to maintain control over the process through a veto. This was also the most commonly cited motivation in de Gaulle's speeches and private utterances of the period. By contrast, there appears to be no documentary evidence whatso- ever to support the conjecture advanced by Camps and many others that the boycott stemmed from de Gaulle's anger over Kennedy's proposals for an MLF.[94]

The continuity of policy—the fact that in many ways de Gaulle's insistence on a veto simply maintained the policies of his Fourth Republic predecessors and passed them on to successors—further confirms the primacy of economic mo- tivations. Fourth Republic governments had sought to place stronger veto rights

---

[90] Ménil, *Who,* 154; Peyrefitte, *C'était,* 2:287–291, 297–299. The feeling was mutual: Hallstein was said to have claimed that he "had not seen politics like this since Hitler."

[91] Stanley Hoffmann, "De Gaulle's Foreign Policy," 303. Also Françoise de la Serre, "The Euro- pean Economic Community and the 1965 Crisis," in F. Roy Willis, ed., *European Integration* (New York, 1975), 150; Hoffmann, "Obstinate," 390–391; Charles Pentland, "Political Theories of European Integration: Between Science and Ideology," in D. Lasok and P. Soldatos, eds., *The European Com- munities in Action* (Brussels, 1981), 546–569.

[92] Peyrefitte, *C'était,* 2:255, 294; Lindberg, Leon N. "Integration as a Source of Stress in the Euro- pean Community," in Joseph S. Nye, ed., *International Regionalism* (Boston, 1968), 238.

[93] Peyrefitte, *C'était,* 2:263, also 264–265.

[94] See Jouve and Peyrefitte, *C'était,* passim; cf. Camps, *European.*

in the Treaty of Rome. In December 1957, just after ratification and *before* de Gaulle entered office, a Quai d'Orsay study had already isolated two means of maintaining de facto unanimity voting after the transition to QMV foreseen for 1966. One was a perpetual veto of the transition to the third stage, the other retention of the national veto on essential questions as a precondition for approving the transition. De Gaulle reviewed these studies and considered both options. The first was difficult as, having already moved to the second stage in exchange for an initial framework agreement on the CAP, it would be difficult to retreat entirely to an intergovernmental system. Thus de Gaulle turned to the second option. In this de Gaulle hardly differed from other governments; he was only more open about his goals. Germany had demanded unanimity voting in certain agricultural matters and, ten years later, a prominent EC report revealed that eight of the nine members of the EC, including France, were satisfied with the Luxembourg Compromise.[95]

Most important, *even if* de Gaulle's motivations in provoking the crisis reflected in part his distinctive geopolitical ideas, the decisive constraint on French tactics in the empty chair crisis remained commercial interest, which forced de Gaulle to compromise. Many argue that the Luxembourg Compromise marked a major victory for de Gaulle and a critical turning point in EC history—a moment when the supranational style of decision-making pursued up to 1966 and desired by France's partners was stunted. De Gaulle himself boasted that "the CAP is in place. Hallstein and his Commission have disappeared. Supranationalism is gone. France remains sovereign." Peyrefitte speaks of "the defense of France's national interest coming before electoral interests." This assessment is exaggerated in every respect. De Gaulle won the electoral battle against farmers but in the end conceded on policy.[96] As we shall see, it is striking how *little* of what de Gaulle sought he achieved and thus how little the crisis diverted the longer-term evolution of the EC. It is perhaps only a slight exaggeration to argue that "the value of the Luxembourg agreements lay precisely in the fact that they had no juridical value, that the legal regulations remained intact, and that they did not restrict in any way [the EC's] future evolution and functioning." Integration took other legal forms; when the governments were prepared to move ahead, they simply reinstated QMV. De Gaulle must himself have agreed with this assessment of the outcome, since he continued to advance proposals for fundamental institutional reform, the most important of which gave rise in 1969 to the Soames Affair.[97]

The main reason for de Gaulle's bargaining weakness was not the overwhelming strength of the diplomatic coalition facing him—though the unwillingness of foreign parliaments to ratify treaty changes and the threat to seek an arrange-

[95] Peyrefitte, *C'était*, 2:255; the German government had already set an important precedent on 3 April 1964 by securing Council acquiescence to its unilateral declaration that subsequent changes in cereal prices be decided only by unanimity. The Dutch had insisted on a similar clause for transport.

[96] Peyrefitte, *C'était*, 2:620, 594, also 356–374.

[97] de la Serre, "EEC," 148; Emile Noël, "Some Institutional Aspects of the Crisis of the Communities," Lecture before the International Faculty for the Teaching of Comparative Law (Brussels, 15 September 1966); Rudolf Lahr, "Die Legende vom 'Luxemburger Kompromise,'" *Europa-Archiv* 38:8 (10 January 1983), 223–232.

ment with Britain mattered—but the weakness of domestic support. Opposition stemmed above all from farmers, who rendered incredible any French threat to withdraw from the EC.[98] De Gaulle and his advisers were painfully aware of the political irony. A policy designed in large part to defend farm interests was interpreted by farmers as a threat. He bitterly criticized "demagogues" among agricultural groups; his major priority thereafter was to restore support, in large part through a generous CAP.[99]

In sum, then, the preponderance of evidence concerning each of the four stages in de Gaulle's European strategy—his views toward the customs union and CAP, the Fouchet Plan, the British veto, and the nature of EC institutions— confirms the primacy of economic concerns. Whether de Gaulle ultimately sought welfare or the grandeur of France does not, in the end, matter; either way, as a democratic leader he was constrained to seek the former. As the General himself put it: "Wealth . . . is the principle object of public concern. No government can afford to ignore these realities. The ambition and efficacy of a nation's policies are bound up with [economic] strength. . . . I was to keep economic and social problems continually in the forefront of my actions . . . — which explains, incidentally, why the accusation of indifference to such matters so obstinately leveled against de Gaulle always struck me as absurd."[100]

Germany: Adenauer's Balancing Act

In the 1960s, as had been the case during the negotiation of the Treaty of Rome, Germany was more strongly influenced by geopolitical concerns than either Britain or France. Adenauer supported strong cooperation with France and the Six, as against British proposals for an FTA. Nonetheless, German policy remained closely in line with its economic interests. Germany favored industrial trade liberalization inside Europe and with third countries but sought to block construction of the CAP and a transport policy. Slow progress toward the CAP was ultimately possible only by employing high EC and German subsidies to maintain the income of German farmers. As during the Treaty negotiations, geopolitical concerns entered only on the margin, tipping Germany away from an FTA and in favor of a geographically narrower but substantively and institutionally deeper customs union.

Geopolitical Interest and Ideology: Adenauer Is "scared stiff"

Adenauer, we saw in chapter 2, held a minority, pro-French view within the German foreign policy establishment. Although Germany's basic geopolitical strategy of closer relations with all the occupying powers did not change during this period, Germany's vulnerability to external threats increased during the four-year Berlin crisis ending in 1961. In particular, the possibility that the

---

[98] Peyrefitte, *C'était*, 2:620; Lindberg and Scheingold, *Europe's*, 256; Camps, *European*, 122; John Newhouse, *Collision in Brussels: The Common Market Crisis of 30 June 1965* (New York, 1967), 89–90, 127–134, 151–155. See pp. 221–222, 228–230 of this book.

[99] Peyrefitte, *C'était*, 2:612–13.

[100] De Gaulle, *Memoirs*, 132.

United States would agree to surrender West Berlin, we saw, "scared Adenauer stiff."[101] Because "de Gaulle's unwavering refusal to negotiate under the pressure of ultimatums . . . prevented the Western powers from uniting on a policy of concessions" in Berlin, one historian has written, cooperation with France was further strengthened as the central priority of Adenauer's European policy. Erhard, the Bundestag more generally, and the SPD opposition took more skeptical views of de Gaulle's motivations and of the geopolitical benefits of Franco-German relations.[102]

Although Adenauer enjoyed considerable influence, particularly in foreign policy, the geopolitical views of domestic groups imposed tight constraints on a one-sidedly pro-French policy. No German government could entirely sacrifice relations with the United States and NATO to relations with France. At the same time, the German political class would perceive any complete repudiation of the connection with France as a major foreign policy "failure," and the battles were all on the margin. Neither German "Gaullists" nor German "Atlanticists" had much room to maneuver. The Bundestag would not accept any compromise of the strong connection with NATO and the United States. Adenauer was forced to retract his initially unqualified support for Gaullist proposals such as the Fouchet Plan. The Bundestag, led by Willy Brandt over Adenauer's vehement opposition, imposed a preamble on the Franco-German Treaty of 1963 reaffirming support for both the EC and NATO.

Yet Adenauer persisted. Many have concluded that his pro-French policy, taken to the extreme in the Franco-German Treaty, was "simply not rational foreign policy."[103] At some risk to his party's electoral viability, Adenauer fought back and fended off efforts to replace him with Erhard by calling attention to Erhard's supposed lack of foreign policy experience, in particular his skepticism about European integration. When Adenauer finally stepped down in 1963, he, Strauss, and other so-called German Gaullists continued to criticize Erhard. As chancellor, Erhard and his foreign ministers supported French troop withdrawals from Germany, yet avoided any outright break with France, which would surely have provoked widespread criticism.[104]

---

[101] Herbert Blankenhorn, *Verständnis und Verständigung: Blätter eines politischen Tagesbuchs* (Frankfurt, 1980), 148ff.

[102] Gordon Craig, "Konrad Adenauer and His Diplomats," in Gordon Craig and Francis L. Lowenheim, eds., *The Diplomats, 1939–1979* (Princeton, 1994), 215, also 217–218. For a contrary view, namely that Germany's power stemmed from the German reunification potion, which was then undermined by the Berlin crisis, see Sabine Lee, "Die zweite Berlinkrise: Deutsche-britische Beziehungen und die Neudefinierung internationaler Beziehungen," in Gustave Schmidt, ed., *Zwischen Bundnissicherung und privilegierter Partnerschaft* (Bochum, 1995), 81–140.

[103] Craig ("Konrad Adenauer," 220) follows even sympathetic biographers like Schwarz and Adenauer's associate, Blankenhorn. Perhaps, he speculates, it was "a malicious attempt to undercut the Atlanticist policy of Ludwig Erhard, his putative successor, and to saddle him with a policy he could not sustain."

[104] Koerfer, *Kampf*, 135; Gabriele Brenke, "Europakonzeptionen im Widerstreit: Die Freihandelszonen-Verhaudlungen, 1956–1958," *Vierteljahreshefte für Zeitgeschichte* 42:4 (October 1994), 606–625; Arnold Heidenheimer, *Adenauer and the CDU: The Rise of a Leader and the Integration of the Party* (The Hague, 1960), 226–229; Wolfgang Dexheimer, *Koalitionsverhandlungen in Bonn: 1961, 1965, 1969* (Bonn, 1973), 52ff.

„Ich esse meine Suppe nicht – nein, meine Suppe ess' ich nicht!"

"I won't eat my soup. Won't, won't, won't!"
Germany refuses to accept French "agricultural integration."
Cartoon by Felix Mussil. *Frankfurter Rundschau*, 2 December 1961.

Economic Interest: Industrial Support and Agricultural Skepticism

The interests of German producers changed very little between 1957 and the 1960s—hence we need only review the structural conditions outlined in greater detail in chapter 2. Although most big business preferred an FTA, organized business in Germany continued to support the EC. Erhard repeatedly tried to convince Adenauer to press France on the FTA and British membership—goals for which the economics minister repeatedly declared himself willing to sacrifice the EC. As in 1957, such efforts were backed by the FDP, small parts of the CDU, and many businesspeople, but not the BDI, still led by Fritz Berg. Berg's group remained officially neutral on the FTA and continued to support Adenauer's pro-French policy, going so far as to rebut Erhard's arguments in public.[105] On other issues, economic interests remained stable as well: sectoral interests continued to oppose cooperation on atomic energy and transport while maintaining a strong commitment to multilateral tariff reductions in the GATT.

Berg's close relations with Adenauer surely played some role, as did political sympathies with the CDU and with European integration. He and other business

[105] Brenke, "Europakonzeptionen," 625.

leaders freely admitted that geopolitical concerns blunted economic objectives. We see tension in a rare breakdown of BDI discipline in 1959, when chemicals and automobile producers circumvented the peak organization and went directly to Adenauer to plead the FTA case.[106] When Erhard replaced Adenauer, Berg announced that the BDI position had become easier. Yet three economic considerations were also important.[107] First, many in business thought the FTA and EEC were compatible; they shared the view of Erhard and his associate Alfred Müller-Armack, who believed de Gaulle could be compelled to accept EFTA expansion or British entry in exchange for the CAP.[108] Second, France had reformed itself economically, providing substantial opportunities for German producers. Berg referred to the 1958–59 reforms shortly after their promulgation as "the most important event . . . in the economic domain since the end of the war" because it reduced the opportunities for French unilateral protectionism.[109] Third, the negative trade effects for exports to EFTA countries predicted by Erhard were modest; to be sure, EFTA trade grew more slowly than EEC trade, but the increase was substantial and the German trade surplus widened. Exports to the EC rose by 324 percent, exports to the EFTA countries by 223 percent. All this meant that, on balance, German business had only a modest incentive to trade the EEC for the FTA and might have faced new risks.[110]

German farmers continued to remain wary of any CAP arrangement that failed to maintain farm incomes, and domestic positions reflected the relative efficiency and competitiveness of producers. As policy proposals became more specific and the costs and benefits more concrete, domestic groups mobilized and the government found itself more constrained. Germany, with high price supports and large net imports, sought to delay liberalization and retain national quota and price systems as long as possible, along with special bilateral arrangements with certain outside importers, notably Denmark. It demanded "equalization of competitive conditions" before any liberalizing measures be taken. A minimal system of optional long-term contracts would have suited German farmers. The power of farm groups was considerable. During the 1950s they had succeeded in securing high, stable subsidization—not least because of the voting power of small farmers in key regions like Bavaria. Moreover, they were widely believed to control the Agriculture Ministry. Erhard and Adenauer consulted regularly with the main farm group, the Deutsche Bauernverband.

Germany would therefore veto any agricultural cooperation without high

---

[106] Gerhard Braunthal, *The Federation of German Industry in Politics* (Ithaca, 1965), 317ff.

[107] Markus Schulte, "Challenging the Common Market Project: German Industry, Britain and Europe, 1956–1963" (paper presented at Oxford University, 22 March 1996), 4–5.

[108] There was little business criticism when the government took the "Bad Kreuznach" decision to end negotiations with the EFTA countries and to move to tariff cutting ahead of schedule. Alfred Müller-Armack, "Politische Führung und Wirtschaftspolitik: Adenauer, die Wirtschaftspolitik und die Wirtschaftspolitiker," *Die Politische Meinung* 20 (1975), 77, cited in Carl Lankowski, "Germany and the European Communities: Anatomy of a Hegemonial Relation" (Ph.D. diss., Columbia University, 1982), 177.

[109] Jeffrey Vanke, "Evolving Expectations, the Emergence of the European Economic Community, and the Foundation of the Pax Europa, 1955–1967" (Harvard University, unpublished paper, 1997), 12.

[110] Schulte, "Challenging," 4–5.

Table 3.2. Relative agricultural prices in EEC countries, 1958–1959

Commodity	Germany	France	Netherlands
Wheat	109.4	74.9	83.0
Sugar	122.3	81.5	99.1
Milk	101.6	92.1	97.8
Beef	101.3	87.8	101.8
Pork	110.0	93.7	90.4
Eggs	109.4	89.8	73.2

NOTE: EEC Average = 100.
SOURCE: Edmund Neville-Rolfe, *The Policies of Agriculture in the European Community* (London, 1984), 500.

support prices. For every major commodity, German prices in 1958–59 lay above the EEC average, whereas those of France and (except in beef) the Netherlands lay below it. The greatest differential existed in cereals, which, however, totaled only 10 percent of German agricultural production; dairy and meat producers were more influential. Although the German government had for some time been seeking to move farmers out of cereal production into high value-added products, a committee of agricultural economists nominated by Germany and the Commission concluded that proposals to harmonize prices at the median level of national prices would cost German farmers some DM1.3 billion annually.[111] Adenauer could compromise some economic interests in order to strengthen the Franco-German relationship, but he could not compromise the core interest of farmers in high support prices.

The Domestic Decision:
From German Gaullism to "Synchronization"

Just as the underlying economic and geopolitical circumstances had changed little since the Treaty of Rome negotiations considered in chapter 2, so German policy on most EEC issues remained essentially unchanged. Germany continued strongly to support internal and external tariff liberalization, resist agricultural liberalization at anything below the German price level, reject atomic energy and transport policies, distance itself from foreign policy cooperation outside NATO, and resist the de jure Treaty changes proposed by de Gaulle in 1965 to weaken supranationalism (though quietly accepting their substance).

Backed by business, the German government strongly supported industrial tariff reductions in Europe and in the GATT. As he had in the Treaty negotiations, Adenauer exploited strong business support to pursue the customs union rather than the FTA. Germany, uncompetitive in transport services, opposed any liberalization measures. In agriculture, German leaders were constrained most fundamentally by pressure from farmers. Plans were continually discussed

[111] Camps, *Europe,* 16; Lindberg, *Political,* 244; Ernst Freisberg, *Die Grüne Hürde Europas. Deutsche Agrarpolitik und EWG* (Cologne, 1965), 132–135, 141–143, 148–150; Gisela Hendriks, "The Creation of the Common Agricultural Policy" (Paper presented at Oxford University, 22 March 1996), 16.

with Edmund Rehwinkel, head of the German farm lobby. Germany, seeking to defend its high-price domestic regimes, saw little advantage in the CAP, which, it was assumed, would reduce domestic support prices and, for the Germans, replace important bilateral quota arrangements with third countries, particularly in Scandinavia. Germany sought to delay and dilute any resolution of the negotiations, as well as the implementation of international obligations to liberalize. German officials backed existing quotas and bilateral arrangements with third countries. Under Treaty of Rome provisions for large bilateral contracts, only one small commodity contract was concluded between France and Germany. In 1959 a "war of eggs" erupted when Dutch eggs were blocked from entering Germany through regulation of their date of freshness—an event that helped turned the Dutch against long-term contracts and toward a centralized CAP.[112] German leaders who favored integration had only two choices: retain the current system or replace it with equally high European prices. No reduction in support prices was possible without full compensation. Even cooperation in constructing a CAP with high prices was possible only under direct threats from France.

Adenauer sought to exploit his power as chief executive to divert policy in a pro-French direction, for example meeting de Gaulle at Colombey in 1958 to pledge support for a French veto of the FTA. Even if he had been so inclined, however, Adenauer could not have pursued a truly Gaullist line with respect to NATO and the United States. Specific proposals stimulated successful opposition from within the CDU, as well as the SPD and FDP—most notably in the case of the Franco-German Treaty, which the Bundestag amended to include references to the EC and NATO.

When Erhard was named to succeed Adenauer as chancellor in April 1963, he chose Gerhardt Schröder, an Atlanticist, as his foreign minister and continued to question the priority of the Franco-German relationship. These two men may well have preferred to abrogate the Treaty and pursue FTA or GATT liberalization instead. Yet they were blocked by Adenauer and his allies, including Franz-Josef Strauss, the powerful Bavarian politician, who criticized Erhard's policies, calling for activation of the Franco-German Treaty clauses on political cooperation, which Erhard initially ignored. Erhard's faction finally won a decisive showdown within the party's executive committee, but victory did not allow him to repudiate close relations with France, block implementation of the Treaty, or threaten France to reopen talks on British membership, much though he and Schröder might have liked to. Both security and economic arguments for integration remained strong, and Erhard was under domestic pressure to demonstrate strong foreign policy leadership in a country where integration remained popular. Hence he actively promoted political cooperation and consistently participated in ongoing EEC agricultural negotiations, subject to linkage with movement in the Kennedy Round of the GATT. Hence the shift from Adenauer

---

[112] François Duchêne, Edward Szczepanik, and Wilfrid Legg, *New Limits on European Agriculture: Politics and the Common Agricultural Policy* (London, 1985), 27; Robert de Bruin, "Le Pays Bas et l'integration européenne 1957–1967" (Ph.D. diss., Institut d'Etudes Politiques de Paris, 1978), 426, 486, 497–506, 639–641; Edmund Neville-Rolfe, *The Politics of Agriculture in the European Community* (London, 1984), 206ff.

to Erhard changed the style but not the substance of German policy. Schröder advanced the concept of "synchronization" of policies: "We should equalize as far as possible the advantages and disadvantages of the measures of the Community as applied to the separate member states. We cannot embark on a system of advance concessions to be made notably by those countries which have already made considerable concessions up to now." Some prominent Germans also believed that if price alignment were postponed long enough, differential inflation would solve the problem by forcing the French to align their prices to prevailing German levels.[113]

During the empty chair crisis, which occurred once Erhard had won a strong electoral victory, he pressed de Gaulle hard, eventually threatening to discuss membership with Britain. Yet even he did not threaten dissolution of the EC. During the crisis the Erhard government organized the Five in defense of the Rome Treaty's QMV provisions, despite a lukewarm attitude toward pooling and delegation. In public Erhard and Schröder maintained appearances, but in private they opposed the Commission proposals for more centralization and appear to have preferred stronger intergovernmental procedures within the Council rather than grant increased power to the Commission in other areas.[114] Marjolin's testimony on underlying support for the Luxembourg Compromise a decade later is telling:

> Whatever certain of [the Five] might be led to say in order to gain the support of parliamentary opinion, [they] did not want the majority vote any more than the French government. . . . Thirteen or fourteen years later when, as part of a task force to investigate a reform of the Community's institutions, I had to talk with the delegations of the member governments, which had increased from six to nine, [none] wanted reestablishment of the majority vote for settling a question that was considered, even by just one government, to be of major importance. A few of them simply asked . . . that the unanimity rule should not . . . be insisted upon when it . . . did not involve a very important interest.[115]

German efforts to impose stronger institutional commitments were limited to those areas, notably foreign trade and competition policy, where more intensive compliance and implementation served its interests.

Shortly thereafter, faced with economic recession, a military scandal, and opposition from the German Gaullists, Erhard was overthrown by his own party and replaced with Kurt Kiesinger at the head of a "grand coalition" of CDU and SPD. Although Kiesinger had been CDU foreign policy spokesman on European matters and favored the Franco-German relationship, little changed in German policy, which remained opposed to French goals but unwilling to make a break. In October 1967 the Germans proposed a new synchronization, link-

[113] Haas, "Technocracy," 77. Also Willis, *France,* 328–332; Camps, *European,* 8–9, 17; Freisberg, *Grüne,* 132–133, 156–158; Camps, *What,* 47–49, 54; Sabine Lee, "Germany and the First Enlargement Negotiations 1961–1963" (paper presented at Oxford University, 22 March 1996), 16.
[114] Newhouse, *Crisis,* 68.
[115] Marjolin, *Architect,* 356.

ing the entrance of new members, fusion of the EC, ECSC, and Euratom treaties, and reinforcement of internal procedures. Despite harsh criticism from the Bundestag, in particular from the SPD, de Gaulle's second veto of British entry went unanswered.

National Preferences: The Primacy of Commercial Interests

The evidence strongly supports the view that commercial interests, not geopolitics, comprised the primary source of national preferences in this period. We have seen that within issue-areas, cleavages formed along similar lines, with business internally split by relative competitiveness. As we have seen, the key arguments in each country were economic not geopolitical—even in France, despite de Gaulle's efforts to legitimate policy geopolitically. EC policy was more consistent with broad foreign economic policies than with politico-military policies: the pursuit of commercial advantage sometimes threatened concurrent geopolitical concerns, such as the Western alliance for Britain and an Anglo-French alliance against supranational institutions. Finally, some conventional arguments for the importance of geopolitical factors—notably the claim that de Gaulle vetoed Britain due to the Nassau deal—are countered by the timing of decisions. As the economic theory predicts, national positions varied by issue, not country, according to the varying competitiveness of national producers rather than geopolitical concerns. France strongly promoted the CAP, supported internal trade liberalization, cautiously permitted external tariff liberalization, and opposed transport policy and the free trade area. Germany strongly supported internal and external trade liberalization, including the free trade area, promoted an EC competition policy modeled on its own, opposed the CAP unless with very high prices, and rejected the transport policy. Britain opposed the CAP, strongly supported external openness, and cautiously supported internal tariff liberalization. The relative position of national preferences remained relatively stable, though their intensity shifted over time in response to the intra-industry trade boom of the 1950s and 1960s and, in France, more rapidly in response to de Gaulle's economic reforms. No government favored social or monetary cooperation.

Pressures from farmers were the most powerful. Even de Gaulle's central ideological goal, the destruction of supranational institutions, was strictly subordinate to economic interests. Farmers were also powerful in Germany, but Adenauer and Erhard could satisfy demands of their farmers with subsidies; the costs fell on unorganized groups, such as taxpayers and third-country producers, and created new export opportunities in the long run. In Britain farmers were much weaker. Macmillan was prepared to override their doubts about the EC, though in the end they supported membership, based largely on the likely level of EC price supports.

The preferences of industry imposed broader constraints. German industry favored both the FTA and the EC, granting Adenauer room to pursue a pro-French policy that Erhard could not fully reverse. In Britain industry favored the FTA but was split over the EC. In France business was split but became enthusiastic about internal market liberalization after devaluation; it came more slowly to accept external openness. On this issue de Gaulle remained more rigid. Perhaps geopolitical ideology led Macmillan to press the issue more quickly than business groups demanded, yet business support also proved stronger than Macmillan had expected. As soon as the government announced its policy, larger, more competitive firms prevailed in domestic debates. By 1961 British officials still feared agricultural groups but were concerned that business groups might punish the government for not moving forward on membership.

I do not rule out geopolitical motivations altogether. Adenauer's choice of the EC over the FTA, de Gaulle's support for more intergovernmental institutions, and perhaps Macmillan's speed in moving toward membership, as well as the constraints he faced in offering nuclear linkages, were surely influenced by geopolitics and ideology. Yet overall, geopolitical ideology remained secondary, entering national calculations only where commercial interests were diffuse, weak, or uncertain. Yet economic inteiests appear sufficient, except in the case of Germany, to explain the policies chosen.

INTERSTATE BARGAINING AND INSTITUTIONAL CHOICES

The EC evolved from 1958 through 1968 through four sets of negotiations. These focused respectively on internal and external tariff liberalization; sectoral and regulatory policies governing agriculture, atomic energy, transport, and competition (antitrust); British accession; and institutional reform. Studies of this period agree almost without exception on the decisive importance of European Commission officials such as Hallstein and Mansholt in consolidating the CAP. For neofunctionalists, commentators, and even skeptics such as Stanley Hoffmann, the period from 1958 through 1966 marked the apogee of successful Commission policy entrepreneurship; it would have continued in the same vein, had Gaullist high politics and the Luxembourg Compromise not interceded. Commission leadership was exercised through the provision of policy initiatives, expertise, mediation, and mobilization that "upgraded the common interest." Such leadership was a necessary condition for the success of the EC in this period.

The historical record decisively disconfirms this view. Information and ideas were plentiful; at no time was there a shortage of policy initiatives, mediators, and social mobilization. The Commission's supranational entrepreneurship was thus generally redundant, often futile, and sometimes even counterproductive. Negotiations were efficient even without supranational involvement. The Commission was successful only when it was pursuing the policies that were emerging from Franco-German discussions. When the Commission failed to conform to their consensus—and sometimes even when it did—governments easily assumed leadership. The result of the Commission's lack of a monopoly on leadership functions and its sometimes technocratic economic objectives was that it lost most major distributive conflicts. Major policies of the EC in this period, most notably the closed, high-priced, comprehensive, and administratively decentralized agricultural policy, were the precise opposite of what the Commission had sought. Distributive outcomes reflected instead the pattern and relative intensity of national preferences. Where governments intensely sought certain policies, as with France on the CAP and Germany on industrial tariff liberalization, they offered concessions and compromises to realize them. Threats of exclusion and exit were effective to the extent they were credible. Cross-issue linkages were limited to the balancing of gains; most concessions were within, not across, issues—all as predicted by intergovernmental bargaining theory. To see how and why the outcomes emerged, we turn now to the negotiation. "The Devil," as Commission President Walter Hallstein was fond of saying, "is in the details."[116]

Harmonizing Internal and External Tariff Policy: Convergent Interests and Acceleration

The creation of an industrial customs union required removal of internal tariffs, harmonization of external tariffs, and a common commercial policy for negotiating with third parties. The first two generated little conflict. The last, due to the threat it posed to French agriculture, was more controversial.

Implementation of internal tariff liberalization according to the Treaty's twelve- to fifteen-year transition schedule proved unproblematic. The Commission's power of proposal counted for little; many governments advanced proposals to accelerate internal tariff removal. There was no outright opposition: Germany was complying unilaterally, and the Benelux countries already had low tariffs. With de Gaulle's reforms, the French position became enthusiastic, simultaneously going far beyond the demands of the Treaty in the area of quota removal—in part to reap profits, in part to head off any FTA. France nonetheless sought to exploit Germany's more intense support for liberalization to secure the CAP. Hence the Commission's proposal for a legally binding agreement to complete the Common Market by 1966 was rejected in favor of a French proposal linking a two-year acceleration to a schedule for adoption of the CAP. In response the Commission abandoned its earlier position and adopted the French one: internal tariffs were to be reduced in the first phase by 50 percent, rather than 30 percent stipulated in the Treaty, and the common external tariff was to be introduced in 1960, six months earlier than planned. The member states added a 20 percent external tariff reduction proposed by the Dutch. In May 1960 the Council of Ministers approved this package; each of the Six complied even in the midst of the 1965 crisis. The last tariffs disappeared on 1 July 1968, eighteen months before the date mandated by the Treaty.[117]

---

[116] Walter Hallstein, *Europe in the Making* (London, 1972), 110.

[117] Lindberg, *Political*, 167–205; Wolfram Hanrieder, *West German Foreign Policy, 1949–1963: International Pressure and Domestic Response* (Stanford, 1967), 167; Hans von der Groeben, *The European Community: The Formative Years* (Luxembourg, 1987), 102. The speed of tariff reduction is sometimes attributed to clear deadlines and detailed policies set forth in the Treaty; this is unlikely, since provisions for safeguards, exceptions, and delays were equally explicit and the drafters of the Treaty in fact expected them to be invoked.

The Treaty of Rome had set levels for the common external tariff for 85 percent of third-country imports by simply averaging the tariffs of Germany, France, Italy, and Benelux. The remaining 15 percent of imports were placed on a list of seventy exemptions from the averaging procedure, called List G; it was soon expanded by 114 new items. France and Italy generally sought to raise tariffs on List G items, whereas Germany, the Netherlands, and the Commission tended to seek lower tariffs, particularly intermediate goods and raw materials. Both sides had an incentive to compromise, the French to prevent a potential FTA, the Germans to participate in GATT negotiations.

Under strong governmental pressure the Commission moved quickly, calling a meeting of national experts in January 1959, assembling information on the tariffs of all member-states, and proposing a negotiating procedure. The Commission did not have a right of proposal in this area and was permitted to chair only on the express condition that it recognize that the responsibility for the negotiations and the decisions rested entirely with the national governments. Even this modest Commission role proved ineffective. By December 1959 agreement had been reached on only twenty-nine products. France and others rejected Commission proposals to close List G and impose across-the-board tariff reductions, turning the negotiations over to the Council of Ministers instead. The Council reached agreement on almost all remaining items within three months. In the first meeting the Commission identified some of the easier products to resolve; thereafter meetings were prepared by the member-states in the intergovernmental Committee on Permanent Representatives (COREPER). National ministers themselves, meeting without national officials, took the most delicate decisions. Agreement on controversial items generally involved either accepting higher protection for the EEC as a whole or permitting exemptions.[118]

The existence of common third-country tariffs necessitated a common policy, as provided for in Articles 110–116 of the Treaty, to conduct multilateral tariff negotiations. Here there was greater conflict in underlying national preferences. To be sure, France initially sought rapid development of a common policy to block Erhard from opening conducting negotiations with EFTA, and Adenauer went along. Once de Gaulle had vetoed the FTA, however, the need to conduct GATT negotiations arose—a matter that brought significant risks for French farm policy, particularly with the CAP only half-implemented. France thus became more demanding. France and the Netherlands held up the EC's mandate for Kennedy Round of GATT negotiations to force German concessions on the CAP; by mid-1963 the Erhard government resigned itself to the linkage, coining the awkward term "synchronization" to describe it. Others spoke of "package deals" that had to include something for every country. The Commission (despite neofunctionalist claims to the contrary) initially opposed such linkages but

---

[118] Camps, *What*, 16–20, 38–39; Lindberg, *Political*, 215; Thomas Rhenisch, "Die Deutsche Industrie und die Gründung der Europäischen Wirtschaftsgemeinschaft" (diss., EUI, 1994), 236–237; Lindberg, *Political*, 197, 206, 212–217. Many existing national quotas with respect to third countries were retained, meaning that such quotas—including Italian and French limits on the importation of Japanese cars—survived into the late 1980s.

was forced to accept them. Only in 1966, after having achieved agricultural price agreements and a considerable measure of industrial modernization, as well as retention of unanimity voting, which protected the CAP, did France finally permit the EC to negotiate seriously in the Kennedy Round, whereupon negotiations were concluded in little more than a year.[119]

During the GATT negotiations, the Commission, which represented the EC in Geneva, repeatedly sought greater autonomy—a move supported by Germany because it was seen as promoting free trade. By contrast, France sought to maintain tight member-state control over the list of "exceptions" (items to be exempted from general tariff reductions or to be negotiated individually at the GATT) and the setting of the Commission's negotiating mandate in Geneva. Although France finally accepted a short list of exceptions as part of a CAP deal with Germany, it insisted on a mandate that left the Commission very little discretion. Hence the Commission often had to wait for necessary renewal or renegotiation of its mandate and was closely overseen during negotiations by the 113 Committee—an oversight committee of governments functioning by unanimity. The French policy was successful: industrial tariff liberalization was extensive, but agriculture remained the one area in which U.S. officials considered the Round a failure. Later in the 1960s the EC began negotiating even further industrial tariff reductions with the seven EFTA countries. In industrial trade, the *Economist* observed, the Common Market in the early 1970s looked "more like an enlargement of the relatively free-trading Germany of Professor Erhard than . . . the protectionist France or Italy of the pre-Common Market days." Yet in agriculture, to which we now turn, protection remained high.[120]

The Common Agricultural Policy: A "straight defeat" for the Commission

While national preferences in industrial tariff removal converged among the Six, permitting smooth negotiations, preferences concerning the CAP were far more conflictual. Accordingly, the CAP accounted for the bulk of the Council's negotiating time in the 1960s and for 95 percent of EC expenditures by the end of the period. Five years were required to agree on a general structure and between seven and twelve, depending on the commodity, to establish specific prices and financing arrangements.

The long delays stemmed from deep conflicts among the member governments, the same conflicts that had prevented the drafters of the Treaty from specifying CAP provisions precisely. In 1958 it was far from obvious that the CAP would emerge at all, let alone what form it would take. The Treaty mandated

[119] Lindberg, *Political*, 196–197; Hallstein, *Uniting*, 66; Camps, *What*, 5–6, 16–20, 32–34, 64, 69–71; Freisberg, *Grüne*, 120; von der Groeben, *European*, 99; Willis, *France*, 337.

[120] David Coombes, *Politics and Bureaucracy in the European Community: A Portrait of the Commission of the EEC* (London, 1970), 170, also 178, 191–197; Prate, *Batailles*, 222–223. The exceptional moments of autonomy were minor. At the very end of the negotiations, the Commission representative appears to have taken initiatives on chemicals, food aid, tobacco tariffs, and self-sufficiency ratios in agriculture and a few other matters. Most, though not all, of these bargains were subsequently confirmed by the Council.

that member-states establish free trade, protection against third countries, centralized financial provisions, and harmonization of national support prices. Variable levies—tariffs calculated as the difference between the current world market price and a specified minimum price—on agricultural imports into the Community, and a corresponding set of export subsidies permitting European farmers to export at world market prices, would bridge the CAP to global markets. An EEC "market organization" would have a mandate to provide technical aid, assist with storage, regulate imports and exports, and above all oversee a "minimum price system."

Yet the Treaty remained vague on details. Five critical issues divided the Six: whether to create a unified system at all; the level of prices; the scope of coverage; incentives for structural adjustment; and whether to centralize oversight and implementation in the Commission. The market organization might have remained a minimalist system of rules, setting a common price for long-term commodities contracts, as foreseen for the transition period. Such an outcome, had it extended to significant proportions of European commodities, might well have been satisfactory to the major beneficiaries of the policy, namely France and the Netherlands. Or the CAP might have become a centralized European organization, establishing low prices, permitting minimal coverage, and encouraging structural adjustment while granting the Commission substantial decision-making power, as the Commission itself proposed. Or it could have become a system to coordinate intergovernmental prices and liberalization among decentralized national policies with high prices, broad coverage, common financing, but cumbersome intergovernmental decision-making, which is what eventually emerged. The role of national quota and subsidy policies remained similarly unclear: would they be preempted entirely by the new system? The final and most important step was the setting of support prices for individual commodities: with differences of 30–50 percent across the Six, prices would determine which national producers prospered and which failed.

In contrast to internal tariff reductions, all of these issues had to be resolved by unanimity vote with no right of proposal for the Commission. This requirement placed recalcitrant governments in a strong position. The issues divided member governments into three groups. The first contained Italy, convinced of the competitiveness of its fruit and vegetable producers, and the Netherlands, with its efficient, high-value-added production. Both were liberalizers: they advocated rapid liberalization even before prices were harmonized and low support prices, limited scope, modest external protection, structural adjustment policies to eliminate uncompetitive producers, and centralization of authority in the hands of the Commission. Germany and Belgium were protectionist: these two countries exported little and opposed any move toward liberalization without prior harmonization of underlying conditions, preferring to maintain discretion to negotiate bilateral arrangements. If there was to be liberalization, it must be accompanied by high support prices and decentralized, only modest structural adjustment policies and flexible administration. France, with nearly 50 percent of the arable land in the Six, found itself between these two groups: it demanded preferential access to the German market for its agricultural goods, along with moderately high prices and external protection.[121] France sought moderate prices and generous export promotion. France sought the minimum amount of centralization necessary to bind the others; it might have been satisfied with long-term contracts, if they had worked, but eventually sought to centralize financing and control over external trade policy. All countries favored continued national discretion over additional subsidies, which preserved the corporatist relations between governments and national farm groups.

The Commission unquestioningly backed the liberal Dutch-Italian position. Sicco Mansholt, EC agriculture commissioner from 1958 though 1970 and a former Dutch minister of agriculture, favored a system favorable to consumers and efficient producers, and open to the outside world. (This had also been the position of Monnet's associate Pierre Uri in the Treaty negotiations.) He vehemently criticized existing "one-sided" systems of "support for prices and markets [that] easily favor overproduction." He reiterated the preeminent importance of an open, market-driven policy, in which "lowering production costs is . . . *an essential factor,*" lest surpluses develop, burdening the system with excessive costs.[122] Supply and demand should be regulated by market price, with state intervention only a temporary safeguard against adverse market conditions. Such an outcome would be possible, Mansholt believed, only if the potential for logrolling among the member-states were limited—which led him to advocate a system of strictly limited subsidies administered independently by the Commission.

The outcome, however, was the opposite: a system of high support prices and external protection at close to the German level, broad coverage eventually extending to 95 percent of EC agricultural production, few incentives for structural adjustment, and decentralized control exercised by the Council. Agriculture, in which farm groups had extremely intense preferences and domination over domestic policy-making, proved resistant to rationalization or even extensive linkage, as favored by the Commission. Instead, it was an area ripe for intergovernmental logrolling, in which national agriculture ministries sought to avoid imposing costs on one another. Efforts to create a CAP were led by those with the greatest interest in doing so, notably France and the Netherlands; Germany was hardly less interested in defending itself. Hence, as intergovernmental theory predicts, the Commission played an active role in the negotiations, but it was not a unique provider of critical information or ideas. Its policy initiatives, expertise, mediation, and mobilization were ineffective or redundant if not counterproductive. Governments could and did fulfill these functions

---

[121] Later in the 1960s, however, unexpectedly rapid growth turned Italy into a net importer of grain and a net debtor to the common fund, while its comparative advantage in fruits and vegetables did not emerge as expected. Hence Italian preferences shifted: after 1963, when prices and financing were discussed, the Italian government began to demand more interventionist policies in its areas of comparative advantage, including products, such as olives, not previously covered.

[122] Joan Pearce, "The Common Agricultural Policy: The Accumulation of Special Interests," in Helen Wallace, William Wallace, and Carole Webb, eds., *Policy-Making in the European Community*, 2d ed. (Chichester, 1983), 149; also Lindberg, *Political*, 243, 264; Institut, *De Gaulle*, 5:180.

whenever interests dictated they do so. Hence the CAP that emerged was a mirror image of the one Mansholt and the Commission sought.

The process was slow. Early efforts by the Commission and national governments to create the CAP failed. A conference at Stresa in July 1958, attended by national delegations of agricultural officials and interest group representatives, generated a Commission report based on discussions chaired by the French, German, and Italian ministers of agriculture. Two Commission proposals and a ringing appeal by Mansholt for greater balance between agricultural and consumer interests elicited only a reiteration of national positions and a final resolution that restated the contradictory goals in the Treaty itself—preservation of family farming, increasing returns to capital and labor in agriculture, greater trade, and the maintenance of a balance between supply and demand.[123]

By 1960 the Dutch and French had grown disillusioned with transitional measures for bilateral long-term contracts with Germany for sales of wheat, sugar, eggs, and dairy products at supported prices. This arrangement might perhaps have become permanent if it had realized key national goals, but German agricultural officials fully exploited their discretion to obstruct bilateral agreements with EC members while preserving existing ones with nonmembers such as Denmark. Piecemeal bilateral harmonization, the French and Dutch concluded, would require detailed negotiations taking far longer than the twelve years foreseen by the Treaty and would preserve many opportunities for indirect protection. Accordingly, they declared in May 1960, any decision to accelerate industrial tariff liberalization would henceforth be linked to a firm schedule for establishing the CAP, starting with the replacement of third-country bilateral quotas with levies. Following explicit veto threats, the Council instructed the Commission to develop proposals, as foreseen in the Treaty, for a more centralized system.[124]

After extensive meetings with experts from national governments and interest groups the Commission presented a 300-page document known as the Mansholt Plan. It proposed a system of variable levies and support prices, as per the Treaty's mandate. More controversial was Mansholt's own contribution. He argued that an efficient, pro-consumer CAP required strict constraints and a centralization of discretionary authority in the Commission to prevent logrolling among member-states. Hence the Council, acting by QMV, would be permitted only to approve broad *criteria* for support prices and variable levies, which would be set by the Commission, subject only to a unanimous Council veto. Each product market would be required to be self-financing, with farmers themselves forced to pay for the disposal of any commodity surpluses. Only a limited number of commodities, totaling 65 percent of EC production, would be included, and of those many would not be eligible for price supports. Finally, the Commission would administer the system, supplanting direct corporatist interaction between

[123] Michael Tracy, "The Spirit of Stresa," *European Review of Agricultural Economics* 21 (Autumn 1994), 357–361.
[124] von der Groeben, *European,* 70–80; Lindberg, *Political,* 247, 271; Freisberg, *Grüne,* 64–66.

national farm groups and their governments. The Commission would also administer a structural adjustment program—Mansholt proposed that it total one-third of EC agricultural resources—to assist smaller, technologically backward, high-cost producers to leave the land and thereby increase productivity. Such a program would preempt all direct national subsidies to agriculture.[125]

National governments, led by agriculture ministers, immediately rejected the Mansholt Plan and reasserted their own collective authority. They created a Special Committee on Agriculture within the Council to represent agriculture ministries. In December 1960, after the French and Dutch had reasserted the linkage between proposals to transform quotas into levies and progress in the GATT, the Council approved a Special Committee report that contained a revised version of the Commission's general proposal for a system of variable levies but ignored Mansholt's proposals for Commission control and more liberal policies. They began to set their own deadlines for decisions and fashion linkages between issues, ignoring Commission pressure.[126]

The Council began by requesting new Commission proposals on specific commodities. During the next three years, Germany consistently withheld support for more detailed programs for specific commodities, whereas France and the Netherlands responded with threats to disrupt industrial trade liberalization if the CAP failed to progress. As each decision to implement the CAP neared, governments escalated their threats. France and the Netherlands first threatened to block agreement on the 10 percent tariff cut, then to veto the move to the second stage of the transition period, to obstruct industrial tariff removal, to deny a negotiating mandate for the Kennedy Round of GATT negotiations, and finally, in the French case, to pull out of the EC altogether—all of this culminating in a walk-out by French agriculture minister Pisani in December 1963, complaining about the persistence of German bilateral quotas.[127]

Germany backed down slowly, each time extracting a quid pro quo. All knew that the imposition of major adjustment costs on German agriculture was electoral suicide; hence the German government's veto threats were credible. On 14 January 1962, after what Hallstein famously described as "137 hours of discussion, with 214 hours in sub-committee; 582,000 pages of documents; 3 heart attacks"—Germany consented to give legal effect to the CAP. The clock was "stopped" for two weeks and the conclusions backdated to meet the symbolic 31 December 1961 deadline. The Commission made no significant new proposals, though it advanced some compromises among national positions.[128] In April 1963 Germany linked progress on the CAP to a Commission mandate on the Kennedy Round. A year later Germany gained a transition period of seven-and-a-half years—very close to the eight it had demanded—in exchange for approv-

[125] von der Groeben, *European*, 76–77, 201; Neville-Rolfe, *Politics* 2, 212–213; Lindberg, *Political*, 240–242.

[126] Hallstein, *Europe*, 65.

[127] Lindberg, *Political*, 234, 251; Alfred Müller-Armack, *Auf dem Wege nach Europe: Errinerungen und Ausblicke* (Tübingen, 1971), 231; von der Groeben, *European*, 101; Neville-Rolfe, *Politics*, 210.

[128] Neville-Rolfe, *Politics*, 218; Camps, *What*, 23; Lindberg, *Political*, 273; Willis, *France*, 288–290.

ing a French proposal to replace its third-country safeguards and quotas with levies.[129] Finally, Germany agreed to an agricultural fund for modest subsidization of third-country export of surpluses, while France conceded Germany special permission to provide direct farm subsidies through 1970. In exchange, the acceleration of industrial tariff removal continued, and the Commission was finally permitted to begin preparing for the Kennedy Round.

With the general structure of the CAP in place, member governments could no longer postpone what one Commissioner recalls as the most important decision, which directly dictated the relative prosperity of farmers in different nations— setting the levels of support prices. The means of financing was less controversial, for taxpayers were considerably less well-organized than farmers.[130] The Commission's initial proposal, advanced in 1962, sought to harmonize cereal prices, basic prices on which other commodities tend to be based, to the arithmetic mean of national prices, which implied a basic wheat price of around DM395/ton—an arrangement, as we have seen, that would have lost German farmers well over DM1 billion annually. In response to continued German delay, the Commission reluctantly modified its proposals in November 1962, now proposing the Belgian wheat price of DM425/ton—relatively high within the EC— and accepted the recommendation of a committee of national experts to grant generous transitional aid to German farmers. The Erhard government continued to resist, citing technical details and invoking agricultural safeguard clauses of the Treaty twice in the first two months of 1964, only to be blocked by the Commission, backed by a Council QMV.

For all their disputing, the governments would not be hurried. When the Commission sought to force a decision by refusing to compromise its proposals further, a rare unanimous Council vote rejected the proposals outright and postponed further discussion of prices. The Commission protested vigorously, but its telegrams went unanswered.[131] More modest Commission proposals were advanced in October 1964, and Paul-Henri Spaak of Belgium assumed the role of mediator between de Gaulle and Erhard. De Gaulle sought to exploit Erhard's vulnerable position *vis-à-vis* the Adenauer and Strauss factions of the CDU/CSU by linking any political cooperation to agriculture. (This striking reversal of roles from the previous year, when France had been pressing for political cooperation, further confirms the symbolic rather than serious nature of geopolitical proposals; they were modified as necessary to gain domestic political support and to press for economic goals.) When Erhard defeated the CDU's domestic Gaullist faction and held firm, however, de Gaulle and French officials repeated their threats to exit the EC. A German official recalls that no one within the government felt that compromises on wheat prices themselves were "in German interest," or that the French exit threats were quite credible. The tactics were effec-

[129] Freisberg, *Grüne*, 102, 105, 108; Lindberg, *Political*, 246–250; 274–276, 278; Camps, *What*, 20–21, 24.

[130] Jean-François Deniau, *The Common Market: Its Structure and Purpose*, 3d ed. (London, 1962), 133–35; Camps, *Europe*, 23; Freisberg, *Grüne*, 130.

[131] Camps, *What*, 47–54; Freisberg, *Grüne*, 132–133, 141–158.

tive, however, because German officials feared that de Gaulle might be capable of "economic irrationality."[132]

In mid-November 1964 Erhard finally accepted a price of DM425/ton—well above what prevailed outside of Germany and Belgium—in exchange for direct transitional aid totaling DM560 million in the first year and special permission to maintain national price support programs through the end of the transition period. Erhard promised German farmers an additional DM840 in 1965 and DM1.1 billion in 1966. This aid more than offset the medium-term losses. At German insistence but without French opposition, it was informally agreed not to change agricultural prices by QMV in the future, as the Treaty mandated. The first fully functioning CAP market organization had been established.[133]

Wheat prices, while relatively high, were modest compared to those of other commodities. The reduction of 9 percent in cereal prices imposed on Germany—but not on German farmers, because of the generous compensation—was more than made up by the high prices subsequently fixed for animal products, which constituted 80 percent of German production. Over strenuous objections by the Commission, the price of milk, a product of particular interest to Germany and the Netherlands, was set slightly *above* the German rate and fully 30 percent above that prevailing in France and the Netherlands. Beef prices, unconstrained by the threat of net EEC surpluses, were similarly high. These outcomes were doubly beneficial to German farmers, since input (wheat) costs were declining and the German government had long attempted to switch farmers out of wheat into higher-value-added products. These shifts were not unwelcome in France either, where de Gaulle had just responded to electoral unrest among farmers by raising milk and beef prices. By 1970 German prices for plant products would rest at 91 percent of their 1958 level, but this decline would be more than offset by an 8 percent increase in the average prices for animal products, which comprised the bulk of German production.[134] Sugar followed. Prices acceptable to high-cost producers (for sugar, Germany and Italy) were combined with a system of quotas to limit excess production—a combination suggested by the Commission in its proposals of March 1966. Yet the rules were

[132] Freisberg, *Grüne*, 163, also 163–168; Camps, *What*, 58; Bruin, *Pays-Bas*, 629, 652ff; Fritz Neef, "Entscheidung für Europa," in Gerhard Schroeder, Alfred Müller-Armack, and Karl Hohmann, eds., *Ludwig Erhard: Beiträge zu seiner politischen Biographie* (Frankfurt, 1972), 337–342.

[133] Erhard made his own late-night decision on the evening of 13 December; it was widely interpreted as reflecting the view that the whole market was more important than the CAP and that, without agreement, the EC might have collapsed. Neef, "Entscheidung"; Neville-Rolfe, *Politics*, 227–228; Hermann Höcherl, "Ludwig Erhard—ein Agrarpolitiker wider Willen," in Schroeder et al., *Ludwig*, 123; Freisberg, *Grüne*, 180–187, 195.

[134] Hans von der Groeben and Ernst-Joachim Mestmäcker, *Ziele und Methode der europäischen Integration* (Frankfurt, 1972), 154; Duchêne et al., *New Limits*, 27; François-Henri de Virieu, *La fin d'une agriculture* (Paris, 1967), 46. Pan-European agricultural groups had little impact. The Comité des Organisations Professionnelles Agricoles de la CEE (COPA), the main pan-European agricultural interest group, called for a higher price of over DM42 per 100 kg., but discipline in COPA broke down, with groups in low-priced countries calling for prices below DM42 and groups in high-priced countries calling for a price above DM42. Biased calculations of transport and delivery costs pushed the real price even higher.

soon changed over Commission objections to accommodate growing surpluses, with French producers compensated through yet another set of payments.[135]

Price rises were matched by expansion in coverage. Italy, whose expected comparative advantage in fruits and vegetables had not emerged, insisted that its net financial benefit be increased and that new products specific to Italy be included in the support price system—a demand it backed by veto threats. In 1964 the Italian contribution to the common fund was reduced by over a third, special price supports were granted to Italian producers, and fruits and vegetables, as well as oils, were added to the price system. Realizing that this arrangement could lead to overproduction within the Community, and a corresponding fall in prices, Italy demanded a special system of government purchasing to maintain support prices. By 1970 several more products not in the Commission's initial proposal had been added, including olive oil, vegetable oil, and oil seeds, with plans to include tobacco, flower bulbs, hops, and fish. The percentage of European agriculture covered by the CAP had risen from 65 percent, the Commission's initial proposal in 1960, to over 90 percent.[136]

The final element in the construction of the CAP was financing. In 1966 the Commission had been instructed by the Council to develop proposals for a central financing system. Germany resisted French and Commission demands for a permanent system of CAP financing based on a centralized EC value added tax of 1 percent. Ad hoc arrangements were employed until the Hague summit of 1969, where France finally achieved agreement in exchange for lifting its veto on British membership. The Commission sought to exploit the opportunity to increase its own role, as well as that of the Parliament, in the budgetary process. A compromise between France and the others was reached whereby, within prior spending limits, the Parliament was permitted to reallocate those funds not expressly allocated by the Council and to veto the overall budget by a 60 percent vote—a victory more symbolic than substantive in the short run.

Looking back in the late 1960s, the CAP had evolved into precisely the system against which Mansholt had warned in 1960. The Commission failed utterly in its effort to tame intergovernmental logrolling. The CAP did not disempower agriculture ministries *vis-à-vis* finance and economic ministries, as intended by technocrats like Mansholt and Uri, but instead created an insulated institutional apparatus with loose budget constraints. Member governments rejected the view that each product area should be self-sufficient, creating instead a single flexible fund. All governments except the Dutch rejected the Commission's suggestion that it alone should set prices; nor did they accept the German proposal that the Council set the rules itself using unanimity for four years and QMV thereafter. A compromise was reached, close to the German position, that permitted annual pricing decisions to be taken by Council vote on proposal from the Commission, with administrative control over implementation retained by

---

[135] Chris Stevens and Carole Webb, "The Political Economy of Sugar: A Window on the CAP," in Wallace, Wallace, and Webb, eds., *Policy-Making*, 321–324.

[136] Freisberg, *Grüne*, 134–135, 153–154, 180–187, 195; Duchêne, *New Limits*, 27; von der Groeben, *European Community*, 200–202.

the member states and the European system reimbursing them. The Commission's attempt to centralize structural adjustment funding failed; about two-thirds of agricultural expenditures remained national, a fact that was to become important in the early 1970s when national programs were expanded in high-price countries such as Germany—veritable "renationalization" of the CAP. All this, finally, preserved many of the old corporatist relations between farmers and the state in Western Europe.[137]

In short, the Commission's initial proposal for a liberal, market-oriented agricultural policy backed by structural adjustment had been transformed by the member-states into its antithesis—system of high support prices, expanded scope, no sector-specific spending caps, and abandonment of the supply-control measures previously imposed by exporting countries. Prices were harmonized at the highest level; European agriculture was effectively shielded from most internal and external market pressures. The CAP not only diverted trade from third-country suppliers to Community suppliers but flooded world markets with subsidized EC exports. In short, there is, three analysts contend, "almost universal agreement on two propositions concerning the CAP . . . it suffers from a chronic condition of oversupply [and second] . . . this is due to high prices, politically determined under the CAP's managed system."[138] All this, as we have seen, was not the result of ignorance; it was continually predicted by Mansholt. Externally, the CAP was more protectionist than the sum of the previous national policies; only one product had been liberalized, oil seed—the result of direct and unyielding U.S. pressure. In sum, the CAP was, in the words of former Monnet associate, "a straight defeat for Mansholt's reforming hope." The Hallstein Commission, one of its members recalled, had begun by thinking that "it should seek rational solutions in matters of agricultural policy," but the "stubborn defense" of national interests made such a course impossible. In the end, even the most critical of its members conceded that the Commission had no choice; it was better to accept an unsatisfactory compromise than to jeopardize progress toward integration.[139]

By 1968 Mansholt was desperate. Observing that price supports meant disorganized markets and intolerable costs, he proposed a radical modernization of agriculture—a second Mansholt Plan. The farming population would be

---

[137] Sir Mark Franklin, "Father of the European Common Agricultural Policy," *Financial Times*, 4 July 1995, 3; Institut, *De Gaulle*, 5:180; von der Groeben, *European*, 72, 200, 202; "Agricultural Decisions of July 1966," *Common Market* 6:11 (November 1966), 241; William F. Averyt, Jr., *Agropolitics in the European Community: Interest Groups and the CAP* (New York, 1977), 110–112. An example of the subtle changes in CAP institutions introduced to preserve domestic political arrangements is a 1966 decision under pressure from France, to alter the Commission's proposal for a common EC grain marketing system under which producers could sell to anyone to a system under which producers were permitted to sell only to a stocking agent licensed by a member-state—thus preserving the French government's compulsory delivery system levy on sales, from which the main French grain producers' group gained most of its dues. Neville-Rolfe, *Politics*, 211–212. "It would be unthinkable," wrote Pierre LeRoy, later a high agricultural official under President Pompidou, "for the [European Community] to intervene directly at the level of payment in the member states. That is why the fund relies on national organizations." Averyt, *Agropolitics*, 53.

[138] Duchêne et al., *New Limits*, 10, also 10–22.

[139] Duchêne et al., *New Limits*, 28; von der Groeben, *European*, 106; Freisberg, *Grüne*, 100–101.

halved, 7 percent of agricultural land would be turned over to forestry, millions of animals would be slaughtered. All this was to be achieved by centralizing and strengthening regional and structural adjustment policies and applying competition policy norms to agriculture. Farmers rioted in the streets of Brussels and national capitals, Mansholt's life was threatened, and agriculture ministers in the Special Committee and the Council, led by Germany, rebuffed the proposal. In the final vote, Commissioner Mansholt was backed, as he had been for a decade, only by his home country.[140]

Transport and Other Sectoral and Regulatory Policies: "Total deadlock"

Policies covering rail, road, and inland waterway transport occupied an ambiguous position in the Treaty. As with the CAP, transport policy lacked specific details. In contrast to agriculture, there was no affirmative duty to act within a particular period. These weaknesses in the Treaty reflected the absence of large-country support for an active transport policy, which also hampered negotiations in the 1960s. A few narrow, unanimously accepted regulations aside, there was little result. The comparison between transport and agriculture, first proposed by Lindberg and Scheingold, is instructive. These scholars attribute at least part of the relative failure on transport to the lack of Commission leadership. Yet the historical record reveals that the Commission provided numerous and varied proposals along the lines employed in creating the CAP, but without success. The key point was that no large country had a sufficient economic interest to promote agreement, nor did Germany have a geopolitical interest in placating the Netherlands.[141]

In 1962 the Commission proposed a grand scheme to do for transport what it sought to do for agriculture, to harmonize national regulatory systems and prices through a centralized organization. National positions reflected sectoral economic interests. Yet in contrast to the CAP, the Dutch alone would clearly benefit from transport deregulation. Dutch producers provided the most competitive ground transport and favored a liberal arrangement, particularly if it granted them privileges to transport goods between two points wholly within other nations (*"cabotage"*). The most important domestic market was Germany. Under existing bilateral quotas, Dutch transporters already controlled 40 per-

[140] Franklin, "Father," 3; Neville-Rolfe, *Politics*, 372–374, 501; Philip M. Williams and Martin Harrison, *Politics and Society in de Gaulle's Republic* (Garden City, N.Y., 1971), 342–346. In 1968, at the last minute before they went into force, Mansholt proposed a 2.6 percent reduction in milk prices after "sharp internal debate over the political wisdom of such action." With dairymen protesting in national capitals and in Brussels, and the French government threatening again to delay industrial tariff reductions if the agreed price was not maintained, Mansholt backed down. The Council then acted without a Commission proposal to further expand milk supports. Further reform proposals in the Commission's structural reform package of 1972 were equally ineffective.

[141] The Treaty mandated provisions to eliminate national discrimination against foreign carriers, and in 1960 the Council passed such a regulation, followed by another banning certain railway tariffs. Stringent Commission enforcement was backed by the member governments. See von der Groeben, *European*, 78; Peter A. Bromhead, "Transport Policy," in Peter Coffey, ed., *Economic Policies of the Common Market* (New York, 1979), 122–23; Leon Lindberg and Stuart Scheingold, *Europe's Would-Be Polity: Patterns of Change in the European Community* (Englewood Cliffs, N.J., 1970), 163ff.

cent of EEC cross-border road haulage. All governments except the Dutch rejected deregulation, and the Council overruled the Commission's unilateral efforts to circumvent opposition by applying competition policy to transport. The Commission then proposed a more regulated system that granted the Dutch a Europe-wide quota of 19 percent, half of what the Dutch already enjoyed, within a more open market. In May 1965, after four years of negotiation, the Council unanimously rejected the proposal and requested proposals limited to the harmonization of frontier procedures and regulation of maximum truck weight. Even these were rejected in 1966, though minimal protections against monopoly pricing were finally approved in 1968. Without effective European legislation, Germany began to impose greater unilateral restrictions on road haulage and Rhine shipping. In sum, all attempts to develop a common policy either failed to gain member-state support or have been dead letters. Even a sympathetic observer, looking back over the first decade, discerned "total deadlock."[142]

In social, industrial, regional, competition, and monetary policy the Commission advanced similarly strong proposals. Yet only in competition policy was there significant support from either France or Germany—and even in competition policy, German support was insufficient to generate more than marginal progress.

Despite numerous proposals from the Commission, no progress was made on regional or industrial policy. The highly centralized French government considered regional policy a national matter and blocked progress. In 1964 the French proposed statutes to facilitate the legal incorporation of European companies and to promote cooperation in scientific research and development, but other member states showed little enthusiasm for the proposal. Not until 1967, when the directorates of Euratom, ECSC, and the EEC merged, was a Directorate General for Industrial Affairs (DG III) created. Industrial policy was not discussed by the member-states until the Hague Summit of 1969.[143]

Hence EC competition policy was, from the very beginning, restricted to the *negative* regulation of business practices, particularly mergers. It was far less successful at dictating acceptable patterns of industrial structures and limiting government intervention, or even controlling monopolies. In competition policy the Treaty granted new powers to central institutions, though their practical import was circumscribed. Articles 85–94 of the Treaty of Rome set out a framework for regulating common competition, mergers (Art. 85), monopolies (Art. 86), dumping (Art. 91), and state subsidies to industry, whether direct or indirect, including preferential public procurement ("state aids," they are termed in Arts. 92–94). The Treaty required the Council to act within three years to establish rules governing mergers. The Treaty permitted the Commission to in-

---

[142] Lindberg and Scheingold, *Europe's*, 165, also 163–167; K. M. Gwilliam, "Realism and the Common Transport Policy of the EEC," in J. B. Polak and J. B. van der Kemp, eds., *Changes in the Field of Transport Studies* (The Hague, 1980), 49–50, 53. This effort to send the Commission new instructions "deliberately bypassed" the Commission's power of proposal. In 1963 the Council suspended application of the competition policy to transport. Finn Jensen and Ingo Walter, *The Common Market: Integration in Europe* (Philadelphia, 1965), 144–45.

[143] von der Groeben, *European*, 106n; Michael Hodges, "Industrial Policy: Hard Times or Great Expectations," in Wallace, Wallace, and Webb, eds., *Policy-Making*, 265–293.

vestigate mergers and make recommendations, but any further action would require Council authorization. On state aids, member governments could act directly by QMV, but they rarely did so until the 1990s.

Commission powers on existing monopolies and state aids remained narrow . Monopolization under Article 86 was not in itself illegal; only abuse of a dominant market position was. In the words of the Commission's major architect of the policy, "only a few cases of undesirable amalgamation can be caught." Even modest steps toward enforcement sparked considerable criticism in France, Germany, and Belgium over what was considered an unduly strict application of EC law. Control of state aids under Articles 92–94 was restricted to a few minor cases. Other nontariff barriers that might have fallen under Articles 92–94, as well as attempts to extend the policy to transport or agriculture, were, as we have seen, blocked. The responsible Commissioner himself concluded that Commission efforts to gain greater authority over mergers and monopolies had failed.[144]

A compromise on merger control was easier, since it pertained entirely to actions that had not yet taken place. Both Germany and France sought to generalize their domestic systems. The German domestic system presumed large concentrations were illegal unless proved otherwise, whereas the French system presumed their legality. When the issue of mergers was debated in 1960 and 1961, the major opposition to assigning appropriate powers to the Commission came from the French, backed by Luxembourg and Belgium. In November 1961, as part of the agriculture package deal, France accepted that the Commission should oversee mergers and that firms should provide timely information on agreements to the Commission. Over the years the Commission has developed effective means of focusing on problematic cases.[145]

The British Question:
"We have to think of new reasons to make your membership impossible."

From 1957 through 1963 Britain and the Six conducted nearly continuous negotiations, with Britain seeking closer connections and the French obstructing negotiations and vetoing agreements. Efforts were renewed in 1967 and twice in 1969. In every case except one of the 1969 episodes, Britain initiated discussions.

The first British membership bid followed the failure of efforts to construct an FTA. Initial negotiations over the FTA opened in the autumn of 1957, immediately following ratification of the Rome treaties. From the beginning French representatives of the Fourth Republic refused to negotiate in earnest, rejecting British suggestions without making counterproposals or raising new issues. When de Gaulle entered office in 1958, he maintained this line. In December 1958, after gaining Adenauer's support, de Gaulle finally vetoed the FTA, calling—

---

[144] von der Groeben, *European,* 108–112, 196–199. Article 91 authorized action to restrict dumping within the Community, but only 14 legitimate cases were reported in the first ten years of the Community, of which the Commission only acted on three.

[145] von der Groeben, *European,* pp. 108–111.

disingenuously—on the British to join the EEC and accept the same obligations as other Community partners. Early in 1960, after the formation of EFTA among seven excluded countries, Britain and some of its new partners announced their willingness to negotiate an EFTA-EC agreement, for which Macmillan unsuccessfully sought U.S. support. Over the next two years it became clear that EC-EFTA negotiations were fruitless. When in early 1961 a British official asked Robert Marjolin, now a Commissioner but rightly considered something of an Atlanticist, what France would do if Britain agreed to all its conditions, Marjolin replied: "We [would] just have to think of new reasons which make your membership impossible."[146]

Anglo-EC negotiations continued from late 1961 through January 1963. We have examined the basic preferences and strategies of Britain, France, and Germany, noting the primacy of commercial interests in all three cases, though geopolitical ideology played a secondary role, particularly in Germany. Britain rightly believed "the real negotiation [was] between Britain and France," as Ambassador Dixon (a man Macmillan considered "the most subtle mind in Whitehall") reported from Paris in 1961. As in the FTA and EFTA-EC negotiations, France stalled. High French officials warned their British counterparts that the relationship between the CAP and Commonwealth preferences was the central issue; without satisfaction on agriculture, France would veto.[147]

Why was the British bargaining position so weak? Why was Britain continuously forced to move down its preference ordering, offering ever greater concessions to the Six? The basic reason is that Britain was more commercially dependent on the Six than vice versa. From 1955 onward British officials accepted that once the EC formed, Britain's bargaining position would be weakened— a consequence of the inexorable postwar shift in commerce away from the Commonwealth and toward Europe. Macmillan and his associates realized by 1959 that they were left, in de Zulueta's words, with "few effective cards to play" in the commercial realm. To be sure, a natural Anglo-German economic alliance existed; if Germany had calculated commercial interests alone, Britain's position would have been much stronger. Yet when Adenauer agreed to back French opposition to the FTA at his first summit meeting with de Gaulle at Colombey in mid-1958—a largely geopolitical commitment, as we have seen, that even Erhard could not reverse—Britain's position was fatally weakened. Adenauer did intermittently intervene to press the Commission toward cooperation with Britain, but he never took Erhard's advice to threaten the French, the only action that might have worked.[148]

British behavior, motivated by Macmillan's domestic caution as well as a misunderstanding of French intentions, seemed initially to support de Gaulle's (and Macmillan's) belief that the British government was too constrained at home to negotiate effectively. Macmillan's strategy, we have seen, rested on a desperate attempt to forge a linkage to geopolitical threats and promises ap-

---

[146] Lamb, *Macmillan*, 166; Lee, "Germany," 12, also 3–7.

[147] Lee, "Germany," 1; Lamb, *Macmillan*, 142–143, also 114, 147–150.

[148] Brenke, *Europakonzeptionen*, 629–631; Wolfram Kaiser, "Wie nach Austerlitz? London-Bonn-Paris und die britische EWG-Politik bis 1961," *Integration* 16:1 (January 1993), 26–27.

peared the only alternative. At Nassau, less than a month before the French veto, Macmillan was still attempting to find a quid pro quo by negotiating a deal with the United States providing Polaris missiles to France. Yet such arrangements were linked to the MLF and did not match even the bilateral terms that Britain had received; they were thus of little interest to de Gaulle. Even if they had been, this strategy floundered on the French concern about agriculture.[149] In the FTA, EC-EFTA, and accession negotiations, Britain began by treating major concessions on the Commonwealth, the common external tariff, and agriculture as explicitly non-negotiable. Macmillan himself made this position clear in the FTA negotiations.[150]

The result was repeated frustration. When Britain called in May 1960 for the resumption of negotiations, this time with the EFTA governments, the government underscored the issue's importance by appointing Reginald Maudling as a special cabinet minister to handle negotiations. Yet the EEC, again under French pressure, refused to negotiate seriously, not least because agriculture was off the agenda. In October 1961 Britain's chief negotiator, Edward Heath, launched accession talks by stressing Commonwealth trade, agriculture, and the status of EFTA countries as the key issues and noted again that the desire for "comparable outlets" for Commonwealth preference commodities was "non-negotiable."[151] Heath did not show flexibility on these issues until May 1962. Only at this point, it appears, did de Gaulle realize that Macmillan might be willing to make concessions, short of a break with the United States, necessary to enter the EC, whereupon he ordered French officials to harden their demands and to issue pessimistic public assessments of the negotiations. As late as December 1962 Heath was still haggling over food imports. Still, it was widely believed that only a few minor agreements on Commonwealth products were needed to conclude the negotiations; failure to reach accord on Commonwealth goods was not the cause of the collapse of the negotiations.[152]

The basic dynamic of the accession negotiations—de Gaulle wary of British membership for agricultural reasons, Macmillan proposing geopolitical side-payments—is reflected in the transcripts of their bilateral summits. In June 1962 at Chateau de Champs, de Gaulle began by emphasizing the absolute French imperative to export agricultural goods and insistently raised the issue of Commonwealth imports, which he termed the "most fundamental" issue. Macmillan insisted on transitional arrangements and hinted several times that Britain would refuse to pay more than its fair share for the CAP. He rejected out of hand de Gaulle's proposal that Commonwealth imports be limited only to tropical products such as cocoa and coffee and mentioned beef and wheat exports. Consistent with his strategy of seeking a geopolitical quid pro quo, Macmillan repeatedly tried to shift the conversation away from economic issues, only to have the General change the topic back.[153]

[149] Horne, *Macmillan*, 2:429–32, 444–447.
[150] Lamb, *Macmillan*, 109, also 107–110.
[151] Lamb, *Macmillan*, 160, 163.
[152] Willis, *France*, 301; Roth, *Heath*, 163; Dixon, *Double*, 299.
[153] Record of a Conversation at the Chateau de Camps, 2–3 June 1962, PREM 11/3775, 7–9.

Only halfway through the session at Chateau de Champs did de Gaulle finally permit the discussion to move to geopolitical issues—whereupon the two statesmen immediately found themselves in much greater agreement! De Gaulle asserted that the Common Market had been created for political ends but that supranational institutions should be replaced by intergovernmental cooperation among the larger powers—a position close to Macmillan's. De Gaulle remarked that for security *vis-à-vis* Russia it would probably be better to have the British in the EC and conceded that "in the last resort" France had more confidence in Britain than in Germany. When the General asked whether Britain was ready to adopt a European attitude, Macmillan assured him that Britain was prepared to strengthen the European end of the alliance. Both explicitly agreed that progress toward political cooperation in Europe was not being made and that the major obstacle to British membership was its "many ties outside Europe" but *not* the British geopolitical preference for the United States over Europe.[154] This dynamic was reiterated at Rambouillet in December 1962, where de Gaulle conceded that the Fouchet Plan had failed and hence British membership would have no influence on foreign policy cooperation. Nonetheless, he continued, it was "not possible for Britain to enter tomorrow." The "main problem," Macmillan noted—for the first time acknowledging the centrality of commercial interests—is "agriculture." France, de Gaulle responded, sought to establish certain EEC policies; once they had been definitively established, Britain and the Scandinavian countries could enter. This, Macmillan noted immediately, was "a most serious statement."[155]

Despite French efforts to delay, by late 1962, just before the veto, nearly all non-French participants saw agreement just around the corner. A marathon session scheduled for January 1963 was expected to resolve outstanding issues; Couve de Murville was clear to the point of tendentiousness that the critical issue was not simply Commonwealth preferences but "financial regulation" of agriculture.[156] This point suggests—consistent with the "prudently audacious" strategy—that it was the imminent success of the negotiations, not their imminent failure, that led de Gaulle to veto British membership explicitly. At his celebrated press conference of 14 January 1963, he announced his unilateral step, which had been decided within the French government almost a month earlier. By this point, British officials themselves agreed that financial regulation of agriculture was the sticking point over which France sought to block formation of an Anglo-German coalition.[157]

Some have argued in retrospect that a more effective British strategy would have made rapid concessions on economic issues. Had Britain facilitated immediate agreement, it is argued, de Gaulle would have been forced to contemplate a veto under far less advantageous circumstances, that is, with an agreement on the CAP not yet in place and with considerable opposition from coalition par-

---

[154] Record of 3 June meeting, 11–14, especially 13; 14ff., 17–18.
[155] PRO, Prem 11/4230; Lamb, *Macmillan*, 166, 192–193.
[156] Horne, *Macmillan*, 2:429–32, 444–447; *Akten 1963* I, Document 17, 30.
[157] Willis, *France*, 299–305; Lamb, *Macmillan*, 196–197, 202.

ties prior to the elections of November 1962. It is possible, moreover, that Macmillan and his closest associates misperceived French interests, failing to grasp the domestic constraints imposed on de Gaulle by farmers. This failure led them to focus on geopolitical linkages, persisting even though both Eisenhower and Kennedy—the latter, Macmillan believed, because of Monnet's influence on George Ball—were unhelpful in nuclear matters. Critics have also suggested that Macmillan was unduly influenced by Treasury, which focused on global monetary issues rather than on trade; too wedded to seeking marginal concessions on Commonwealth trade; a geopolitician inexplicably unwilling to invoke geopolitical arguments in domestic debates; or simply a politician overly cautious in the management of domestic public and elite opinion but one who could have exploited his large majority to override domestic opposition.[158]

Certainly a strategy of rapid economic concessions would have held more promise, yet those who criticize British strategy in retrospect overlook two factors. First, Macmillan's worries about domestic opposition were widely shared. In his diary Macmillan termed his ability to gain unchallenged support on the EC "a miracle, a miracle." Other politicians in Britain felt that domestic opposition over farm subsidies and the Commonwealth was potentially fatal. Second, Macmillan could have increased the costs of the General's veto, but it is questionable whether such a tactic would have held it off entirely. The interests of France and Britain were diametrically opposed on agriculture, and de Gaulle had many options for delaying the negotiations. British officials, after all, fully intended to block the CAP if they could. Within the British government this was a major reason to seek membership rapidly. No commitment to support the CAP could be credible until after it was firmly embedded in the *acquis communautaire*. Only German willingness to link the completion of the CAP to British membership— as Erhard proposed—might have fundamentally altered the bargaining situation. Yet this Adenauer was unwilling and Erhard unable to do—for both economic and geopolitical reasons. Nor would any of this have been possible without a delay of several years, during which anything might have happened.[159] Indeed, Macmillan's European statecraft must be judged in many ways an extraordinary act of leadership. He reversed British policy and engineered massive concessions with remarkably little domestic opposition, all *before* British trade patterns had completed their shift toward the Continent. Perhaps the most important weakness in his conduct of policy, namely his tendency to discount the import of de Gaulle's underlying economic motivations, is an error that most subsequent analysts are hardly in a position to criticize.

Between de Gaulle's first veto and British accession in 1973, the fundamental objective of Britain's policy toward Europe was, as we have seen, to avoid commercial exclusion from European markets at the lowest possible cost. Whatever their geopolitical views, subsequent British governments pursued the same ob-

---

[158] See, for example, Lieber, *British;* Kaiser, *Using;* Piers Ludlow, *Dealing with Britain: The Six and the First British Application* (Cambridge, 1997); Horne, *Macmillan,* 2:430–450; Harold Macmillan, *At the End of the Day, 1961–1963* (London, 1973), 111, 475–476.

[159] Horne, *Macmillan,* 2:358; Lamb, *Macmillan,* 186–187.

jective. A permanent financial settlement for the CAP was not reached until 1969; hence Wilson government's attempt to reopen negotiations in 1966–67 was foiled by a second Gaullist veto. In February 1969 de Gaulle approached the British about an intergovernmental alternative to the EEC, and the Foreign Office (whether deliberately or by accident, we do not know) took its revenge, embarrassing the General by leaking the initiative, which forced him to repudiate it. Not until 1969–70, after de Gaulle had been replaced by Georges Pompidou, were serious negotiations opened; Pompidou was confident that de Gaulle would support him.[160] As we have seen, Pompidou's sole condition for opening negotiations with Britain was not geopolitical; it was creation of the permanent financing system for the CAP.

Institutional Choices

Institutional choices during this period resulted in changes in the formal structure of the EC unforeseen in the Treaty. The most significant of these led to the growth in intergovernmental rather than supranational influence. It resulted from the strengthening of the Council bureaucracy and the limitation of QMV through the Luxembourg Compromise. The 1960s witnessed three major reforms.

Reform of the Council: "Dispossessing the Commission"

A series of institutional reforms strengthened the role of intergovernmental bodies at which governments were directly represented at the expense of the Commission. First was an expansion of the Committee of Permanent Representatives, at which diplomats from the member-states meet to prepare Council decisions. By the end of the 1960s the Council was meeting twice as often and COREPER three times as often as the Commission, and the number of expert meetings held by the two was nearly equal. National ministers often acted alone, then instructed COREPER to work out details, proposals, and procedures. Explicit recognition of the role played by COREPER was one of two formal changes in the Treaty during the 1960s, though it merely "put the official stamp on positions which already existed."[161]

Second was the establishment in September 1960 of the Special Committee on Agriculture, a committee composed of officials from national agriculture ministries and permanent diplomatic representatives unforeseen in the Treaty. The Special Committee bypassed even COREPER, the customary forum for all other matters, in which foreign ministries were represented. France and the Netherlands unsuccessfully sought to avoid a monopoly on representation by agriculture ministries by naming Mansholt to head it, but Germany and Belgium insisted on a rotating presidency and sent their agricultural ministers to repre-

---

[160] For further discussion, see chapter 4 of this book.

[161] Émile Noël and Henri Étienne, "The Permanent Representatives Committee and the 'Deepening' of the Communities," in Ghita Ionescu, ed., *The New Politics of European Integration* (London, 1972), 104, also 112, 123.

sent them. This arrangement eventually spawned twenty-eight subcommittees for preparing and reviewing proposals. Since the Council had yet to institute majority voting, there was little to stop it from modifying Commission proposals by the same unanimity required to pass them.[162] Other issue-specific committees, including the Medium-Term Economic Committee, were employed to develop new policies independently of the Commission. The Article 113 Committee, mentioned in the Treaty, oversaw trade negotiations with much tighter constraints than expected, and it permitted the Commission neither to make nor to respond to proposals without prior approval.

Third was the imposition of management committees to oversee the daily administration by the Commission. This system was imposed in agriculture in 1962 and extended to other areas. The committees kept governments informed of Commission activities and could vote to send specific decisions to the Council for reconsideration. In agriculture, oversight over daily operations was maintained by one "management committee" per commodity, composed of national and Commission representatives. If the management committee disapproved of a Commission decision (by majority vote), its application would be suspended for one month, during which the Council could reverse the decision by majority vote. Hallstein sought without success to organize Assembly opposition to their creation.[163] The system was extended in 1968, over the strong opposition of the Commission, to foreign tariffs, veterinary controls, and harmonization of domestic regulations, with tighter controls through a system of "regulation committees." From the perspective of the original treaty the effect, according to the Parliament, was to "dispossess the Commission of powers in accordance with the spirit of the Treaty."[164]

The Failure of the Fouchet Plan

The Fouchet Plan has customarily been treated as an attempt to organize foreign policy cooperation among the Six. No doubt de Gaulle would have been pleased to supplant some of NATO's functions with a European arrangement. Yet, as we have seen, de Gaulle's real ambition was to seduce pro-European groups into silence while he gained agricultural concessions and, secondarily, to reform European institutions.

Discussion of the Fouchet Plan was launched in July 1960 in Rambouillet, at one of the increasingly cordial summits between Adenauer and de Gaulle. After suggesting a bilateral treaty, which Adenauer rejected, de Gaulle proposed intergovernmental cooperation based on periodic meetings by heads of state and

---

[162] Stanley Henig, *Power and Decision in Europe: The Political Institutions of the European Community* (London, 1980), 34; von der Groeben, *European*, 78, 103, also 101; Lindberg, *Political*, 244–245, 257, 260.

[163] Freisberg, *Grüne*, 101–102; Lindberg, *Political*, 246–250.

[164] Claude Lassalle, Les Comités et l'évolution institutionnelle de la CEE," *Cahiers de droit européen* 4:1 (1968), 406; also Noël and Étienne, "Permanent," 106–120; Hans von der Groeben, Jochen Thiesing, and Claus-Dieter Ehlermann, eds., *Kommentar zum EWG-Vertrag* 4th ed. (Baden-Baden, 1991), 4332–4335.

a set of subordinate intergovernmental commissions for political, cultural, economic, and military affairs. These commissions would be overseen by a permanent secretariat charged with preparing consultations and implementing decisions, and a common assembly of members of national parliaments. Adenauer immediately signaled his approval and, though resisting de Gaulle's proposals for a European referendum on the Fouchet Plan, helped legitimate the effort by arranging reciprocal visits with de Gaulle in 1962. Most spectacular among them were a ceremonial *Te Deum* at Rheims cathedral and enthusiastic receptions for de Gaulle in Germany, at which the General delivered extemporaneous speeches in passable German.[165]

Domestic opposition, however, soon forced Adenauer to demand clarification, signaling that the German government would not entirely support any policy that undermined NATO. Thereafter he was more cautious, agreeing to endorse the French proposal only in exchange for acknowledgment that "the closest possible cooperation" with NATO was "vital to the defense of the free world."[166] Initially the French seemed to offer a narrow agreement on foreign policy; as we have seen, the French draft of fall 1961 excluded economic affairs and included a modest Belgian "revision clause" calling for future integration of foreign policy into the EC. Only the Dutch remained opposed outright. Yet the sudden French decision to substitute a tougher second draft was made at a meeting among Couve, Debré, and de Gaulle just four hours after the agricultural decision of January 1962. Thereafter they offered no compromise. As we have seen, this was consistent with de Gaulle's "prudently audacious" plan. De Gaulle considered it unlikely that others would accept the plan; he was unwilling to make any economic compromises to achieve it, which suggests the primacy of goals other than geopolitical cooperation against the superpowers. With the success of the agricultural negotiations a few hours previously, de Gaulle was able to reassert the underlying French position.

The hardening of the French position ended the isolated Anglophile opposition to the Fouchet Plan conducted by the Netherlands. "A bad day for Europe, a good day for the Netherlands," one Dutch correspondent observed.[167] Other national leaders, with the notable exception of Adenauer, now saw de Gaulle as unalterably opposed to existing EEC institutions.[168] Spaak, abandoning hope that the French would accept supranational cooperation, backed Dutch demands for British participation; the German and Italian governments withheld support. The five other governments drafted an alternative text reiterating the importance of NATO and the EEC, providing for a Court of Justice and independent secretary general, watering down unanimity voting (though in a way sufficiently vague as to make no commitments), reestablishing the revision clause, and mentioning direct election to the Assembly. Subsequent negotiations, with Italian mediation, were unable to reach agreement. By mid-1962 Monnet—who had

---

[165] Bodenheimer, *Political*, 76–102; Ménil, *Who*, 65, 76–77; Silj, *Europe's*.
[166] Ménil, *Who*, 67; Silj, *Europe's*, 5–8, 112; Soutou, "Général," 135–136, 139.
[167] Bodenheimer, *Political*, 171n. Also Willis, *France*, 297.
[168] Silj, *Europe's*, 16, 42ff.

initially been seduced into supporting the plan—broke with de Gaulle, and all five ministers from Monnet's MRP party in the Debré government resigned. International leaders termed the negotiations a "resounding failure," and by October even Adenauer had given up hope. When de Gaulle tried to organize tripartite collaboration in January 1963, excluding Benelux, Italy withdrew.[169] This left only France and Germany, who signed a bilateral agreement, the Franco-German Friendship Treaty, in February 1963. This—we should recall—had long been a Gaullist goal. Yet the Treaty was "empty of significant political content," a symbolic document without any binding provisions.[170] Neither France nor Germany suggested more than regular consultation on foreign policy, youth exchanges, and a coproduction project for military aircraft. It was, Alfred Grosser observed, "a treaty based on wishful thinking. In general, a treaty establishes procedures or agreements; here we find established the *desire* to arrive at agreement."[171] And even this anodyne agreement did not, as we have seen, survive ratification in Germany without the addition of a pro-NATO preamble.

Both de Gaulle and Adenauer acted in any case as if the text did not exist: de Gaulle had just vetoed British entry without consulting Germany, and, in the weeks following, Adenauer accepted the MLF without consulting the French. At the Franco-German summit in June 1964 de Gaulle, now facing the Erhard government, blocked all political negotiations and announced that he would pursue an independent policy with respect to the Soviet Union, thus undermining support from many German Gaullists like Franz-Josef Strauss. This may have been a unilateral act of geopolitical strategy, but most participants saw it primarily as a means of pressuring Erhard to accept lower agricultural prices, which de Gaulle announced as his major concern. The Franco-German treaty changed little in European foreign policy-making, languishing in obscurity until resurrected, by Brandt, as a symbolic counterweight to *Ostpolitik*.[172]

Majority Voting, the Commission, and the "Empty Chair" Crisis

Among institutional issues de Gaulle focused his attention above all on majority voting and Commission initiative. These elements of EC institutions were scheduled to become much more important in 1966, when, with transition to the third stage foreseen in the Treaty, QMV would be introduced in some decisions concerning the CAP, the external tariff, and transport policy.

De Gaulle would surely have raised the issue in any case, but President Hallstein of the Commission gave him a pretext by linking proposals on the financing of agriculture, requested by the Council and much desired by France, to its own proposal for centralizing control over future spending from external tariffs and agricultural levies in the Commission and the Parliament. There would be considerable discretion, since the funds in question, about 8 percent of the government spending of the Six, greatly exceeded current obligations. More

---

[169] Silj, Europe's, 7n, 17–24, 31–33, 110; Soutou, "Général," 142, 191.
[170] Craig, "Konrad," 221.
[171] Grosser, *French*, 74.
[172] Willis, *France*, 332–336.

broadly, the Commission sought a first step toward a long-run transformation of the Council into the upper house of a European federal parliament.[173] Hallstein and Mansholt knew that the Commission's strategy was controversial but failed to heed widespread warnings. Marjolin had made it clear that it would provoke French retaliation. Yet the moment seemed propitious, a last chance to exploit leverage stemming from de Gaulle's desire for the CAP. De Gaulle, moreover, faced elections. In order not to lose the initiative, Hallstein and Mansholt prepared their proposals in secret, initially even from the other Commissioners, departing from the standard practice of holding hundreds of preliminary meetings with high national officials and COREPER before issuing a proposal.[174]

The French government rejected the proposal outright, refusing to discuss anything except short-term agricultural financing. Despite public expressions of support, no government (except perhaps the Netherlands) supported the budgetary proposals in private. French and German officials quickly agreed to a compromise, postponing the issue until 1970. With an eye to the Bundestag, Erhard and Schröder proposed that the Assembly be permitted to suggest alterations in the distribution of funds between budget items but not changes in budget totals. On the final evening of the negotiation the German Bundestag passed a resolution—apparently worked out between "Europeanists" in the German, Dutch, and Italian parliaments, the European Movement, apparently including Monnet, and the Commission—supporting the Commission's proposals. The Dutch and German governments, though ultimately willing to accommodate France, felt it important for domestic reasons not to appear to concede too easily. When the Germans called for postponement, however, Couve de Murville refused as chair to "stop the clock," as had happened before in such circumstances, declared the negotiations a failure, and returned to Paris.[175]

A few days later the French government announced that it had withdrawn its permanent representative from Brussels and was boycotting any Council meetings concerning new policies. The French stayed out when, on 22 July, the Commission dropped its earlier proposals and retreated to "the lines of consensus of the Council." After a delay of two to three months, coinciding with the traditional summer recess, the French government proposed a brisk schedule for catching up on Community business and for resolving basic issues—subject, however, to a series of demands, among them that the Commission change its name, refrain from running an information service, abandon accredited diplomatic missions, stop sending representatives to international organizations, cease

---

[173] For overviews of the crisis, see Newhouse, *Crisis;* John Lambert, "The Constitutional Crisis, 1965–1966," *Journal of Common Market Studies* 7:3 (May 1966), 195–228; Lindberg, "Integration"; Émile Noël, "Témoignage: L'administration de la Communauté européenne dans la rétrospective d'un ancien haut fonctionnaire," in Erik Volkmar Heyen, ed., *Die Anfänge der Verwaltung der Europäischen Gemeinschaft* (Baden-Baden, 1992), 145.

[174] Von der Groeben, *European,* 180–81; Lambert, "Constitutional," 206; Marjolin, *Architect,* 349–353; Spinelli, *Eurocrats,* 74, 76.

[175] All governments, even those of the Benelux, appear to have been much less federalist in private than in public. Lambert, "Constitutional," 206; Jean-Marc Boegner, "1958, le Général de Gaulle et l'acceptation du traité de Rome," *Espoir* 87 (December 1992), 33; Newhouse, *Collision,* 68, 111–118.

criticizing the policies of member-states in public, submit proposals to the Council before publicizing them, end mobilization of domestic groups, and draft vaguer directives so as to limit its own discretion and maximize that of national officials.

If de Gaulle's goals were audacious, his tactics remained prudent. Unable to risk destroying the EC or jeopardizing the CAP, he never so much as hinted at withdrawal. Top French officials assured their counterparts that France could envisage no alternative to membership. The French ambassador departed, but his assistant remained; written procedures kept essential business moving. French diplomats boycotted Council and COREPER meetings on new policies, such as fiscal harmonization, but not study groups and management committees concerned with existing policies, such as the CAP, GATT negotiations, even the association of Greece and Turkey. At home the French government defended the EC, largely on economic grounds, against those who favored an opening to Eastern Europe and the USSR. The government prepared its domestic budget for the planned reduction in internal EC tariffs, which it carried out on schedule at the end of the year despite the boycott. In short, far from challenging economic integration, de Gaulle was *exploiting* its irreversibility to press others for institutional reform.[176]

De Gaulle's intransigence provoked previously unreachable consensus among the Five, led by Germany, based on defense of the Treaty.[177] During the crisis COREPER met twenty-two times to transact business without the French; the Court and Commission continued their normal activities. In late October the Five issued a statement, based on an even more explicit secret agreement, defending the basic provisions of the Treaty. They were close to transacting normal Council business without France when de Gaulle, electorally embarrassed at home and diplomatically isolated abroad, came back to the table. The Five also "made no secret of the fact that they were thinking of approaching the British if the French continued their boycott."[178]

The final settlement was an agreement to disagree. The French got some but not much of what they had requested. The Council was to be represented alongside the Commission in EC foreign policy and press activities. No concessions were made on formal QMV, but an extra-legal document called the Luxembourg Compromise codified the agreement to disagree.[179] A first clause, proposed by

[176] John Newhouse, *De Gaulle and the Anglo-Saxons* (New York, 1970), 47; Ménil, *Who*, 135; Lindberg, "Integration," 253–256; Newhouse, *Collision*, 119–120, 130–134, 151–153; Lambert, "Constitutional," 210–213. Anne Jaumin-Ponsar, *Essai d'interprétation d'une crise* (Brussels, 1970), 104–105, 124, points out that de Gaulle's election rhetoric was strikingly pro-EEC.

[177] Newhouse, *Collision*, 148–149; Spinelli, *Eurocrats*, 212–213; Lindberg, "Integration," 239–241. The most widely cited analysis of the elections is that of the Gaullist commentator Pierre Drouin in *Le Monde* of 14 January 1966; though his evidence that the farm vote decisively influenced the outcome was weak, de Gaulle evidently believed it and was shocked into action. Peyrefitte, *Trouble*, 50–52.

[178] Camps, *European*, 122; Newhouse, *Collision*, 89–90, 130–134, 151–153, 155; Noël, "Institutional"; Jaubin-Polmar, *Essai*, 98; Rudolf Lahr, "Die Legende vom 'Luxemburger Kompromiß.'" *Europa-Archiv* 38:8 (10 January 1983), 223–232; de Bruin, *Pays-Bas*, 72off., 734, 755.

[179] Noël, "Institutional"; Newhouse, *Collision*, 130–134, 151–153; Lindberg, "Integration," 255, 264; Jaumin-Ponsar, *Essai*, 143–145.

Schröder, stated that all countries agree that, where majority voting threatens the vital interests of a state, member-states will seek for a reasonable time a solution acceptable to all—a position not unwelcome, as we have seen, in Germany.[180] A second clause noted that France "considers that . . . discussion must be continued until unanimous agreement is reached" in matters of vital national interest.[181] In retrospect many have seen the Luxembourg Compromise as an essential turning point, a marked slowing of the momentum gained during the early 1960s. Yet it would be incorrect to stress unanimity voting. All of the rapid movements of the 1960s were, after all, decided by unanimity. Even without the compromise, moreover, the Treaty unambiguously stated that all new policies—notably regulatory harmonization under Article 100—had to be approved unanimously. As one commentator noted at the time, "as regards the long-term issues of the federalist-nationalist conflict, the 1965–66 crisis changed nothing."[182]

Left out of all this was the Commission, whose initial proposals were forgotten by all except the Dutch, whose resolution for strengthening the Assembly was rejected. Hallstein became the scapegoat: de Gaulle forced him to resign the presidency after one year, despite the German government's half-hearted effort to mount a defense. Hallstein, his usefulness at an end, chose an immediate but dignified retirement. The Commission, one analyst noted, "acted rashly in the spring of 1965 and . . . the Commission played no part in the settlement of this crisis. The governments of the Five handled the crisis, and they handled it very well."[183]

Explaining Bargaining Outcomes

For neofunctionalists and even skeptics, the 1960s were the heyday of Commission policy leadership, until Gaullist high politics and the Luxembourg Compromise interceded. Hallstein's description of the Commission as the "engine of European integration," Haas wrote in 1967, had been correct "until 1965."[184] Such analysts maintain that the Commission fulfilled essential functions in policy initiation, mediation, and mobilization. This was bolstered by the fact that in these decisions the Commission had some formal powers of initiative and amendment; Hallstein himself claimed in retrospect that this empowered the Commission to act as both "initiator" and "honest broker."[185] The Commission is said to have enjoyed "important advantages in EEC policy-making by virtue of its rights of initiative." Vice-President Mansholt and the Commission, it is argued, "guided the [CAP] negotiations, . . . [hence] the final regulations do not differ markedly from the Commission's initial proposals." Only the Commission could

[180] Jaumin-Ponsar, *Essai*, 99, 113, 132.

[181] Newhouse, *Collision*, 156–157, 159–161; Lindberg, "Integration," 267.

[182] John Lambert, *Britain in Federal Europe* (London, 1968), 138.

[183] Camps, *European*, 124. Also Willis, *France*, 361.

[184] Ernst B. Haas, "'The Uniting of Europe' and the Uniting of Latin America," *Journal of Common Market Studies* 5:4 (June 1967), 323–324.

[185] Hallstein, *Europe*, 32.

fulfill the unique role of "representing the Community interest." The Commission was also a critical mediator. Generally "only . . . institutions representing the 'general interest' are in a position to mediate between the national viewpoints effectively." The inability of governments to agree on "precise formulas forced them to delegate the task of formulation to the Commission," without whose "mediating and brokerage functions . . . a decision would not have been achieved." A particular example is the Commission's "ingenuity" and "skill" in proposing "package deals," for example linking "the French interest in the completion of the CAP and the German . . . interest in progress on the Kennedy Round." Finally, the Commission was a critical mobilizer. It exploited "its direct access to the European Parliament and to the press and other opinion-forming media" to promote integration. In short, the Commission's ability to "upgrade the common interest" in these ways was *a* necessary condition, and quite possibly *the* necessary condition, for the striking success of integration during the 1960s.[186]

Empirical support for such conclusions drawn from supranational bargaining theory rests almost entirely on three observations. First, the Commission was closely involved in most negotiations. Second, it made many proposals that were accepted. Third, it often helped draft final agreements. All three points are true, though far from universally so. Yet when we pose more rigorous questions, namely whether Commission involvement was *necessary* or *decisive* for agreement, or whether the outcome resembled the Commission's *initial* proposals, we find that its role was weak. Commission entrepreneurship was, almost without exception, redundant or futile if not counterproductive.

We uncovered, to begin with, no cases in which Commission officials enjoyed privileged access to vital legal, political, or technical information. The theoretical consensus notwithstanding, this is unsurprising. Governments possessed equal or superior information about each issue. The Commission comprised fewer than 2,500 officials, and so was smaller than most national ministries, let alone national governments. It possessed limited capacity to collect information and little technical expertise, relying instead on committees of outside experts, most selected by their home governments. "The preponderant influence exercised by the national government experts," one study at the time concluded, "is explicable by the well-known fact that the government experts summoned by the Commission at [the initial] stage are often the same persons with whom it will have to negotiate its proposals."[187] Nor did Commission meetings of experts provide a unique conduit of information; the intergovernmental Council simultaneously held as many parallel ones.

Nor are there prominent cases in which the Commission, by virtue of its central position, demonstrated particular insights into national preferences and power. To be sure, close ties existed between particular Commissioners and national governments—Hallstein had been Adenauer's closest foreign policy col-

[186] Lindberg, *Political,* 210, 235, 244–245, 274; Camps, *What,* 43–44; Camps, *European,* 6, 35.

[187] Christoph Sasse, Edouard Poullet, David Coombes, and Gérard Deprez, *Decision Making in the European Community* (New York, 1977), 209.

laborator, Marjolin met weekly with de Gaulle's foreign minister—but most information appears to have flowed from the Commission to governments. We have no evidence of the Commission's particularly informed or acute political judgment, let alone any systematic manipulation of information.[188] Indeed, many of the Commission's proposals in transport, agriculture, and external trade, not least the 1965 proposal to link CAP financing to centralized control over finance, were extraordinarily impolitic. In the latter case, Hallstein and Mansholt ignored concrete prior warnings from those, among them Commissioners Marjolin and von der Groeben, who possessed the appropriate political information. Unconnected and unconcerned with democratic politics, Hallstein and Mansholt grew overconfident after a few apparent successes—a pattern, perhaps characteristic of officials not under direct democratic control, that we have already observed with Monnet and will encounter again with Jacques Delors.

National leaders had assessments of one another's preferences superior to those of the Commission; these were, moreover, usually uniform across governments, with little evidence of informational asymmetries. Sometimes leaders were unaware of domestic constraints on other governments, but in general only when foreign leaders were unsure of their own domestic consensus. Only de Gaulle remained somewhat opaque to his counterparts, in large part because he adopted a strategy of deliberate deception. Both German and British leaders tended to see de Gaulle as primarily a geopolitical ideologue, not a defender of French commercial interests. Hence the German government made concessions on the CAP for fear the General would "irrationally" withdraw from the EC, and British leaders focused on geopolitical carrots rather than assuage de Gaulle's fears about the CAP or exploit his domestic political weaknesses. (Even in this case, as we have seen, more rapid British or German concessions may not have deterred de Gaulle.) Yet, as the empty chair crisis demonstrates, the Commission was even less well informed about de Gaulle's motives than were national governments.

There is equally little evidence that bottlenecks impeded efficient bargaining. *In not a single significant case* did the Commission intervene to propose policies, mediate among governments, or mobilize domestic groups in a way unavailable from other actors and that resulted in a politically viable agreement. Despite the weakness of the Commission, negotiations appear to have been efficient—further evidence that transaction costs were low relative to interests. No clearly Pareto-improving deals were "left on the table," and there is no correlation between Commission involvement and efficient bargaining. Commission proposals were often ignored and, in the empty chair crisis, so ill-judged that many believed they nearly destroyed the EC.

The Commission did, as supranationalist theory predicts, often advance proposals in the "general" interest, that is, the interest of the consumer or of economic efficiency, as well as some package deals. Yet as one commentator concluded, "it is difficult at present for the Commission to gain support from the

---

[188] Marjolin, *Architect,* 264; Craig, "Konrad," 219.

national governments unless it can appeal to their self-interest. . . . A generalized appeal based on the need to advance European unity has little effect."[189] Commission proposals were rarely unique, and even its CAP ideas were identical to the Dutch position at Stresa. (Monnet, still active with his Action Committee, was erratic, supporting then opposing the Fouchet Plan, advancing no unique and viable proposals.) Proposals that were unique, as in transport policy and the empty chair crisis, proved futile. Only those proposals previously or simultaneously initiated by the most interested national governments were successful, as intergovernmental theory predicts: agricultural initiatives came from France and the Netherlands, foreign trade and competition initiatives from Germany, free trade initiatives from Britain. When proposals displeased governments, national leaders simply revised them or circumvented the Commission entirely, often ignoring its formal powers. Where greater coordination was required, the power to prepare proposals was swiftly transferred to intergovernmental bodies such as the Special Committee in agricultural matters or COREPER in the case of List G external tariff negotiations. Supranational mediation was ineffective in large part because governments already had an accurate notion of one another's preferences. When negotiations grew difficult, key compromises could be reached at bilateral Franco-German summits or in the Council of Ministers, with occasional mediation by leaders such as Spaak from smaller countries. By contrast, the Commission was ineffective and repeatedly sidelined—the empty chair crisis being only the most extreme example of a common phenomenon.

Commission efforts to mobilize transnational groups enjoyed similarly little success. Only in agriculture was a unified interest group active at the European level, but it had little discipline over its members and immediately fragmented into competing national groups over the question of prices. One study concluded that "there is no evidence that a French organization . . . has ever been able directly to promote a particularly cherished objective with success on the Community level."[190]

Since efficiency was easily assured, even without supranational intervention, distributional conflict was the primary concern of negotiators. In comparison with the Treaty negotiations, the stakes became more transparent, making negotiations more difficult. As Hallstein noted, "pricing and marketing policy increasingly formed the centre of gravity of the practical political work that was done," and so the scope for package deals was restricted in any case.[191]

The Commission's influence on distributional outcomes was equally marginal, consistent with its lack of privileged access to information and ideas. As neofunctionalists rightly assert, the Commission often (though by no means always) advanced the final proposals on the basis of which agreement was reached. Perhaps the simplest and strongest piece of evidence against the thesis that the

[189] Camps, *What*, 56.
[190] Hanns Peter Muth, *French Agriculture and the Political Integration of Western Europe* (Leyden, 1970), 210.
[191] Hallstein, *Europe*, 186.

Commission was influential is the simple fact that the outcomes in the most important areas were the opposite of what the Commission *initially* sought. Transport integration was an outright failure, and the CAP was close to the opposite of the Commission's ideal. Institutional arrangements in external trade policy were uncomfortably constraining, though German influence resulted in the mandate's permitting tradeoffs. Only in the acceleration of internal tariff removal, where Commission proposals were clearly redundant, was the outcome close to the Commission's ideal. The observation that the Commission sometimes advanced successful proposals, which lies at the center of previous studies, tells us little about its influence. The observation that it achieved its preferences *only* when they were consistent with those of major governments, as we are about to see, tells us a good deal.

Distributional outcomes reflected instead the relative power of governments, defined in terms of asymmetrical interdependence. Where interests converged, as in internal tariff reductions, side-payments were modest and debate was limited to the scope of acceleration. Governments such as that of Germany which strongly favored acceleration offered concessions to get it. Where commercial conflict of interest was great and no geopolitical interests offset them, as in transport, monetary, and social policies, no significant agreement resulted, despite Commission activism.

Within each issue-area the relative power of government—and hence the pattern of compromises and side-payments—reflected preference intensity, with the governments most favorable to the core of a sectoral policy compromising most on the margin to achieve it. Thus to gain access to German agricultural markets, its major goal, France was forced to accept prices at the German level and a more forthcoming policy toward the GATT. Britain, desperate to avoid commercial exclusion, was willing to pay virtually any price short of a complete break with the United States in order to gain membership. Germany, to achieve both internal market and general geopolitical gains, its highest priorities, accepted less than optimal outcomes on external trade policy and British accession.

Threats of exit and exclusion were, as predicted by intergovernmental theory, effective where credible. The most credible threat was levied by France and Germany against Britain; escape from exclusion dominated British policy for a decade. By contrast, the British threat to pull out of NATO was not credible, as British officials recognized, and was immediately dismissed. Germany's exit threat was weak because of strong economic interests and Adenauer's geopolitical beliefs; even in the empty chair crisis Germany blocked Dutch efforts to open discussions with Britain. French policy-makers were aware of the threat of an Anglo-German link, which helped bring them back to their empty chair in 1966.

Yet the hypothesis about exit and exclusion does face one apparent anomaly: the apparent success of de Gaulle's threats to withdraw if Germany did not make concessions on the CAP and EC institutions. This threat was not rationally credible, which both French and German governments understood. De Gaulle could not afford to jeopardize the CAP and would have been disadvantaged more than Germany by dissolution of the customs union into an FTA or a GATT arrangement. So why was the threat effective? We have seen that de Gaulle's deliberate deception led German leaders to believe he might be economically irrational and British leaders to focus on geopolitics rather than try to undermine the economic basis of his domestic support. Beneath the surface, moreover, there was considerable support among other governments, particular that of Germany, for some of de Gaulle's demands, not least his opposition to QMV. Between Erhard and de Gaulle the disagreement was as much symbolic as substantive, and therefore the true risks for de Gaulle were correspondingly lower; Erhard was in any case too weak domestically to take risks. Yet perhaps the most profound insight is that, appearances notwithstanding, the threat was not in fact particularly effective. Far from achieving a wholly reformed institution, as he sought from 1960 onward, de Gaulle achieved an agreement to disagree. During the empty chair crisis, we have seen, de Gaulle never called French EC membership into question. When domestic and international opposition coalesced, he quickly compromised, accepting informal rather than legal changes in decision-making.[192]

Finally, the potential for package deals was, as intergovernmental theory suggests, quite limited. Linkages could not impose large absolute losses on major interest groups. Linkage was instead largely restricted to balancing out gains across sectors or facilitating agreement *within* large, growing sectors with intra-industry trade—both cases that did not create large net winners and losers. Industrial tariffs are an example. Where there were large net winners and losers with undisputed control over domestic policy-making—agriculture, List G— little linkage was possible. Then logrolling generated policies that benefited producer groups at the expense of diffuse, unorganized, or unrepresented constituencies. In the CAP, for example, French and German farmers received higher average support prices, paid for by European consumers and taxpayers, as well as North American and EFTA farmers newly excluded from European markets.

Explaining Institutional Choice

As in the negotiation of the Treaty, institutional pooling and delegation through QMV or Commission autonomy are most consistent with the credible commitments approach, whereas ideological factors played a secondary role and technocratic considerations explain almost nothing.

National positions on delegation were not coherent, as an ideological explanation predicts, but reflected issue-specific imperatives, as credible commitment concerns predict. Where a government expected to be in the minority, as did Germany in the CAP, it resisted QMV; where it expected to be in the major-

---

[192] Keohane and Hoffmann compare this threat of exit to the threat to exclude Britain in 1985– 86, arguing that exit or exclusion was still possible to contemplate in the 1960s but not in the 1980s. Hence France gets its way and Britain compromises. This study suggests, instead, that exit was costly in both periods and the outcome was similar. Cf. Robert Keohane and Stanley Hoffmann, "Institutional Change in Europe in the 1980s," in *The New European Community: Decision-Making and Institutional Change* (Boulder, 1991), 21.

ity, as did Germany on GATT issues, it supported QMV. This was true even of Gaullist France. Backed by the Netherlands, France insisted in the early 1960s on moving beyond long-term contracts to a centralized CAP; Gaullist governments also insisted that authorization of bilateral quotas and price-setting be institutionalized, with substantial Commission input. De Gaulle and Pompidou insisted after 1966 on moving from an ad hoc intergovernmental mode of financing to a VAT centralized in Brussels. In each case centralization was to lock in implementation of and compliance with the CAP—initially to block persistent efforts by German agriculture officials to circumvent the CAP in favor of bilateral agreements and later to assure permanent financing of the CAP at generous levels before British entry. As the French foreign minister noted, his government became "the guardian of the Treaties" when it suited its interests.[193] Germany employed the same tactics in external tariff and competition policy. After France blocked a flexible negotiating position in the GATT, Germany sought greater Commission autonomy from the 111 and 113 committees. Even antifederalist Britain included QMV in various free trade plans, primarily for fear that France would exploit any veto and safeguards.

Ideology played only a secondary role. To be sure, the empty chair crisis was in part ideologically motivated within constraints set by economic interests. Germany was more willing to accept rhetorical commitments to majority voting and an active parliament. Such issues were distinguished, however, by their lack of predictable material consequences. Yet even on purely institutional issues, much ideological rhetoric was simple posturing. The Erhard government was prevented by the Bundestag from making an immediate compromise but in fact the underlying German position was not so different from that of France. Both remained skeptical about QMV and quietly colluded to maintain unanimity for decades after the Luxembourg Compromise. In the end the compromise reflected de Gaulle's willingness to water down his ideology to retain the economic benefits of integration.

Governments paid closer attention to the autonomy of international institutions when the results were predictable. In general, they granted autonomy in inverse proportion to scope. The most striking institutional innovations in the 1960s were in fact designed primarily to limit supranational power. Member-states either exploited ambiguities in the Treaty or circumvented the Treaty outright, as with the Special Committee on Agriculture and the Luxembourg Compromise. Administration of the CAP and conduct of foreign trade negotiations were both expressly limited by oversight committees, limits on scope, and alternative institutions. Governments delegated only within carefully circumscribed limits, usually concerning daily management and isolated enforcement decisions, where a neutral body was necessary to avoid noncompliance.

By the late 1960s the construction of the customs union foreseen in the Treaty of Rome was complete. The process of market integration had reached the point of no return. Germany and France, Gaullist concerns notwithstanding, were committed in practice to policy-making within the EC, for which they were willing to sacrifice other economic and geopolitical objectives. The consolidation of the customs union was not an unintended consequence of previous decisions; it was instead the result of deliberate efforts both by those who drafted the Treaty in the 1950s and by those who elaborated it in the 1960s. All governments contributed, not least Gaullist France, which defended the Treaty as the only means to achieve its predominant goal, agricultural integration. In this there was much policy continuity: the major priorities and preferences of governments in the 1950s were, for the most part, their priorities and preferences in the 1960s. The issues debated during the 1960s, such as the elaboration of the CAP and the commercial policy—were those inherited from the incomplete Treaty of Rome negotiations. The few shifts in policy—a movement in British strategy from opposition to membership and a sudden intensification of French preferences for industrial tariff liberalization—were not, for the most part, shifts in preferences. Instead, they simply accelerated trends foreseen by those who signed the Treaty or responded to slowly evolving economic constraints. Behind it all was the rapid expansion of industrial trade among developed countries, regardless of international institutional affiliations. In the decades to come, European leaders would turn to other economic issues occasioned by worldwide trends, among them the rise of new regulatory concerns and a series of exogenous macroeconomic changes. In the next chapter, we turn to the most important of these policy responses, monetary integration.

CHAPTER FOUR

Divergence and Convergence:
Toward Monetary Integration, 1969–1983

> [Some say] it is a mistake to treat . . . European construction [as] traditional diplomacy, since [it] is a movement of true integration . . . [But] this was exactly what we tried to do in the monetary field. . . . We failed, and had to realize that traditional diplomacy was the game successfully played by the others.
>
> —Luigi Spaventa, Italian economist and policy-maker (1980)

The most significant development in the EC during the 1970s and early 1980s was the emergence of European monetary integration. Three decisions were particularly salient: the creation of the European Exchange Rate Agreement or "Snake" in 1973, the making of the European Monetary System (EMS) in 1979, and the "hardening" of EMS constraints on France between 1982 and 1986. The Snake and EMS created adjustable peg systems that stabilized exchange rates but functioned in an "asymmetrical" manner by apportioning the costs of domestic macroeconomic adjustment disproportionately to weak-currency countries such as France, Italy, and Britain (which had to tolerate relatively high interest rates and overvalued currencies) rather than to strong-currency countries like Germany. The institutional rules of the EMS were minimal: supranational authorities were weak and financial obligations modest, though a norm emerged that unanimous consent was required for parity changes. Monetary negotiations were linked at times to other issues, including successful British accession, weak CAP financing and reform, an expansion of regional but marginal social policies, direct elections to the European Parliament beginning in 1979, failed efforts to promote greater qualified majority voting (QMV), and the creation of the European Council, a forum in which EC chief executives hold regular summit meetings.

Many explanations of these decisions stress "high politics," that is, the geopolitical and ideological motivations of national leaders. In France, Georges Pompidou and Valéry Giscard d'Estaing are said to have promoted the Snake and the EMS, as well as British membership, in order to offset German *Ostpolitik*; François Mitterrand, to have strengthened the system out of commitment to European ideology. In Germany, Willy Brandt is said to have sought to match *Ostpolitik* with a Western initiative, while Helmut Schmidt aimed to realize a federalist vision as a joint European response to dependence on an unreliable

United States in defense matters.[1] Other commentators stress domestic partisan politics and distinctive economic ideologies.[2] Finally, some analyses emphasize the political entrepreneurship of Commission President Roy Jenkins in promoting the EMS.

My argument is instead that economic interests were a predominant motivation for national decisions in each episode, that bargaining outcomes reflected the relative power of states rather than supranational entrepreneurship, and that the minimal nature of institutional commitments reflected the unwillingness of powerful governments, notably Germany, to constrain their macroeconomic autonomy. The decline of Bretton Woods and rising capital mobility, both of which undermined domestic macroeconomic autonomy, triggered a search for regional arrangements to stabilize exchange rates. Yet agreement was neither immediate nor automatic. Effective cooperation among large countries began only in the mid-1980s. Willingness to cooperate varied considerably across countries and across time. This, I argue, reflected above all the differentials in the transitional costs of moving to fixed exchange rates, which in turn stemmed from the desire of producers of international traded goods for competitive exchange rates and particular national macroeconomic preferences, as predicted by the theory of exchange-rate policy outlined in chapter 1. Major monetary agreements emerged out of a quid pro quo between strong-currency countries, led by Germany, and weak-currency countries, led by France. Successive German governments sought to dampen appreciation of the deutsche mark (DM) and expand domestic room for macroeconomic stimulation; in France, Giscard and Mitterrand sought to dampen currency volatility and bolster the economic and political credibility of domestic anti-inflationary policies. Cooperation was possible, however, only after prior decisions had led to a convergence of macroeconomic performance and policy, thereby reducing the costs of cooperation to the tradable sector of the economy—as was the case under Schmidt and Giscard in the late 1970s, as well as Mitterrand and Kohl after 1983. Greater policy convergence, more than rising interdependence, explains the greater success of the EMS than of the Snake; the persistent Franco-German support and Anglo-Italian reticence regarding monetary cooperation; and the particular conditions that strong- and weak-currency countries sought to impose on one another.[3]

---

[1] E.g., Michele Fratianni, and Jürgen von Hagen, *The European Monetary System and European Monetary Union* (Boulder, Colo., 1992); Jeffrey Sachs, and Charles Wyplosz, "The Economic Consequences of President Mitterrand," *Economic Policy* no. 2 (1986), 261–313; Haig Simonian, *The Privileged Partnership: Franco-German Relations in the European Community, 1969–84* (Oxford, 1985).

[2] Jonathan Story, "The Launching of the EMS: An Analysis of Change in Foreign Economic Policy," *Political Studies* 36 (Autumn 1988), 397–412; Kathleen R. McNamara, *The Currency of Ideas: Monetary Politics in the European Union* (Ithaca, 1998).

[3] This argument is consistent with but different in emphasis from existing work on the EMS. John Goodman, *Monetary Sovereignty: The Politics of Central Banking in Western Europe* (Ithaca, 1991), places greater emphasis on domestic institutional commitments; McNamara, *Currency*, on the role of ideas; and Jeffry A. Frieden, "Making Commitments: France and Italy in the European Monetary System, 1979–1985," Center for German and European Studies *Working Paper Series 1.14* (Berkeley, Calif., 1993), on the final steady state, rather than inflationary divergence during the transition to fixed exchange rates. Nor do these works treat the dynamics of bargaining or institutional commitment.

On related issues—notably CAP reform, British membership, and greater regional subsidies—each government continued to pursue the narrow commercial interests that had led it to create and consolidate the EC in the 1950s and 1960s. In all this geopolitical interests and ideology mattered only on the margin: geopolitics was exploited by chief executives like Schmidt and Giscard to legitimate monetary cooperation but trumped economic interests only in Margaret Thatcher's lonely and ultimately futile opposition to British participation in the EMS after 1984. Only in pure areas of institutional reform—the formation of the European Council and direct elections to the Parliament—do we see consistent attention to geopolitical interests and ideology.

Despite substantial convergence among national preferences, the extent to which those preferences converged is often exaggerated. Important distributional issues remained. The outcomes of bargaining over these issues reflected (to an even more striking degree than in the 1950s and 1960s) the initiative and relative power of national governments rather than the desires of supranational entrepreneurs. Both strong- and weak-currency countries sought to transfer adjustment costs to one other. The result was a series of disputes over the "symmetry" of the system. Both the Snake and the EMS marked victories for Germany in that they imposed commitments to adjust at the expense of domestic stability on weak-currency countries, while leaving macroeconomic policy in strong-currency countries essentially unfettered. This outcome did not result from pressure by supranational entrepreneurs in the Commission, whose proposals tended to be either unoriginal or ineffective; on most controversial issues, notably the symmetry of the system and the provision of finance, the Commission sought the opposite of the outcomes finally reached. Instead the EMS was decisively constrained by the ratifiability of agreements in Germany (Germany's "win-set").[4] Particularly important was the extraordinary domestic influence of the Bundesbank, which meant that the governments of strong and weak-currency countries, both of which would have preferred a more symmetric system, were faced with a credible threat to reject any arrangement that undermined German macroeconomic autonomy.

The choice whether to delegate and pool monetary sovereignty in international institutions, I argue finally, was motivated by the substantive preferences of governments concerning monetary cooperation and their resulting willingness to be constrained by commitments. The provision of technocratic information and underlying geopolitical ideology, by contrast, played little role. Here too there was disagreement. In European monetary affairs, despite a long history of extensive information exchanges, weak-currency governments sought genuine pooling and delegation of sovereignty in the hope it would curb German unilateralism. Germany refused. Snake and EMS decision-making was conducted instead within intergovernmental ministers, as Germany preferred, not in more

---

[4] This interpretation is consistent with the general theoretical analysis, though not all empirical conclusions, of Dorothée Heisenberg, "The Mark of the Bundesbank: Germany's Role in European Monetary Cooperation (Ph.D. diss., Yale University, 1996). See also Peter Ludlow, *The Making of the European Monetary System* (London, 1982).

supranational institutions proposed by France.[5] Both positions reflected economic interests. External controls were imposed on weak-currency countries, but these were modest and tended to increase the credibility of domestic policies. Similarly, the institutionalization of summitry within the European Council was designed to increase the agenda-setting power of national governments and, if secondarily, to strengthen national executives *vis-à-vis* domestic groups. Ideological concerns were reflected only in the establishment of elections to the Parliament, the substantive consequences of which were uncertain. In short, a combination of economic interest, relative power, and concerns about credible commitments explains the essential nature of European monetary cooperation from 1969 through 1983.

NATIONAL PREFERENCE FORMATION: "ECONOMISTS" VS. "MONETARISTS"

From conflicts within the European Payments Union (EPU) in the mid-1950s to disputes over reform of the EMS in the mid-1980s, the positions of European governments on questions of exchange-rate stabilization remained remarkably stable. They divided into two basic camps.[6] The first, termed the "economist" position, was characteristic of countries with strong currencies, low inflation, and persistent trade surpluses: Germany, the Netherlands, and until 1970 Italy. It held that economic convergence should precede monetary integration and should be asymmetrical, with the costs of exchange-rate stabilization borne primarily by weak-currency countries. Monetary union should be the "coronation" of a long process of economic convergence and integration, in which such aggregates as inflation, debt, and interest rates move toward hard-currency country (in this case, German) standards; and free movement of goods and capital should be assured. Such an arrangement favors strong-currency countries because it reduces the costs to exporters of currency appreciation, increases domestic macroeconomic flexibility, and assures stable trading patterns. The second, "monetarist" position—misleadingly named, for it has little to do with monetarist economic theory—was espoused by countries with weaker currencies, higher inflation, and persistent trade deficits: France, Britain until 1980, Belgium and Italy after 1970, backed by the Commission. In this view, monetary cooperation should precede economic convergence and, with the costs of exchange-rate stabilization borne equally or primarily by strong-currency countries. Positions on every major issue of monetary integration—obligations to intervene, levels of currencies, financial transfers, speed of integration—evince this central cleavage (see Table 4.1).

[5] This argument is consistent with John T. Wooley, "Capital, and the EMS: Policy Credibility and Political Institutions," in Alberta Sbragia, ed., *Europolitics: Institutions and Policy-Making in the "New" European Community* (Washington, D.C., 1992), 157–190; Francesco Giavazzi and Alberto Giovannini, *Limiting Exchange-Rate Flexibility: The European Monetary System* (Cambridge, Mass., 1989).

[6] Loukas Tsoukalis, *The Politics and Economics of European Monetary Integration* (London, 1978); Kenneth Dyson, *Elusive Union: The Process of Economic and Monetary Union in Europe* (London, 1994), 65–67.

Table 4.1. Monetary cooperation and related issues, 1969–1983: Preferences and outcomes

Issue-area	Germany	France	Britain	Commission	Outcomes
Monetary policy	Prefers adjustable-peg exchange-rate system to dampen DM appreciation and stimulate economy, particularly strongly during periods of dollar depreciation (1969–73 and 1977–79). Yet the system must remain "asymmetrical," in that intervention rules and financing obligations impose only a minimal domestic constraint in strong-currency countries.	Prefers adjustable-peg system to support disinflationary policies, particularly in 1976–1980, but prefers a "symmetrical" or "monetarist" system in which intervention rules and generous financial transfers shift burden of domestic adjustment toward strong-currency countries.	Opposes participation in adjustable-peg system. Before 1979 accepts membership only with intervention rules and very large financial transfers that strongly favor weak-currency countries, though prefers to avoid outright exclusion. After 1979 supports even stronger unilateral domestic discipline than EMS provides. By 1985 cabinet, parliament, and business press for EMS on "economist" terms.	Consistently prefers the British 1978–79 position: a "symmetrical," "monetarist" system backed by major financial transfers ("fiscal federalism").	1969–1978: German "economist" position prevails in the Snake. France and Britain leave.

1979–1983: German position prevails in the EMS, backed by an unkept promise to reconsider in two years and modest one-time side-payments. France joins; Britain opts out. |

CAP reform	Prefers higher unilateral price supports to offset monetary fluctuations (MCAs), a reduction in third-country export subsidies. Resists renegotiation of British share.	Prefers higher export subsidies, reduction of price supports to moderate levels, elimination of MCAs. Strongly favors permanent CAP financing. Resists renegotiation of British share.	Once a member, opposes export subsidies, prefers continued price subsidies, renegotiation of British share.	Prefers CAP reform with low prices and structural adjustment.	No change.
Regional policy	Opposes until British referendum.	Skeptical.	Strong support.	Strong support.	Modest transfers until British referendum, then increase.
Institutional reform	Prefers strong European Council and direct elections to EP. Skeptical of more QMV and centralization of CAP finance.	Prefers centralized CAP finance and strong European Council. Weak support for EP elections. Opposes QMV.	Prefers strong European Council, skeptical of EP elections, opposed to QMV. Probably opposes centralized CAP finance.	Strongly prefers centralized CAP finance, more QMV, standardized direct elections to EP. Skeptical of strong European Council.	Centralization of CAP finance, creation of moderately strong European Council, unstandardized direct elections to EP, no formal change in QMV.

Germany: Balancing Internal and External Stability

From 1965 through 1985 the German government consistently supported deeper European monetary cooperation, even monetary unification, provided it did not threaten domestic monetary control. It espoused the economist position, whereby monetary integration would proceed on the basis of prior economic convergence to Germany's low-inflation standard. On this basis, German leaders repeatedly initiated or backed exchange-rate stabilization during periods of dollar weakness such as 1969–73 and 1977–79, as well as the late 1980s. The timing was not coincidental: dollar depreciation generated unpleasant upward pressure on the DM. Throughout, German policy was based not, as most analysts assume, on the strict anti-inflationary preferences of the Bundesbank, but on a compromise between concern about inflation, on the one hand, and concerns about export competitiveness and domestic economic stimulation, on the other. On other prominent issues, German policy remained stable. Germany supported enlargement to include Britain and high CAP price supports, even when they violated EC rules, but opposed high CAP export subsidies and large outlays for regional and social funding. In institutional matters, Germany favored direct elections to the European Parliament and closer cooperation among chief executives in the European Council.

Geopolitical Interest and Ideology: Ostpolitik and "Memories of Auschwitz"

Upon entering office in 1969, Willy Brandt's major priority in foreign policy was *Ostpolitik*, the normalization of relations with East Germany and the Soviet Union. Brandt sought to employ monetary cooperation as part of an active *Westpolitik* aimed at assuaging foreign fears of "a second Rapallo" and securing French acquiescence to a renegotiation of the status of Berlin. Legislation authorizing Ostpolitik eventually passed the Bundestag by only one vote, and overt foreign opposition might have tipped the balance in the other direction. A July 1970 Cabinet meeting on Ostpolitik directly linked the goal of a German-Soviet treaty renouncing the use of force to "dynamic" German initiatives concerning European integration of particular concern to France.[7]

Many analyses of Schmidt's motivations ascribe to him primarily geopolitical motivations, grounded either in concern for European political independence from the United States or in general, European federalist sentiments. By the late 1970s, it is true, Schmidt was angry with Jimmy Carter over handling of relations with the East, and he was to be damaged by Carter's waffling on the neutron bomb. An ambivalent passage from Schmidt's memoirs, published ten years later, is often cited as evidence of geopolitical motivation. Schmidt claims to have "regarded the EMS *not only* as a mere instrument to harmonize economic policies . . . *but also* as part of a broader strategy for the political self-determination of

---

[7] Willy Brandt, *Begegnungen und Einsichten* (Hamburg, 1996), 322. Arnulf Baring, *Machtwechsel: Die Ära Brandt-Scheel* (Stuttgart, 1982), 319–321; Lankowski, *Germany*, 308–309, 316–317; Henning, *Currencies*, 183. Electoral pressure to show a foreign policy "success" may have played a role. Cf. Story, "Launching," 408, who underestimates the narrowness of Brandt's mandate.

Europe"—though the passage literally states that economic policy was dominant.[8] Schmidt had been involved in European integration since the 1940s and had served on Monnet's Action Committee since the 1950s, as well as maintaining close relations with Robert Marjolin, Raymond Barre, and others. Schmidt also publicly endorsed occasionally (and after leaving office, increasingly) the view that European or Franco-German cooperation has helped guarantee Franco-German peace after wars "from Napoleon to Hitler."[9] He wrote the introduction to the German edition of Monnet's memoir. On the basis of this evidence—there is no more—many analysts speculate that such ideological concerns were predominant in Schmidt's mind.[10]

Yet Schmidt's Euro-enthusiasm should not be exaggerated. His Europeanism was constrained by pragmatism, and his primary concerns, as we shall see, remained economic. When Schmidt spoke of world power, it was economic power to which he generally referred. He had opposed the Treaty of Rome because it excluded Britain and had not been active on European issues, in particular monetary issues, until economic conditions dictated such a course. Like Giscard, he disliked visionary plans and, even more than Brandt, displayed in private a consistent skepticism, bordering on disdain, for core European policies such as the CAP, for exuberant expressions of European ideology, and for supranational officials. Of the Commission, Schmidt once remarked: "Let the realists who know what they are talking about look after Europe, and spare us the opinions of people who could not even run a tram company for more than two years without running a deficit. Like his British and French counterparts, Schmidt strongly supported proposals to supplant the Commission with more intergovernmental procedures.[11] When Spinelli's Draft Treaty was proposed in the early 1980s, Schmidt grumbled: "So we have to identify ourselves with Europe now . . . I don't believe in it."[12]

Economic Interests: "Every third German" Lives from Exports

We have seen in previous chapters that postwar West Germany pursued a strategy of export-led growth, one element of which was a persistently undervalued

[8] Fratianni and Van Hagen, *European*, 17–18, citing a 1990 article in *Die Zeit*.

[9] Helmut Schmidt, *Weggefährten: Erinnerungen und Reflexionen* (Berlin, 1996), 258, also 252–262.

[10] Fratianni and von Hagen, *European*, 16–19.

[11] Carr, *Schmidt*, 96. Also Emminger, *D-Mark*, 364; Roy Jenkins, *European Diary, 1977–1981* (London, 10), Roy Jenkins, *Life at the Centre* (New York, 1993), 474; Timothy Garten Ash, *In Europe's Name* (New York, 1994), 95; Gaddum, *Deutsche*, 197ff. Did Schmidt pursue this as an electoral tactic to demonstrate his global status as a statesman? It appears to have been the opposite; both Schmidt and Giscard sought to advance initiatives *after* elections. See interviews in Wolfram F. Hanrieder, ed., *Helmut Schmidt: Perspectives on Politics* (Boulder, Colo., 1982). Schmidt, *Die Deutschen und ihre Nachbarn* (Berlin, 1990), 241–242, is blunt about the primacy of political economy: "For the decision to simply cut through the knot, there was one important reason: Giscard and Barre were convinced that the EMS was necessary to realize their own economic policies; I was equally convinced of this." References to the United States concern not the *geopolitical* leadership position of European countries but Europe's need to oppose what Schmidt considered a disastrous U.S. interest- and exchange-rate policy.

[12] Carl Otto Lenz, "The Draft Treaty Establishing the European Union: Report on the Federal Republic of Germany," in Roland Bieber, Jean-Paul Jacqué, and Joseph H. H. Weiler, eds., *An Ever Closer Union?* (Brussels, 1985), 213.

currency. The monetary effects of this were offset by the Bundesbank, which held down inflation to a level lower than that prevailing elsewhere in Europe. The result: regional monetary tension. Upward pressure on the DM was matched by downward pressure on other European currencies. German policy-makers responded though a series of ad hoc measures, including capital exports, domestic absorption of the remaining liquidity, and occasional border controls. Within the relatively stable, low-inflation world of Bretton Woods, such policies were adequate to stabilize exchange rates, but with the weakening and collapse of Bretton Woods, the German government began to lose control. At the international level, the policy divergence—and divergence in price levels—between Germany and its neighbors raised the question of who would adjust their domestic macroeconomic policy in order to stabilize exchange rates.[13]

The essence of the German position was that the burden of adjustment to stable exchange rates should fall on weak-currency countries, while strong-currency countries should remain protected against either imported inflation or demands to finance foreign deficits. Hence Germany embraced the economist perspective, which mandated that macroeconomic convergence should precede any surrender of monetary sovereignty. From a political perspective, Germany's adherence to the "economist" position was a stable and relatively advantageous compromise between the two entrenched domestic coalitions that disputed exchange-rate policy throughout the postwar period, regardless of the external institutional environment.

The first coalition included tradables producers, particularly exporters, large banks, and many unions and Social Democrats, all of whom favored a fixed external value for the DM, even at the risk of slightly greater inflation, in order to assure a competitive exchange rate. While increased inflation might also undermine export competitiveness, it was preferable to business, since, one analyst noted, "imported inflation affects the export-oriented industries' foreign and domestic prices before their domestic costs ,[hence] such lagged inflation would be insufficient to remove the comparative advantage of German exports."[14] Moreover, as long as German inflation was lower than that of its neighbors, nominal exchange-rate stability would result in real DM depreciation, which exporters favored. Social Democrats also favored greater macroeconomic flexibility and lower interest rates, which could be achieved by fixing a more competitive exchange rate. Large banks, closely connected to industry through equity

---

[13] Interpretations of German foreign economic policy consistent with this analysis of its European monetary preference include Michael Kreile, "West Germany: The Dynamics of Expansion," in ed., Peter Katzenstein, *Between Power and Plenty: Foreign Economic Policies of Advanced Industrial States* (Madison, Wisc., 1978), 191–224; William Wadbrook, *West German Balance of Payments Policy: Prelude to European Monetary Union?* (New York, 1972); Carl Lankowski, "Germany and the European Communities: Anatomy of a Hegemonial Relation" (Ph.D. diss., Columbia University, 1982); Herbert Giersch, Karl-Heinz Paqué, and Holger Schmiedling, *The Fading Miracle: Four Decades of Market Economy in Germany* (Cambridge, 1992; C. Randall Henning, *Currencies and Politics in the United States, Germany and Japan* (Washington, D.C., 1993).

[14] Wadbrook, *West*, 80; Daniel Gros, and Niels Thygesen, *European Monetary Integration: From the European Monetary System towards Monetary Union* (London, 1991), chap. 2.

holdings and long-term relationships, generally supported this strategy. Other motivations for external monetary stability, such as dampening exchange-rate volatility, appear to have been secondary.

The second, opposing coalition included firms and unions connected with domestic, nontradables sectors, such as construction, domestic banks and state services, some consumer interests, many German economists, and above all the central bank, the Deutsche Bundesbank. This coalition favored price stability even at the expense of real DM appreciation, which implied floating rates or a flexible pegged-exchange-rate system that did not impose obligations on strong-currency countries. The Bundesbank was a powerful actor not simply because of its institutional independence but because of its strong anti-inflationary mandate, grounded in public and elite opinion. It toppled at least two postwar chancellors, seemingly heedless of their party: Erhard, of whose fall in 1966 Bundesbank president Blessing remarked that "we had to use brute force to put things in order," and Schmidt, whose policies I examine below. Its actions contributed to the fall of at least one more.[15] At the international level, the Bundesbank contended that price stability required that it maintain autonomy to temper capital inflows with currency appreciation, whatever the consequences for competitiveness. The shift to floating rates in the early 1970s accorded the Bundesbank even greater de facto independence, tempered only by the selection of its presidents, by threats to alter its legislative statute, and by formal international agreements, which, once properly ratified, supercede German law.

There has been intermittent conflict between these two coalitions since the founding of the Federal Republic. Germany's "economist" position on European monetary cooperation—cooperation to keep the exchange rate down insofar as it did not threaten domestic inflation—reflected a stable compromise between these two groups. Germany's strong competitive position and credible anti-inflationary institutions generally permitted a relatively attractive unilateral policy compromise to be struck, resulting in low inflation and continuous trade surpluses. The currency was consistently undervalued, but whenever significant depreciation threatened, for example after the second oil crisis, the Bundesbank moved strongly to shore up the DM. The compromise was threatened only when the twin goals of export competitiveness and low inflation came into direct conflict, which occurred whenever the dollar weakened. This was visible already under the European Payments Union in the mid-1950s, then at an accelerating pace with the decline of Bretton Woods, thus in 1959–61, 1968–69, 1971–73, 1977–79, and 1986–88 and 1995–97. In each case, dollar depreciation triggered inflows of capital into Germany and outflows of capital from its weak-currency neighbors, pressuring Germany either to inflate domestically or to revalue the DM upward. Proposals for even modest revaluation unleashed such bitter domestic conflict between the two coalitions and, in particular, such virulent opposition from industry, as to render revaluation, in the words of one economic historian, "a practically unavailable alternative" during

---

[15] David Marsh, *The Bundesbank: The Bank That Rules Europe* (London, 1992), 187, also 168–195.

the 1960s. The result was a cumulative DM undervaluation over the decade of almost 15 percent, leading to international pressures on the parities of weak-currency countries.[16]

European monetary integration, as leading German bankers and policy-makers made clear, was primarily a means to preserve this policy in the face of international monetary turbulence. If European currencies were coordinated, dollar depreciation would be less likely to trigger depreciation among neigh-boring currencies and capital flows would be less likely to target Germany. Yet any commitment to European cooperation would be opposed and likely blocked by the Bundesbank if it threatened higher inflation. (Business was also con-cerned that higher inflation might lead to real DM appreciation, as occurred af-ter the modest 1961 revaluation.) German officials were particularly concerned about a situation of moral hazard, in which unlimited support would encourage other countries to run indefinite deficits while forcing Germany to accept higher inflation. The result was the economist position: Germany agreed to accept con-straints on its own monetary policy only if other countries fulfilled two precon-ditions: macroeconomic convergence to low inflation, and capital liberalization. The German government first announced this policy in 1965.[17]

Whenever dollar depreciation placed upward pressure on the DM, the export and banking coalition was strengthened against the Bundesbank, smaller bank-ers, and nontradable producers. With the decline of Bretton Woods, such con-flicts became more common. In 1968–69, with both the dollar and the franc weakening, capital began flowing into Germany and there was considerable in-ternational pressure for a DM revaluation. The prospect was supported domes-tically by the Bundesbank, the Deutsche Sparkassen- und Giroverband (the Ger-man equivalent of savings and loans), small banks primarily involved in domestic finance, the main union federation, the DGB, and the Council of Economic Advisers. Opposition to revaluation and floating came from farmers and indus-try, represented by the BDI (still headed by Fritz Berg), with allies in the Eco-nomics Ministry. Berg, backed by machine-tool, electronics, chemicals, and au-tomobile manufacturers, stressed that floating would disrupt the "calculus" of

---

[16] Wadbrook, *West*, 129, also 125–134; Henning, *Currencies*, 180ff; Marsh, *Bundesbank*, 170–171. The continuity of the policy combination of high *nominal* exchange rate and a low *real* exchange rate, along with the international difficulties that arose, is striking. The dynamics of the Euro-pean Payments Union in the 1950s, before the founding of the EC, already hint at same factors that would influence policy forty years later—even though direct capital flows were controlled. See Monika Dickhaus, "Zwischen Europa und der Welt: Die internationale Währungspolitik der deutschen Zentralbank, 1948–1958" (diss., EUI, 1995), 253–260. The revaluation debate between 1959 and 1961 revealed the same domestic split, though with the Bundesbank in a more ambivalent role; the outcome, a 5 percent revaluation, was too little, too late to offset the DM undervalua-tion. By the late 1960s, however, the Bundesbank consistently preferred appreciation to inflation. Hugo M. Kaufmann, "A Debate over Germany's Revaluation 1961: A Chapter in Political Economy," *Weltwirtschaftliches Archiv* 103 (1969), 190–195; Otto Emminger, *The D-Mark in the Conflict between Internal and External Equilibrium*, Princeton Essays in International Finance no. 122 (Princeton, N.J., 1977).

[17] Ludlow, *Making*, 15; Wadbrook, *West*, 75–77, 273n, 275, 279–280; Marsh, *Bank*, 212; Jonathan Carr, *Helmut Schmidt: Helmsman of Germany* (London, 1985), 140–141. By strengthening other Euro-pean currencies, moreover, modest amounts of European monetary cooperation may have bolstered the Bundesbank's ability to manage the major external source of domestic instability, the DM–dollar relationship.

German export industry, from which, he argued, "every third German lives." The powerful Bavarian politician Franz-Josef Strauss, backed by farm groups, pointed out that revaluation would depress CAP agricultural prices. Karl Schiller, minister of economics and finance, argued that appreciation would dampen inflation by reducing export surpluses and shifting resources to public spending. The anti-revaluation group triumphed for nearly a year, as the French government expended considerable sums in fruitless defense of the franc. Even after a franc devaluation, pressures induced by capital inflows could not be resisted indefinitely. In August 1969, as one of its first actions, the incoming government of Willy Brandt finally revalued the DM.[18]

The 1968–69 experience was repeated in the next decade during two major periods of dollar weakness.[19] Each time case Bundesbank intervention provided only short-term relief before purchases of DM inflated the money supply; the result was a domestic tightening and DM appreciation. The same coalitions formed as before, but with higher stakes; coalitions for floating and fixed rates replaced those for and against revaluation. Supporters of fixed rates within Europe were led by the BDI. Fiscal tightening was not politically feasible, so policy-makers sought to strike a balance between tightening and currency appreciation, on the one hand, and higher inflation and currency stability, on the other. In 1973, with net capital inflows totaling eight times the current-account surplus, the German government was forced to float free of Bretton Woods constraints, reestablishing domestic control at the expense of substantial appreciation. The same pressures arose in 1977–78, as a softening dollar and DM appreciation led to support for monetary integration from exporters, led by the BDI and the large banks. The BDI also noted that the Bundesbank's new freedom might restrict government spending. Sheltered sectors, represented by the Deutsche Industrie- und Handelstag (DIHT) and smaller banks, were neutral. Critical of Schmidt were economists, led by all five of the major German economic institutes; the opposition CDU/CSU, whose attacks were vehement enough to "question Germany's traditional bipartisan approach to major EC questions"; and, above all, the Bundesbank. In addition, Schmidt faced growing pressure from unions and the SPD for expansionary policies and greater job creation. An internal memo to the chancellor called on him to exploit the moment to stimulate the economy prior to the 1980 elections.

During this period monetary cooperation was linked to other issues, but the

[18] This paragraph and the next follow Carr, *Helmut*, 141; Dorothée Heisenberg, "Mark of the Bundesbank," 59ff; Lankowski, *Germany*, 292–295, 299–301, 313–315; Otto Emminger, *D-Mark, Dollar, Währungskrisen: Erinnerungen eines ehemaligen Bundesbankpräsidenten* (Stuttgart, 1986), 357–367; Valéry Giscard d'Estaing, *Le Pouvoir et la vie* (Paris, 1988), 143–144; Great Britain, House of Commons, *The European Monetary System*, First Report from the Expenditure Committee, 1978–1979 (London: HMSO, 1978), 62; Ludlow, *Making*, 135–137, 267; Story, "Launching," 401–402; Henning, *Currencies*, 187–189; Karl Kaltenthaler, "The Sources of Policy Dynamics: Variations in German and French Policy toward European Monetary Cooperation," mimeo. (Memphis, Tenn., 1996).

[19] Josef Ertl, *Agrarpolitik ohne Illusionen: Politische und Persönliche Erfahrungen* (Frankfurt, 1985), 45–50; Eckart Gaddum, *Die deutsche Europapolitik in den 8oer Jahren: Interessen, Konflikte und Entscheidungen der Regierung Kohl* (Paderborn, 1994), 102–103, 113. A gentlemen's agreement between Giscard and Schmidt to cut CAP support prices and limit MCAs was ignored by Ertl, who replied: "I don't take orders from the Chancellor." Kohl aggressively pursued the farm vote in the mid-1980s and hence made few compromises.

underlying political economy of the German position changed only slowly, if at all. On the British question, Germany continued to press for accession, a position still near unanimously supported by business. On the CAP, German farmers insisted on continued high prices. Schmidt was personally skeptical about CAP agricultural subsidies—he went so far as to seek a gentleman's agreement with Giscard to cut them, but the effort was immediately quashed by his FDP agriculture minister Josef Ertl (a staunch Bavarian advocate of small farmers' interest), backed by the FDP, the opposition CDU/CSU, and even the parliamentary faction of his own SPD. By the end of the 1970s Germany had become the sixth-largest agricultural exporter in the world, almost entirely within the protected European market. Cuts in support prices, essentially impossible in 1966, were no more feasible ten years later. Finally, there was considerable suspicion of regional subsidies, which involved net transfers from Germany to its neighbors.

The Domestic Decision:
"We stand under the primacy of economic policy"

We begin with the Brandt government, which took its first steps toward monetary integration in 1969, against a backdrop of continuous upward pressure on the DM. As we have seen, Brandt himself was motivated primarily by geopolitics, in particular the need to provide Western support for Ostpolitik. Yet the necessary domestic support for any commitment to monetary cooperation had to be grounded in economic interest. Brandt recognized that the impact of DM appreciation on export industries was a "particularly decisive factor" favoring monetary cooperation. Domestic constraints tied him to the economist position and prevented him from courting favor with weak-currency countries by accepting invasions of sovereignty that favored them, such as the pooling of reserves, expanded short-term stand-by agreements, and automatic German obligation to support weak foreign currencies. The Bundesbank argued that even if weak-currency countries simply financed public-sector deficits on general capital markets, the result would be a transfer of real resources. European monetary integration must therefore create a "stability community" or no community at all. Between 1969 and 1974 the dominant force in German international monetary policy-making was Finance Minister Helmut Schmidt, whose support for the economist view found near-unanimous backing within the bureaucracy and government, even among high officials in the Economics Ministry who accepted greater inflation as an "integration sacrifice" that Germany had to make for "Europe." The economist position was formally ratified by a Cabinet meeting in October 1972. Thereafter key supporters of political cooperation in the Foreign Ministry and Chancellor's office were replaced with pragmatists, including Karl-Otto Pöhl, later Bundesbank president.[20]

During this period, German officials repeatedly pressed for European monetary integration, as well as for stronger IMF control over the United States, as alternatives to floating. Schmidt and the Cabinet—acting, he later recalled, in response both to U.S. pressure and to imposing the costs of DM revaluation on

[20] Lankowski, *Germany*, 311, also 318–319; Baring, *Machtwechsel*, 660–687.

German exporters—initially resisted floating but were ultimately forced to adopt it for lack of viable alternative.[21] Schmidt's resistance led to the first among many clashes between Schmidt and Emminger; only U.S. devaluation averted an all-out governmental crisis. The change in U.S. policy led the German government to propose and negotiate a joint European float, with both Schmidt's and Emminger's support, which went into operation in March 1973, just a few days after Germany announced it could no longer defend the Bretton Woods parities.[22]

After succeeding Brandt as chancellor in 1974, Schmidt remained a pragmatic advocate of European monetary cooperation. He repeatedly offered unilateral financial support to France, Italy, and Britain, the legality of which was dubious under German law, in unsuccessful efforts to convince them to remain in the Snake.[23] His speeches in this period, like those of his finance minister, Hans Apel, were characteristically blunt, leaving little doubt that his primary goal was to insulate Germany against the commercial implications of currency instability: "It would be unwise to break out of the Snake; then, indeed, one would not have to support the others, but then one would also lose influence over the EC partners, in that they would pursue economic and stabilization policies which would cause their own currencies to fall." The result: whereas German exports as a percentage of GDP had registered a 1 percent decline between 1969 and 1972, they rose by 4.8 percent between 1972 and 1976.[24]

Yet by 1977–78 the withdrawal of France, Italy, and Britain had eroded the Snake's effectiveness. Between October 1977 and February 1978 the dollar depreciated by 12 percent against the DM, leading to upward pressure. These events created for Germany a situation that Commission president Roy Jenkins, one of the few international leaders who enjoyed Schmidt's close confidence, described as follows:

[Germany] would either have to let the mark rise into the stratosphere, with disastrous results for exports . . . investment [and] employment, or the Bundesbank would have to buy vast quantities of dollars to keep the exchange rate down, an action that would increase the German money supply and involve serious inflationary dangers. Chancellor Schmidt therefore had strong incentives to look for a sys-

[21] Harold James, *International Monetary Cooperation since Bretton Woods* (New York, 1996), 215–216. Also Helmut Schmidt, *Weggefährten: Erinnerungen und Reflexionen* (Berlin, 1996), 174; Lankowski, *Germany*, 316–317. Henning argues that the failure to revalue demonstrates the interest of the Bundesbank, and in particular its president, Karl Klasen, former president of Deutsche Bank, in competitive exchange rates. Yet the conventional view, namely that the Bundesbank switched sides in 1972 when capital controls proved ineffective, seems at least as plausible, given that the Bundesbank had supported revaluation in 1969.

[22] Heisenberg, *Mark*, 70–73; Emminger, *D-Mark*, 365 cites Klaus Dieter Arndt, president of the Deutsche Instituts für Wirtschaftsförderung and in 1968–70 Schiller's parliamentary state secretary: "Wir müssen Stabilitätsöpfer für Europa bringen." Also Lankowski, *Germany*, 340–341, 368–369; Baring, *Machtwechsel*, 670ff; James, *International*, 242.

[23] Kathleen Burk and Alec Cairncross, *Goodbye Great Britain: The 1976 IMF Crisis* (New Haven, Conn., 1992), 65ff.

[24] Lankowski, *Germany*, 357, also 341–342, 352–354. Fritz Scharpf attributes to Schmidt a "learning process" whereby he came to understand that floating exchange rates were no panacea; but he seems to have resisted floating from early on. Cf. Scharpf, *Crisis and Choice in European Social Democracy* (Ithaca, 1991), 126.

tem in which changes in the dollar rate would be less disturbing to the stability of exchange rates vis-à-vis Germany's main trading partners.[25]

Jenkins termed this an "unacceptable situation."

The major G-7 conflict at the time was similar. It pitted surplus countries like Germany against the United States, and Schmidt was forced to agree to DM appreciation—a promise he did not keep. Instead, beginning in late 1977 or early 1978, Schmidt became convinced of the need for fiscal stimulation and monetary loosening. Even Anglo-American pressure was unlikely to lead the Bundesbank to accommodate such policies. Emminger signaled publicly that any further stimulation would be met by monetary tightening—a stance, Schmidt later claimed, with "neither Keynesian nor monetarist foundations [but] motivated by missionary zeal for the price stability of the DM."[26] In April 1978, in an effort to gain international support for his domestic policy, Schmidt took up discussions with Giscard on European monetary cooperation. His proposals, which eventually led to the EMS, contained financing provisions for weak-currency countries, mandatory interventions, and a system built around a European unit of account. Yet French and German insiders realized that the "kernel" was exchange-rate stabilization and the rest "symbolic."[27]

Most analyses—particularly, it seems, those by economists—speculate that Schmidt (and Giscard) were geopolitically motivated. They stress Schmidt's anger at what he perceived as Carter's mismanagement of transatlantic affairs, his European federalist beliefs, and his concern to prevent future wars in Europe. Michele Fratianni and Jürgen von Hagen conclude flatly that "the overriding explanation for the EMS . . . is the desire of policy-makers on the European continent to use monetary integration to achieve political union."[28] Yet almost no primary evidence (beyond a few ambiguous quotations from Schmidt's

[25] Roy Jenkins, in Commission of the European Communities, *Hommage à Émile Noël, Secrétaire général de la Commission européenne* (Luxembourg, 1988), 23. Also Simonian, *Privileged*, 278–280; Story, "Launching," 406.

[26] Schmidt subsequently blamed the Bundesbank for hounding him out of office. Also Emminger, *D-Mark*, 364–365; Daniel Biron and Alexandre Faire, "Le Marc souverain," *Le monde diplomatique* (18 November 1978); James, *International*, 293–296; Scharpf, *Crisis*.

[27] Clappier, the head of the French central bank and Giscard's personal representative, saw it so. Story, "Launching," 405.

[28] Fratianni and von Hagen, *European*, 221, also 17–18, a more nuanced formulation on 19. For similar arguments, Sachs and Wyplosz, "Economic Consequences," 261–313; Bernard Connolly, *The Rotten Heart of Europe: The Dirty War for Europe's Money* (London, 1995), 6, 11, 19. Ironically, it is economists who most consistently advance explanations based on geopolitics. They rightly point out that no general welfare explanation for monetary policy preferences is adequate, then often default directly to a geopolitical, rather than a political economy explanation. In part this reflects an absence of primary research. Fratianni and von Hagen's confident assertion of the "predominance of political considerations" in Schmidt's motivations, to take an example from an otherwise insightful economic analysis of the EMS, is backed by three pieces of evidence: an undocumented conjecture by Samuel Brittan that, on closer inspection, actually concedes the primary of political economic reasoning; the fact that Schmidt sought to keep both the Bundesbank and Brussels uninformed (which, as we have just seen, makes sense in political economy terms); and one quotation cited above, at best ambivalent, from a newspaper article by Schmidt over a decade later in which he calls the EMS "*not only* . . . a mere instrument to harmonize economic policies . . . *but also* part of a broader strategy for the political self-determination of Europe."

memoirs and speculation by those without direct contact to Schmidt) favors this conjecture. The preponderance of direct evidence—justifications cited by closely involved participants, patterns of domestic coalitions, timing, and policy consistency—confirms that Schmidt's personal commitment to the EMS and that of the German government were driven primarily by the potential economic consequences. Geopolitical and ideological concerns played a secondary, if not entirely negligible, role.

Almost without exception Schmidt's own statements, as well as contemporary and subsequent testimony from those closest to him—including his assistant Manfred Lahnstein, Emminger, Giscard, James Callaghan, Dennis Healey, and Jenkins, and the Deutsche Bank's chief economist—suggest that the primary purpose of the initiative was to dampen DM appreciation by helping weak-currency countries impose macroeconomic discipline rather than either devalue or impose trade restrictions.[29] This in turn would permit higher German growth, which, economist Robert Triffin argued at the time, would serve general European interests.[30] Schmidt clearly saw that economics and politics were closely related, but his own secret strategy documents of the time privileged economic motivations: "Never since the world economic crisis of the thirties have domestic political, foreign political, and political-economic actions of the rulers (and of the parliament) of Germany had such a strong mutual dependency . . . as in the last years. That would seem to be no less true, indeed perhaps more so, *for the year 1977, which will again stand under the primacy of economic policy.*"[31] To be sure, Schmidt criticized Carter for mishandling the Euromissile affair, but nowhere does he link monetary policy explicitly to these security issues. His criticisms of U.S. policy in this context are primarily aimed at U.S. foreign *economic* mismanagement, and in particular its monetary policy, not simply or even primarily defense.[32]

For Schmidt, the exploitation of European institutions and ideology was tactical, a deliberate deception. A confidential SPD strategy document drafted by

[29] A fine example of the situation typical of EC studies, noted in chapter 1: at least one quotation from a "participant" or "contemporary commentator" can be construed so as to favor any of several plausible motivations, yet the preponderance of hard primary evidence decisively supports one hypothesis. See Jenkins, *European*, 224; Denis Healey, *The Time of My Life* (London, 1989), 489; James Callaghan, *Time and Chance* (London, 1987), 492; Commons, "European," 144ff, 158; Helmut Schmidt, "The European Monetary System: Proposals for Further Progress," *The World Today* 41, 5 (1985), 87–91; Schmidt, interviews, in Hanrieder, *Helmut*; Schmidt, *Deutschen*, 249; Schmidt, *Wegge-fährten*, 268–269, cf. 262; James, *International*, 289ff; David Marsh, *Germany and Europe: The Crisis of Unity* (London, 1994), 141. Only a few participants, none well positioned to judge, believed geopolitical factors important, let alone decisive. Bernard Clappier, the French Central Bank president, subsequently speculated that "Schmidt's launch of the EMS was his response to Carter's shelving of the neutron bomb"—a speculation for which there appears to be no documentary evidence. Emminger later guessed that Schmidt may have been influenced, but only secondarily, by Monnet's European federalism. See Story, "Launching," 397; Ludlow, *European*, 82–85; Barring, *Machtwechsel*, 688.

[30] For a retrospective assessment, see Robert Triffin, "Summary and Conclusions," in Jacques van Ypersele and Jean-Claude Koeune, *The European Monetary System: Origins, Operation and Outlook* (Luxembourg, 1985), 11. See also fn 67 of this chapter.

[31] Cited in Ash, *Europe's*, 85.

[32] No evidence corroborates Giscard's claim that Schmidt supported defense cooperation rather than Giscard's proposal for monetary cooperation. Cf. Giscard, *Le Pouvoir*, 136.

Schmidt during the previous year—the "Marbella paper"—defends a European policy on the assumption that "under the primacy of economic policy" Germany would be thrust inevitably into a leadership position and required ideology to mask its actions:

> [Due to] the revival of memories not only of Auschwitz and Hitler but also of Wilhelm II and Bismarck [it is necessary to] operate not nationally and independently but in the framework of the European Community and the Alliance. *This attempt to cover our actions multilaterally will only partially succeed.*[33]

European institutions were instruments for promoting the German interests, though these may also be the interests of other European countries. To this day Schmidt denies outright all "supranational" motivations for monetary integration, asserting instead that it was a matter of "German national interest."[34]

Domestic divisions around Schmidt's proposal, as we have seen, were consistent with economic incentives, resembling those that had consistently formed in Germany for two decades over decisions about revaluation and floating, inside and outside the EC. DM appreciation in 1977–78, one analyst noted, shifted "indifference" among "representative spokesmen of mainstream German official opinion" into cautious support for cooperation. By contrast, the Foreign Ministry was not closely involved in the negotiations, though Hans-Dietrich Genscher did support them, perhaps for geopolitical as well as electoral reasons.[35] There was no domestic debate about the geopolitical implications of the EMS.

Schmidt's major concern was to overcome opposition from the Bundesbank, which he feared would either kill the proposal at the bureaucratic level or "orchestrate" business and partisan opposition. To this end he skillfully exploited international institutions in a "two-level" strategy that involved considerable secrecy, the threat of legislative revision, and exploitation of the executive's initiative in foreign affairs. It was "essential," he later recalled, to manage the proposal in the chancellor's office, which had responsibility for foreign policy and international exchange-rate agreements, and "to get a big head of steam behind the plan" before going public. This tactic required the chancellor to circumvent standard EC procedures, since the Bundesbank president normally participates in Cabinet discussions of monetary questions and often represented Germany at formal EC (ECOFIN) meetings. For the first four months, Schmidt directed policy through a small team composed of Chancellery and Finance Ministry officials, employing a personal representative as a negotiator. Institutionally, the EC shifted domestic-policy initiative from the Bundesbank to the government. Bundesbank president Otto Emminger was "systematically excluded from the circle of the initiated" and informed about the details only in the last days before the July meeting of the European Council in Bremen, when "the Franco-German

---

[33] Ash, *Europe's*, 87.

[34] Schmidt remarks, at the Conference on Jean Monnet, Paris (May 1997).

[35] Andrew Shonfield in Commons, "European," 58, also 62; Emminger, *D-Mark*, 357–367; Henning, *Currencies*, 187–189; Marsh, *Bundesbank*, 194–195. Giscard d'Estaing, *Pouvoir*, 143–144.

plan was already complete and all [he] could do was insist that the Chancellor should not enter into any binding commitments."[36] Schmidt also threatened the Bundesbank with legislative revision, although the threat was hardly credible, given his modest parliamentary majority which depended on support from the more austerity-minded FDP. Any major change in the Bundesbank's powers—and the definition of what constituted such a change lay in part in the Bundesbank's hands, but certainly included establishment of the a common fund and the more symmetrical intervention requirements foreseen by Schmidt for the second stage—would require potentially difficult parliamentary ratification. After international agreement was reached, Schmidt maintained domestic initiative by circumventing parliamentary assent, creating the EMS through an extra-legal resolution of the European Council rather than through treaty revision, which would have required Bundestag assent.[37]

The Bundesbank retained de facto veto power, however, because of its potential to mobilize substantial opposition and because without statutory revision it was responsible for implementing the arrangement on a day-to-day basis. Schmidt was forced to make concessions. He paid an unprecedented visit to a Bundesbank Council meeting and, after considerable correspondence, accepted three Bundesbank conditions, each of which reinforced the economist position. Obligations to intervene should be "asymmetrical," that is, place greater burdens of adjustment on weak-currency countries. The obligation to intervene or lend DMs to other central banks would be triggered only when governments reached the edge of their bands, not on an everyday, "intra-marginal" basis—just when weak-currency countries are vulnerable. Finally, Schmidt wrote a secret letter—secret, that is, until leaked, officially denied, referred to in Emminger's memoirs and several histories, then produced in 1992 to justify Bundesbank nonsupport for the Italian lira—attesting to the Bundesbank's right to refuse even "mandatory" intervention if it threatened domestic price stability and other governments refused to devalue. Pöhl, later Bundesbank president, later bragged of having "turned the original concept on its head by making the strongest currency [not the ECU] the yardstick for the system."[38]

---

[36] Ludlow, *Making*, 95; Carr, *Helmut Schmidt*, 141; Henning, *Currencies*, 186–187; Emminger, *D-Mark*, 358–366; Healey in Commons, "European," 64–65; James, *International*, 283–285; Ludlow, *European*. For a more detailed treatment, see Andrew Moravcsik, *Why the European Community Strengthens the State: International Cooperation and Domestic Politics*, Harvard Center for European Studies Working Paper Series no. 52 (Cambridge, Mass., 1994). The timing of German or French actions is inconsistent with a strong motivation to stabilize Italy or France politically against an internal Communist threat. Neither acted in more than an ad hoc way to ease external constraints on Italy during the critical period surrounding the June 1976 parliamentary elections, in which the Communists were expected to do well. In the end, they backed the IMF. Schmidt thought it necessary to wait until *after* the Left lost elections in France to act on the EMS.

[37] Ludlow, *Making*, 136; d'Estaing, *Pouvoir*, 143–145; Jenkins, *Life*, 480–483; Emminger, *D-Mark*, 357–358; Heisenberg, *Mark*, 122; Carr, *Helmut*, 141. In France, where the central bank was apparently more reliable than the finance minister, Giscard named the central bank governor, Clappier, as his personal representative.

[38] Marsh, *Bundesbank*, 233; Emminger, *D-Mark*, 357–361, who argues that Schmidt perhaps sought to "save his political capital to alter the treaty later to accommodate a second agreement, which he was already planning, including a European fund to finance intervention and payments im-

Policy consistency also suggests the importance of political economy. Schmidt's eight years in office were not characterized by other major European initiatives; nor did his actions in the G-7 focus on defense issues. Schmidt simultaneously pursued the same two-level strategy in institutions other than the EC. At the G-7 Bonn summit of 1978, only ten days before the Bremen summit on the EMS, he accepted G-7 obligation to reflate the German economy. His simultaneous criticism of President Jimmy Carter's "locomotive" proposal was apparently designed to cast Carter as a scapegoat and to deflect U.S. demands for DM revaluation. Subsequent interview-based research concludes that Schmidt let "himself be pushed into a policy that he probably favored on domestic grounds but would have found costly to pursue . . . without the summit." Schmidt, we have seen, also sought to extend unilateral assistance.[39] Similarly, was certainly aware that the EMS might "mean that we have to expand our money supply somewhat more rapidly."[40]

Timing similarly confirms the predominance of political economic concerns. The precipitating cause of the German initiative was rapid dollar depreciation in late 1977 and early 1978, which drove the DM up relative to other European currencies. In this period, moreover, revaluation followed a recession that had left the exchange rate overvalued and German industry with little room for further rationalization. Nor was there room for monetary manipulation. Bundesbank intervention could provide only short-term relief before purchases of DM started to inflate the money supply.[41] By contrast, there is no coincidence of timing with major foreign-policy decisions. The major geopolitical events that threatened to undermine Ostpolitik and spark U.S.–Germany acrimony—the "two-track" decision, the Soviet invasion of Afghanistan, the Polish crisis—did not arise for a year or more *after* the EMS had been negotiated. Schmidt and Giscard, unlike their predecessors and successors, did not take any important steps toward an EC foreign policy and defense cooperation, retaining instead the institutions and practices they had inherited from Brandt and Pompidou.[42]

This is not to say, however, that European ideology and institutions were irrelevant. Faced with strong opposition, Schmidt sought to exploit international institutions—the G-7 and the EC—to expand his domestic autonomy on the margin; in the language of two-level games, he "cut slack." This course was possible

---

balances." Also Heisenberg, *Mark*, chap. 4; Kaltenthaler, "Sources," 18; Wilhelm Nölling, *Unser Geld: Der Kampf um die Stabilität der Währungen in Europa* (Berlin, 1993), 55ff; Alain Prate, *Quelle Europe?* (Paris, 1991), 254–255; Henning, *Currencies*, 189.

[39] Robert D. Putnam and C. Randall Henning, "The Bonn Summit of 1978: A Case Study in Coordination," in Richard Cooper et al., *Can Nations Agree? Issues in International Economic Cooperation* (Washington, D.C., 1989), 67, based on interviews with "those closest to Schmidt." The "scapegoat" analysis is Raymond Barre's interpretation as well. Story, "Launching," 405.

[40] 1978 interview cited in Heisenberg, "German Financial Hegemony," mimeo (Yale University: 1996), 6. Also Heisenberg, "Mark," 289; Henning, *Currencies*, 205–209.

[41] Jenkins, in Commission, *Hommage*, 23; Ludlow, *Making*, 76–77; Lankowski, *Germany*, 404–405; Simonian, *Privileged*, 279–281.

[42] Afghanistan and Poland came later. Schmidt was aware of the missile issue from 1977 onward, but a tightening of Franco-German military cooperation did not begin until much later. Schmidt maintained that economics was the basis of the Giscard-Schmidt friendship; *Weggefährten*, 258, 266ff.

for both ideological and institutional reasons. Ideologically, the EC legitimated Schmidt's policy, providing additional protection against domestic criticism. The FDP, led by Hans-Dietrich Genscher, apparently supported the proposal for geopolitical and ideological reasons. Even the conservative *Frankfurter Allgemeine Zeitung* and the opposition CDU/CSU, though substantively critical, were compelled to compliment Schmidt's European "leadership" and "vision."[43]

Despite Schmidt's efforts, the EMS failed to realize his domestic goals. Between 1979 and 1982 Schmidt, backed by substantial segments of banking and industry as well as the SPD, sought depreciation, lower interest rates, and more fiscal reflation. He was blocked by the Bundesbank. Faced with an unexpected tightening of U.S. monetary policy and the second oil shock, the DM weakened in 1979–80, inflation crept up, and the Bundesbank responded by raising interest rates to unprecedentedly high levels, triggering a deep recession. The EMS renegotiation and deepening scheduled for 1981 never took place. In the end, as Schmidt had long feared, Bundesbank pressure helped hound him from office by driving up interest rates. The final straw was the neoliberal FDP's defection from the governing coalition in September 1982.[44]

A new government formed under the leadership of the CDU's Helmut Kohl. With the dollar rising and the DM rebounding, the Bundesbank eased interest rates—just in time to secure electoral success for the new coalition in March 1983. Business and finance continued to support monetary cooperation and the EMS grew increasingly effective; with the dollar strong, Germany enjoyed an extended period of real DM depreciation during which lower interest rates and dampening DM appreciation were low-priority concerns. During the string of realignments after 1982, the Bundesbank and the government, led by the Finance Ministry, worked closely together to maintain a tough negotiating position yet were prepared to compromise on the margin to encourage continued French membership. The conservative Kohl government probably had less interest in macroeconomic stimulation than did that of Schmidt, but still there was more continuity than change. By the end of his term in office Schmidt had grown quite critical of Mitterrand; Kohl continued Schmidt's policy of tolerating controlled French devaluations. Like all governments since Erhard's, however, Kohl linked continued EMS membership and financial support for weak-currency countries to the moderation of EMS realignments and the imposition of domestic austerity. He made no effort to deepen the system. In these years the system imposed little constraint on the Bundesbank's control over domestic monetary policy. Indeed, it may in fact have enhanced Bundesbank control by stabilizing exchange rates, strengthening the DM during its brief periods of weakness, and diffusing pressure from the dollar.

During the entire period from 1969 through 1983, German preferences concerning issues to which monetary policy was linked—agriculture, EC redistributive policies, British membership, institutions—remained relatively stable. As

---

[43] Ludlow, *Making*, 267; Story, "Launching," 401–402.
[44] Scharpf, *Crisis*, 150–157; Eric Owen Smith, *The German Economy* (London, 1994), 166, also 191–192; Henning, *Currencies*, 191–195.

it had earlier, Germany supported British entry but was not willing to contemplate substantial changes in the *acquis communautaire* to achieve it. On agriculture Brandt, Schmidt, and Kohl resisted any reduction in nominal prices, a non-negotiable position; though skeptical of export subsidies, they were not positioned to reduce them. The major German contribution to CAP reform during this period ran in the opposite direction: the introduction, first unilaterally then regionally, of higher domestic subsidies in the form of Monetary Compensation Accounts (MCAs), an extra price subsidy to offset shifts in exchange rates. MCAs essentially preserved the side-payments that Erhard had offered German farmers in 1966 as part of the deal on grain prices. German Agriculture Ministry reports in 1973 concluded that Germany should renationalize price policy through a permanent border tax system; MCAs achieved the same goal. When Giscard linked abolition of MCAs to the EMS proposal in the late 1970s, the SPD and FDP factions in the Bundestag responded by voting to maintain MCAs until the final stage of the EMS. By 1976 the prices paid German wheat producers were some 10 percent *above* the basic EC price, leading to a German agricultural export boom. Because of the product mix, however, domestic farmers had no objection to Germany's support for rapid Iberian accession—a region where German industrial exporters had important interests.[45]

During this period the EC considered various forms of redistributive transfer from richer to poorer regions of the EC, the most important event being realization of the regional policy authorized by the Treaty of Rome. Many technical justifications for regional payments were concocted, but few were convincing. Brandt's generous impulses in this area were blocked by his financial experts. Germany would of course be a donor country, and Schmidt, never one for euphemisms, observed that regional policy was in fact a bribe covered only by "swimming trunks with "regional policy" written on them."[46] Given the German government's commitment to austerity in the 1970s and the spiraling costs of the CAP, Schmidt was prepared to provide financial transfers only in exchange for policy quid pro quos, such as British membership and participation in the EMU or higher CAP prices. Schmidt included small sums in the EMS proposal to win over Ireland and larger ones to influence the outcome of the 1975 British referendum—the real source of the EC regional policy—but was unwilling to go further. Both Schmidt and Kohl sought, moreover, to centralize regional aid in a single fund with more rigorous, EC-wide criteria managed from Brussels.[47]

[45] Simonian, *Privileged*, 178, 288–290; Michael Tracy, *Farmers and Politics in France* (Enstone, 1991); Bernard May, *Kosten und Nutzen der Deutschen EG-Mitgliedschaft* (Bonn, 1982), 103. Support prices were calculated in ECU. When exchange rates shifted, the support price in the devaluing country's currency would increase, and the support price in the revaluing country would decrease, necessitating use of a parallel set of "green" exchange rates to keep domestic prices stable. MCAs were a complex set of compensation paid to offset the resulting disparities. German farmers were particularly vulnerable, due to the low price elasticity of demand and the high number of small, marginal farmers.
[46] Simon Bulmer and William Paterson, *The Federal Republic of Germany and the European Community* (London, 1987), 35 and sections on regional and social policies.
[47] Lankowski, *Germany*, 248–250, 320–323, 362ff, 365–366, 416–422. In 1971 Brandt advanced a major proposal for an EC social policy, including EC guidelines for employee rights for social security; norms for working conditions, collective bargaining and Mitbestimmung; regional and environmental policies; and the right of initiative to the EC's Economic and Social Committee. Even the

Finally, Germany took a differentiated position on institutional questions. Like other large country leaders, Brandt and particularly Schmidt supported the deepening of intergovernmental European summitry; Schmidt was a particular proponent of this form of international negotiation, conducted by chief executives. In addition, German parliamentarians consistently supported direct elections to the European Parliament, though leaders such as Schmidt or Kohl appear to far have been less enthusiastic.

In sum, economic interest offers a consistently powerful explanation for Germany's stance on integration issues during the 1970s. This claim is true across each dimension of national preferences. Economic interest accounts for Brandt and Schmidt's initiating role in and consistent support for negotiations about monetary integration; Germany's support since 1965 for an "economist" ("asymmetrical") monetary arrangement; the nature of domestic coalitions and the justifications German officials gave, in private and public, for the policy; differential levels of policies support across monetary policy, agriculture, regional policy, and British accession; and the timing of German initiatives.

France: External Support for Internal Rigueur

In contrast to the economist position espoused by Germany, weaker-currency countries, backed by the Commission, adopted the "monetarist" perspective, which mandated that common commitments to support parities, finance other governments, and centralize monetary decision-making should precede macroeconomic convergence. In this view, sovereign powers over monetary decision-making should be transferred to central institutions relatively quickly, driving and facilitating economic convergence. During this process strong-currency countries would bear a burden of adjustment equal to or greater than that of weak-currency countries. The burden takes the form of higher inflation, a reduced trade surplus, and intervention or financing to support weak currencies. Such an arrangement favors weak-currency countries because it reduces the costs and perhaps increases the credibility of domestic adjustment.

Geopolitical Interest and Ideology: "Centrist, liberal and European"

Two geopolitical concerns are often cited in explanations of French policy on Europe during this period: the "German problem," and European federalist ideology.

Worries about the preponderance of German power are often cited as motives for Gaullist moves toward monetary cooperation. Some have asserted that the exchange-rate crisis in 1968–69 set General de Gaulle himself thinking seriously about the need for British membership in the EC as a counterbalance to Germany, though he left office before any effective initiative could be taken. The same fear was shared by Georges Pompidou, Jacques Chirac, and Michel Jobert in the 1970s, occasioned by Brandt's Ostpolitik and trade competition with the

---

DGB did not support such an extreme proposal, and Schmidt soon killed it. Germany later blocked efforts to establish a centralized incomes policy.

East, as well as hints of monetary and agricultural independence. At worst, French leaders feared, Germany might go neutral. Even Giscard, not a Gaullist, argued publicly that in a world where economic power had become decisive, France could no longer emulate Britain but must now follow the German example of monetary probity. Creation of a "big four" of industrialized economies was necessary, he argued, "because it would not be good for Europe to be dominated by one country."[48]

Pro-European forces in France grew more influential. The Gaullist coalition proved weak after the General's resignation and, in order to prevail in a three-way presidential race, Pompidou was forced to negotiate electoral alliances, most important with the Giscardian center-right. Giscard was still a strong advocate of monetary cooperation, and among his principal demands in exchange for support was said to be a pro-European line. Although the sources of Giscardian Europeanism may have been ideological, they were also economic and electoral. Giscard was at the time believed to be the primary representative of modern, internationalized big business, whereas Gaullist support tended to come from small business, agriculture, and older, more nationalist voters. Giscard campaigned in 1974 on the platform "Centrist, Liberal and European." Mitterrand, too, could claim European credentials dating back to the 1948 European Assembly and, particularly after 1984, spoke often of a "European vocation."[49]

Though there is no evidence that large numbers of voters supported either Giscard or Mitterrand for European reasons, the stance appears to have been successful. In the 1970s Chirac failed to mobilize Gaullist opposition to European federalism for electoral purposes. Chirac resigned in 1976 as prime minister, ostensibly over the issue of direct elections to the European Parliament, though most observers saw his resignation as a means of avoiding responsibility for difficult economic policy decisions. In November 1978 Communists and Gaullists joined forces to defeat the EC budget in the Assemblée Nationale. In the European elections of 1979 Chirac and the Gaullists sought to exploit anti-European sentiment by playing on suspicions about French identity and concern among farmers about Spanish, Portuguese, and Greek membership. The result was so disappointing, yielding only 16 percent of the vote, that the anti-European experiment was not repeated.[50]

Economic Interest: The Politics of Policy Failure

By the late 1970s both business and government in France experienced an acute sense of domestic policy failure. Productive investment had stagnated for over a decade, during which French production costs grew faster than its competitors' and devaluation became the principal way to keep French export prices in line with those elsewhere. These trends in domestic political economy are critical for understanding the motivations of French statesmen for their foreign economic policy. By the early 1980s, after the overt failure of the Socialist experiment, there seemed to be no alternative to disinflation through monetary discipline.

[48] Simonian, *Privileged*, 179–192; Michel Jobert, *L'autre regard* (Paris, 1976), 347ff.
[49] Andrew Knapp, *Gaullism since de Gaulle* (Aldershot, 1994).
[50] On Chirac see Knapp, *Gaullism*, 57, 420, 452.

Out of this experience came two competing programs for economic revival. The first was that of Giscard and his technocratic prime minister, Raymond Barre. With a 20 percent depreciation just behind them and the fear of inflation ahead, Giscard and Barre sought to restore growth and investment without increasing public debt or imposing trade protection. The key was to be a long-term reduction in inflation and greater industrial productivity. The model was Germany, which had adjusted relatively smoothly to the first oil shock—a fact not unnoticed in the Ministry of Finance. These goals were to be achieved through the Plan Barre—the introduction of monetary targeting, restrictions on direct government credit, fiscal restraint, and downward pressure on wages, including government sanctions against wage increases. The primary aim was economic modernization through higher value-added exports and lower inflation. In this view, one that Giscard had held for many years, the lesson of the period from 1969 through 1976 was that Keynesian stimulation and devaluation were no longer effective tools to achieve sustainable economic growth. The same view was held by moderates within Pierre Mauroy's government under the Mitterrand presidency.[51]

It had always been the case, of course, that in the short run the trade effects of devaluation were costly to some. The J-curve, the delayed adjustment of trade volumes and debt payments to changes in exchange rates, as well as France's structural propensity to import more for each unit of exports than did Germany, tended to worsen deficits in the short term, before the positive benefits of devaluation came into play. Sudden devaluations could also disadvantage producers with long-term contracts and drive up inflation. In practice, a certain amount of financial support was required to support devaluation, but still devaluation was hardly ineffective. Even those French policy-makers who favored a strong currency, including Barre and Jacques Delors, moderate among French ministers, conceded that devaluation was often necessary. Throughout his term as finance minister, Delors favored greater devaluation *vis-à-vis* the DM than was actually achieved.[52]

More important, rising capital mobility and the de facto weakening of capital controls meant that domestic interest rates could not be shielded from the consequences of depreciation, and in particular the imposition of risk premia. During the 1970s France experimented with various schemes to shield domestic interest rates from international markets through credit rationing; none was satisfactory or effective in the long run. Capital controls, while imparting short-term stability to domestic interest rates, were eventually circumvented and anyway reduced the confidence of international investors. A risk premium began to be charged on francs, and French domestic interest rates began moving toward and above world market rates. Businessmen complained. There was wide-

---

[51] Patrick McCarthy, "France Faces Reality: Rigueur and the Germans," in David Calleo and Claudia Morgenstern, eds., *Recasting Europe's Economies: National Strategies in the 1980s* (Lanham, Md., 1992), 56; Michael Loriaux, *France after Hegemony: International Change and Financial Reform* (Ithaca, 1991), 199–207, 230–232, 248–250; McNamara, *Currency*.

[52] Peter A. Hall, *Governing the Economy: The Politics of State Intervention in Britain and France* (New York, 1986), 196–199; Loriaux, *France*, 230–232; Goodman, *Monetary*, 111–115; McCarthy, "France," 56; Michel Develle, *Vive le franc* (Paris, 1988), 164ff.

spread agreement on the need for fundamental financial liberalization. Logic demanded that under capital mobility, the government must choose between pegged exchange rates and monetary sovereignty.[53]

Moreover, persistent fiscal and trade deficits made the strategy so successfully pursued by de Gaulle, backing devaluation with fiscal austerity and downward pressure on wages, more difficult to achieve. A growing consensus among French economists and officials believed that devaluation encouraged increases in wages and government spending, leading to a spiral of rising inflation and decreasing competitiveness. Officials began to contemplate the use of monetary policy to impose disinflation and fiscal austerity.

The Giscard-Barre strategy and EMS membership received some support from big business in France, with primary opposition from the Left and more radical labor unions. The alternative to the view of Giscard and Barre and the moderates under François Mitterrand was a Keynesian view espoused by the more radical majority in the incoming Socialist government and, a few years earlier, by the Gaullist prime minister under Giscard until 1976, Jacques Chirac. They held that the problem in France was insufficient demand, which could be overcome through fiscal stimulus and monetary accommodation, backed if necessary by protection and devaluation. This macroeconomic strategy was tried twice and perceived a failure. The Socialist stimulus was more modest than what Chirac pursued in the mid-1970s, its failure more striking. With nearly all other OECD governments pursuing contractionary policies, the French economy was increasingly constrained by inflation, which rose rapidly; capital flight, totaling an estimated 1 percent of GDP; and a yawning current account deficit, mostly with other EC countries, greater than the domestic stimulus in 1981–2. By mid-1982 investment was stagnant and speculative pressure on the rise. Devaluations followed in October 1981 and June 1982, though the total was modest— only two-thirds of what even a moderate like Delors thought necessary at the time. Mauroy was "given the green light to break inflation," in order to avoid "ending up like Harold Wilson under the thumb of the IMF." A wage and price freeze was implemented, but no corresponding fiscal measures were taken, leaving a government deficit of 2.9 percent of GDP in 1982. External deficits increased, and the French government took a $4 billion loan from private banks as well as arranging central bank swaps with Germany. By early 1983 the vast majority of observers agreed that French policy was unsustainable. The result was a move to disinflation and austerity.[54]

---

[53] This paragraph and the next draw on John Goodman and Louis Pauly, "The Obsolescence of Capital Controls? Economic Management in an Age of Global Markets," World Politics 46 (October 1993), 50–82; Dyson, *Elusive*, 67; McCarthy, "France," 57–58; Loriaux, *France*, 199ff; Christian de Boissieu and Marie-Hélène Duprat, "French Monetary Policy in the Light of European Monetary and Financial Integration," in Heidemarie Sherman, ed., *Monetary Implications of the 1992 Process* (New York, 1990), 78; David Begg and Charles Wyplosz, "The European Monetary System: Recent Intellectual History," in *The Monetary Future of Europe* (London, 1993), 29–35, review the literature; Kalthenthaler, "Sources," 17–18.

[54] Subsequent studies suggest that in 1981 the economy was already at close to its nonaccelerating inflation rate of unemployment, hence there was little room for a demand expansion. Sachs and Wyplosz, "Economic," 285ff; Harold van Buren Cleveland, "Europe in the Economic Crisis of Our Time: Macroeconomic Policies and Microeconomic Constraints," in Calleo and Morgenstern,

There is good reason, as we shall see, to believe that these policy lessons were sufficient to convince French policy-makers to impose monetary discipline. Yet some scholars argue that the lessons were augmented by two cognitive factors. The first was the example of Germany in the 1970s, whose virtuous circle of declining inflation and lower real interest rates suggested a "Modell Deutschland," which was often mentioned by Barre and Giscard, albeit in different words. The second was a shift in the reigning policy paradigm toward monetarist economic theories. Neither account explains coalitions or timing.[55]

Whatever its sources, greater austerity, if it meant more flexibility in social charges and lower government spending, attracted active support from big business leaders in the CNPF, who applauded efforts to reorganize industry on a more competitive basis, and from the largest moderate union, the CFDT, which shifted in 1977 to support austerity.[56] The Socialists entered government with the intention of reversing this policy, but by mid-1982 it had become clear that there was no alternative. Mitterrand began meeting secretly with top businessmen, discussing measures to increase investment, lower taxes, reduce social reforms, and halt the reduction of the workweek at 39 hours. Yvon Gattez, head of the CNPF, held ten meetings with the president during this period; he subsequently maintained that these meetings marked "the psychological turning point for the left with regard to business."[57]

On other issues, economic interests in France had become far more favorable to EC liberalization. Business and agriculture did not oppose Pompidou's opening to Britain, as they had in the early 1960s. French industry was now far more competitive vis-à-vis the United Kingdom, while agriculture was protected by the *acquis communataire*. Once agriculture was secure, moreover, the British might be useful allies in opposing the expansion of supranational institutions.[58] Farm groups favored British accession, as long as the CAP was secure, campaigned strongly for the abolition of MCAs, which offered German farmers extra protection, and favored the maintenance of high export subsidies.

In closing, we must note that extravagant claims have been made for the linkages between the EMS and some other issues, notably the CAP: one analyst concludes that "French withdrawal from the EMS would have jeopardized the CAP." Yet this issue was almost never raised in French (or Italian) domestic politics— quite the opposite, it was farmers whose opposition delayed the formation of the

---

Recasting, 175–177; Alain Fonteneau and Pierre-Alain Muet, *La gauche face à la crise* (Paris, 1985), 119–121. Pierre Favier and Michel Martin-Roland, *La décennie Mitterrand: Les ruptures (1981–1984)* (Paris, 1990), 1:413, 419, 428–429, 442, 498; Kaltenthaler, "Sources," 17–18; David R. Cameron, "The Colors of a Rose: On the Ambiguous Record of French Socialism," paper presented at the Center for European Studies, n.d., 18–20.

[55] Loriaux, *France,* 218–220; Goodman, *Monetary;* Ton Notermans, "Monetary Integration and Political Economy: A Short Overview," *ARENA Working Paper* no. 24 (Oslo, November 1996); McCarthy, "France," 56; McNamara, *Currency.*

[56] Robert Flanagan, David Soskice, and Peter Lange, *Unionism, Economic Stabilization, and Income Policies: European Experience* (Washington, D.C. 1983), 620, 637, 640–642.

[57] Pierre Favier and Michel Martin-Roland, *Le décennie* Mitterrand (Paris, 1990), 1:413, 419, 428–429, 442, 498.

[58] Alain Peyrefitte, "L'Europe vers la monnaie unique: Sauver l'euro, la livre, le mark, le franc et les autres," *Le Figaro* (26 July 1996), 26, calls these concerns "decisive."

EMS—and the CAP survived decades of currency fluctuations. At most it is true that farmers were probably well-disposed to monetary integration because it would limit conflict over MCAs.[59]

The Domestic Decision: Locking in Austerity

From the late 1950s through 1973 French policy-makers achieved high levels of export-led growth through a strategy more interventionist than that pursued by Germany. The allocation of credit, ownership of firms, and nature of trade policy were heavily influenced and often directly mediated by the state. During the 1950s and 1960s France's robust economic growth, tight fiscal policy, and judicious if initially aggressive use of devaluation kept economic growth high and domestic inflation under control. Unit labor costs remained largely constant relative to those of major trading partners.[60]

As finance minister under de Gaulle, Giscard advocated a greater degree of European monetary coordination, a view backed by the Ministry of Economics and the Central Bank. The franc came under pressure as the dollar weakened in the early 1960s, but in this period France ran trade surpluses and de Gaulle was able to stabilize the economy. Monetary independence was a matter of pride and prestige, and de Gaulle could side with Michel Debré and economist Jacques Rueff, opponents of Bretton Woods and advocates of a return to the gold standard. In the turbulence leading up to the collapse of Bretton Woods, however, the declining dollar placed more severe strains on French macroeconomic policy. The *événements* of May 1968, de Gaulle's referendum defeat, the rising electoral threat from the Left, the oil crisis, and subsequent slower growth created an increasing temptation to cushion the effects of economic adjustment by offering abundant credit to firms, accommodating high wage settlements to workers, and providing more generous government benefits. U.S. dollar depreciation tended to depress the franc against the DM as capital flowed into Germany and dollar-denominated goods grew more competitive. By 1968–69 the franc was under enormous pressure vis-à-vis the DM—a crisis that French officials soon interpreted as the first to be induced by capital movements. In the face of tension between DM and franc, de Gaulle initially refused to devalue—even though this decision ironically forced him to seek support from global multilateral institutions, European central banks, and the U.S. government—but instead tried to force a German revaluation. When Germany refused, the General voiced bitter recriminations: "France has been deserted: more than anyone else, I helped restore Germany to her rightful place in international relations. But . . . the Boches will always be Boches—humble when they are beaten and arrogant as soon as they feel strong again."[61] In April 1969, after de Gaulle's resignation,

[59] Cf. Sachs and Wyplosz, "Economic"; McNamara, *Currency*.

[60] Loriaux, *France*, 186ff.

[61] Philippe Alexandre, *The Duel: De Gaulle and Pompidou* (Boston, 1972), 244, 247–248, also 245–249; Schmidt, *Deutschen*, 242–243; Dyson, *Elusive*, 69–70; Alain Prate, *La bataille économique de Général de Gaulle* (Paris, 1978); L. Tsoukalis, *Politics and Economics*, 70–71; Jenkins, *Life*, 264ff; Loriaux, *France*, 246–248. The French realized the critical role of the dollar early on. In discussions with de Gaulle and Macmillan in 1962, Pompidou noted that dollar depreciation created pressure against which "no currency would hold." Record of a Conversation at the Chateau de Champs, 3 June 1963 (PREM 11/3775), 19.

Pompidou assumed the presidency and soon ordered an 11 percent devaluation, resolving the crisis. Thereafter he sought to preserve the commercial advantages that accrued by avoiding any appreciation of the franc.

In July 1969 Pompidou proposed a linked set of negotiations on three issues: CAP financing, British entry, and monetary coordination—what he termed the "triptych" of completion, enlargement, and development. Pompidou's priorities were unambiguous: a permanent financing arrangement for the CAP was the non-negotiable prerequisite for British entry. As we saw at the conclusion of chapter 3, the decision to link British entry to a permanent financing arrangement for agriculture embedded in the *acquis* was not a new departure for French policy but the culmination of a policy pursued consistently for more than a decade. With agriculture secure and GATT negotiations subject to unanimous vote, the French no longer had any reason to exclude Britain.

Some have interpreted the transition from de Gaulle to Pompidou as a change in ideology. Yet on concrete issues, particularly institutional questions, Pompidou remained a strong opponent of supranationalism, whether it came in the form of a strong political secretariat for EPC, strong monetary institutions, majority voting, or a democratically elected parliament. This opposition was disguised by his rhetoric, as deliberately deceptive as that of de Gaulle. One illustration is the phrase "European Union"—a goal Pompidou purported to support. When Michel Jobert of the Elysée staff inquired of Pompidou's close associate Edouard Balladur what the phase meant, the latter reportedly replied: "Nothing . . . but then that is the beauty of it." Pompidou himself called it "a vague formula . . . in order to avoid paralyzing doctrinal disputes." At a Council meeting the French representative called the term "idiotic," prompting one of his foreign counterparts to remark that it was the first time he had heard a French foreign minister select this adjective to describe the president of the Republic![62]

On other issues Pompidou, like Giscard and Mitterrand after him, pursued the enduring interests of French industrialists and farmers. As French industry grew relatively more competitive and its British counterpart relatively less, British accession no longer seemed the threat it had been ten years earlier. Pompidou's advocacy of British membership in the early 1970s raised, in contrast to the uncompromising hostility in the 1950s, little controversy among economic interest groups. Indeed, moves during the last few months of de Gaulle's presidency had suggested a new openness toward British accession, as well as monetary integration, even from the General himself. Pompidou was sufficiently confident not to fear criticism from the General in retirement.[63]

Some speculate that Pompidou permitted the British to enter to balance the Germans in the monetary area, a claim for which there is little solid evidence though it cannot be ruled out. Yet monetary policy was clearly less important to Pompidou than were agriculture and British entry. The French president may have felt that after the currency crisis of 1968–69, cooperation might stabilize

---

[62] Garret Fitzgerald, *All in a Life: An Autobiography* (London, 1991), 133; Jobert, *L'Autre,* 164; Christian Franck, "New Ambitions: From the Hague to the Paris Summits (1969–1972)." in Roy Pryce, ed., *The Dynamics of European Union* (London, 1987), 130–148, especially 144–145.

[63] Michel Jobert, *Mémoires d'avenir* (Paris, 1976), 182; Knapp, *Gaullism,* 417–418.

exchange rates and provide an instrument by which to influence German policy. Of a desire to stabilize the CAP, there is little evidence. It seems more likely, given Pompidou's coalitional and electoral weaknesses, that domestic politics was dominant. Giscard, we have seen, made pro-European policies a condition of the coalition. Pompidou sought to act strongly in European policy, lest the Assemblée and ministers make a move for greater power over foreign policy. Two conclusions are clear. If France was balancing Germany, the threat was likely economic, and no move could have been contemplated without secure CAP financing, whatever the motivation.[64]

In any case, Pompidou was neither ideologically nor economically prepared to move forward with monetary integration. Under pressure from the Gaullist right, Pompidou backed away from the supranational institutions recommended in the Werner Report. His French government was uninterested in imposing the *rigueur* required to support fixed exchange rates; instead it established a double rate, with an appreciated exchange rate for capital transactions and another fixed to the weak dollar for trade. Facing the threat of unilateral German action, France did enter the Snake in 1973; but elections loomed in which the Left was favored, and so Pompidou refused to restrict either government spending or wage increases. Devaluation was rendered inevitable by growing domestic consumption, the oil shock, and rising German interest rates. France exited the Snake in January 1974 and floated the franc, hoping to reenter later with French industry in a more competitive position.[65]

Upon his election to the presidency in May 1974 after Pompidou's sudden death, Giscard moved to impose austerity, backed by renewed participation in the Snake. In 1974 he restricted credit and raised taxes, triggering a recession but bringing the trade balance back into surplus within a year. He immediately reentered the Snake, overriding objections from the Finance Ministry and Banque de France, only to see Prime Minister Jacques Chirac initiate a strong pro-cyclical increase in government spending (a stimulus larger than the Socialists generated after 1981) that undermined the current-account balance and forced France to quit the Snake again in 1976.[66]

In August 1976 Giscard replaced Chirac with the liberal economist Raymond Barre, a technocrat with European experience rather than a party politician, who was given a strong mandate (underscored by his simultaneous appointment as finance minister) to impose economic austerity. As we have seen, Barre and Giscard sought to reduce wage inflation and restrict government credit and debt while increasing productive investment.

French support for the EMS over the next few years was aimed primarily at providing external support for Giscard and Barre's domestic economic plan. The EMS provided an anti-inflationary anchor; internal documents of the time referred to it as "une solution de rigueur" and argued for EMS as a means to reduce the costs of austerity. Dollar depreciation increased pressure on the franc,

---

[64] Cf. Simonian, *Privileged*, 90–91, 104–105; Jobert, *Mémoires*, 183; Eric Roussel, *Georges Pompidou* (Paris, 1984), 318, 344ff.

[65] Simonian, *Privileged*, 78–79, 83.

[66] Boissieu and Duprat, "French," 51–98.

and Giscard and Barre sought to secure the Plan Barre by strengthening the franc, thereby disciplining French firms into greater competitiveness—a move widely interpreted as an attempt to emulate the German austerity of the early 1970s.[67] The precise timing of the international initiative reflected domestic electoral concerns. Giscard called for a revival of monetary integration in early 1977 and had reportedly been considering it for longer but did not seize the initiative until after a surprisingly strong showing in the parliamentary elections of early 1978. With no elections scheduled until 1981, moment was propitious to embark on a reform plan.

While Giscard and Barre were attempting in some ways to emulate Germany, their preferences concerning the form of monetary integration were far from identical to those of the German government. Giscard sought currency stability and external discipline but preferred a symmetrical system in which strong-currency countries would share the burdens of adjustment—precisely as the political economy theory predicts. This thread was consistent through the Fourcade Plan of 1974, Giscard's proposals of April 1976, and French proposals during the EMS negotiations. Giscard refused to reenter the Snake after 1976 for this reason. The weakness of his negotiating position, however, was that he had already committed to austerity and thus, though favoring a symmetrical arrangement, preferred an asymmetrical system to no cooperation at all. He was fully aware, at latest by September 1978 and probably well before, that symmetry was an unrealistic negotiating goal and that the EMS would therefore "effectively mean Europe's becoming a Deutsche Mark zone," much like the Snake. He was "nevertheless ready to go along." The Gaullist leader Jacques Chirac went along as well, despite similar doubts.[68]

There is, by contrast, very little evidence that Giscard was motivated by geopolitical goals. He was, like Schmidt, an economic pragmatist suspicious of supranational institutions and European federalism. While Giscard's supporters were pro-European, there is little evidence that monetary cooperation was a sufficiently important issue to highlight for electoral reasons alone. Whether motivated by Gaullist pressure or by personal commitment, he advanced initiatives aimed at expanding the power of the European Council at the expense of the Commission. Jenkins described him as desiring "to cut down the power of the

---

[67] Ludlow, *European Monetary System*, 82–85, 200ff; Goodman, *Monetary*, 118ff; Ralf Joas, *Zwischen Nation und Europa: Die europapolitischen Vorstellungen der Gaullisten 1978–1994* (Bochum, 1996), 133; Schmidt, "Die Bürokraten ausgetrikst," *Die Zeit* (24 August 1990), echoes his interviews and memoirs: "Giscard and Barre were convinced that they absolutely needed the EMS to realize their own economic policies; I was similarly convinced . . . France had left the Snake hoping to free itself from the strict discipline imposed by exchange rates, and yet maintain a equilibrium by imposing capital controls. . . . This had only very unsatisfactory success . . . the dependency of European monetary policies on the dollar, dollar interest rates and dollar speculation, was particularly destructive."

[68] This paragraph and the next draw on Callaghan, *Time*, 492; Loriaux, *France*, 252–259; James, *International*, 300; Biron and Faire, "Le marc"; Raymond Barre, *Une politique pour l'avenir* (Paris, 1981), 21–38, 69–78, 115–120, 125, 178–180; Story, "Launching," 410–411. Some have argued Giscard was trapped by his own rhetoric: Unable to soften the EMS, he was compelled to go forward with a project that had become a symbol of "keeping up with the Germans." I found no empirical evidence for this conjecture. Callaghan's conversations with Giscard, the public debate, as well as the rapid willingness of Giscard to compromise suggest suspicion. Cf. Heisenberg, "Mark of the Bundesbank," 107, 265.

Commission, . . . our political role [and] our connection with Parliament . . . to amalgamate us with the Council Secretariat and with COREPER, and thus to make us all servants of the European Council."[69] While the available evidence does not permit us to know for sure, there is little evidence that he saw European ideology as something more than an ex post justification to promote concrete arrangements of advantage to France. As with Schmidt, no simultaneous geopolitical initiatives were taken and, in any case, Giscard was by French standards something of an Atlanticist. European defense or political identity seems to have interested him only a little, perhaps due to constraints imposed by Gaullist coalition partners. Nor is there much evidence that Giscard's occasional rhetoric about Franco-German cooperation against the U.S. dollar and the restoration of French power as one of the "big four" countries was more than a line aimed at his Gaullist coalition partners. In fact, neither France nor any of its partners proposed the coordination of exchange-rate policy *vis-à-vis* the dollar. What we know of internal deliberations accords neither European ideology nor Franco-German relations much importance; such references were reserved for public events. Neither European ideology nor the Franco-German relationship is mentioned more than occasionally in Giscard's memoirs; neither provides an explanation of the timing, negotiating positions or domestic coalitions behind the EMS.

Technocrats in national governments and the Commission, as well as some subsequent commentators, viewed the French decision as driven by increasing trade interdependence, which required governments to reduce risk for traders. Other observers see the EMS as a means to preserve French interests in the CAP by reducing the effect of MCAs. Yet neither explanation enjoys much evidentiary support. Giscard did occasionally mention rising trade interdependence but it tells us little about timing, nor why currency stability should suddenly be more important than currency competitiveness after years of the contrary policy. The CAP and MCAs appear to have played little role in the negotiations; nor was there much expectation that the EMS would resolve the issue. Indeed, French farmers were the one group that mobilized actively *against* the EMS, jeopardizing the negotiations for ten weeks by holding out for abolition of MCAs; if they expected the EMS to reduce the importance of MCAs, this activity made little sense.[70]

This is not to relegate European symbolism and geopolitical arguments to complete insignificance. Such arguments were employed as ex post justifications to reduce the political cost of austerity by "shifting blame" and "locking in" policies. According to Alain Prate, a governor of the French central bank and a participant in the negotiations, Giscard was concerned that domestic ratification would allow ministers, parliamentarians, and judges to obstruct ratification. It was thus useful to create the system through a "resolution" of the European Council—short of a formal revision of the Treaty of Rome—which required no

---

[69] Jenkins, *European*, 311.
[70] Cf. Kathleen McNamara, "Common Markets, Uncommon Currencies," in Jack Snyder and Robert Jervis, eds., *Coping with Complexity in the International System* (Boulder, Colo., 1992), 303–327; Loriaux, *France*, 255–257.

domestic ratification. EMS membership gained the approval of both Mitterrand and Chirac.[71]

Giscard and Barre's policy of stabilization, like Schmidt's policy of reflation, was only partially successful. The franc grew stronger, yet balance of payments surpluses were nonetheless achieved in 1978 and 1979; the franc rose 10 percent between 1979 and 1981, but as the presidential election loomed and the Left surged, it grew politically more costly to refuse the fiscal and financial demands of firms and voters. Giscard and Barre, fearing electoral challenges from Chirac on the right and Mitterrand on the left, capitulated. The provision of credit was not constrained as significantly as planned, and enterprises faced less incentive to restructure. Inflation remained high.[72] Despite this retreat from austerity, Giscard lost the election of 1981 to Mitterrand and the Socialists.

Giscard's opponent, François Mitterrand, entered office at the head of a Socialist-Communist coalition committed to the view that fiscal and monetary policy should be used to stimulate growth by placing money in the hands of consumers. Some macroeconomic models employed at the time suggested that the economy was being held down by restrictive policies and weak demand; they also predicted global recovery. A Keynesian reflation would generate higher growth. The new government immediately faced a run on the *franc*, but—in a decision subsequently criticized—did not devalue. The failure of the expected recovery to materialize and fear of expropriation, taxation, and inflation led to considerable capital flight, a yawning trade deficit, repeated devaluation, dwindling reserves, and low domestic investment. The fact that the United States and most other European governments were pursuing contrary policies increased the pressure on France. In response to external imbalances Mitterrand's first instinct was to propose a system of capital controls and coordinated reflation at the EC level, which proved infeasible due to German and British fears that they would simply be asked to bail out the French. By early 1983 observers agreed that French policy was unsustainable. The issue arose whether to devalue again and impose austerity inside or outside the EMS.[73]

Mitterrand vacillated. The future of the Socialist experiment was debated at weekly ministerial meetings and among small groups of formal and informal ad-

[71] Prate, *Quelle,* 255; Commons, "European," 83.

[72] Loriaux, *France*; Goodman, *Monetary,* 103–111, 121–129; Flanagan, Soskice, and Lange, *Unionism,* 620, 636–637, 640–642, 644ff. Whereas credit rationing worked well in a period of high growth, the system generated moral hazard in a period of structural adjustment, when the government was particularly vulnerable to demands from politically powerful groups to employ its discretion to extend subsidies.

[73] Of those among Mitterrand's advisers who argued against devaluation, only Delors appears to have mentioned the EC. According to Prime Minister Pierre Mauroy, the decisive consideration was symbolic: the Socialists sought to reassure economic actors by avoiding the divisive policies of the interwar Left. Mitterrand's cryptic remark at his inauguration—"We will not devalue on a day like today"—seems consistent more with this explanation than with concern about Europe. Goodman, *Monetary,* 129–130; Pierre Mauroy, *C'est ici le chemin* (Paris, 1982, 17ff; Thierry Pfister, *La vie quotidienne à Matignon au temps de l'union de la gauche* (Paris, 1985), 245ff; Philippe Bauchard, *La Guerre des deux roses: Du rêve à la réalité* (Paris, 1986), 26–30; cf. Jean Peyrelevade, "Témoignage: Dallait-il dévaluer en mai 1981?" *Revue politique et parlementaire* 87 (May–June 1985,) 128–131; Jacques Attali, *Verbatim, 1981–1986,* vol. 1 (Paris, 1993), 403–406.

visers. Mitterrand postponed the decision until the two rounds of local elections of early 1983. In those elections the Communist party—the Socialist government's coalition partner—suffered a disastrous setback. This outcome required a political adjustment but did not force monetary discipline; instead the outcome was viewed primarily as an indictment of *rigueur*. Accordingly it initially strengthened Mitterrand's commitment to exit, as he told Mauroy a few days later. The decline of the Communist party undermined political support for the status quo, forcing a decisive choice on Mitterrand, but it did not dictate the direction of that choice.[74]

Shortly thereafter, in March 1983, Mitterrand finally rejected floating the franc in favor of austerity and EMS membership. He delegated Delors to negotiate a face-saving realignment with Germany, which wiped out the cumulative inflation differential with Germany since 1979. (Though much discussed, the precise terms of the realignment, whether Germany and others revalued or France devalued, were more symbolic than substantive, since international markets tended to set the level of the DM autonomously.) Thereafter the French government embarked on a policy of more sustained *rigueur*, resulting in lower inflation, higher unemployment, and stabilization of the franc.

The causes of the 1983 "turnaround" and the resulting decision to consolidate the EMS have been much debated. Early analyses, particularly those by economists, argued that Mitterrand and the Socialists remained in the EMS for geopolitical and ideological reasons. This view persists.[75] Yet—though the historical record of this decision remains incomplete—the preponderance of circumstantial and hard primary evidence suggests that macroeconomic considerations dominated the decision, with ideology and geopolitics playing a secondary role.[76] The timing of the turnaround, we have just seen, suggests the primacy of economic concerns. The year 1983 was not particularly salient from a geopolitical perspective, but it marked the definitive end of the Socialist economic experiment. Some policy adjustment was compelled by the constraints imposed by capital mobility on French policy, which narrowed the range of viable economic choices.

The nature of domestic cleavages and deliberations and the consistency of the decision with unilateral French policy suggests the preeminence of economic concerns. The debate within the French government revealed a cleavage between two groups recapitulating two basic views along economic lines. Defenders of autarky, the so-called Albanians (including Jean-Pierre Chévène-

[74] Hall, "Economic," 56; Pierre Mauroy, "La nuit de la rigueur," *Le nouvel observateur* 1594 (18 May 1995); Favier and Martin-Roland, *Le décennie*, 1:466.

[75] Sachs and Wyplosz, "Economic," 294–295. For a similar linkage argument, which hints at economic sources of ideological preferences, see Frieden, "Making," 32–33. Neither offers direct evidence.

[76] For overviews of this interpretation, see Peter A. Hall, "The Evolution of Economic Policy under Mitterrand," in George Ross, Stanley Hoffmann, and Sylvia Malzacher, eds., *The Mitterrand Experiment: Continuity and Change in Modern France* (New York, 1987), 56ff; David Andrews and Thomas Willett, "Financial Independence and the State: International Monetary Relations at Century's End," *International Organization* 51 (Summer 1997), 496–498.

ment, Pierre Bérégovoy, Mitterrand's close friend and head of the multinational firm Schlumberger Jean Ribout, and until the last moment Laurent Fabius), argued for macroeconomic accommodation of public industrial investment, a temporary strategy of inflation and devaluation to reduce internal public and private debt, withdrawal from the EMS, and the erection of trade and capital barriers. After restoring its competitiveness, France might reintegrate into European institutions. Moderates, backed by a group comprising Delors, Mauroy, Michel Rocard, Jacques Attali, Elisabeth Guigou, and numerous Treasury officials, pushed for austerity and devaluation within the EMS. These officials believed external constraints (trade deficits and, more important, capital outflows) were imposed primarily by excessive internal demand *vis-à-vis* Germany, not the exchange rate—a view supported by subsequent studies. While they would have preferred a greater measure of German economic stimulation as a solution to balance French austerity, they saw the wholesale imposition of trade barriers and capital controls proposed by the Albanians as risky. Devaluation was to be welcomed but would not solve the underlying problem.[77]

In 1983 Mitterrand chose the path that was expected to impose the lowest medium-term economic costs. The decisive piece of information, insider testimony confirms, was an assessment provided by the French Treasury, backed by central bank and Elysée officials, who maintained that leaving the EMS would not significantly loosen the short- and medium-term costs of austerity and monetary tightening. Michel Camdessus, the Treasury director, predicted that withdrawal from the EMS might lead to a 20 percent devaluation and require 20 percent interest rates to stabilize the currency—a point apparently decisive for Mitterrand. Reserves were inadequate to defend the currency in a float for more than fifteen days—a point apparently decisive for Mauroy. (Yet short-term concerns were not dominant: the policy of *rigueur* was reiterated and reinforced later in the year when Mitterrand—who may initially have intended to stay within the EMS, then withdraw later—again opted to remain within the EMS.) Even the Albanians conceded that their alternative would impose greater costs than staying within the EMS. Finally, there was little confidence that the proposals of the Albanians for stimulation would work. Delors added that the active industrial policy advocated by the Albanians would require borrowing from foreign sources, which would only further tighten the external financial constraint.[78]

Whether this assessment was correct has been debated, with some hinting that Mitterrand was deliberately misinformed. To be sure, even Delors saw further depreciation of the franc as an attractive policy, but only if a credible austerity

---

[77] Favier and Martin-Roland, *Le décennie,* 438–445, 453–460.

[78] It was expected that DM and dollar imports would drive the external deficit from FF 50 billion to FF 70 billion. It was argued that it would be difficult to stabilize the currency at less than a 10–15 percent devaluation without greater fiscal and monetary austerity, that such a devaluation might have destructive short-term inflationary effects due to rising import costs. Accounts based on participant testimony include Prate, *Quelle,* 262–263; Mauroy, "La nuit de la rigueur," *Le nouvel observateur* (18 May 1995); Attali, *Verbatim,* 1:402–413; Favier and Martin-Roland, *Le décennie,* 1:438–445, 452–453; Philippe Bauchard, *La Guerre des deux roses: Du rêve à la réalité* (Paris, 1986), 34ff; Serge July, *Les Années Mitterrand: Histoire baroque d'une normalisation inachevée* (Paris, 1986), 85, 94–97.

plan were imposed at the same time, as de Gaulle had done in 1958. (As late as the currency crisis of 1992–93, France favored depreciation, but only if it took the form of a unilateral German revaluation.) Maintaining the credibility of such a scheme without international support, as the British Labour government discovered in 1976, was difficult. In inner circles the concern was repeatedly raised that failure to establish credibility would simply push France into the hands of the IMF. Even if the more disastrous scenarios had been inaccurate, the critical point remains unchallenged that a unilateral policy of draconian capital controls, seen as a necessary corollary to leaving the EMS, would have been at least as costly as remaining within the EMS.[79]

By contrast, no direct evidence has emerged that Mitterrand or anyone in his government thought seriously about the consequences for French geopolitical prestige or for European ideals. Mitterrand appears to have begun internal discussions over EMS membership not with an apparent desire to find a way to stay in the EMS, as geopolitical ideology would predict, but with an inclination to leave it. He appears to have retained this inclination until he received the economic information cited above. Participants in internal debates report no discussion of federalism, the Franco-German relationship, the geopolitical importance of "tying Germany into Europe," or the Euromissiles controversy. Only when the president faced the television cameras to announce the devaluation did he invoke European ideology.[80]

[79] Olivier Jean Blanchard and Pierre Alain Muet, "Competitiveness through Disinflation: An Assessment of the French Macroeconomic Strategy," *Economic Policy* 14 (1993), 11–44, suggest that a larger devaluation would have been effective in the long-run, but only on two conditions: (1) the maintenance of stringent fiscal discipline; (2) the tolerance of significant short-term costs, which (the authors argue) might have called the credibility of French policy into question. See also Andrews and Willett, "Financial," 495. Some challenge this analysis, arguing that the arguments put forward by French officials concerning the costs of devaluation were deliberate misrepresentations—a bluff collectively carried out by Elysée, Treasury, and central bank officials. Of this there is little hard evidence. Macroeconomic models support the view that there would have been severe short-term difficulties.

[80] After reviewing much of the primary evidence, David Andrews and Thomas Willett term the appeal to geopolitical and ideological motivations an "ex post facto justification." See "Financial," 496. An ambiguous exception appears to be Mitterrand's off-hand remark in early 1983 reported by Attali: "I have two ambitions: the construction of Europe and social justice. The EMS is necessary to achieve the former, but limits my ability to achieve the latter." Attali also reports that Mitterrand wandered into his office shortly before the devaluation and asked whether Attali would have recommended entering the EMS in 1983 if France were not already a member. Attali, *Verbatim*, 1:399, 413, also 420–431. Even this is consistent with a weak version of the economic argument, namely that Mitterrand pursued geopolitical goals only when his economic options were constrained. See also Philip H. Gordon, *A Certain Idea of France: French Security Policy and the Gaullist Legacy* (Princeton, 1993), 124–134; Patrick McCarthy, "France Faces Reality: *Rigueur* and the Germans," in David Calleo and Claudia Morgenstern, eds., *Recasting Europe's Economies: National Strategies in the 1980s* (London, Md., 1990), 67, who claims France "could hardly have exhorted the Germans to accept the Pershing missiles in January 1983 and then withdrawn from the EMS three months later." This is speculation, and implausible on its face. Of the many spectacular turnarounds in Mitterrand's long political career, surely this would not have been the most difficult. For an earlier attempt to employ "Europe" as the glue of an anti-Communist, center-left alliance, see Jean-Jacques Servan-Schreiber, *Les fossoyeurs* (Paris, 1993), 2:182–183. Mitterrand may also have recalled the similar tactic employed by the Mollet government, in which he served, during the Treaty of Rome negotiations, described in chapter 2. Insofar as French prestige was concerned, the only major concern appears to have been avoiding loss of control over the economy and the embarrassment of IMF intervention.

The most to be said for geopolitical ideology is that it provided an expedient way for Mitterrand to justify the abandonment of the Socialist experiment. He exploited Europe as an ideological cover for the switch to domestic macroeconomic *rigueur* and as an appeal to pro-European centrist groups, long the core of French support for the EC—a gambit he had considered at least once before in his long political career.[81] This would permit systematic "blame avoidance"; with withdrawal, the blame might have fallen squarely on the president. Yet even so, ideology appears to have counted for little until Mitterrand was convinced that disinflation was inevitable and that a unilateral policy had no material advantages. At most, then, Mitterrand's effort to refashion his political image and discourse as a "European" became important only where economic incentives were balanced; more likely, it was an adaptation to the only economic course perceived as realistic.

In agriculture, both Giscard and Mitterrand pursued traditional French interests. Each supported export subsidies and sought to abolish MCAs. Giscard and Mitterrand both considered lowering support prices, even drastically, which would have decreased the profit per unit of French commodity production, but simultaneously would have increased French penetration of the German market; Mitterrand succeeded to a very limited degree in dairy products, but only in exchange for large side-payments. Giscard, less beholden than the Gaullists to farmers, appears personally to have shared Schmidt's suspicion of support prices, but government studies evaluating a more free-market agricultural policy revealed that it would benefit only 40 percent of French farmers, mostly specialty producers competitive on world markets, while imposing large costs on the rest. In the end, the idea gained little political support and was dropped. Opposition to MCAs was an issue of the highest importance in France: successive presidents, prime ministers, and foreign ministers took a personal interest in the issue. The farm lobby blocked ratification of the EMS for several months in order to press for their abolition. Giscard, though he championed Greek accession, delayed Spanish and Portuguese accession, much more costly to French farmers.[82]

Finally, on institutional matters Pompidou, Giscard, and for the most part Mitterrand all remained skeptical of greater supranationalism, whether in the form of expanded Commission powers, direct elections to the parliament, or more majority voting. The Gaullists particularly opposed elections, an issue that Chirac sought unsuccessfully to exploit in the 1979 elections but subsequently dropped when it generated little public interest. Giscard also resisted elections but accepted them as part of a linkage. Like Schmidt, Giscard was skeptical of the Commission and made special efforts to deny it international status and the advantages of majority voting—or perhaps he was forced to do so by Gaullist pressure. Pompidou and Giscard both accepted the need for a new institutional impulse for integration, for which purpose they preferred the creation and ex-

---

[81] As the Socialist majority declined, center parties may have viewed a public commitment to Europe and the EMS as enhancing the credibility of Mitterrand's policy reversal, thereby increasing their incentive to cooperate tacitly with the government.

[82] Tracy, *Farmers*; Knapp, *Gaullism*, 376; Ertl, *Agrarpolitik*, 45–50; Simonian, *Privileged*, 179–181.

pansion of the European Council. Giscard proposed replacing Commission initiative with, at least in part, European Council guidance. Mitterrand showed little interest in European institutions until the Single European Act, when he cautiously accepted majority voting for the single market—a topic we take up in chapter 5.[83]

Britain: Monetary Cooperation as a "second-best course"

After an abortive six-week effort in 1973 to participate in the Snake under the Conservative government of Edward Heath, Britain remained aloof from participation in exchange-rate arrangements. Aware that the others would go on without it, Britain made no effort to block monetary integration efforts such as the EMS, but similarly no serious effort to join them. Until the mid-1980s, the very end of this period, British non-participation was relatively uncontroversial domestically, largely, I argue, because it was seen as economically infeasible for a high-inflation country without massive dislocation. Only in the 1980s, in the face of declining macroeconomic control in the face of international mobile capital, a disastrous experience with sterling appreciation, and, more important, a convergence of inflation rates to continental levels, did the weight of business, partisan, and ministerial pressure turn toward participation. As on the continent, these supporters saw the EMS primarily as a device to avoid currency misalignment and increase the credibility and predictability of domestic policy. Any move toward membership remained blocked, however, by the increasingly isolated opposition of the ideologically antifederalist prime minister, Margaret Thatcher.

Geopolitical Interests and Ideology:
From Indifference to "deep-seated prejudice"

At no point from 1969 through 1985 were geopolitical or ideological arguments in favor of monetary cooperation widespread in Britain. To be sure, the Foreign Office generally felt that participation in the EC and EMS would improve Britain's diplomatic position in Europe—the traditional argument about "remaining at the heart of Europe"—but there is no evidence that such concerns had much influence.

Geopolitical ideology, in particular British antifederalism, did however account for some British opposition. Both the extreme left of the Labour party and the extreme right of the Tory party harbored substantial doubts about European federalism. Left Labour opposition helped to dissuade Callaghan from entering the EMS, though their geopolitical arguments were drowned out by economic ones, which alone were sufficient to keep Callaghan out. With the decline of the Commonwealth, right-wing Tory opponents of Europe on sovereignty grounds had been reduced to a recalcitrant minority. Such voices would have had little influence were it not for the personal beliefs of Thatcher herself. She proved to be a formidable opponent of monetary integration, at least in part, it seems, on

[83] Jenkins, *European*, 313, Fitzgerald, *All*, 133.

ideological grounds. There is unanimous agreement that Thatcher displayed at all internal meetings on Europe a "deep-seated prejudice" against the EC.[84] While no British government would have joined the EMS before 1983, during the following few years Thatcher was increasingly isolated—as we shall observe in more detail in chapter 6—as one after another of her ministers declared themselves convinced by the political economic arguments in favor of participation in the ERM.

Economic Interest: "A preference for exchange-rate stability does not override views about its level"

The primary concern of British business at the beginning of the period considered here, as it had been a decade before, was to overcome exclusion and seek EC membership. In 1971 a survey of the 500 largest businesses in Britain found that 85–86 percent believed EC membership would be good for the country and for themselves, by 1974, after entry, 415 of a sample of 419 heads of major companies favored remaining in. In large part this reflected direct commercial interest. There was agreement that in industrial trade lay the major British advantage from membership. British trade with the Six had increased rapidly in the early 1960s, Commonwealth trade continued to decline; its stagnation thereafter was attributed to exclusion.[85]

The peak industrial interest group, renamed the Confederation of British Industry (CBI), was led by larger exporting firms and increased pressure for membership. With the rise of monetary cooperation, the City, relatively uninvolved, began to advocate membership strongly. The CBI was closely connected with the negotiations, as was the National Farmers' Union, which despite some difficulties on detail favored membership, which would lead to considerable increases in farm incomes. Opposition arose due to residual concerns about Commonwealth products and the Labour belief that accession would constrain autarkic socialist economic policies. Transport unions were "particularly strongly" opposed to membership but abstained in the 1972 party vote to avoid a Labour party split. Strong business support was forthcoming even though economic forecasts predicted only a small increase in net national welfare. Welfare gains were dampened by the inefficiencies of the CAP and tighter balance-of-payments constraints.

In assessing exchange-rate policy, the CBI considered "competitiveness" to be "paramount."[86] A more competitive exchange rate, which implied lower inter-

---

[84] Michael Butler cited in Lord Gilmour, "The Thatcher Memoirs," *Twentieth Century British History* 5:2 (1994), 272.

[85] This section follows Butler and Kitzinger, *1975*, 10ff, 69ff, 83; Christopher Lord, *British Entry to the European Community under the Heath Government of 1970–74* (Aldershot, 1993), 16–17, 30–31, 86–89, 102, 104–105, 112–113, 118, 122; Lewis Minkin, *The Contentious Alliance: Trade Unions and the Labour Party* (Edinburgh, 1991), 171–180, also 453–456; Simon Z. Young, *Terms of Entry: Britain's Negotiations with the European Community, 1970–1972* (London, 1973), 103ff, 110–111. Even where geopolitical concerns were invoked, a major argument held that an independent military and armaments policy was unaffordable without economic integration.

[86] This paragraph and the next are based on CBI testimony in House of Commons, Treasury and Civil Service Committee, "International Monetary Arrangements" (London: HMSO, 12 July 1982), 181, also 175–193; (28 June 1982), 84–114; (26 July 1982), 199. Optimal, the CBI argued, would

est rates as well as export prices, was seen as necessary to avoid considerable weakening of industry. Even large multinational firms with U.K. commitments, such as Ford Motor and Unilever, pressed for a competitive exchange rate. Optimal, the CBI argued, would be a significant depreciation against the currencies of other European countries, against whose firms Britain primarily competes, and a more modest depreciation against the dollar. (Since other European competitors also must purchase dollar-denominated imports, import prices mattered less for competitiveness.) For British-based multinationals, the major virtue of exchange-rate cooperation was greater pressure on strong-currency countries to revalue and to provide financing for weak-currency countries like Britain.

For CBI members other goals remained secondary. Reduction of volatility in exchange rates was a relatively minor matter; business surveys revealed that "a preference for stability does not override views about the desirable level for sterling." Business was particularly unconcerned about short-term volatility, as their open positions tended to be small. Insofar as business favored greater stability in real exchange rates, misalignments, big industrial firms argued, were worrisome only when they implied overvaluation. Lower inflation, in particular fewer increases in wages, was similarly secondary; an increased risk of inflation was well worth the recommended depreciation, though CBI groups were relatively indifferent whether real exchange-rate stability was achieved through nominal stability or through depreciation. Financial groups in the City, as well as the Bank of England, were slightly more supportive of exchange-rate targeting and remained concerned about U.K. exclusion. The Bank of England and the government were slightly more concerned about inflation than was business, which favored more competitive exchange rates.

When Britain debated the EMS in 1978, the major argument against membership stressed in private and public economic analyses alike was that any such arrangement would impose an asymmetrical burden on weak-currency countries, leading to severe constraints on growth and government spending. James Callaghan and Denis Healey, his chancellor of the exchequer, realized that the fundamental question was whether inflation could be dampened sufficiently within the EMS to render British participation viable. "Surely," observed Healey, "the clash between domestic and international responsibility is at the heart of the whole subject." From this perspective the moment was judged inauspicious. From Edward Heath's abortive effort to participate in the Snake, the Treasury drew the lesson that greater convergence was required between high British inflation rates and those on the Continent. Membership, it was estimated, would

---

be significant depreciation against the currencies of other European countries, against whose firms Britain primarily competes, and a more modest depreciation against the dollar, in which intermediate imports were denominated. Yet since other European competitors also had to purchase dollar-denominated imports, import prices mattered less. (Similar concerns were voiced by French analysts.) Banks not dependent on interest rates took a similar position. For example, accepting houses—banks that traded government debt on a fee-for-service basis—argued that Britain's structure of trade (oil production) and deep, highly liquid markets for government debt made the EMS inappropriate even if technical modifications made it more symmetrical.

require a cut of £1.5 to £2 billion in government spending during the first year; other estimates were higher. Sterling was already floating considerably above its proper value, from the combined effects of high interest rates and North Sea oil revenues, and many felt it should not be kept artificially high. Increasingly observers doubted that rapid devaluation would offset shocks, though estimates still suggested that devaluation would have a modest positive effect.[87]

With these economic fundamentals, hardly any interest group or political party in Britain favored immediate participation in an adjustable-peg monetary arrangement. Among business groups, the CBI strongly opposed EMS membership. Surveys revealed that CBI members recognized the existence of a trade-off between the disciplining of wages and costs via real exchange-rate appreciation and the shift in price competitiveness due to depreciation. Hence the CBI officially supported membership in the EMS only if Britain entered at a competitive rate, remained free to alter parities, shared the adjustment burden with Germany, and received adequate credits—a set of demands surely known to be unrealistic. The TUC echoed CBI concern about deflation, as well as the destabilization of monetary relations with third countries.[88]

Only multinational corporations tended to favor greater exchange-rate stability even if it meant modest appreciation. Unilever, Shell, Dunlop, ICI, and Imperial Tobacco favored immediate membership. The Association of British Chambers of Commerce (ABCC), comprised of more export-oriented firms, was also supportive, advocating EMS membership as a means of to impose external discipline on inflationary forces in the domestic economy, in particular limiting government spending and aggressive wage claims. Even these firms, however, argued that obligations must be symmetrical; hence they opposed the Franco-German proposal. Some argued for rapid transition to a single currency, to avoid dominance by the DM. The ABCC also took the opportunity to press for further policy changes, including the removal of nontariff barriers (NTBs), capital controls, taxation harmonization, CAP reform, and more equal distribution of public spending.[89]

The most consistent support came from the large London clearing banks. In the 1960 the City had traditionally treated monetary integration with skepticism, but with the collapse of Bretton Woods, its position changed. In testimony before the Commons concerning the EMS proposal, the chairmen of three of the Big Four London banks—the fourth dissented—were "dead against staying out completely." Their underlying argument was not transaction costs gains, which would remain minimal unless Europe established a single currency, but

---

[87] Commons, "European," 61–62, also 2–5, 8–9, 10–60, 68–69, 82–83, 129; Callaghan, *Time*, 492–494; Carr, *Schmidt*, 142.

[88] See Commons, "European," 1ff, xxvii–xviii, 120–122, 140–143. The claim by major bankers that British business welcomed EMS membership was greeted with open amusement in the committee chambers. Also Helen Thompson, "The UK and the Exchange Rate Mechanism, 1978–80," in Brian Brivati and Harriet Jones, eds., *From Reconstruction to Integration: Britain and Europe since 1945* (Leicester, 1993), 228; Jenkins, *Life*, 470.

[89] Commons, "European," 115–118, arguing that the EMS cannot work in the United Kingdom without direct controls on wages.

instead the fear that exclusion would undermine London's role as an international financial center. Moreover, the EMS would impose "extra discipline" on inflation and stabilize exchange rates by creating a "public relations" deterrent to depreciation. Finally, though one suspects this argument was for public consumption, Britain should not exclude itself from future EC negotiations over compensatory transfers, resources, or adjustment. While recognizing the trade-off between disinflation and price competitiveness, the bankers asserted that unemployment would not necessarily increase. On balance, they conceded that "it must be an act of faith [that] the balance of advantage" lay with membership, though the positive experience of the Snake countries was cited.[90]

Yet even the clearing banks did not, on balance, advocate immediate membership. One chairman, Robin Leigh-Pemberton of National Westminster, later head of the Bank of England, noted that the convergence of domestic policies toward greater priority on low inflation and the buoyant effect of North Sea oil created a propitious moment to join the EMS, but stopped short of advocating immediate entry. The other two stressed the need for "transitional" measures "special arrangements" over two to five years for weaker-currency countries, at least until the dollar strengthened and greater macroeconomic convergence had been achieved among potential member countries. All realized that the system should be "symmetrical" for British membership to be sustainable; they were skeptical of an asymmetrical system or one that permitted easy adjustment.[91]

During the early 1980s the CBI and large firms continued to oppose immediate EMS membership. British industry was hit hard by Thatcher's disinflationary policies, which exacerbated the unexpectedly massive appreciation of the pound. Unit labor costs increased by over 25 percent in two years. Accordingly, the CBI and Institute of Directors rejected entry at prevailing high levels, though they were prepared to reconsider if inflation fell: "The advantages of exchange-rate stability are so widely cited by businesses, however, that there would be a case for the Government to reconsider full EMS entry if the technical problems [asymmetries] could be overcome and . . . if there was clear evidence that the level of the exchange rate against other European currencies was competitive." The consensus in the business community was that nominal exchange-rate flexibility should be maintained unless it became clear that slower wage increases and rising productivity would lead to labor costs similar to those of major European competitors. This position was backed by the Treasury, financial firms in the City of London, and the Bank of England, though representatives of the last quietly noted the "impressive . . . degree of exchange rate stability" achieved by the EMS. Industrialists close to the Conservative party pressed the prime minister and Parliament for relief, yet in 1982, with the exchange rate falling and

[90] Commons, "European," xiv–xv, 5, 77, 85–87, 90–101; Ludlow, *Making*, 222–223. The banks argued that while they profited from exchange-rate transactions connected with floating rates, stability was more important, particularly in trade finance. Some were skeptical of any composite currency, which would generate high transaction costs.

[91] Morse, in Commons, "European," 92–93, 96, 99–100. Bankers were unconcerned with the potential for rising unemployment. An argument often used was that Britain should maintain its bargaining power in areas such as the CAP and budgetary issues.

elections looming, CBI members voted down a resolution condemning Conservative Party interest-rate and exchange-rate policy.[92]

In 1984 the CBI suddenly reversed its position on ERM participation. Fear that the extended misalignment of sterling over the preceeding five years might be repeated and the fall of sterling to an acceptable level might be achieved were cited by CBI surveys as the major causes for this "marked change." The CBI leadership added the need for greater influence over critical EC trade and monetary negotiations over issues such as border controls, standards, satellite broadcasting, and the EMS itself. The immediate impact on competitiveness was expected to be minimal.

The Domestic Decision: "The argument rests on political judgment"

As a weak-currency country increasingly employing depreciation as a tool of policy, British concerns about monetary policy had been remarkably stable since the late 1950s. British politicians had long complained in private about what they considered irresponsible behavior on the part of Germany, which refused to revalue the mark or to lend abroad to support other currencies.[93] Edward Heath's government took Britain into the EC in the early 1970s, but continued to struggle with the balance of payments. Heath briefly sought to participate in the Snake, but, with France and Italy, was quickly driven out. The second Wilson government and that of his successor, James Callaghan, initially embraced depreciation as a strategy for boosting competitiveness. British inflation raged at an average annual rate between 1970 and 1978 of 12.7 percent, close to Italy's 15.1 percent and well above France's 9.5 percent and Germany's 5.3 percent. Wilson had opposed European monetary integration on the ground that it would impose subservience to German policy priorities and hence, under British conditions, severe recession. Callaghan never seriously considered rejoining the Snake; political opposition to the EC and high inflation rendered it impossible. In 1976 Britain was driven to the IMF, convincing many moderate Labour supporters that Keynesian demand management had become ineffective in an open economy.[94]

---

[92] This paragraph and the next rest on Commons, "European," 100, also 78, 1:xxi–xxxiii, 2:1–17; Wilhelm Schönfelder and Elke Thiel, *Ein Markt—Eine Währung: Die Verhandlungen zur Europäischen Wirtschafts- und Währungsunion* (Baden-Baden, 1994), 60–61; OECD *Economic Outlook* 58 (December 1995), A46. On the subsequent evolution of business views, see chapter 6. For a detailed analysis of business views, see James I. Walsh, "Global Finance, Domestic Politics: International Monetary Policies in Britain, France and Italy" (Ph.D. diss., American University, 1997), 94–101, chap. 6; Stephen Blank, "Britain: The Politics of Foreign Economic Policy, the Domestic Economy, and the Problem of Pluralistic Stagnation," in Katzenstein, ed., *Between Power and Plenty*; Henning, *Currencies*, chap. 1.

[93] Macmillan called German policies "shortsighted and selfish" in Memorandum by the Prime Minister, 29 December 1960/3 January 1961, PREM 11/3325, 9–10; Ben Pimlott, *Harold Wilson* (London, 1992), 465ff; Edward Heath, *Old World, New Horizons* (Cambridge, Mass., 1970), 52.

[94] Andrew Britton, *Macroeconomic Policy in Britain, 1974–87* (Cambridge, 1991), 149; Peter A. Hall, "The Movement from Keynesianism to Monetarism: Institutional Analysis and British Economic Policy in the 1970s," in Sven Steinmo, Kathleen Thelen, and Frank Longstreth, eds., *Structuring Politics: Historical Institutionalism in Comparative Perspective* (Cambridge, 1992), 90–113.

Early statements and papers from the government of James Callaghan, who became prime minister in 1978, suggest that it may have briefly considered EMS membership as a means of imposing macroeconomic discipline. The Foreign Office added that membership would strengthen Britain's position within the EC. Callaghan was constrained, however, by domestic opposition. Substantial elements of the Parliamentary Labour Party and the National Executive Committee were openly critical, in part on grounds connected with belief in the virtues of economic autarky. Most moderate groups, such as the Labor Committee on Europe, favored British entry only on condition that the system be symmetrical enough to permit pressure from France, Britain, and Italy to moderate German policy. If this condition were met, it was argued, membership in the EMS would weaken speculative pressures against sterling and permit British input on future developments. If it were not, British competitiveness would be undermined.[95]

The Callaghan government's negotiating position clearly shows the importance of the economic calculation of the consequences for competitiveness and interest rates. That position, public and private, was that Britain could not enter the EMS unless symmetrical obligations were imposed on its members, particularly Germany, and exchange-rate flexibility was permitted; in private discussions with Schmidt, precisely this concern about the appreciation of sterling was central. At one Treasury press briefing, Ken Couzens, Britain's representative in the preliminary discussions, described it as "little more than a means of holding down the mark and imposing restrictive policies on Germany's partners." Denis Healey, chancellor of the exchequer, who had been told by Manfred Lahnstein that the EMS was meant to keep the DM down, complained that it would lead to trade deficits and excessive deflation in weak-currency countries. Callaghan labeled Germany's refusal to reduce its "anti-social" surpluses "an act of German self-interest," one "thinly disguised by a veil of Community spirit." This view supported by a number of those testifying before the House of Commons. This view was backed by the Bank of England. Callaghan declared that he was "simply not prepared to preside over the de-industrialization of Britain."[96]

Even before the Bremen meeting, British representative Couzens had withdrawn from the discussions. Callaghan may have toyed with the idea of using EC regional funding to square the circle, that is, to offset the deflationary effects of the monetary peg. According to the British Green Paper on the EMS, resource transfers were necessary to avoid dampening growth, shifting capital and labor out of tradable sector and cutting budgets within the time lag between monetary

---

[95] Commons, "EMS," 120–122, 140–143; Jens Henrik Haahr, *Looking to Europe: The EC Policies of the British Labour Party and the Danish Social Democrats* (Aarhus, 1993), 75–79. Callaghan may have toyed with imposing discipline through the exchange rate; in 1979 he announced that Britain would seek to keep the pound in the EMS's 2.5 percent bands even if it was not a formal participant. The government's Green Paper argued that anti-inflationary benefits outweighed loss of competitiveness.

[96] Commons, "European," 4, 65, also 71; Ludlow, 113; Healey, *Time*, 438–439. Also Schmidt, *Weggefährten*, 280–281, Ludlow, *Making*, 111–114, Callaghan, *Time*, 492–494; Carr, *Schmidt*, 142; James, *International*, 301–302. Callaghan continued to advocate the locomotive theory and transatlantic cooperation rather than the EMS. Some internal documents suggest that concern for the stability of the multilateral, IMF-based system figured in British opposition, but I follow James (302) in discounting such concerns as an *ex post* justification not consistently represented in key internal discussions.

arrangements and the suitable reduction of inflation rates. In the end, however, such financing did not shift Callaghan's view; it seems doubtful that any reasonable amount would have. Aware that the others would move ahead with or without the British, Callaghan and Healey's major concern was to avoid exclusion from future decisions by joining the institutions while declining to participate in the exchange rate mechanism (ERM). This followed the demands of business groups. Some speculated that Callaghan sought to exploit anti-European sentiment during the election but was prepared to enter the ERM if Labour had won the upcoming election, but this, as we shall see in more detail in chapter 6, remains speculation.[97]

Monetary integration was linked to a number of other issues. On almost all such issues, British preferences during the 1970s and early 1980s remained unchanged, varying across issues with specific economic interests. Britain sought, above all, EC membership. When opportunities arose to press for entry, as in 1967 and 1971, British leaders of all major parties were quick to pursue them. Whatever residual sense held that Britain should forgo economic advantages in order to maintain foreign policy "independence" from Europe, whatever that might mean, had all but disappeared by 1970. Edward Heath, while concerned with economic interests, appears to have felt that Britain's geopolitical status now depended on entry. The more consistent concerns of policy-makers were, however, economic. Britain's relative economic decline had led to a "near obsessive" citation of GNP growth statistics by ministers and officials—though some politicians also argued that this was not connected with exclusion from the EC. A content analysis of Parliament speeches on membership reveals that the most commonly mentioned point by proponents in both parties was economic advantage, as were a majority of the top five points mentioned by Conservative supporters; economic arguments also figured prominently, if less so, among opponents.[98]

The most consistent pressure for entry, however, came from big business. Business concerns about the economic costs of exclusion from Europe, as we have seen above, intensified during the 1960s, as trade continued to shift away from the Commonwealth toward Europe. Among social groups, big business was the strongest supporter of membership. In the 1975 referendum, the European League for Economic Cooperation, loosely connected with the European Movement but funded largely by the City, mobilized influential individuals in favor. Contributions to "Britain in Europe," the umbrella group supporting a yes vote on the 1975 referendum, were led by major multinationals such as Shell, Ford, and IBM. The Yes campaign outspent its opponents tenfold. While there was now little effort to defend Commonwealth access, there remained concern, for

[97] Commons, "European," 65, also 67–68, 74–76. Also Heisenberg, *Mark*, 109; Schmidt, *Weggefährten*, 280–281; Ludlow, *Making*, 134–158, 173; *Green Paper on the European Monetary System*, Cmnd 7405 (London: HMSO, November 1978); Roy Jenkins, "Britain in Europe: Left Behind Again?" *Royal Bank of Scotland Review* 162 (June 1988), 3–8; Haahr, *Looking*, 77–78.

[98] This section follows Butler and Kitzinger, *1975*, 10ff, 65ff, 83; Lord, *British*, 15–20, 30–35, 69ff, 83, 86–89, 102, 104–105, 112–113, 118, 122; Young, *Terms*, 103ff, 110–111. It was in any case becoming clear that an independent military and armaments policy was unaffordable without economic integration. Minkin, *Contentious Alliance*, 171–180 and on the 1980s, 453–456.

example in the Treasury, about British industry, which had grown relatively less competitive than it had been in 1960.

There was considerable cross-issue variation. While favoring industrial trade liberalization, the British government remained skeptical of agricultural cooperation. The CAP, like the EC fisheries policy, had been designed by the Six and carefully insulated from British influence. As a net contributor to the budget and a marginal agricultural exporter, Britain gained little. Britain sought a relatively slow transition to the CAP and would have sought exemptions if they had been possible. Yet farmers were not opposed and the rapid decline in Commonwealth trade meant that third-country preferences were no longer a source of British opposition, as they had been in the early 1960s. Hence the CAP had a negative effect on public opinion, but did not significantly influence government policy. When France made it a non-negotiable quid pro quo for membership, Britain accepted. British concern about costs for taxpayers and consumers did not matter until the referendum, when deficits offered a convenient foil for ideological antifederalists. Its deficit status drove Britain's aims on regional policy. Realizing its powerlessness to impose fundamental reform on the CAP, the British government, though generally opposed to centralization, pressed for expanded financial transfers to offset the budgetary drain.[99]

Finally, on supranational institutions, the bulk of the Labour party and even the relatively pro-European Conservative party remained skeptical of the increased powers for the European Parliament and Commission. Under Heath and Callaghan, however, Britain supported increased coordination among chief executives through the European Council, which was seen, at least by the former, as a means of increasing the domestic autonomy of chief executives.

The success of the EMS led the British government to repeatedly consider membership in the ERM, support for which had become near-unanimous among British businessmen and economic ministers by the mid-1980s. Two major debates were held within the Thatcher government in the early 1980s, one in 1981, the second in 1985. The primary internal justifications advanced for participation in the ERM were economic, although the Thatcher's opposition, surely in part ideologically motivated, postponed entry for five years. Nearly all references to decision-making on ERM in this period by participants—Howe, Lawson, Thatcher—mention the influence of strong business pressure; many refer to concerns about avoiding exclusion from EMU. Splits within business, we have seen, reflected economic interests as well. Howe appears to be the only leading politician in the government ideologically committed to Europe.

During the late 1970s, while still in opposition, the Tories had criticized Callaghan's lack of leadership in the EMS negotiations. When Callaghan decided against participation, Thatcher proclaimed it "a sad day for Europe." Upon entering office, Thatcher initially moved to support the system, placing 20 percent of reserves into the European Monetary Cooperation Fund. Yet she took no further steps to participate more fully after 1979. Given the definitive failure of incomes policy, only the unilateral targeting of monetary aggregates, while

[99] Young, *Terms*, 58ff.

permitting the exchange rate to float freely, could force disinflation: "Significant foreign exchange market intervention could prejudice the achievement of
monetary targets, so if the latter were sacrosanct there was no room for the former."[100] Roy Jenkins recalls:

> Within six months of each other, Mr. Callaghan and Mrs. Thatcher told me, in
> the same room as it happened, why they each had to stay out [of the ERM].
> Mr. Callaghan said it was because he was afraid of being locked in at too high a
> rate, which would prevent his dealing with unemployment. Mrs. Thatcher said it
> was because she was afraid of being locked in at too low a rate, which would pre-
> vent her dealing with inflation.[101]

Between 1980 and 1983, the combination of tight monetary policy, North Sea oil,
and the second oil shock led to a devastating combination of recession and currency appreciation. By 1981, with inflation much lower, the government had reversed course and was loosening monetary policy and letting sterling depreciate.

In a 1981 policy review the Foreign Office and the Bank of England supported participation in the ERM, whereas the Treasury remained skeptical.[102]
Among the few within the Treasury strongly favoring membership was a young
official named Nigel Lawson, who saw the EMS primarily as a means of reducing the domestic political costs of disinflation. In 1981 he wrote to Chancellor
Geoffrey Howe:

> [ERM participation] is in many ways a second best course. . . . Straightforward
> monetary discipline is superior. But . . . as the election approaches, when the po-
> litical pressures for the relaxation of monetary discipline will start to mount . . . we
> may . . . be able to enforce and maintain a greater degree of effective financial dis-
> cipline if we were to embrace the exchange rate discipline. This is particularly ap-
> posite given that those of our colleagues who are most likely to be pressing for re-
> laxation of monetary discipline, are those who are keenest on the UK joining the
> EMS. In other words, we turn their sword against them. . . . At the end of the day
> the argument rests on political judgment.[103]

The argument was economic in the (political economic) sense the term is employed in this book—Lawson was acting to achieve a set of political economic
goals, not to realize geopolitical interest or ideology—although the tactic of exploiting European ideology was clearly important. Thatcher, evidently more
confident politically and apparently seeking to avoid the uncomfortable rhetorical turnaround that a shift to exchange-rate targeting would require, rejected

---

[100] Richard Brown, "British Monetary Policy and European Monetary Integration," in Heidemarie
Sherman, ed., *Monetary Implications of the 1992 Process* (New York, 1990), 110.

[101] Jenkins, "Britain in Europe," 6. He adds, "Britain then proceeded under both of them to enjoy for several years a higher combination of unemployment and inflation than any participating
member."

[102] Nigel Lawson, *The View from No. 11: Memoirs of a Tory Radical* (London, 1992), 112ff.

[103] Lawson, *View*, 111–113; also Thompson, "UK," 229–230.

Lawson's plea and others like it. Participation in the ERM, she argued, would restrict rather than expand her freedom of maneuver.

When the CBI shifted from opposition to support for ERM membership in 1984, Lawson, now chancellor of the exchequer, was initially displeased but quickly reversed course. By January 1985 the government's lax attitude toward the exchange rate had led to a depreciation of sterling (albeit *vis-à-vis* an overvalued dollar). The inflationary consequences were beginning to be felt, and Lawson switched to a de facto policy of targeting the exchange rate, to which there was little opposition within the government. "Benign neglect," Lawson's 1985 budget statement declared, "is not an option."[104]

The debate over ERM participation naturally arose again. Many supporters of ERM membership argued that it would offer greater anti-inflationary discipline with only slightly less monetary autonomy, since exchange rates tended to overshoot. A policy debate ensued, in which Lawson led the fight to enter the ERM, based on largely economic reasoning. In a 1985 memo to Thatcher, he argued that macroeconomic policy management through monetary targeting had grown technically impossible, although too much political capital had been invested to risk a public renunciation. Howe recalled that monetarism, in the sense of reliance *solely* on domestic monetary targets, "moved almost beyond the frontiers of attainability during the second half of the 1980s"—a situation he attributes to the unintended consequences of financial liberalization and the elimination of external capital controls, which led exchange rates to overshoot their targets. "We had to undergo the less than exhilarating experience of admiring French success in hitting with increasing accuracy broad monetary targets, in containing inflation at an increasingly credible low level . . . and achieving respectably sustainable economic growth. . . . Far from easing the external constraint, free exchange rates meant that policy makers were obsessed with the need to please the markets."[105]

Participation in the ERM, Lawson continued, would reinforce anti-inflationary credibility with "a beneficial long-term influence on interest rates." The basic problem facing the United Kingdom, in his view, was rising unit labor costs, which the government could in theory combat either by devaluation or by greater wage restraint; by removing the possibility of the former, he argued, the ERM would compel the latter. Capital markets, moreover, were imposing rising costs on nonmembership, which appeared to signal the willingness to devalue. The year 1985 was also said to be auspicious, because the exchange rate was low, the next election relatively distant, inflation converging toward Continental levels, and the dollar strong. Finally, Lawson expected a pre-election flight from sterling in several years, which would be "marginally easier" to handle inside the ERM than outside: it would occur later and could be pinned more easily on po-

[104] Commons, "European," 16; Lawson, *View*, 476; William Keegan, *Mr. Lawson's Gamble* (London, 1989), 144–160; Walsh, *Global*, 101–102.

[105] Sir Geoffrey Howe, "The 364 Economists: Ten Years On," (n.p., 1991), 100–101; also interview with former British Chancellor of the Exchequer; Malcolm Crawford, *One Money for Europe? The Economics and Politics of Maastricht* (London, 1993), 282–290; Lawson, *View*, 500, 664; Brown, "British," 121–122; Thompson, "UK," 231; Britton, *Macroeconomic*, 306.

litical threat from Labour rather than a lack of confidence in Conservatives. (Lawson, perhaps looking forward to a pre-election boom, speculated that Britain might take a "temporary leave of absence" at that time.) Nothing could be done about unemployment, he argued, which reflected labor market failures. In short, "the EMS establishes fundamental credibility."[106]

Lawson was supported by Treasury officials, the governor of the Bank of England, the past chancellor (Howe), the Foreign Office, an overwhelming majority in Cabinet, the CBI, and a sizable majority of the parliamentary Conservative party. By November 1989 even the Labour Party would come out in favor. While the pressure for participation in the ERM reflected economic interests (Howe excepted), the British government's continued rejection of ERM membership until 1990 must be attributed primarily to the obstinacy of the prime minister herself, who rejected Lawson's arguments and sought to close debate with the chancellor by force of will: "I do not want you to raise the subject ever again. I must prevail."[107] Thatcher's actions were not driven entirely by nationalism; she also rejected Lawson's alternative proposal for an autonomous Bank of England. Her central response to Lawson's plea was economic: the strength of sterling and tightness of current policy, she argued, meant that ERM participation would commit the government to *higher* inflation.[108] We take up this debate again in chapter 6.

Explaining National Preferences

These patterns of national positions, timing, and domestic support suggest that national preferences are best explained with reference not to geopolitical ideology but to economic interest. These interests reflect a combination of commercial imperatives and institutionally mediated macroeconomic goals. In Germany and Britain the evidence reveals that direct pressure from business groups played a predictable role; in France there is less evidence of direct business involvement, though the government's actions were consistent with it. European governments agreed that monetary sovereignty, fixed exchange rates, and capital mobility—the "inconsistent trio"—could not be maintained simultaneously. Hence pegged exchange rates under conditions of capital mobility required governments to harmonize to a similar standard of macroeconomic performance. The Snake and the EMS were attempts to craft a bargain between strong- and weak-currency countries. The core of that bargain was that strong-currency countries would receive protection against currency appreciation, while weak-currency countries would receive support in disinflation. Both would receive relief from currency volatility, in particular upward overshooting, which harmed producers and undermined macroeconomic control.

The role of the decline and collapse of Bretton Woods in triggering efforts to find a European substitute is too obvious to dwell on. But how should we explain

[106] Lawson, *View*, 857, 1055–1059.

[107] Gilmour, "Thatcher," 274, also 272–273. Gilmour, a participant, speculates that Thatcher's opposition was motivated by constraints on her domestic macroeconomic discretion.

[108] Lawson, *View*, 867ff; Walsh, *Global*, 187.

national variations in preference, over time and across countries? At the level of national preferences, cooperation had three key preconditions. The first was that the preferences and policies of weak-currency countries shifted toward lower inflation. Without substantial disinflation, a currency peg would have imposed too great a cost in terms of eroded competitiveness and high interest rates. The second was a preference on the part of strong-currency governments to stimulate the economy and dampen currency appreciation. The third was that obstacles to the realization of these convergent ambitions could be circumvented through policy coordination. For both weak- and strong-currency countries, coordinated intervention could heighten policy credibility on international markets and alter specific domestic macroeconomic institutions and practices.[109]

This shift in attitudes was not a straightforward result of direct "spillover" from rising trade interdependence. We have seen that almost no evidence supports the view that the stability of CAP prices or the maintenance of the customs union—often cited by the Commission and occasionally by national leaders—significantly influenced national monetary preferences.[110] Such arguments are inconsistent with patterns of support for policies. Rising trade independence alone cannot explain why business in weak-currency countries should favor pegged exchange rates. At most the stability of the common market was invoked as a justification for policies pursued for other reasons.[111]

Insofar as rising interdependence created support for monetary integration, the important element was greater capital mobility. Rising capital mobility undermined efforts to maintain artificially low real interest rates, thereby eliminating one of the major justifications for retaining full monetary sovereignty. Moreover, capital mobility made it more difficult to maintain parities unilaterally, as the Germans, French, and British all learned in the late 1960s and early 1970s. Each episode of dollar depreciation pushed the DM upward, while the franc and lire were pulled downward, importing inflation into both types of country.[112] The most important lesson was that currency depreciation, though not inefficacious, was no substitute for discipline. In Britain, France, and Italy, depreciation in the 1970s failed to lead to sustained growth and lower real interest rates, but it did stoke inflation. This realization, combined with more convergent inflation rates, led industrialists in France, Italy, and Britain to back currency appreciation as a means of dampening wage inflation and of shifting resources away from the public sector. This is not to say that the exchange rate

[109] For analyses see Samuel Brittan, "The European Monetary System: A Compromise That Could Be Worse than Either Extreme," *World Economy* 2 (1979); Giavazzi and Giovannini, *European Monetary System*.

[110] For a "spillover" view of this kind concerning agriculture, see McNamara, "Common," and more broadly, Barry Eichengreen and Jeffrey Frieden, "The Political Economy of Monetary Integration: An Analytical Introduction," *Economics and Politics* 5 (July 1993), 85–104.

[111] In addition to the evidence above, see McNamara, *Currency*, chaps. 1–3.

[112] On capital mobility, see David M. Andrews, "Capital Mobility and State Autonomy: Toward a Structural Theory of International Monetary Relations," *International Studies Quarterly* 38, no. 2 (1994), 193–218; Andrews, "Capital Mobility and Monetary Adjustment in Western Europe, 1973–1991," *Policy Sciences* 27 (1994), 425–445; McNamara, *Currency*. On the role of the dollar, C. Randall Henning, "European Monetary Integration in Its Global Context," *International Organization* 47 (1993).

did not matter: Lawson still sought to keep the pound down, Delors to increase French devaluations, and Schmidt to avoid DM appreciation. Yet increasing capital mobility does appear to have given depreciation a smaller and somewhat more erratic effect on domestic interest rates, undermining one of its traditional benefits.[113]

The evidence clearly suggests that the EMS did not cause disinflation; instead, a substantial commitment to disinflation was a precondition for monetary cooperation. Shifts in domestic policy precede and appear to have been largely independent of shifting international institutional commitments.[114] The decline of Bretton Woods, the rise of franc-DM tensions, and the move to floating predate the construction of the Snake. The EMS was created to defend Schmidt's fiscal objectives and those of the Plan Barre, not the reverse. Mitterrand's decision to impose *rigueur* predates his commitment to remain in the EMS. At the heart of the success of the EMS was, therefore, the trend toward low-inflation policies throughout Europe which began around 1977 to 1979. This trend occurred regardless of whether the country in question was inside or outside the EMS. Jean-Jacques Rey of the Belgian central bank recalls:

> The decisive change of mood came about after 1982, when countries like Belgium, Denmark and France decided to operate major economic policy adjustments, involving a clear switch toward a DM exchange-rate target. The change in policy orientation did not occur because of EMS, but [because] the costs of economic divergence within the ERM had become obvious, and they were unlikely to disappear simply by opting out of the system. . . . Admittedly, participation was also seen to entail feedback effects . . . but the first-round sequence goes from the basic policy reversal to ERM sustainability, not the other way around.[115]

In accordance with this view, cross-national studies suggest that average disinflation was no swifter in EMS countries than in non-EMS countries such as

---

[113] In Denmark the shift occurred in 1982–83; in Ireland in 1981; in France in 1978–79, then again in 1982–83. In Italy, incremental steps during the 1980s led to a more autonomous central bank. The hard lira policy came incrementally. Efforts to use devaluation and wage indexation (the *scala mobile*) to shift resources toward the tradable sector supported by the peak industrial group, Confindustria, only encouraged greater wage demands and public spending. Boissieu and Duprat, "Recent," 71; Massimo Russo and Giuseppe Tullio, *Monetary Coordination within the European Monetary System* (Washington, D.C., 1988), 303; Goodman, *Monetary Sovereignty*.

Some maintain that this sequence reflected above all lessons learned from the German example in the 1970s and, more broadly, the spread of monetarist ideology. It is certainly true that some national leaders, notably Giscard and Barre, cited the German case as a model. Yet Giscard and Barre had supported such domestic policies since the mid-1960s, whereas others, particularly Socialists, switched as the result of overt domestic policy failure. Consistent French support for the "monetarist" position suggests that this explanation cannot be taken too far. Finally, there is much evidence that monetarism as an ideology was treated with skepticism, even in Germany. Nonetheless, this conjecture cannot be definitively rejected. For a sophisticated treatment, see McNamara, *Currency*.

[114] Willett and Andrews, "Financial," 20ff.

[115] Jean-Jacques Rey, cited in Francesco Giavazzi, Stefano Micossi, and Marcus Miller, eds., *The European Monetary System* (Cambridge, 1988), 138–139. Also, Rainer Masera of the Banca d'Italia argues that the key remains "convergence of economic fundamentals," 403; Tsoukalis, "Money," 128; Schmidt, *Deutschen*, 220, 233.

Table 4.2. Average annual inflation rates (%) (CPI)

Country	1970–1979	1980–1986	1984–1986
Germany	5.2	3.3	1.5
France	9.2	9.0	5.3
Britain	13.2	7.7	4.8
Italy	12.8	13.9	8.4

SOURCE: *OECD Economic Outlook* 58 (December 1995), A18.

Britain.[116] Nor did the *relative* inflation performance of member and nonmember governments change significantly, though those who chose to participate tended to have lower inflation (see Table 4-2). Disinflation, in sum, appears to have been more cause than consequence. EMS membership was not a substitute for disinflation, nor a necessary condition for it. It was instead a particular way to institutionalize disinflation so as to reduce its perceived costs, economic and political.

Why choose international cooperation rather than a unilateral peg to the DM or to an appropriate currency basket, as Austria, Sweden, and Britain did at times? The historical record suggests, though it cannot definitively confirm, four reasons, each of which focuses on the expectations of domestic economic and political actors for the EMS commitment.

The most commonly cited yet least important reason was the hope that the EMS might at some future date—whether by the revision in 1981 or a shift to a single currency—transform into a more symmetrical arrangement. Yet this must have been secondary, since we have seen that Giscard and Mitterrand accepted EMS membership even though they realized that such a transformation was not imminent; the British, having discussed the matter with the Germans and French, never even entertained such illusions.

A second reason for the EMS was to dampen exchange-rate volatility, thereby providing a more stable environment in which to manage monetary policy and discouraging the sort of overshooting that characterized U.K. and U.S. policy during the early 1980s. Under floating exchange rates and with high capital mobility, consistent macroeconomic management proved difficult, if not impossible. In Britain, even convinced monetarists like Nigel Lawson had decided by 1985 that a pegged exchange rate was the only credible macroeconomic policy target; Howe, as we saw above, thinks it was for just this reason. Clearly this was the concern of British business, which quickly swung to support of membership in the EMS after its experience with massive exchange-rate appreciation and re-

[116] This point is disputed, but the preponderance of evidence supports the lack of direct impact. Fratianni and von Hagen, *European,* 48–53, 68–71, 221–222; Francesco Giavazzi and Alberto Giovannini, *Limiting Exchange-Rate Flexibility: The European Monetary System* (Cambridge, Mass., 1989); Daniel Gros and Niels Thygesen, *European Monetary Integration: From the European Monetary System towards Monetary Union* (London, 1991); cf. Frieden and Eichengreen, "Political," 28. For the Commission's counterargument, see Michael Emerson et al., *One Market, One Money* (London, 1992), 210ff.

duced inflation. Similarly, Bundesbank support for currency pegs—even if the support was almost never invoked—may have dissuaded speculators. There is strong evidence that the EMS did indeed dampen exchange-rate volatility.[117]

A third reason was that many believe pegged exchange rates bolstered the credibility of domestic disinflation, thereby reducing its economic cost. The EMS arranged external finance, currency swaps, and coordinated intervention in support of currency pegs. The European political symbolism was thought to bolster confidence in national currencies among international financial markets, thereby reducing risk premia, and among domestic economic actors, thereby reducing the output cost of disinflation. There is in fact little evidence of this: output costs of disinflation appear to have been no lower in EMS than in non-EMS countries. Yet such claims were widely believed.

The fourth reason is that the EMS offered justifications that, for some governments, reduced the political costs of unpopular austerity policies. In short, governments "cut slack" domestically. Use of the EMS reinforced institutional control over monetary policy, avoided blame for costly austerity by scapegoating the EC and foreign governments, and provided ideological legitimation for monetary stabilization by linking monetary cooperation to underlying economic and geopolitical purposes (everything from the maintenance of trade liberalization to the prevention of Franco-German war).[118] Except during the Socialist experiment from 1981 through 1983, the chief executives of France, where inflation was traditionally moderate and European integration popular, grasped at the EMS as an instrument to legitimate and sustain a centrist coalition around austerity. Both Giscard and Mitterrand exploited the symbolic and institutional significance of the EC to justify the imposition of *rigueur*. This interpretation is more convincing than the conventional geopolitical view that the EMS commitment was "paramount" because of France's desire to deepen its participation in the EC.[119]

These considerations, along with underlying inflation rates, help explain the cross-national patterns in policy and process. Ability and willingness to partici-

---

[117] Gros and Thygesen, *European*. Randall Henning and James Walsh attribute differences in exchange-rate policy between Germany and France, on the one hand, and Britain, on the other, to closer links on the Continent between banks and business, which in turn influence the respective central banks—an argument advanced also by Stephen Blank with respect to British policy generally and Alan Milward with respect to the Treaty of Rome. Walsh maintains that in Britain, as opposed to France and Italy (and implicitly Germany), a relatively weak relationship between business and finance undermined "consensus among senior policy-makers" (particularly central bankers) for competitive exchange rates. This, he argues, explains large fluctuations in exchange rates and the weakness of British support for EMS. This view cannot be dismissed, but I have not found much confirming evidence. Despite loose ties, British business, finance, and the central bank were almost perfectly aligned in the 1980s. All three, excepting one bank, were publicly opposed before 1982–83, all publicly in favor by 1984. Despite close bank-industry links in Germany, business and the Bundesbank consistently took opposed positions. Cf. Henning, *Currencies*; Walsh, "Global."

[118] Roland Vaubel, "A Public Choice View of the Delors Report," in Vaubel and Thomas Willett, eds., *The Political Economy of International Organizations: A Public Choice Approach* (Boulder, Colo., 1991), 306–310; Jeffry A. Frieden, "Making Commitments: France and Italy in the European Monetary System, 1979–1985," in *Center for German and European Studies Working Paper Series 1.14* (Berkeley, Calif., 1993).

[119] Moravcsik, "Why the European Community." Cf. Frieden, "Making," 38–39.

pate in a fixed-rate regime was an inverse function of underlying inflation. In founding the EMS, Schmidt sought to stimulate growth while reducing exchange rate instabilities, whereas Giscard after 1976 sought to facilitate the domestic adjustment required to bring French inflation into line. Both leaders felt their ambitions, unattainable through domestic institutional means, might be realized through international cooperation.[120]

Cooperation remained weak during periods when governments pursued divergent macroeconomic policies. The Snake and the EMS were relatively ineffective when the inflation rates of France, Britain, and Italy diverged and the domestic political will to impose austerity was absent. The British government, by contrast, faced more entrenched inflation, could draw on weaker public support for European integration, and in the 1980s was led by a more confident and resolutely antifederalist chief executive. Thatcher, in overt opposition to many of her advisers, preferred to disinflate by confronting and conquering rather than circumventing domestic opposition, whatever the short-term costs. She pursued rigorous disinflation and crafted nationalist rather than European appeals. Nonetheless, those in Britain who did favor membership, notably Nigel Lawson, argued on precisely the grounds sketched above.

Even where policies converged enough to generate a shared interest in exchange-rate stabilization, persistent differences in inflation rates between hard- and soft-currency countries sparked significant distributive conflict. While Schmidt sought a lower exchange rate and greater macroeconomic flexibility, he was unable to push the Bundesbank very far; German preferences were relatively narrowly defined. Hence the paradoxical result that Germany initiated most of the negotiations yet was not forthcoming in distributive negotiations, for no agreement could sacrifice German monetary sovereignty; no large move toward accommodating expansion was permitted. The German win-set was correspondingly narrow.[121] For their parts, the Giscard government, and even more so those of Callaghan and Giulio Andreotti in Italy, were limited in their ability to impose domestic austerity and discipline, even with external support. Hence France, Britain, and Italy sought lower inflation, but none waited to converge entirely on German levels. This basic cleavage between hard- and soft-currency countries drove the dispute between "economists" and "monetarists" that characterized European monetary discussions from the early 1950s to the end of the period in question. Each side sought to reduce the costs of domestic policy adjustment: France, Britain, and Italy sought arrangements that would reduce inflation with minimal austerity and discipline, whereas Germany sought to avoid appreciation without undermining domestic monetary control.

Variation across other issues linked to monetary policy, such as British accession, CAP reform, and regional policy, reflected narrow commercial interests even more strongly. France linked British entry to agriculture, Germany imposed

[120] Story, "Launching," 401; Begg and Wyplosz, "European Monetary System," 21–23.

[121] Roland Vaubel, "The Return to the New European Monetary System," in K. Brunner and A. Meltzer, eds., *Monetary Institutions and the Policy Process,* Carnegie-Rochester Conference Series 13 (Amsterdam, 1980).

MCAs in the CAP, donor countries permitted increases in regional funding only as explicit side-payments. Only in defining preferences over institutional matters, the most uncertain issue, did geopolitical ideology play a major role. The geopolitical argument is least plausible in the case of agricultural policy and in regional and social transfers. Even German institutional preferences concerning the Council and Commission can be interpreted, as we shall see, as a credible commitment mechanism to achieve specific economic goals. Only in institutional matters with no clear consequences, such as direct elections to the Parliament, is there strong evidence for the primary importance of ideology.

By contrast, attempts to promote cooperation for purely geopolitical or ideological reasons—Brandt's proposals for a monetary fund, Jenkins's fiscal federalism, and perhaps some symbolic proposals on Pompidou's part—were quickly scaled back to fit within the perceived economic interests of major governments. Yet this is not to ignore geopolitical interests and ideology entirely. Schmidt and Giscard exploited European ideology to justify policies they pursued primarily for economic reasons. Antifederal ideology also did have a strong, independent effect on Thatcher's policies, which reflected to a large extent her personal antipathy regarding European integration. Yet even in the British case an economic explanation tells us as much about British preferences than does a geopolitical one. But for Thatcher's personal antipathy, Britain would have joined the ERM in the mid-1980s, when business and the Conservative party were firmly in favor. As we shall see in the next chapter, Thatcher could not forever resist the combined pressure of ministers, British business, and the City.

INTERSTATE BARGAINING

Given the different preferences among various governments concerning the nature of monetary cooperation, as well as such related issues as agricultural reform, British entry, and regional policy, as well as varying views concerning the proper institutions in which to embed these substantive issues, intense negotiations were required to reach agreement. In monetary policy, negotiations were conducted in three stages: negotiations on the Snake between 1969 and 1973, negotiations on the EMS in 1978 and 1979, and negotiations within the EMS.

Beyond the Common Market: The Snake, 1969–1973

Despite numerous proposals, starting with the Spaak Report in 1956 and including suggestions from Monnet's Action Committee, private economists like Robert Triffin, the European Parliament, and the Commission, which in 1965 made monetary coordination a major objective, no concrete momentum toward monetary cooperation occurred during the 1960s. The Council of Ministers did, however, agree to create EC committees to discuss monetary, financial, and macroeconomic issues. The most important of these was ECOFIN, at which finance and economics ministers met monthly with members of the Commission present. In January 1968, with the dollar under downward pressure, proposals for monetary cooperation began once again to proliferate. A leading Luxembourg politican, Pierre Werner, submitted a plan for monetary union, which was followed, one month later, by a less ambitious Commission memorandum and later by a proposal from Giscard. Raymond Barre, who had replaced Robert Marjolin as Commissioner for economic and financial affairs, called for "realistic" steps, such as agreed growth-rate targets, consultations on short- and medium-term economic policy, the provision of unconditional short-term credits to members facing balance of payments problems, and the provision of conditional medium-term financing to members with persistent deficits—a cautious proposal tilted slightly toward French "monetarist" priorities. The Council accepted Commission proposals establishing a consultation procedure and affirming short-term support for balance of payments in principle, but surplus countries (Germany, the Netherlands, and Italy) refused to move beyond limited central bank swaps.[122]

Momentum toward monetary agreement picked up only after July 1969, when Pompidou proposed linked negotiations on British entry, monetary integration, and agricultural financing, to be discussed at a summit meeting among chief executives at The Hague. The French insisted that agriculture be resolved first; after a marathon ministerial session, a system of centralized EC financing for the CAP, based on 1 percent of national VAT receipts, was established. As a quid pro quo the French government accepted the opening of negotiations over British accession and limited new budgetary powers for the European Parliament concerning noncompulsory expenditures but successfully resisted pressure for direct elections to the Parliament. In addition, there were agreements on intergovernmental cooperation on foreign policy and regular summit meetings in the European Council.[123]

By contrast, monetary policy was relegated to the rhetoric of the final communiqué, whereby the Six undertook to complete Economic and Monetary Union. Brandt was unwilling to move beyond short-term swaps to a European Reserve Fund without prior economic convergence, whereas Pompidou called for immediate steps to create short-term support, coordinate external monetary policy, and, in a departure from previous French policy, pool reserves. In March 1970 the member-states called for study by a group of national politicians and experts chaired by Pierre Werner, Prime Minister of Luxembourg.[124]

The Werner Report, which appeared in October 1970, sought compromise between deficit and surplus countries. It proposed an "irrevocable fixing of parity rates," perhaps with a single currency, and "the complete liberalization of capital," all within a system operated by an EC system of central banks modeled on the U.S. Federal Reserve. Transition was to take place in three stages. The first two would employ narrower exchange-rate bands and a medium-term fund managed by national central banks. Only in the final stage would parity changes

---

[122] Dyson, *Elusive*, 65–71; Tsoukalis, *Politics*, 53, 82–90; Schmidt, *Deutschen*, 240–242; Franck, "New," 138–139.

[123] Franck, "New," 130–135.

[124] Tsoukalis, *Politics*, 82–90; Coffey and Presley, *European Monetary Integration*, 37–38.

be prohibited and sanctions imposed for noncompliance. Controls over fiscal policy were particularly strict, with authority over national budgets, as well as expanded EC regional and structural funds, overseen by the Parliament.[125]

The report was greeted with magnificent rhetoric but little concrete action. An ECOFIN resolution of March 1971 proclaimed the launching of the first stage. In May 1971, six weeks after the ECOFIN resolution, the German and Dutch governments responded by temporarily floating the DM and the guilder, despite opposition from both the French and within Germany, from the Bundesbank. At the Paris summit of October 1971 it was agreed to complete "European Union" by 1979 and "Economic and Monetary Union" by 1980; the plan was endorsed again one year later. The chief executives simultaneously proclaimed goals in science and technology, environmental and social policy, as well as calling for deeper cooperation in foreign policy. Yet in practical discussions at a Franco-German summit and various meetings during 1971, the member states were more cautious, reaching agreement close to the lowest common denominator. The German government, under Bundesbank pressure, insisted on strict convergence and a safeguard clause that would permit the monetary measures of the first stage to be reversed after five years if economic convergence had not been achieved; the French, under Gaullist pressure, rejected explicit mention of transfers of sovereignty in the final stage. Agreement was reached on only a few concrete steps: closer consultation among central banks, modest medium-term financial aid, and nonbinding coordination of short-term policies. Germany continued to press for a joint float against the dollar but France rejected the plan and Italy refused, fearing that their currencies would simply follow the DM upward.[126]

The April 1972 Basle Agreement, reached among central bankers meeting at the Bank for International Settlements (BIS), created the "Snake in the Tunnel." This arrangement permitted European currencies to deviate within bands of ±2.25 percent. It was organized outside formal EC institutions, and five nonmembers—Sweden, Norway, Denmark, Britain, and Ireland—were participants. The Snake remained a pure exchange-rate agreement. Germany rejected Commission and French proposals for a joint reserve fund, regional policy, and centralized redistribution, insisting on prior economic convergence. Further action could be taken only by finance ministers voting unanimously in the ECOFIN Council. In March 1973 the joint peg to the dollar became a joint float; when the German government threatened to go ahead on its own, Pompidou chose to follow. A modest European Monetary Cooperation Fund was cre-

---

[125] Tsoukalis, *Politics*, 103–104; Gros and Thygesen, *European*, 12–14, 24–26. Although divergent inflation rates were not yet a major problem, the Werner Commission foresaw the potential difficulties and called for massive transfers of power: "The center of decision for economic policy will exercise independently . . . a decisive influence over the general economic policy of the Community. . . . public budgets [will] be decided at the Community level . . . the creation of liquidity throughout the area and monetary and credit policy will be centralized; monetary policy in relation to the outside world will be within [its] jurisdiction." Cited in Tom de Vries, "On the Meaning and Future of the European Monetary System," *Princeton Essays in International Finance* (Princeton, N.J., 1980), 7.

[126] Tsoukalis, *Politics*, 104–106, 110–113; Gros and Thygesen, *European*, 16.

ated, yet it was without real authority. By 1974 the Commission could recommend little except for more frequent meetings.[127]

The Snake did not dissuade European governments from pursuing specific national priorities. Within six weeks of its creation, speculation forced out the British pound and the Irish punt; the Italian lira followed in early 1973.[128] The remaining countries soon split into strong and weak currencies, with Germany, the Netherlands, and Norway in the first group, and France, Belgium, Sweden, and Denmark in the second. For a time, weak-currency countries tried to avoid unilateral devaluation against the DM, resorting instead to external financing and capital controls. Yet unilateral capital controls proved ineffective, and Germany rejected a European system of two-tiered exchange rates proposed by France and Belgium. In January 1974, with devaluation inevitable and elections approaching, the French government withdrew. Schmidt's offer of a DM 9 billion loan to keep France in—an act of questionable domestic legality—was rejected; the French government had already accumulated a large debt keeping the franc in the joint float, and the prospect of more was unappealing. France rejoined in December 1975, only to exit again the following year after Chirac's reflation. Schmidt pressed the British and, in August 1974, offered the Italians a $2 billion loan to finance their return. Both efforts were futile. Neither country was able to stabilize its exchange rates, and in 1976 both negotiated IMF stabilization agreements.[129]

By 1976 the Snake functioned only among small northern European countries contiguous with Germany—the Netherlands, Belgium, and Denmark—with Sweden and Norway as associate members.[130] Nine exchange-rate adjustments occurred, and the Bundesbank intervened on several occasions in favor of smaller currencies. Yet in general the Snake did not discipline devaluations, unilateral requests were not challenged, and no common policy developed toward the dollar. The Marjolin Committee report on monetary integration concluded: Europe is no nearer to EMU than in 1969. In fact, if there has been any movement, it has been backward. The Europe of the 1960s represented a relatively harmonious economic and monetary entity which was undone in the course of recent years; national economic and monetary policies had never

---

[127] Gros and Thygesen, *European*, 20–21. Also Tsoukalis, *Politics*, 114–118, 126, 128, 139–141, 144–150, 155; Lankowski, *Germany*, 326ff, 340ff, 361; Dyson, *Elusive*, 85; Loriaux, *France*, 248–249.

[128] In public France and Germany called on Britain and Italy to rejoin, but privately discouraged them from doing so—the entire tactic apparently aimed at postponing decisions on side-payments. The movement to the "second stage" of EMU, proclaimed in 1973, contained no concrete measures. Germany offered to guarantee the British sterling balances, and Heath was apparently willing to take sterling into the float on these terms; but he was dissuaded by the Treasury. Gros and Thygesen, *European*, 30–33.

[129] Tsoukalis, *Politics*, 115–118, 139–141, 154–168; Lankowski, *Germany*, 360; Carr, *Schmidt*, 89–94.

[130] Tsoukalis, *Politics*, 129, 152–157; Ludlow, *Making*, 2–12. Switzerland proposed to join the Snake in 1975 but withdrew its application when confronted with stiff French conditions. During this period Italy, though continuing to run a current account surplus, suffered from large capital outflows. Fearing a run on the lira, they joined the French camp on this issue. The French, however, desiring financing but having relatively large reserves, were suspicious of proposals that would undermine national control over reserves.

been in 25 years more discordant, more divergent, than they were at that time.[131] As two commentators observed, "the Snake was only a limited, though significant exception to Europe's lapse into more divergence than at any time since the very first postwar years."[132]

Relaunching Exchange-Rate Cooperation: The European Monetary System, 1977–1979

Monetary integration, Helmut Schmidt observed in 1977, was "in the air." There was no shortage of initiatives. Over a dozen proposals for EC reform had been advanced by member governments, professional economists, and expert committees, and were suggested by numerous reports on the state of the EC more generally. Among these were reports from the Commission and Parliament focused particularly on an expansion of EC activities under strong, centralized institutions for budgetary approval and codecision by an elected Parliament and the Commission; groups appointed by the Council focused primarily on improving intergovernmental institutions.[133]

Such official EC proposals had little impact, however. Not atypical was the fate of the monetary proposal advanced by Roy Jenkins, the former Labour minister who was named to the Commission Presidency in 1976 at the suggestion of Schmidt and Giscard. In a series of lectures beginning in October 1977, Jenkins made closer monetary cooperation the centerpiece of his EC program for the next four years. This decision, a surprise to most observers, reflected—so he later recalled—his assessment that it was the issue most likely to be accepted. Schmidt sought expansion, and stabilization programs had been introduced by Callaghan in Britain, Andreotti in Italy, and Barre in France—thereby creating a convergence of interests.[134]

Jenkins later downplayed his own contribution to the 1978 Franco-German proposals, arguing that he had contributed relatively little. The definitive primary-source study of the negotiations concludes that, in the minority of areas where his proposals resembled those finally accepted, Jenkins was simply "lucky that events appeared to point in the same direction as his own arguments"; Jenkins himself notes that Monnet "taught me always to advance along the line

---

[131] Marjolin Committee Report, cited in Gros and Thygesen, *European*, 20, also 17–21, 35.

[132] Gros and Thygesen, *European*, 25.

[133] Schmidt, *Deutschen*, 221. These included an April 1974 Commission proposal for the pooling of reserves; the Marjolin Committee report of March 1975 calling for a $10 billion Exchange Stabilization Fund and a common currency unit as a reserve asset and means of financial settlement; the May 1975 plan of French finance minister Fourcade for a more symmetrical system of adjustment based on a currency basket and a joint policy *vis-à-vis* the dollar; the Commission Report on European Union of June 1975, which called for a common currency for determination of exchange rate margins (the "Europa"); the November 1975 report of nine independent economists (the "All-Saints' Day Group") calling for the use of a parallel currency; two OPTICA reports of the Commission, published in 1976 and 1977, proposing a parallel currency; the February 1976 plan of the Dutch finance minister Duisenberg for greater consultation and policy coordination; and the 1976 Tindemans Report advocating a two-track system and greater domestic policy coordination.

[134] Jenkins, *European*, 20–25.

of least resistance."[135] The only proposals not widely advanced outside of Jenkins's speeches were those concerning fiscal federalism, which the Commission had nonetheless proposed since 1971. Administration of government spending, excluding social welfare and law and order but including all structural and sectoral spending, regional policy, external relations, foreign aid, and perhaps defense and unemployment, totaling 5–7 percent of GDP, was to be centralized at the EC level. Such proposals for supranational centralization were treated almost universally, and not just in Germany, as politically naive. Chief executives reaffirmed their rhetorical commitment to EMU at the December 1977 meeting of the European Council, but concrete steps included only a few studies and a slight increase in regional subsidies.[136]

It was thus left to two chief executives, Schmidt and Giscard, to assume the role of "principal architects" of the EMS. A close personal relationship and the combined influence of their two countries made Schmidt and Giscard effective allies. In January or February 1978, during one of their numerous conversations, they decided to support a new initiative on European monetary integration. Though neither explicitly claims exclusive parentage, Schmidt appears to have taken the greater initiative. According to him, the proposal was deliberately scheduled after the French elections to ensure a "strong government" in France—that is, one free of Communist influence. The two leaders carefully planned the agenda for the Copenhagen European Council summit on 7 April.[137]

To their counterparts in Copenhagen, Schmidt and Giscard stressed the need to insulate a West European bloc from monetary fluctuations emanating from Japan and the United States. Schmidt called for creation of a European Monetary Fund (EMF) to take over financial dealings connected with the Snake and other EC financial institutions; the pooling of 15–20 percent of official reserves; official intervention in EC currencies rather than the dollar; and the increased use of a common currency unit in central bank transactions, with its eventual employment as a reserve asset or common currency. Some top French and Ger-

---

[135] Cites from Ludlow, *Making*, 61; Jenkins in *Hommage*, 23, Jenkins, *Life*, 463. Also Schmidt, *Die Deutschen*, 221. Ludlow observes: "Both men had reasons of their own for acting as they did . . . and it would be absurd to suggest that they embarked on their course simply because of the promptings of the Commission president."

[136] Ludlow, *Making*, 37–50, 57–60, 97–101. This figure was based on the so-called MacDougall Report, entitled *The Role of Public Finance in European Integration*—the work of Jenkins staffer Michael Emerson, inspired by the economist Robert Triffin. The report contrasted this option with three alternatives: the status quo with about 1 percent of GDP spent by the Community; a program of regional, structural reform policies totaling about 2½–3 percent of GDP; or a set of responsibilities on par with major federal countries, which would spend 20–25 percent of GDP. The outcome was well below even the first option.

[137] Edmund Dell, "Britain and Origins of the European Monetary System," *Contemporary European History* 3 (1994), 29–30; Emminger, *D-mark*, 357; Ludlow, *Making*, 88–89, also 63–87; Jenkins, *European*, 224. Heisenberg, "Mark," 91–92, argues it was Schmidt. Schmidt says he cannot remember. *Deutschen*, 221, 249. Asked about parentage, Giscard is coy, quoting Napoleon: "En matière de paternité, Monsieur, il n'y a que des hypothèses," though he hints that he had promoted it more forcefully than Schmidt, who instead favored defense cooperation. To support this conjecture, we have seen, no evidence was found. Giscard, *Pouvoir*, 136, 142.

man officials felt from an early date, however, that these elements were mostly "symbolic"; the "kernel" of the initiative remained exchange-rate stabilization.[138]

No formal proposal or decision was made at Copenhagen. With Schmidt and Giscard's strong support, a declaration proclaimed the need for "concerted" European stimulation. At a confidential breakfast the next morning, however, Schmidt, Giscard, and Callaghan agreed to launch secret discussions among personal representatives: Schmidt's assistant Horst Schulmann, Banque de France head Bernard Clappier, and a British Treasury official. (Ken Couzens attended only a few meetings, and by June the British had withdrawn.) Schmidt and Giscard, perhaps also Callaghan, were convinced that monetary diplomacy must be conducted in secret to impede opposition from central bankers and finance ministries, most important Bundesbank president Emminger. Schmidt subsequently observed that for the reason the EMS would never have emerged through formal channels—that is, through the committees of the EC's Council of Ministers of Economics and Finance. Clappier, Emminger's French counterpart, withheld information from the Bundesbank president. The other six national chief executives, their finance ministers, and central bank presidents, as well as senior officials meeting in the Monetary, Central Bank, and ECOFIN committees, were left in complete ignorance. The Danish prime minister, responsible for setting the Council agenda, heard nothing and assumed plans had been abandoned.[139]

Schmidt was unable to convince Callaghan to join the EMS. Aware that the others would go ahead without him, Callaghan sought instead to block formation of a "two-tiered Europe" with a threat to raise such issues as the CAP, regional policy, and "the sore question of the British army on the Rhine" at the upcoming Bremen summit in July—an echo of Macmillan's tactic almost two decades earlier. Yet the promise of funds for coordinated intervention and regional policy, as well as the sympathetic attitude of the Benelux countries, permitted Schmidt and Giscard to "establish total dominance over the Council." At Bremen, it was agreed to make the initiative public and to prepare a draft agreement by the end of October. Not long thereafter Callaghan, after fruitless discussion with Andreotti about a coordinated Anglo-Italian position, decided definitively to forego the EMS. Giscard, whose position on substantive issues was closer to that of the British, arranged with Callaghan that Britain, even if not participating actively, would be an institutional member and party to any further discussions.[140]

After the Bremen summit, negotiations on technical details were transferred to various standing and ad hoc committees of senior officials and ministers un-

[138] Ludlow, *Making*, 91–92; Schmidt, *Deutschen*, 231–232, 237.

[139] Ludlow, *Making*, 82–93, 94–117; Gros and Thygesen, *European*, 35–36, 43; Schmidt, *Deutschen*, 221.

[140] Ludlow, *Making*, 82–117, 222–225, 245–247, especially 114, 126; Schmidt, *Deutschen*, 225–226, 231–237; Gros and Thygesen, *European*, 35–36, 43; Callaghan, *Times and Chance*, 492–493; Healey, *Time of My Life*, 438–440; Giscard, *Pouvoir*, 147–152. There is no evidence that greater satisfaction of Callaghan's demands for resource transfers would have changed his view. Cf. Taylor, "Interdependence," 380–381.

der ECOFIN. Senior officials were told to "work out the details" of the plan rather than "questioning fundamentals." When the committees were unable to reach compromises, ministers and executives of the member governments held final negotiations between November 1978 and March 1979. Though EC institutions served to legitimate cooperation, supranational actors played little role as mediators or mobilizers. Jenkins's initial hope for fiscal federalism aside, the Commission's only concrete concern was a proposal to eliminate MCAs—an issue raised again, unsuccessfully, by Giscard late in the negotiations. The only compromise proposal of note developed by actors other than France and Germany was a final compromise proposed by Belgium.[141]

Yet EC institutions were not entirely irrelevant. Their most important role was to legitimate the arrangement by assuaging the psychological and political unease that might have arisen from the first overt act of German political leadership in the history of European integration—which we have seen, Schmidt considered the primary reason for employing European institutions, albeit informally. In neither France nor Germany did EMS entry require Treaty amendment. Nonetheless the final conclusion was delayed as Giscard faced down opposition from farmers seeking abolition of MCAs. Schmidt dryly referred to this demand, non-negotiable on the German side, as "an unavoidable need to temporarily pay tribute to French agricultural interests," waiting for ten weeks until Giscard prevailed over agricultural unrest and Gaullist opposition.[142]

Andrew Shonfield observed of the EMS that "rarely in the business of international politics do the technicalities so clearly express the essential points at issue."[143] Each of the four major technical issues that occupied negotiators mirrored the fundamental conflict between weak- and strong-currency countries concerning the costs of adjustment. Germany, followed by Denmark and the Netherlands, insisted on the continued existence of rules like those of the Snake, in which obligations to adjust fell asymmetrically on weak-currency countries; France, Belgium, Italy, and Britain sought to reconfigure the system to create more symmetrical obligations.

Germany supported an asymmetrical *obligation to intervene* that fell primarily on deficit countries, whereas France, Italy, and Britain preferred symmetry. This dispute took the form of a technical debate over "divergence indicators," the most important issue from the very beginning of negotiations to its resolution in September 1978. Deficit countries argued that the margins within which currencies were to move should be defined with reference to a "currency basket," later termed the European Currency Unit (ECU), and any single currency, strong or weak, that diverged from the ECU would be obligated to adjust. The arrangement would work to French advantage because, as Clappier described the Snake, "three out of four problems had arisen because the strongest cur-

[141] Commons, "European," 158; Ludlow, *Making*, 195, 251.
[142] Ludlow, *Making*, 282, also 263–264, 280–282; Schmidt, *Deutschen*, 228–229; Prate, *Quelle*, 255; Jenkins, *Life*, 470.
[143] Andrew Shonfield, in Commons, "European," 59.

rency, in almost every case the DM, had reached its upper limits."[144] Surplus countries, led by Germany, favored a "parity grid" system, whereby two countries were obliged to intervene, as under the Snake, when the maximum permissible distance between their two currencies was reached. The parity grid appeared more symmetrical, since two governments were obliged to intervene simultaneously, but the de facto obligation was asymmetrical. Creditor countries could adjust by selling their own currency, an operation that generally could be sustained if not sterilized or reversed and so maintained for an extended period without policy adjustment. Deficit countries, by contrast, had to sell foreign reserves, a course that could not be sustained without a shift in domestic policy. With Germany ready to abandon the project if its demand was not met, Giscard conceded the parity grid system at the Aachen summit of mid-September 1978 — but public perceptions, as we shall see, were carefully managed to disguise the concession. The compromise was reached on German terms, and the divergence indicator was reduced to a "bureaucratic nicety offering jobs for computers and statisticians."[145]

Even these asymmetrical obligations to intervene troubled the Bundesbank. The Bundesbank insisted that the EMS be designed as a system of bands not fixed parities, with the obligation to intervene triggered only when currencies reached their margins (and so when weak currencies are at their most vulnerable). Absence of a clear standard granted the Bundesbank considerable de facto discretion. There was no commitment to joint policy-making or central control either of monetary and fiscal policy or of policy toward the dollar; the latter role fell by default to the Bundesbank. The EMS functioned as a "two-track" or "variable geometry" system, in that it was the first institution in the history of European integration to formally impose differential obligations. The Italians and Irish demanded broad (6 percent) bands, which meant that the EMS would place only marginal constraints on domestic policy; the British opted out. Even with these limitations, the agreement was not, as it were, "ratifiable" within Germany; the Bundesbank, as we have seen, received a letter permitting it to exempt itself from intervention and lending requirements.[146]

France, Italy, and Belgium advocated extensive *balance of payments financing* for deficit countries. Germany resisted. Schmidt himself had begun the negotiations strongly in favor of a European Monetary Fund, with some pooling of reserves, but the "fundamental reservations" on the part of the Bundesbank placed a "severe constraint on the discussions," which translated into a watered-down agreement close to the Bundesbank ideal.[147] EMS arrangements slightly expanded the short-term financing provisions of the Snake but avoided open-

[144] Jocelyn Statler, "EMS: Cul-de-sac or Signpost on the Road to EMU?" in Michael Hodges and William Wallace, eds., *Economic Divergence in the European Community* (London, 1981), 117; Ludlow, *Making*, 161.
[145] Ludlow, *Making*, 163, generally, 162–164.
[146] Ludlow, *Making*, 134–158, 173, 251–273; Gros and Thygesen, *European*, 52–53; Emminger, *D-Mark*, 361ff.
[147] Ludlow, *Making*, 166.

ended, longer-term commitments. Like the Snake, the EMS included a "very short term financing facility" to grant nearly unlimited loans over periods of forty-five days. It also expanded the "short-term" and "medium-term" facilities of the Snake but only to a level roughly the same as a country's IMF quota. (Recall, moreover, that Schmidt's letter limited the extent to which the Bundesbank was bound by an international commitment.) On this point, one the participant noted later, agreement was "temporary, almost fictitious."[148]

Italy, Ireland, and initially Britain, concerned about the deflationary consequences of membership, backed proposals by the European Parliament and the Commission for *more generous regional subsidies,* which Germany, the principal potential donor, was hesitant to provide. In retrospect, even large regional transfers would probably have been unsuccessful in persuading Callaghan to enter. Giscard sided with Germany against Irish and Italian demands, declaring that "France cannot upset her own financial arrangements in order to ensure the adhesion of those for whom membership ought to be an act of political will rather than a question of cash." On the side, however, he quietly negotiated special arrangements for the Irish, who entered in exchange for a modest bilateral arrangement totaling ECU 66 million annually. (The Irish calculated that Britain would soon enter, after which a side-payment would be more difficult to negotiate.) Long-term financing, in part through the European Investment Bank, was both modest and redundant. The Italians, having negotiated 6 percent bands, accepted a symbolically small sum of approximately ECU 133 million.[149]

With their demands for symmetry frustrated, France and its allies called for *prompt reconsideration and revision of the EMS structure.* Germany agreed at Aachen to "consolidate" the system within two years, including creation of a European Monetary Fund (though with unspecified powers) and the "full utilization of the ECU," but specific commitments were deliberately vague. Germany maintained throughout the negotiations that prior economic convergence and permanent, centralized control over national budget deficits were preconditions for further monetary integration—a precondition codified in the Aachen agreement. In February 1980 Schmidt and Giscard agreed to postpone the second stage "indefinitely." On the creation of the EMF, the German government—here the Bundesbank was unambiguous—was unwilling to create an autonomous organization without adequate guarantees, which would have required formal Treaty revision. At a heated meeting in 1981 the Bundesbank official in charge of international affairs reportedly dismissed the matter with four words: "We don't want it."[150] Schmidt, in domestic political trouble, was in no position to resist. The only public complaints about reversion to the old system came from the Commission, which submitted a set of proposals to the Council of Ministers.

---

[148] Gros and Thygesen, *European,* 49, also 48–50; Statler, "EMS," 122–123; Ludlow, *Making,* 240.

[149] Gros and Thygesen, *European,* 43; Ludlow, *Making,* 252–261; Fitzgerald, *All,* 343–344; Statler, "EMS," 119–121, 125–126. On Italy and the role of ideology, see Paul Taylor, "Interdependence and Autonomy in the European Communities: The Case of the European Monetary System," *Journal of Common Market Studies* 18 (June 1980), 381–383.

[150] Connolly, *Rotten Heart,* 23; Gros and Thygesen, *European,* 54–55.

These proposals, politically ill-advised and widely viewed as technically inferior, were ignored.[151]

The distributional bargaining outcomes could not have been clearer. Each of the four major issues generated nearly identical interstate coalitions of strong- and weak-currency countries, and each produced a nearly identical outcome—an asymmetrical one closely approximating the German position. The system did not impose domestic adjustment on Germany. Despite its pretense to be a new, more symmetrical system, the EMS was "basically a geographical extension of the Snake."[152] Both Giscard and Callaghan, as well as Schmidt, were quite aware of its true nature.

Yet the system was cleverly packaged, exploiting fully the ambiguity and complexity of monetary cooperation, as well as large doses of European symbolism, to *appear* more symmetrical—a tactic that has misled subsequent commentators, such as Joseph Grieco, even several decades later, who see the EMS as successful because it was less asymmetrical and thus involved fewer "relative gains" than did the Snake.[153] From after-dinner speeches at bilateral summits to carefully staged events like the Aachen summit in November 1978, Giscard and Schmidt, like Brandt and Pompidou before them and Kohl and Mitterrand later on, constantly reminded those around them that the Franco-German relationship and the European Community were "sanctioned by history, underpinned by the necessity to overcome the self-destructive conflicts of the past"—and so attempted to disguise the basic issues at stake.[154] At Aachen, press officials of both governments stressed the historical reverberations of Schmidt and Giscard's joint visit to the throne of Charlemagne and a concert in the cathedral of Aix-la-Chapelle, deliberately evoking (albeit in a less Roman Catholic form) memories of the celebrated meeting between Adenauer and de Gaulle at Rheims nearly two decades earlier. The substance of the Aachen agreement was kept secret and received relatively little notice, though it eventually leaked out. In response to direct questions from the press, Schmidt denied the existence of any disagreement. He waxed uncharacteristically about "our old and dear continent." Giscard added: "Perhaps when we discussed monetary problems, the spirit of Charlemagne brooded over us."[155]

This was a deliberate deception. The EMS was also designed to appear more to French interests. Giscard proposed that the new money be called the ECU, an English acronym ("European Currency Unit") that corresponded to the *écu*, a French coin from the time of the Valois. The appearance of French negotiating success was preserved by including *both* the ECU-based system and the parity grid system in the agreement, though insiders in both Germany and France

[151] de Vries, "Meaning," 28; Tommaso Padoa-Schioppa, *Money, Economic Policy and Europe* (Luxembourg, 1985), 51, also 81–83.

[152] Gros and Thygesen, *European*, 48.

[153] Cf. Joseph M. Grieco, *Cooperation among Nations* (Ithaca, 1989), 222–223.

[154] The quotation is Ludlow's paraphrase of after-dinner remarks at the Franco-German summit at Aachen in September 1978. Ludlow, *Making*, 184.

[155] Ludlow, *Making*, 182; Carr, *Schmidt*, 145.

understood that the ECU system could not possibly influence de facto obligations. Such measures, Giscard and Schmidt agreed, would "better permit the 'selling' of the policy in France." *Le Monde* even reported German concessions at Aachen.[156]

Consolidating the EMS, 1980–1985

Between 1979 and 1981 the EMS functioned very much like the old Snake. A year after Aachen, at the first biannual meeting to assess the system, the French government quietly abandoned any pretence of an ECU-based or hybrid standard, officially reducing the new currency unit to a marginal role as an accounting value for certain EC transactions. Numerous Commission proposals were ignored.

The financing and intervention mechanisms of the EMS were rarely employed, a situation that suited the Bundesbank. Facilities for EC financial support were hardly used. Medium-term EC credits proved unattractive, since similar Euromarket loans were available without conditionality. The enlarged credit facilities were used only twice, by France in 1983 (the loan proved inessential and was paid back ahead of schedule) and by Greece in 1985. Use of the new unlimited, very-short-term financing (VSTF) facility was also rare. Intramarginal interventions, discouraged by the EMS agreement, proliferated even though they did not qualify for VSTF funding but were financed by the weak-currency countries. Germany successfully resisted attempts to extend VSTF financing to intramarginal interventions, "due to the desire to maintain control of domestic monetary policy, which would otherwise be impaired by "symmetric" monetary base interventions."[157]

For weak-currency countries, the EMS initially imposed few direct restrictions on domestic economic policy; instead it registered parity changes ex post facto. This outcome was due in part to weakness of the DM. After devaluation of the Italian lira in February 1981, however, the EC Monetary Committee reaffirmed that parity changes would have to be approved unanimously, with the aim of controlling and conditioning devaluations.[158] France, still governed by Giscard and Barre, evidently sought to limit devaluations by countries with even weaker currencies. Shortly thereafter, Germany began to challenge proposed parity shifts more aggressively, leading to tougher negotiations and smaller than requested devaluations for weak-currency governments. The French devaluations of 1981–82, for example, totaled 18.5 percent against the DM, as opposed to the 23–29 percent that Delors—the most moderate in the government on this

---

[156] Giscard d'Estaing, *Le pouvoir*, 151–152; Heisenberg, *Mark*, 107–108.

[157] Rainer S. Masera, "An Increasing Role for the ECU; A Character in Search of a Script," in D. E. Fair and C. de Boussieu, eds., *International Monetary and Financial Integration: The European Dimension* (Dordrecht, 1988), 129–131, 146. See also Horst Ungerer, Owen Evans, and Peter Nyberg, *The European Monetary System: The Experience, 1979–82* IMF Occasional Paper no. 19 (Washington, D.C., 1983), 15ff. Economies with little hope of short-term convergence—the Italian, Irish, and Danish—employed wide (6 percent) bands, which imposed little constraint.

[158] Goodman, *Monetary*, 197–199. On this speculative point, I draw on discussions with David Andews.

issue—claimed was appropriate. By mid-1982 Mitterrand was thoroughly disillusioned with Schmidt, who could not deliver the Bundesbank. In the third devaluation of March 1983, German negotiators offered 5 percent, the French countered with 10 percent, and they agreed on 8 percent—finally offsetting the accumulated inflation differential since 1979. There was little opposition in Germany to a modest devaluation, for the French threatened to exit the EMS and establish trade barriers. But Germany imposed conditions, including tax increases and spending cuts, which prompted one sympathetic French observer to label the EMS a "soft version of the IMF," even though most were moves that the French government was externally constrained to pursue in any case.[159]

Negotiations over British entry, agreed to at The Hague in 1969 and launched in June 1970, raised many of the same issues as nine years earlier, under Macmillan. Resolution was, however, more rapid because of more conciliatory attitudes on both sides. Britain gained entry but was forced to make concessions on most other issues. In particular, acceptance of the new CAP financing arrangements was an absolute French precondition. The British demanded a long-term quid pro quo for the disproportionately small gains they would gain from the CAP, but these demands were rejected. Instead, a modest transitional arrangement was extended. British payments would rise from 9 percent to more than 20 percent of the EC budget over five years. And Britain was forced to abandon demands for other exceptions. France was unrelenting in pursuing its interests, threatening at one point to require Britain to repatriate sterling balances if the British did not concede on other issues.

Germany initially refused any further side-payments, setting its initial offer on regional policy deliberately low so as to discourage serious bargaining. The 1975 British referendum—a credible threat of "involuntary" exit—induced generosity. A more extensive program of regional subsidies, carefully designed to include substantial British participation, was created.[160] This pattern—an initially weak bargaining position for new entrants, followed by regional or structural funding if they could threaten to veto an important initiative or involuntarily exit—would be repeated immediately after Greek accession in 1979 and Iberian accession (Spain and Portugal) in 1985. In each case, payments came primarily from Germany, whose exporters and investors benefited from accession with relatively little dislocation, and they went to those countries most disadvantaged. Hence in exchange for participation Ireland and Italy received side-payments, symbolic in the Italian case, in the monetary arrangements established by Germany and France. Greece received funding not on accession but after threatening to veto proposals soon afterward. And Greece, Italy, and France received funds to offset losses from Spanish and Portuguese accession.[161]

---

[159] Favier and Martin-Roland, *Le décennie*, 415; Barre, *Politique*, 76. Which currencies revalue and devalue is largely symbolic. The rate *vis-à-vis* currencies outside the EMS is generally dictated by the DM; so what matters most is the differential. Connolly, *Rotten*, 25; interview with member of the Delors Committee.

[160] Young, *Terms*, 103ff; Butler and Kitzinger, *1975*, 77ff; Franck, "New," 136–137.

[161] David Allen, "Cohesion and Structural Adjustment," in Helen Wallace and William Wallace, eds., *Policy-making in the European Union* (Oxford, 1996), 209–234.

By contrast the CAP itself, the major source of the imbalances that had to be offset by regional policy, remained with two important exceptions unchanged. The first exception, we have seen, was the establishment of the permanent financing arrangement, whereby a tax at 1 percent of VAT revenues, along with centralized pooling of levies, provided centralized EC funds ("own resources"). The second was the recognition of MCAs—automatic price offsets for currency shifts—on which Germany insisted and against which the French protested vehemently. A very young Joseph Ertl, recently named German minister of agriculture, recalls a critical moment around 1970 when the venerable Maurice Schuman, then French foreign minister, summoned him for a face-to-face meeting. Schuman criticized Ertl for acting like a German nationalist rather than a "European" (an interesting accusation from a Gaullist) and demanded that MCAs to be made temporary lest France withdraw from the CAP. Ertl, apparently acting without authorization, responded that he was of a younger generation, had not fought in the war, and therefore could not be shamed. When he told Brandt what he had said—the chancellor in a dentist chair—Brandt gave his support, and the French government backed down. MCAs, combined with enormous direct national support systems, "cordoned off" national markets, essentially "renationalizing" the CAP prices almost as soon as they were finally harmonized.[162]

Explaining Bargaining Outcomes

The historical record suggests that interstate bargaining reflected the power and preference intensity of national governments rather than the desires of supranational entrepreneurs. This interpretation provides the most plausible explanation of the distribution of information among actors, the pattern of outcomes, the nature of interstate quid pro quos, the greater success of the EMS as compared to the Snake, and the provision of policy initiation, mediation, and entrepreneurship.

Turning first to the efficiency of negotiations, it is clear that even in the absence of supranational entrepreneurship, the outcomes of Snake and EMS negotiations were extremely efficient at the international level—though perhaps less so, as we shall see, at the domestic level. The necessary initiation, mediation, and mobilization were provided almost entirely by powerful domestic actors—mostly chief executives, ministers, and central bankers—with only inessential, intermittent, and generally ineffective participation by supranational actors. Thus the Snake and EMS conformed to the pattern set in other major postwar international monetary initiatives, such as Bretton Woods and Rambouillet, whereby the

---

[162] Ertl, *Agrarpolitik*, 35–43, 96–98, 106ff. The incident is striking. A meeting between a senior and a junior minister was itself rare, signaling the importance attributed to the issue by the French government. Brandt's solo, off-handed style of decision-making suggests there was no question of compromising farm interests for European ideals. Ertl, among others, has asserted that MCAs were responsible for the extraordinary expansion of German agricultural exports during the 1970s—leading finally to Germany's becoming the world's sixth-largest agricultural exporter, almost entirely within the protected EC market. The structure established in 1966 survived, as did substantial national subsidies; for Germany in 1984, they totaled DM20 billion. On exports, see Winfried von Urff, "The Common Agricultural Policy," in C. C. Schweitzer and D. Karsten, eds., *Federal Republic of Germany and EC Membership Evaluated* (New York, 1990).

primary initiators of negotiations were the chief executives of the two largest and most influential countries.[163] Pompidou and Brandt launched the Snake, Schmidt and Giscard the EMS, France and Germany negotiated the 1983 French turnaround. Each exploited what "executive slack" was at hand, moving soon after favorable elections in 1969, 1978, and 1983.[164]

Commission proposals were either redundant, such as the narrow and conservative Barre proposals in 1969, or futile, as in the case of Jenkins's advocacy of financial transfers. Many of the most innovative and influential documents, notably the Werner Report, were drafted by national politicians. Committees of central bankers and finance ministers provided useful technical support, but their decisions directly reflected their accustomed domestic role, not a particular transnational function. At no time between the late 1960s and the mid-1980s does there appear to have been a bottleneck or bias in the provision of viable proposals for monetary integration, dozens of which came from private economists, ministers, central bankers, and chief executives. Commission proposals for CAP reform, regional policy, and social programs fared the same.

Once negotiations were launched, national governments continued to dominate the proceedings. "Few," Peter Ludlow reports, "doubted that it was in the French and German capitals that the crucial decisions were and would be taken." The negotiations themselves proceeded unmediated among chief executives, ministers, and top national officials; there is no evidence they were inefficient. As for mobilization, the problem was not to mobilize support but avoid the possibility that supranational institutions, transnational bureaucratic committees, and official mediators would compromise secrecy—and secrecy was a necessary condition, Schmidt argued later, for the success of the EMS negotiations. Demobilization, not mobilization, of domestic and transnational interests was critical. There is no reason to believe that selective mobilization would have facilitated greater agreement at any point.[165]

The Commission possessed no apparent expertise in monetary affairs comparable to, let alone superior to, what was available from national sources. Each chief executive drew on expert manpower outside his or her own staff, Giscard from the Elysée, Matignon, and Banque de France, Schmidt from the Finanzministerium and Kanzleramt. The Commission intermittently contributed proposals and studies, or assembled groups to discuss monetary cooperation, but its actions added little. National leaders were well-informed about the longer-term consequences of the decisions they were making, for example, that the EMS would function, if at all, as a "DM zone" with implications for bilateral trade balances and domestic macroeconomic constraints. Little evidence supports the widespread assertion that asymmetry was an unintended consequence.

We have seen that distributional conflicts between strong- and weak-currency

---

[163] James, *International,* 300.

[164] Loukas Tsoukalis offers no hard evidence to support his intriguing claim about the 1970s that "long-term close contact among senior officials of the member countries over a long period" constituted "a necessary but not sufficient condition for the implementation of schemes for intra-EC cooperation, such as the Snake and later the EMS." Certainly it does not seem to apply to the initiation of the EMS. Tsoukalis, "Money," 117.

[165] Ludlow, *Making,* 196.

countries concerning the symmetry or asymmetry of the system were resolved in favor of Germany. The resulting system imposed no financial or policy commitments without prior economic convergence toward low-inflation policies. How is this distributional outcome to be explained?

We may dismiss supranational bargaining theory. The Commission possessed no specific information or ideas and fulfilled no specific functions that permitted it to influence the efficiency of negotiations over monetary, agricultural, or regional policies. Roy Jenkins himself estimates that the member states enacted no more than perhaps 25–30 percent of what he had proposed. That 25 percent, moreover, was redundant. Where Jenkins, like Barre and others in the late 1960s and early 1970s, took a distinct position on distributive issues—on symmetry of the EMS, opposition to MCAs, "two-track" monetary integration, fiscal federalism, and agricultural price reform—his actions failed to counter the will of Germany.[166]

Instead the evidence strongly supports intergovernmental bargaining theory, with its focus on relative preference intensity and the size and shape of national win-sets. The process in Germany leaves little doubt that, because of the veto position of the Bundesbank, the only ratifiable agreement, at least until full economic convergence and institutional guarantees of low inflation at the EC level, was one that left the Bundesbank's domestic autonomy essentially intact. The Bundesbank's domestic legitimacy—not least among industrialists—made its assent essential for domestic ratification of any monetary agreement and its assistance required for implementation. Germany, we have seen, had a "kinked" win-set: any compromise beyond a certain threshold would quickly render the agreement unratifiable, despite what some German governments construed as a net national interest in greater symmetry. This internal division explains not just German bargaining power but the *seemingly* contradictory and incoherent nature of German strategy. Brandt and Schmidt consistently *initiated* monetary negotiations and offered large compromises and side-payments, yet adopted an uncompromising position on essential issues, insisting on an asymmetrical system with "economist" preconditions for any future transfer of sovereignty. Germany's narrow win-set limited its major partners to France after 1983, excluding Britain and Italy from effective participation.

This explanation of bargaining outcomes is surely more convincing than a conventional view of Germany as a European monetary hegemon.[167] Views drawn

---

[166] Jenkins, *Hommage*, 22–25.

[167] For hegemonic explanations, see Andrei Markovits and Simon Reich, *The German Predicament: Memory and Power in the New Europe* (Ithaca, 1997), chap. 8, who base their assessment of hegemony on the existence of German trade surpluses. For criticisms, Matthias Kaelberer, "Hegemony, Dominance or Leadership? Explaining Germany's Role in European Monetary Cooperation," *European Journal of International Relations* 3 (March 1997), 35–60; Dorothée Heisenberg, "German Financial Hegemony or Simply Smaller Win-Sets? An Examination of the Bundesbank's Role in EMS and EMU Negotiations," paper delivered at the conference of the American Political Science Association (1–4 September 1994); McNamara, *Currencies*, chaps. 1–2. McNamara shows that Germany was only slightly larger than its neighbors, marginally more wealthy per capita, lacked deep capital markets, and did not dominate European trade as the United States did after World War II. However, it did run persistent trade surpluses, and the DM was the major currency into which speculative capital tended to flow during exchange-rate crises. Also, unilateral actions by the German government may

from variants of hegemonic stability theory treat Germany as a unique, low-cost provider of one or more of four public goods: financial side-payments, the externalities of macroeconomic adjustment, access to extensive reserves, and an anchor currency with unique anti-inflationary credibility. Was Germany able to prevail in negotiations because it controlled such assets?

We have seen that Germany provided neither significant financial side-payments nor desired macroeconomic adjustment. Offers of large loans to Britain, France, and Italy in exchange for exchange-rate stability under the Snake were refused; in any case, they replicated support available from other sources. Financial inducements to Italy to join the EMS were marginal; only Irish participation might reasonably be traced in part to them. As for macroeconomic adjustment, it appears to be true that German policy had a disproportionate influence on its neighbors, meaning that German concessions might have been more valuable than those of others. Still, in neither the Snake nor the EMS did Germany significantly adjust its policies in order to support exchange-rate stabilization, despite consistent pressure from other governments to do so. As one Bundesbank official noted in 1988: "External considerations are not permitted to dictate monetary policy over any length of time, as this might conflict with the primary objective of price stability."[168] Far from providing the macroeconomic adjustment others desired, Germany deliberately exploited the EMS to avoid it.

Hence an argument about asset-based hegemonic power must rest on the remaining two factors, Germany's large reserves and its reputation for low inflation. Clearly French and British officials believed that these assets might help stabilize the system against speculative attack and increase the credibility of pegged exchange rates. This was probably true. Yet German influence should not be exaggerated. The EMS was managed primarily through intramarginal intervention from which the Bundesbank abstained. In a crisis the prospect of Bundesbank intervention may have increased the credibility of weak-currency pegs; but with the possible exception of the French turnaround in 1983 (when the low level of reserves appears to have been viewed in France as an important short-term constraint on policy), the provision of such support in the form of swaps, intervention, and balance of payments support does not appear to have imposed binding constraints on French or British policy. Instead, the binding constraint was the willingness to tolerate high interest rates or competitive disadvantage. A similar caution applies to Germany's anti-inflationary reputation. Certainly the desirability of a peg to the DM did *not* stem from some technical necessity for weak-currency countries to link to a strong currency, as some accounts imply.[169] It was equally possible to peg, unilaterally or collectively, to a currency basket; indeed, most EMS governments overtly favored such a system.

Yet while Germany's reputation, reserves, and status as a global currency assured it would wield influence in monetary negotiations, there is no reason to

---

have imposed larger negative policy externalities, in the form of macroeconomic constraints and an undervalued currency, on its neighbors than they on it.

[168] Begg and Wyplosz, "Recent," 26.

[169] Dyson, *Elusive*, 16; Kaelberer, "Hegemony."

believe that these assets were "objectively" more valuable for Germany than was abstention from depreciation. The fact that Germany could provide credibility without "seriously endangering [domestic] monetary stability" should have made it *more* willing to compromise. The key determinant of bargaining outcomes was not Germany's larger assets; in fact, the concentration of power in German hands made agreement *more* difficult to reach.[170] From the perspective of an SPD government and of many domestic businessmen, Germany benefited as much as or more than its partners from exchange-rate cooperation, gaining competitiveness and enhancing macroeconomic autonomy, not to mention geopolitical advantages.[171] The fact that German political and economic institutions did not weight such concerns equally with those of low inflation was critical.

The outcomes of negotiations over other substantive issues similarly confirm intergovernmental bargaining theory. In agricultural policy, other governments acceded to Pompidou's demand (backed by the threat of veto over British accession) for a centrally financed CAP. Both German and French preferences had converged substantially since 1960: France was now agnostic toward or even supportive of British accession, though it still favored accession less than other governments did, whereas Germany increasingly tolerated, even supported, the CAP, though similarly less than other governments. Under such circumstances, and unlike during the 1960s, linkage was finally possible. France threatened to withhold acceptance in exchange for an agricultural financing agreement. At roughly the same time, the German government unilaterally imposed MCAs to assure continued high support prices to its farmers. The French government threatened to withdraw from the CAP, but that threat was no more credible in 1970 than it had been in 1965. Hence MCAs became a permanent part of the CAP. No agreement was possible in areas such as industrial policy, where national interests diverged—as we shall see in more detail in Chapter Five.

Explaining Institutional Delegation

In each of these major areas—agriculture, monetary integration, and reform of decision-making—important steps were taken toward pooling and delegating sovereignty.[172]

The pattern of delegation and pooling within and across areas is most consistent with concern about the credibility of intergovernmental commitments; ide-

---

[170] Rolf Caesar, "German Monetary Policy and the European Monetary System," in Fair and de Boissieu, eds., *International Monetary*, 22. The critique is related to those that stress the "will" or preferences rather than the "power" of the hegemon as key. In the asymmetrical interdependence view proposed in this book, in contrast to the hegemonic view, disagreements over realignments would have been *less* difficult to resolve if "the German authorities had not been so strongly committed to meeting their money-supply targets." The words are Peter Kenen's in Giavazzi, *European*, 391.

[171] Nor is there evidence for the claim, often heard among French economists, that German exports are less price-sensitive, allowing Germany to better tolerate currency appreciation. This is surely not evident in German domestic policies, where the value of the DM has long been a central concern.

[172] Regional policy, little specified in the original Treaty, had to be established ad hoc through application of the all-purpose Article 235. Helen Wallace called its implementation "little more than an exercise in pork barrel politics." See David Allen, "Cohesion and Structural Adjustment," in Wallace and Wallace, eds., *Policy-Making*, 212.

ology played a secondary role, and the need to provide technocratic information little at all. We observe, as the credible commitments approach suggests, governments resisting delegation and binding rules where they benefit from autonomy, but delegating and pooling sovereignty where they benefit by locking in foreign (and sometimes future domestic) governments. By contrast, the technocratic view predicts a general interest in centralizing expert functions proportional to the complexity of the issue, and the ideological view predicts a coalition of "federalist" states—Italy, Germany, and the Benelux, one would presume— in favor of supranational authority. The predictive power of the credible commitment view is proportional to the certainty about material interests. On agricultural and monetary policy, positions on institutional delegation track positions on issues. On most decision-making issues, such as creation of the European Council and strengthening of supranational institutions, large and small countries split. Only where substantive consequences are hardest to predict, direct elections to the Parliament, does federalist ideology appear to have been important—precisely as the credible commitment view itself predicts.

In agriculture, institutional changes made the provisional permanent. In order to institutionalize the central agricultural bargain of the 1960s, which had given the French preferential access to German agricultural markets in exchange for extensive subsidization of German farmers, a simultaneous centralization and fragmentation took place. The protection of farm income meant that Germany sought to guarantee especially high domestic prices, whereas France sought to assure large export subsidies. In 1969–71, each end of this log-rolling bargain was vulnerable, in particular after British accession, so there was an incentive to "lock in" cooperation through new institutions. Pompidou successfully promoted a permanent CAP financing system based on centralized EU taxes ("own resources"), making the financing of agriculture an integral part of the *acquis communautaire*. In linking this proposal to British accession, we have seen, he was quite frank about potential hostile coalitions including Britain. At roughly the same time, Germany unilaterally imposed MCAs, not only brushing aside repeated French efforts to negotiate them away but successfully pressing for their multilateral recognition. Noncredible French threats to withdraw from the CAP were ignored. This move undermined a key principle of the CAP, namely de facto uniformity of domestic prices, and thus marked a substantial "renationalization" of the CAP almost as soon as it was in place.

Similarly, monetary cooperation under the Snake and EMS was designed to lock in the Franco-German bargain: international institutions would provide credibility for France and other weak-currency countries, and domestic autonomy for Germany. A few information and consultation matters aside, the requirement of unanimous consent for exchange-rate realignments was the only limitation on formal sovereignty imposed by monetary integration during this period. This rule, which imposed disproportionate constraints on weak-currency countries in crises, offered Germany a quid pro quo in exchange for its limited support of weak currencies.

France, Italy, and Britain had sought tighter rules binding Germany to macroeconomic adjustment through higher inflation or financing, and the Commission persistently asserted that supranational objectives required the transfer of sovereign powers to centralized institutions. Yet any agreement restricting the Bundesbank's autonomy could have been neither ratified nor implemented in Germany. Hence implementation was left in the hands of intergovernmental committees comprised of finance ministers and central bankers, reflecting existing domestic influence in most countries.[173] Until 1986, and even then only symbolically, no European monetary agreement was recognized as a legal instrument under either EC or domestic law. The only conceivable alternative might have been agreement on the basis of the Werner Report's economist terms for the third stage—namely, with sanctions for noncompliance, controls over fiscal policy, and central authority over national budgets (more or less as would be agreed in 1991)—but only after economic convergence and capital liberalization. In any case, Pompidou was disinclined to impose austerity and compelled to reject supranational institutions because of Gaullist opposition.

The major innovation of the period was the creation of a new institution, the European Council, where chief executives meet regularly. Its major consequence was to transfer policy initiation away from the more rule-governed Commission and Parliament. The creation of the European Council reflected a close understanding among leaders of the three largest EC member states, though federalists such as Altiero Spinelli and Monnet himself voiced support as well. Schmidt, Giscard, and both Heath and Wilson were willing to go further, supporting proposals for a directorate of chief executives of the large countries alone, the creation of an intergovernmental secretariat, replacement of the Council of Ministers by the European Council under certain circumstances, limitations on Commission participation, and, at least Giscard was tempted to argue, recognition that the European Council was the *only* body that could give guidance to the EC—replacing functions of the Council of Ministers as well as the Commission.[174] These proposals were rejected by smaller countries. The final communiqué from a 1974 summit called for triannual meetings of the chief executives, to be called the European Council, in exchange for which smaller countries gained a series of studies, most important one of direct Parliament elections sometime after 1978, and also an EC passport, renunciation of unanimity voting in the Council of Ministers except on the most important issues, and other proposals to rejuvenate European institutions.[175]

Over the Council, countries tended to divide into stable coalitions as predicted by both the credible commitments and the technocratic views, with large countries, including Britain, France, and Germany, favoring concentration of power in a "directorate," and smaller countries, notably the Netherlands, Belgium, Ireland, and Italy, preferring stronger, rule-governed supranational institutions, in particular the Commission, along with qualified majority voting in the Coun-

---

[173] Members were permitted to sterilize reserve flows and manage reserves, interest rates, and fiscal policy independently. European monetary institutions "were not designed to bypass the sovereignty of individual countries' monetary authorities." de Vries, "European," 8.

[174] Fitzgerald, *All,* 132–139.

[175] Simon Bulmer and Wolfgang Wessels, *The European Council: Decision-Making in European Politics* (London, 1986), 35–41.

cil of Ministers. Large countries favored the European Council because it expanded the ability of chief executives to bargain free of domestic constraints while preserving the ability of large countries to take major initiatives—the EMS being a clear example. Heath recalls that the primary purpose of the Council was to permit chief executives to propose compromises, issue linkages and side-payments that ministers, bureaucratic factions, or domestic groups might otherwise block.[176] These interests encouraged creation of an institution that was exclusive, nontransparent, flexible, and open-ended.

Over the next decade the Commission "no longer played the active role of policy initiator that was envisaged . . . the lack of political weight behind Commission initiatives necessitated a stronger political body for steering the EC."[177] Chief executives exploited the Council to become "deeply involved in all the major constitutional decisions of importance to the Community." Initiatives were taken on issues such as environmental policy, proposed in 1972 and 1975, the EMS, and direct elections. This permitted a round of issue expansion and institutional change to take place without a discrete set of Treaty-amending negotiations, as was to occur with the Single Act and Maastricht treaties in the 1980s and 1990s. Smaller countries, skeptical of such plans, settled for a commitment to study parliamentary power and the rejuvenation of QMV.[178]

Only on the powers of the European Parliament, the most symbolic of the institutional issues and one in which the political and economic consequences were highly uncertain and the proposed transfer of power modest, did ideological factors play an important role. Federalists criticized the Council's antidemocratic form, achieving a minor increase in the budgetary powers of the Parliament, as well as direct elections. Denmark joined Britain and France in opposition to direct elections, and Germany joined Italy and Benelux in favor.

As part of the same bargain, an agreement to employ QMV where the treaty required it was reached, subject to prior agreement by the member states. Nearly all decisions during this period, the only exceptions being some common commercial policy and agricultural matters, were in any case unanimous under the Treaty. Callaghan's lone opposition to the division of Council issues into those that required unanimity and those that could be decided by QMV—evidently with linkage between agriculture and the budget in mind—was enough to block any general change. Nonetheless, two small countries, Belgium and Ireland, exploited their turns as president to invoke QMV with some limited success, in par-

---

[176] Edward Heath, "At the Heart of Europe," in Geraldine Price, ed., *A Window on Europe: The Lothian European Lectures 1992* (Edinburgh, 1993), 215. The European Council was quite accurately criticized by many European federalists in the Parliament as lacking both legal and democratic justification. Bulmer and Wessels, *European*, 43–45 and 114–115, where they report: "Given that much time and effort is invested into putting together package deals at the European Council, there is an aversion to re-opening matters in the Council of Ministers for the sake of the Parliament. . . . The MEPs often found themselves being given a summary of the proceedings of the most recent European Council by a junior minister who had not even been present himself!"

[177] Bulmer and Wessels, *European*, 113.

[178] Fitzgerald, *All*, 133, 138–139, 155, who hints that the Council provided an incentive for chief executives, particularly current EC presidents, to advance proposals that might generate high-profile diplomatic agreements, for which they could claim credit.

ticular to circumvent British budgetary objections to the passage of agricultural financing.[179] Yet this did not directly affect major reforms, such as the agenda for removing NTBs under the SEA in the mid-1980s, which would in any case have required unanimity. There remained little support as the Marjolin Report revealed, for abolishing the Luxembourg Compromise.

The 1970s are often portrayed as a period of stagnation in European integration, yet this characterization is true only from a federalist perspective that focuses on the institutional centralization of administrative and democratic decision-making. From the perspective of substantive policy-making, the 1970s was a decade of both consolidation and innovation.

Agreements on permanent CAP financing and British membership at The Hague are often seen as beginning a new era, but along with MCAs they were, in fact, the final steps in the consolidation of a Franco-German bargain that had taken over a decade to negotiate. That bargain, we saw in Chapter 3, moved trade liberalization forward, first among the Six and then through GATT negotiations and enlargement, as quickly as France could stand it. At the same time an agricultural policy was created that maintained high prices for German farmers, export subsidies for French farmers, and preferential market access for both. Permanent CAP financing, MCAs, even British entry secured this bargain rather than revising it.

Monetary integration, by contrast, was an area of substantial innovation. Its outcomes confirm the importance of economic interests, relative power, and credible commitments. The Snake and EMS were created to handle new substantive problems occasioned by the decline of Bretton Woods and by macroeconomic divergence among European countries. We have seen that membership reflected a convergence of policy preferences around a particular form of domestic disinflation; only as weak-currency countries committed themselves to disinflation by means of monetary discipline, resulting in real currency appreciation, did cooperation become possible. The precise bargain around which the two organizations formed reflected the relative preference intensity of governments, which in turn reflected the tight constraints that the Bundesbank imposed on the German government. Delegation and pooling of sovereignty in institutions reflected the willingness of governments to lock in policies; they bound Germany loosely and weak-currency countries somewhat more tightly.

These decisions had two important legacies. First, monetary integration under the Snake and EMS differed from market integration under the Common Market and the CAP in that it was never intended to apply uniformly to all EC members—the first of an increasing number of such variable-geometry or multi-track policies. Despite Commission pressure for participation of all members and substantial fiscal federalism, member governments created a de facto "two-track" Europe, dividing those within the "DM zone" from those outside. The

---

[179] Decisions permitting majority voting were so rare that Fitzgerald had to wait five months for an appropriate opportunity. Fitzgerald, *All*, 147–148.

Snake excluded Britain, Italy, and, apart from a few periods, France, while it included non-EC members such as Norway and Sweden. The ERM did not include Britain until 1990; Italy and others joined with wide bands; Austria shadowed the DM for years without formal membership.[180] The creation of the European Council, a flexible, executive-led forum with an ambiguous legal relationship to the EC, was the institutional counterpart of multitrack policies. Despite the formal institutional innovations and the tolerance for informal institutional processes required, EC governments were able to agree on new forms of substantive cooperation.

Neither the German government nor, in particular, the French and Italian governments were entirely satisfied with the asymmetrical compromise imposed upon them by the Bundesbank. The goal of the Mitterrand government became reform of the EMS to render it more symmetrical, not exit from it. But further reform was impossible until a substantial number of countries had fulfilled the conditions set forth by Germany in 1965 for monetary union, namely capital liberalization and economic convergence. When these conditions were met, in the late 1980s, demands for monetary union would arise again.

---

[180] To be sure, MCAs had already "renationalized" the CAP almost as soon as common prices were established, but the basic policy remained uniform across countries. Gisela Hendricks, "Germany and the CAP," *International Affairs* (Winter 1988), 87.

CHAPTER FIVE

Relaunching Integration: The Single European Act, 1984–1988

> The real significance of the Single Act [was] that when the chips were down, the great majority of Member States [would] go along with the ultimate development of the Community. Those who chose not to . . . would simply be left behind.
>
> —Lord Arthur Cockfield, former Commissioner for Internal Market Affairs (1994)

In the late 1980s the European Community experienced its most important period of trade liberalization since completion of the Common Market in 1968.[1] This new impulse toward European integration—the "relaunching" of Europe, the French called it—was unexpected. The late 1970s and early 1980s were an era of Europessimism and Eurosclerosis, during which politicians and academics alike lost faith in European institutions. A few years later, optimism and institutional momentum had replaced malaise and stagnation. The source of this transformation was the Single European Act (SEA), a document approved by European heads of government in 1986.

The SEA linked further liberalization of European trade with procedural reform. The liberalization half of the package, incorporating 279 proposals contained in a 1985 Commission White Paper, aimed to create "an area without internal frontiers in which the free movement of goods, persons, services and

---

[1] This chapter draws on my article "Negotiating the Single European Act: National Interests and Conventional Statecraft in the European Community," *International Organization* 45:1 (Winter 1991), 19–56. From the extensive general literature on 1992, the best negotiating history of the Single European Act, written by an intelligent insider who took comprehensive notes, remains Jean De Ruyt, *L'Acte unique européen: Commentaire* (Brussels, 1987). Other useful histories, collections, and commentaries include Peter Ludlow, *Beyond 1992: Europe and Its Western Partners* (Brussels, 1989); Michael Calingaert, *The 1992 Challenge from Europe: Development of the European Community's Internal Market* (Washington, D.C., 1988); Angelika Volle, *Grossbritannien und der europäische Einigungsprozess* (Bonn, February 1989), 46–76; Wayne Sandholtz and John Zysman, "1992: Recasting the European Bargain," *World Politics* 42 (October 1989), 95–128; Jochen Thies and Wolfgang Wagner, eds., *Auf dem Wege zum Binnenmarkt: Europäische Integration und deutscher Föderalismus* (Bonn, 1989); Roy Pryce, ed., *The Dynamics of European Union* (London, 1987); George Ross, *Jacques Delors and European Integration* (Oxford, 1995). On mutual recognition, a critical source is Kalypso Nicolaïdis, "Mutual Recognition among Nations: The European Community and Trade in Services," diss., Harvard University, 1995.

capital is ensured."[2] To realize this goal, European leaders committed themselves to eliminate nontariff barriers. They had to tackle comprehensive liberalization of trade in services and the removal, partial harmonization, or mutual recognition of domestic regulations that acted as NTBs. In the package proposed then and added to over the next few years were the elimination of customs procedures and other border formalities; the minimal harmonization of regulatory nontariff barriers, particularly industrial standards and regulations in the food-processing industry; the liberalization of trade and investment in financial services; the abolition of exchange controls and other limits on international capital movements; the harmonization of taxation systems; and the suppression of preferential public procurement.

The institutional half of the SEA involved three reforms. First was the introduction of qualified majority voting under Article 100. Before the SEA, Article 100 of the Treaty (governing harmonization of regulations) specified unanimity voting. In addition, as we saw in chapters 3 and 4, the use of QMV had been limited by the Luxembourg Compromise, France's unilateral and extra-legal assertion in 1966 that any member state could veto a proposal in the Council of Ministers by declaring that a "vital" or "very important" interest was at stake. The result was de facto unanimity voting even where QMV was authorized. The SEA formally expanded the use of QMV in the Council of Ministers to regulatory issues connected with the realization of the internal market under Article 100, but it also deliberately created the informal expectation that voting would be practiced as conceived before 1966.

The second institutional reform was the so-called new approach based on "mutual recognition"—a politically uninvasive but substantively demanding form of liberalization whereby only minimal standards are harmonized and governments must accept any imports from other member states in compliance with them. Related to the "new approach" was the "delegation to standards" procedure, employed in some matters involving industrial standardization, whereby governments mandated minimal levels of regulatory protection and delegated the setting of precise standards to existing, voluntary European standards-setting bodies. The new approach marked a significant shift in regulatory strategy, avoiding the detailed and uniform standards that had proved often fruitless during the 1970s; it reduced the legislation required to achieve liberalization by over two-thirds.

The third reform granted slightly greater powers to the European Parliament under the so-called cooperation procedure. The Parliament was granted the power to propose amendments which, if accepted by the Commission, would be sent back to the Council of Ministers for consideration under a favorable set of voting rules.[3]

The SEA returned European integration to public prominence. Yet regulatory market liberalization was hardly the only EC reform that could have emerged during the mid-1980s. Jacques Delors and François Mitterrand had sought to

---

[2] Article 8A of the Treaty of Rome, as amended by the Single Act.

[3] George Tsebelis, "The Power of the European Parliament as a Conditional Agenda-Setter," *American Political Science Review* 88 (1994), 128–142.

deepen monetary integration. The Parliament had pressed for greater democratization and institutional development, codified in a European constitution. The German and Italian foreign ministers had proposed stronger cooperation on foreign policy. Many French officials had spoken of defense cooperation. Some multinational firms had advocated more active industrial and infrastructure policies. Britain had sought fundamental budgetary and agricultural reform. And of course governments might simply have muddled through without any basic reform at all, concentrating their efforts on unilateral or global multilateral policies. What accounts for the timing and the content of the reform that relaunched European integration after years of disappointment?

Journalistic reportage, academic analysis, and oral histories reveal a bewilderingly wide range of alternative explanations for the Single Act and the White Paper—from opposition to the U.S.–USSR bargain at Reykjavik to legal precedents set by the European Court of Justice to pressure from rising U.S. competition. Nearly every potential cause has provoked extensive speculation. As a French official in Brussels quipped, "When the little boy turns out well, everyone claims paternity!"[4]

Among scholars and commentators, however, a conventional wisdom has emerged about the origins of the SEA. It derives from supranational bargaining theory. The decisive impulse stemmed from far-sighted Commission officials like Etienne Davignon, Jacques Delors, and Arthur Cockfield, who combined the technocratic voluntarism said to be characteristic of francophone politics (Delors and Davignon) with the pragmatism said to be characteristic of English politics (Cockfield). Participants seem particularly inclined to embrace this view. As we saw in chapter 1, Cockfield himself confidently asserts that strong entrepreneurial leadership was a sufficient condition for reform: "If the Commission is ineffective, as tragically it was during the Thorne Presidency, the Community languishes. Where you have a forceful and visionary President, as Jacques Delors has been, backed by a strong and effective Commission, the Community makes progress."[5] Numerous leading academic analysts follow the same line.[6] Supra-

---

[4] Interview with EC official, January 1989. For a comprehensive and sympathetic review of potential factors, see Sandholtz and Zysman, "1992." John Ardagh, "Will the New Europe Please Sit Down," *New York Times Magazine* (10 May 1991), 49–59, cites the failure of Reaganomics, the rise of Japan, the emergence of Gorbachev, concern about the German Question, the rise of global finance, the emergence of the Green Movement, rising travel, and the general fear of global disintegration.

[5] Lord Cockfield, *The European Union: Creating the Single Market* (London, 1994), 111. For similar arguments, see Ross, *Jacques*; Sandholtz and Zysman, "1992." Delors's own assessment, as we shall see, is far more measured.

[6] Whereas only a few analyses assert the extreme claim that supranational entrepreneurship was a "sufficient" condition—though the assertion that preferences can be fundamentally manipulated leads in this direction—most nonetheless advance the strong claim that it was a "necessary" condition. For representative variants of an enormous literature, see Sandholtz and Zysman, "1992"; Ross, *Jacques*; Neill Nugent, "The Leadership Capacity of the European Commission," *Journal of European Public Policy* 2:4 (December 1995), 603–623, 1995; Geoffrey Garrett and Barry Weingast, "Ideas, Interests and Institutions: Constructing the European Community's Internal Market," in Judith Goldstein and Robert O. Keohane, eds., *Ideas and Foreign Policy: Beliefs, Institutions, and Political Change* (Ithaca, 1993), 173–206; Daniel Wincott, "Liberal Intergovernmentalism and Integration: Towards an Everyday Critique," *Journal of Common Market Studies* 33:4 (December 1995).

national officials, it is further argued, were backed by a coalition of visionary multinational businessmen who, strongly supportive of market liberalization, convinced or circumvented reluctant national leaders.[7]

The historical record suggests an alternative view based on a convergence of national economic preferences, intergovernmental bargaining among national leaders, and the design of new international institutions based on the aim of more credible commitments. This convergence stemmed from a combination of structural economic trends toward higher rates of international trade and investment, including more multinational production, and perceived policy failures. After the reversal of French economic policy in 1983, single market reform emerged as the only basis on which European integration could have moved forward. The SEA assembled a set of liberalized measures demanded by business, widely viewed as inevitable, and, to a large extent, already being implemented unilaterally and bilaterally. National leaders were also motivated by geopolitical ideologies, but economic interests remained primary in the sense that no major government—not even that of Germany—was willing to sacrifice a major economic interest for the sake of ideologically desirable integration.

Far from being in the thrall of clever supranational entrepreneurs, moreover, national chief executives—Helmut Kohl, François Mitterrand, and Margaret Thatcher—were the critical decision-makers, maneuvering domestically to remove obstacles to agreement. Governments initiated most of the major proposals (which were plentiful), conducted and mediated most of the negotiations, and mobilized domestic support. In fact, unilateral, bilateral, and non-EC multilateral initiatives were well under way by the time the EC first considered the SEA. By contrast, Commission officials like Delors, most European Parliamentarians, and leading multinational businessmen had quite different priorities. They would come to accept the SEA as a second-best outcome. Insofar as the activities of Commissioners and Europarliamentarians enhanced the efficiency of negotiations, they did so by increasing the saliency of internal market issues, formulating concrete proposals, and mobilizing business support—tasks largely complete before Delors and Cockfield entered office.

The most important institutional reforms—expanded QMV and the new approach to NTB removal—were designed to enhance the credibility of commitments and the efficiency of decision-making. They responded to unsatisfactory experience with harmonization negotiations in the 1970s. Only in areas where consequences were difficult to judge, notably increased powers for the Parliament, did ideological factors—pro-European sentiment and attitudes toward domestic parliamentary power—influence national positions. There is little evidence that a perceived need for centralized, technocratic decision-making had any impact on the choice of institutions; indeed, the "new approach" was a profoundly decentralizing policy.

[7] Maria Green Cowles, "The Politics of Big Business in the European Community: Setting the Agenda for a New Europe," diss., American University, 1994.

NATIONAL INTERESTS AND THE SINGLE EUROPEAN ACT

After 1983 national preferences in Germany, Britain, and France converged toward support for single market liberalization. Britain was its strongest supporter, followed by Germany and France. In one other area, the greater formal use of QMV, France and Germany were in agreement, whereas the British remained reluctant. In all other substantive areas, including industrial policy, agricultural subsidies, monetary union, foreign and defense cooperation and pure institutional reforms, no two governments agreed. What explains this pattern of national preferences?

I argue that these national preferences primarily reflected economic interests, and in particular increasing global and regional trade and investment, which exacerbated concerns about international competitiveness. In the 1960s a large majority of multinational firms in Europe had been based in the United States or Britain; by the 1980s there were many Continental multinationals. The decade saw increased transnational capital flows in the form of foreign direct investment (FDI) and lending. Beginning in the mid-1970s FDI rose rapidly, led by investment from other European countries, which increased from 25 percent to 40 percent of total inward stock. Over 50 percent of this investment entered France, Spain, Italy, Portugal, and Belgium. Intra-industry trade among European nations also continued to increase with income: in Greece and Portugal it totaled 30–40 percent of trade; in Denmark, Spain, Italy, and Ireland approximately 60 percent; and in the others 75–85 percent. This trade boom was not unique to Europe; to a greater extent than ever before, European firms focused on global, not just regional, competitiveness. Intra-European exports as a percentage of consumption expanded from 19 percent to 25 percent between 1980 and 1990, with third-country exports rising even faster, from 14 percent to 19 percent. Mergers and acquisitions rose from $9 billion in 1986 to $52 billion in 1989; transatlantic flows increased even faster.[8]

Surveys of industry in 1986–88 reveal broad-based business support in all countries for the SEA as a tool to increase the global competitiveness of firms. Over 90 percent of top European corporate executives saw the fragmentation of the European market as an important inhibition on competitiveness, second only to labor inflexibility. In Britain it was considered the most important factor. This view focused on economic benefits to business: only 1 percent of the executives stressed political union. Around 60 percent of executives and owners felt the single market would improve their firm's performance, 65 percent that it

---

[8] Jean Savary, *French Multinationals* (Geneva, 1984); Maria Green Cowles, "The Rise of the European Multinational," *International Economic Insights* 4 (July/August 1993), 15–18; Cowles, *Politics*, chaps. 1–2; Robert Z. Lawrence, *Regionalism, Multilateralism, and Deeper Integration* (Washington, D.C., 1996), 58–59; André Sapir, "Regional Integration in Europe," *Economic Journal*, November 1996; Sapir, "Regionalism and the New Theory of International Trade: Do the Bells Toll for the GATT?" *The World Economy* 16 (July 1993), 423–438. Intra-European exports as a percentage of total European exports increased from under 40 percent in 1955 to around 55 percent in 1970, but then remained stable until rising to 60 percent during the second half of the 1980s. Yet the latter increase reflected primarily the expansion of agricultural trade. Augusto de la Torre and Margaret R. Kelly, *Regional Trade Arrangements*, IMF Occasional Paper no. 93 (Washington, D.C., February, 1992).

would increase exports, up to 80 percent that it would increase opportunities within Europe, but fewer, only around 50 percent, that it would improve "national performance." Service providers emphasized competitiveness *vis-à-vis* foreign, non-EEC firms within the European market; under 15 percent saw global competitiveness in third markets as the major purpose of the initiative.[9]

These structural economic conditions translated into diffuse business support, spearheaded by multinationals, for single market liberalization across the three major countries. It was strongest in Britain, where multinational firms were still disproportionately important; it was slightly weaker in Germany, which had strong exporters and a growing multinational presence; and it remained uneven in France, where liberalization was seen as difficult but necessary to assure future competitiveness.

Britain: "We relished the idea of a Europe . . . frontier-free"

Britain was from the start an enthusiastic supporter of liberalization, which accorded with long-standing demands of British industry, the competitiveness of British service providers, and Thatcherite ideology. By 1985 Britain had already implemented many of the reforms in the White Paper, including capital liberalization, service deregulation, and simplification of customs procedures, and had proposed them repeatedly at the European level. Only on institutional issues did Thatcher hesitate, seeking to avoid formal Treaty changes—in part for ideological reasons, in part due to the fear that an open-ended negotiation would lead to the uncontrolled extension of QMV to social and environmental regulation. Britain also supported, perhaps only for tactical reasons, a modest extension of political cooperation. How is this pattern of preferences to be explained?

Geopolitical Interest and Ideology: Still a "deep-set prejudice" against Federalism

With the exception of the discussions of political cooperation and institutional issues, at no point do objective geopolitical calculations appear to have played a significant role in British thinking on the SEA. The initiative was not a means of maintaining British influence in Europe, managing security externalities, or responding to security threats. Such claims are largely absent from commentaries on Britain in Europe during the 1980s. The British government favored a

---

[9] Neil Fligstein and Peter Brantley, *The 1992 Single Market Program and the Interests of Business*, Center for German and European Studies Working Paper 1.27 (Berkeley, 1994); Booz-Allen & Hamilton/Wall Street Journal Survey Results, European Panel of Chief Executives, "1992 Harmonization," "Europe's Fragmented Markets," "Company Restructuring," n.d. (1986–1988); IFO Institut für Wirtschaftsforschung. "An Empirical Assessment of Factors Shaping Regional Competitiveness in Problem Regions" (Munich, 1989). Fligstein and Bentley found, however, that support did not vary with capital-intensity or measures (though rough) of the potential to exploit increasing returns to scale, and the total r-squared for all firms was relatively low, between .15 and .25. Export-oriented sectors included textiles, fibers, and clothing in Italy; textiles, metals, mechanical engineering, computers, automobiles, precision engineering in Germany; and computers and autos in France. The IFO, however, reported that expected benefits did vary positively with firm size, exports, and activity in the investment goods and business services sectors.

Table 5.1. The single European Act, 1981–1988: Preferences and outcomes

Issues	Britain	Germany	France	Commission	Outcome
Internal market	Actively prefers liberalization from the late 1970s onward, particularly in services.	Prefers liberalization of border controls, industrial standards, government procurement, and industrial subsidies. Strongly prefers to protect some high domestic standards in environment and elsewhere.	Actively prefers liberalization of industrial and processed food standards, and prefers joint financial deregulation and elimination of border controls.	Favors automatic mutual recognition without prior harmonization or safeguards, balanced by social policy. This is initially a low priority for Delors.	QMV introduced into Article 100, but with safeguards (Article 100A4) and sometimes prior harmonization. No significant social policy.
CAP and budget	Prefers to eliminate CAP, seeks to reduce net contribution through a rebate, and seeks to cut EC export subsidies.	Prefers to raise or maintain prices and MCAs while cutting EC export subsidies and stabilizing German fiscal contribution. Favors rapid Iberian entry.	Prefers modest price increases, high export subsidies, elimination of MCAs, no increase in net French contribution, and a long transition period for new Iberian entrants.	Favors large price reductions, modest British rebate, rapid Iberian entry, elimination of MCAs.	No major CAP reform. Costs continue to rise. Modest dairy price reduction offset by side-payments and rise in other prices. Substantial British rebate. MCAs reformed but remain significant. Long transition for many Iberian products.

Industrial policy	Supports minimal, decentralized R&D program on a strict *juste retour* basis.	Supports minimal, decentralized R&D program on a strict *juste retour* basis.	Prefers extensive program with EC funding.	French position.	Minimal, decentralized, *juste retour* R&D program.
Monetary policy	Opposes participation in ERM despite growing domestic support.	Opposes deepening unless capital liberalization and economic convergence.	Strongly and actively supports more symmetrical monetary cooperation.	French position.	Brief rhetorical commitment to future consideration.
Foreign policy	Opposes any formal deepening, particularly in defense.	Supports deeper cooperation if consistent with NATO.	Supports formal cooperation, even if it challenges NATO.	Supports any deepening.	No action.
Institutions	Strongly opposes increase in QMV or EP powers, though willing to compromise on internal market.	Strongly supports expanded EP powers and QMV in a limited range of areas.	Opposes increase in EP powers and supports limited QMV.	Supports centralization and QMV across to board; modest support for EP powers.	QMV in Article 100 and a few other areas. Informal acceptance of mutual recognition and "new approach." Modest increase in EP powers.

strengthening of European political cooperation, but only insofar as it was possible without empowering an independent bureaucracy. Foreign policy cooperation was comfortably intergovernmental in form, and within it Britain's traditionally professional Foreign Office had come to play a prestigious role.[10]

If geopolitics influenced British policy, therefore, it was primarily through the ideological beliefs of the Prime Minister. Thatcher herself was, we saw in chapter 4, a virulent antifederalist. Famously hostile to the Foreign Office, she had little use for the traditional British desire to make sacrifices to "be at the heart of Europe." She was wary of attempts to strengthen supranational institutions and to expand EC competence into areas, such as indirect taxation and social legislation, not immediately linked to trade. Like most British Conservative politicians, she was reflexively more Atlanticist than European on questions of regional security and foreign policy; Atlantic arrangements also granted Britain disproportionate influence. She firmly opposed formal changes in Council procedures—perhaps in part because of the antifederalism common to British political culture—though she understood the need for some movement away from unanimous decision-making in order to implement single market reform effectively. For this reason the British government sought a stronger European Court. Hence the Thatcher government favored *informal* means of encouraging QMV but opposed any treaty changes that might undermine the sovereign prerogatives recognized by the Luxembourg Compromise.[11]

Economic Interest: A "genuine Common Market"

The Confederation of British Industry and other British business groups, we have seen, had long supported liberalization of European trade. This position reflected the CBI's more multinational membership and an internal structure unique among European peak business associations, one which encouraged individual firms to express views independently of sectoral associations. In the mid 1970s the CBI had already begun to promote EC standardization, the removal of nontariff barriers, and the reform of public procurement; in 1977 it added R&D policies to the list. Yet the differential and diffuse impact of NTBs across sectors long prevented the CBI from achieving consensus on a coherent single market proposal.[12]

The CBI finally adopted an official, public position in March 1980, in conjunction with the Department of Trade and Industry. In a joint statement with the Institute of Directors, the CBI noted its concern about the declining competitiveness of Europe *vis-à-vis* the Pacific Rim and called for the creation of a "genuine common market," including liberalization of goods, services, and transport, simplification of the Common Market, and elimination of nontariff barriers. Majority voting was to be used where the treaty allowed it, with suspension of the right to veto only for proposals "clearly designed only to develop the in-

---

[10] Interview with British foreign minister, 1992.

[11] Margaret Thatcher, *The Path to Power* (London, 1995), 470–472.

[12] Keith Middlemas, ed., *Orchestrating Europe: The Informal Politics of the European Union, 1973–1995* (New York, 1995), 715n; Cowles, *Politics*, 133–139. The CBI was not comprised of sectoral associations, which permitted more flexibility in representing the majority concerns, in this case that of export-oriented ones.

ternal market." Beginning in 1983, the Institute of Directors called for completion of the EC single market within five years. At roughly the same time, the CBI argued that "unification of the internal market . . . must be the major policy objective," while any proposals that might lead to a "two-tier Europe" must be resisted; this objective, the CBI argued, required QMV, at least "where the treaty allows it."[13] On some specific issues, however, such as limitations on takeovers, business split down the middle, and here, some analysts maintain, "the government's liberal bias [was] decisive."[14] Although British industry does not appear to have mounted a major campaign for the 1992 agenda or to have scheduled regular consultations, the British government appears to have been fully aware and supportive of business interests. There was, however, little business support for more radical federalist schemes; hence business groups did not plan to make the European Parliament's Draft Treaty a major issue or push the government on behalf of it.[15]

Support among businessmen for liberalization in services was particularly strong. London had long been the preeminent European center of international financial and transport services, and bankers and insurance firms based in the City continued to wield strong influence on British foreign economic policy. London-based subsidiaries and firms had been at the heart of the rise of Eurocurrency markets in the 1960s and 1970s. In British financial services, a decade of domestic reform (the Big Bang or the City Revolution), beginning with the Banking Act of 1979 and culminating in the Financial Services Act of 1988, was already nearly complete when the EC's pathbreaking Second Banking Directive was approved in 1988. These changes were designed to increase price competition, particularly in domestic markets, and to impose, for the first time, detailed governmental licensing and oversight on what had been an informally regulated and highly cartelized sector. The decisive moment came when the Bank of England shifted to the pro-reform camp, a move based, one leading commentator argues, on "the perception that reform was needed to safeguard London's postwar position as an international financial centre by adopting American institutional patterns."[16]

The result of unilateral liberalization and sectoral competitiveness was strong business support for liberalization of European service markets, particularly in banking, insurance, and securities trading, as well as transport. In particular,

---

[13] David Edward, Robert McAllister, and Robert Lane, "The Draft Treaty Establishing the European Union: Report on the United Kingdom," in Roland Bieber, Jean-Paul Jacqué, and Joseph H. H. Weiler, eds., *An Ever Closer Union?* (Brussels, 1985), 295ff.

[14] Stephen Woolcock, Michael Hodges, and Kristin Schreiber, *Britain, Germany and 1992: The Limits of Deregulation* (London, 1991), 100.

[15] Ibid., 109–110; Bieber, Jacqué, and Weiler, *Ever,* 295–299.

[16] Michael Moran, *The Politics of the Financial Services Revolution: The USA, UK and Japan* (London, 1991), 72–78, 85–87, also 124–126, 132–134. Large and more internationally oriented firms supported liberalization, while small and more domestically oriented firms favored continued regulation. This split permitted the government to act with more independence, confident that the most powerful segment of the industry would support liberal policies. David Marsh, and G. Locksley, "Capital: The Neglected Face of Power?" in Marsh, ed., *Pressure Groups: Interest Groups in Britain* (London, 1983), 43. More generally, Stephen Blank, "Britain: The Politics of Foreign Economic Policy, the Domestic Economy, and the Problem of Pluralistic Stagnation," in Peter J. Katzenstein, ed., *Between Power and Plenty: Foreign Economic Policies of Advanced Industrial States* (Madison, Wisc., 1978), 89–137.

since British finance (along with that of Luxembourg) is widely conceded to be internationally competitive and constitutes twice the percentage of GDP of any other EC country, Britain was widely considered to be the strongest beneficiary from financial deregulation. The abolition of exchange controls in 1979 freed British institutional investors to move funds abroad and heightened the competitive pressure on domestic service providers. Even before capital liberalization, British investors devote a greater proportion of GNP to overseas investment than their counterparts in any other major capitalist nation. The Thatcher government had also begun liberalization of telecom services with the Telecommunications Act of 1981 and three years later followed the United States in legalizing competition in basic phone service. Thatcher encouraged further deregulation of international air transport. The government set about privatizing utilities and introducing competition in the public procurement of largely capital goods, including transportation, energy, and armaments systems.[17]

By contrast, British agricultural interests had changed little since the 1970s. With its small, efficient agricultural sector concentrated in areas, such as sheep husbandry, not generously subsidized by the CAP, Britain gained little from agricultural programs that comprise 70 percent of the EC budget. Thus Britain found itself by far the largest per capita *net* contributor to the Community budget. A more equitable arrangement was a consistent goal of British governments in the 1970s and 1980s.

The Domestic Decision: Britain Is "Enthusiastic"

The preponderance of evidence strongly supports the conclusion that Thatcher's European policy was driven primarily by economic interest; it was an extension of her domestic regulatory reforms.[18] Only on secondary issues was geopolitical ideology influential. The British government was "enthusiastic" about Lord Cockfield's 1985 White Paper, which, one commentator observed, "set out an essentially Thatcherite agenda for 'deregulation' and 'enhanced competition' throughout the EC."[19] The White Paper mirrored Thatcher's own

[17] Many perceived the immediate gains as small, particularly after the details of the provisions actually enacted under the SEA became clear. In a survey of the U.K. financial service industry conducted in 1989, service providers argued that the European wholesale market for financial products had already been substantially liberalized through private activity. Retail markets, limited by pre-existing consumer loyalties and host country restrictions on business practices such as advertising and fund composition, would change only slowly. Woolcock et al., *Britain*, 78–79, 84–85; Loukas Tsoukalis, *The New European Economy: The Politics and Economics of Integration*, 2d ed. (New York, 1993), 112; Moran, *Politics*, 11–12; Marsh and Locksley, "Capital," 38; Sir Geoffrey Howe, "The 364 Economists: Ten Years On," lecture at the Annual Meeting of IFS (20 May 1991), 95–97; Heather D. Gibson, *The Eurocurrency Markets: Domestic Financial Policy and International Instability* (New York, 1989), 84–97.

[18] In some areas, Thatcher's reforms rendered Britain more vulnerable to exploitation by foreign governments. The British economy had long been more open to cross-border takeovers, for example, than its neighbors'. Thatcher's liberal policies meant that "access to the British market has been granted unilaterally anyway, so British entrepreneurs might as well seek equivalent access to the rest of the EC market"—not only in the financial sector but also in industrial sectors and deregulated utilities, where among EC members "the market for corporate control [was] truly open only in Britain." Woolcock et al., *Britain*, 99–100, also 94–99.

[19] Robert Skidelsky, "Britain: Mrs. Thatcher's Revolution," in David Calleo and Claudia Morgenstern, eds., *Recasting Europe's Economies: National Strategies in the 1980s* (Lanham, Md., 1990), 128.

moves toward privatizing industry, eliminating obstacles to foreign takeovers, opening public procurement, reducing regulatory controls, introducing competition among alternative suppliers of public services, and deregulating the provision of financial services.[20] British demands to retain unanimity were limited to areas of particular British idiosyncrasy, such as border controls, or of particular Thatcherite sensitivity, like the regulation of small business and fiscal harmonization. As Geoffrey Howe later observed: "Broadly we relished the idea of a Europe that was frontier-free. . . . In the end we obtained . . . as close as possible to achieving that prospect."[21] By contrast, the Labour party and the TUC continued to favor a stronger EC industrial and social policy, as well as unanimity voting, while remaining somewhat skeptical of the SEA.[22]

British policy had continuously pursued external economic liberalization while paying little attention to European integration for its own sake. Thatcher was an early advocate of most of its provisions. In 1981 and 1982 her government called for pan-European telecommunications and transport deregulation, publicly promised to lower European airfares, and submitted proposals for pan-European removal of NTBs, starting with services.[23] The British government's September 1983 memorandum proposed liberalization of financial services (especially insurance), transport (especially air transport), the simplification of frontier controls, mutual recognition of professional qualifications, a joint policy to stimulate European high-technology industries, and the elimination of nontariff barriers through European standardization. The British government supported a "single-passport" system for financial services, in which a firm based in any member-state could provide services throughout the Community. In July 1984 the British moved unilaterally to simplify customs procedures. Support for banking reform and the abolition of exchange controls placed Britain firmly on the side of Germany and the Benelux countries in favor of the elimination of capital controls.[24]

Geopolitical interests and ideology played a secondary role. The traditional British geopolitical concern ("being at the heart of Europe") swayed Thatcher not at all. She also did not permit her own ideological opposition to Europe to influence the basic direction of British policy. During the SEA negotiations she confided to one of her closest advisers on European issues that had she not been prime minister, she would have taken a more strongly anti-European view, but she was constrained by the views of the parliamentary party and of business. The same adviser recalls that he advised that decisions be made solely on the basis of British

[20] Woolcock et al., *Britain*, 97–99.

[21] Sir Geoffrey Howe, *Conflict of Loyalty* (London, 1994), 456–7. Howe adds: "The idea of a Europe that was frontier-free for goods, services and capital, but not for (criminal or non-European) people nor for (dangerous or infected) animals and plants."

[22] Edward, McAllister, and Lane, "Draft," 295–299.

[23] The Conservative government promoted EC deregulation during the British presidency in 1981. United Kingdom, House of Lords, *Debate on ECC 17th Report: Internal Market* (1982–83), 427; House of Lords, *Report of the European Communities Committee: Internal Market* (1981–82), H.L. 204; Roger Morgan, "Vereinigtes Königreich," in W. Weidenfeld and W. Wessels, eds., *Jahrbuch der europäischen Integration* (Bonn, annual), 1982 (p. 462), 1983 (p. 367), and 1984 (p. 388).

[24] *European Report*, 21 September 1981; Woolcock et al., *Britain*, 78–79, 84–85; Louis W. Pauly, *Opening Financial Markets: Banking Politics on the Pacific Rim* (Ithaca, 1988), 174.

economic interests and that such advice was invariably accepted. (Thatcher's perception of economic interests may have in some measure reflected her personal brand of economic liberalism.) The government consulted often with business. Several Whitehall offices reviewed all proposals in the White Paper drafted by Thatcher's former colleague, Cockfield; the general conclusion was that few could harm British economic interests. Thatcher read every word of the SEA text, underlining sections, and was prepared to debate particular clauses or demand particular changes at summit meetings.[25]

Geopolitical ideology, in this case Thatcher's own antifederalism, mattered most on institutional questions. Thatcher strongly opposed formal treaty changes to provide QMV or to repeal the Luxembourg Compromise, in part for ideological reasons and in part because it might lead other issues, such as environmental and social policies, to receive similar treatment. Britain was strongly opposed to expansion of the role of the Commission or Parliament in the process of EC legislation or implementation, and objected to expansion of the substantive scope of judicial review by the ECJ but not, apparently, to increases in its effectiveness. In short, Thatcher consistently sought to secure maximum liberalization while limiting centralization of power in Brussels and to avoid spillover in the form of more intensive regulation or increased financial commitments. Thatcher similarly opposed provisions to strengthen or formalize monetary cooperation in the form of Economic and Monetary Union (EMU)—a position backed throughout this period by economic analysis and, until around 1985, business opinion.[26]

The other major British concern in the period, as it had been since 1973, was the EC budget. With accession, Britain had been forced to accept the agricultural and budget policies as part of the *acquis communautaire*. British farmers remained less numerous and more competitive than their Continental counterparts, generating a lower level of EC spending. Upon entering office, Thatcher campaigned to get "her money back" from the EC, demanding that two-thirds of the British deficit in recent years be rebated and that permanent adjustments be made to limit agricultural spending and to prevent future budgetary disequilibria.

West Germany: Quiet Liberalism

The major impetus for reform in Germany came from Foreign Minister Hans-Dietrich Genscher, soon followed by Chancellor Helmut Kohl, who sought to promote European integration, more efficient EC institutions, and cooperation

---

[25] Interview with former British prime minister's chief adviser on European issues, 1997. British policy was also more centrally coordinated than in most countries; representatives of up to fourteen Whitehall offices meet daily under Cabinet Office chairmanship. Mark A. Blythe, "Internal Market Measures: Policy Coordination by the United Kingdom," in Jürgen Schwarze, ed., *Legislation for Europe 1992* (Baden-Baden, 1989), 111–113.

[26] Bieber et al., *Ever*, 290–291; Howe, *Conflict*, 458. British initiatives, notably the 1984 bilateral Anglo-Italian initiative for a modest strengthening of foreign policy cooperation, appear to have been primarily tactical, aimed at splitting the Franco-German couple. See Malcolm Rifkind in *Hansard* (27 June 1984), Col. 988 and (21 March 1984), Col. 452.

on foreign policy in order to realize geopolitical, ideological, and partisan goals. Yet economic interest remained the key constraint. Neither geopolitical ideology nor partisan competition led Kohl and Genscher to pursue policies that compromised German economic interests. Hence the German government welcomed internal market reform, though it did not propose many concrete measures; but vetoed stronger monetary, R&D, and regulatory policies. It proceeded cautiously on agricultural reform.

Geopolitical Interest and Ideology: Ostpolitik and Electoral Competition

The most prominent proponent of further integration in Germany was Foreign Minister Genscher, leader of the Free Democratic party. Genscher strongly supported European cooperation, particularly in the area of East-West relations and foreign policy, which he viewed as a vital complement to Ostpolitik and essential to an activist foreign policy.[27] In 1980, still under the Schmidt government, serious planning began in the Foreign Ministry for a European *relance.* The primary focus was on foreign policy cooperation, as is clear from the early history of the 1981 Genscher-Columbo initiative: only Italian pressure appears to have induced Genscher to include economic issues, including "further development of the EMS." The German government remained suspicious, however, of proposals in the mid-1980s for a European defense organization.[28]

In Germany a partisan consensus (excepting only the Greens) had persisted since the late 1950s in favor of European integration. Federalist ideas enjoyed considerable parliamentary, as well as public, support. Some major German proposals, such as an expanded role for the Parliament and strengthened foreign policy cooperation, were widely viewed, not least within the Bundestag, as desirable steps toward eventual political union. The Bundestag voted almost unanimously in favor of the Parliament's Draft Treaty—a position far more radical than any national government would adopt.[29] Schmidt, even with Genscher as foreign minister, had paid most attention to monetary policy, but the CDU coalition government headed by Helmut Kohl, which took power in 1982, was generally more favorable to Genscher's geopolitical agenda. Kohl was also very likely personally pro-European. The first issue Kohl raised after being elected CDU-Chief, back in 1973, had been European integration, with particular attention to the single market, free movement across borders and the need for streamlined decision-making to achieve it. To be sure, he presented the single market agenda as a response to economic stagnation, but his speeches, like those of Adenauer, consistently presented integration as a solution to the perennial "German problem." Initially upon entering office he did not promote European initiatives, but within a few years, reportedly spurred by electoral competi-

[27] For a retrospective overview, see Hans-Dietrich Genscher, *Erinnerungen* (Berlin, 1995), 362ff.

[28] Genscher, *Erinnerungen,* 364–365; Gaddum, *Deutsche,* 243, 297; Elizabeth Z. Haywood, "The French Socialists and European Institutional Reform," *Journal of European Integration* 12 (Winter–Spring 1990), 124. See also Marina Gazzo, "Introduction," in Gazzo, ed., *Towards European Union: From the "Crocodile" to the European Council in Milan* (Brussels, 1985), 2:28–29, 39–40.

[29] Bieber et al., *Ever,* 213.

tion from Genscher (the most popular among Germany's major politicians) the Chancellor began actively promoting integration in high politics.[30]

Economic Interest: "Open and unhindered access"

Although German big business and banks did not play the prominent role in developing proposals for trade liberalization that their British, Benelux, and extra-EC counterparts did, a large majority supported the 1992 program. German industry, dependent on EC markets for nearly half its exports, remained relatively competitive through the difficult 1970s and tended to favor trade liberalization, including regulatory harmonization. The percentage of exports in GNP was higher than for any other European country; German growth was export-led even during the recession of 1980–82. Unlike France, which preferred liberalization behind EC protectionist barriers, Germany favored global openness.[31] "Open and unhindered access" to and suppression of subsidies in Southern markets were vociferously advocated by German peak organizations. In 1982 the Bundesverband der deutschen Industrie came out in favor of single market liberalization, particularly opposing foreign subsidies to uncompetitive industries. In 1985 the BDI reiterated its support for liberalization by supporting QMV and the White Paper. A point-by-point analysis of the White Paper detected few threats to German interests. A similar view was held regarding Spanish and Portuguese accession. The Deutscher Industrie- und Handelstag had come out with a similar analysis in 1981. Unions, generally positive, varied with level of exports; unions that represented strong capital-goods exporters, such as IG Metall, were more positive.[32]

Within business, liberalization proposals triggered familiar splits along lines of competitiveness. Capital goods producers—automotive, machine tool, chemical, and electronics firms—were optimistic, though some evidence suggests that many placed a low priority on liberalization, figuring that they would benefit with or without 1992. Some were concerned about rising Japanese competition; for example, auto producers feared that restrictions on imports of low-priced

---

[30] Gaddum, *Europapolitik*, 223–233; interview with Kanzleramt official; Werner Filmer and Heribert Schwan, *Helmut Kohl* (Düsseldorf, 1985), 255–257; Pierre Favier and Michel Martin-Roland, *Le décennie Mitterrand* (Paris, 1990), 2:213.

[31] F. Franzmeyer, "Mehr Gemeinsamer Markt bei verschärftem Außenschutz der EG—Die Bundesrepublik in Handelspolitischen Dilemma?" in Rudolf Hrbek, ed., *EG-Mitgliedschaft: Ein vitales Interesse der Bundesrepublik Deutschland* (Bonn, 1984), 71–87.

[32] BDI, *Was bringt der EG-Binnenmarkt?* 2d ed. (Cologne, 1990); BDI, *Einheitliche Europäische Akte: Auf dem Weg zum Gemeinsamen Binnenmarkt—Weiterentwicklung der Gemeinschaftspolitiken* (Cologne, April 1987); BDI, *Completion of the Single European Market: Consequences for the European Community's External Economic Relations—German Industry's View* (Cologne, 1989); Werner Weidenfeld, *Binnenmarkt '92: Perspektiven aus deutscher Sicht* (Gütersloh, 1989), 94–95, 207–212; Christian Deubner, "The Southern Enlargement of the European Community: Opportunities and Dilemmas from a West German Point of View," *Journal of Common Market Studies* 18 (March 1980), 229–245; H. Kramer, "Bundesrepublik Deutschland," in Weidenfeld and Wessels, *Jahrbuch* 1982, 315–318; *Nichttarifäre Handelhemnisse im innergemeinschaftlichen Warenverkehr* (Bonn, 1981). On unions, Andrei S. Markovits and Alexander Otto, "German Labor and Europe '92," *Comparative Politics* 24 (January 1992), 168–174, suggest the complexity of the considerations in the minds of unions. I contend, however, that their data do not fully support their claim about the "primacy of ideology" (p. 178) in the calculations of unions, not least because the issues on which unions differed, such as transnational union collaboration, played a relatively minor role in the SEA.

automobiles would force Japanese firms into the luxury market, threatening German producers. A substantial minority, concentrated in sheltered sectors such as coal mining, electrical power generation, shipbuilding, aircraft, and food products, as well as sectors dependent on public procurement and product lines subject to detailed norms and standards, as in food processing, opposed liberalization and sought to maintain high German NTBs. One study showed that of only seven among hundreds of German sectors threatened by liberalization, five were in food processing and defended current regulations on the basis of consumer safety. Similarly, German farmers remained wary of any significant reduction in prices.[33]

There was widespread fear of liberalization in service sectors, notably finance, telecommunications, insurance, and transport, particularly trucking, where many smaller firms existed or competition was impeded by cartels, interlocking patterns of corporate control, and limitations on hostile takeovers. Still, it was unclear whether liberalization under the SEA would change these practices, and so the norm was closer to apathy than opposition. The big three banks were reportedly optimistic about financial deregulation. In assessing German finance, one analyst concluded: "With the possible exception of Britain, no other Community member would appear to have more to gain from the creation of a single EC banking market. . . . Frankfurt might well find itself the continent's leading financial centre, ranking perhaps second only to London." A more differentiated situation prevailed in insurance.[34]

In its policies toward international money and capital flows, Germany was heavily influenced, as we have seen, by a domestic consensus led by the Bundesbank against any monetary integration without prior economic convergence. In 1981 the Bundesbank bowed to rising pressures and eliminated controls on inflows of capital, traditionally employed to restrict foreign use of the DM—a step that has been attributed to the increasing internationalization of German banking and industry.[35]

The Domestic Decision: "Endorsement without excitement"

Throughout the 1970s and 1980s the German government consistently favored trade liberalization and regulatory harmonization that did not threaten existing high German standards for social and environmental protection—yet

---

[33] Weidenfeld, *Binnenmarkt '92*, 207ff; Markovits and Otto, "German," 168–174; Hans-Eckart Scharrer, "The Internal Market," in Carl-Christoph Schweitzer and Detlev Karsten, eds., *The Federal Republic of Germany and EC Membership Evaluated* (New York, 1990), 8–9; Peter Katzenstein, ed., *Industry and Politics in West Germany: Toward the Third Republic* (Ithaca, 1989), passim; Thomas R. Howell et al., eds., *Conflict among Nations: Trade Politics in the 1990s* (Boulder, Colo., 1992), 175; interview with the director of the insurance industry association, Bonn, 1989; Eckart Gaddum, *Die deutsche Europapolitik in den 8oer Jahren: Interessen, Konflikte und Entscheidungen der Regierung Kohl* (Paderborn, 1994), 175; DIHT, *Competitive and Adaptation Strategies of German Companies in the Single European Market: Results of a Corporate Survey* (Bonn, 1989).

[34] Woolcock et al., *Britain*, 88–92, also 81–84, 101–106. Germany could afford to liberalize since traditionally close relations between large banks and industry, including substantial holdings by banks, provided a comparative advantage for German banks and protection for firms, which had little to fear from hostile takeovers.

[35] John Goodman and Louis Pauly, "The Obsolescence of Capital Controls? Economic Management in an Age of Global Markets," *World Politics* 46 (October 1993), 50–82.

it did so without great enthusiasm. Internal market initiatives were included in German proposals for reform; Kohl and the Economics Ministry provided strong, perhaps decisive, support for Commissioner Karl-Heinz Narjes's efforts in the early 1980s to establish an EC internal market council. In September 1983 a German memorandum on ESPRIT proposed a long list of measures to liberalize the internal market. Though Genscher remained motivated primarily by geopolitics, the CDU proved more interested in liberalization than the outgoing Schmidt government had been. Yet regulation was still favored by many businesses. As one analyst concludes, "while German officials universally endorse European integration, they have displayed a palpable lack of excitement over the EC 1992 process itself."[36]

The government's ambivalence reflected Germany's ambivalence about economic regulation. On the one hand, the Kohl government entered office convinced that numerous sections of the German economy were overregulated and oversubsidized, in part because of the influence of unions. Accordingly, the government initially sought public support for domestic deregulation. Supply-side tax cuts reduced the public-sector percentage of GNP from 50 percent to 46.5 percent. A commission was appointed to examine deregulation of transport, telecommunications, and insurance. On the other hand, Germany is a wealthy country with strong business and popular support for regulation. Efforts to translate deregulatory prescription into policy were abandoned due to opposition from public-sector bureaucracies, unions, and small business. Some within the CDU saw the White Paper and SEA as an alternative means to achieve deregulation. The German telecommunications reform commission, for example, worked closely with EC officials to deregulate and liberalize the German sector, thereby overcoming efforts by the Bundespost, backed by the unions, to defend its monopoly. Using 1992 in part to force domestic deregulation, but recognizing the delicacy of such issues as environmental and social standards, the German government was a quiet supporter of the SEA but not a leader.[37]

With the exception of German reunification, all major EC decisions taken under the Kohl government were prepared in small cabinet meetings with Kohl, Genscher, the finance and agriculture ministers, and other ministers only as needed. Most decisions were actually reached earlier among the coalition partners: Kohl, Genscher, and the CSU leader. Active promotion of integration therefore tended to emerge not from economic ministries but from the Foreign

[36] One analyst concludes: "In contrast to the leadership role taken by the British in some key areas of the 1992 programme, the Germans have tended to be followers." Woolcock et al., *Britain*, 101–106. This stance is belied by an interview with Commissioner Karl-Heinz Narjes (Brussels 1991). Also Heinz Kramer, "Bundesrepublik Deutschland," in Weidenfeld and Wessels, eds., *Jahrbuch 1981*, 410, 419n; Kramer, "Bundesrepublik Deutschland," in Weidenfeld and Wessels, eds., *Jahrbuch 1982*, 315–317; Thomas R. Howell and Gregory I. Hume, "Germany," in Howell et al., *Conflict among Nations*, (Boulder, Colo., 1992), 175, more generally, 160ff; *European Report*, 29 September 1983.

[37] Rudolf Morawitz, "Industrial Policy," and Joachim Scherer, "European Telecommunications Policy: Some Political Costs and Benefits," both in Schweitzer and Karsten, *Federal Republic*, 14–21, 253–261; Woolcock et al., *Britain*, 81–84; Rüdiger Soltwedel, *Deregulierungspotentiale in der Bundesrepublik*, Kieler Studien no. 202 (Tübingen, 1986); Bundesrepublik Deutschland, *Bericht der Deregulierungskommission* (Bonn, n.d. [1985]).

Ministry and the Chancellor's Office. There was little difference between them, though the Chancellor's Office gave slightly greater emphasis to domestic economic constraints. Given the high visibility and the electoral popularity of the issue, however, Kohl and Genscher competed to exploit European issues and so to present themselves as statesmen. Both sought to capture the issue by taking public initiatives, sometimes without fully considering their content. This competition intensified after early 1987. European integration and Ostpolitik were again linked as Genscher began to call for an opening to Gorbachev which would require solidification of the EC. There was little potential benefit to be gained from highlighting market liberalization, so the German government remained quiet on trade liberalization itself.[38]

On CAP issues Kohl aggressively competed with the FDP for the farm vote and so would brook no compromises in defense of agricultural interests. Germany remained skeptical of many CAP reforms. As we have seen, Germany had grown dependent on protected agricultural markets. With the change in party, even the impotent hostility to high agricultural prices evident under Schmidt—the so-called Preisdruck-Politik—disappeared entirely. Kohl strongly supported the continuation of MCAs or their equivalent. In 1985 Kohl supported his agriculture minister in invoking the Luxembourg Compromise, the first German veto in EC history, against reductions in agricultural prices. At the same time Germany backed British efforts to achieve a more equitable sharing of budgetary costs.[39]

The result was a series of high-level political proposals in which Germany played a leading role but for which economic integration was subordinate. The Genscher-Columbo initiative, concerned primarily with foreign policy cooperation, came from the Foreign Ministry. In February 1984 the Kanzleramt floated the idea of a Franco-German union with an independent parliament and government. Yet when France and Germany moved forward instead with a bilateral agreement to reduce customs controls and regulatory barriers, opposition from the Finance and Interior ministries undermined implementation.[40]

The German government was an early supporter of treaty amendments. The Kanzleramt and Foreign Ministry agreed in 1984 that the Dooge Committee (to prepare them) should be given prominence and intended to propose a well-known politician, Karl Carstens, as its head. They also agreed, in preparation for Dooge Committee discussions, on a program to extend QMV, institutionalize EPC, bolster the European Parliament's role through direct negotiations (conciliation procedures) with the Council of Ministers, deepen economic integra-

[38] Genscher, *Erinnerungen*, 368–369, 374–375, 383; Wolfgang Bickerich, *Helmut Kohl: Kanzler der Einheit* (Düsseldorf, 1995), 185ff; Gaddum, *Deutsche*, 233ff; interview with Kanzleramt official.

[39] Franzmeyer, "Mehr," 71–76; Gaddum, *Deutsche*, 113–120, 155ff; Gisela Henricks, "Germany and the CAP: National Interests and the European Community," *International Affairs* 65 (Winter 1988–89), 75–87. This is often painted by those unfamiliar with the German domestic situation as a situation in which the agricultural ministry secretly colluded against its own government to achieve higher prices, but the history of the negotiations makes it clear that Kohl cooperated with and backed Agriculture Minister Kiechele throughout.

[40] Heinz Kramer, "Bundesrepublik Deutschland," in Weidenfeld and Wessels, eds., *Jahrbuch 1984*, 334.

tion and harmonization, strengthen environmental policy, and expand high-technology policy. The German government stole the spotlight on foreign policy cooperation and preempted the British by promoting common Franco-German foreign and security policy.[41]

At no point, however, did the commitment to a federal Europe lead Germany to support cooperation that contravened its economic interests. Germany pressed strongly for a clause in the SEA permitting governments with high regulatory standards to derogate upward from harmonization agreements in order to maintain high levels of regulatory protection. On monetary policy, Kohl backed the Bundesbank position of strict economic convergence before any further move toward EMU. He compromised only slightly, evidently because of last-minute pressure from Genscher, to include a rhetorical reference to monetary integration but no substantive concessions. On R&D policy, Germany was willing to cooperate only as long as no significant net financial transfers were involved. Finally, the room for CAP reform was minimal.[42]

France: A Socialist or a Conservative Europe?

The French position in the SEA negotiations was characterized by a curious combination of caution about the single market project and enthusiastic support for European reforms. French EC policy reversed between 1981 and 1986, from support for domestic industrial policy and reflation through construction of a "Socialist Europe" to support for liberalization and openness consistent with domestic *rigueur* and internationalization. This shift reflected the economic and political consequences of the failure of the French Socialist experiment. Economically, the French government had to cope not only with longer-term trends toward trade and factor liberalization, which placed competitive pressure on France, but with the need to craft an alternative economic strategy. Backed by business leaders, the French government committed to international liberalization, for which Europe served as a technocratic means and as a source of political legitimation. By 1984–85 many of the reforms foreseen in the SEA were already being contemplated in French unilateral or bilateral policy. These economic concerns appear to have been sufficient to generate weak French support for liberalizing decisions. Surprisingly, however, Mitterrand quickly became not just a reluctant supporter of liberal policies but an enthusiastic activist for European integration. He, like Delors, preferred monetary union as an EC goal, but he lent powerful support to the single market plan. This enthusiasm is best explained as a result of Mitterrand's personal effort to exploit Europe to recast his political, partisan, and electoral identity after the failure of Socialist policies—a tactic decided independently of (and perhaps at the long-term expense of) the French Socialist party. The substance of the reform was dictated by economic interest.

[41] Gaddum, *Deutsche*, 240–247.
[42] Interview with Kanzleramt official.

Geopolitical Interest and Ideology: "Mitterrand on the road to Damascus"

Most analyses of the geopolitical ideology underlying French policy has focused on the personal convictions of the French president—in part because he clearly instigated the pro-European turn in French policy after 1983. About the "true" personal beliefs of Mitterrand—a "notoriously Machiavellian" politician of whom it is said that "his greatest constant is inconsistency"—we can only speculate. Mitterrand himself claimed to be European and could trace his involvement in the European movement back to the 1940s. Typical of his remarks concerning the turnaround was the following: "I have two ambitions: the construction of Europe and the promotion of social justice. The EMS is necessary to achieve the first, but limits my ability to achieve the second."[43]

This is accurate. Whatever its roots and however strong it was, Mitterrand's commitment to Europe was clearly subservient to what he termed the promotion of social justice—that is, to Socialist economic management. Thus, though rhetorically pro-European, Mitterrand (and the French Socialists) all but ignored the EC during the first few years of his presidency, limiting activities to calls for socialism on a European scale. Mitterrand's own pro-European activism emerged only in 1983–84, after the Socialist experiment had been abandoned. There is, as we saw in chapter 4, no evidence that Mitterrand advocated pro-European positions in internal debates; he opposed European economic cooperation until circumstances forced his hand. Nor, despite Mitterrand's tendencies to exploit the Fifth Republic constitution, did the French government show interest in broad foreign-policy initiatives such as the Genscher-Columbo proposal, which the French immediately criticized. André Chandernagor, the French minister for European affairs, observed sarcastically before the Assemblée Nationale that some Europeans were trying to build Europe "from the roof down." Foreign policy cooperation, central to Genscher's purposes, seemed initially not to interest Mitterrand at all.[44]

Under Mitterrand, moreover, the government remained hostile toward strengthening the Court, Commission, and Parliament. Giscard had been particularly concerned by the Court's political activism and called for action at the May 1980 Dublin summit "to do something about the European Court and its illegal decisions." The French government proposed that each of the large countries be permitted to name an additional justice. Yet Giscard had at least pi-

[43] Tony Judt, "Truth and Consequences," *New York Review of Books*, 3 November 1984, 8, 12. The quotation on the turnaround is from Jacques Attali, *Verbatim, 1981–1986* (Paris, 1993), 1:399. On the view that Mitterrand was genuinely pro-European, see Alistair Cole, *François Mitterrand: A Study in Leadership*, 2d ed. (London, 1997), 131, 150. Certainly Mitterrand had earlier taken strikingly pro-European stances, such as a threat in the 1970s to withdraw from the Socialist party if it voted an anti-EC position. Some speculation links French European policy in this period to fears about German neutralism or U.S. unilateralism, but I was able to locate no direct evidence to support a link to policy.

[44] Gabriel Robin, *La Diplomatie de Mitterrand ou le triomphe des apparences, 1981–1985* (Paris, 1985), 219 and passim; Gianni Bonvicini, "The Genscher-Columbo Plan and the 'Solemn Declaration on European Union' (1981–1983)," in Pryce, *Dynamics*, 174–187; Joseph Weiler, "The Genscher-Columbo Draft European Act: The Politics of Indecision," *Revue d'Intégration Européenne* 6 (Spring 1983), 129–154.

oneered the intergovernmental European Council and participated in creating the EMS. The Socialist party view, promulgated in the elections of 1979 and 1981 and in government statements between 1981 and 1984, was that no institutional reform was necessary. On the Luxembourg Compromise, Mitterrand maintained Giscard's position: explicit support for the Compromise itself and advocating the use of QMV on smaller issues. Thus it came as something of a surprise when France quietly backed efforts to override the threatened British veto of the cereal price package in May 1982 and, more broadly, the principle that the Council, rather than the vetoing state, should determine what constitutes a "vital interest" under the Luxembourg Compromise. Yet France, backed even by pro-EC countries such as Italy, immediately reasserted the integrity of the Compromise. The Socialist party itself split over the European Parliament Draft Treaty, with the centrists (Rocardians) in favor and left-wingers (CERES) opposed. As late as the Luxembourg conference of mid-1985, Mitterrand opposed strengthening the Commission or Parliament.[45]

If European ideology was significant, it seems most likely that it was so because it provided Mitterrand's legitimation for economic turnaround—and a way of profiling himself as a statesman and idealist. We saw in chapter 4 that the 1983 policy reversal appears to have stemmed primarily from economic calculations, with geopolitics and ideology employed as *ex post* legitimation of the inevitable. With the French EC presidency in early 1984 Mitterrand—perhaps true to his European idealism but undoubtedly also conscious of political advantage—announced a major diplomatic initiative for the "relaunching" of Europe a few months before elections to the European Parliament. The decision was announced suddenly, even to his closest associates, on the flight back from the EC Athens summit in December 1983. The moment gave Mitterrand maximum personal political advantage. It was a few months before elections and the eve of the French presidency of the EC. The shift was backed by Mitterrand's decision to replace Europe Minister André Chandernagor with the more experienced Roland Dumas, to whom he gave a wide mandate. The decision was immediately recognized by the German Foreign Ministry as an important signal. Hints were soon dropped in speeches.[46]

Yet Mitterrand himself had yet to establish clear goals. Careful not to commit France rashly to new policies, his utterances were at first just symbolic. His May 1984 speech before the EP was "intended . . . to create an impression of approval for the draft treaty, [while] the actual wording was more ambiguous."[47] While supporting "a new treaty," he added that "it should not of course substitute for

---

[45] Hjalte Rasmussen, *On Law and Policy in the European Court of Justice: A Study in Comparative Judicial Policy-Making* (Leyden, 1986), 354, also 357. Also R. Formesyn, "Europeanisation and the Pursuit of National Interests," in Vincent Wright, ed., *Continuity and Change in France* (London, 1984), 237–241; Haywood, "French," 121–136. Cf. Attali, *Verbatim*, 1:886ff.

[46] Some participants believe Mitterrand deliberately undermined the Athens summit so that a major breakthrough could be achieved in the French presidency. Michael Butler, *Europe: More than a Continent* (London, 1986), 118.

[47] Haywood, "French," 133–134; Bieber et al., *Ever Closer*, 222; Genscher, *Erinnerungen*, 367; Attali, *Verbatim*, 1:723.

the existing treaty, but extend it to new fields, as in the case of a political Europe." He distinguished the "inspiration" of the Parliament's Draft Treaty, which France supported, from the Draft Treaty itself. French nominations of Commissioners to the new Commission in 1984 were decided with careful consideration of the areas France sought to control, not with general idealism.[48]

There is little evidence of genuine idealism. Mitterrand had repeatedly rejected federalist proposals; he had been particularly hostile to the Treaty on European Union proposed by the venerable Italian federalist and Europarliamentarian Altiero Spinelli. Behind the scenes Mitterrand remained committed to intergovernmental institutions—French proposals on the Commission and Parliament were modest. Yet Mitterrand's speeches contained precisely the sweeping pronouncements and grand projects—at once idealist and opportunist— that had characterized his political career. At a stroke, his rhetoric positioned him in the center, constructed a new identity for the Left, and split the Right. The initiatives appear to have come from the Elysée, without discussion with or direct pressure from others in the party, but Mitterrand was surely aware that the idea had some resonance in the center of the political spectrum, where Delors, Rocard, Giscard, and others clearly favored Europe. By adopting a high profile on the issue, moreover, Mitterrand could increase his domestic stature as an international statesman. "Gaullism by any other name," Stanley Hoffmann termed the tactic. Once the Socialist domestic program had failed, as Alfred Grosser observed, Europe "afforded [Mitterrand] a sort of "fuite en avance," assuring his stature in the one area still available." Or, as one senior French diplomat observed dryly: "Monsieur Mitterrand's term as president of the European Council became his road to Damascus."[49]

Economic Interest: "Modernize or decline"

A combination of rising economic interdependence and the perceived failure of state-led French policies gave French business and government strong incentives to liberalize. As late as early 1983 a radical policy of closure, devaluation, and subsidization was still being actively considered. By 1984 substantial liberalization of trade and investment was viewed as inevitable—the imperative was "Modernize or decline." The question remained only what form it would take.

In the face of rising trade and investment in Europe, documented at the start

---

[48] Cole, *François*, 126–127.

[49] Stanley Hoffmann, "Mitterrand's Foreign Policy, or Gaullism by Any Other Name," in George Ross and Hoffmann, eds., *The Mitterrand Experiment: Continuity and Change in Modern France* (New York, 1987), 301–302; Cole, *François*, 126; Robin, *La diplomatie de Mitterrand*, 145, also 219. If a ploy for the upcoming European elections, it was singularly inept; although carefully crafted in advance and "certainly no spur of the moment decision," it "came as a bombshell . . . [which] could not fail to make [the Socialists] look rather foolish during the election campaign." Haywood, "French," 133, also 132–135, 147. See also George Ross, "Machiavelli Muddling Through: The Mitterrand Years and French Social Democracy," *French Politics and Society* 13 (Spring 1995), 51–59. For an equally ironic but more positive assessment, see Philippe Moreau-Defarges, "'. . . J'ai fait un rêve . . .': Le président François Mitterrand, artisan de l'union européenne," *Politique Etrangère*, Fall 1985.

of this chapter, France, like Germany and Britain, saw intense discussion in the early 1980s about declining relative competitiveness, particularly in high-technology sectors, *vis-à-vis* third countries: Japan, the United States, and newly industrializing countries. Speeches by French leaders in this period make constant reference to international competitiveness and "reconquering the internal market." A new generation of business entrepreneurs—the "young Turks"—assumed control of the peak association of employers, the CNPF, aiming to direct it toward less state-centered policies. Robert Faroux of Saint Gobain, for example, was particularly close to Mitterrand and sought to convince him to forsake intervention and permit French firms to compete unhampered.[50] Many other businessmen close to Mitterrand remained interventionist.

Particularly important was the globalization of finance and services, which helps explain why deregulation in financial services, not initially the central part of Cockfield's White Paper, became a French priority. With the liberalization of U.S. and British finance, a new, internationally deregulated environment was emerging in which first-mover advantages could be of lasting importance for financial competitiveness. Government studies established that France was the world's second-largest exporter of services after the United States. France, one civil servant noted, "had a lot to gain [and] at the EC level we stood to gain the most."[51] France, though a latecomer to domestic financial liberalization, sought to establish Paris as an important financial center. Thus there was interest to "catch up with the leading countries in the field of financial innovation (the United States, the United Kingdom, Canada, etc.) in order to maintain the competitiveness of the French banking system and the role of Paris as a financial center."[52] Unfavorable regulation would undermine the comparative position of banks in international markets. By the late 1970s capital controls had grown more costly and less effective, and the elimination of capital controls implied adjustments in taxation, reserve requirements, liquidity rations, and other regulations. These changes in France led to splits between more and less competitive banks. Hence the Treasury launched reforms without consistent support from the banking community.[53]

There was, in addition, rising concern in France about the effects of NTBs, particularly those imposed by Germany, where legal standards backed by organizations of manufacturers were significant barriers to imports. The processed food sector, which in this period had generated considerable EC litigation, remained a particular source of concern. In late 1982 France suggested that the Commission compile a list of internal barriers, based on voluntary submissions, though internal market initiatives remained linked to more external protection.

---

[50] Alain Lipietz, "Governing the Economy in the Face of International Challenge," in James Hollifield and George Ross, eds., *Searching for a New France* (New York, 1991), 32–34; Thomas R. Christofsen, *The French Socialists in Power, 1981–1986* (Newark, Del., 1991), 101–110; Cowles, *Politics,* 230.

[51] Nicolaïdis, *Mutual,* 295–296.

[52] Christian de Boissieu and Marie-Hélène Duprat, "French Monetary Policy in the Light of European Monetary and Financial Integration," in Heidemarie Sherman, ed., *Monetary Implications of the 1992 Process* (New York, 1990), 57, also 50–61.

[53] Goodman and Pauly, "Obsolescence," 50–82; Christian de Boissieu, "Recent Developments in the French Financial System," in Boissieu, ed., *Banking in France* (London, 1990), 21–23.

Between 1982 and 1984 the French government pressed for bilateral agreements with Germany concerning customs formalities and nontariff barriers—a set of discussions that spawned two bilateral treaties and the multilateral Schengen agreement.[54]

Beyond concerns about German NTBs, this period witnessed important changes in the relative competitiveness of French agriculture, which shifted French support for the Common Agricultural Policy. Export subsidies and preferential access remained essential, generating a large agricultural trade surplus, but France was no longer a large net beneficiary from the EC budget, with even bleaker prospects after the entry of Spain and Portugal.[55] Moreover, the percentage of the population employed in agriculture had been declining steadily. While the government continued to support moderately high prices and export subsidies, it had slightly more room for reform. Still, France did continue to benefit from the preferential trading arrangement at the core of the EC and opposed any British attempt to reduce its liabilities under the system. Claude Cheysson, the French foreign minister, declared in 1982, "the United Kingdom [seeks] *juste retour*, which is not a Community idea. We and the British are not speaking of the same community."[56]

Yet these challenges of competitiveness and interdependence did not unambiguously point toward trade liberalization. An alternative was to strengthen traditional state intervention. The Socialist government, elected in 1981, looked to nationalization and industrial subsidies. Those on the Left of the Socialist party advocated a defense of domestic policy through collective European industrial policy and, if necessary, closure of the French market. Leading figures in the CNPF did support liberalization, but still it is implausible to explain the major policies of the Mitterrand government as a direct reflection of business pressure. In any case, many less competitive firms resisted greater competition.

Commercial concerns alone might have had only a modest effect were it not for a more fundamental crisis in the traditionally statist French system of industrial management. With slower growth across the OECD after 1973, discipline had to be imposed on costs and wages—a task to which the French system was unsuited. Business accepted state subsidies but resisted state management. In the 1970s, under the *encadrement de crédit*, the government responded to tight conditions by rationing credit to, in declining order of priority, the Treasury, state-owned enterprises, private financial institutions, and private nonfinancial firms—with financial intermediation continuing to provide 80 percent of finance. Preferential rates were extended to privileged sectors, including exports, housing, and agriculture, totaling 40 percent of bank lending. In the resulting

[54] Joan Pearce, John Sutton, and Roy Batchelor, *Protection and Industrial Policy in Europe* (London, 1985), 6, 14, 47–48, 66, 140–141; Ralf Joas, *Zwischen Nation und Europa: Die europapolitischen Vorstellungen der Gaullisten 1978 bis 1994* (Bochum, 1996), 174–176, 224.

[55] Although the French government became more accommodating of agricultural reform and French ministers spoke out occasionally about overgenerous support—as agriculture minister, Michel Rocard even adopted an activist stance toward dairy subsidies—they remained relatively staunch supporters of export subsidies. Paul Taylor, "The New Dynamics of EC Integration in the 1980s," in Juliet Lodge, ed., *The European Community and the Challenge of the Future* (London, 1989), 6.

[56] Paul Taylor, *The Limits of European Integration* (London, 1983), 240–241.

"overdraft economy," nonfinancial firms, which borrowed through bank credits rather than rely on capital markets or self-financing, faced a chronic shortage of funds. With increasing capital mobility and financial competition, borrowers and lenders disadvantaged by government policy were able to move outside the system. To prevent this, the French system of managed credit had traditionally relied on exchange controls, yet these proved porous. The late 1970s saw a large increase in foreign indebtedness by French firms—most strikingly in the financial sector itself. Increased domestic competition from foreign banks forced French banks to take government pressure to internationalize, which they had been ignoring, more seriously.[57]

The French government's microeconomic urge to discipline or direct firms had macroeconomic implications as well: the system undermined government control over monetary policy. By separately regulating money market rates, interest rates, and quantitative credit restrictions, the Bank of France sought to stabilize exchange rates, promote investment, and control the money supply. Yet fighting inflation through monetary targeting—adopted in 1976 and only briefly loosened between 1981 and 1983—required that public-sector deficits be financed through nonmonetary means. Monetary tightening was coming to be viewed throughout Europe as a substitute for a credible incomes policy, but it remained impossible as long as the government rationed credit. By the early 1980s it had become apparent that a market-based monetary policy that would avoid both debt and credit shortages required broader and deeper private capital markets.[58]

Again there were two responses to this crisis. The Barre government, whose rhetorical goal was to "adapt France to the conditions of the new world economy," sought to overcome these problems through an external monetary peg, which would commit France to microeconomic austerity and macroeconomic discipline—"the major precondition for healthy development." Externally, the goal was to increase French competitiveness in specific international markets by encouraging less price-sensitive, high-technology export industries such as aerospace, automobiles, transportation systems, and electronics; rationalizing large, traditional industries such as steel, nuclear power, and telecommunications; and fostering an orderly contraction in labor-intensive sectors like textiles. To force adjustment, the government would increasingly expect firms to seek finance at market rates. Part of this program was an effort to expand stock and bond markets, encourage corporate borrowing on private markets, and expand the direct role of households in finance.[59]

From the mid-1970s onward the retreat from industrial policy had gone hand-

[57] Michael Loriaux, *France after Hegemony: International Change and Financial Reform* (Ithaca, 1991; Boissieu and Duprat, "French," 52–54, 62–63, 78–79; Stephen S. Cohen, James Galbraith, and John Zysman, "Rehabbing the Labyrinth: The Financial System and Industrial Policy in France," in Cohen and Peter A. Gourevitch, eds., *France in a Troubled World Economy* (London, 1982), 49–75; Goodman and Pauly, "Obsolescence."

[58] Loriaux, *French;* Boissieu and Duprat, "French," 57–66, 81. One potential response was to develop new instruments for handling government debt, but such indebtedness became increasingly expensive over time.

[59] Lipietz, "Governing," 30–31.

in-hand with financial innovation and liberalization. In July 1978 the Monory Act offered tax incentives for the development of the stock market. In July 1979 mutual funds were created, followed in September 1981 by new types of short-term assets and in June 1982 new financial instruments for the low-income population. The Socialist interlude created a brief countertrend, but by 1983 the marketization and securitization of corporate financing came to be seen, as under Giscard and Barre, as the only way to attract needed industrial invest-ment. The Delors Act of January 1983 created new instruments for capitalizing private and nationalized firms, followed the next month by the creation of an unlisted securities market and, later in the year, by new industrial development funds. Corporate financing from capital markets, stocks, and bonds increased from approximately 25 percent in 1981 to around 75 percent in 1986.[60]

We have seen that Giscard and Barre had been unable or unwilling to cut government employment or industrial subsidies significantly. Credit was still rationed, particularly among smaller corporate borrowers; private opportunities for larger companies grew up alongside the existing system. Intervention con-tinued, with French firms wishing to invest abroad finding it difficult to do so, and some foreign firms wishing to invest in France being refused permission. All in all, the Giscard-Barre policy failed to stimulate corporate activity; in 1980 pri-vate investment remained stagnant.[61]

Mitterrand and the Socialists came to power with an alternative policy: na-tionalization, subsidization, and, if necessary, external closure aimed at full em-ployment. In industrial policy most members of the Socialist government ar-gued that intervention to create vertically integrated *filières*, linking the entire production process from raw material to finished product, would increase pro-ductivity. More moderate Socialist ministers such as Delors were skeptical of such policies well before they entered office, arguing instead for deregulation, reduced state intervention, and increased autonomy for business managers. Indeed, the Socialists quickly discovered that nationalized industries were a lia-bility; they posted enormous losses in 1981, and subsidies appeared to have little effect. As minister of industry, Jean-Pierre Chèvènement discovered that na-tionalization did not fundamentally alter these dilemmas. Plans to turn around steel, coal, and shipbuilding failed; paper, machine tools, and automobiles were in trouble. Labor costs rose much faster than in Germany. Chèvènement's highly interventionist policy generated loud protests among executives and workers alike, and his resignation followed a rebuke from Mitterrand at a February 1983 Council meeting for not allowing managers enough autonomy. The public sec-tor aside, business investment was still flat.[62]

[60] Boissieu and Duprat, "French," 55–57, 62–63.

[61] Cohen, Galbraith, and Zysman, "Rehabbing," 49–55, 65–66; Vincent Wright, "Introduction: The Change in France," in Wright, *Continuity*, 18, 20–21.

[62] Favier and Martin-Roland, *Décennie*, 1:450, 455–456; Christoffsen, *French*, 101–110, 131–134; Loriaux, *French*; Michael Loriaux, "States and Markets: French Financial Interventionism in the Seventies," *Comparative Politics* 20 (January 1988), 175–193. Of particular relevance here, see Franco Archibugi, Jacques Delors, and Stuart Holland, "Planning for Development," and Delors, "The Decline of French Planning," in Holland, ed., *Beyond Capitalist Planning* (New York, 1978), 184–202, 9–33. Delors argues that problems with planning had been resolved through inflation and that

With no fiscally viable alternative, the Mitterrand government opted for austerity, which implied a policy of liberalization. In his first speech after replacing Chèvènement as minister of industry in 1983, Laurent Fabius signaled a strengthening of *rigueur*, parallel to the decision to remain in the EMS, announcing that "the state does not intend to become a substitute for the role of enterprises and entrepreneurs."[63] Under the motto "Modernize or decline" (later, under his prime ministership, altered to the more gentle "Moderniser et rassembler"), Fabius announced that nationalized firms would henceforth be expected to become profitable; those that did not would perish. The role of banks as intermediaries was not immediately limited, but the government began to offer credit at closer to market terms.

Fabius followed Delors's lead by creating additional instruments for firms to borrow on private capital markets. He laid great rhetorical stress on competitiveness in foreign markets, a turnaround from the initial Socialist policy of recapturing the internal market. After the shift the CFDT supported *rigueur* even more strongly than the government.[64] Mitterrand's press conference of April 1983 signaled his own willingness to pursue this line—a shift seen by many as indicative of a "Bad Godesberg" experience for the Socialist party.[65] One analyst observed, "the Socialist experience . . . confirms the existence of constraints on policy, the importance of which was such that the government [sacrificed] much of its discretionary power over the allocation of credit."[66]

The reforms extended to financial markets as well. In 1984 the French government returned to accommodating foreign investment and capital flows and accelerating the trend toward the liberalization of finance and equities. In the first half of 1984 a flurry of deals involved cross-investment between French nationalized firms and U.S. multinationals, although France continued to block foreign investment in sectors with surplus capacity.[67] On replacing Delors as finance minister in the Fabius government, Pierre Bérégovoy moved decisively to extend the liberalization of financial markets. Delors had already introduced new forms of shareholding and investment, as well as opening a "second market" for small enterprises, which Giscard and Barre had left under the *encadrement* system. In November 1984 a reform of the entire financial system eliminated credit ceilings amid capital controls and created new money, bond, and futures markets.[68] In April 1985 Bérégovoy began to decontrol bank rates, permitting more interbank competition. In early 1985 negotiable certificates of deposit were authorized, followed the next winter by markets for commercial

---

France had to move toward a less statist mode of industrial management, one more selective in providing finance and offering greater autonomy to managers. French planning was appropriate to a situation in which governments manage production of basic commodities but was inappropriate to a more internalized economy.

[63] Christoffsen, *French*, 131–134.
[64] Loriaux, "States," 186.
[65] Philippe Bauchard, *La Guerre des deux roses: Du rêve à la réalité* (Paris, 1986), 290–294; Christoffsen, *French*, 100–101, 108, 132–133, 137–138.
[66] Loriaux, "States," 189.
[67] Pearce, Sutton, and Batchelor, *Protection*, 72–73.
[68] Goodman and Pauly, "Obsolescence," 73–74.

paper, negotiable treasury bills, notes issued by specialized financial institutions, and financial futures. "The stock market," observed one commentator, "had never done so well as under the Socialists." The years 1987 and 1988 saw the introduction of an options market, individual retirement accounts, and futures contracts on the stock index.[69]

In sum, by the mid-1980s the traditional French system of extensive industrial subsidies, controlled credit, and closed financial markets was well on the way to being replaced with more market-oriented, open arrangements. Perhaps even more important, the two alternatives to liberalization and deregulation, namely a policy of autarky and nationalization, initially pursued by the Socialists, and a policy of "muddling through" with piecemeal government discipline, pursued by Giscard and Barre, had been discredited. The stage was set for multilateral reform.

The Domestic Decision: Mitterrand's "fuite en avance"

Throughout the 1980s the French government sought to create a Europe economically and politically supportive of its domestic economic and partisan objectives. In the early years of the Mitterrand presidency, the French government paid little attention to Europe; insofar as it did, the goal was a Socialist Europe. The most important French initiatives of this period, one in October 1981 on "un espace social européen" and another in autumn 1983 on "un espace industriel européen," though relatively minor and utterly futile, reflected this goal.[70]

At his first European Council meeting in 1981 Mitterrand proposed a package including Euro-loans for new industries, promotion of the computer and energy industries on a European scale, examination of means to reduce the workweek, recognition of the overriding importance of social objectives, expansion of cooperation with the developing world, and an anti-unemployment program of fiscal stimulation—all culminating in the creation of a "powerful European social area" billed as the first step toward a "socialist Europe." Concessions on British demands for budgetary reform were linked to German and British support for coordinated reflation through the EMS, EC social and investment financing, and funding for R&D and energy projects. Mitterrand also proposed a two-tier system of capital controls to insulate Europe from the American economy and an extended period in which to stimulate the French domestic economy free from external constraints. All these efforts at European summitry, like efforts to establish an EC industrial policy in the 1970s, gained little support in Bonn and London and were never seriously discussed. In the end, they only served to teach Mitterrand, in his own words, "just how conservative Europe really was." Yet such failures appear to have caused Mitterrand and the Socialist party little concern.

The turning point clearly coincided with the domestic policy turnaround of 1983–84, after which French policy moved cautiously in a more liberal and more

[69] Bauchard, *Guerre*, 326–327; also Loriaux, "States," 188; Cohen, Galbraith, and Zysman, "Rehabbing," 53–55; Boissieu and Duprat, "French," 57–58.
[70] Pearce, *Protection*, 6, 14, 47–48, 66, 140–141, 198; Favier and Martin-Roland, *Décennie*, 1:367. The Mitterrand quotation is from an interview with an Elysée official in 1992.

European direction—which suggests an underlying economic motivation. We have seen in Chapter 4 and above that the failures of the Socialist experiment were failures of economic management. Mitterrand's motivations for the 1983 turnaround were dictated, above all, by the economic unsustainability of his monetary and industrial policies.

First consequences of this domestic turnaround in European policy were hesitant. The French initiative in September 1983 pointed to a crisis of European competitiveness *vis-à-vis* the United States in most high-tech sectors. The French offered support for EC technology policies, along with industrial policy, public works, and external protection. Although the memo also mentioned regulatory harmonization, standardization, and liberalization of public procurement, these matters were less prominent. Some of these proposals—with the exception of regulatory harmonization—may well have been influenced by contacts with the European Roundtable of Industrialists (ERT), which had several high-level meetings with Mitterrand and his aides during 1983 and 1984, in which it strongly advocated industrial subsidies.[71] By 1984 and 1985 the *discours* in France on the Community had become more liberal, and the French government embraced the internal market program. Catherine Lalumière, secretary of state for European affairs, stressed that "the proposal for the establishment of a large internal market . . . is the most important proposal for our firms and citizens. Colbert's descendants took some time to throw off the cultural shackles of protectionism."[72] Within this new strategy, financial and industrial deregulation, greater openness to foreign investment, a higher priority on greater competitiveness, and rising concern about foreign NTBs led to significant policy changes. In financial services France sought to *accelerate* European reforms in order to achieve competitive advantage. Bilateral agreements with Germany and the Schengen Accord—an ad hoc agreement to end border controls—recognized the French interest in thorough liberalization. In short, by the end of 1984 France was unilaterally, bilaterally, and multilaterally seeking to implement much of what was to be in the Single Act two years later.[73]

This shift in foreign policy was connected in two ways with the failure of the Socialist experiment. The more straightforward was simply that the domestic shift created an incentive to pursue supportive international economic policy. If the state did not assure finance and adjustment, there was less reason to oppose international markets doing so. Of the domestic changes, fundamental was financial reform, which, as economist Jacques Mélitz has observed, future historians may well call the most important precondition for the acceptance of the SEA. Without it, France could neither have agreed nor implemented the agreement.[74] Policy failure gave a second impetus to major change. French economic priorities remained consistent with its global market position and policy style: moderate agricultural reform and pressure for the removal of NTBs particularly

[71] Pearce, *Protection*, 6.
[72] "Interview with Catherine Lalumière, Secretary of State for European Affairs," *Speeches and Statements*, French Embassy in London, CTL/DISCOM/180/85 (31 October 1985), 3.
[73] Goodman and Pauly, "Obsolescence," 50–82.
[74] Jacques Mélitz, "Financial Deregulation in Europe," *European Economic Review* 34 (1990), 394–395.

in the food sector, monetary reform on "monetarist" terms to loosen French macroeconomic constraints, difficult state-led movement toward financial and trade liberalization, and support for a collective industrial policy.

Yet the failure of the Socialist experiment had a second, more subtle consequence: it forced Mitterrand to seek an alternative geopolitical *grand projet* and a partisan identity disassociated from the Communist Party. There is no evidence, internal or external, that a reconsideration of geopolitical threats took place in this period. Only the need for political legitimation can explain Mitterrand's sudden enthusiastic embrace of European rhetoric and his high-profile activism. He was open to pressure even from the Gaullist Right, led by Chirac, which would seek to wrest control of the European issue from him during the period of *cohabitation.* With his Parliament speech in early 1984, Mitterrand began to adopt the rhetoric of European federalism, calling for a reconsideration of the Luxembourg Compromise and advocating procedural reform as long as it was limited to the Council and the Commission and did not imply a radical democratization of EC politics.[75]

From that point on, Mitterrand played a decisive role in promoting European integration. He pursued European reform even though he appears personally to have had significant doubts about liberalization; like Delors, he preferred monetary union as a European agenda. On the eve of the Luxembourg conference, Mitterrand, with the backing of Delors, continued to seek a link between the single market, which he continued to see as an essentially Anglo-German proposal, to a more fundamental French concern: German concessions on monetary policy.[76]

Explaining National Preferences

With the reversal of French economic policy in 1983, single market liberalization emerged as the only substantive issue that could command consensus from the major EC governments. Britain had supported it since well before the Conservative government took office in 1979, Germany had long been passively supportive, and France moved from support for industrial policy to support for trade liberalization in 1983–84. Still, governments differed concerning the relative importance of single market reform vis-à-vis other substantive issues and the institutional form such a reform should take.

Variations in cross-national and cross-issue preferences confirm the primacy of economic interests. The issues on which the White Paper focused—food products, industrial standards, service deregulation—were precisely those highlighted in bilateral efforts among member governments and pressure from

---

[75] Gazzo, ed. *Towards,* 1:82–85; Cole, *François,* 128–130.

[76] On the plane to the Luxembourg summit of December 1985, Mitterrand is reported to have considered prospects for the French proposals for coordinated fiscal reflation, monetary cooperation, social policies, and industrial policies as poor. Despite close Franco-German relations, Mitterrand described France as facing a tacit Anglo-German alliance of free-market liberals. Mitterrand did impress upon his advisers the importance of remaining part of Europe. Favier and Martin-Roland, *Décennie,* 2:216–217; Attali, *Verbatim,* 1:887.

business executives. National preferences registered economic interests, with each country outlining distinctive priorities. Germany supported market reform as well as regulatory cooperation, imposing clear limits on CAP reform, monetary cooperation, and R&D cooperation, and remaining cautious on service liberalization. Britain promoted CAP reform, market liberalization, and particularly service deregulation, but strongly opposed monetary integration, R&D policies unless strictly *juste retour*, and common regulatory policies in areas such as the environment. France supported monetary and R&D cooperation, advocated prudent market liberalization and services deregulation, remained very cautious on CAP reform, and ambivalent about environmental cooperation. Each government sought to protect sensitive areas: fiscal harmonization and small business for Britain, high regulatory standards and MCAs for Germany, executive authority vis-à-vis Parliament for France. By contrast, though all three governments ostensibly favored foreign policy cooperation, none suggested or seriously considered significant commitments. Defense cooperation was never seriously discussed.

Domestic decision-making processes further support the economic view. The most highly mobilized social groups were big business interests, particularly multinational firms, and cleavages reflected competitiveness. In Germany and Britain, support from manufacturing firms was driven primarily by international competitiveness: the more export-dependent a firm or sector, the more optimistic it tended to be about the effects of market liberalization. In France, there is insufficient evidence to be sure. Larger firms and those with disproportionate exports or investments overseas, tended to be most favorable. The service sector—led by telecom, transport, finance, and insurance—were the most optimistic of all. Although capital intensity itself did not correlate with support for liberalization, large multinational firms in capital-intensive sectors spearheaded efforts to promote liberalization. A secondary influence on business views was state ownership: executives in sectors with government-owned firms (disproportionately in non-exporting sectors) viewed liberalization of regulatory standards and public procurement most unfavorably.[77] Throughout Europe, MNCs were particularly prominent supporters.

Yet if business support was broad, it was also thin; business did not take a proactive role. This may reflect the diffuse nature of the benefits—a conjecture consistent with polls at the time. Outside the Benelux countries, the great majority of businessmen believed that the effects of 1992 on corporate costs would be small—much less even than modest Commission estimates. Though industrial restructuring was viewed as inevitable, removal of trade barriers was an unimportant factor, for most European MNCs were already organizing on a Continental scale. There were pockets of intense concern and opposition, particularly in small business, which most European executives expected to be net losers from 1992. And only one quarter of executives thought 1992 would boost employment. Businessmen had relatively little confidence that discriminatory pub-

[77] Fligstein and Brantley, "1992"; Booz-Allen and Hamilton, "European Panel"; IFO, "Empirical Assessment."

lic procurement, levels of taxation, or state intervention would actually be restrained, or that the "Europe 1992" program would be implemented on time.[78]

Chief executives justified the SEA largely on grounds of competitiveness. The statements of politicians and executives confirm that the 1992 plan was in part a response to Europe's declining industrial competitiveness. Most accounts of the SEA point out that in the late 1970s and early 1980s many European leaders were concerned with Eurosclerosis—a combination of persistent high unemployment, low growth rates relative to other OECD countries, a technological lag in many sectors, and declining international competitiveness. In high-technology, European leaders feared long-term decline *vis-à-vis* the United States and, particularly, Japan in industries such as electronics and telecommunications. Even more striking was the effect of foreign competitive pressure and increased capital mobility on the financial service and transport sectors. Deregulation in the United States and, perhaps more important, in the United Kingdom and some smaller countries posed a challenge to other national service providers. Economic crisis and external competition provide a convincing explanation for specific policies: standardization and R&D subsidies in high-tech sectors, and the liberalization of financial and transport services.[79]

Left-wing opposition aside, the SEA provoked little partisan debate, limiting our ability to reconstruct motivations from cleavages. Europe remained a low-priority issue for the voters of all three countries. In Germany, CDU leaders concluded that there was a permissive consensus in favor of European integration but no active agitation for it. The issue of the Draft Treaty "played no part in the election campaign." In France, observers of French politics agreed that "the Union Treaty was hardly mentioned by candidates for the European elections." In Britain, the two major political parties did not consider the issue important enough to take official positions on the Draft Treaty.[80] Partisan opposition from the French Communists, left-wing French Socialists, and the left of the British Labour party was certainly predictable on economic grounds but not significant.

It is clear, however, that electoral competition in essentially pro-European electorates gave Genscher, Mitterrand, and Kohl an important reason to present themselves—particularly while their countries held the presidency—as pro-European. Geopolitical ideology provided an incentive for national leaders to focus their attention—and the attention of publics—on the EC, which in turn increased their incentive to make concessions that would secure agreement. On the Continent, diplomatic success in Europe added to a politician's stature, sometimes independently of purpose. In Germany, moreover, a strong elite consensus favored integration. German parliamentarians supported political inte-

[78] Booz-Allen and Hamilton, "European Panel."

[79] Evidence is summarized in Sandholtz and Zysman, "1992." Interviews with CEO of Philips (Eindhoven, 1991).

[80] Carl Otto Lenz, "The Draft Treaty Establishing the European Union: Report on the Federal Republic of Germany," in Bieber, Jacqué, and Weiler, *Ever Closer*, 214; Jacques Genton, "Ratification and Implementation of the Draft Treaty Establishing the European Union: Constitutional and Political Implications for France," in Bieber, Jacqué, and Weiler, *Ever*, 221; Edward, McAllister, and Lane, "Draft," 295–299.

gration: the German commitment to QMV and Parliament powers, for example, appears to have been largely independent of, though not in contradiction with, its substantive goals. Indeed, the Bundestag would likely have ratified Spinelli's Draft Treaty had the opportunity arisen. Much of Thatcher's opposition reflected skepticism about EC social regulation from a relatively right-wing government in a (relatively) low-income country. Yet there was also little popular or parliamentary support for integration. Even the pro-European Liberal–Social Democratic Alliance Manifesto for the European elections opposed Treaty amendments.[81] The ideological status of Europe in domestic politics or in the minds of leaders accounts for the consistency of German support for supranational institutions and general reform, for Genscher and Mitterrand's pro-European activism before they knew what substantive results might be, and for Thatcher's opposition to supranational institutions despite support for liberalization.

Nonetheless, economic interests remained primary in the sense that no major government was at any time willing to sacrifice significant economic interests for the sake of ideology or "high politics." The closest thing was the French turnaround, but as we have seen, this resulted primarily from economic failure not geopolitical imperatives. Geopolitics proved more malleable than economics. Where economic and geopolitical interests came into conflict, as with Thatcher's views on QMV and Gaullist support for liberalization, economic interest seemed to prevail. The predominance of economic concerns is also evident from the consistency of national policies across a range of domestic and international forums. Unilateral policy shifts, bilateral Franco-German negotiations, and the Schengen Agreement all preceded EC efforts. They were linked by no geopolitical interest or ideology but by a common economic program.[82]

In all three countries, the timing of change also confirms the economic view. A shift in domestic preferences to lessen state intervention—the failure of the Socialist experiment in France, modest deregulation under Kohl in Germany, the Thatcher revolution in Britain—immediately preceded EC discussions. This trend was pan-European. For example, Britain had eliminated capital controls in 1979, Germany in 1981, and France was moving to do so in 1984.[83] The most

[81] Lenz, "Draft," 213; Edward, McAllister, and Lane, "Draft," 295–299.

[82] Much has been made of the Japanese threat in sparking European cooperation in the 1980s, and it was clearly important, particularly in electronics. Yet the French share of global exports remained roughly constant from 1950 to 1980, with the striking increase in the Japanese share of global exports (from 3.4% to 15.4%) more than matched by the even more striking decline in the British share (25.5% to 9.9%). If there was a single commercial challenge to France in the 1980s, it stemmed from Germany. During the 1970s and 1980s, as German agriculture reached grater levels of self-sufficiency and German importers sought cheaper sources in third countries, the trade balance with Germany worsened. J. R. Hough, *The French Economy* (New York, 1982), 202.

[83] During 1984–1985, for example, Benelux banking was liberalized, leading to increased opportunities for foreign banks. Swedish banking was liberalized when it became clear that multinational banks and firms were willing to move abroad to seek cheaper capital. Pauly, *Opening,* 175–176; Goodman and Pauly, "Obsolescence," 57, 78; Cowles, *Politics,* chap. 3; Sandholtz and Zysman, "1992," 109; Manfred Wegner, "Preparing the 1990s—A Three-Pronged Strategy," in Wolfgang Wessels and Elfriede Regelsberger, eds., *The Federal Republic of Germany and the European Community* (Bonn, 1988), 115–124. Perhaps the only area in which national governments clearly lagged Commission proposals was in telecommunications, where Davignon began proposing privatization and greater competition in 1979, before any government, except perhaps Britain, had moved forward. Yet even here, national action in the major countries often predated the passage of Council directives on the subject.

salient difference between this and previous episodes of concern about external competitiveness, such as "le défi américan" of the late 1960s, was that unilateral policy alternatives were perceived to have failed, leading to convergent EC preferences. By contrast, there is little evidence of significant structural changes in the geopolitical situation of Europe during this period. Explanations based on French concern about German neutralism, conflict with Russia, or U.S. unilateralism lack empirical support and do not explain the persistence of interest in single market liberalization beyond the early 1980s.

Interstate Bargaining

The SEA was not the sole proposal considered by the member states during this period. Varied proposals included not just plans for internal market liberalization but initiatives for a deeper industrial policy, monetary union, intensive defense and foreign policy cooperation, and institutional reform. What explains the outcomes of interstate bargaining over single market reform? Did successful negotiations require, as most analysts have argued, decisive intervention by supranational and transnational political entrepreneurs? How was the SEA linked to QMV—an institutional innovation opposed by the British government?

My analysis challenges existing accounts of the SEA, which emphasize the activities of supranational and transnational entrepreneurs, including the Court, various Parliamentary groups, transnationally organized business, and above all Delors, Davignon, and other Commissioners. Most analyses see some combination as "necessary" conditions for the SEA. I conclude that such influence remained secondary and that the negotiations confirm intergovernmental bargaining theory. Well-informed national governments dominated the process. Proposals were plentiful and national leaders themselves acted as political entrepreneurs, initiating negotiations, mediating compromises, and mobilizing domestic support. Outcomes reflected above all the convergence of national interests rather than the goals of supranational actors. Successful bilateral and multilateral initiatives predated EC bargains. The few cases where governments, notably Britain, accepted policies they did not favor involved an explicit, credible threat of exclusion. Nonetheless, it might be argued that supranational actors had a slightly larger influence on outcomes than in other grand bargains we have examined. Governments had targeted internal market reform and QMV as areas ripe for reform, and numerous proposals had been advanced for internal market liberalization, but no government had outlined a package of reforms like the White Paper. Supranational entrepreneurship speeded reform, whose main outlines were firmly set by enduring national interests.

Support for reform grew steadily during the early 1980s, but a backlog of seemingly intractable issues blocked its consideration. The critical element was Mitterrand's new activism, which permitted repeated Franco-German threats to exclude Britain—first in a revival of QMV on CAP issues, then on budgetary matters, finally on the decision to call an IGC. The first steps toward reform involved renegotiation of the EC budget and the structure of CAP financing to satisfy Britain. Resolution of these issues was so decisive that it was a de facto

François Mitterrand takes Margaret Thatcher for a ride.

precondition for launching other reforms, including the SEA. France, Germany, and the Benelux countries first turned to QMV and the threat of exclusion to secure Thatcher's agreement.

From Rebate to Relance: "Stand up and be counted"

From the start, Germany was willing to contemplate reform. A clear signal of German intent was sent by the Genscher-Columbo initiative of 1981—a Council resolution proposed by the German foreign minister, later joined by his Italian counterpart and backed by the Commission, calling for greater movement toward European unity. The Genscher-Columbo initiative focused on foreign policy-making but also included proposals for internal market reform. The two foreign ministers justified the initiative by reference to economic recession and institutional malaise in the EC. To address the completion of the internal market, discussed in the Council almost continuously since the completion of the Common Market in 1968, the Council set up an ad hoc group to draft a report to the Stuttgart summit in June 1983.[84]

Yet the "Solemn Declaration on European Union" issued at Stuttgart by chief

---

[84] Based on declarations of this sort, David Cameron rightly argues that the roots of the Single Act can be traced back to the 1970s, yet before 1983 no internal market and decision-making initiative was considered seriously by the three major governments. Cameron, "The 1992 Initiative: Causes and Consequences," in Alberta Sbragia, ed., *Europolitics: Institutions and Policymaking in the "New" European Community* (Washington, D.C., 1992), 23–74.

executives on the basis of the report remained vague, with symbolic clauses to satisfy each government but none mandating anything of substance. The Declaration reaffirmed the desire to reinforce both economic and security cooperation and called for the completion of the internal market alongside coordinated reflation, social programs, reinforcement of the monetary system, and a European industrial policy. A general consensus recognized that internal market liberalization was the most promising, but no concrete steps were taken. It was also agreed that if EC institutions were to be strengthened, the next step must be to restore QMV and restrict use of the veto under the Luxembourg Compromise. Yet substantial opposition precluded anything more than the suggestion that member states voluntarily abstain rather than veto. Even this informal proposal elicited from France, Britain, Denmark, Ireland, and Greece immediate *procès-verbaux* reaffirming the Luxembourg Compromise. Shortly thereafter, Prime Minister Pierre Mauroy publicly attacked the Stuttgart Declaration and reasserted the veto right.[85]

The only concrete outcome of the Stuttgart summit was, therefore, agreement that the EC could not move forward until it resolving three related problems— the British rebate, the need to increase EC funds, and the entry of Spain and Portugal—and a proposal by Genscher to resolve them as a package was approved. The British budgetary contribution had been a constant concern since Britain's accession in 1973. At the time, as we saw in chapters 3 and 4, Britain was forced to accept the *acquis communautaire*, although the CAP was particularly disadvantageous to it. The result was a large net budgetary deficit, almost as large as that of Germany, to the benefit of farmers in the Netherlands, France, Italy, and even Germany itself. Attempts to offset this net deficit through regional policy side-payments, as demanded by Edward Heath in the early 1970s, or by adjusting British payments to the EC downward, as demanded by Harold Wilson and James Callaghan, had only a marginal long-term effect. Unanimous approval of the nine member governments was difficult to secure, and the result was a persistent British liability.

Immediately on entering office, Margaret Thatcher sought a permanent rebate and, if possible, limits on CAP spending. She spoke bluntly of getting "my money back." To achieve this end, however, she required bargaining leverage. Between 1979 and 1984 she was repeatedly persuaded by Cabinet colleagues and backbenchers that an attempt to withhold funds would generate an immediate and undoubtedly successful legal challenge as well as EC retaliation. So, at her first European Council meeting, she linked the deficit to CAP price decisions, over which Britain wielded a de facto veto. One year later, Britain gained a generous three-year proposal rebating more than two-thirds of its net contribution. The other member governments, however, rejected Commission proposals for a permanent solution through limits on agricultural subsidies and an increase in regional policy benefits to Britain—yet another futile attempt to achieve the Commission's original vision of a liberal, lower-cost CAP.[86]

---

[85] Robin, *La diplomatie*, 219; De Ruyt, *L'acte*, 35, 315–324.

[86] Margaret Thatcher, *The Downing Street Years* (New York, 1993), 60–65; Ludlow, *Beyond*, x–xi; Geoffrey Howe, "The Future of the European Community: Britain's Approach to the Negotiations,"

When the three years were nearly up, Thatcher sought to employ the same tactic to achieve another multiyear bargain. But the others had had enough. In mid-May 1982 the Belgians, then holding the presidency of the Council, responded by proposing to pass the new agricultural prices by QMV—an unprecedented but (strictly speaking) legal step accepted by six governments over British, Danish, and Greek opposition. British efforts to invoke the Luxembourg Compromise were rejected, for the linkage was not deemed a "vital interest." Pressure on Britain was heightened by an explicit threat to institutionalize a "two-track" Europe and create a "special status" for Britain. A one-year bargain, relatively unfavorable to Britain, was the result. The following year, 1983, an even smaller British rebate was offered. Thatcher's efforts to force a permanent solution to the budgetary imbalance seemed stalled.[87]

After 1983, however, the negotiating situation shifted in favor of Britain and against France, because of the latter's need for increased CAP funding. First, the 1 percent VAT ceiling was no longer sufficient to fund agricultural commitments; in October 1983 CAP payments were delayed for lack of funds. The need to raise the VAT percentage simply to maintain the status quo gave Britain a de facto veto without invoking the Luxembourg Compromise. Thatcher promised to block any funding increases until the budget issue was resolved. Second, Germany threatened to veto VAT increases until accession negotiations with Spain and Portugal, long blocked by France, were concluded. Germany imposed 1985 as a deadline. As Mitterrand stated in internal discussions, with Iberian accession France would cease to be a large net CAP beneficiary; limitations on CAP spending were now in its long-term interest.[88]

With the EC fiscal situation growing more perilous and French interests shifting, Mitterrand opted for a *fuite en avant*. His intention, clearly stated in confidential discussions by the end of 1983, was to exploit the French presidency to achieve a high-profile breakthrough on enlargement, agriculture, and the budget.[89] Mitterrand's extraordinary personal involvement in the six-month presidency prompted one French observer to call him a "one-man orchestra." He began the year with a personal tour of all the European capitals to seek a basis on which to relaunch the EC, followed by "shuttle diplomacy" between Paris, Bonn, and London. He announced that he would complete the enlargement negotiations by September 1984 and called for a conference to "preserve Europe." His speeches, most notably in May before the European Parliament, underscored

---

International Affairs 60 (Spring 1984), 188–189; Lord Gilmour, "The Thatcher Memoirs," *Twentieth Century British History* 5 (1994), 266.

[87] Robin, *La diplomatie,* 215. The linkage to the Falklands crisis may have played a minor role, but the broadly accepted view is that the British were isolated and extended the definition of "vital interest" beyond what was acceptable. This argument is supported by two facts: the move to QMV was a long-term trend in the EC between 1980 and 1985, and Thatcher was unable to achieve a significantly better bargain in the preceding years; things changed only in 1983 when new funding had to be voted by unanimity.

[88] Robin, *La diplomatie,* 215. The Mitterrand government had reversed its opposition to budgetary increases after the pro-European turn and announced that it would complete the enlargement negotiations by September 1984.

[89] Favier and Martin-Roland, *Le décennie,* 2:198–202.

the economic nature of the current crisis and elaborated a vision of the future EC as an instrument to combat the economic decline of Europe. "Europe," he warned, "is beginning to look like an abandoned building site." He proposed political cooperation, technological programs, and CAP reform. Two constant refrains were decision-making and internal market reform.[90]

From early on, the core of Mitterrand's strategy had been to isolate the British and threaten to move ahead without them if they did not compromise. These tactics were repeatedly discussed by top officials in France and Germany; threats were made, deliberately and consistently. This tactic was first used to moderate Thatcher's demands for a rebate. Mitterrand and Kohl repeatedly threatened to move toward a two-tier Europe ("Europe à deux vitesses"), whereby those willing to move ahead with European integration would conclude their own agreements and leave dissenters behind. Mitterrand called for a conference to discuss relaunching the Community among those member states who would "stand up and be counted." In his May 1984 speech to the European Parliament, he picked up the thread again, speaking frankly about the need for a Europe "à geométrie variable." Dumas announced that if budget agreement were not reached, his government would call a meeting without the British to discuss various proposals for reform; he boldly raised the possibility of a two-track Europe during Thatcher's visit to the Elysée. For his part, Kohl announced shortly thereafter that the "decisive conditions had been created" to move toward completion of the European market and majority voting in the Council. He called for movement toward greater European unity within a year, whether or not all countries agreed.[91]

The threat of exclusion was not a bluff. Mitterrand's position paper for the Fontainebleau summit, prepared by Jacques Attali, foresaw two possibilities: if agreement was reached on the budget, Spanish and Portuguese accession and the relance would be discussed; if no agreement was reached, discussions would begin on how those, excluding Britain, who were willing to adopt a positive attitude might move ahead. The Franco-German threat was deliberately leaked to raise doubts among the British negotiators. The British press picked up the theme, and a House of Commons report called for a more conciliatory negotiating position.[92]

Within a year, the agricultural and budgetary issues had been resolved, because of the British linkage and the new French willingness to compromise. Thatcher, backed by the Netherlands, sought a formal agreement binding governments to limit future increases in CAP spending; Germany sought the same goal as a gentlemen's agreement. The French government put its farmers on notice that, as Agriculture Minister Michel Rocard stated, the revitalization of agri-

---

[90] "Speech of François Mitterrand before the Netherlands Government (7 February 1984)," released by the French Embassy in London, CTL/DISCOM/29/84.

[91] Interview with Kanzleramt official, 1991; Corbett, "1985," 268–269; Françoise de la Serre, *La Grande-Bretagne et la Communauté européenne* (Paris, 1987), 193–194, 207–209; Favier and Martin-Roland, *Le décennie*, 2:198–202; Paul Taylor, "New."

[92] Kohl speech in Gasso, ed. *Towards*, 98; Favier and Martin-Roland, *Le décennie*, 2:200–202; House of Commons, *Third Report from the Foreign Affairs Committee* (Session 1983–1984), "The Forthcoming Fontainebleau Summit" (London, April 1984), xxi–xxx; *Le Monde*, 18 March and 5 May 1984.

cultural policy could no longer serve as the instrument of European unification. Under Rocard's direction, a modest compromise was reached in March 1984. Rocard also proposed limits on dairy subsidies and, with Mitterrand's backing, employed QMV to get them through. France agreed for the first time that the British net contribution should be cut permanently to reflect Britain's lower per capita income but kept up the pressure by blocking the 1983 British rebate totaling £457 million. Britain and Germany overrode the vociferous protests of Commission President Gaston Thorn and rejected Commission efforts to create "budgetary peace" by raising the VAT to 2 percent and to authorize future increases in spending without domestic parliamentary ratification.[93]

At the Brussels summit in March 1984, the heads of government agreed to agricultural spending in a way that would keep any growth in British contribution roughly in line with its percentage of Community GDP. Yet the budget rebate for 1984 and following years remained unsettled, with the others offering ECU 1 billion and Thatcher demanding ECU 1.5 billion. After 36 hours of negotiation at Fontainebleau in May 1984 and an explicit, credible threat to exclude the British from future decisions, a compromise was finally reached on a permanent annual rebate totaling two-thirds of its annual net contribution. The French assumed a disproportionate portion of the necessary financing, since Kohl insisted that the German contribution be strictly limited. Moreover, the Council agreed to generalize the principle of *juste retour*: no member state should be required to sustain a "budgetary burden which is excessive in relation to its relative prosperity." An effort was made to phase out MCAs, in exchange for which German farmers received massive compensation (5 percent) of VAT payments through 1988, and the German government was granted authority to provide additional subsidies.

With the CAP issue and accession out of the way, Fontainebleau marked the moment when momentum began to gather toward a package deal of internal market and decision-making reform. The heads of government called for internal liberalization, coordinated stimulation, and collaborative research designed to give the Community "an economic impulse comparable to that given by the Common Market in the 1960s." They further agreed that customs controls would eventually be abolished.[94]

These decisions at Fontainebleau reflected a consensus among member states; even staunch defenders of the Commission concede that the package had little to do with Commission entrepreneurship.[95] Though some call these declarations meaningless, the simultaneous actions of governments indicate the seriousness of internal market efforts. Mitterrand sought immediate agreement on expanding QMV and obliging governments to justify vetoes; yet he had to settle for the creation of two ad hoc committees—a back-up position agreed in advance between Italy, the Netherlands, Germany, and France. The first, the Ad

[93] De Ruyt, *L'acte*, 47–49; Press Conference with Mitterrand, 2 April 1984; Robin, *La diplomatie*, 69–81, 133–145, 211–229, especially 145, 212; Favier and Martin-Roland, *Le décennie*, 2:210; John Newhouse, "One against Nine," *New Yorker*, 22 October 1984, 74–78, 89.

[94] De Ruyt, *L'acte*, 261.

[95] David Williamson, "The Package: Making a Success of the Single Act," *Common Market Law Review* 25:3 (1988), 486.

Hoc Committee on a People's Europe (later the Adonnino Committee), was to investigate those aspects of the Community directly visible to the common citizen: customs formalities for individuals, equivalence of university diplomas, the creation of European symbols, European volunteer programs. The second and far more significant committee, the Ad Hoc Committee for Institutional Affairs (later the Dooge Committee, after its Irish chairman), had a mandate to consider institutional, political, and economic reform. It was at this point also, as we have seen, that Mitterrand and Kohl demonstrated their commitment to internal market reform by entering ad hoc parallel negotiations that would soon lead to the Schengen Agreement, eliminating border formalities among European countries.

Origins of the Single Market Initiative: A "dull and boring" Proposal?

Why a single market initiative? Why, in particular, the White Paper? Between 1980 and 1984 the elimination of NTBs rose on the EC agenda, not least due to pressure from the Commission and Parliament. In explaining the proposal for internal market liberalization, claims have been made for the decisive importance of supranational entrepreneurs, including the Court, the Parliament, the Commission, and various national governments as well as transnational business.

Much attention has been paid to the Court's 1979 *Cassis de Dijon* decision, which promulgated the principle of "mutual recognition." The conventional argument is not that the ECJ had a direct effect on opening markets—such an effect would have required decades—but that it inspired the Commission to generalize the principle into a program for minimal regulatory harmonization under Article 100. This argument rests on the conjecture that cooperation had been hamstrung by the absence of some random "focal point" around which states could coordinate.[96]

Yet the evidence does not confirm the view that *Cassis*, though later exploited by the Commission, was a "necessary" condition for the SEA, or that it provided a "focal point," nor even that any such coordination problem existed. Proposals for more aggressive regulatory liberalization in services, for example, were blocked not for lack of an appropriate institutional solution but because of resistance to pressure from countries with less competitive providers to demands by the two major service exporters, Britain and the Netherlands.[97] *Cassis*, moreover, was not the first ECJ decision establishing a principle of overruling national regulations to permit EC trade, nor the most extreme, nor the most ambitious. Indeed, it represented something of a *retreat* from previous ECJ jurisprudence. Mutual recognition was not a new innovation for the Commission but a long-recognized procedure, employed in EFTA and parts of the Treaty of Rome. Discussions of employing mutual recognition date back to 1967 and in 1973, over a decade before the SEA, when Commissioner Ralf Dahrendorf (with

---

[96] Garrett and Weingast, "Ideas"; Lawrence Gomley, *Prohibiting Restrictions on Trade within the EC* (Dordrecht, 1985), 267; Daniel Wincott, "Institutional Interaction and European Integration: Towards an Everyday Critique of Liberal Intergovernmentalism," *Journal of Common Market Studies* 33 (December 1995), 597–610.

[97] Nicolaïdis, *Mutual*, 189–194. See also fn. 140 of this chapter.

strong support from the British government) set forth a program for regulatory harmonization based on a new model of mutual recognition. The Commission had moved aggressively but unsuccessfully on this basis in the area of professional services—suggesting both that the mutual recognition was not new in 1985 and that its use was not sufficient to generate cooperation. Finally, mutual recognition was a modest part of the White Paper and SEA agenda; many regulations still needed to be harmonized. For all these reasons, Cockfield himself does not even consider mutual recognition to be a fundamental innovation of the single market initiative, pointing instead to the "reference to standards" procedure and the extension of mutual recognition to services.[98]

The evidence much more strongly supports the view that the level of member state demand, not the supply of particular institutions—mutual recognition, the reference to standards procedure, and majority voting, for example—explains the timing and motivations for cooperation. The move to mutual recognition reflected the realization that if member governments, inspired by economic policy failure and big business pressure, were serious about liberalizing the internal European market, mutual recognition was the only remaining institutional procedure with a chance of succeeding. There was a limited range of institutional alternatives. By the early 1980s it was clear that a *laissez faire* system of "national treatment" simply condoned rising NTBs. Twenty years of negotiations over "harmonization" had proven ineffectual. Only mutual recognition remained. Carefully documented studies of the link between ECJ jurisprudence, Commission entrepreneurship, and the SEA conclude therefore only that *Cassis* may have at most *accelerated* the single market program, not that it was a necessary condition; the willingness of governments to accept more radical liberalization was the critical factor.[99] Comparison with the other major policy technology introduced by the "new approach" of 1985, namely the "reference to standards" procedure, is equally instructive. It had been introduced in the Low Voltage Directive of 1973, yet its existence did not lead to more directives of its kind for a decade and a half.

[98] Lord Arthur Cockfield, "The Real Significance of 1992," in Colin Crouch and David Marquand, eds., *The Politics of 1992: Beyond the European Single Market* (Oxford, 1992), 7; Nicolaïdis, *Mutual*, 151–154, 247–261, 280; Jacques Pelkmans and Ad Vollebergh, "The Traditional Approach to Technical Harmonization: Accomplishment and Deficiencies," in Jacques Pelkmans and Marc Vankeheulen, eds., *Coming to Grips with the Internal Market* (Maastricht, 1986), 9–30; interview with a Campo; all point out that there were other areas, such as testing, in which the Commission long proposed mutual recognition. The idea was not new but was not considered viable, due to opposition from member governments. A number of different legal forms had been attempted, including one, "minimal harmonization," in which minimal standards would be reached—an even *less* stringent variant of the combination of harmonization and mutual recognition employed in the SEA. *Cassis* appears to have shifted the focal point of scholars more than the focal point of practitioners.

[99] For refutation of the claim that *Cassis* was decisive, Nicolaïdis, *Mutual*, 195–287. Nicolaïdis also rejects the view that member states were forced to act in order to keep control of a process, which cannot explain the success of service deregulation although the Court had limited the scope of mutual recognition in services. See also Karen J. Alter and Sophie Meunier-Aitsahalia, "Judicial Politics in the European Community: European Integration and the Pathbreaking *Cassis de Dijon* Decision," *Comparative Political Studies* 26 (January 1993), 555; Claus-Dieter Ehlermann, "The 1992 Project: Stages, Structures, Results and Prospects," *Michigan Journal of International Law* 11 (Summer 1990), 1102.

Others argue that the decisive sources of the single market initiative lie in the lobbying of multinational business groups. According to Dr. Wisse Dekker, CEO of Philips and an activist in this period, European integration in the 1950s was initiated by politicians, whereas in the 1980s it entered a new, "industrial" phase, led by business leaders. This, it is argued, was part of a deeper trend whereby larger, multinational and export-oriented firms were establishing independence from national organizations dominated by smaller, national, and often more protectionist firms.[100]

Most who stress the role of multinational business point to the exclusive and influential European Roundtable of Industrialists, founded in 1983 by Pehr Gyllenhammer, CEO of Volvo, which brought together the heads of a small number of Europe's largest multinationals and which pressed for internal market liberalization from 1985 onward. Davignon may have had an indirect influence on the formation of this group. In 1981 he brought together large European information technology firms (the "Thorn-Davignon Commission") to develop proposals for technology programs and European technical norms, after which they reportedly discussed market liberalization. Davignon reportedly suggested formation of a private group. Yet the ERT did not originate single market proposals. Indeed, it initially opposed them, relegating reductions in border formalities and greater standardization to secondary status. The ERT agenda supported instead an expansion of the industrial policy proposals advocated by Davignon and the French government, with which the ERT maintained close relations. The ERT's first memo to the Commission in June 1983 focused on open public procurement, R&D tax credits, elimination of fiscal and legal impediments to mergers and subsidiaries, greater cross-border flows of people and information, reform of the regional and social policy, monetary cooperation, and industrial standardization—all reflected in the French memorandum of September 1983 calling for an EC industrial policy. The ERT paid greatest attention to the establishment of large European venture capital projects, including networks of mobile communications, electronic banking, and a high-speed rail, each of which would be "godfathered" by one of its corporate members. Its first detailed proposals, advanced in December 1984 and October 1985, concerned a trans-European infrastructure network (the key element of which was later abandoned in favor of the Chunnel) and creation of a European technology institute of interest to pharmaceutical companies.[101]

Given their focus on these transnational "grands projets," ERT leaders were slow to embrace the White Paper, initially proclaiming it a "dull and boring" document, in which "no one was interested." They sought instead to persuade the Commission to pare it down to a small number of proposals and to focus on

---

[100] Wisse Dekker, "Europe's Economic Power—Potential and Perspectives," speech at the Swiss Institute for International Studies (Geneva, 25 October 1988). Indispensable is Cowles, *Politics*, especially 163ff.

[101] Cowles, *Politics*, 218–224, 232. Cowles argues that multinational firms favored a "European" social democratic model of society. Certainly business, for example in the ERT, supported an agenda of industrial policy and public-sector spending, and came to support regulatory harmonization, service liberalization, and elimination of customs formalities only after initial skepticism and opposition.

their preferred agenda. Only in December 1984 did ERT representatives sit down for the first time with the Monnet Committee. By June 1985, when the ERT finally adopted the report on the internal marked drafted by Wisse Dekker, chairman of Philips, and hand-delivering copies to Attali and Mitterrand, the member states had already opted for the program and Delors was conducting informal discussions with individual firms. From December 1986 on, however, the ERT did run a "watchdog" committee to press for implementation.[102]

Another oft-cited business influence on the White Paper agenda was a series of speeches delivered in the autumn of 1984 and early 1985 by Dekker, also a participant in Davignon's Committee and a founding member of the Round-table. Dekker proposed a plan he called "Europa 1990."[103] Many details of Europa 1990—its focus on internal market liberalization, division of tasks into categories (reform of fiscal, commercial, technical, and government procurement policies), ideology of economies of scale, recognition of the link between commercial liberalization and tax harmonization, and identification of the ultimate goal with a particular date—resembled Delors's proposal before the European Parliament a few months later, as well as the White Paper of June 1985. Yet the originality of Dekker's proposal should not be exaggerated. Dekker only presented his proposals in late 1984, around the same time that member governments told Delors that internal market policy was the only area in which they were prepared to move. Dekker was in close contact with officials from the Council, Commission, and Parliament, and he followed the detailed proposals for the simplification of customs formalities and standardization they had developed over the past three years, though he added proposals for electronic border formalities and fiscal harmonization.[104]

Other groups of MNCs were no more innovative. The Union of Industrial and Employers' Confederation of Europe (UNICE), the leading EC industrial interest group representing national peak organizations, called for more majority voting in February 1984 but did not develop internal market proposals, though it would subsequently support them. A similar, though more informal, group was founded at the same time by André Bénard, a managing director of Royal Dutch Shell, but advanced no proposals. On balance, the most that can be said for European multinationals is that they offered vocal support in 1985–86 once others had developed proposals for internal market liberalization. They raised the salience of the program and backed it with threats of disinvestment. In each case, business groups, while providing essential support, reacted to initiatives from the Commission and the Parliament, as well as member governments.[105]

---

[102] Cowles, *Politics*, 244–245, also 174–180, 211ff, 232; Sandholtz and Zysman, "1992," 117; Wolfgang Streeck and Philippe C. Schmitter, "From National Corporation to Transnational Pluralism: Organized Interests in the Single European Market," *Politics and Society* 19 (June 1991), 133–165. Middlemas, *Organising*, 716n; Cowles, *Politics*, 234–238, 214–249; interview with a Campo.

[103] "Europe 1990: An Agenda for Action" (Eindhoven, 13 November 1984). The four aspects of the Dekker plan were administrative simplification of border formalities, harmonization of indirect taxation, standardization of technical norms, and liberalization of government procurement.

[104] Interviews with Émile a Campo and Fernand Braun.

[105] Sandholtz and Zysman, "1992," 108, 116–120; Axel Krauss, "Many Groups Lobby on Implementation of Market Plan," *Europe Magazine*, July/August 1988, 24–25; Ludlow, *Beyond*, 27–30;

A more important source of proposals than either the Court or the multinationals was the European Parliament. Since 1980 parliamentarians had issued resolutions and reports supporting two programs—one "maximalist," one "minimalist." The maximalists, including many Italians and quite a number of Germans, were European federalists. They advocated broad expansion in the scope of Community activities, backed by procedural reforms, focusing particularly on increased power for the Parliament.[106] Following a Europarliamentary penchant for animal names, these activists called themselves the "Crocodile group," after the Strasbourg restaurant where they first met. Led by the venerable Altiero Spinelli, a founding father of the Community, their efforts culminated in the European Parliament resolution of February 1984 proposing a "Draft Treaty Establishing the European Union"—a new, more ambitious document to replace the Treaty of Rome.

The minimalists turned out to be more influential. Skeptical of federalism and parliamentary reform, they preferred working with national leaders to liberalize the internal market. Founded late in 1981 the "Kangaroo Group" (named for the Australian marsupial's ability to hop over borders) was funded by a group of sympathetic (largely British and Dutch) business interests, and counted Basil de Ferranti, a leading British industrialist and Tory parliamentarian, among its leaders. French proponents of market liberalization thought the name too silly to attract influential support and founded their own group.[107] The Kangaroos encouraged parliamentary studies on economic topics and in 1983 launched a public campaign in favor of a detailed EC timetable for abolishing administrative, technical, and fiscal barriers, reference to which was included in the Draft Treaty. An August 1983 Parliament report (the Albert-Ball Report) stressed for the first time the "costs of non-Europe."[108]

The Kangaroo Group increased the salience of internal market issues among British businessmen and is said to have influenced Thatcher government proposals for market liberalization in 1982 and 1983. Along with Commission and Council officials, it made contact in early 1984 with the Brussels representative of Philips, who helped develop Dekker's "Europa 1990" initiative.[109] Beyond this, however, there is little evidence that the Kangaroos significantly increased sup-

---

Calingaert, *1992*, 8; Wallace, "Making," 7. Interviews with a Campo, Braun, and von Moltke; Cowles, *Politics*, 174–180, 211ff.

[106] For strong claims, Marina Gazzo, "Introduction," in Gazzo, *Towards*, 7–10. Direct elections to the European Parliament in 1979 are said to have endowed the body with democratic legitimacy and given European federalists new impetus.

[107] Various issues of the publication of the Kangaroo Group, *Kangaroo News*, on file in office of the Kangaroo Group, London; interview with administrator of the Kangaroo Group, 1989.

[108] Michel Albert and James Ball, *Toward European Recovery in the 1980s: Report to the European Parliament*, Washington Papers, no. 109 (New York, 1984).

[109] Basil de Ferranti, who created the Kangaroo Group, had worked on the CBI Europe Committee in the 1970s, communicated with British and Dutch business in 1981–83, and worked with Council officials to form the groups. At a spring 1984 meeting with a Philips representative, an Action Committee member, parliamentarians and Council officials suggested a program, including a precise timetable with precise planks, which came to Dekker, who then named a task force and came up with "Europe 1990" by Autumn 1984. The program was presented in January 1985 in coordination with Delors. Interview with Wisse Dekker; a Campo, 1991.

port for internal market reform. In Britain the CBI, we have seen, was already pressing for internal market reform starting in 1977; Dutch business had traditionally been favorable. Nor did the Kangaroos develop specific proposals or play a prominent role in public debates; throughout this period the maximalists in Parliament garnered far more publicity.

Most influential of all nongovernmental entrepreneurs was the Commission itself. The Commission's decision to move toward the single market proposal reflected the failure of prior efforts to develop an EC industrial policy, promoted by the Commission and supported by France and Italy. During the 1970s Commissioner Altiero Spinelli favored a broad initiative, Commissioner Ralf Dahrendorf sought a more modest one, and various committees suggested alternatives. Yet all such proposals met with British and German opposition. Of numerous industry-led efforts only Airbus succeeded. Etienne Davignon, internal market commissioner from 1976 through 1984, did finally manage to establish a program for international research consortia called ESPRIT, which emerged in 1982 as a pilot program and was expanded in 1984. ESPRIT did not seek to establish a centralized EC industrial policy, but simply coordinated national programs under a strict *juste retour* arrangement, whereby each government received from each project precisely the funding it put in. Such an arrangement was the maximum Britain and Germany would accept.[110] Yet even ESPRIT remained relatively minor and did not become the core of the single market initiative. Any influence Davignon might have had on the SEA remained indirect, through his efforts to mobilize European transnational business groups.

During the 1970s internal market liberalization had also been an important if secondary concern of Commission and Council secretariat officials. With the completion of the Common Market, the Commission had proposed comprehensive programs to harmonize regulatory barriers to trade under Article 100 of the Treaty. In 1968 the Commission tabled a program of 281 proposals with a proposed deadline of eighteen months for completion. Yet harmonization proceeded slowly. Four years later another deadline, 1977, was set. By 1986, nearly twenty years later, several hundred directives had been passed, but most were modest and required an excruciatingly long time to negotiate. By the late 1970s NTBs were coming into force faster than the EC was negotiating them away. Overall, moreover, the issue of regulatory harmonization, a highly technical matter influencing a fragmented set of domestic bureaucratic interests, remained obscure.[111]

From 1980 to 1984 Commission officials, led by Commissioner for Industry Karl-Heinz Narjes, developed a comprehensive plan to overcome NTBs. Starting with the harmonization agenda of 1968, Narjes added the reduction of customs

---

[110] Wayne Sandholtz, *Hi-Tech Europe: The Politics of International Cooperation* (Berkeley, 1992), 95–97, 159, 170–171, 305. Sandholtz concludes from the study of ESPRIT that *juste retour* is a "necessary" condition for cooperation, but in this regard ESPRIT was exceptional, in large part because some governments were not strongly committed to the program. At about this time, the French foreign minister defended the *acquis communautaire* in agriculture, for example, by arguing that "*juste retour* is not an EC idea."

[111] Nicolaïdis, *Mutual,* 137–141; interview with a Campo.

formalities and a plan for deregulation of services and transport, the latter endorsed by the European Council in December 1982. The next year, with strong personal support from Kohl, Narjes and Council officials secured agreement on a special Council of Ministers for internal market matters. This was critical, for NTB issues tend to be highly technical and were discussed in the general Council of Ministers. Ministers tended to be bored and had little incentive to overrule business and bureaucratic opposition to obscure proposals; a Council official with decades of experience recalls never seeing a minister attend Council discussions of harmonization issues before 1984.[112]

Later that year, Narjes gained approval of a directive calling for a "standstill clause" requiring prior notification of any new standards. He discussed future plans with business groups and just before leaving office in December 1984 released a comprehensive document summarizing the necessary proposals. By the time Delors and Cockfield entered office in January 1985, many of the early steps toward liberalization had been taken. Cockfield's White Paper of June 1985, detailing almost 300 proposals for internal market liberalization, was comprised almost entirely of materials in the files of top Commission officials. Indeed, at the time Cockfield assembled them, one-third of the proposals were already under consideration.[113]

The most effective steps to eliminate administrative and regulatory barriers to trade during this period, however, were taken not by supranational officials or transnational interest groups but by national governments themselves. In early 1984 the British government set forth an agenda for the removal of "all" EC trade barriers. The French government, concerned that German standards were blocking imports, and the German government, concerned that France would close its borders because of balance of payments difficulties, successfully pressed for a bilateral Franco-German arrangement to simplify and eventually eliminate border formalities—a step that would force a measure of de facto mutual recognition. In Saarbrücken shortly after the Fontainebleau summit of May 1984, Kohl and Mitterrand agreed to negotiate the abolition of all controls on normal goods traffic, harmonization of domestic veterinary and sanitary legislation, free movement of people, and common streamlined administrative procedures—an accord codified in the Treaty of Moselle. Another agreement was signed in July. The German government also agreed to bilateral negotiations and to recognize French standards where possible. Meanwhile discussions continued on food products, though implementation on the German side was, as we have seen, disappointing. Belgium, the Netherlands, and Luxembourg, which had long since

---

[112] Interviews with a Campo, von Moltke; interview with Karl-Heinz Narjes, 1992. Heinrich von Moltke, "Binnenmarktpolitik," in Weidenfeld and Wessels, *Jahrbuch 1982*, 149–153, and "Binnenmarktpolitik," in *Jahrbuch 1983*, 141–53. Karl Kaiser et al., *The European Community: Progress or Decline?* (London, 1983), 14–15, 45–47. This policy document, drafted by the heads of leading national research institutions, demonstrates the range of the consensus at the time that "the single most important action the Community can take in response to rising unemployment and falling GDP" is to endorse the plan for unity of the internal market, including deregulation of services and transport— backed by majority voting. Even during the period of Europessimism, contemporary observers noted the increase in momentum in internal market matters.

[113] Interview with Braun; a Campo; Cockfield, *European*, 29, 42; von Moltke, "Binnenmarktpolitik" (1994).

eliminated border controls, argued that their arrangement should be generalized; Kohl and Mitterrand called for eventual accession to the Benelux customs union. The idea was to create a "super EEC," promoting trade liberalization while renewing the threat of a two-tier Europe. By December 1984, before Delors entered office, a tentative accord had been reached that would soon result in the Schengen Agreement eliminating customs checks.[114]

British Exclusion and the Call for an Intergovernmental Conference: "A test of truth"

We have just seen that the SEA emerged from a confluence of the desire for institutional changes in the EC in general, as demonstrated in the Genscher-Columbo initiative, and the substantive agenda of single market reform. In the preparations for Fontainebleau, national leaders were thinking ahead to just such a package. As Geoffrey Howe declared at the time: "The negotiation launched at Stuttgart and continued at Athens in December 1983 is not just about the budget and the CAP. It is about the whole future shape and direction of Europe." Mitterrand and Kohl proposed QMV, the removal of frontier controls, and internal market liberalization; Thatcher exhibited a newly positive spirit, circulating a paper entitled "Europe: the Future" outlining the British government's vision for Europe. At the head of her list of priorities was liberalization of the internal market, particularly in services, and cooperation on foreign policy. Foreign Minister Howe proposed the removal of "all—and I mean all, economic barriers," suggesting 1990 as a deadline. "Europe: the Future" also called for informal QMV where the Treaty provided for it. On the Luxembourg Compromise, nations should be able to veto "where a very important national interest is at stake" but "should be required . . . to set out their reasons fully" before the European Council.[115]

Kohl and Mitterrand grasped the initiative and backed their demands for formal treaty amendments with renewed threats to create a "two-track" Europe. They sought to construct expert committees along the lines of the Spaak Committee of 1955–56 that had led to the Treaty of Rome; indeed, it was often informally termed "Spaak II." The leaders aimed to give the committee a high profile by naming Karl Carstens as its head, but through a diplomatic misstep the Irish prime minister named his compatriot James Dooge instead. Mitterrand signaled grand ambitions by appointing Maurice Faure, the French lead negotiator for the Treaty of Rome negotiations, as his personal representative. Faure arrived at the second meeting of the committee with a proposed draft report approved by Mitterrand himself (over the objections of the Quai d'Orsay), which

---

[114] Heinrich von Moltke, "Binnenmarktpolitik," in Weidenfeld and Wessels, *Jahrbuch 1984*, 143–154; Pearce, Sutton, and Bachelor, *Protection*, 6, 14, 47–49, 66, 140–141; Helen Wallace and William Wallace, *Flying Together in a Larger and More European Union* (The Hague, 1995), 71; Geoffrey Howe, "Grossbritannien und die Bundesrepublik Deutschland als europäische Partner," *Europa-Archiv* 39 (10 November 1984), 637.

[115] Howe, "Future," 190; "Europe: The Future—United Kingdom Memorandum (June 1984)," in Gazzo, *Towards*, 86–95.

became the working text. He was made rapporteur and immediately convinced the committee to act by majority vote, further isolating the British and other skeptics.[116]

The committee viewed procedural reform as its "real task" but was unable to agree on the two decisive issues: QMV and veto rights. The British delegation arrived expecting to find themselves located comfortably in the center of the spectrum, alongside France and perhaps Germany. France, however, joined Germany in calling for an "intergovernmental conference" (IGC) to negotiate formal treaty changes establishing QMV on internal market issues—a position backed by all except Britain, Greece, and Denmark, which supported only reiteration of the voluntary, informal steps to encourage majority voting already acknowledged in the Stuttgart Declaration. The Dooge Committee agreed to disagree, with the position of the seven recorded in the text of its report and the dissent of the three in the footnotes. On substantive matters, however, the British fared better. The report contained many originally British proposals, such as common EC standards, liberalization of transport and insurance services, and open public procurement. By late 1984 the momentum toward internal market reform was clear to inside observers.[117]

As the Dooge Committee deliberated, it came time to name a new European Commission and its new president. France and Germany, seeking to expedite the *relance* by giving the position political prestige, pressed for a president from a large country. Domestic coalitional politics appears to have prevented Germany, whose informal turn it was, from nominating a candidate. Etienne Davignon, the self-nominated front-runner, lacked national political experience and was considered by some insufficiently inspiring, though he was apparently one of Thatcher's first choices. Claude Cheysson, proposed by Mitterrand, was rejected by both Kohl and Thatcher as too intemperate. Delors, freed from the post of minister of finance just in time by a reshuffle in France, was nominated at the last minute. Delors's stature as a politician with senior ministerial experience, his years as a member of the EC Economic and Social Committee, and his reputation for sensible economic policy-making led Germany and Britain to signal immediate approval. Thatcher nonetheless took the sensible precaution of naming Lord Cockfield—selected for his Cabinet-level experience and, Howe later remarked, his "single-mindedness in our cause"—as a liberal, free-trade counterweight. On 17 July 1984 Delors accepted the post.[118]

When Delors assumed the presidency, internal market reform was not foremost in his mind. His own preferences were not unlike those pursued by the French government: he favored a European social policy (his first major initiative

---

[116] "Conclusions of the European Council at its Meeting in Fontainebleau" (26 June 1984), reprinted in Gazzo, *Towards*, 96–97; Haywood, "French," 137–138; Favier and Martin-Roland, *Le décennie*, 2:211–212.

[117] Haywood, "French," 138–139; *Financial Times*, 30 November 1984, 3 December 1984, 22 March 1985, and 10 May 1985; *Le Monde*, 30 March 1985; Corbett, "1985," 269; von Moltke, "Binnenmarktpolitik 1984" (1985), 143–154.

[118] Howe, *Conflict*, 405. Many are said to have proposed Delors. Grant, *Delors*, 58; Fitzgerald, *All*, 588; Howe, *Conflict*, 404; Ross, *Jacques*, 28; Bauchard, *Guerre*, 266.

as president), a stronger European industrial and technology policy, and, above all, deeper monetary integration. Yet before assuming office, Delors embarked on a trip to ten capitals, sounding out member governments on different "big ideas" to relaunch the EC. Member states differed over political cooperation, monetary policy, defense, and procedural reform, but all (possibly excepting Greece) were in substantial agreement only about the need for internal market liberalization—a fact already reflected in the Fontainebleau communiqué. Delors also spoke with a business group led by Max Kohnstamm, an old Monnet associate, who suggested that internal market reforms would require an extension of QMV.[119]

In his maiden speech before the European Parliament on 14 January 1985, Delors announced the goal of completing the internal market by 1992—a date coeval with two four-year terms of the Commission—aiming to render it irreversible by 1988 and complete by 1992. Yet he remained skeptical. Not until late 1985, however, did this become the core of his reform program. Just before the Milan summit in mid-1985, after the Dooge Committee had completed its work, he (somewhat reluctantly) proposed a link between QMV and internal market liberalization. Yet the Commission, fearing failure, remained lukewarm; even then, equally important priorities appear to have been a doubling of R&D funding and monetary reform.[120]

Despite personal doubts, Delors was not one to waste an opportunity. When the Council "endorsed the goal of a single market by 1992 and called upon the . . . Commission to draw up a detailed program with a specific timetable," Delors passed the Council request to Cockfield, the internal market commissioner, who interpreted his mandate broadly and drafted a White Paper. In lieu of a firm definition of a "completed internal market," Cockfield's White Paper set forth nearly 300 specific proposals, including VAT harmonization, service deregulation, standardization, and mutual recognition in various areas, accompanied by a brief philosophical defense of free trade. Cockfield claims in retrospect to have sought deliberately to limit the ability of governments to analyze the White Paper by sending it only ten days before Milan—though, as we have seen, this tactic was not successful—then leaking it strategically to the press.[121]

Meanwhile the member states had become more active. In preparation for the

---

[119] Interviews with Delors, 1989–1996.

[120] Attali, *Verbatim*, 1:718. Among Delors's own priorities appears to have been creation of a European Technological Community; upon assuming the Commission Presidency, Delors also took the monetary portfolio for himself. Grant, *Delors*, 66–67; interview with Jacques Delors, 1996. Maria Green Cowles argues on the basis of interviews that his major concern was institutional reform, but others contest this. Delors appears to have been cautious about linking internal market and institutional change in 1995 but was convinced "after six months . . . the institutional question cannot be avoided." Press conference of 26 June 1985, cited in Ken Endo, "Political Leadership in the European Community: The Role of the Commission Presidency under Jacques Delors, 1985–1995," thesis, Oxford University, 1995, 63. Also Ross, *Jacques*, 31; Cockfield, *European*, 53–54; *Bulletin EC 3–1985*, pt. 1.2.4.

[121] Cockfield, *European*, 29, 33, 42, 48–52, 82–83; interviews with Braun and a Campo. Meanwhile Genscher and Dumas worked to propose the EUREKA project. Genscher, *Errinerungen*, 376–377.

Luxembourg and Milan summits of March and June 1985, Germany proposed to relaunch the Community by limiting the Luxembourg Compromise, extending EC competence in foreign affairs, and completing the internal market—a package based on the Dooge Report. France proposed a new Article 235 permitting some countries to move ahead without others ("flexibility"). Germany rejected the clause, along with any formal commitments on monetary policy without ratification by national parliaments. The French government called the German demand "a retreat from the current situation," since it sought progress within the EMS only by intergovernmental agreement.[122]

The British government, supporting economic reform but nonetheless hoping to channel momentum away from treaty amendments, launched a counteroffensive. Britain tied its previous proposal for internal market reform, first announced before the Fontainebleau summit and now codified in the White Paper, to gentlemen's agreements to abstain rather than invoke the veto. This procedural proposal now included two new elements: voluntary restraint in invoking the Luxembourg Compromise at lower levels of the Council once the chiefs of state had set an objective (similar to a French proposal several years earlier) and a separate treaty codifying principles of informal political cooperation. One of the two French papers for the conference called for more or less the same thing, adding the old French proposal that vetoes must be justified in writing before the Council.[123]

As the Milan summit opened, the heads of government unanimously approved the White Paper. They also immediately accepted the British proposal on informal improvements to decision-making; but most countries sought to go further. The British, Danes, and Greeks rejected Delors's proposal for immediate amendment of the Treaty to provide for QMV on Articles 99–101. Genscher proposed a return to the decision-making procedure which existed before the Luxembourg Compromise and QMV on internal market issues, but some (presumably including Thatcher) found renunciation of the Luxembourg Compromise unacceptable. Even watered down with British amendments, the text was rejected.[124]

Anxious to avoid a failure under its presidency, the Italian government called unexpectedly—at least for some participants—for a majority vote on whether to convene a formal IGC under Article 236. The Commission and in particular Émile Noël reportedly worked on the proposal with Foreign Minister Andreotti, who was competing with Prime Minister Craxi to be seen as pro-European. Germany and the Benelux countries immediately supported Italy, France and Ireland cautiously joined them, and Britain, Denmark, and Greece were left in opposition. British protests (on procedural grounds) against invocation of a first-ever majority vote in the European Council were dismissed, and the conference was called. Thatcher returned from Milan in a fury but within a few days allowed

---

[122] Attali, *Verbatim*, 1:896–897.

[123] De Ruyt, *L'Acte*, 57–59; Haywood, "French," 142–143; Gazzo, *Towards*, reprints British proposals.

[124] Grant, *Delors*, 70–74; De Ruyt, *L'Acte*, 60–61; Haywood, "French," 143; Gazzo, *Towards (Supplement)*, 3–8; Commission document, COM (85) 352 (26 June 1985).

herself to be persuaded, by Howe among others, that Britain should attend the IGC. Two related considerations appear to have influenced British thinking.[125]

First, Britain had little to lose from QMV on White Paper issues and other Article 100 matters such as service deregulation. A careful, proposal-by-proposal study by Thatcher's associates concluded that British interests could be threatened in only a few areas. Nor was the British government deaf to constant reminders that some procedural changes were needed to assure implementation of the internal market plan. Howe recalls that "soon the irritations of Milan faded into history . . . the UK still formally challenged the need for any Treaty changes at all . . . [but] we were in truth eager to hammer into place the Cockfield single market program."[126]

Second, Britain faced a renewed threat of exclusion. By the time of the Milan conference, public statements by Dutch, French, German, and, to a lesser extent, Italian politicians suggested considerable support for exclusion. Mitterrand called the decisions at Milan "a test of truth." As we have seen, Mitterrand and Kohl had exploited the threat of exclusion with great finesse. The threat was credible: France had long promoted "two-track" initiatives, especially in high-tech, and during this period a two-track EC had found prominent exponents among European academics and commentators. Article 82 of the European Parliament's Draft Treaty on European Union proposed it as an alternative, and legal experts seriously evaluated it as a legal expedient. Inside observers at the time agree that the British interest in liberalization combined with a credible threat of exclusion to decisively influence British policy. Britain attended the IGC, accepted the inevitability of formal Treaty amendment, and played a skeptical but ultimately constructive role.[127]

The Intergovernmental Conference: A "clear and decisive" Victory

A draft of the SEA was set forth during the first month of the IGC, remaining details were worked out among foreign ministers and chief executives at five meetings between 21 October and 1 December, and the document was signed in February 1986. The draft introduced QMV under Article 100, as well as ar-

---

[125] De Ruyt, *L'Acte*, 60–61; Haywood, "French," 143; interviews with Kanzleramt official, Commission officials; British Prime Ministerial official; Gazzo, *Towards (Supplement)*, 3–8; Howe, *Conflict*, 446–448. The procedure for Treaty amendment under Article 235 offered two advantages to the recalcitrant: it excluded the Parliament and required unanimity. The latter limited the possibility of "two-track" decisions, particularly in comparison with the Parliament's proposal for a wholly new treaty.

[126] Howe, *Conflict*, 447, also 408–409, where Thatcher is portrayed as "enthusiastic," even before Milan; Cockfield, "Real," 5. British officials were also concerned that formal treaty changes in an IGC might encourage movement beyond single market issues. Interview with former Prime Ministerial adviser, 1997.

[127] Interview with British Prime Ministerial official; von Moltke, "Binnenmarktpolitik 1984"; Cockfield, "Real." See Helen Wallace with Adam Ridley, *Europe: The Challenge of Diversity* (London, 1985), especially chap. 5; Eberhard Grabitz, ed., *Abgestufte Integration: Eine Alternative zum herkömmlichen Integrationskonzept?* (Kehl am Rhein, 1984); Bieber, Jacqué, and Weiler, eds., *Ever*, 167–175; Corbett, "1985," 242.

ticles governing services, transport, relevant external tariffs, capital movements, and right of corporate establishment.[128]

From the beginning all governments agreed on internal market reform along the lines of the White Paper agenda; the negotiations defined the terms under which the reform would take place. From the maximalist perspective, the SEA was a process of limiting the scope and intensity of reform to those procedural and substantive changes needed to liberalize the internal market—a process necessary to secure the assent not only of Britain but of other member states who, when it came to drafting a document, suddenly proved more jealous of their sovereignty than their public rhetoric might have suggested. In addition, side-payments were promised to poorer countries which otherwise threatened to veto the arrangement.

Pressure from Britain and other governments exempted certain internal market functions. Fiscal harmonization remained subject to unanimity, and the rights of employees and free movement of persons remained outside EC jurisdiction. In substantive areas other than internal market policy, the lack of consensus reduced commitments to a minor or symbolic level. The Luxembourg presidency asked the Commission to prepare texts, an opportunity that Delors, still unreconciled to reform focused predominantly on single market policy, exploited to introduce materials on monetary cooperation, technology, the environment, culture, and cohesion—only to see them removed once again. New clauses concerning political cooperation, social policy, technology policy, cultural policy, human rights, development aid, and energy did not go beyond a codification of current practice; environmental policy, a new area, remained under unanimity.[129]

Monetary cooperation was most contentious. It had long been a personal interest of Delors and had been his first choice as a substantive vehicle for reform. Commission proposals subjected progress toward a common monetary fund to unanimous approval *of those who chose to participate*—a two-track proposal that would have accorded EC legitimacy to any effort by a smaller group to proceed on its own. Consistent with the monetary preferences outlined in Chapter 4, France and Italy felt that the Delors proposal was too weak, whereas Germany, Britain, and the Netherlands opposed any mention of monetary policy. When Germany and Britain lost patience and tied monetary cooperation to the complete liberalization of capital markets by the end of 1986, the others quickly agreed to a compromise that included no concrete steps beyond existing policies. Commission activism was curbed shortly after the opening of the conference by an informal meeting of the ministers of economics and finance, who insisted—largely at German insistence—that they be consulted before any further monetary proposals were made to the conference.[130]

---

[128] Gazzo, *Towards*, 2:56ff.

[129] De Ruyt, *L'Acte*, 67–91; Corbett, "1985," 249–250, 259; Noël, "Single," 8. The Commission and a number of governments sought to exploit the negotiations to expand EC legal competences to include many general functions under Article 235.

[130] Corbett, "1985," 247–248; Gazzo, *Towards*, 2:24, 86. Also Gazzo, 1:38; Ludlow, *Beyond*, vi.

In a formal sense the SEA left member governments no closer to EMU and perhaps further away. Opposed by Thatcher but pressured by Genscher, Kohl accepted a rhetorical reference suggested by Delors to the "progressive realization" of EMU in the preamble to the revised treaty. Delors saw the clause as a legitimating device, but Thatcher argued that the words "did not change anything. If they did, I would not have agreed to them." Subsequently she second-guessed her own decision, but the evidence suggests she was initially correct; the rhetoric itself had no effect. In addition, for the first time Britain gained legal recognition within the Treaty of its veto power over monetary integration, which it could use to prevent incremental, extra-Treaty developments toward EMU. Indeed, some argued that progress toward monetary union "seem[ed] likely to be checked rather than encouraged." Even Delors would state only that the revised treaty makes "allowance for . . . evolution when this becomes necessary."[131]

Governments agreed on the need for significant exemptions and escape clauses. Poorer states feared the imposition of high standards. Article 8C directed the Commission to keep in mind the concerns of poorer countries in drafting directives. Richer countries, notably Germany and Denmark, feared QMV would force them to lower environmental, safety, or social standards. In this context, the negotiators deliberately avoided discussing the Luxembourg Compromise or the procedures for calling a majority vote (the latter determined later by the Council itself). Instead, Germany proposed that the government with the highest standards be accorded a veto. This qualitative veto was rejected, but the final Treaty instructed the Commission in Article 100A(3) to take into account high standards and, more important, retained a weaker veto. Article 100A(4), written by the chief executives themselves in the final summit session, permits nations outvoted in the Council or wishing to invoke a safeguard clause to retain their domestic regulations under Article 36.[132]

The SEA introduced a cooperation procedure whereby Parliament could intervene late in the legislative process to veto legislation or to add amendments which, if approved by the Commission, would be placed before the Council under voting rules similar to those governing Commission proposals. From the perspective of the Commission and the member states, this procedure increased the participation of the Parliament without infringing on the formal powers of either the Commission or the Council.[133] To be sure, Germany and Italy consid-

---

[131] Gazzo, *Towards*, 1:8, also 25–26; Thatcher, *Downing*, 741; *Economist*, 30 November 1991, 47; De Ruyt, *L'Acte*, 272; Corbett, "1985," 268. The SEA included language limiting the EMS to its present functions. The view that the outcome reflected "a triumph" for British negotiators has been most cogently argued by Taylor in "New."

[132] Under Article 100A(4), it is now the Court and, to a lesser extent, the Commission—no longer the member-states, as under the Luxembourg Compromise—that ultimately determines what constitutes proper justification for exempting a state from a Community internal market decision. Implementation has subsequently emerged as an important area of conflict. De Ruyt, *L'acte*, 172ff; Haywood, "French," 146.

[133] Here I follow the critics of Tsebelis's formal analysis of Parliamentary powers, which deliberately overlooks the element of the procedure viewed as most critical by Commission officials at the time, namely the need for the Parliament to gain Commission approval, as well as informal pressures and the threat to veto, which are decisive. Cf. Tsebelis, "Power."

ered it inadequate; both sought to institutionalize face-to-face negotiations between Council and Parliament—a non-binding "conciliation" or binding "codecision" procedure. Britain and Denmark opposed any increase in parliamentary powers. The balance was held by the Benelux countries, which sought to maintain the current powers of the Commission, which they viewed as a guardian of small state interests. The new cooperation procedure was extended to Article 100 and certain social, technological, and environmental decisions, but not to other areas such as liberalization of services, capital movements, and transport policy. Largely at German insistence, EP consultation was required for all legislation, and EP assent was required for the accession and association of new countries. Efforts to require assent for amending the Treaty, for new rules on EP elections, and for the creation of new financial resources were blocked by one or more of Britain, France, and Germany—in the case of financial resources, by all three.[134]

One final provision essential to the passage of the internal market program was the expansion of "structural funds"—infrastructural funding for poorer regions of the Community. This so-called convergence policy was necessary not because it was an essential element of economic liberalization, as the Commission at times claimed, but because it was the political price of support from Greece, Ireland, and Italy, and later Spain and Portugal. As the report of the intergovernmental committee that prepared the negotiations (the Dondelinger Group) made clear, "some delegations [considered] appropriate provisions . . . *a condition for the acceptance of the proposals on the Internal Market.*"[135] The richer countries hesitated to offer anything immediately but agreed that regional, structural, and development funds would be "significantly increased in real terms within the limits of financial possibilities"—a phrase that laid the foundation for a sizable increase in funding approved in 1988.

Delors was active in managing the negotiations over the structural funds. In 1987 he linked solutions to the structural, agricultural, and budget problems into a single negotiation. Agreement on structural funds, viewed skeptically by Thatcher, showed the willingness of Germany and France to threaten Britain once again with exclusion. This threat is often incorrectly attributed to Delors and a Commission threat to resign, but as usual the power behind the threat was quietly but firmly wielded by Kohl himself. He agreed to provide some of the extra funds, then faced down Thatcher in a late night "confessional" by threatening to issue a four-point communiqué announcing that the EC would henceforth do business without Britain.[136]

Domestic ratification was unproblematic, though delayed in Denmark and Ireland, where constitutional obligations required a referendum, and in Italy,

[134] Interview with Delors; De Ruyt, *L'acte,* 124ff. A Commission proposal to grant itself extensive implementing powers, to be overridden only by unanimous vote of the Council, was summarily rejected.

[135] Gazzo, *Towards,* 2:58.

[136] Interview with Kanzleramt official, who made transcripts available. For incomplete treatments, Ardagh, "Will," 44; Ross, *Jacques,* 40–43.

where the SEA was criticized for not going far enough. Italian prime minister Craxi voiced doubts that the SEA included enough of the maximalist agenda and promised support only if the European Parliament approved it—which it had no choice but to do. In the wake of the Luxembourg summit, Kohl and Mitterrand stated—though the statement was perhaps for posterity—that they would have been prepared to go further on the powers of the Parliament and monetary policy respectively, as well as on QMV. In Britain, by contrast, Whitehall studies termed the outcome a success on "all the points which were of real importance," and Thatcher hailed the results as "clear and decisive."[137]

Explaining Interstate Bargaining: "Staying in the game"

The conventional wisdom accords decisive influence on the SEA to the political entrepreneurship of visionary, activist EC officials, judges, parliamentarians, and transnational interest groups. This view is grounded, explicitly or implicitly, in the assumptions of supranational bargaining theory, namely that information and ideas are scarce commodities vital to international cooperation and that supranational officials have a comparative advantage in providing them.

The most extreme support for this position comes from participants, notably Lord Cockfield, who claims, as we have seen, that the major difference between the successful SEA and previous reform efforts was the existence of an activist Commission. Academic analysts have followed him. The central conclusion of George Ross's study of the Delors Commission is that the SEA would have been impossible without the particular French tradition of technocratic political voluntarism found in the person of Delors: "The political lucidity of the Commission's proposals and the shrewdness with which they have been presented have been central variables in Europe's forward movement. . . . The Commission had the power and the institutional right to pick and choose among possible courses. . . . The right choices . . . could set the Community in motion again. Bad political work . . . would have wasted the opportunity."[138] In the same vein, Wayne Sandholtz and John Zysman insist that structural conditions were "contingent" and "indeterminate"; therefore supranational entrepreneurship was required to "create a common European interest and construct bargains."[139] Making the informational assumptions more explicit through game theory, Geoffrey Garrett and Barry Weingast speculate that ECJ decisions may have provided a necessary focal point, permitting governments finally to coordinate on a common set of liberalizing policies.[140] Others argue that mobilization of transnational business groups—either spontaneously or with supranational encouragement—was decisive because it permitted interested parties to persuade or bypass reluctant national governments.[141]

[137] Interview with British Prime Ministerial Adviser; Howe, *Conflict*, 457.
[138] Ross, *Jacques*, 3, 12.
[139] Sandholtz and Zysman, "1992," 128.
[140] Garrett and Weingast, "Interests," 189. On p. 190, however, they concede that this is a "one-sided theory that overlooks the power and functional interests of major governments."
[141] Cowles, *Politics*; Sandholtz and Zysman, "1992."

Claims for the importance of supranational entrepreneurship are, I argue, much exaggerated, not least because they are based simply on the facts that supranational officials were active and the negotiations successful, not on a methodologically sound evaluation of their influence. Instead, the data confirms a view more consistent with intergovernmental bargaining theory. Throughout the negotiations, national chief executives—Kohl, Mitterrand, Thatcher—were active, well-informed participants. Many actors, not least the most interested national governments, were willing and able to perform critical negotiating functions—advancing initiatives, mediating among governments, and mobilizing interested social groups. By the first half of 1984, at the latest, single market liberalization was recognized as the only program likely to command consensus among the major governments. Where distributional disagreements emerged, the preferences of major member governments imposed strict limitations on possible bargains. Governments vetoed agreements they opposed, threatened to exclude others from those they supported, and offered side-payments to cinch the deal. By contrast, Commission officials, Europarliamentarians, and many business groups viewed the SEA as a second-best alternative to monetary integration, democratization, industrial policy, or foreign policy cooperation. In short and as intergovernmental theory predicts, demands by powerful governments, not the supranational supply of proposals, imposed the binding constraint on cooperation. The decisive evidence is reviewed below.

The most fundamental constraints on reform were convergent national demands for liberalization, not the supply of proposals. By 1983 national preferences had converged sufficiently that the three major governments were willing to move beyond the existing level of European integration and supported single market reform as the optimal way to do so. After resolving accession and budget wrangles, they turned their attention to this project. Viable proposals were numerous, coming from governments, supranational actors, and private groups. Indeed, successful bilateral Franco-German negotiations and multilateral discussions (the Schengen Accord) on nontariff barriers and customs formalities predated the launching of discussions within the EC. Some transnational and domestic interests mobilized spontaneously. Other proposals, such as service liberalization, were advanced by the British. By 1985, when the SEA came under serious consideration, some EC reforms were already in place, including creation of the Internal Market Council and the standstill agreement. Governments were sufficiently mobilized that most Commission proposals responded to specific requests from member states. After 1983 internal market liberalization emerged as the most consistent target for reform in government proposals from all three major governments; QMV was supported by two of the three. The direct result was pressure for single market reform and a credible threat of exclusion to achieve QMV.

The decisiveness of changing demand rather than shifting supply is most clearly seen if we compare the SEA to previous Commission proposals. Throughout the late 1960s and 1970s Commissioners had proposed many of the same items as part of various packages, often with similar deadlines, only to see governments reject or ignore them. Narjes revived this agenda in the early 1980s, pressing for similar institutional and regulatory changes. By assembling all this history into a coherent proposal Delors and Cockfield made the most of a favorable situation, but they were doing what others had tried before. Narjes himself believes in retrospect that "a strong proposal like a program for internal market liberalization and a change in the treaty was unthinkable [*nicht denkbar*] before Fontainebleau. The Delors project of 1984–85 would have been a complete failure in 1981–82."[142] Genscher, Kohl, and Mitterrand clearly understood the same point, for between 1981 and 1984 they deliberately cleared the table of existing problems in order to make room for a "relance."

Evidence from negotiations underlines the importance of national governments. Throughout, governments were relatively well-informed and specific policy proposals were plentifully available, whether from national governments themselves or from supranational officials, Europarliamentarians, transnational interest groups, multinational firms, or domestic interest groups. The French government, as well as the Luxembourg presidency, submitted entire draft treaties; each government submitted draft proposals on individual issues. To be sure, 60–70 percent of final provisions were based on Commission wording, but much of it was essentially technical or legal drafting. Governments examined the White Paper in detail, both domestically and in joint sessions, subjecting particular elements to frank criticism; 30–40 percent of the clauses were altered accordingly. Many examples of Commission agenda-setting noted by analysts, by contrast, are marginal: for example, the Commission's ability to retain the wording "an area without frontiers" in the SEA.[143] Another example is the widespread description of what one journalist termed Delors's "intuitive flair for marketing," which is said to have led him to link the single market package to the "magic number" of 1992.[144] This decision, often treated by commentators unfamiliar with the EC as a particularly effective entrepreneurial innovation, was in fact obvious and oft-employed. As we have seen, most major Commission programs contained similar deadlines, as did private plans like Dekker's. Indeed, just a few months earlier, Narjes had drawn up an eighteen-month plan for a common EC customs document, gradual elimination of frontier controls, a uniform method of collecting VAT on imported goods, and an increase in meetings of the Internal Market Council. As Cockfield recalls, the idea was so obvious that the major problem was settling disagreements over whose date to choose: "All sorts of people had proposed all sorts of dates."[145] In sum, the only regularity

---

[142] Interview with Narjes.

[143] De Ruyt, "L'Acte," 70–90; interviews with Delors; Grant, *Delors*, 75; Corbett, "1985," 245; Richard McAllister, *From EC to EU: A Historical and Political Survey* (London, 1997), 162–183, esp. 176–180.

[144] Cf. Ardagh, "Will," 45–46.

[145] Cockfield, *European*, 33; Pearce, Sutton, and Bachelor, *Protection*, 48. A deadline was in any case no guarantee of success. Many EC plans with deadlines failed, including Pompidou's 1982 deadline for "Union Politique," monetary plans promulgated by Barre when he was at the EC, various EURATOM and energy sector plans not achieved, the Commission's various proposals for nontariff barrier removal in the 1970s, and the Parliament's deadline of 1982 for direct elections. Indeed, such plans failed so regularly that Monnet advised against ever setting such deadlines. Martin Holland, "Jean Monnet and the Federal Functionalist Approach to European Union," in Philomena Murray and Paul B. Rich, eds., *Visions of European Unity* (Boulder, Colo., 1994), 93.

that stands up is that every major proposal given serious consideration had strong national sponsors.

Nearly all of the SEA was negotiated by traditional means: chief executives, ministers, diplomats, and personal representatives made proposals, shuttled among capitals, hammered out bargains. Bargaining was either unmediated or was mediated through the Council secretariat or third countries. All governments were active although, on economic interests alone, one would have predicted somewhat stronger British participation. Delors himself stresses the importance of Mitterrand's shuttle diplomacy, recalling that he met six times (once a month) each with Kohl and Thatcher during the 1984 French presidency alone. Proposals, drafting, and other transactions were handled, as they would be in the Maastricht Treaty discussions, by what Geoffrey Howe termed a "tiny but immensely efficient Luxembourg machine," backed not by the Commission officials but by the intergovernmental Council of Ministers secretariat headed by Niels Ersbøll, which polled member governments, kept the agenda manageable, and presented the European Council with dozens of alternative proposals.[146]

Where the Commission participated, it did so largely at member state discretion. Member states accepted Commission initiation and mediation because it favored their interests, but they rejected a similar role for the Parliament, essentially ignoring the maximalist agenda. Parliamentary reform proposals had been circulating since the Kirk Report of 1974, without success; their ideas did not appear in European Council resolutions—supranational theory tells us nothing about the timing of the SEA. National governments viewed the Parliament's proposals as too open-ended ("real reform . . . requires a treaty encompassing all Community policies and the institutions needed to implement them"), too democratic (the powers of the Parliament should be "extended to new spheres of activity"), and too automatic (the Draft Treaty would have gone into effect without unanimous Council approval). In Germany international discussions were under way before the parliamentary draft treaty; the Parliament's actions had little influence on their course.[147]

Government representatives, abetted by the Commission, deliberately excluded independent MEPs from decisive forums after Fontainebleau, ignoring the Parliament's continuous protests against the emasculation of the Draft Treaty and its exclusion from the "real participation" in the discussions. Though a few countries sent MEPs to the Dooge Committee as representatives—recall that the Committee's importance had been downgraded due to a Franco-German diplomatic misstep—one of its first actions was to reject the Draft Treaty and to begin negotiations with a French government draft instead. The ease with which the member states parried EP pressure also casts doubt on any argument that the SEA was necessary to coopt rising demands for even more thorough institutional reform. In the end, the Parliament overwhelmingly passed a resolution

---

[146] Howe, *Conflict*, 454; McAllister, *From EC*, 180–183.

[147] Citations are from the European Parliament's July 1985 formal opinion regarding the working proposal for an Intergovernmental Conference. See Gazzo, *Towards*, 2 : 13–14. Also Gaddum, *Deutsche*, 247; Michael Burgess, *Federalism and European Union: Political Ideas, Influences and Strategies in the European Community, 1972–1987* (London, 1989), 120–123.

protesting that the Single Act "in no way represent(s) the real reform of the Community that our peoples need," but had to accept the *fait accompli*.[148]

As an initiator and a mediator, Delors made his most important contributions not from his ability to intervene but from his keen awareness of the extreme constraints under which he was acting. Delors's most statesmanlike judgments concerned the proper moment to compromise. In September–October 1985 he finally dropped strong advocacy of monetary and social reform—his personal priorities, but policies unacceptable to the United Kingdom and, in the case of monetary policy, Germany—and instead stressed the links among internal market reform, majority voting, and the increases in structural funds needed to win over Greece and the other southern countries, as well as environmental policy, a traditional concern for Denmark. Delors's conciliatory move may have facilitated political compromise, but it did so precisely because his position was closely circumscribed by the views of the major states. Indeed, his elimination of monetary reform from the package resulted, as we have seen, from the direct pressure of domestic officials.[149]

All this said, it might plausibly be argued that supranational political entrepreneurs played a significant if secondary role in assembling a particular package of concrete single market proposals and mobilizing transnational interests—a greater role than in any other episode in this book. No government as steadily and successfully promoted a package of single market initiatives as did Narjes and later Cockfield in the Commission and the Kangaroo Group in the Parliament. Most of this work had been completed before Delors and Cockfield arrived. Nevertheless, they succeeded in reintroducing many issues that the EC had been discussing for decades, presentation as a package directed at solving the growth crisis, the mobilization of transnational business around that package, and relentless publicity for it may have been essential in making reform possible. Something similar might well have emerged in time—after all, the White Paper was a response to an explicit request from the European Council—but supranational and transnational entrepreneurs surely speeded it along.[150]

Perhaps even more important, the Kangaroo Group and the ERT, as well as Dekker's initiative, were all developed with strong encouragement from supranational officials or parliamentarians. These groups of multinational, export-oriented firms focused on EC-level liberalization, so they circumvented the more traditional, nationally oriented representation of other European business groups. The latter, though supportive of liberalization, were limited in that national organizations—which more strongly represented import-competing,

---

[148] De Ruyt, *L'Acte*, 56, also 85; Gazzo, *Towards*, 2:17–20, 27, 30, 41, 104; 1:11–17.

[149] Noël, "Single," 7–9; Corbett, "Single," 248ff; De Ruyt, *L'Acte*, 70ff; *Financial Times*, 9 October 1989; interview with Jacques Delors, Harvard University, 1989, and Jacques Delors, *Our Europe* (London, 1992), 25–29. Also Calingaert, *1992*, 9. The initial draft amendments submitted by the Commission to the Intergovernmental Committee went far beyond the final settlement (except on the powers of the Parliament), and Delors compromised only under pressure—a fact which hardly lends credence to Delors's claim that he foresaw all in January 1985. This may, however, underestimate Delors's skill in setting the agenda, where aggressiveness may have paid some dividends.

[150] This is a similar conclusion, we have seen, to that reached by the most reliable studies of the impact of Court decisions on the SEA.

small business, and nontradables producers—had to approve actions. There was relatively little spontaneous mobilization of such groups. Some British and German business groups openly favored single market liberalization even before 1980, and some transnational groups, notably the ERT, initially opposed the single market initiative as second-best. Still, vocal support from these groups was quickly forthcoming, and it contributed to the momentum in favor of full implementation of the "Europe 1992" plan. In chapter 7 we return to the reasons for the unique role of supranational actors in the SEA negotiations.

The remarkable efficiency of the negotiations, their speed and comprehensiveness, might be attributed in part to supranational entrepreneurship, the distributive outcomes themselves clearly reflected the preferences of member states. Single market liberalization was the only substantive area that enjoyed support from all three major EC governments; Delors ascertained this before entering office and accorded it decisive importance, though he repeatedly tried to overcome these constraints. The White Paper agenda was close to a lowest common denominator. The Anglo-German veto of monetary and defense integration and the Anglo-French veto of institutional development for its own sake left only the internal market initiative as a feasible basis for reform. It may well be that Delors's actions as finance minister of France contributed as much to the SEA as did his actions as president of the Commission. Efforts by Delors and others to realize uniquely supranational and transnational preferences tended to be futile. The incoming Commission president had sought monetary and social integration, and leading Parliament groups had proposed institutional reform; the most prominent transnational business groups initially opposed the White Paper agenda in favor of a centralized EC industrial and infrastructure policy; even the ECJ had sought general application of "mutual recognition" rather than a broad package of reforms linked to QMV.

The substance of the SEA, as intergovernmental theory predicts, reflected above all the national priorities of the most recalcitrant countries. Germany, the Netherlands, and the United Kingdom rejected outright any monetary cooperation that would require institutional changes. The French threatened to veto any package without a monetary clause, but the result was no more than rhetoric in exchange for Mitterrand's agreement in principle to move toward capital liberalization. (Thatcher might have vetoed but was convinced that the clause would have little effect.) [151] Exclusive focus on the single market, without a large expansion of technology programs, secured British support. Danish opposition killed Commission proposals for cultural policy but encouraged the environmental proposals. Genscher proposed strengthening the Parliament; Delors tried to exploit the issue to expand the Commission's power, but his efforts were rejected by a large majority of governments. Exceptions to QMV reflected individual national concerns: in general, exceptions supported by one or more large countries, such as Anglo-German opposition to QMV on fiscal and taxation mat-

---

[151] In an oft-cited quotation from her memoirs, Thatcher herself later treats this as a decisive mistake, but in fact there is no evidence that the vague SEA treaty clause in any way forced or facilitated future movement on monetary policy. Thatcher, *Downing*, 555, 740ff.

ters, tended to be sustained, whereas those backed by smaller countries, such as Irish opposition to QMV in banking matters, tended to be rejected.[152] Thatcher's success in negotiating a fundamental revision of the rules for calculating net obligations to the EC budget in effect concluded negotiations over the terms of British accession begun in 1970. The agricultural *acquis communautaire* inherited from the 1960s was a Franco-German deal, but the new agreement reflected more closely the new *trilateral* balance of power within the EC, which Britain achieved by linking its demands to obstruction on other issues. It also marked an important move in the direction of *juste retour* in agricultural matters, a solution similar to that adopted in R&D policy. To be sure, the Commission quietly slipped some new issues, such as R&D and environmental programs, into the revised treaty. Yet most concerned functions that the EC had been handling under indirect authorization for years; there was little opposition from member-states to a concrete mandate to cover them.[153]

Yet the agreement was not entirely at the lowest common denominator. Threats to veto and exclude had two consequences. First, the single case of a government accepting a reform it did not support—British acceptance of formal treaty changes mandating QMV—was achieved through the explicit threat of exclusion. The British were particularly vulnerable not simply because exclusion would be costly but because the Thatcher government strongly supported internal market reform. This threat worked because, as we have seen, the Franco-German threat of exclusion was credible and was repeatedly employed from 1983 through 1985. Paul Taylor observes: "British diplomacy . . . had to balance two objectives: that of satisfying specific interests, and that of staying in the game. A measure of compromise in the former [became] necessary to achieve the latter."[154] A similar threat—with consequences more diffuse and vague—secured Thatcher's acceptance of increased structural funding.

Second, veto threats came, predictably, from those countries that gained least from the agreement. Poorer countries—with less interest than Britain in agreement—could more credibly threaten to veto or obstruct it. The result was Article 8, directing the Commission to take account of the special needs of poorer countries in proposing directives, and a promise of side-payments—provided in cash, which imposed costs on unorganized taxpayers rather than on powerful interest groups.

In sum, the evidence strongly supports the intergovernmental view that demand for liberalization, that is, the preferences and power of states, not the supply of policy innovations from informed and inventive entrepreneurs, that was decisive for integration during the mid-1980s. Commission and Parliament entrepreneurship failed to shift any major aspect of the interstate bargain and contributed only modestly to its efficiency; outcomes reflected credible threats of veto and exclusion. At most supranational entrepreneurs increased the effi-

---

[152] De Ruyt, *L'Acte*, 75–80; 135ff; Corbett, "1985," 245ff.

[153] Indeed, some such shifts, as in environmental policy, were designed to in part *avoid* the automatic introduction of QMV under Article 100.

[154] Taylor, "New," 3. Also Haywood, 135–136; Cockfield, "Real," 5.

ciency of the negotiations—speeding agreement and increasing the scope of internal market reform—by packaging existing proposals, presenting them as an active response to economic decline, and helping to mobilize groups that, after initial hesitation, came to support reform.

Explaining Institutional Choice

The SEA reform package included various reforms designed to pool and delegate sovereignty. These included the extension of qualified majority voting for single market issues and a few other areas; the introduction of more automatic procedures for liberalization, notably "mutual recognition" and "reference to standards"; and the involvement of the Parliament in the legislative process through the "cooperation procedure." Numerous other institutional reforms, primarily suggested by the Commission and Parliament, were rejected.

What explains these institutional choices? The historical data reveal a combination of concern for the credibility of commitments and ideological commitment to Europe, with the former accounting for the details and scope of delegation, the latter altering the willingness of governments to pool and delegate sovereignty on the margin. By contrast, technocratic motivations for delegation appear insignificant.

Cross-issue variation confirms the importance of credible commitments. Article 100, where governments introduced QMV, was not an area of particular technical complexity or symbolic salience, as technocratic and ideological theories predict. Instead, governments chose an area in which numerous related issues were linked, with considerable joint gains from compliance but concerns about obstruction. Only in the case of the "reference to standards" procedure, employed in about a dozen of the White Paper issues, is it plausible to argue that technical complexity required delegation to specialized industrial regulators—but here the desire for credible commitment provides an equally plausible explanation. The speed of decision-making also increased significantly.[155] Governments, moreover, sought to manipulate QMV so as to exclude those areas where they were likely to find themselves isolated in opposition. Hence the British Tory government succeeded in exempting fiscal harmonization, some environmental policies, and social security; Germany and Denmark supported the revised Article 100A4, which granted safeguards to high-standard countries. Even where the consequences of institutional decisions were uncertain, as in the powers of the Parliament, governments remained cautious, restricting the scope of the cooperation procedure to core areas already subject to QMV.

Cross-national variation supports either ideology or credible commitments, but disconfirms the technocratic view. Smaller or poorer governments—Ireland

---

[155] Wolfgang Wessels, "Verwaltung im EG-Mehrebenensystem: Auf dem Wege zum Megabüro-kratie?" in Markus Jachtenfuchs and Beate Kohler-Koch, eds., *Europäische Integration* (Opladen, 1996), 165–192. Wessels finds, intriguingly, that the total number of legislative acts did not increase significantly in the late 1980s, though their importance may have—particularly if we assume, with Cockfield, that the "new approach" employed one five-page directive where ten fifty-page directives would previously have been needed. Cockfield, "Real," 6.

and Greece, even Britain—were not more favorable to delegation, as the technocratic perspective predicts. The credible commitments view predicts that all governments, led by Britain and the governments of small and wealthy countries, should favor QMV. The Benelux countries were indeed supportive, but Britain and Denmark were not. Despite its strong support for internal market liberalization, Britain favored an *informal* norm without Treaty amendments, though it quickly backed down in response to a threat of exclusion. British ambivalence is explicable in part because, as the poorest of the large countries and an opponent of the CAP, Britain was concerned about spillover to issues in which high standards (or high CAP prices) might be imposed upon it. Antifederalist ideology surely played a role. Yet in the end Britain backed down in large part because it valued substantive gains.

Ideology best explains, as even the credible commitments view concedes it should, variation in the willingness of countries to promote and accept institutional delegation in areas where the consequences were highly uncertain and relatively minor—notably, increased powers for the European Parliament. Here the geopolitical ideology of chief executives, parliamentary parties, and publics appears to have been decisive. Pressure for greater EP powers came from countries with a tradition of European federalism and with strong domestic parliamentary systems: Germany, Italy, and the Benelux countries. Opposition came from countries, such as Britain, France, and Denmark, with a tradition of skepticism about European federalism and/or strong executives. Both France and Britain defended domestic systems in which the executive was strong vis-à-vis parliament. Neither Britain nor Denmark had a strong tradition of European federalism, and the latter's government was under the tight control of a parliament whose prerogatives the governments defended.[156]

The justifications given by participants are consistent with both an ideological and a credible commitments account. Ideological motivations for institutional choice are suggested by timing: Genscher and Mitterrand were proponents of QMV before they were sure to which issues it would apply, whereas Thatcher was instinctively an opponent. At the same time, however, QMV (along with mutual recognition and the removal of customs controls) was perceived as a means to avoid decision-making deadlock, log-rolling, or noncompliance—thereby overcoming the deadlocks and delays that had plagued regulatory harmonization in the 1970s. Indeed, QMV was emerging as an informal practice to circumvent opposition by recalcitrant governments—notably Britain, Greece, and Denmark—even before the SEA. Through precommitment, the veto power of isolated governments and recalcitrant domestic constituencies was reduced. Even the creation of the Internal Market Council in 1983 was viewed not primarily as a means of increasing the informational efficiency of decision-making through specialization, but as a means of attracting the attention of economics ministers, thus creating political support for reform.[157]

---

[156] Alberta Sbragia,"Mastricht, Enlargement, and the Future of Institutional Change," manuscript (University of Pittsburgh, 1993).

[157] Alan Dashwood, "Majority Voting in the Council," in J. Schwarze, ed., *Legislation for Europe 1992* (Baden-Baden, 1989), 79; Thomas Sloot and Piet Verschuren, "Decision-Making Speed in the Euro-

By contrast, there is no evidence that the SEA was viewed as a means of centralizing information in a regulatory bureaucracy. To the contrary, the SEA recognized for the first time that centralized direction was *inefficient.* Cockfield estimated that one five-page "reference to standards" directive, such as the Low Voltage Directive, replaced ten directives totaling 500 pages; even federalists saw this as the true advantage of the "new approach."[158] The principle of mutual recognition has been heralded as a great breakthrough for European political integration, but Giandomenico Majone reminds us that it "works in large part because it represents a permanent abdication of responsibility by the Commission to national regulation." At the same time it would be misleading to see mutual recognition as posing less of a challenge to national sovereignty than harmonization. Mutual recognition requires more trust among nations, because governments precommit themselves to permit imports under minimal collective standards, thereby privileging liberalization over continued regulation. Its major advantage is that it permits more efficient collective decision-making.[159]

National governments tended to be jealous of their sovereignty where no clear practical purpose for cooperation was at hand. They resisted efforts by the Commission to slip in provisions expanding its own autonomy. Generally, the extent of delegated discretion remained inversely proportional to its substantive scope. Extensive delegation was governed by tight rules, and open-ended delegation was avoided. National governments rejected Commission proposals for a procedure to authorize future increases in funding without Treaty changes or national parliamentary ratification. The Commission was granted power of implementation, as was customary under EC practices, but Commission proposals to expand its own powers of implementation were rejected.

In sum, the pattern and process of transferring sovereignty suggest a combination of ideological and instrumental motivations. The major governments that negotiated the SEA were clearly willing to promote European institutions in part for reasons of geopolitical ideology, a particularly potent force where the consequences of delegation and pooling were uncertain and relatively minor. Where the consequences were calculable and significant, a combination of ideology and credible commitments best explains the pattern of institutional choice. Governments were unwilling to delegate or pool sovereignty for its own sake, but where such delegation and pooling served a substantive purpose, ideologically federalist governments proved significantly more willing to do so.

Convergence of economic preferences, relative power, and concerns for credible commitment were the most important forces determining the outcome of

pean Community," *Journal of Common Market Studies* 29 (September 1990), 75–85. It had always remained standard practice in the budget council. Butler, *Europe,* 162; A Campo and Narjes interviews.

[158] Interview with Delors, 1989; Cockfield, "Real," 6.

[159] Giandomenico Majone, "Introduction," in Majone, ed., *Deregulation or Reregulation? Regulatory Reform in Europe and the United States* (New York, 1990), 3–4. On Britain, see Helen Wallace, "Bilateral, Trilateral and Multilateral Negotiations in the European Community," in Roger Morgan and Caroline Bray, eds., *Partners and Rivals in Western Europe: Britain, France and Germany* (Aldershot, 1986), 158–159.

the SEA negotiations. Policy convergence resulting from policy failure and global competition, intergovernmental bargaining using threats of veto, exclusion, and exit, and the need for QMV to "lock in" reform and undermine future domestic opposition explain the fundamental shape of the reform. Two factors play a significant but secondary role. First, geopolitical ideology—in particular the split between federalists and nationalists—helps explain a somewhat greater willingness to support both substantive reform and transfers of sovereignty in France and Germany, as well as the Thatcher government's instinctive opposition to sovereignty transfers despite their instrumental advantages. Second, supranational entrepreneurship from Commission and Parliament failed to alter the distributional outcomes of the negotiations, but it may have increased their efficiency. Existing governments and interest groups were somewhat less able to spot and support proposals than in earlier cases. Throughout, and this was consistent with the changed institutional dynamics of the EC since the early 1970s, the focus was on the periodic summit meetings of the chief executives in the European Council, from which emerged key requests, decisions, and deadlines.

The SEA rejuvenated the EC and its single market. A flood of significant legislation was passed and a new liberalizing spirit prevailed. As the British government foresaw—but perhaps to an extent Thatcher herself had not fully expected—these measures reregulated, as well as deregulated, the single market. Before the implementation of the White Paper agenda had truly begun, however, France and Germany were moving toward deeper integration in the monetary area, to which we now turn.[160]

---

[160] Majone, "Introduction"; Nicolaïdis, *Mutual Recognition.*

CHAPTER SIX

Economic and Monetary Union: Negotiating the Maastricht Treaty, 1988–1991

> We should be under no illusions—the present controversy over the new European monetary order is about power, influence, and the pursuit of national interests.
>
> —Wilhelm Nölling, president, Hamburg Landeszentralbank (1992)

The Treaty on European Union, negotiated for one year ending with agreement at Maastricht in December 1991 and ratified by each member-state in the following year, set a timetable and conditions for the transition to economic and monetary union (EMU). EMU entailed "irrevocably locked currencies" for qualifying countries—a transition that was to occur automatically by 1999 even if only a few governments qualified. Plans were set for a European central bank (ECB), which would enjoy greater independence than any national central bank today. Political control would be imposed only over exchange-rate cooperation *vis-à-vis* third countries. To qualify, countries would have to meet a stringent set of criteria, including stable exchange rates, low inflation, and reduced deficits.

Parallel negotiations on "political union," initiated after governments had agreed to discuss EMU and linked to it, generated modest results. Governments agreed to deepen existing intergovernmental coordination of foreign policy. They hinted at future defense cooperation (the "second pillar") and established intergovernmental procedures to coordinate police and immigration policies (the "third pillar"). They modestly expanded majority voting and modified the legislative procedure to provide in some cases for "codecision," in which the European Parliament negotiates directly with the Council of Ministers over its proposed amendments. An arrangement for coordinating social policy was created among eleven governments, with Britain opting out. The Treaty was ratified after unexpectedly contentious referenda in France and Denmark, a smoother one in Ireland, and the imposition of important legal conditions by the German constitutional court.

The coincidence of timing between German unification and the Maastricht negotiations, as well as the revolutionary content of the Maastricht Treaty, has led most observers to explain Maastricht as a response to the geopolitical revolution of 1989. "Considerations of security and geopolitics," says one commentator, "once again became the driving force of European integration."[1] The governments of France and other neighboring countries, with the cooperation of German leaders, allegedly sought a means to lock post-unification Germany into an integrated Europe. Without "French fears of a united Germany," one analyst asserts, "Maastricht would not have happened."[2] Others maintain that a weakened Germany was forced to offer a monetary quid pro quo in exchange for Western assent to unification.[3] Still others point to the ideological beliefs of strong European leaders such as Kohl and Mitterrand, who are said to have exploited political momentum resulting from the success of the SEA.[4] It is nearly impossible, many scholars maintain, to find significant support for EMU among economic interest groups, particularly in Germany.[5] Even those who argue that Maastricht reflected a concatenation of contingent conditions so complex that there is little prospect of finding support for any theory of national preferences, lay significant weight on German unification.[6]

Similar consensus reigns in treatments of interstate bargaining and institu-

[1] Michael J. Baun, *An Imperfect Union: The Maastricht Treaty and the New Politics of European Integration* (Boulder, Colo., 1996), xii, 2, also 156, 160. Baun maintains as a "central theoretical claim" that "the end of the Cold War and German unification have made European integration once again primarily a matter of 'high politics.'"

[2] Keith Middlemas, *Orchestrating Europe* (New York, 1995), 157. Also Wayne Sandholtz, "Choosing Union: Monetary Politics and Maastricht," *International Organization* 47:1 (Winter 1993), 31–34; Joseph Grieco, "The Maastricht Treaty, Economic and Monetary Union and the Neo-Realist Research Programme," *Review of International Studies* 21 (1995), 21–40.

[3] E.g., Geoffrey Garrett, "The Politics of Maastricht," *Economics and Politics* 5:2 (July 1993), 105–124; Karl Kaltenthaler, *Germany and the Politics of Europe's Money* (Durham, N.C., 1998); Alan S. Milward and Vibeke Sørensen, "Interdependence or Integration? A National Choice," in Milward et al., *The Frontier of National Sovereignty: History and Theory, 1945–1992* (London, 1993), 29; Elizabeth Pond, *Beyond the Wall: Germany's Road to Unification* (Washington, D.C., 1993), 154–155, 159; Margaret Thatcher, *The Downing Street Years* (New York, 1993). Among dissenters are Peter Ludlow, "Reshaping Europe: The Origins of the Intergovernmental Conferences and the Emergence of a New European Political Architecture," in *Annual Review of European Community Affairs 1991* (London, 1992), 395–447; David Andrews and Thomas D. Willett, "Financial Interdependence and the State: International Monetary Relations at Century's End," *International Organization* 51:3 (Summer 1997), 499–500; John Newhouse, *Europe Adrift* (New York, 1997), 76–106; and Guido Carli, *Cinquant'anni di vita italiana* (Rome, 1993), 405; Steven Weber and John Zysman, "Why the Changed Relation between Security and Economy Will Alter the Character of the Europe Union," *BRIE Working Paper 99* (Berkeley, Calif., April 1997).

[4] Thomas Risse, "Between the Euro and the Deutsche Mark: German Identity and the European Union," Georgetown Center for German and European Studies Working Paper Series PS 1.3 (Washington, D.C., 1997); Kjell Goldmann, "Nationalism and Internationalism in Post-Cold War Europe," *European Journal of International Relations* 3:3 (September 1997), 259–290, especially 269; Peter Katzenstein, "United Germany in an Integrating Europe," in Katzenstein, ed. *Tamed Power: Germany in Europe* (Ithaca, N.J., 1997), 11–15, 24–29, 41–45; Thomas Banchoff, "National Identity and the Politics of Maastricht" (mimeo, Georgetown University, 1994).

[5] Kathleen R. McNamara, *The Currency of Ideas: Monetary Politics in the European Union* (Ithaca, N.Y., 1997), 37–42; Dorothée Heisenberg, *The Mark of the Bundesbank: Germany's Role in European Monetary Cooperation* (Boulder, Colo., forthcoming). Thomas Risse considers the costs and risks for Germany to give up its "cherished" DM so obvious that he declines even to provide evidence about the perceptions of government and business of their economic interests. Risse, "Between," 2. None of these studies conducts systematic, primary source–based research into the preferences of national industrial groups.

[6] Sandholtz, "Choosing," 36–39, cites five necessary conditions for preference formation and hints that an even greater number would be required to explain supranational leadership and bargaining outcomes.

tional delegation. Turning from preferences to bargaining outcomes and institutional choices, many analysts portray Germany as having fared badly in the negotiations because it gave up the Deutsche Mark without ironclad guarantees of low inflation or offsetting movement on political union. The supranational entrepreneurship of Jacques Delors or the power of transnational coalitions of central bankers and financial technocrats, it is said, undermined German opposition to EMU.[7] Finally, choices to delegate and pool sovereignty—including creation of the European Central Bank, expansion of QMV, and establishment of parliamentary codecision—tend to provoke explanations that stress ideology. The conflict between federalist Germany and France, on the one hand, and antifederalist Denmark and Britain, on the other, are said to have defined the cleavages on institutions.

In sum, German reunification, agenda-setting by supranational officials, and federalist ideology form the core of most existing interpretations of the Maastricht negotiations. In this chapter I challenge each element of this conventional explanation. While none is wholly incorrect, each requires substantial revision in light of the available historical evidence.

National preferences, I argue, were driven primarily by the enduring structural economic interests of strong- and weak-currency countries under conditions of increased capital mobility and macroeconomic convergence. They were essentially unchanged by German reunification. Firm commitments by France and Germany to move decisively forward with EMU—and opposition by Britain to that goal—predate the fall of the Berlin Wall and remained unchanged after unification was completed in August 1990. As in most previous EC bargains, economists by and large rejected EMU, but it had a clear political economic justification.[8] The conditions under which governments would be willing to move to EMU, as well as the pattern of disagreements among them, had been relatively stable since the late 1960s, but economic conditions changed. Shifts in national strategies during the late 1980s reflected convergence in European macroeconomic policies, liberalization of trade and capital movements, dollar depreciation, a desire for macroeconomic loosening by major governments, particularly that of Germany, and a desire to reduce exchange-rate volatility if it could be achieved with little loss of competitiveness—similar factors to those, we saw in chapter 4, which triggered initiatives for European monetary cooperation in the 1970s. The national position was, contrary to what most analysts have concluded, consistently supported by a decisive majority in peak business groups in both France and Germany.[9] In Britain, with much higher inflation, business opposed an immediate commitment to EMU but insisted on avoiding decisive exclusion if others went forward. Despite ideological misgivings on the

---

[7] George Ross, *Jacques Delors and European Integration* (Oxford, 1995).

[8] Barry Eichengreen and Jeffry Frieden, "The Political Economy of European Monetary Integration: An Analytical Introduction," in Eichengreen and Frieden, eds., *The Political Economy of European Monetary Integration* (Boulder, Colo., 1994), 5; Paul Krugman, "Policy Problems in a Monetary Union," in Paul de Grauwe and Loukas Papademos, eds., *The European Monetary System in the 1990s* (London, 1990), 62.

[9] E.g., business leaders in *Financial Times* (hereafter *FT*), 28 July 1989, 22, and citations below.

Table 6.1. Economic and monetary union negotiations, 1988–1992: Preferences and outcomes

Elements of EMU	Germany	France	Britain	Commission	Outcome
Single currency (EMU)	Prefers EMU with no "opt-out" but demands a parliamentary vote to "opt-in."	Prefers EMU with no "opt-out."	Opposes EMU. All countries have to opt-in explicitly but cannot be excluded.	French position.	EMU with British and Danish opt-out and unilateral German opt-in.
Strict convergence criteria ("two-speed" EMU)	Favors prior but flexible macroeconomic convergence, criteria; prior autonomy of national central banks; and full capital liberalization.	None.	Unclear.	French position.	German position prevails.
Schedule and procedure for the transition	Favors automatic movement in 1999, with QMV to decide which countries qualify. In the interim, a weak EMI, headed by a central banker.	Favors rapid movement in 1997 or before by simple majority vote. Strong interim EMI starting in 1993, headed by an EU official.	Favors maximal delay. Weak transitional EMI headed by a central banker.	French position.	Final transition in 1997 if a majority qualify, 1999 automatically, with QMV to determine membership. Weak interim EMI headed by a central banker.

ECB autonomy, mandate, and voting procedure	Prefers autonomous bank, except for multilateral exchange-rate policy, firm anti-inflationary mandate, and simple majority decision-making.	Favors political control, particularly over exchange rates, balanced mandate, and decisions by simple majority.	Opposes EMU but apparently argues that the ECB should be autonomous with a strong anti-inflationary mandate.	French position, plus even stronger Commission role.	German position prevails.
Location of ECB and name of currency	Frankfurt; Euro.	Paris, maybe Brussels; ECU.	London; ECU.	Brussels.	Frankfurt; Euro (decision later).
Domestic budgetary controls with sanctions	Yes, by simple majority.	No.	No.	No.	Yes, decision by QMV (later).
Financial transfers	No bail-outs, no financial transfers.	No financial transfers.	No financial transfers.	Fiscal federalism: large, permanent financial transfers.	No bail-outs or federalism, but temporary increase in structural funds (decision later)

Table 6.2. European political union negotiations, 1988–1992: Preferences and outcomes

Issues	Germany	France	Britain	Commission	Outcome
Overall structure	Single structure.	Three pillars.	Three pillars.	Single structure.	Three pillars.
CFSP procedure	Favors QMV and active Commission role.	Favors QMV only on implementation, no formal role for the Commission, and independent secretariat.	Favors unanimity, no Commission role, comes to support independent secretariat.	Same as Germany.	Anglo-French position prevails.
WEU and defense cooperation	Prefers WEU as a bridge between EU and NATO.	Prefers WEU subordinate to EU.	Prefers WEU subordinate to NATO.	Same as France.	Symbolic advisory role for EU in advising WEU.
Justice and home affairs	Prefers strong policy with QMV and Commission role.	Prefers weak policy without QMV or Commission role.	Opposes any policy.	Commission view even stronger than that of Germany.	Policy is created but with QMV on only a few issues and no formal role for the Commission.
Social policy	Strong social policy on nonfinancial issues.	Strong social policy on nonfinancial issues.	No social policy.	Strong social policy on many issues.	Britain opts out and Eleven move ahead with weak cooperation on nonfinancial issues.

Other new policies or expansion of QMV	Favors generalizing QMV to economic issues, including environment and research, but with many exceptions: industrial policy, professional qualifications, indirect taxation. Seeks to restrict education and culture policy.	Favors new industrial policy, as well as QMV on research, but restrictive clauses on culture and environment.	Favors no new policies.	Favors uniform QMV and Commission involvement, except in consumer safety. Opposes any restrictive clauses.	Consumer safety, some environmental and public health clauses added (most already conducted under Article 100). Restrictive culture and education clauses forbid harmonization.
EP powers and the legislative process	Favors Parliamentary initiative at Commission's expense, and advocates both "co-decision" and limits on the right of the Commission to amend or withdraw proposals.	Opposes any increase in EP powers.	Opposes any increase in EP powers, except oversight over Commission.	Favors Parliamentary powers insofar as Commission prerogatives intact.	Modest increase in issues subject to cooperation procedure and introduction of codecision. Commission powers unchanged, except EP votes on its nomination.
Strengthen ECJ	Yes	Yes	Yes	Yes	Yes
Oversight of Commission ("comitology")	Status quo.	Status quo.	Status quo.	Major priority is greater autonomy.	Status quo.

part of leading Conservative politicians, the British government adopted the same position. On other economic issues—social policy, immigration, and industrial policy, for example—each government similarly sought to realize enduring economic interests.

The Maastricht negotiations witnessed a resurgence of the intergovernmental negotiating style that had dominated EC bargains before the SEA. Supranational and transnational entrepreneurship tended to be ineffective, redundant, even counterproductive; governments and a handful of officials at the Council working with the Italian, Luxembourgeois, and Dutch presidencies, along with the efforts of major governments, placed a wide range of proposals on the table and mediated among them. Only a handful of officials in the intergovernmental Council Secretariat or in monetary bodies were consistently involved. The outcomes of distributive conflict, I shall argue, consistently reflected the preferences of Germany—the country with the tightest domestic win-set and the most to give up in the monetary negotiations. Threats of exclusion secured the participation of recalcitrant governments such as Britain's. All this confirms intergovernmental bargaining theory and rather decisively disconfirms supranational theory.

Finally, the choice of institutions reflected above all the need for credible commitments, in particular Germany's desire to "lock in" a guarantee of low inflation by creating an autonomous ECB, by far the most contentious issue in the negotiations. Positions on ECB autonomy reflected the distribution of economic costs and benefits. Nothing in this act of delegation was technocratically necessary; governments in weak-currency countries favored, and had long practiced at home, a monetary policy based on control by political authorities. And only in general institutional matters, such as the role of the Parliament, did ideology influence national positions.

In sum, a combination of enduring economic interests, asymmetries of interdependence, and the desire to coordinate policy within a structure that assured more credible commitments best explains the conduct and outcome of the Maastricht negotiations.

NATIONAL PREFERENCE FORMATION

By 1988 France and Germany were agreed to move toward EMU; both pressed aggressively, despite domestic controversy. In Britain, Margaret Thatcher's outright opposition to EMU was replaced by John Major's caution. While doubting that immediate participation and support was feasible, the British government was under strong pressure from business to dampen currency volatility and to avoid outright exclusion from any Franco-German arrangement. On the form of EMU, traditional splits between strong- and weak-currency countries reemerged, with Germany calling for an independent central bank and other anti-inflationary guarantees while France and the Commission sought a central bank under greater political control. Britain remained divided, supporting anti-inflationary protection but seeking delay on the transition to EMU. On other issues, Germany and France supported deeper cooperation in some specific areas, whereas Britain opposed integration across the board.

Germany: A "European Germany" or a "German Europe"?

Modern German politicians ritualistically recite Thomas Mann's celebrated quotation: "Our aim is not a German Europe, but a European Germany." Yet the two goals are closely connected, and nowhere more clearly than at Maastricht. Germany supported a single European currency, a "European Germany," in exchange for which it demanded the creation of European institutions of German choosing such as an independent central bank, capital mobility, and prior macroeconomic convergence—a "German Europe." What motivations underlay Germany's acceptance of monetary union at this time and on these terms?

The most commonly advanced explanation rests on a linkage between EMU and objective geopolitical shifts, in particular German unification. Germany is said to have conceded EMU to reassure its neighbors about unification. Such a connection was highlighted in the rhetoric of Chancellor Helmut Kohl and Hans-Dietrich Genscher during the negotiation of German unification, from November 1989 to August 1990. If German unification played an important role, however, we should observe a major shift in German policy in late 1989 and, perhaps, a shift in the opposite direction in late 1990. We should also see, in contrast to longstanding German policy, inattention to the specific economic content of EMU as well as the consequences of economic issues, and decisive concern with political union. Finally, domestic coalitions and discourse should be dominated by geopolitical rather than economic considerations. Since we observe none of these, we have good reason to be skeptical of claims about some causal link between unification and EMU.

The historical record disconfirms an objective geopolitical explanation, but both political economic factors and geopolitical ideology offer more plausible candidates. Political economic theory predicts that the German negotiating position at Maastricht, like that in negotiating the EMS, would reflect not the uncompromising anti-inflationary position of the Bundesbank (supported by some public and business opinion) but a compromise between the Bundesbank's anti-inflation and the demands of German business interests and the Chancellory for a competitive exchange rate and macroeconomic stimulation. Whereas the Bundesbank's power and position remain constant, pressure from the government and business (led by big financial firms and export interests) for a looser monetary policy and exchange-rate stability should be proportional to pressure from dollar depreciation and the government's desire for macroeconomic stimulation; both factors were present in the late 1980s and early 1990s. (In addition, the German government perceived threats to the stability of the existing EMS and the convergence of foreign governments to German macroeconomic norms.) The conflict between these two domestic coalitions, the political economic theory predicts, will also dominate domestic divisions and discourse. On balance, however, given the advantages of the EMS (despite threats to its stability), the German economic interest in EMU should be only modest and the risks

Table 6.3. Annual percentage change in consumer prices, 1984–1992

Year	Germany	France	Britain
1984	2.4	7.4	5.0
1985	2.2	5.8	6.1
1986	−0.1	2.7	3.4
1987	0.2	3.1	3.4
1988	1.3	2.7	4.9
1989	2.8	3.6	7.8
1990	2.7	3.4	9.5
1991	3.5	3.2	5.9
Average (1984–91)	1.9	4.0	5.8

relatively significant; hence we expect support from economic interests will be less than enthusiastic. We therefore expect Germany to demand strong concessions in exchange for "giving up the Deutsche Mark"; EMU is likely to be possible only in conjunction with relatively strong anti-inflationary guarantees—the traditional "economist" position we encountered in chapter 4. Anything more than modest compromises on this score is likely to render EMU unratifiable.

Even those who accept the predominance of economic interests cannot dismiss entirely the role of geopolitical ideology, in particular the European federalism of Kohl, Genscher, members of the Bundestag, and the German public. If European ideas (or the electoral advantages of espousing them) were decisive, we should expect steady support for EMU throughout the period in question— at least through the 1990s. We should observe the foreign minister and chancellor taking the initiative and strongest support from political parties and public opinion rather than from economic interests; domestic cleavages should reflect the relative strength of federalist convictions in various parties, and discourse should focus on ideological and symbolic issues, such as the prevention of future European wars and the symbolic desirability of European union. We should observe a German negotiating position uniform across economic issues and relatively little attention being paid to the economic conditions under which integration proceeds. If popular support for Europe is decisive, we should see strong European moves preceding elections, not after them.

The balance between economic and ideological motivations is difficult to judge precisely, given the absence of primary documentation and the continuing controversy surrounding the issue. On balance, however, the historical evidence presented below—cross-issue variation, timing, policy consistency and negotiating tactics, domestic cleavages and discourse, and internal deliberations—offers slightly stronger support for the importance of political economic motivations than for geopolitical concerns. Overall the most plausible conclusion is the following: economic conditions were largely favorable, German business was firmly (albeit not enthusiastically) supportive, and the economic consequences of EMU were at best uncertain, so the Kohl government enjoyed a certain autonomy to pursue its European federalist ambitions. This context may help to explain the active role Germany took in moving monetary integration beyond the EMS, a status quo that was relatively attractive for Germany. Still, Germany remained on the whole less able to compromise away from its ideal economic outcome than was France, and it employed what bargaining power it had almost exclusively to promote its preferred economic outcome rather than deeper political union. In sum, the preponderance of evidence suggests that in German preference formation, economic interests were at least as important as European federal ideology and probably more so. Nonetheless both may have been necessary for significant forward movement.

Geopolitical Interest and Ideology: A "political task of historic dimensions"

Claims that German preferences in the Maastricht negotiations reflected geopolitical interests and ideology take two basic forms. Most geopolitical explanations highlight *objective* concerns, notably the sudden opportunity after November 1989 to promote German unification, which required Germany to give France the diplomatic quid pro quo of EMU and neutralized domestic opposition to EMU. Some others point to *ideological* concerns: the personal beliefs of Genscher and Kohl and the electoral competition between the two before a pro-European public. Kohl's personal commitment is often treated as decisive; one analyst writes that "only Kohl, virtuoso and one-man band, could have maneuvered monetary union to acceptance in Germany. If he isn't widely popular, he is widely trusted." [10]

There is little doubt that the geopolitical strategy of German leaders linked German and European integration. The connection between East-West relations and integration had, of course, long been central to Genscher's variety of Ostpolitik, and Kohl had mentioned it in private discussions as early as 1983. [11] There is little doubt that German unification took precedence in the minds of Kohl and Genscher. Kohl proceeded unilaterally, often without international consultation, in 1989–90. The fall of the Wall and the prospect of more rapid unification raised two concerns that made linkage to Europe even more salient. First, European support might be required to negotiate with the Soviet Union. Horst Teltschik, Kohl's closest adviser, observed that the chancellor "was in a situation of having to approve practically every French initiative for Europe," the most novel of which was the European Bank for Reconstruction and Development (EBRD). [12] Second, unification required formal changes within the EC to define the status of the new territory, resolve changes in German and EC law, and establish appropriate exceptions to existing rules. Acceptance did not, at first, seem automatic. In the first years of the transition it was widely believed that unification would strengthen Germany; Belgium and Luxembourg sup-

[10] Newhouse, *Europe*, 102–103.

[11] Timothy Garten Ash, *In Europe's Name: Germany and the Divided Continent* (New York, 1993), 361n; Peter Ludlow, "The Politics and Policies of the European Community in 1989," in Ludlow, ed., *Annual Review of European Community Affairs 1990* (London, 1991), xlix.

[12] Horst Teltschik, *329 Tage: Innenansichten der Einigung* (Berlin, 1991), 61; Stephan Haggard and Andrew Moravcsik, "The Political Economy of Financial Assistance to Eastern Europe, 1989–1991," in Robert O. Keohane, Joseph S. Nye, and Stanley Hoffmann, eds., *After the Cold War: Politics and Institutions in Europe* (Cambridge, Mass., 1993).

ported rapid reunification, but Britain and the Netherlands were openly skeptical and France more discreetly so.

Kohl and Genscher had consistently supported European objectives even before reunification was on the agenda. The precise mixture of personal conviction, electoral calculation, and diplomatic strategy is difficult to ascertain. Foreign Minister Hans-Dietrich Genscher, we have seen, had long promoted European integration; his overall diplomatic conception had long involved embedding Germany in international institutions. Kohl had long offered rhetorical support for integration, which he often justified as a means to prevent future European wars. Many have linked this support to his training as a historian and to his being the last leading German politician with personal memories of World War II.[13] In private discussions soon after he replaced Schmidt as chancellor in 1982, Kohl termed new German efforts to bring about European unification "a political task of historic dimensions." Ten years later he was calling for movement to what "the founding fathers of modern Europe dreamed of following the last war: the United States of Europe."[14] Here, in contrast to the case of Schmidt, there is little evidence of underlying skepticism about supranational institutions or federalist ideas.

Another influence on Kohl and Genscher appears to have been electoral. The period after 1987 was characterized by competition among party leaders, led by Kohl and Genscher, for prominence in foreign policy. European activism was politically advantageous, and there is considerable evidence that both politicians focused, sometimes obsessively, on such concerns. Genscher's stature in foreign affairs helped to make him the most popular of Germany's leading politicians. At critical points between 1988 and 1991, Kohl and his advisers explicitly considered how foreign policy activism might influence the chancellor's electoral standing; this was a primary concern, though it was German unification that captured their immediate attention. European integration was popular in Germany, enough so that it neutralized some skepticism about EMU. Still, a surrender of the DM was constrained by the right-radical Republican party and the CSU, both of which might exploit EMU in parliamentary elections, notably those scheduled for December 1990. Kohl and Genscher appear to have agreed to cooperate on European issues to avoid electorally dangerous treaty negotiations before 1991.[15]

German governments tended to favor foreign policy cooperation more generally. Kohl and Genscher, like Schmidt before them, realized that German unilateralism had to be embedded in multilateral institutions in order to secure the support from neighboring countries. Even in unilateral initiatives, such as Ostpolitik, the "ten-point plan" for German unification, and the recognition of former Yugoslav republics, simultaneous recommitment to multilateral institu-

---

[13] Wolfgang Bickerich, *Helmut Kohl: Kanzler der Einheit* (Düsseldorf, 1995), 177–178; Helmut Kohl, *"Ich wollte Deutschlands Einheit,"* compiled by Kai Diekmann and Ralf Georg Reuth (Berlin, 1996), 483.

[14] Thatcher, *Path*, 481.

[15] Ash, *Europe's*, 361; Ludlow "Policies," xlix, also liv. Interview with Kanzleramt official (Bonn, 1992).

tions served to reassure allies. Hence the German government had long supported a strengthening of the EPC mechanism and looked favorably on efforts to deepen European defense cooperation, as long as they did not directly challenge NATO. In January 1988 France and Germany had agreed to create a Franco-German Council on Security and Defense, as well as a Franco-German brigade. The foreign and defense policy positions on which France and Germany agreed in March and April 1990 were comprised of longstanding German proposals.[16]

On institutional questions, Germany maintained its traditional support for the principles of QMV and expanded Parliament powers. German advocacy of a stronger Parliament reflected in large part the position of the Bundestag, whose members consistently supported greater political integration. Kohl had a more nuanced view, in which institutional issues were secondary. The government's long-term if unstated goal was to strengthen both the Council and the Parliament, if necessary at the expense of the Commission. Early in negotiating Maastricht, the CDU and FDP factions in the Bundestag announced they would not ratify EMU without movement toward political union. The SPD threatened to oppose Maastricht at the last minute if the Parliament voted against it. For its part, the Bundesrat, representing the regions, announced that it would refuse to ratify the treaty without a subsidiarity clause. Germany had good substantive as well as ideological reasons to favor expanded QMV and parliamentary powers, which in general favored the passage of higher EC regulations—though this support did not extend to areas of particular national sensitivity such as fiscal harmonization. Germany peppered its proposals for QMV with numerous exceptions. Finally, Germany publicly supported a unified EC institutional structure rather than the three-pillar structure favored by France and Britain, which hived off sensitive areas for intergovernmental treatment.[17]

Economic Interest: EMU Only on "non-negotiable" Terms?

From 1987 through 1991 (and thereafter), peak business groups in Germany consistently though less than enthusiastically supported continued monetary integration, albeit subject to traditional German "economist" conditions. The German experience with the EMS had been largely positive. The EMS had contributed to the undervaluation of the DM, which in the late 1980s created large trade surpluses, while only marginally limiting Bundesbank autonomy. German business viewed monetary integration as in its interest, but the EMS status quo was also relatively attractive, perhaps more so than EMU was. So German business could afford to insist on preconditions for EMU. Thus in October 1988,

---

[16] Teltschik, *329*, 176; also 106, 369; Christa van Wijnbergen, "Germany and European Political Union," in Finn Laursen and Sophie Vanhoonacker, eds., *The Intergovernmental Conference on Political Union* (Maastricht, 1992), 49–50; Reinhardt Rummel and Wolfgang Wessels, "Federal Republic of Germany: New Responsibilities, Old Constraints," in Christopher Hill, ed., *National Foreign and European Political Cooperation* (London, 1983), 34–55.

[17] Interview with Kanzleramt official; JoEllyn Fountain, "The German Länder and the EC: Federalism as a Source of Regional Influence," paper presented at the International Conference of Europeanists, Chicago, 31 March–2 April 1994.

60 percent of German industrialists supported further monetary integration; though the lowest percentage in the EC, where support averaged 90 percent, it was still a significant majority.[18]

Little direct evidence about the sectoral distribution of business preferences is available from the late 1980s, but such views can be inferred from two sources: the views of peak interest groups, and polls conducted in the mid-1990s. These reveal that large banks were EMU's strongest supporters; they supported union not to reduce foreign-exchange transactions—which would in fact impose losses on them—but apparently because integration would lock in open markets, permitting them to expand domestic and European market share at the expense of smaller counterparts. Business support was not based primarily on the desire to reduce transaction costs of managing exchange rates or eliminating the cost of exchanging currencies. Eighty percent of German exports were denominated in DM, and the relative gains from currency stabilization were viewed as modest. Instead, support derived from the desire to assure free movement of investment and financial capital and to dampen DM appreciation. Accordingly, larger firms and those in export sectors (automobiles, electrical machinery, machine tools) were particularly favorable.[19]

Business concerns about currency appreciation would intensify during the 1990s, as German export competitiveness continued to decline under the combined pressure of the large fiscal costs of reunification, the collapse of the ERM, and the devaluation of the pound, peseta, and lira. By 1996 a BDI committee dominated by Germany's major exporters—Krupp, Merck, Hoechst, AEG, Daimler-Benz, Siemens, Trumpf—was stressing competitiveness: "The dramatic appreciation of the DM in past years has already worsened our position relative to our foreign competitors. Since 1989, about one third of the price rise in labor costs is homemade, two-thirds resulted from currency shocks. Such a situation should not repeat itself [for] distributional maneuvering room has be-

---

[18] Statistics from the Association for Monetary Union in Europe.

[19] BDI President Hans-Olaf Henkel, "Entlasten statt entlassen wäre richtig: Hohe Staatsquote führt zu hohe Arbeitslosigkeit," *Süddeutsche Zeitung*, 17–18 February 1996; and poll results in "Führungskräfte sagen ja zum Euro, ohne an den Terminplan zu glauben," *Süddeutsche Zeitung*, 14 March 1996, which shows 77 percent support of EMU, rising rapidly in a period of DM appreciation. Also, Deutsche Industrie- und Handelstag, "Deutsche Unternehmen und Europäische Währung" (Bonn, September 1995); BDI, *Der Euro: Chance für die deutsche Industrie—Report des Industrieforums EWU* (Cologne, 1996). Some of these polls of business combine stability and the level of the currency into one measure termed "volatility," but interviews suggest the greater importance of the level. For evidence that business statements in support of monetary integration stressed the benefits of market liberalization rather than the direct benefits of monetary stabilization, see Carsten Hefeker, "Germany and European Monetary Union," *Center for European Policy Studies Paper* no. 69 (Brussels, 1997); Committee for the Monetary Union of Europe, *A Programme for Action* (Paris, 1988).

[20] BDI, *Euro*, 9, also 8–11. Mark Duckenfield, in research conducted some years after Maastricht, reports that for German exporters, the issue is not a 1–2 percent savings on transaction costs in currency charges but DM 415.2 billion in exports to EU members, which might suffer under the deleterious effects of currency instability in general and an appreciating currency in particular. Verband der chemischen Industrie, "European Monetary Union: Economic Assessment," in *European Monetary Union* (Frankfurt, 1996), 8, cited in Mark Duckenfeld, "Getting EMU Off the Ground: The Politics of Monetary Union in Germany and Britain," paper prepared for the Annual Meeting of the American Political Science Association (August 28–31, 1997).

come narrow."[20] This position was also held by producers of nontradable goods, such as the construction industry, who thought that EMU would benefit export industries and lead to a general loosening of macroeconomic constraints.[21]

Business incentives were translated directly into political demands. Public pressure for EMU came from business and unions, conditional on a commitment to low inflation—which would protect the competitive real value of the Deutsche Mark. The Bundesverband der deutschen Industrie (BDI), Germany's major industrial interest group, praised the Delors report in 1989 and issued public statements in support of monetary union in 1990 and 1991. In the late 1980s the Deutsche Industrie- und Handelstag (DIHT), the other major group, proposed a three-stage plan for EMU closely resembling what the German government later advocated. Support also came from the Association for Monetary Union in Europe, founded in late 1986 by Giscard and Schmidt to unite representatives of big business and banking across Europe. In April 1988 the association published a detailed blueprint for monetary union and later in the year presented survey results revealing big business support for EMU. Though some have argued that this group did not engage in direct lobbying, Alfred Herrhausen of Deutsche Bank praised the Delors report in its name. Yet on balance, one review of interest group positions during and after the Maastricht negotiations concludes, "the balance among . . . important interest groups . . . tips in favor of, and in many cases takes the form of active lobbying for, monetary union." Above all, this is because "events in exchange markets have shown that the German export industry is sensitive to large adverse exchange rate movements." Business support for EMU, however, remained conditional on adequate anti-inflationary safeguards. Business groups insisted that European monetary institutions be autonomous and that all member countries first establish independent central banks—an idea that had emerged early from German business circles. Industry had an incentive to favor a larger EMU, as long as it remained stable and anti-inflationary, in order to prevent competitive devaluation on the part of outsiders.[22]

Unions were also strongly supportive; farmers weakly so, if at all. The Social Democratic party and the unions, led by the Deutsche Gewerkschaftsbund, backed business in support of EMU. The DGB and BDI issued joint statements in favor of EMU in July 1989 and August 1990; union support was steady. The SPD may have sought to loosen German monetary policy, which it felt was slowing growth. Alternatively the SPD and DGB may also have shared the big business assessment of the economic benefits of export promotion through mone-

---

[21] European Construction Industry Confederation, *Construction Activity in Europe* (1996), cited in Duckenfield, "Getting," 31. One Bauindustrie official explained, "We knew these cuts were coming with or without monetary union. The convergence criteria just make it easier for the politicians to pretend to be good guys." Interview with official from Hauptverband der Deutschen Bauindustrie, Bonn, August 12, 1996. Nontradable goods producers would have reason to support any policy likely to promote macroeconomic stimulation in Germany.

[22] The conclusion is from Hefeker, "Germany," 55. Schönfelder and Thiel, *Markt,* 49–53, also 125–126; Connolly, *Rotten,* 243; Karl Kaltenthaler, *Germany and the Politics of Europe's Money* (Durham, N.C., forthcoming); Hefeker, "Germany," 14–16. For a skeptical view of transnational groups, though one not based on detailed study of national interest groups, see McNamara, *Currency.*

tary integration. In either case, dissent within the SPD was stronger than within the CDU/CSU. Some Social Democrats voiced concerns that the French and others might pull out of the EMS if asymmetries persisted—an action hinted at in French and Italian government statements.[23] German farm groups tradition- ally opposed or remained lukewarm toward EMU; they were slightly more posi- tively inclined during the Maastricht negotiations. It is often asserted that farm groups should support EMU because they are affected by shifting agricultural prices, but this narrowly functionalist view ignores the distributional implications of various subsidies designed to offset such shifts. On balance, German farmers have benefited disproportionately from such subsidies and thus have never per- ceived an interest in EMU, though their view might have been changing in the mid-1990s as EC member governments, including their own, became less will- ing to provide subsidies.[24]

In addition, the Kohl government had its own macroeconomic reasons to side with business in favor of EMU. Like the Schmidt government a decade ear- lier, the Kohl government was continuously pressing the Bundesbank in this period to loosen monetary policy, first in response to the dollar depreciation of the late 1980s, then in response to the shock of German unification. In 1987 the Kanzleramt called for lower interest rates, backing the Louvre Accord, but the Bundesbank raised them—an act believed in retrospect to have contributed to the "Black Monday" stock market crash. By early 1989 Bonn and Frankfurt were clashing again over macroeconomic policy. Then, when Kohl announced in February 1990 his intention to move toward *German* monetary union—a move certain to create inflationary pressures—he set the stage for yet another round of conflict. Thereafter Kohl associates repeatedly attacked the Bundesbank for exceeding its mandate by seeking to influence taxation, government spending, and wages, as well as for failing to support the government's European policy— a complaint backed by explicit reminders that the Bundesbank statute could be changed and that its current mandate "does not contain the obligation that sta- bility be achieved through a deep recession." In short, the Kohl government in the late 1980s and early 1990s, like the Schmidt government a decade earlier, experienced the classic postwar German conflict between a chancellor favoring monetary accommodation of dollar depreciation and higher domestic spending through higher inflation and a Bundesbank favoring monetary tightening, lower inflation, and DM appreciation.[25]

The opposition to EMU was led, as it had been in the case of the EMS and as predicted by the political economic theory, by the Bundesbank, backed by academic economists, the domestic banking sector, and a substantial portion

[23] Eckart Gaddum, *Die deutsche Europapolitik in den 8oer Jahren: Interessen, Konflikte und Entschei- dungen der Regierung Kohl* (Paderborn, 1994), 346–349; Wilhelm Schönfelder and Elke Thiel, *Ein Markt—Eine Währung: Die Verhandlungen zur Europäischen Wirtschafts- und Währungsunion* (Baden- Baden, 1994), 29–39; Karl Kaltenthaler, "International Institutions and Domestic Politics: Under- standing the Relationship between German Domestic Politics and the EMU Initiative," Washington University *Political Science Paper* 242 (St. Louis, Mo., 1994), 14–16; Hefeker, "German," 1996, 16–17.
[24] Hefeker, "Germany," 54.
[25] Connolly, *Rotten,* 92–96, also 37–42, 83–85, 242–243; Middlemas, *Orchestrating,* 171, 722n.

of public opinion. The Bundesbank Council was split over the issue. Some members, particularly SPD members such as Claus Köhler, appear to have been somewhat more sympathetic to EMU, whereas others, led by vice-president Helmut Schlesinger, defended absolute priority for domestic stability. The balance seems to have been held by a centrist faction, initially including President Karl-Otto Pöhl, Leonhard Gleske, responsible for international affairs, and Lothar Müller, the Bavarian regional bank president. This group did not express public opposition to "irrevocably linked" exchange rates but nonetheless questioned whether the proper preconditions could possibly be met. Pöhl, as we shall see below, was unwilling to oppose EMU outright. Moreover, though skeptical about a single currency, he and other Bundesbank officials were even more strongly opposed to British proposals for a parallel currency, which they believed would undermine monetary control.

Whatever their differences, Bundesbank officials agreed that economist preconditions must be imposed; their conception of such preconditions was stricter than that of either business or the Chancellery. Through a series of plans and commentaries issued between 1989 and 1991, the Bundesbank publicized its "unconditional and non-negotiable preconditions" for EMU. Among these were a European central bank at least as independent as the Bundesbank, full economic union including capital liberalization, and a lengthy transition based on strict convergence criteria rather than an explicit timetable. During 1990 the Bundesbank, acknowledging the momentum toward EMU, argued that if a binding commitment were made, it should be to a "two-track" system, with governments entering only if they met specific economic preconditions. In 1990 Schlesinger added a fourth precondition: political union with centralized controls on fiscal policy.

Still, the Bundesbank was not entirely opposed to EMU. Pöhl's ambivalence aside, Hans Tietmeyer, Kohl's handpicked nominee to the Bundesbank Board, became increasingly influential after joining the board in 1989. He took over the Bundesbank presidency in 1993 after the retirement of hard-liner Helmut Schlesinger, who had succeeded Pöhl in 1991. Tietmeyer could move only modestly in the government's direction, in part by exploiting arguments about the need to defend German competitiveness. It was Tietmeyer, even before he assumed the presidency, who publicly threatened unruly British and Danish voters with exclusion, arguing that if the Maastricht Treaty were not ratified, the subset of countries that favored its provisions should conclude a parallel agreement.[26] Still, the German Council of Economic Advisers, the Finance Ministry, and the Advisory Council of the Economics Ministry all backed a strict economist position. Only some members of the Bundestag supported a softer position, and even among them there remained considerable skepticism about naming a European currency the "ecu" (which sounded too French) and about too great a compromise of the preconditions.[27]

---

[26] Connolly, *Rotten*, 282; David Marsh, *Germany and Europe: The Crisis of Unity* (London, 1994), 146.

[27] David Marsh, *The Bundesbank: The Bank That Rules Europe* (London, 1992), 212–219. See also Gaddum, *Deutsche*, 298–305; Smyser, *German*, 292, also 278–279; Richard Corbett, *The Treaty of*

Pressure from German business on other economic issues discussed at Maastricht remained essentially unchanged, reflecting Germany's traditional economic interests. Completion of the European single market, not regulatory or monetary harmonization, remained the major business concern. Business, labor, and public opinion favored regulatory harmonization that would bring other EC members up to the relatively high standards prevailing in Germany but refused to forego the SEA right to derogate upward to protect domestic standards. On social policy, German business was ambivalent, tending to favor cooperation to "level the playing field" but not extensive European-level intervention in collective bargaining. Widespread skepticism concerning full liberalization on professional qualifications reflected strong domestic interests. Germany's particular vulnerability to flows of migrants from the East, the fact that Germany took a disproportionate percentage of migrants and refugees to the EC, and the domestic political limitations imposed on restrictive policies imposed by Social Democratic opposition—all of which stoked extreme right-wing opposition, threatening to the governing CDU and FDP parties—suggest that the government would favor a European policy in the area of immigration and asylum that would help manage and legitimate more restrictive policies. Characteristically, economic groups said little about political union.

The Domestic Decision: Reasserting the "Economist" Compromise

Both economic and geopolitical factors appear at first glance to have contributed to German preferences in the Maastricht negotiations. What does the evidence reveal about their relative contribution?

The conventional view, we have seen, is that German support for EMU—in particular Kohl's willingness to move ahead at Strasbourg with a schedule for an IGC—reflected new geopolitical circumstances after the fall of the Berlin Wall on 9 November 1989. Kohl, it is argued, offered EMU as a quid pro quo for French support of German unification or, alternatively, unification and economic opportunities in former East Germany were required to overcome skepticism from business and the Bundesbank, which had forced Kohl to water down the 1987 Basel-Nyborg Agreement and the 1988 agreement creating the Franco-German Economic Council. Two pieces of evidence are commonly cited in favor of this geopolitical linkage: the coincidence of timing between the agreement to hold an IGC, which was reached a month after the fall of the Berlin Wall, and the German willingness to "give up" the Deutsche Mark.[28]

Geopolitical concerns seem at first glance to explain Kohl's dynamic leader-

---

Maastricht (Harlow, U.K., 1993), 40–41; Wayne Sandholtz, "Monetary Bargains: The Treaty on EMU," in Alan Cafruny and Glenda Rosenfeld, eds., *The State of the European Community* (Boulder, Colo., 1993), 133; Hefeker, "Germany," 20; Ludlow, "Policies," xlii; *Europäische Währungsordnung: Gutachten des Wissenschaftlichen Beirats beim Bundesministerium für Wirtschaft*, Studien-Reihe 61 (Bonn, 1989); Connolly, *Rotten*, 251; Detlev W. Rahmsdorf, "Währungspolitik," in Werner Weidenfeld and Wolfgang Wessels, eds., *Jahrbuch der europäischen Integration 1991/92* (Bonn, 1992), 126.

[28] Risse, "Between," 2.

ship in November 1989. On November 20, he met with close advisers to plan strategy for the marathon of elections scheduled over the coming year. The chancellor found himself in the weakest electoral position of his career, and his advisers concluded: "The Chancellor's high international reputation must be exploited domestically and the German question was a bridge to improve his image."[29] Only the next day did the German government perceive the first hints that the Soviet leadership might really be willing to accept radical change on the German question. German unification was to be the instrument. Kohl's November 28 address before the Bundestag, in which he presented a ten-point plan for eventual German unity embedded within an "all-European process," came as a surprise to all except CSU chief Theo Waigel; its content was kept from Genscher as well as from all foreign governments except the United States. Teltschik recorded in his diary that the speech was a "great success" because "the Chancellor has taken over opinion leadership on the German question." Both Genscher and the SPD were outmaneuvered and quickly followed suit. Genscher recalls a discussion with François Mitterrand shortly thereafter in which both stressed the linkage between German and European unification, focusing in particular on the need for movement on EMU to convince France and others not to actively balance against Germany.[30]

Yet this coincidence of timing is superficial; the sequence of events in fact helps us *dismiss* the possibility that linkage to German unification was decisive. Instead, timing strongly supports the economic explanation. The decision to move ahead on EMU through an IGC *predates* the fall of the Wall by at least three months and probably three years, depending on how one reads the evidence, and continued long after reunification was completed. Though reunification did not become a focus of German policy until November 1989 or an immediate possibility until late January 1990, Kohl and Genscher had been consistently if cautiously promoting EMU from, at the very latest, the Hanover summit of mid-1988. Yet in March 1987, shortly after the SEA came into force, Genscher was already calling for deeper monetary cooperation. He was supported by the economics minister, Martin Bangemann, also from Genscher's FDP. The response was a series of informal discussions and proposals. The German government sought to respond to criticisms that monetary integration was asymmetrical and established new institutions: the 1987 Basel-Nyborg agreement permitted intramarginal intervention and stronger financing provisions, a Franco-German Economic Cooperation Council created in 1988 provided a forum for bilateral cooperation. By seeking to structure both to constrain the Bundesbank, Kohl and Genscher went well beyond the minimum necessary to maintain Germany's

[29] Teltschik, *329*, 41–44. Also François Mitterrand, *De l'Allemagne, De la France* (Paris, 1996), cited in *Le Monde*, 23 April 1996, 15.

[30] Teltschik, *329*, 58; Bickerich, *Kanzler*, 130; Barbara Lippert et al., *German Unification and EC Integration: German and British Perspectives* (London, 1993), 11. For an overview of the great power diplomacy, though without direct documentation on EC issues, see Philip Zelikow and Condoleeza Rice, *Germany United and Europe Transformed* (Cambridge, Mass., 1995), 120–121; Hans-Dietrich Genscher, *Erinnerungen* (Berlin, 1995), 677–680.

European image. Though the Bundesbank successfully limited the scope of both reforms, the proposals signaled the intent of the chancellor and foreign minister.[31]

In February 1988, in response to French and Italian proposals for a more symmetrical monetary arrangement, Genscher offered a proposal for rapid movement toward EMU, hinting that some sacrifice of domestic stability might be necessary. He suggested that a committee of "wise men" be named to study the issue. Kohl endorsed Genscher's proposal in a speech before the European Parliament. Thereafter Kohl and Genscher moved relentlessly toward the calling of an intergovernmental conference, the only purpose of which could be a treaty amendment to create EMU. This movement was matched the following month by a memo from Finance Minister Gerhardt Stoltenberg, less enthusiastic but not entirely negative, and a month later by a Bundesbank paper and a press conference by President Pöhl, foreshadowing many ideas subsequently to appear in the Delors Report. These contributions reasserted the need for free capital flows and anti-inflationary guarantees in exchange for any further German commitments.[32]

From 1988 onward Kohl and Genscher looked to exploit the instruments at their disposal, to increase domestic pressure on Bundesbank and Finance Ministry officials. At the Hanover European Summit of June 1988, working with Delors, they realized Genscher's proposal for a committee to discuss monetary reform proposals, though Kohl insisted on a committee of central bank presidents chaired by Delors. Pöhl initially agreed to serve on the committee only if it were comprised solely of central bankers and was mandated to propose limited technical reforms in the EMS or to assess the *general* desirability of further monetary integration. At the last minute, however, Kohl, Mitterrand, and Delors agreed that the group would be chaired by Delors and would prepare concrete proposals for EMU. Pöhl, cornered, considered immediate resignation but was reportedly convinced by Bundesbank colleagues to "participate constructively" since this was the only way the Bundesbank position would be taken seriously. To prod the committee further, Kohl issued a statement jointly with eight other center-right heads of government calling for an intergovernmental conference on EMU. When the Delors Committee reported, Kohl maneuvered for rapid acceptance of its recommendations at the Madrid Summit of June 1989. At the Madrid discussions Kohl had signaled unambiguously that he supported a rapid move to set a firm date for the IGC; Genscher sought to move even faster.[33]

---

[31] Schönfelder and Thiel, *Markt*, 66; Bickerich, *Kohl*, 108–109, 116–117, 131–134; Kohl, *Wollte*, 39–44; Frank Elbe, *Ein runder Tisch mit scharfen Ecken: Der diplomatische Weg zur deutschen Einheit* (Baden-Baden, 1993), 44ff. Before December 1989, the consensus view in the German government—shared by CSU chairman Theo Waigel and top Kohl aide Teltschik—remained that unification was a realistic goal only over a ten-year period. Zelikow and Rice speculate that Teltschik did not fully understand Kohl's true motivations. Zelikow and Rice, *Germany*, 34–35, 79–81, 92–93, 105, 122–123.

[32] Schönfelder and Thiel, *Markt*, 22–30. Gaddum, *Deutsche*, 312.

[33] Marsh, *Bundesbank*, 214n. Pöhl later called this decision an error; once on the committee, he argued, he was less able to defend German interests, either by opposing proposals within the committee or by criticizing the report afterward. Gaddum, *Europapolitik*, 351–353; Charles Grant, *Delors: Inside the House That Jacques Built* (London, 1994), 119–120; David M. Andrews, "The Global Origins

The preceding month Kohl, Genscher, Theo Waigel (who had replaced Stoltenberg as finance minister), and Helmut Schlesinger, who had replaced Pöhl at the Bundesbank, had met in committee to hammer out a common German position. EC governments, with or without Britain and Denmark, would meet within the year to set a date for an IGC. Germany would support calling the IGC, but on the basis that EMU could proceed only through creation of a federal European bank with full autonomy, a clear commitment to price stability, strict limits on the monetary financing of government deficits, and prior irrevocable fixing of national currencies. These principles were summarized in a position paper, "The German Position on Economic and Monetary Union," drafted by the Finance Ministry and approved by the Bundesbank. Already in spring 1989, then, the Bundesbank apparently recognized, as it had with the Delors Committee, that direct opposition would exceed its constitutional prerogatives and might not be politically justifiable. Bundesbank support may have been based, some have since suggested, on an underestimate of France's willingness to comply with stringent institutional and economic preconditions. The critical point is, however, that all agreed that convergence was a sufficient condition for German support of EMU.[34]

Thereafter German decision-making was centralized in the hands of the party leaders, though they kept a wary eye on the Bundesbank. Decisions relevant to Europe under the Kohl government, as we saw in the last chapter, were generally made by party chiefs and ratified in the Cabinet by the chancellor and senior ministers. As leaders of the three coalition parties—Kohl of the CDU, Stoltenberg and Waigel of the CSU, Genscher of the FDP—were closely involved in the negotiations, Bundestag rejection of the treaty was unlikely, even when Kohl ultimately failed to get significant movement on political union.

By October 1989 Kohl had added the final element to the German negotiating position. He insisted that EMU be linked to deeper political integration, particularly to greater use of QMV, wider powers for the Parliament, and closer cooperation on foreign policy—longstanding priorities for the Bundestag and for German public opinion. These demands were fleshed out early in 1990, after the fall of the Berlin Wall, but only a few additions were new: a subsidiarity clause demanded by the German regions and more detailed proposals for cooperation on asylum, visa, and law enforcement policy. From mid-1989 onward the German position—EMU only on the traditional economist preconditions of capital mobility, economic convergence, central bank independence at home and abroad, and simultaneous movement toward closer political cooperation—remained constant.[35] German support for EC enlargement and concerns about

---

of the Maastricht Treaty on EMU," in Cafruny and Rosenthal, *State*, 111; Schönfelder and Thiel, *Markt*, 56–57, 66–67; Ludlow, "Policies," xliv–xlv.

[34] Heisenberg, *Mark*, 164–165; Schönfelder and Thiel, *Markt*, 54–57; Ludlow, "Policies," xlii.

[35] Andrews, "Global," 112; Schönfelder and Thiel, *Markt*, 42–54. The Bundesbank did remain relatively quiet during the first half of 1990, during which the focus was on criticisms of *German* monetary union. By the second half of 1990 and during the year 1991, Bundesbank officials reemerged as vocal critics and provided specific proposals that Kohl generally accepted over opposition from France and the Commission. *Economist*, 7 December 1991, 52; Lippert et al., *German*, 45, 120.

immigration, which arose at the same time, might be explained either on economic grounds or as a defense against social disruption.[36]

By mid-1989 differences within the German government concerned not *whether* to call an IGC but *when* to do so. The government's negotiating position on conditions was approved internally during discussions in the spring and summer. In June and July 1989 Kohl agreed with Mitterrand in principle to set a date for the IGC; French and German finance ministry officials met in September 1989 to prepare the announcement of the IGC for Strasbourg. Over the next month Kohl met with top business executives and secured their support; meanwhile Pöhl, Mitterrand, and Delors publicly predicted that a final decision on the timing of an IGC to negotiate EMU would be set at the Strasbourg Council. To be sure, Kohl consistently demanded that the starting date of the IGC be delayed, but it would be wrong to ascribe this demand to some fundamental opposition to EMU or the absence of domestic support in Germany. The bulk of the evidence suggests instead that Kohl was driven by fear of extreme right-wing opposition in the elections in late 1990—a motivation signaled to French officials and acknowledged by his closest associates, as well as Genscher, who had every incentive not to reveal that Kohl had taken the lead. Kohl refused to compromise this domestic political objective, as the geopolitical account suggests he did. The IGC was convened only after the December 1990 elections, in keeping with Kohl's consistent demand. In sum, as the chief Foreign Ministry official responsible for EMU later observed, unification did not fundamentally change the German policy consensus. It led only to a "redoubling of previous efforts."[37]

Nor was subsequent German negotiating behavior consistent with a linkage to unification. To be sure, Kohl's public rhetoric does suggest such a link. He assured Germany's allies that any steps toward reunification would be taken within Europe. As early as October 1989 Kohl sought to dampen media speculation that Germany might seek a neutralist solution and pressed President George Bush to stress the link between Western solidarity and progress in the East. Although he unveiled the "ten-point" plan for German unity in late November without consulting European allies, Kohl quickly renewed efforts to deflect in-

---

[36] "Our Algeria lies to the East," one journalist reports Germans as saying. John Newhouse, *Europe Adrift* (New York, 1997), 124. For the economic argument, see Haggard and Moravcsik, "Political."

[37] Schönfelder and Thiel, *Markt*, 22, also 20–22; Hubert Védrine, *Les mondes de François Mitterrand: à l'Élysée 1981–1995* (Paris, 1996), 420, 428–429. Genscher, despite his best efforts to emphasize his own role, remembers telling Mitterrand "with a good conscience" on November 30 that "we have already reached a decision" to set a date. The only difficulty, Genscher recalls, was that the CDU wanted to delay the IGC long enough to avoid any conflict with parliamentary elections scheduled for late 1990. Genscher, *Erinnerungen*, 679–680. See also Ludlow, "Politics," xlii–xlv; Wolfgang Schäuble, *Der Vertrag: Wie ich über die deutsche Einheit verhandelte* (Stuttgart, 1991), 20–27; Bickerich, *Kohl*, 139; David Buchan, *Europe: The Strange Superpower* (Aldershot, 1993), 32–33; interviews with Jacques Delors (1992–1996). Even those biographers who attribute the most foresight to Kohl do not place his move for unification any earlier than June 1989; most place it much later. E.g., Christian Müller, *Helmut Köhl* (Frankfurt, 1996); Zelikow and Rice, *Germany*. Kaltenthaler asserts that EMU was "dead in the water" before the situation was "fundamentally transformed" on 9 November 1989. Yet this conclusion rests only on public statements showing that before 9 November Kohl had assured domestic constituents that political union and anti-inflationary guarantees were necessary corollaries to EMU. This position did not change after 9 November, when Germany moved ahead. Kalthenthaler, *Germany*, 107–108.

ternational criticism. In every major foreign policy speech and at European summits over the last two months of 1989, he explicitly linked German unification to European integration.

Yet this reassurance was rhetorical; it left Germany's bargaining position on major EC issues unchanged. If the linkage-to-unification thesis were correct, we should expect sudden German concessions to France or a significant loosening of domestic constraints after the Berlin Wall fell. Yet the German negotiating position *hardened* between November 1989 and August 1990: Kohl insisted the IGC should start no earlier than December 1990, repeatedly rejected foreign appeals to accelerate the timetable, demanded a parallel IGC on political union, and reiterated economist demands. Moreover, if Kohl and Genscher had been compelled to support EMU in 1989 by a quid pro quo, they could have reversed policy when unification was concluded in August 1990, a year earlier than expected. Yet Kohl not only failed to do so, he continued to exploit every opportunity to promote EMU. He did not demand, for example, weighted voting in the ECB, prior convergence before setting a schedule, or a more flexible transition arrangement, even though he could easily have done so simply by siding with Britain and the Bundesbank against France or by remaining silent. All this is precisely the opposite of what a causally critical linkage to unification would imply.

Although we can reject the linkage between unification and the German position on EMU, it is more difficult to disentangle the relative influence of pro-European ideology and economic interest. On balance, economic interests appear to explain more—particularly the timing, domestic cleavages, and specific negotiating demands behind the German position—but we cannot dismiss the role of pro-European ideology (whether in the minds of leaders or in their partisan calculations) in tipping the government to favor a rapid move to EMU.

Only economic motivations can account for the core of the German "economist" position on EMU—prior convergence, capital mobility, central bank independence—which had remained essentially unchanged since 1965. This position, as we have seen, reflected a domestic compromise between business and government, on one side, favoring a competitive currency and macroeconomic flexibility, and the Bundesbank, backed to a certain extent by public and business opinion, on the other, which privileged low inflation. Policy consistency also supports the economic view. The Kohl government pursued similar economic objectives across different forums—it supported the Louvre Accord, challenged the Bundesbank domestically, and pursuing a bilateral arrangement with France before and during the Maastricht negotiations; an explanation based on Kohl's belief in European federalism has difficulty explaining such consistency of policy, even outside the EC. Despite a modest movement toward a Franco-German brigade, there was no parallel movement in German preferences and strategies concerning security relations.

The economic explanation, which predicts that dollar depreciation, macroeconomic convergence, and capital liberalization should promote monetary integration, also best accounts for the timing of the Franco-German initiative, which increased momentum after 1988, when all three factors were present. We observe in this period a willingness on the part of France and some other weak-currency countries, Britain excepted, to converge to German low-inflation standards. In addition, the French government threatened to obstruct capital liberalization and hinted at withdrawal from the EMS if concerns about asymmetry were not addressed—certainly this is what none other than Delors was advising the French government to do. In addition, as we have seen, business support for EMU, while not overwhelming, was solid and more positive than public opinion. The consistency of German policy across international forums—simultaneous efforts to strengthen the Louvre Accord at the global multilateral level, to work bilaterally with France in the Basel-Nyborg process and the Franco-German Council, and unilateral efforts by the Chancellory to place independent pressure on the Bundesbank—suggests that German international monetary policy was not linked specifically to European ideology. Neither the linkage-to-unification view nor an ideological explanation can provide a plausible account for German bargaining positions, domestic cleavages, or timing.

Cross-issue variation in German support for integration also falls into a pattern predicted by economic and functional motivations rather than the uniformly positive attitude predicted by a geopolitical explanation. Longstanding opposition to French proposals for industrial policy stemmed from German competitiveness without such aid and commitment to its traditional, indirect modes of subsidization. Germany also opposed the extension of majority voting to areas of particular economic sensitivity, including indirect taxation and the recognition of professional qualifications. A mixture of geopolitical and economic concerns was visible in German attitudes toward the coordination of criminal policing, asylum, and visa matters. The fall of the Wall increased the incentives for Germany—with borders to the East and a large proportion of the EC's refugees—to act in these areas. Such issues reflected a particularly delicate domestic problem for Kohl, for Germany exhibits powerful domestic sentiments concerning responsibility to grant asylum and equally strong right-wing, anti-immigrant feeling. European cooperation offered not just a way to share the burden but perhaps also potential support for measures to restrict immigration to levels that would assure domestic political stability. These were the last substantive issues to be demanded by Kohl. In addition, a more purely geopolitical matter, German opposition to cultural policy reflected the absence of any specific gains, as well as skepticism from regional governments.[38]

Both the issue-specific and geopolitical linkage theories predict that geopolitical concerns would dominate German positions, as they appear to do, in those areas without clear and certain economic implications, such as support for stronger Parliament and foreign policy cooperation. Objective geopolitical and ideological constraints on a unilateral German foreign or defense policy induced preferences for deeper cooperation; Bundestag and public opinion had

---

[38] Grant, *Delors*, 193. At the June 1991 summit, Kohl called for common immigration and police cooperation, apparently because Germany's liberal constitution limited its ability to deal with these problems unilaterally.

long favored greater powers for the European Parliament. Regional governments pressed for a Council of Regions, though this step, opposed domestically
by the federal government, proved more symbol than substance. Yet perhaps the
most striking aspect of German policy is that the government did *not*, in the end,
insist upon significant movement toward political union as a quid pro quo for
EMU. It appears that the EMU bargain was stable on its own.

Yet domestic deliberations and cleavages—in particular the early support of
Genscher for EMU and the enthusiastic position of government as compared to
business—prevent us from dismissing federalist ideology entirely. To be sure,
the German government explicitly refused to take significant steps toward EMU
until 1988, when a combination of economic convergence, dollar depreciation,
and Franco-Italian threats increased the economic incentive to do so. We have
seen, moreover, that business and labor, perhaps also farmers, supported EMU
from the start and that internal divisions were those predicted by economic theory. Yet Genscher and Kohl appear to have been strongly predisposed toward
integration, even in advance of a clear economic justification for it. The earliest
and most consistent support for deepening monetary integration came from
the foreign minister, not from economic authorities. Beyond Genscher, whose
role should not be exaggerated, stood Kohl. Thus momentum toward EMU was
maintained, even accelerated, after Kohl triumphed electorally and Genscher
had lost first the domestic political initiative and later his position. Electoral
concerns may have played a role, but the surrender of the Deutsche Mark was
hardly popular, and Kohl postponed negotiations until after elections. The most
enduring source of ideological support for EMU appears to have been Kohl's
own beliefs.

Public and parliamentary support for European federal goals may also help
explain the success of the Maastricht Treaty provisions for EMU after the failure
of the more modest Basel-Nyborg and Franco-German Economic Council agreements of 1987 and 1988. The link between EMU and a federalist vision may
have bolstered public and parliamentary support for the Maastricht Treaty by
helping to shield it from Bundesbank opposition. Appreciation of such constraints may help explain, for example, Pöhl's conciliatory behavior on the Delors
Committee. Yet the European idealism of the German government was tightly
constrained by economic interests and parliamentary skepticism. Ratification
was unproblematic, yet the Bundestag and Bundesrat did not pass it entirely as
Kohl wanted. Kohl sought a constitutional change to transfer Bundesbank functions to a supranational body. Schlesinger intervened directly, eventually watering the proposal down to a clause permitting such actions only within the conditions for EMU set forth in the treaty. And strong opposition came from the
German Supreme Court, which required that final implementation of EMU be
ratified by another parliamentary vote.[39]

For Germany the most important purposes of EMU were economic: to depress and stabilize the real exchange rate and to provide the government with

---

[39] Connolly, *Rotten*, 135n.

greater macroeconomic flexibility by undermining Bundesbank control. On balance, the timing, process, policy consistency, negotiating demands, and cross-issue variation of German preference formation are more consistent with this economic account than with any involving geopolitical interests or ideas. As political economic theories predict, moreover, support for deeper monetary integration on this basis intensified at a time of dollar depreciation and pressures for higher spending as well as convergence to German norms by other countries. The particular balance of economic concerns—pressure for an autonomous central bank and prior economic convergence by Germany's neighbors, on the one hand, and for limitations on foreign depreciation and EMU even without full anti-inflationary guarantees, on the other—was similar to that which had arisen in previous European monetary negotiations. This domestic compromise was then translated directly into policy. The two sides were represented bureaucratically and agreed on a compromise negotiating position; the government slightly relaxed these conditions in the last days of the negotiations.

The result: Germany supported an EMU that fulfilled most if not all of the "economist" preconditions demanded by Bundesbank and public opinion while paving the way for a larger EMU and a softer Euro, an outcome good for German exporters. Yet the economic theory also predicts uncertainty and skepticism about the net benefits of EMU, particularly *vis-à-vis* the existing and relatively attractive EMS. Support for EMU in Germany would thus be neither enthusiastic nor uncontroversial. The weakness of economic support had two implications. First, the domestic win-set in Germany was narrow. Despite important differences of degree, business, parliament, and the Bundesbank were united in support of a relatively autonomous European central bank, moderately tight convergence criteria, and centralized budgetary controls. Second, however, within the relatively narrow constraints of the win-set, European ideology—though not German unification—appears to have motivated German policy on the margin. Kohl and Genscher's enthusiasm for integration helped to define German positions where allowed by the permissive parliamentary and public consensus and the weakness and divisions among economic interests (as compared to, say, German views on the SEA or CAP).

France: "Franc fort" and Frankfurt

The paradox of French international monetary policy since 1988 has been its extraordinary continuity in the face of deep and persistent domestic conflict. From 1984 onward French governments consistently advocated a deeper and more symmetrical form of European monetary cooperation; after 1987 they recommended EMU—a position maintained to the present day, regardless of which party is in power. There is considerable disagreement over the sources of this policy, with some citing concerns about German unification, others European federalist ideals, and still others a particular French economic strategy of domestic discipline and a pegged exchange rate—the *franc fort* policy.

Each explanation offers distinctive predictions about the nature of French preferences and the process of French preference formation. If the German threat were decisive, we should see a decisive shift in French policy in late 1989, discourse and domestic divisions dominated by geopolitical concerns, and a relatively undifferentiated set of French negotiating demands aimed at locking Germany into Europe through political union. If European ideology were decisive, we should see a stable French policy over this time period, a set of symbolic goals connected with federal Europe, and little attention to the precise economic terms of the final agreement. If economic interests were decisive, pegged exchange would impose real currency appreciation and domestic tightening for a country with moderate inflation, which could be offset only by establishing more symmetrical international monetary arrangements. Hence we should observe pressure for monetary cooperation steadily increasing through inflationary convergence and accelerating with dollar depreciation in 1987–88 (and again in the mid-1990s), domestic divisions and discourse dominated by economic concerns such as competitiveness and macroeconomic performance, strong support from business, and French negotiating demands aimed at establishing looser, less autonomous European monetary rules, as traditionally supported by "weak-currency" countries.

On balance the historical record consistently disconfirms the importance of German unification and most supports the economic explanation; yet we cannot dismiss the ideological explanation entirely. Although support from French business and the concern of the government for greater macroeconomic flexibility were clearly predominant and led to the predicted set of internal cleavages and external negotiating demands, European ideology and the traditional desire of French governments to play a leading role in Europe may well have established a legitimating permissive consensus within public and partisan opinion, as well as offering President François Mitterrand yet another opportunity to sign agreements that profiled his leadership role.

Geopolitical Ideology and Interest:
Is François "always dancing with the wrong woman"?

The task of understanding France's geopolitical goals and perceptions with respect to Germany is complicated by French president François Mitterrand's distinctive style of governance, which involved the cultivation of numerous policy options through the simultaneous pursuit of parallel policies for a time— each often shadowed by a separate team of internal advisers, often unknown to the others—followed by a swift presidential decision. The opaque and superficially contradictory quality of French foreign policy was exacerbated by Mitterrand's insistence, which he shared with his predecessors, on maintaining foreign policy as a presidential "domaine reservé" to be conducted from the Elysée.[40] Still, we can isolate three geopolitical factors that may have influenced French preferences in the Maastricht Treaty negotiations.

One was Mitterrand's desire to bolster *the prestige of France* by maintaining an active French role at the center of Europe and in defense of European federal ideals. This was not, as we have seen, initially of primary importance to him.

[40] Védrine, *Les mondes,* 30–43, 51–54.

Remembrance of glories past.
Louis XIV, Napoleon, de Gaulle, and Mitterrand in diminishing order.
Cartoon by Kevin Kallaugher. *The Economist*, 8 July 1989. Used with permission.

Neither the EC nor its supranational institutions, we saw in chapter 5, played a significant role in the first years of Mitterrand's presidency, but they emerged as an ideological alternative once the Socialist experiment had failed. From this perspective, Mitterrand's desire to appear "European" in the Maastricht negotiations might be seen as a continuation of his decade-long effort to split the right wing of the French political spectrum and bolster the sagging electoral fortunes of the Socialist party—by the late 1980s further weakened by a recent *cohabitation* with the right. A strong move toward integration would, at the very least, exploit pro-European sentiment and profile Mitterrand himself as a world leader. Whatever its role in determining French policy during the negotiations, this motivation was clearly reflected in Mitterrand's decision, over the objections of all but one of his top officials, to call a referendum on the Maastricht Treaty in 1992. In 1987 and 1988—just before Mitterrand's reelection but also around the time that momentum toward EMU began to pick up again after the French failure to include stronger monetary provisions in the SEA—Mitterrand also began pressing for the signing of a new Elysée Treaty, with provisions for closer military cooperation, though the French government was careful, despite German pressure, to exclude nuclear weapons.[41]

A second geopolitical motivation stemmed from *traditional Gaullist ideology*, now shared by the Socialists, which combined an important role for na-

[41] Védrine, *Les mondes*, 55, 120–130, 273, 295, 409–415, cf. 126; Anand Menon, "Continuity and Change in French European Policy, 1981–1997," paper delivered at Harvard University, 2 October 1997. For more detail, see chapters 4 and 5 of this book.

tional executives, a unilateralist desire for independence from the United States, and opposition to supranational institutions, particularly the European Parliament. Accordingly, France favored strengthening the European Council, opposed greater powers for the Parliament, and advocated a bicameral parliamentary system with a Senate made up of national legislators—though this last notion was probably an effort to generate a legitimate if nonviable alternative to Germany's proposals. France, a long-time supporter of a "European security identity" within the EC, also spoke in favor of deeper defense cooperation independent of NATO. How much of this activity was symbolic, like the 1991 expansion of the joint Franco-German brigade—a step reportedly taken neither with substantial input from foreign and defense ministries nor with much attention to military effectiveness—remains unclear. In this regard, Mitterrand's defense of France's traditional prerogatives, like his executive-led style of foreign policy-making, was in fact quite traditional; Stanley Hoffmann has termed it "Gaullism by any other name."[42]

The third and most commonly cited geopolitical motivation was to meet a *renewed German threat*. French policy-makers had long spoken of the need to maintain parity with Germany and to offset German dominance institutionally in order to retain French influence in Europe and, some commentators argue, in such global multilateral forums as the GATT and G-7.[43] The fall of the Berlin Wall in November 1989 and the prospect of a unified Germany with an independent policy toward eastern Europe appeared to rekindle such concerns. Kohl's announcement of his ten-point plan for unification in November 1989 without consulting EC partners and his conduct of direct negotiations with Gorbachev in July 1990 led in France to consternation and occasionally what appeared hysteria. Among the more measured pronouncements was that of the French ambassador to Germany, who stated in late 1989 that the real danger of unification was that it "would give birth to a Europe dominated by Germany, which no one, in the East or West, wants."[44] European integration could help offset such concerns.

Consistent with Mitterrand's opaque and contradictory leadership style, the initial French response to German unification combined two contradictory strands. On the one hand, Mitterrand appears to have worked behind the scenes to impede unification by cooperating with Russia, Poland, and East Germany—most spectacularly in his December 1989 joint declaration with Gorbachev that border changes were premature and in his open support for an "East German identity." He sought to establish a pan-European confederation, a policy that

[42] Enrico Martial, "France and European Political Union," in Laursen and Vanhoonacker, *Intergovernmental Conference*, 121–122. Interview with French Cabinet Minister (May 1994); Stanley Hoffmann, "Mitterrand's Foreign Policy, or Gaullism by Any Other Name," in George Ross, Hoffmann, and Sylvia Malzacher, eds., *The Mitterrand Experiment: Continuity and Change in Modern France* (New York, 1987).

[43] Christian de Boissieu and Jean Pisani-Ferry, "The Political Economy of French Economic Policy and the Perspective of EMU," in Barry Eichengreen and Jeffry Frieden, eds., *The Political Economy of European Integration: The Challenges Ahead* (Ann Arbor, Mich., 1997).

[44] Alistair Cole, *François Mitterrand: A Study in Leadership*, 2d ed. (London, 1997), 152, also passim; David Yost, "France in the New Europe," *Foreign Affairs* 69:5 (Winter 1990), 107–128.

had the added advantage of possibly forestalling entry of East European countries into the EC, an event Mitterrand is said to have hoped to delay for decades. The French also considered bilateral military and even nuclear cooperation with Britain as a counterbalance.[45] On the other, Mitterrand kept open the possibility of deeper cooperation with Germany. In public he treated unification as natural, even desirable. He pressed Kohl to offset unification with a deepening of monetary integration. Beginning in February 1990, his top officials were in constant contact with their German counterparts over a proposal for political union.[46] German leaders were nonetheless frustrated by Mitterrand's two-pronged geopolitical strategy, as one anecdote suggests. During the period in which Mitterrand remained indecisive, the other European heads of government were waiting for the French president to arrive at a summit—the French president insisted on arriving last, a diplomatic prerogative that his status as a head of state, rather than head of government, permitted—when Kohl turned to another prime minister and remarked: "Poor François, always off dancing with the wrong woman!"[47]

Yet the contradictions were soon clarified. The refusal of Russia, Poland, and the United States to oppose Germany and the massive GDR vote for unification in mid-March 1990 forced a resolution of the contradictions in French policy. In March 1990 the French government dropped bilateral discussions with Britain, on the eve of an important speech on defense cooperation by Douglas Hurd in Paris, and turned definitively to Germany. Mitterrand's sole goal became to secure a monetary quid pro quo for France, backed by whatever concessions on political union were required. By mid-April Mitterrand and Kohl had drafted a joint letter in which both leaders called for parallel negotiations on monetary and political union. It is commonly asserted that the French government viewed Franco-German cooperation as a means to offset growing German power and, therefore, as a substitute for possible alliances with Britain or the Soviet Union.[48]

Economic Interest: "Germany was *the* determinant of our economic policy"

From 1988 onward, polls revealed consistent 80–90 percent support among French businessmen for EMU—among the highest levels in the EC. Business began to favor cooperation to reduce exchange-rate fluctuations and assure cheaper and more flexible sources of finance but assumed that EMU would not undermine French competitiveness—the primary concern of business. Thus the CNPF embraced a strengthening of EMS or a transition to EMU, as well as convergence criteria and fiscal constraints, while seeking to assure that EMU

[45] Interview with French Minister, 1994; interview with adviser to Margaret Thatcher, 1997.

[46] For an analysis that stresses this side, see Védrine, *Les mondes*, 393–479.

[47] Interview with European prime minister, April 1997.

[48] Baun, *Imperfect*; Grieco, "Maastricht"; Sandholtz, "Choosing"; Cole, *François*, 154–155; Grant, *Delors*, 133; Zelikow and Rice, *German*, 206–207, 234–235; Claire Tréan, "La France et le nouvel ordre européen," *Politique Etrangère* 56 (Spring 1991), 81–90; John Laughland, *The Death of Politics: France under Mitterrand* (London, 1994), 238ff; Martial, "France," 116. In October 1990 Mitterrand instructed his defense minister, Jean-Pierre Chévènement, to improve nuclear capabilities but did not allocate funds for the purpose.

was not too strict. This concern took various forms. Smaller firms and traditional sectors stressed the need for looser convergence criteria to assure that weak-currency "outsiders" would not depreciate against the franc, undermining French competitiveness. Others in business, particularly those in aerospace and other export sectors dependent on the dollar exchange rate, supported EMU on the condition that the Euro be set at a competitive rate *vis-à-vis* the dollar—or the franc entered EMU at a particularly competitive rate. As the value of the franc rose in 1992 and 1993, after the fiscal shock of German reunification, higher interest rates led French industry to call for depreciation, though it continued to support EMU. Support for EMU surged upward again in the mid-1990s, as it appeared that the Euro would not be as strong as some had feared.[49]

The Conseil National de Patronat Français, the leading French business interest group, translated these preferences into demands. The CNPF supported EMU but called for political controls over the ECB to prevent too harsh an anti-inflationary regime. The organization split over the Maastricht Treaty and therefore took no official position on the referendum, though its president, representing larger and more competitive firms, spoke out in favor. Reluctance to give strong support to the arrangement evidently stemmed primarily from its social policy provisions, which business believed to be unnecessary and disadvantageous, particularly without the full participation of Britain. This ambivalence may also have reflected discomfort with the independence of the ECB. Large banks favored EMU as well, though the president of Paribas, André Lévy-Lang, an advocate of EMU, pointed out that its effects would be "marginal," since wholesale banking was already integrated and retail banking would not be integrated for twenty to thirty years. Banks apparently saw a significant comparative advantage, however, if Britain did not participate and demanded that the ECB limit access to its refinancing facilities to participants in EMU. In the mid-1990s leading French and German industrialists cooperated to publicize their support for EMU with a competitive rate *vis-à-vis* the dollar. (French firms were somewhat more vulnerable than their German counterparts to world market pressure from dollar-denominated products, but the difference was not as great as is often thought.) Prominent supporters of EMU with close ties to business, among them former president Valéry Giscard d'Estaing, called for a weaker franc against the dollar and, implicitly, against the DM.[50]

The cautious and conditional support of business for EMU was echoed by Socialist and Gaullist governments alike, which recognized that financial liberalization, capital mobility, and convergence toward low inflation had increased the benefits and reduced the costs of exchange-rate stabilization. The financial deregulation and budgetary reform required for convergence was occurring

---

[49] For polls and other data on French business, see Pisani-Ferry, "France," 28–29; Amy Verdun, "Does European Economic and Monetary Integration Limit Policy-Making Autonomy?" *Essex University Working Paper* (Colchester, 1996); interview with French cabinet minister, 1994. Also Philippe Bauchard, *Deux ministres trop tranquilles* (Paris, 1994), 151ff; Blanchard and Muet, "Competitiveness"; Connolly, *Rotten,* 107–108, 111–112; Laughland, *Death,* 15–16.

[50] Pisani-Ferry, "France," 15–20, 30, and previous note.

unilaterally. The Gaullist government from 1986 to 1988 was particularly supportive of privatization, but even Socialist governments favored greater liberalization and deregulation of finance and industry. Like Britain, the Benelux countries, and Scandinavia, France relaxed restrictions on the activities of foreign banks, with the Paris-based Eurobond market reopening in 1985. With the striking failure of highly interventionist industrial policy, the government was abandoning direct financing of industry and committed itself to greater autonomy for managers. By 1988 France was well on the way to eliminating capital controls; the French government later advanced the timing of full capital liberalization to an earlier date than EC rules required. These moves were supported by business. The "young Turks" in control of the CNPF continued to press for more market-oriented policies—though some remained skeptical about the strong currency policy.[51]

By the late 1980s a combination of technological developments, cross-border investment, and liberalization had further reduced the cost-effectiveness of capital controls, except in the very short term. Increasing capital mobility during this period reduced the scope for the domestic manipulation of interest rates, thereby shifting the trade-off between exchange-rate stability and domestic monetary autonomy in favor of the former. Where this trend was interrupted—notably by Keynesian reflation, as in France, Belgium, Sweden, and Norway after the second oil shock—inflation spiraled upward and external disequilibria induced policy reversal (a politically and economically costly process we traced in chapter 4). By 1986 there was strong evidence that remaining real interest rate differentials between France and its neighbors reflected little more than risk premia imposed on weak currencies.[52]

French macroeconomic performance, particularly inflation, was also converging to German levels. In this regard, the French situation seemed sharply different from that of either Italy or Britain.[53] This change, along with weak oil prices, robust economic growth during the late 1980s, and a temporary dip in unemployment, made EMU under German terms appear feasible at relatively low cost. Lower inflation and progressive stabilization of the franc was matched after 1987 by falling unemployment during an upswing of the business cycle. The dollar's decline after 1986 placed downward pressure on the franc, but the continuing overvaluation of the dollar meant that the pressure did not grow severe for a few years. When it did, French officials argued that macroeconomic pressures on France stemmed from the threat of speculative attacks rather than from divergence in underlying economic fundamentals; this was certainly the

[51] Interview with official in the French Treasury, 1989; Louis W. Pauly, *Opening Financial Markets: Banking Politics on the Pacific Rim* (Ithaca, N.Y., 1988), 174; Christian de Boissieu and Marie-Hélène Duprat, "French Monetary Policy in the Light of European Monetary and Financial Integration," in Heidemarie Sherman, ed., *Monetary Implications of the 1992 Process* (New York, 1990), 62–63; J. R. Hough, *The French Economy* (New York, 1982), 209. See also chapters 4 and 5, above.

[52] Capital liberalization was not a direct consequence of EC commitments. David M. Andrews, "Capital Mobility and Monetary Adjustment in Western Europe, 1973–1991," *Policy Sciences* 27 (1994), 432–33; Boissieu and Duprat, "French," 78–79.

[53] On unit labor costs, *OECD Economic Outlook 58* (Paris, November 1995), A16.

lesson that leading government officials appear to have drawn from the 1987 EMS realignment.[54]

In this regard, EMU was seen as the continuation of longstanding French international monetary goals by other means. The French economic argument for EMU was as follows: policy was in any case converging toward low inflation, market-driven interest rates, and greater capital mobility—in short, France was committed to liberalization and the *franc fort*. In this context, the more symmetrical EMU appeared to offer advantages over the more asymmetrical EMS, including lower risk premia and exchange-rate volatility, greater political legitimation, and, above all, more symmetrical obligations *vis-à-vis* Germany, which would translate into looser constraints on macroeconomic policy. This was not, as some have argued, the result of a complete ideological conversion of French policy-makers to the German doctrine of low inflation and monetary discipline, leading to a near-total convergence of French and German interests.[55] To the contrary, the French government, like French business, maintained the traditional French support for monetary union on "monetarist" terms—that is, with looser convergence criteria, greater political control over the ECB, a relatively large number of members, an explicit mandate to target employment and growth, and a weaker European currency than that favored by Germany.

Like the EMS, EMU was an effort to overcome an underlying Franco-German asymmetry that stemmed ultimately from Germany's strong export performance and the autonomy of the Bundesbank. Unlike the EMS, however, EMU took place after the French economy, and those of many other EC member-states, had converged toward German macroeconomic standards. The EMS did not create this convergence—as some who stress that EMU was only the result of spillover from the EMS seem to suggest. Nearly all European countries, whether or not they were members of the EMS, converged toward lower inflation and more stable exchange-rate policies during the 1980s and suffered from asymmetry insofar as they sought to stabilize exchange rates. David Andrews rightly observes that "monetary authorities in Paris and Rome were obliged to pursue increasingly Germanic monetary policies throughout the 1980s not *because* policy coordination with Germany had been formally institutionalized, but in spite of it."[56]

---

[54] Connolly, *Rotten*, 36–40, 107–109; Jacques Attali, *Verbatim* (Paris, 1993), 1:429; McCarthy, "France," 58; interview with French Cabinet Minister.

[55] Sandholtz, "Choosing Union"; McNamara, *Currency*.

[56] Andrews, "Capital Mobility," 431. The stability of French preferences over time and the similarity of pressures facing non-EMS and non-EC members call into question another widespread view, namely that French preferences at Maastricht stemmed from the success of the SEA. In an influential essay, "Choosing Union," Wayne Sandholtz revives the neofunctionalist claim that state preferences are fundamentally path-dependent, that is, the primary determinants of state preferences are prior integrative decisions in other areas. The boost in public support for the EC following the SEA was a "necessary" condition, he conjectures, without which Maastricht would have been a "ritual invocation." He also notes that the SEA's provisions for capital liberalization created strong pressures to move to EMU. Yet the French government supported greater symmetry in the EMS and movement toward EMU from the 1985–87 period onward, predating the SEA's rise to public prominence by some years. Similarly, while the move to EMU was clearly linked to capital liberalization—the French

Within this new context of convergence and liberalization, EMU promised to expand French macroeconomic flexibility by imposing greater symmetry between France and Germany. Inability to shield French interest rates from external pressures and the fall of inflation to just above German levels suggested that in order to reduce real interest rates any further, one needed to alter German policy.[57] EMU was expected to *loosen* constraints on French macroeconomic policy by eliminating risk premia and loosening German policy. The result would be a weakening of the European currency *vis-à-vis* the dollar and perhaps a more competitive position for France *vis-à-vis* Germany.[58] As one French policymaker put it concerning the G-7 in this period: "Germany was absolutely *the* determinant of our economic policy and yet it was sometimes difficult to work with them, especially [with] the Bundesbank. [Macroeconomic coordination] was a good way for us to . . . pressure Germany so they would accept more growth, a more dynamic fiscal policy, and a reduction of interest rates."[59]

Yet the economic case for EMU in France still rested on a gamble, namely that the consequences of a more symmetrical Franco-German relationship, new capital market conditions, and reduced volatility under EMU—a stable Euro relatively competitive against the dollar—would offset the costs of convergence and the residual benefits of maintaining the discretion to let the franc depreciate under current arrangements. The policy was under constant attack from those who bore the brunt of the *franc fort* policy. Unions and the far left and National Front took the lead, but even French industry did not advocate a strict anti-inflationary regime of the kind favored by the Bundesbank. Although the public discourse of French elites suggests that they accepted that EMU would impose a measure of economic modernization on France, it is clear that they consistently rejected the view that this would best occur through a fully independent central bank patterned after the Bundesbank.[60]

Preference Aggregation: "At least I'll have a vote"

We have seen that prima facie arguments can be advanced for three explanations of French preferences. The French government may have seen Maastricht

---

government attempted to link the two in negotiations—there is no evidence that the preference for EMU was a response to the unintended consequences of the EC's subsequent capital liberalization directives.

[57] Pisani-Ferry, "France," 16.

[58] It may seem perverse to argue that the French sought lower interest rates and a more permissive policy, given the French reticence to devalue even in the face of manifest disequilibria that emerged after German reunification. Yet the latter was tactical, aimed at bolstering credibility; subsequently French government officials agreed that they had made a serious mistake by failing to devalue unilaterally once they had failed to force unilateral revaluation of the DM. Pisani-Ferry, "France," 8–10. For a critique of the *franc fort* policy, see Olivier Jean Blanchard and Pierre Alain Muet, "Competitiveness through Disinflation: An Assessment of the French Macroeconomic Strategy," *Economic Policy* 16 (1993), 12–56.

[59] Yoichi Funabashi, *Managing the Dollar: From the Plaza to the Louvre* (Washington, D.C., 1988), 125–126.

[60] Pisani-Ferry, "France," 12–13, 26, 30–32, also cites criticism by Alain Juppé and others. Pisani-Ferry argues that French pressure for European fiscal coordination and pressure to soften the stability pact reflect French traditions and do not challenge the independence of the ECB.

as a means to tie a unified Germany into Europe; to promote Mitterrand's European federal vision; and to realize commercial and macroeconomic objectives: lower interest rates and more stable and competitive exchange rates. Each interpretation seems plausible. Arguments consistent with each were advanced in the Maastricht referendum debates. In the historical record, how important does each motivation appear to have been in the formation of French preferences concerning the issues discussed at Maastricht?

The historical record does not support the view that French preferences in the Maastricht negotiations were decisively influenced by German unification. An objective geopolitical explanation would predict that French preferences would shift in 1989, but in fact preferences remained stable after 1985, despite the unification of Germany and the dissolution of the Soviet Union. Major French initiatives came in 1987 and 1988, several years before the fall of the Wall; by early 1989 the French government had already signaled a willingness to accept German "economist" conditions. In the discourse and domestic cleavages within France, there is essentially no direct evidence—elements of the referendum rhetoric, which included all possible arguments, aside—that top French policy-makers saw themselves as "enmeshing" Germany in order to limit its geopolitical ambitions. Foreign Minister Roland Dumas, for example, justified stronger EC institutions not as a geopolitical counter to unification but as a way to constrain the independent central bank supported by Germany.[61] It is true that in the period December 1989 through June 1990, Mitterrand and Kohl both spoke publicly of EMU as a counterpart to German reunification, yet there is little evidence that this was more than an effort to pressure the Bundesbank and other opponents within Germany.[62]

Nor does the cross-issue variation in French preferences support an objective geopolitical explanation. If German unification were a driving force behind the French position, we would expect strong French support for political integration. Yet here too the French position remained unchanged: in striking contrast to its active initiation of discussions on EMU, the French government sought to *avoid* discussions of political union, including foreign and defense policies, the powers of the European Commission or Parliament, and immigration. There were few French innovations and little willingness to compromise; political union was viewed by both parties as a concession to Germany in exchange for EMU. Defense cooperation was an exception, but it is unclear whether the extreme French position was meant to be taken seriously; one German diplomat claims the German government viewed the weak defense provisions of the Maastricht Treaty as no more than a means to let France "save face."[63] Finally, although the French

[61] Patrick McCarthy, "France Looks at Germany, or How to Become German (and European) While Remaining French," in McCarthy, ed., *France-Germany, 1983–1993: The Struggle to Cooperate* (New York, 1993), 51–72; Laughland, *Death*, 246ff; Martial, "France," 117–120; *Agence Europe*, 20, 23–24 April 1990; interview with French Minister.

[62] Direct evidence about confidential French deliberations during this period is scant and unreliable, hence we are thrust back on softer sources. Given the intensity and partisanship of the French debate to this day, it is unclear how reliable the sources would be, even if a comprehensive analysis were feasible.

[63] Cole, *François*, 158–160.

government appears to have panicked briefly in the face of German unification, there is little evidence that domestic groups mobilized around the issue. French public opinion remained relatively sanguine about German reunification. Though nearly every possible argument was aired, the German threat played a role in the Maastricht referendum debates that was relatively minor compared to macroeconomic policy and general concerns about sovereignty.

It is more difficult to disentangle the relative importance of ideological and economic motivations, though on balance the historical record appears more consistent with economic motivations. The timing of French initiatives in 1987 and 1988 supports both views: it might be attributed to Mitterrand's willingness to support any pro-European initiative after early 1984, when the French launched bilateral efforts to redress asymmetries in the EMS, or to economic convergence and dollar depreciation after 1987.

Domestic discourse and cleavages appear also to have run along lines of economic beliefs and interests rather than partisan or personal commitment to the European idea. Certainly Mitterrand believed—as late as his decision in 1992 to call a referendum—that a high profile in EC initiatives would bolster his own standing and that of the Socialist party in public opinion, yet those who supported (and those who criticized) monetary union appear primarily to have been concerned with the economic benefits and costs of the *franc fort* policy.[64] This is particularly true of French initiatives in 1987–88, which were taken, after all, by Gaullists. The French aide-mémoire of 1988, like its Italian counterpart, called for the elimination of asymmetries in the EMS and complained that the DM was "structurally undervalued," generating large German surpluses. The Italian memo threatened to invoke escape clauses, limit capital liberalization, and impose harmonization requirements if asymmetries in the operation of the EMS were not redressed. Even Delors recommended that the French withdraw from the EMS if its asymmetries were not redressed. French central bank governor Jacques de Larosière observed in 1990: "Today I am the governor of a central bank who has decided, along with his nation, to follow fully the German monetary policy without voting on it. At least, as part of a European central bank, I'll have a vote."[65] Mitterrand defended the treaty by stressing that the ECB board would be under the control of the Council and its members individually responsible to national concerns. Jacques Attali was more succinct: the treaty's central purpose was "to get rid of the D-Mark."[66] Conflicting assessments of the cost-effectiveness of the *franc fort* policy were a prominent part of the referendum debate, though sovereignty concerns also played an important role. Some prominent Gaullist politicians, though not Jacques Chirac, took up the criticisms, which focused on the defense of social security and economic prosperity, but did not confront European ideology directly. Pierre Bérégovoy, the

---

[64] Interview with French Minister.

[65] Cited in *Washington Post*, 25 October 1990. Bérégovoy told Lawson that he had been skeptical about EMU but had been talked around to it by de Larosière. Lawson, *View*, 913. See also Daniel Gros and Niels Thygesen, *European Monetary Interaction: From the European Monetary System towards Monetary Union* (London, 1991), 311–313. On withdrawal, interview with Delors.

[66] David Marsh, *Germany and Europe: The Crisis of Unity* (London, 1994), 144; Connolly, *Rotten*, 141–142; interview with French official.

French finance minister for the Socialists during much of the period, later turned against the treaty, resentfully reflecting that he had been forced to play along with "that huge con trick, the Maastricht Treaty."[67]

The pattern of French negotiating tactics and positions across various issues tends to confirm the predominance of economic concerns. France was far from uniformly favorable or opposed to economic integration, as an explanation grounded in European ideology would predict. The distinctive French "monetarist" position—support for a less autonomous ECB, a larger number of participants, and a rapid transition—remains unexplained, as are other traditional economic concerns of France, including a strong European social policy, a strong employment law, and industrial policy—all areas where relatively generous French policies rendered France vulnerable within the relatively liberal EC. As both geopolitical and economic theories predict, it was only in purely institutional matters with vague, uncertain, or weak substantive consequences that geopolitical ideas clearly drove French preferences. France sought a modest role for the European Parliament as compared to the European Council, an independent defense identity, and cooperation on foreign policy that preserved a large measure of sovereignty. Such policies reflected instead traditional French ideological concerns, most notably the desire to limit the centralization of supranational power. French priorities also included strengthening national parliaments while strongly opposing a regions committee and enhancement of Commission and parliamentary powers. The three-pillar model, insulating foreign and interior policy-making from traditional EC procedures, was a French innovation. This might be explained as an ideological preference or as an objective geopolitical calculation: unilateral French defense and foreign policies were viable as compared with those of Germany, hence French suspicion of supranational institutions.[68]

Perhaps the most striking evidence in favor of an economic rather than an ideological interpretation is the consistency of French policy inside and outside the EC. The central French economic goal—greater macroeconomic flexibility through restraints on the Bundesbank and multilateral financing of central bank intervention—remained the same regardless of whether the forum was regional, bilateral, or multilateral. This is flatly inconsistent with the claim that French policy was driven by geopolitical ideas, which would imply a sharp distinction between symbolically significant Franco-German and EC cooperation, on the one hand, and cooperation elsewhere, on the other. French policy toward EMU, we have seen, was consistent with the unilateral *franc fort* policy. France supported initiatives to these ends in 1979 and 1981 during EMS negotiations and abortive reform efforts, in 1982 as an element in a G-7 proposal, in 1984 within the EC, in 1985 during the SEA negotiations, in 1987 as an aim of the Basel-Nyborg reforms of the EMS, and in 1988 as part of bilateral discussions about a Franco-German Economic Council; and continuously from 1988 through 1991 as part of proposals for EMU. The uniformity of the French com-

---

[67] Laughland, *Death of Politics*, 119; Connolly, *Rotten*.
[68] Interviews with Permanent Representative and Council Secretariat official (Brussels, 1994); Attali *Verbatim*, 3:651.

mitment to a particular international monetary policy—whether the negotiating environment was unilateral, bilateral, regional, or multilateral—is inconsistent with a geopolitical explanation.

Events after Maastricht, in particular French behavior during the currency crises of 1992–93, provide one final source of evidence that the French government pursued its European monetary policy for economic reasons independent of EC rules rather than purely ideological reasons. The French government defended the credibility of its commitment to the *franc fort* policy in 1992–93, *even where EC rules did not require it*—suggesting that the French commitment to the underlying economic policy was steady even where it was possible to maintain European credentials in other ways. During the franc-DM crisis of August 1993, France refused to devalue (as seemed appropriate to offset macroeconomic divergence induced by the fiscal shock of German reunification) even when it was possible with Germany's blessing and fully within the EMS. France called instead for a DM revaluation in an effort to shift the onus onto Germany alone. When the Netherlands, followed by Belgium and Denmark, announced they would follow Germany, thereby isolating the franc, the French government preferred moving to wider bands, thereby essentially rendering EMS constraints meaningless. Once within those wider bands, which would have permitted a 15 percent devaluation within the system, the French government neither loosened policy significantly nor depreciated the franc.[69]

In sum, evidence concerning French domestic discourse, cleavages, and negotiating strategy tends decisively to disconfirm the causal importance of German unification and rather strongly to confirm the predominance of economic interests in French policy. However, we cannot dismiss entirely a secondary but significant role for European ideology. As in Germany, the role of ideology appears to have reflected the weakness or ambivalence of economic incentives. Although decision-makers appear to have been concerned primarily with relaxing constraints on French macroeconomic performance, the risks and the general technical and political uncertainty surrounding monetary policy may well have meant that neither policy was clearly superior. It is undeniable that French businesses strongly supported EMU, but it is less clear that they had a compelling structural reason to do so. The Maastricht referendum debates revealed deep splits over the proper course between adherents of the *franc fort* and muddling through with some variant of *l'autre politique*. French policy-makers later came to believe, we have seen, that the government pursued nominal exchange-rate stability to the point of obsession, foreswearing devaluation in the mistaken view that establishing the credibility of the franc and persevering with a policy of "competitive disinflation" was the best course.

We cannot, therefore, dismiss the possibility that European federalist ideas

---

[69] On these events, see Peter Norman and Lionel Barber, "The Monetary Tragedy of Errors That Led to Currency Chaos," and "The Day Germany Planted a Currency Time Bomb," *FT*, 11–12 February 1992, 2. Also interview with French Minister (Cambridge, 1994). In Italy, industry supported efforts to limit government spending and wage settlements by keeping interest rates high and the currency strong. James I. Walsh, "Global Finance, Domestic Politics: International Monetary Policies in Britain, France and Italy," (diss., American University, 1997), 211.

held by some policy-makers in a relatively autonomous French state may well have intervened in an important way between structural economic pressures and policy.[70] In the absence of conclusive evidence concerning internal French deliberations surrounding EMU—an issue that remains controversial—we cannot dismiss the possibility that, given two highly uncertain policy options, strong public support for Europe integration, and commitments by both the Gaullist and the Socialist parties, it was ideological support for Europe that rendered EMU and the *franc fort* the more attractive option. European ideals provided political legitimacy, a wider range of justifications, and a set of scapegoats not just for economic adjustments that appeared inevitable, as with the EMS negotiations, but for continuation of the *franc fort* policy.

Britain: A "rat bag of proposals" from "cloud-cuckoo land"?

Britain opposed nearly every policy contained in the Maastricht Treaty except those that strengthened the European Court's enforcement powers, provided for a weak Common Foreign and Security Policy, called for greater subsidiarity, and made the European Central Bank independent. It opted out of the social policy entirely and EMU provisionally. Between 1985 and 1991 Britain did join the EMS, but only within relatively loose 6 percent bands—by 1992, after a series of policy errors, it had fallen back out.

The geopolitical theory predicts that such a negative position across the board might emerge as the consequence either of British antipathy toward Germany or of British ideological opposition to European federalism fostered by an extreme nationalist prime minister, Margaret Thatcher. EMS, less threatening to British sovereignty than EMU, might be marginally acceptable, but EMU under no circumstances. Similarly, Britain would oppose the transfer of sovereignty to the European Parliament and, because it had a viable unilateral national defense policy, would join France in opposing any foreign policy or defense cooperation, The political economic theory, by contrast, predicts that the British would accept only cautious commitments toward monetary integration—a loose commitment to the EMS but not EMU—favored by business groups, because of Britain's incomplete economic convergence with the low inflation and stable exchange rates prevailing on the Continent. Business concerns about the slide in competitiveness that might result from any firm commitment to stable exchange rates would be decisive; yet business would at the same time seek to avoid any permanent exclusion from monetary arrangements, for exclusion was perceived as undermining the global position of British industry and, above all, finance.

On balance the evidence supports the economic explanation of British preferences more strongly but not decisively. In the few places where the two generate strikingly divergent predictions—as in Britain's attitude toward exclusion from EMU—Britain tended to follow its economic interests as they were perceived by business interest groups and economic ministers. Still, there is sub-

---

[70] Some attribute these ideas to a French desire to emulate German policy, though the evidence remains inconclusive. McNamara, *Currency*.

stantial evidence to suggest the importance of Thatcher's Euroskeptical geo-political ideology, which delayed for quite some time the adoption of policies advocated by powerful economic interests and nearly all Cabinet ministers.

Geopolitical Interest and Ideology:
"We have surrendered enough sovereignty"

Two geopolitical concerns may have played a role in Britain's European pol-icy during this period: concern about German unification and Thatcher's ideo-logical opposition to federalism, the latter supported by increasing numbers of parliamentary Euroskeptics.

The first factor, German unification, need not detain us long. It is difficult to see precisely how it might have influenced British policy. In Britain as in France and Germany, there is little evidence to support a link between European pol-icy and the revolutionary events of 1989. There were, to be sure, those—in-cluding some Euroskeptics in Parliament and even members of Thatcher's inti-mate circle, such as Nicolas Ridley—who indulged in anti-German diatribes. Yet whenever they stated their position concretely, their concerns proved to be eco-nomic rather than military—indeed, the economic nature of the threat appears to have been the source of some frustration among traditional Tories. EMU, Ridley charged in a celebrated passage, was "a German racket designed to take over the whole of Europe. . . . The DM is going to be the strongest currency . . . I'm not sure I wouldn't rather have the shelters and the chance to fight back than simply being taken over by . . . economics."[71] Ridley was, it should be added, fired for uttering such comments. Overall, there is no evidence of a link between politico-military goals and economic integration.

Nor did the prospect of German unification forge such a link. Like Mitterrand, Thatcher tried initially to impede German unification; she sought alliances with eastern countries, particularly with the USSR and Poland, around the principle of the sanctity of existing borders. She proposed closer Anglo-French coopera-tion. Hurd and the Foreign Office went some way toward negotiating military (including nuclear) cooperation with France. Yet Thatcher, unlike Mitterrand, never claimed (even rhetorically) that European integration could substitute for cooperation against Germany. When German reunification went forward any-way, and the French reversed policy on bilateral and regional cooperation with Germany, Thatcher had little interest in supplanting a balancing policy with a European one. Instead she accepted it as "one instance in which the foreign pol-icy I pursued met with unambiguous failure." She continued to oppose EMU as she had before. In short, German unification came and went, leaving British policy, like that of France, unchanged.[72]

If the roots of British policy were geopolitical, they must therefore have in-

---

[71] Dominic Lawson, "Saying the Unsayable about the Germans: An Interview with Nicholas Ridley," *Spectator*, 14 July 1990, 8; interview with Patrick Robertson, founder and director of the Bruges Group, 1992.

[72] Margaret Thatcher, *The Downing Street Years* (New York, 1993), 813. For an overview of Thatcher's policies toward the Soviet Union and German reunification in this period, Paul Sharp, *Thatcher's Diplomacy: The Revival of British Foreign Policy* (London, 1997), chaps. 10–11.

volved not an objective geopolitical threat but a particular geopolitical ideology. Thatcher's "root and branch" opposition to EMU and many aspects of federalism reflected her own brand of British nationalism, which predisposed her to reject any proposal for centralizing power at the European level; over time this view was supported by increasing numbers of Euroskeptical MPs. Aggressive efforts by Delors and Arthur Cockfield to expand Commission activities to areas such as tax harmonization only heightened Thatcher's suspicion. The ability "to run an independent monetary, economic and fiscal policy," she proclaimed, "lies at the heart of what constitutes a sovereign state. . . . Taxation, fiscal and monetary matters [go] to the heart of the control of the executive." A celebrated speech at Bruges in 1988, aimed directly at Delors, set forth Thatcher's vision of European integration as "preserving the different traditions, parliamentary powers and sense of national pride [that have] been the source of Europe's vitality through the centuries . . . [not] some sort of Indentikit European personality."[73] She believed also, an associate recalled, that Britain had unusual influence due to "historical distinction, skilled diplomacy and versatile military forces"; though she appears to have disliked and distrusted the Foreign Office's tendency (so she believed) to seek diplomatic accommodation that would bring Britain "closer to the heart of Europe."[74] British sovereignty was the fundamental issue. "In my view," she concluded in the Bruges speech, "we have surrendered enough."[75]

These ideological concerns suggest one prima facie explanation for the British government's extreme opposition to nearly all proposals considered in the Maastricht negotiations, not least EMU—a tendency shared with the Danes and Greeks, similarly inclined ideologically.[76] Although John Major took a somewhat more moderate line, his own views remained far less open to Europe than those of Geoffrey Howe, Michael Heseltine, Douglas Hurd, and other leading Tory politicians—though hardly as extreme as the growing Euroskeptic opposition within the parliamentary party.

On specific issues of geopolitical or ideological import, notably CFSP and the powers of the European Parliament, Britain voiced its traditional support for intergovernmental arrangements. Britain supported French proposals for a multipillar design separating foreign policy from the EC institutional structure but seemed from the start willing to compromise slightly in the direction of strengthening and expanding the WEU (though not where core NATO functions were at stake). Britain backed French skepticism about expanding the powers of the Parliament, though it signaled early on a willingness to make modest compromises such as a binding vote by the Parliament on the investiture of the Commission.[77] Though it involved a transfer of national sovereignty, support for stronger enforcement by the European Court appears not to have troubled the Euroskeptics.

---

[73] Sharp, *Thatcher's*, 168–170, also 171–172; Thatcher, *Downing*, 750.

[74] Interview with Thatcher adviser, September 1997; Lord Gilmour, "The Thatcher Memoirs," *Twentieth Century British History* 5:2 (1994), 257–264.

[75] Sharp, *Thatcher's*, 176–177; Margaret Thatcher, *The Path to Power* (London, 1995), 473–480.

[76] Thatcher, *Downing*, 751.

[77] Hugo Young, "The Prime Minister," in Dennis Kavanagh and Anthony Seldon, eds., *The Major Effect* (London, 1994), 23.

Economic Interest: "The prime minister has achieved exactly what business needs"

The statements of British industry concerning monetary integration suggest that its preferences reflected three considerations. On balance, business sought, in declining order of importance, continued reciprocal access to European markets, competitive exchange rates, and low interest rates. In addition it opposed a strong EC social policy. These considerations led British peak business groups to advocate cautious involvement in EMU, but only if the exchange rate was competitive and inflation low. Although peak business groups did not support immediate or automatic participation in the single currency scheme, they adamantly insisted on avoiding exclusion from it.

In chapter 4 we left British industry and banking in 1985 just after their shift to support for ERM participation, which was expected to stabilize exchange rates at a competitive level. Support steadily increased throughout the remainder of the decade. CBI surveys showed that business, particularly big business, was concerned more about the exchange rate than about the interest rate; a competitive value for sterling was seen as essential to industrial profitability. In 1988, as the downside of Nigel Lawson's macroeconomic boom was becoming evident and the government starting to raise both interest rates and the value of sterling to dampen inflation, the CBI and the Institute of Directors reiterated their support for exchange-rate stabilization. It was thought at the time that ERM membership might bolster the credibility of British policy, thereby permitting lower interest rates. Given the alternatives—higher interest rates or taxes, lower spending, or incomes policy—ERM membership seemed an attractive option, particularly if (as all assumed at the time) the exchange-rate peg was a flexible one within 6 percent bands, as was the case for Italy. By 1990, with interest rates nearly 15 percent, inflation close to 10 percent, and sterling at a moderate value, 93 percent of British business leaders supported participation in the ERM, and 50 percent believed it should have happened long ago—albeit within wide bands. Finally, the CBI continued to oppose any permanent exclusion from the EMS or EMU, for fear of disadvantaging British finance. CBI documents repeatedly mentioned the need to be influential in future EC economic negotiations, including Maastricht, which business and government alike perceived as requiring serious participation in the EMS.[78]

Thus the CBI supported the government's entry into the ERM in late 1990, though it remained skeptical of the high rate the government chose. CBI leaders had hoped to delay British entry until inflation was going down, but support for ERM membership was so overwhelming that temporary overvaluation was overlooked. Yet inflation and competitiveness remained the most

[78] Walsh, *Global*, 211, also chap. 6; William Keegan, *Mr. Lawson's Gamble* (London, 1989), 198–229; Helen Thompson, "The UK and the Exchange Rate Mechanism, 1978–80," in Brian Brivati and Harriet Jones, eds., *From Reconstruction to Integration: Britain and Europe since 1945* (Leicester, 1993), 236; Universal News Services report, 11 October 1990. Exchange rates were a less important influence on investment decisions—other costs and proximity to customers dominated such calculations—but once in place had a significant influence on profitability. *FT*, 28 July 1989, 22. Interview with Patrick Robertson.

important concerns. The Institute of Directors, less influenced by large multi-national firms, remained more skeptical, noting that inflation remained high, and even the CBI increasingly criticized the high interest rates required to maintain the parity. A Labour motion critical of the resulting macroeconomic stringency gained surprising support among Conservative MPs. Such pressures, along with concern from homeowners, contributed to the Major government's break with the ERM in September 1992, which followed a period in which the Bank of England spent nearly £10 billion in a fruitless defense of sterling. Among the lessons the government learned from the experience, Chancellor Norman Lamont reported, was that membership in the ERM required greater macroeconomic convergence between Britain and Germany.[79]

About EMU and a single currency, the CBI remained more cautious. Although 70 percent of businesses surveyed thought EMU would assist exports and sourcing and half thought it would assist distribution and marketing, their primary concern remained competitiveness. The CBI noted that inflationary convergence was much more important for EMU than for EMS, since devaluation could not offset any reduced competitiveness. Entry should thus be not immediate but "the culmination of an evolutionary process" of inflationary convergence. Doubts were voiced about both strict convergence criteria and fiscal freedom, though an autonomous ECB attracted general support. A second concern of business, particularly in the financial sector, was the threat of exclusion from a "two-tier" EMU. Nearly all business leaders, including the CBI, stressed that this outcome would be worst of all. Market liberalization remained the major priority for British business, both in industry and in services, which provided market opportunities and contributed to high flows of FDI into Britain. EMU was expected to influence financial and industrial firms; the government should therefore make every effort to "remain in the game." Hence once the treaty was signed, the CBI strongly recommended rapid ratification, followed by EMU membership. These ambiguities were reflected in the CBI position, which endorsed the government's alternative parallel currency plan (the "hard ecu") but "unequivocally" disassociated itself from the Major government's opposition to a single currency. "Only when a single currency is established," the CBI argued, "will business reap the full benefits of economic and monetary union." The more cautious Institute of Directors endorsed only the "hard ecu" proposal, citing transaction cost gains.[80]

Outside of monetary policy, the major concern was EC social policy, of which

[79] CBI, *European Monetary Union: A Business Perspective* (London, 1989), cited in *FT*, 10 November 1989, 10; House of Commons, Treasury and Civil Service Committee, *The 1992 Autumn Statement*, Minutes of Evidence (Session 1992–93, 16 November 1992), 38–40; Walsh, *Global*, 191; Reuter Business Report, 5 October 1990; Universal News Service, 5, 11 October 1990.

[80] *FT*, 6 July 1990, 11, and 5 November 1990, 1, 22; also 5 March 1991, 9; 23 June 1990, iii; 20 May 1993, 19; Verdun, "European," 19; *Economist*, 19 May 1990, 97; Alexander Italiener, "Mastering Maastricht: EMU Issues and How They Were Settled," in Klaus Gretschmann, ed., *Economic and Monetary Union: Implications for National Policy-Makers* (Maastricht, 1993), 68–70; Universal News Service Report, 22 July 1992, 14 June 1990; *FT*, 6 July 1990, 7 November 1990, 11, and 5 November 1991, 11; Sarah Hogg and J. Hill, *Too Close to Call* (London, 1995), 153ff. The social charter continued to enjoy strong public opinion support, even among Conservative voters.

business was skeptical. Yet with collective bargaining and social welfare excluded, social policy was viewed as a relatively minor affair. Again the result was ambiguity: CBI public statements remained critical, but the confederation reluctantly followed the UNICE position of supporting modest reform—a position that evidently caught the Major government by surprise. For its part, the Trades Union Congress was skeptical of German proposals, favoring instead stronger political control over the ECB and greater fiscal freedom, but it supported ratification, citing the social policy provisions. The Labour party strongly support the social charter. The CBI also called consistently for stronger enforcement by the European Court of Justice, a position adopted by the government.

In sum, British business supported the Major government's policy of cautious movement toward monetary cooperation and avoidance of any exclusion. As the CBI director general stated the day after Maastricht, "the Prime Minister achieved exactly what business needs: agreement on economic and monetary union, which has left the way open for UK participation in a single European currency, steps to secure more even enforcement of Community legislation, and no extension of Community powers (e.g. social policy) that could threaten international competitiveness."[81]

The Domestic Decision: "The issue is British jobs, British sales, Britain's future"

The last half of the 1980s witnessed rising domestic pressure to participate in the ERM. Increasingly isolated, Thatcher resisted but finally entered in 1990. British skepticism of the EMU remained constant, though both the Thatcher and the Major governments were careful to avoid any result that would trigger permanent exclusion. As regards political union, Britain resolutely opposed everything—increased powers to the European Parliament, more supranational foreign, defense, and interior policies, an extended social policy, and expansion of qualified majority voting. The only exception was increased enforcement power on the part of the European Court. We have seen that both geopolitical and economic theories offer explanations of this essentially negative position regarding the Maastricht negotiations. What more does the historical record of decision-making reveal about the relative influence of economic interest and geopolitics?

We may reject the influence of the salient geopolitical event of the period, German unification. British policy does not change in this period, neither toward economic integration nor toward foreign and defense policy integration; no linkage is drawn between monetary integration and security affairs. Objective geopolitical factors explain, at most, British policy toward European defense and foreign policy cooperation. Given the relative prestige and viability of its unilateral political and military policies—not least its permanent seat on the UN Security Council, highly regarded diplomats, independent military capabilities, and nuclear weapons—both the geopolitical and the (issue-specific) economic theories predict that Britain, like France, would be skeptical of supranational institutions in this area. This skepticism is precisely what we observe.

---

[81] Universal News Service Report, 11 December 1991.

Regarding the decisions to join the ERM and to oppose EMU, it is more difficult to disentangle the relative importance of antifederalist ideology and economic interest. On balance the evidence more strongly supports economic motivations, but it is far from unambiguous.

On this point the evidence concerning the ERM is clearest. Here the pattern of domestic cleavages and the nature of domestic discourse clearly reveal economic interests favoring participation arrayed against Thatcher's consistent, but in the end futile, ideological opposition. In 1989–90, the issue of ERM membership arose again, as it had in 1981 and 1985.[82] As before, the primary internal justifications for participation by domestic officials and ministers (except Geoffrey Howe) were economic not geopolitical. Descriptions of decision-making on ERM by such participants as Howe, Lawson, and Thatcher all mention strong business pressure; many speak of avoiding the economic costs of exclusion from EMU. Howe appears to have been the only leading politician in the government ideologically committed to Europe. Against was arrayed Thatcher's personal opposition, surely in large part ideologically motivated. Thatcher was able to forestall entry into the ERM for five years following the formation of a clear governmental and interest group consensus. In the absence of party and business opposition, Thatcher claimed retrospectively, she would have taken an even *more* overtly anti-European stance, as she did after leaving office.[83]

During the second half of the 1980s Thatcher's room to indulge her personal views narrowed; unilateral British policy moved in the direction consistently recommended by Lawson and Howe. Between 1986 and 1988 Lawson secretly "shadowed" the DM at a rate of £1 sterling to DM 3 for a year, reducing interest rates and employing direct intervention to avoid appreciation. Before the Madrid summit of July 1989, Lawson and Howe threatened to resign if their demands, backed by silent majority in both cabinet and Parliament, were not met. Thatcher announced her willingness to join the ERM when inflation fell, capital markets liberalized, and the single market was completed. In October 1990, though Lawson and Howe were now gone, Thatcher entered the ERM. Thatcher and Major (now her chancellor) were apparently thinking ahead to the 1992 elections and sought to dampen opposition within the party and to lower inflation without higher interest rates or spending cuts. Some British officials advanced tactical arguments for entry. Foreign Secretary Hurd, following Howe and Lawson, was concerned that British opposition to EMU would be undermined without participation in the ERM, a view backed by Leon Brittan and Thatcher's confidant, Dutch prime minister Ruud Lubbers. They concluded that the best option yet untried was a public commitment to the ERM. This conclusion was reached even though economic conditions were inauspicious: inflation was rising, sterling was weak, and a recession seemed imminent.[84]

Sterling entered the system at DM 2.95, a rate aimed at dampening inflation

---

[82] See chapter 4.
[83] Interview with Chancellor of the Exchequer; interview with Thatcher adviser; Thatcher, *Path*, 473ff.
[84] Walsh, *Global*, 102–106; Keegan, *Lawson's*, 156ff; Lawson, *View*, 915, 930ff; Thatcher, *Downing*, 710; Connolly, *Rotten*, 69; *FT*, 23 October 1990, 14; *Independent*, 23 October 1990, 4; interview with prime minister.

but moderately costly to industry. The negative effects on growth were compounded by the unilateral nature of the British recession and the monetary spillover from German unification. The U.K. government did not consult other ERM members before entering and ignored Bundesbank warnings about the unsustainability of the policy. Thatcher's close advisers understood that the rate was high, as Pöhl warned them at the time. Drawing on the experience of the EMS during the 1980s, however, they advised her that Britain could easily change parity in the future—a piece of advice one of her closest advisers later termed "my biggest mistake." Britain did, however, employ a wide fluctuation band, which gave some room to maneuver. In the end the rate proved unsustainable, and the lesson learned by the British government was, we have seen, not to fix exchange rates until there was "a greater degree of monetary convergence" with Germany.[85]

Turning from the ERM to EMU, we see a quite different picture. Support within the government for ERM membership was intense, but preferences concerning EMU were split, with a considerable majority opposed. Numerous pro-ERM officials rejected EMU, among them Lawson, for whom "transaction costs and exchange rate uncertainties [were] insignificant compared with the real economic and, still more, political issues at stake."[86] Robert Leigh-Pemberton, governor of the Bank of England, similarly opposed EMU; his reaction had something to do with the fact he was a Thatcher appointee whose appointment, one analyst has noted, was "more blatantly political than most."[87] Business groups opposed membership. Britain proposed instead a plan, developed by a former ambassador now working in the City, for an "evolutionary approach to monetary union"—namely, a scheme for a parallel currency to float alongside the national currencies and possibly eventually replace them—though many around Thatcher conceded to journalists that British support was predicated on the assumption that EMU would *not* lead to a single currency. Of top Tory politicians, only Howe openly supported EMU.[88]

Cross-issue variation (or lack thereof) in British preferences is consistent with the predictions of both a geopolitical explanation and one stressing issue-specific, largely economic motivations, but it may slightly favor the latter. Let us consider first noneconomic issues. On foreign and defense policy, as well as the European Parliament—issues without clear economic implications—both theories predict negative positions. Indeed, Britain opposed QMV in foreign policy and demanded a safeguard authorizing unilateral noncompliance. This demand, which reportedly angered almost all other governments, is what one would ex-

[85] Interview with former Thatcher adviser; Commons, *1992 Autumn*, 38. Also interview with British Treasury official, 1997; Walsh, *Global*, 189–191; Lawson, *No. 11*, 112–113, 485–493, 1029; Connolly, *Rotten*, 138–141; Marsh, *Germany and Europe*, 158–159. Thompson ("UK," 238, also 234–238) concludes that "the UK government entered the ERM without having a clear conceptual idea of what ERM membership meant, not as an expedient action for itself but as a participant in a system which had evolved without it."

[86] Lawson, *View*, 1060.

[87] Keegan, *Mr. Lawson's*, 153.

[88] Sir Geoffrey Howe, *Conflict of Loyalty* (London, 1994), 533–534.

pect from a government with viable unilateral alternatives and a strong position in existing organizations such as NATO. Britain's traditional defense of parliamentary sovereignty and suspicion of federal institutions dovetailed with the Conservatives' fear that the European Parliament might be dominated by Social Democrats. More broadly, the British government supported the French proposal for a decentralized and supranational "three-pillar" design as in part a means to limit the Court and other supranational bodies to economic issues; at the same time, the government adopted British business' only major institutional demand, namely stronger enforcement powers for the Court *within* the economic realm.[89]

British preferences on most economic issues were consistent with both motivations. On immigration, results predicted by two theories are similarly difficult to distinguish. Britain, with few problems controlling its own borders (it has only twenty-four legal points of entry), did not face the difficulties in managing the movement of people that other governments faced and therefore saw no need to mention migration in the treaty. This issue was also of some ideological importance. On social policy the British government threatened to veto any agreement committing Britain to a common social policy, as one would expect given both Britain's economic status as a moderately poor EC member and the ideology of the Conservative government. Since most social policy concerns with direct financial implications were not under active consideration, the issue quickly became partisan and symbolic, with extreme positions taken by parliamentary and cabinet Euroskeptics, on the one hand, and the Labour party opposition, on the other. (Yet even the Tony Blair government, while joining the Social Chapter, did not seek to expand its provisions.) [90] On the all-important issue of monetary policy, Britain remained skeptical of any commitment to EMU, which position is consistent both with the low level of convergence and with British antifederalism. As we have seen, even moderate Tory ministers were skeptical of the convergence criteria; Hurd argued publicly that by restricting fiscal deficits, Germany sought to create "a fitness club which would keep everyone underweight forever."[91]

One critical aspect of the British position does, however, distinguish the two theories. The British concern to *avoid exclusion from EMU*—the most vulnerable spot in its negotiating position—can only have reflected fears about the potential economic costs of commercial exclusion; it served no evident geopolitical purpose. Compare the British position in social policy, where an opt-out was acceptable, even desirable for economic reasons—it would enhance British competitiveness. The Thatcher and Major governments consistently sought the option to join any EMU proposal; but the decisive limitation on them was that a veto would encourage others to move ahead on their own. In the Delors Committee, for example, Leigh-Pemberton announced opposition to a single

[89] *Economist,* 7 December 1991, 52–53.

[90] Interview with British Ambassador, 1996; Hogg and Hill, *Too Close to Call,* 257–260; *FT,* 6–12 December 1991.

[91] Newhouse, *Europe,* 92.

currency and to any plan for what was being termed an "irreversible process" toward it, yet was forced to discuss details of the Franco-German plans in order to maintain any influence at all. In the end, he rejected Thatcher and Lawson's instructions to dissent from the Delors Report.[92]

The pattern of domestic cleavages and discourse reinforces the importance of economic calculations concerning exclusion. The critical difference between Thatcher and economic interest groups was not opposition to EMU, which both shared, but the prime minister's preference for exclusion over participation in any agreement. She considered permitting the other eleven member governments to sign a separate EMU treaty. On this point Thatcher was overruled; a majority in Cabinet was unwilling to court exclusion and sought a compromise in order to "remain in the game." Critical were concerns about the economic costs of exclusion, particularly to British finance.[93] Some expected Major to soften Thatcher's negotiating stance and restore flexibility to the British position, but the shift proved minimal. Top advisers from the Treasury and Britain's permanent representative in Brussels pointed out that Britain could not afford to be excluded entirely from EMU because of the financial consequences for the City—a view reportedly accepted by Major though later called into question by the continuing expansion of British finance. Nonetheless, once the treaty had been ratified even in Denmark, the CBI harshly criticized any delay, a view reiterated by Major, who declared that "the issue is British jobs, British sales, Britain's future."[94] This unwillingness to be excluded contrasts with Major's conduct on social policy, where he saw no reason to retain a British right to participate and opted out entirely. The critical differences can be explained only if economic interests, including partisan views of the economy, are decisive.[95]

Public divisions and debate over ratification confirm the importance of both ideological and economic motivations, with Euroskeptical opponents setting the tone with discussion of British sovereignty. Thatcher criticized the erosion of sovereignty and termed the result of discussions over political union a "rat bag of proposals," whereas advocates of a European policy responded that effective modern diplomacy required the "pooling" of sovereignty.[96] Yet on concrete economic issues, domestic divisions and discourse tended to turn toward underlying commercial concerns. Social policy generated widespread skepticism. Differences between Conservatives, virulently opposed to any social policy, and Labour, moderately favorable, resulted from competing preferences over the provision of public goods; geopolitical ideology, interest, and attitudes to-

---

[92] Interview with Thatcher adviser; interview with two members of the Delors Committee, 1991, 1996; Connolly, *Rotten*, 79–80; Lawson, *View*, 907–909; Ross, *Jacques*, 80–85; Thatcher, *Downing*, 707–708; Howe, *Conflict*, 576–577; Walsh, *Global*, 157–158.

[93] Thatcher, *Path*, 483–484; Thatcher, *Downing*, 724–725; *FT*, 23 October 1990, 14; interview with former top prime ministerial adviser.

[94] Michael Angus, president of the CBI, cited in *FT*, 20 May 1993, 19; interview with Thatcher adviser.

[95] Interview with British ambassador, 1996; interview with Thatcher adviser, 1997. In retrospect, it is unclear whether this argument was correct. Since 1991 activities in the City have expanded greatly, consolidating its position. Yet the fear was clearly prevalent at the time.

[96] Sharp, *Thatcher's*, 178, also 179–182.

ward sovereignty cannot explain this cleavage. (If the subsequent actions of the Blair government are any guide, there was opposition across the board toward extensive social legislation at the European level—a position consistent with Britain's structural economic circumstances.) Major signaled a clear willingness to entertain compromises on core geopolitical issues such as foreign policy, the European Parliament, and even defense, yet he threatened to veto agreement over more economic issues, including labor law, immigration policy, social policy, and EMU.[97]

Economic interests appear to have had just as significant an influence on discussion of the critical question of EMU. To be sure, Thatcher proclaimed that those who thought nation-states would accept the limitations of EMU were living in "cloud cuckoo land"; there is little doubt that she objected to the implied loss of sovereignty. (At times Thatcher and some of her closest associates conceded that she opposed ERM and EMU membership also in order to maintain executive control over whether to employ reserves to defend parity or raise interest rates.) Even Ridley, with his virulently hostile rhetoric about rising German power, rejected monetary integration for primarily economic reasons: Britain could not meet German productivity rates, hence exchange-rate stability would require wage cuts. The British, like the French and Italians, were aware that the EMS functioned asymmetrically. Major appears to have opposed immediate commitment to a single currency and any "irreversible" plan for achieving it primarily because the British economy had converged insufficiently with those of its neighbors and only secondarily because of passionate parliamentary opposition—or so he told Mitterrand near the end of the negotiations.[98]

On balance, the evidence on the sources of British preferences regarding the Maastricht Treaty permits us to dismiss German unification as an important factor and to restrict the influence of other objective geopolitical concerns to the determination of British foreign and defense policy.[99] It is more difficult, however, to determine the relative importance of geopolitical ideology and economic interest. The most one can conclude is that economic factors appear slightly more important, particularly in the long term on what was by far the most significant issue of the period: monetary cooperation. Thatcher's outright ideological opposition to any participation in the EMS and EMU could delay British cooperation but could not block it indefinitely. We see the greater force of economic motivations also on the issue of strengthening the European Court and

[97] *Economist,* 7 December 1991, 52. Major was similarly uncompromising on the symbolic issue of the term "federal."

[98] Sharp, *Thatcher's,* 178; interview with Thatcher adviser. Also Sharp, *Thatcher's,* 174; Walsh, *Global,* 154; Attali *Verbatim,* 3:691–2; *FT,* 28 July 1984, 22; interview with British ambassador; *EuroWatch,* 31 May 1993, 5.5. Arguments in Cabinet for joining the ERM were either economic or diplomatic, the latter aimed at influencing future economic decisions.

[99] The timing of policy shifts appears to support both theories. The major change between 1982 and 1985 is an increase in support among economic actors and government officials for ERM participation. This shift is readily explicable as the result of more competitive exchange rates, as business groups stated at the time. However, we also see an increase in overt parliamentary opposition to EMU within the Conservative party as Thatcher's supporters assumed control, though this move of course left basic British skepticism about the scheme unchanged.

perhaps also in the generally more uncompromising British opposition to concessions on social and immigration policy than on the powers of the European Parliament or the European Central Bank.

Explaining National Preference Formation

In each of the three major EC members a preponderance of evidence shows that economic interests were at least as important as geopolitical concerns in defining national preferences in the Maastricht negotiations. Most evidence suggests that economic concerns were considerably more important. Although the evidence permits some tentative conclusions, in particular the rejection of objective geopolitical factors in motivating the move to EMU, a more precise and reliable determination of the relative weights of economic interest and European ideology in each country must await the availability of more primary sources. In each country records of the preferences and tactics of business groups and the deliberations of national executives remain incomplete.

The available evidence strongly disconfirms what is perhaps the most widespread hypothesis about national motivations for the Maastricht Treaty, namely that national preferences were dictated by the need to tie Germany into Europe after unification. In all three countries, timing, national negotiating tactics, and domestic discourse and cleavages are inconsistent with a pervasive concern about the geopolitical impact of unification. Most strikingly, British, French, and German preferences are stable throughout the period from 1988 onward, unchanged either by the fall of the Berlin Wall in November 1989 or by the conclusion of German unification in August 1990. Objective geopolitical factors only appear to explain policies toward foreign and defense policy: Britain and France, with viable unilateral policies, nuclear weapons, and UN representation, opposed a strong common policy with supranational institutions.

It is more difficult to assign relative weights to geopolitical ideology and economic interest—that is, to varying commitments to European federalism and the varying commercial and macroeconomic preferences of strong- and weak-currency countries in the face of economic interdependence. In each country, to be sure, the bulk of the evidence supports an economic explanation. German support for monetary integration with "economist" conditions reflected the traditional domestic compromise among economic interests: business, the chancellor, and the Bundesbank. Germany sought to maintain the benefits of the EMS, dampen the appreciation of the DM, and loosen domestic macroeconomic constraints in the face of dollar depreciation and the fiscal burden of German unification. This policy was consistently supported by business, labor, large banks, the major opposition party, and, it appears, even farmers. France also favored wresting control over German monetary policy away from the Bundesbank in order to relax domestic macroeconomic constraints and reduce risk premia; movement toward EMU was a quid pro quo for capital liberalization and, so French leaders hinted, continued participation in the EMS. Rising capital movements and inflationary convergence made such a goal possible for France (as for Germany) in a way it had not been a decade earlier. As in Germany, so in France EMU enjoyed strong support from business and finance. Consistent French pressure for a less autonomous ECB, looser convergence criteria, and greater political control over common exchange-rate policy suggest that French policy was not the result of ideological conversion to German-style macroeconomic policy. In Britain, where inflation was raging at close to 10 percent in 1990, economic interest groups and economic officials did not support EMU, fearing that fixed exchange rates might swiftly become uncompetitive, yet the overriding concern was nonetheless to avoid outright exclusion, which was expected to have a negative impact on industry and finance.[100]

The evidence clearly suggests that these economic considerations imposed critical constraints, but alone they may have been insufficient to determine the pattern of national preferences—namely, an enthusiastic Franco-German move toward EMU opposed by Britain. Even in Germany and France EMU was controversial, and support among economic groups, though clearly positive, was not enthusiastic. The Maastricht referendum debate in France and the continued controversy in Germany further suggest that unilateral alternatives or continued cooperation within the EMS remained viable options within both countries.

We should not, therefore, dismiss the possibility that European federal ideas played a secondary but significant role in shaping national positions toward the Maastricht negotiations. An ideational explanation of national preferences would stress the ways in which ambitious leaders pursue their own federalist or nationalist beliefs about integration or seek to profile themselves electorally by appealing to such beliefs among the public or parliamentarians. The distribution of such ideas is broadly consistent with national positions—Franco-German support, backed by Benelux and Italy, and British opposition, backed by Denmark and Greece. Mitterrand in France and both Kohl and Genscher in Germany sought to profile themselves as European statesmen, whereas successive British prime ministers were motivated in part by strong personal or parliamentary Euroskepticism.

Let us not forget the limitations of an explanation based on geopolitical ideology. It tells us little about the timing of movement toward EMU (1987–88), the reasons for doing so, the domestic cleavages surrounding the decision, or enduring international conflict between "economists" and "monetarists" over the structure and conditionality of the ECB. Nor can the support of more federalist countries be attributed to the weak provisions for political union, which occasioned considerable criticism in Germany. The near-uniform negativism of the British position seems at first glance to support an ideological interpretation, but such an account cannot explain the decisive weakness of the British position, namely, that Britain was consistently forced to make concessions to head

---

[100] The generally positive role of Italy is anomalous. It is, moreover, troubling that the public assessments of the French and German governments appear to rest on slightly different assumptions about the probable economic consequences of EMU. Though both favored a loosening of Bundesbank policies, more members, and political control of the ECB, the rhetoric of French politicians implied that EMU had been more successful at achieving this goal than did that of their German counterparts. This suggests a possible intervening role for economic ideas. More research is required to sort out these considerations.

off exclusion. Finally, geopolitical ideology fails to account for varying positions on other economic issues: French support for and Anglo-German opposition to industrial policy, Franco-German support for and British opposition to deepening of social and environmental cooperation, ongoing British support for liberalization of service markets, and varying national positions on concurrent negotiations over agricultural reform.

Still, European ideology appears to help explain at least two aspects of preferences. First, as both economic and geopolitical explanations predict, ideology appears to have played a particular role in areas with no immediate economic implications, such as codecision for the European Parliament and cooperation in foreign and defense policy—though in the latter case objective geopolitical factors offer an adequate explanation. The British and the French tended to support strengthening of the Council, the Germans supported the Parliament. The British were most unilateralist on foreign policy, the French less so, the Germans least, a reflection of the viability of their respective unilateral policies. Second, European federal ideas and their nationalist counterparts appear to have been responsible for general national tendencies for or against integration, which created, at the very least, considerable leads and lags. In Britain, Thatcher's opposition, probably ideological in origin, delayed British entry into and adjustment to the EMS by five years. In Germany, Kohl and Genscher enthusiastically promoted monetary integration after 1988, despite considerable economic risk and before the macroeconomic benefits of doing so had become fully evident. Absent enthusiastic support from the French and German governments and a permissive public consensus in both countries, it is possible that economic arguments for EMU could not have triumphed.

Negotiating the Maastricht Treaty

We have seen that by the late 1980s, as French and German macroeconomic performance and policies converged, the level of agreement between the two countries concerning the desirability of EMU rose; neither was true of Britain. Nonetheless, significant differences remained, even between France and Germany. As had been the case in the Snake and EMS negotiations, France sought a looser, more "politicized" monetary arrangement and Germany a stricter, more "autonomous" monetary arrangement (though not one as strict as that favored by the Bundesbank). Britain sought to avoid any monetary arrangement at all but to avoid exclusion from any that was created. Also, as traditionally had been the case, Germany favored strong steps toward political union, including cooperation on interior affairs, foreign policy, and defense cooperation, as well as stronger powers for the Parliament; France sought more modest, intergovernmental steps toward political union, with particular attention to a common defense, social policy, and a stronger European Council; whereas Britain favored no major movement toward political union at all, though it signaled a willingness to compromise on foreign policy and new powers for the European Court.

The bargaining outcomes included a strong EMU largely on German terms, weak provisions for political union, an expansion of EC activities to include police and immigration affairs, a modest social policy from which Britain opted out, and new codecision powers that disappointed supporters of the European Parliament. How are these outcomes to be explained? Intergovernmental bargaining theory predicts that the outcome would reflect the relative intensity of national preferences in each area, with entrepreneurial functions (policy initiation, mediation, social mobilization) carried out by the most interested governments and those that intensely seek agreement making the largest concessions. Supranational bargaining theory predicts that the outcomes would reflect the inability of governments to bargain efficiently and the entrepreneurial intervention of supranational officials in the Commission, Parliament, and Court as policy initiators, interstate mediators, and mobilizers of social support.

We shall see that, after the case of the SEA, in which supranational officials played as important a role as they ever had, Maastricht marked a return to the intergovernmental bargaining style that had traditionally characterized EC negotiations. Bargaining was initiated, mediated, and mobilized by governments, and it was efficient. The intervention of Commission officials, led by Jacques Delors, was generally redundant and occasionally counterproductive. Distributional outcomes consistently reflected the relative opportunity costs of agreement, in particular the relative satisfaction of Germany with the monetary status quo, which accorded the German government dominant bargaining power. In exchange for surrendering monetary autonomy, Germany was able to dictate to a very large extent the form and function European monetary arrangements.

Monetary Integration: A German Europe

The question underlying negotiations was whether Germany should adjust through higher inflation or the others through deflation. Formally and normatively, the system remained flexible.[101] Nothing implied that the French, Italian, and British governments must refuse to alter parities in response to repeated suggestions from the Bundesbank and others, but in practice national policies converged toward a more rigid position.

German unification altered the economic fundamentals. Germany's demand boom meant that German adjustment had to occur either through currency revaluation or through higher inflation. The first was blocked by German fears of lost competitiveness and Anglo-French-Italian fears of a loss of credibility; the second, by Bundesbank opposition. The result: adjustment could take place only through a collapse of fixed rates or through the maintenance of high interest rates and low inflation in Germany's neighbors. This tension placed considerable strain on the system.[102]

---

[101] David and Peter Marsh, "Lessons of Europe's Currency Turmoil," *FT*, 30 April 1993, 3; interview with French minister.

[102] Connolly, *Rotten*, 274–275; interview with French minister, 1994.

European leaders at sea on monetary integration.
Cartoon by Oliphant copyright © 1991 Universal Press Syndicate. Reprinted with
permission. All rights reserved.

Agenda-Setting and the Delors Committee:
"Pöhl . . . could not stop the process"

Consideration of EMU began almost immediately after currency pressures
unleashed by dollar depreciation led to the highly contentious EMS realignment of January 1987. The French demanded German reflation, the Bundesbank responded with a realignment. (A comparison of French and German
economic fundamentals gave good reason to think that German policy was
too restrictive.) The French government, as we have seen, searched for means
of exerting international pressure on Germany. Edouard Balladur, Gaullist prime
minister Jacques Chirac's finance minister, called for a more intensive system of
macroeconomic surveillance with the aim of a more "appropriate sharing of
adjustment efforts." His demand was quickly echoed by Delors, who called in
March 1987 for a "more symmetric system." In the same month Genscher called
for institutional deepening of monetary cooperation. Informal discussions were
initiated.[103]

Yet the Bundesbank managed to frustrate efforts by French and German governments to create an institutional structure in which more symmetrical policies
would be possible. French initiatives in the G-7 came to nothing. The so-called
Basel-Nyborg Agreement, which reflected the Bundesbank's strong influence

---

[103] *FT*, 17 June 1987; *Le Monde*, 1 April 1987; Schönfelder and Thiel, *Markt*, 22–30.

over the Committee of Central Bank Governors, permitted intramarginal interventions but created no new binding obligations on surplus countries. France and Germany agreed in November 1987 to creation of a Franco-German economic council, which would permit finance ministers and central bank presidents to meet to set policy objectives. Repeating Schmidt's tactics of a decade earlier, the Kohl government excluded the Bundesbank from the negotiations and informed it of the contents of the agreement only days before the signing in January 1988. Yet the Bundesbank presented a legal analysis purporting to show that the arrangement violated the Bundesbank statute—not so subtly threatening noncompliance.[104]

Having failed to solve the problem of asymmetry by reforming the EMS through multilateral, bilateral, or regional means, France turned to more radical proposals. In October 1987 Mitterrand, who had already sought stronger monetary provisions in the SEA, called for a European central bank. After the Franco-German Economic Council was watered down, the French president was quickly followed by Balladur, who proposed a most intensive cooperation in January 1988. One month later a memo from Balladur's Italian counterpart Giuliano Amato reiterated the demand. Asymmetries in the EMS, they argued, "structurally undervalued" the DM and enlarged German current-account surpluses. The Italian memo threatened to invoke escape clauses in the process of capital liberalization, then under consideration, as well as implement various protective domestic regulations, if current asymmetries in the operation of the EMS were not redressed.[105] The Kohl government, having backed French efforts over the preceding year, responded positively. Genscher called almost immediately for rapid movement toward monetary union, hinting that some sacrifice of domestic stability might be required and proposing a committee of "wise men" to study further monetary integration. Kohl quickly endorsed the proposal in a speech before the European Parliament. A March memo from Finance Minister Stoltenberg was less enthusiastic but did not shut the door.

The Commission was also active as were private groups. Delors's primary priority back in 1984 had been deeper and more symmetrical monetary integration. When Britain and Germany had blocked French efforts to deepen monetary cooperation, Delors finally pursued internal market liberalization instead, preserving no more than references to monetary policy. A December 1987 Commission report linked EMU to capital liberalization and informally canvassed governments about the possibility of forming an expert committee. Yet Delors, doubting that an interstate consensus existed, waited until March 1988, after the French and Italian initiatives and the German response, whereupon the economist Tommaso Padoa-Schioppa finally convinced him to call publicly for EMU. In early 1988 Delors reportedly gave a speech within the Commission saying "Let us not speak of EMU for two years," because of his misplaced skepticism about the German commitment. Numerous private and semipublic groups also

[104] Ellen Kennedy, *The Bundesbank: Germany's Central Bank in the International Monetary System* (London, 1991), 93ff.
[105] Gros and Thygesen, *European*, 311–313.

proposed monetary union. Most prestigious among them was the Association for Monetary Union in Europe, comprised largely of bankers and business-people, founded in late 1986 by Giscard and Schmidt. In April 1988 the group published a detailed blueprint for monetary union and between 1988 and 1990 presented annual survey results revealing substantial big business support for monetary union.[106]

At the European Council of Hanover on 27–28 June 1988, where the final element of the SEA bargain, a financial transfer to the southern countries (the "Paquet Delors"), was concluded, the major governments agreed to set a timetable to lift exchange controls and to consider future steps toward EMU. Thatcher, quite aware of what was happening, had terms such as "central bank" and "single currency" removed from the communiqué, but her belief that she had thus "sidelined" EMU was, as Lawson and the Labour opposition both observed, illusory. She failed to block the proposal on which Mitterrand and Kohl had focused their attention: the naming of a committee to discuss monetary integration—chaired, as Lawson later pointed out, by of all people Delors.[107]

Kohl and Mitterrand carefully attended to the nature of the Delors Committee. Earlier in the month Kohl had agreed to move forward on monetary union in exchange for French acceptance of a date for liberalizing capital movements. Two aspects were critical: membership and mandate. After careful advance discussions with Balladur, Kohl, and Genscher, Delors backed Genscher's proposal to create a committee of five independent experts, presumably academics or "wise men," but Kohl and Stoltenberg, backed by Thatcher, insisted that the committee involve national central bank governors acting in their personal capacity. Kohl suggested Delors chair the committee; Delors and the French, seeing this as biasing the committee toward German preferences, were able to secure only the participation of three private experts.[108] Even more important was the committee's mandate, which instructed it to propose a concrete plan for EMU. The committee thus had to recommend major reforms rather than marginal improvements. We have seen that this mandate, deliberately inserted at the last minute by Kohl and Mitterrand to pressure the Bundesbank, nearly led Pöhl to resign. Pöhl later termed his participation a "mistake": "If I had boycotted it I could not have stopped the process, but I could have slowed it down. I would have been freer to criticize the Delors Report." Yet it is unclear whether

---

[106] Grant, *Delors*, 118–120; Ross, *Jacques*, 80–81; Gros and Thygesen, *European*, 312–314; Ken Endo, "Political Leadership in the European Community: The Role of the Commission Presidency under Jacques Delors, 1985–1995 (diss., St. Anthony's College, Oxford, 1996), 84; 102, chap. 7; Gaddum, *Deutsche*, 312; Committee for the Monetary Union of Europe, *Programme*. Gros and Thygesen, *European*, 315, lists numerous other private and academic conferences and groups.

[107] Gros and Thygesen, *European*, 316–317; Lawson, *View*, 902–904; Thatcher, *Downing*, 708, 740–741; Grant, *Delors*, 119–120; Ross, *Jacques*, 81; Schönfelder and Thiel, *Markt*, 38–40.

[108] Interview with Delors and member of the Delors Committee. The idea of central bank governors has been variously attributed to Thatcher, Kohl, and Delors. At the time, it appears that more aggressive pro-EMU actors, such as Delors, Mitterand, and Genscher, favored an independent group, whereas a more cautious group, including Kohl and Thatcher, favored central bank governors. On the quid pro quo with capital liberalization, Vedrine, *Mondes*, 416–418.

this claim is realistic; his advisers at the time feared that if he did not serve, he would be excluded from critical debates over the details of the scheme.[109]

Launching the Negotiations:
Kohl and Mitterrand "confront and isolate" Thatcher

Between the Hanover summit and the convening of the IGC in late 1990, a wide range of monetary alternatives was introduced and then reduced to a few viable options. This process occurred in three stages: in June 1989 the Delors Committee report was approved; the Strasbourg summit of December 1989 decided to convene an IGC in late 1990; and monetary negotiations were formally linked to discussions on political union in June 1990.

On the Delors Committee, Pöhl was universally recognized as the decisive voice, because the Bundesbank enjoyed an important voice in the critical state. Agreement would be possible only if his skepticism of EMU and his personal disdain for Delors, which he displayed by reading newspapers through the first meetings of the committee, could be overcome. It was understood that he would reject outright any proposal with an anti-inflationary commitment significantly weaker than that of the Bundesbank. In addition, Leigh-Pemberton of the Bank of England had been instructed by Thatcher and Lawson to enlist Pöhl's aid in blocking any move toward a central bank or a single currency. Delors, the Italian and French central bankers, and the three civilian members adopted a diametrically opposed position, favoring a single currency with weaker guarantees against inflation.[110]

Early on, the committee accepted all Pöhl's demands. Major concessions were made by the French, including the acceptance of budgetary convergence criteria, no transfers of sovereignty during early stages of the transition, and the prior independence of national central banks. No objection was raised to Pöhl's demand that the Eurofed have greater independence and autonomy than existing national central banks. In exchange, Pöhl, over the objections of Bundesbank hardliners, approved a single currency. Perhaps, he later hinted, he thought the conditions would never be met. In the end only Leigh-Pemberton remained reluctant, but his counterproposal for a parallel currency was discussed and rejected by all participants in January 1989. Pöhl was unwilling to contemplate uncontrolled monetary creation and remained skeptical of Thatcher's entirely negative attitude toward monetary integration. Believing that unilateral opposition would be even more costly than acceptance, Leigh-Pemberton added his signature.

Delors lent his name to the proceedings but played a modest role through-

---

[109] Grant, *Delors*, 121, also 118–120; Ross, *Jacques*, 80–81; Attali *Verbatim*, 3:35; Gros and Thygesen, *European*, 312–314; interviews with two members of the Delors Committee.

[110] For this paragraph and the next, I use interviews with two members of the Delors Committee, 1991, 1996; Steven Solomon, *The Confidence Game: How Unelected Central Bankers are Governing the Changed World Economy* (New York, 1995), 476. Pöhl was not as opposed to EMU as his Bundesbank colleagues, who insisted that he rescind some concessions at Stage II of the transition during the last few meetings of the committee.

out, eschewing ambitious proposals or political entrepreneurship. Instead, he later recalled, he encouraged professional discussions and permitted the central bankers to dictate the "substance" of the report. Although the committee may have gained modest prestige by bearing Delors's name, his concrete role was that of a secretariat: he drafted compromise texts but, according to one committee member, neither proposed nor blocked any major element of the final report. His only distinctive proposal was identical to that advanced by Roy Jenkins in the EMS negotiations, namely increases in structural funding; it met the same fate. The resulting three-stage plan was very similar to the Werner Report of 1969, albeit with greater anti-inflationary protection. Yet the report was intentionally unclear on the most critical points: no one, not even Delors, dared press Pöhl or Leigh-Pemberton to commit to a firm schedule or a specification of concrete transitional stages for achieving EMU.[111]

The report was approved by the heads of government at the Madrid European Council of June 1989. Prime Minister Gonzalez toured the capitals in advance and brokered a compromise among conflicting positions; Kohl and Mitterrand coordinated closely. Kohl was in "complete agreement" with Delors and Mitterrand, according to one analyst who examined the transcripts. Gonzalez concluded after his tour that Mitterrand and Delors would insist on acceptance of the Delors Report. The first stage would begin on 1 July 1990, and an IGC would be convened. Mitterrand's proposal to set precise schedule for stages two and three of the transition, or for the IGC itself, received little support. Thatcher hoped that the lack of explicit approval for the report, as well as language insisting that "full and adequate preparations" must precede the IGC, would slow further movement. Yet the Germans and French were committed to move forward. Genscher and Dumas agreed that the French presidency in the second half of the year would set precise terms, and they convened a committee under Elisabeth Guigou, to meet whether the British participated or not, with a mandate to provide a report to serve as the basis for an IGC. Guigou's committee was instructed simply to summarize key issues rather than attempt to resolve issues left open by the Delors Report. Horst Teltschik, Kohl's closest aide on such questions, informed his French counterpart, Jacques Attali, that Kohl would be prepared at that time to "confront and isolate" Thatcher on EMU and launch an IGC.[112]

[111] Grant, *Delors* 120–124.
[112] Ludlow, "Politics," xliii–xliv; Attali *Verbatim*, 3:239, also 263, 297. Also Jim Cloos, Gaston Reinesch, Daniel Vignes, and Joseph Weyland, *Le Traité de Maastricht: Genèse, analyse, commentaires* (Brussels, 1993), 38–42, 92ff; Gros and Thygesen, *European*, 323; Thatcher, *Downing*, 750–752; Schönfelder and Thiel, *Markt*, 66–67; interview with French minister, 1994. Michael Garthe, "Bundesrepublik Deutschland," in Werner Weidenfeld and Wolfgang Wessels, eds., *Jahrbuch der europäischen Integration 1988/89* (Bonn, 1989), 303, reports that Kohl mediated between Thatcher and Mitterrand, calling for a conference on changing the treaty only once the steps in the Delors Report had been considered. Some criticize the Guigou Committee, named to achieve this end, as inadequate, but participants reveal that it was a deliberate attempt by politicians to precommit to further cooperation and coordinate French and German policy before raising controversial issues. Mitterrand's assistant Vedrine makes it appear as if Mitterrand convinced Kohl at the summit itself and even mentions a link to German unification, but this is not corroborated elsewhere. Even this account, however,

The French government, now holding the rotating EC presidency, kept the momentum going, resulting in an agreement at Strasbourg in December, where the chief executives publicly accepted a monetary IGC to begin in December 1990. This date, proposed by Germany for nearly a year, was the earliest Mitterrand believed he could achieve. The British government had hoped that at Strasbourg the Germans would call for "further preparations," but Germany instead moved forward with plans to support France. By October high-level Franco-German discussions were well under way to prepare the Strasbourg meeting on the basis of agreement between Kohl and Mitterrand that an IGC would be launched in 1990, completed in late 1991, and ratified in 1992. Mitterrand and Pöhl both gave speeches in October predicting that Strasbourg would set a date for an IGC to negotiate the transition to EMU. Mitterrand and Delors wanted negotiations to begin within six months, but Kohl insisted that they be delayed until after the German elections of November 1990—consistent with his longstanding effort to dampen the right-wing electoral challenge. Kohl underscored the "principal German objectives": according to French officials, these were to have preparations handled by finance ministry and central bank officials, the independence of national and European central banks, a clear commitment to price stability, prior economic convergence, and simultaneous movement toward political union. France opposed every one of these objectives, but Mitterrand signaled French willingness to make concessions in exchange for German acceptance of EMU. In November and December the central bank governors met in Basel and endorsed Pöhl's recommendation that national central banks remain or become independent under the new system.[113]

German willingness to move toward EMU and set a date for the IGC at Strasbourg in December 1989 is generally attributed to the sudden opportunity for unification following the fall of the Berlin Wall. The German government was forced to offer a quid pro quo to remove French opposition to unification; some allege that other governments suddenly had a greater incentive to lock Germany into Europe. Yet such claims are based on no more than Mitterrand and Kohl's public rhetoric and the apparent coincidence of timing. To be sure, the Hungarian decision in September to permit East Germans to move west, and the fall of the Berlin Wall on 9 November 1989, did change French and German rhetoric. In their speeches, Mitterrand and Kohl increasingly linked German unification and EMU. Mitterrand privately warned Genscher that if European unification did not precede German unification, Germany would face a triple alliance of France, Britain, and Russia; the French government issued sharp warnings

---

clearly shows that Kohl supported an IGC but was concerned about the timing *vis-à-vis* German public opinion. Vedrine, *Les mondes,* 419–421.

[113] Thatcher, *Downing,* 760. Pöhl's speech in October was cautious but noted that the IGC would take place and, in an extemporaneous aside, predicted that the final decision would be taken at the Strasbourg Council meeting in December. Ludlow, "Politics," xliv–xlv. More generally, Grant, *Delors,* 131–150, especially 144; Attali *Verbatim,* 3:322, 326, 367–368, but see 349; Schönfelder and Thiel, *Markt,* 58–69; David Buchan, *Europe: The Strange Superpower* (Aldershot, 1993), 32–34.

that failure to set a date for negotiations on EMU would be viewed as evidence that Germany was backing away from Europe. His spokespersons criticized German demands for political union as a disguised effort to delay EMU.[114]

Yet there was no shift in concrete positions consistent with an "EMU for unification" bargain. As we have seen, Germany and France had been planning to move forward at Strasbourg for months. Although Kohl was clearly concerned not to alienate Mitterrand, he in fact made no further compromises between 9 November 1989 and 1 August 1990. To the contrary, he went ahead with prearranged plans to set a late-1990 date for an IGC at Strasbourg and *upped* German demands, requiring parallel negotiations on political union—ignoring warnings from Delors that this linkage would lead to a crisis. During this period, Delors efficiently moved forward with preparations to include the former East Germany in the EC—streamlining accession in a way that avoided potential conflict.[115]

Nor is there evidence of any quid pro quo on the part of Germany's neighbors. They remained "tough," refusing to do more than reiterate existing treaty agreements on the German question. Mitterrand continued to seek cooperation with East Germany or Russia to slow unification (though characteristically keeping his options open), Thatcher sought to exploit military cooperation to block unification (characteristically leaving herself no good fallback position), and other European leaders voiced worries. American and German leaders exploited the opportunity to press for unification without waiting for agreement on an increasingly integrated EC. French concessions to Germany on political union occurred only once unification was a *fait accompli*. In mid-March, Kohl renewed his demand for a simultaneous acceleration of political union (still viewed skeptically by France).

Only at the time of the East German elections of 18 March, in which Kohl's coalition gained a significant victory, did the French government publicly reverse position, conceding to Germany a second negotiation on European political union. When Franco-German discussions in late March resulted in a bilateral agreement explicitly proposing an agenda for political union, Delors dropped his open opposition to it. The Dublin summit of 28 April, by which time European governments had reconciled themselves to German unification, approved the second IGC on political issues and beginning arrangements for the inclusion of eastern Germany in the EC. During the remainder of 1990, the governments prepared the IGC. Again, Germany made no concessions.[116]

Preparations for the IGC stimulated a range of official proposals. In November

---

[114] Thatcher, *Downing*, 795–796; Attali *Verbatim*, 3:343, 352–354; François Mitterrand, *De l'Allemagne, De la France* (Paris, 1996), 79–99; Baun, *Imperfect*, 40; interview with Delors; Zelikow and Rice, *Germany*, 95–98, 116–117, 133–138, 145ff, 234–235.

[115] Interviews with Delors.

[116] Teltschik, *329*, 106, 172ff, 176, 369; Attali, *Verbatim*, 3:375, 449; Baun, *Imperfect*, 40–45; Kiessler and Elbe, *Tisch*, 59ff; Smyser, *German*, 278–279. In confidential discussions with Bush, Kohl stated that he overrode the Bundesbank on EMU in order to tie Germany to Europe and thus earn the trust of Mitterrand, whom he considered more far-sighted than Thatcher, and discussed integration as part of a diplomatic strategy to dampen opposition to unification.

1990 the Committee of Central Bank Governors responded to a request from the Rome summit by proposing draft statutes for a European System of Central Banks (ESCB). The central banks granted strong powers to the ESCB and ECB, particularly in exchange-rate policy, monetary creation, and prudential supervision, but left other major issues to the IGC. Germany continued to push for low-inflation guarantees; the March 1990 European Council decision affirmed the need for convergence criteria—specific macroeconomic preconditions that all participants in the EMU must meet.[117]

While French officials saw strict convergence criteria as an inevitable if unfortunate quid pro quo that Germany could exact for EMU, Delors did not. Throughout this period, the Commission's central and largely futile goal remained to undermine German insistence on strict conditionality and a two-speed Europe. Pöhl and others in Germany denounced Delors's proposals as undermining domestic monetary discipline; even poorer countries rejected them as pressing the tempo too quickly and neglecting regional aid. At the meeting of finance ministers in September, only France, Belgium, Italy, and Denmark defended Delors, who reportedly "left the meeting in a state of shock." When the IGC opened a few months later, the finance ministers began by criticizing Delors's proposal. German finance minister Waigel immediately reinserted criteria for prior macroeconomic convergence. Delors persisted in a futile challenge to Germany's insistence on convergence criteria, comparing their definition to medieval debates about the sex of angels.[118]

Among futile Commission interventions found, for example, in its August 1990 opinion on EMU, reportedly written by Delors himself, and a Commission draft treaty of December 1990 were the use of the names "ecu" for the currency and "Eurofed" for the bank, a short transition period, Council and Parliament involvement in naming the ECB's executive board, international representation in monetary affairs by a troika of supranational officials and the Council president rather than finance ministers, Eurofed supervision of economic policies during the transition, generous financial assistance in the form of both loans and grants, attendance by Commission officials at meetings in various institutions, democratic accountability of the ECB before the Parliament, a decision by special majority of eight whether the preconditions for movement to EMU were satisfied, and no automatic enforcement of prohibitions on monetary financing, public debt guarantees (bailouts), and excessive budget deficits. Each of these conditions proved unacceptable to Germany and was rejected. Only Commission proposals for Council control over foreign-exchange interventions, advisory status for the Monetary Committee, sanctions against excessive national deficits, and multilateral surveillance were accepted.[119]

---

[117] Schonfelder and Thiel, *Markt*, 63–64.

[118] Grant, *Delors*, 147, also 148–151; Baun, *Imperfect*, 49–51.

[119] See "Intergovernmental Conferences: Contributions by the Commission," *Bulletin of the EC* (Supplement 2/91); Ludlow, "Reshaping," 423–425; Robert Wester, "The European Commission and European Political Union," in Laursen and Vanhoonacker, eds., *Intergovernmental*, 205–214; Grant, *Delors*, 151.

Other governments slowly converged on the German position, which in fact hardened as the details of the agreement became clearer. From October 1990 onward, with German reunification and parliamentary elections completed, governments moved away from Commission materials and began to converge around a Dutch proposal to set dates on the basis of prior economic convergence. This plan formed the basis for agreements reached at summit meetings in Rome in October and December 1990. Kohl now pushed forward, signaling his willingness to announce a date for the beginning of the second stage of EMU. In the discussions, as well as in official conclusions and press briefings, it became clear that the eleven were prepared to move ahead to monetary union without Britain. With this threat in place, the member governments reached a compromise, setting 1 January 1994 as a starting date for Stage Two, and agreeing that a single currency would be an early element in Stage Three and that simultaneous negotiations on political union would be conducted. The date 1994 was earlier than the German government had previously proposed, but the significance of this concession was minimal because German opposition had stripped the transitional system, under the European Monetary Institute, of any decision-making power. When formal negotiations began in mid-December 1990, the major contours of a feasible bargain were already visible. Germany again rejected British schemes for a parallel currency and insisted, over French and Commission objections, on ECB autonomy, strict convergence criteria, budgetary controls, modest financial transfers, weak second-stage institutions, and parallel movement toward European political union in exchange for a firm commitment to a single currency on a specified date.[120]

The EMU Negotiations: France and the Commission "lose the game"

Although the broad lines of EMU had been decided, key details remained to be negotiated. Accordingly, the negotiations began with what one analyst termed a "flurry of position papers as most of the major players made their opening negotiating gambits and outlined their preferred vision of EMU."[121] Every delegation introduced detailed textual proposals. France and Germany each submitted a full draft treaty, and Britain and Spain provided detailed proposals for the second stage of EMU. Private groups also remained active. A proposal issued by the Association for the Monetary Union of Europe, for example, set out plans for the transition in considerably greater detail than the Delors Committee had provided.[122]

Governments established tight control over the negotiations. The Luxembourg government, having assumed the rotating EC presidency, managed the plethora of proposals by adopting a procedure developed in the SEA negotiations, whereby a committee from the Luxembourg presidency, the Secretary

---

[120] Ludlow, "Reshaping," 428; Gros and Thygesen, *European*, 324.

[121] Corbett, *Maastricht*, 39.

[122] Interview with national chief negotiator, 1994; Schönfelder and Thiel, *Markt*, 119–121; Italiener, "Mastering," 68–70.

General of the Council, and the Commission developed open-ended drafts with alternative texts in controversial spots. Most of the work was carried out by fewer than a dozen officials of the Council Secretariat and the Luxembourg government; the Commission was not directly involved, though in March it submitted its own draft. By April the Luxembourg presidency and Council Secretariat presented their draft treaty. Overlap with the Commission's draft from the previous month was limited to relatively uncontroversial provisions; the Luxembourg draft was sufficiently dissimilar to spark strong Commission criticism. In mid-1990 governments had begun to transfer authority from ECOFIN and the Monetary and Central Bank Committee to the foreign ministers and heads of state, whose personal representatives, assisted by the secretary general of the Council, led the negotiations. The final details were worked out in November at ministerial meetings, as well as two Kohl-Major summits, and at Maastricht itself.[123]

By spring 1990 the British government was the lone remaining opponent of movement to a single currency. It resubmitted its proposal for a "hard ECU" proposal with a parallel "13th currency," which would coexist with existing currencies, perhaps replacing them in the long term. Spain initially favored the idea but backed away when most other governments rejected it. Studies known to all governments showed that businesspeople would not switch to the hard ECU without the prospect of its rapidly becoming Europe's single currency. Polls revealed that business strongly supported a single currency; only some banks dependent on foreign-exchange transactions, disproportionately located in the City of London, favored a parallel currency. Pöhl reiterated his earlier attacks on the proposal, stating that it would impede control over the money supply and pointing out that it had already been rejected twice, once in the Delors Committee and once in Rome. So governments set about hammering out the details of the transition to a single currency, with Britain playing a cautious role.[124]

Intergovernmental bargaining theory predicts that Germany, whose alternative to a single currency, given asymmetries in the EMS and domestic support for its current macroeconomic arrangements, was the most attractive among its supporters, should benefit on net from side-payments and compromises. Anything less than a "German" EMU would simply be vetoed at home, whereas greater compromise was possible in neighboring countries. This was indeed both the perception of participants and the result of objective analysis, though many, perhaps most, political scientists have sought to argue that Germany came away badly from the negotiations. If we take EMU with a single currency as a given and examine the eight most important distributional issues that surrounded it, all but one favored Germany. These were (1) the right to opt out, (2) "convergence" criteria for participation, (3) the schedule and procedure for the transition to EMU, including "two-speed" provisions, (4) the nature of transitional or "second-stage" institutions such as the European Monetary Institute, (5) the autonomy, mandate, and voting procedures of the ECB, (6) the site of the ECB

[123] Ludlow, "Reshaping," 429, 445; Grant, *Delors*, 184.
[124] Corbett, *Maastricht*, 40; interviews with two members of the Delors Committee.

and name of the currency, (7) controls and sanctions on excessive national deficits, and (8) provisions for bailouts and other financial transfers.[125] These issues are summarized in Table 6.1.

Overall, the outcomes tended to be closest to Germany's initial negotiating position, that is, a variant of the "economist" position. On all issues except the last two, German compromises were slight, despite pressure from France, the Commission, and other governments. On controls and sanctions on excessive deficits, later termed the "stability pact," Germany gained much of what it wanted, though sanctions would be imposed by QMV not the simple majority vote that German hardliners preferred; weaknesses in the treaty were later corrected. On the final issue, financial transfers, Germany successfully resisted bailouts and fiscal federalism but later, along with France and Britain, conceded an increase in structural funds, agreed at the Edinburgh summit of December 1992. Let us consider each issue in turn.

Opt-Out Clauses. Denmark and Britain initially demanded a generalized opt-out clause, which the Netherlands presidency obligingly proposed. The other ten ministers and Delors took the opposite view, fearing that Germany might later invoke it. Kohl himself threatened to veto any agreement with a general opt-out. The details of opt-out clauses were not determined until a meeting of finance ministers just before the Maastricht summit. Led by Germany, the ten pressured Denmark to abandon its position, leaving only Britain, which negotiated an exceptional opt-out clause.[126] Later the German Constitutional Court and the Danish parliament unilaterally imposed requirements for parliamentary ratification of the final move to EMU.

Convergence Criteria. Governments agreed early on the need for "mutual surveillance" and convergence guidelines overseen by the Council. The Germans, supported by the Danes, Dutch, and British, went further, favoring strict convergence criteria specifying inflation rates, deficits, debts, interest rates, and exchange rates. Weak-currency countries realized that EMU with high underlying inflation would be costly, but they also feared exclusion from a "two-track" scheme in which some members could move ahead without the others. Hence Spain, Greece, Portugal, Ireland, Italy, and the Commission, though interestingly not Britain, opposed convergence criteria. Delors went so far as to allege that any such criteria would constitute a betrayal of German promises at the Rome summit—a claim that elicited an angry denial from Kohl. French leaders favored a looser arrangement as well but understood that for Germany, strict convergence criteria were nonnegotiable; they opposed them publicly. Finance Minister Bérégovoy's spokesman hinted at an underlying deal when he recalled that "Germany totally backed us from the moment we made it clear that we would not be lax on implementing the criteria for countries to get into EMU."[127]

---

[125] For a more fine-grained analysis, see Italianer, "Mastering."

[126] Grant, *Delors*, 182; Ross, *Jacques*; Agence Europe, *Bulletin*, 26–27, 29, and 30 October 1991 and 5 December 1991, 9.

[127] *Agence Europe*, 11 December 1994; Sandholtz, "Monetary," 136–137; Lorenzo Bini-Smaghi, Tommaso Padoa-Schioppa, and Francesco Papadia, "The Policy History of the Maastricht Treaty: The Transition to the Final Stage of EMU," Banca d'Italia mimeo (Rome, 1993), 24.

So German demands were met. Convergence criteria were set close to EC averages, the Germans keeping one eye on the participation of Italy—potentially costly in German domestic politics. Participation was to be limited to those governments of countries where the inflation rate was within 1.5 percent of the three lowest rates, long-term interest rates fell within 2 percent of the three lowest, budget deficit was less than 3 percent of GDP, national debt was less than 60 percent of GDP, and the currency had remained within the ERM with no devaluations for two years. The final stage would begin in 1997 if a majority of EC members met these conditions, otherwise in 1999. National central banks would be made independent and capital would circulate freely. Weak-currency countries secured only a provision providing for a "flexible" interpretation of the criteria by the European Council, including "trends" in debts and deficits. The German decision to accept this compromise, proposed by Belgium, was made by Kohl himself, overriding some German officials. Yet even the German Finance Ministry and Bundesbank were not wholly opposed: at the September 1991 meeting of ECOFIN, Waigel and Schlesinger had already stressed the complete agreement among finance ministers that the convergence criteria provided "adequate room for political evaluation," a position Kohl and Genscher clearly favored.[128]

Schedule and Decision Procedure for the Transition. With French support, the Commission sought rapid, unconditional commitments; Delors proposed 1993 for the third stage and 1995 for the second. Denmark and Britain, on the opposite end of the spectrum, opposed any firm schedule at all. Other governments favored an intermediate solution. Many advanced proposals, but the German position was decisive. By siding with Britain and Denmark, Germany could at any time have blocked agreement on a final date, an outcome favored by the Bundesbank. Yet Kohl and Genscher consistently sought to "lock in" the agreement, though they delayed doing so until the Maastricht summit itself. It was agreed, on the basis of a compromise proposed by Spain and France, there that there would be two opportunities to move forward, first in 1997, second in 1999.[129]

Mitterrand and Kohl accepted from the start that transition to the third stage would be decided by majority vote. The final arrangement, based on Dutch and French compromise proposals, established that the 1997 decision on whether a majority of countries met the criteria would be reached by unanimous vote, followed, if necessary, by *automatic* movement forward in 1998–99, with governments voting by simple majority on which countries qualified. The automaticity of the 1999 decision reflected a personal decision by Kohl, who, his associates and British counterparts surmised, sought to assure a transition to EMU even in the face of domestic opposition. All votes were to be cast by heads of state and government, meeting in the European Council, not by ministers of finance, cen-

---

[128] Sandholtz, "Monetary" 135–136, 142; Schönfelder and Thiel, *Markt,* 135; *AE,* 5 December 1991, 10, and 30 October 1991, 8.

[129] Interviews with two national representatives, 1994, 1996; Ludlow, "Reshaping," 425. Since the German government, as opposed to the Bundesbank, had long favored setting a date, it is misleading to conclude that "the Commission and French would eventually win the date struggle" (Ross, *Jacques,* 246) or to speak of a Franco-Italian "ambush" at Maastricht (Marsh, *Germany and Europe,* 147).

tral bankers, or parliaments, a provision that preserved the executives' domestic initiative. Governments committed themselves not to hinder other qualifying governments from moving forward.

Second-Stage Institutions. The transition was critical since, if the French got their way, multilateral surveillance and standard-setting would begin to infringe on Bundesbank autonomy even before the transition to a single currency. Many proposals for the transition were explored. France, Italy, Belgium, Luxembourg, Greece, and the Commission sought to establish a central bank as soon as possible and to codify ERM rules within the treaty, with the hope of imposing symmetrical adjustment on Germany before creation of the single currency. The Commission took the lead, advancing proposals for a symmetrical EMS in 1990. In February 1991, shortly after the Bundesbank publicized its plan, Kohl announced that Germany opposed the creation of a European central bank before the third stage, after convergence criteria had been met and participants chosen. Again Delors's angry attacks had no effect on Kohl.[130] Germany carried the day, and the discussion shifted to the nature of an interim organization, the European Monetary Institute (EMI). France, Italy, Spain, Greece, and Portugal wanted the EMI to be headed by an EC official and granted powers to oversee and promote the development of a single currency, but Britain and Germany successfully promoted a separate board of central bankers and stripped the EMI of any power over policy. Having done so, Kohl was in a position to accept a Spanish proposal to launch the now essentially meaningless second stage relatively early—in 1994 as promised at the Rome summit, though not in 1993 as the Commission and France advocated.[131]

ECB Autonomy, Mandate, and Voting Procedures. The German government was particularly insistent that the ECB remain autonomous and be granted a strong anti-inflationary mandate. Though rejecting a prominent role for the Commission, the French government sought to strengthen the Council of Ministers as a counterweight by granting it joint responsibility for economic policy. Germany resisted French, Italian, and Commission demands for the inclusion of macroeconomic priorities other than inflation (e.g., unemployment, growth targets) in the ECB mandate, and for the head of the ECB to be drawn from outside the ranks of central bankers. Only Belgium and the Netherlands showed support for empowering the Commission, Court, or Parliament.[132]

---

[130] Vociferous opposition from potentially excluded countries, backed by the Commission, was overridden. The Dutch proposal that any six countries that met the criteria in 1996 could move ahead alone was initially supported only by Germany. After the fact, Delors and his associates claim that this did not undermine the "real purpose" of Stage 2, which had always been to signal commitment. Schönfelder, *Markt* 133–142, 152–157; Italianer, "Mastering," 95ff; Ross, *Jacques*; Sandholtz, "Monetary," 137; Grant, *Delors*, 183–184.

[131] Connolly, *Rotten*, 167–169; Bini-Smaghi, Padoa-Schioppa, and Papadia, "Policy," 14–21. Evidence of the German government's commitment is that when France and the Commission proposed that in 1997 the governments set a date for the transition by consensus, whereupon the ECOFIN would assess convergence and provide detailed plans by a qualified majority of 8 (of 12), whereupon those governments who were to move forward would vote unanimously on the exchange rates at which their currencies would be linked, Germany criticized the result as too *weak*, since it permitted governments that would not or could not move to veto the progress of those who sought to move forward.

[132] Ross, *Jacques*, 84–89, 153–156, 185–188; interview with French minister; Ludlow, "Reshaping," 398–399.

Again Germany triumphed. In no aspect of EMU was the Commission granted the unique power of proposal it enjoyed elsewhere; in two relatively minor areas it shares proposal rights with the ECB. The Parliament can be consulted but was accorded no formal role. Article 109, concerning control over exchange-rate policy, remains vague, with overlapping competence for the Council of Ministers and the ECB; it was nonetheless generally understood that exchange-rate policy would remain in ECB hands. The Commission's demand for formal participation was rejected. There remained some risk that pan-European societal pressures on the ECB might lead to policies laxer than those pursued by the Bundesbank, but this possibility was offset by the fact that the Maastricht treaty went even further than German domestic law in insulating the central bank from political control. François Lamoureaux of the Commission observed bitterly: "There will be an EMU in the treaty [but] we've lost the game on economic policy. Policy coordination, such as it will be, will be intergovernmental, [the Commission's] voice will be small."[133] Yet voting procedures in the ECB were to be on a one-nation, one-vote basis. Germany and other large countries neither demanded nor received weighted votes. This issue elicited little controversy or discussion, but one experienced chief negotiator termed Germany's quiet willingness to concede equal votes "the greatest concession he has ever experienced at an international meeting."[134]

ECB Location and Currency Name. Germany pressed for the ECB to be located in Frankfurt and resisted the name "ecu" for the currency, viewing it as too French. Decisions on site and name were not resolved at Maastricht but were instead postponed. Several years later, the bank was placed in Frankfurt and the currency was named the Euro, as the Germans had advocated.

Budgetary Constraints. There was near-unanimous rhetorical agreement on the need to monitor and constrain budget deficits. Among central bankers and finance ministers, a "near consensus" felt that the EC must intervene where debt/GDP ratios exceed 60 percent, a "majority" supported action where deficits exceed 3 percent of GDP, and "many members" favored action where budget deficits exceeded investment. The real debate concerned the strength of enforcement mechanisms and, in particular, the use of sanctions. From the beginning the German government, led by Waigel, supported stringent sanctions, including withholding EC funds, prosecution in European Court, and suspension of EC membership, for budget deficits. At various times the Dutch presidency, Germany, and the EC Monetary Committee supported punishment by simple majority. Support from Bérégovoy, who initially approved of the strict provisions in the Delors Report, was weak, though the French government did not overtly oppose sanctions. A curious alliance of Delors and Britain, backed by Italy and Belgium, opposed sanctions outright, arguing that friendly pressures, market forces, or more flexible criteria were sufficient.[135]

---

[133] Ross, *Jacques*, 156. Also Reimut Jochimsen, "EMU: A German Central Banker's Perspective," in Klaus Gretschmann, ed., *Economic and Monetary Union: Implications for National Policy-Makers* (Maastricht, 1993), 202–203.

[134] Interview with ambassador of a member-state, 1994.

[135] Corbett, *Maastricht*, 43; *Economist*, 7 April 1991, 88, 20 October 1991, 60, and 9 October 1991, 5–6; Grant, *Delors*, 183.

The outcome approximated German preferences. Monetary financing of deficits was banned, as were excessive deficits or public debt, as determined by the Council acting by qualified majority. Multilateral surveillance was imposed. Sanctions could be imposed on a sliding scale, starting with peer pressure, publicity, and market forces through to fines and suspension of EC payments. On the stringency of punishment, German hardliners like Waigel compromised only slightly, in that full suspension of EC membership was not included.[136] Delors aide François Lamoureaux lamented that "the 'budgetarists' have won."[137] Looking ahead, even this relatively favorable agreement was not enough to quell domestic anxiety in Germany, and within a few years Kohl and Waigel secured even more explicit budgetary controls—the so-called stability pact, imposing a procedure for sanctioning EMU members with "excessive" fiscal deficits.

Financial Transfers. Poorer countries, more likely to be excluded from EMU or, if admitted, placed under considerable macroeconomic strain, sought side-payments in exchange for their assent. (Analysts have also linked these side-payments to the acceptance of social policy provisions.) Spain was boldest, making public its demand for a quid pro quo to EMU. Germany, Britain, and France refused to make such side-payments explicit in the treaty, perhaps for fear of jeopardizing ratification, and they rejected Commission proposals for permanent increases in the Community budget. Nonetheless, a month before the final summit Delors had met with the Greek, Irish, Portuguese, and Spanish foreign ministers, quietly promising them large increases in structural funding—ECU 6 billion for Ireland alone—if they signed the Maastricht Treaty. It is hard to imagine that this promise would have been possible, let alone credible, in the absence of coordination with the major donor countries who informally approved a large increase in structural funding, the Delors II Packet, at the Edinburgh summit the following year.[138]

These eight elements comprise a Franco-German bargain, excluding the British and ignoring the Commission, on German terms, the only exception being side-payments to poorer countries. Germany committed itself to a single European currency and one-country, one-vote arrangements at a specified date under a series of conditions that it dictated—an outcome that favored France. In exchange Germany received extensive concessions concerning the form and substance of monetary union. The result was a two-track system limited to countries able to withstand prior convergence and domestic reform, willing to forgo bailouts and risk penalties for subsequent fiscal deficits, all led by an unprecedentedly autonomous central bank with a strong anti-inflationary mandate.[139]

These monetary arrangements nonetheless elicited objections from extreme

---

[136] Corbett, *Maastricht*, 43; Ludlow, "Reshaping Europe," 397ff; Connolly, *Rotten*, 271. Controversial issues were the following. The Monetary Committee proposed no monetary financing of debt and no bail-outs, and that the avoidance of "excessive deficits" should become "a key principal of EMU." On the latter issue, eleven countries were willing to grant the Council power to decide by majority vote, with Britain resisting. Weak-currency countries favored lax sanctions for violators; strong-currency countries favored tougher ones.

[137] Ross, *Jacques*, 156.

[138] Thatcher, *Downing*, 763. Connolly, *Rotten*, 198; Ludlow, "Reshaping," 398.

[139] For a parallel conclusion employing even more detailed data, see Italianer, "Mastering."

elements on the spectrum of German opinion, notably Bundesbank officials and Bavarian politicians, who criticized the surviving discretion in interpreting convergence criteria, setting exchange-rate policy, and conducting fiscal policy. For the most part, however, the treaty satisfied even their demands, and much that did not was revised toward the Bundesbank position after the treaty had been signed. To satisfy parliamentary and public opinion, however, Kohl dictated one more precondition for agreement, namely a deepening of political integration. To this matter we now turn.

The Intergovernmental Conference on Political Union

The negotiations on political union were a sideshow to the monetary negotiations. They began much later, at German insistence, largely as a means of domestic political legitimation for the controversial monetary bargains. France was never supportive; Britain at times was virulently opposed. After setting the agenda and despite, if anything, a surfeit of entrepreneurial agenda-setting by governments, Germany and its federalist allies encountered difficulty translating monetary power into political concessions. France and Britain made compromises where they were most affordable—on institutional matters—but outcomes on other issues, such as foreign and defense policy cooperation, social policy, and immigration policy, were either close to a lowest common denominator or were limited by opt-outs and flexibility clauses.

Initiating Negotiations: Germany Sets the Agenda

Political union was placed on the agenda in response to the German government's proposals. Since mid-1989 Kohl had argued that the Bundestag would demand progress on foreign policy and the powers of the Parliament in exchange for ratification of a monetary agreement. Thereafter its support would be consistent. Until the spring of 1990 Mitterrand ignored the German initiatives; Thatcher, too, remained utterly skeptical. Just before Kohl's stunning victory in the 18 March East German elections, however, Mitterrand and Kohl's respective staffs entered high-level negotiations, swiftly hammering out a preliminary agreement. The joint "political integration" initiative called for reform of joint foreign policy and internal decision-making institutions. On 18 April the French and German governments forwarded a joint request for a parallel conference on political union to the Irish presidency.[140]

In contrast to monetary negotiations, which focused from the start on a clear goal, the negotiations on political union were completely open-ended. A deluge of proposals ensued, including a full draft treaty from Germany. The Parliament offered five widely differing reports. Each country advanced distinctive, often longstanding proposals. Germany, backed cautiously by France, sought cooperation on foreign policy. Germany also pressed for cooperation on policing and immigration, and, backed by Italy and Belgium, it favored increased Parliament powers. France proposed an independent European defense identity. Spain and

---

[140] Ross, *Jacques*, 89–106; Zelikow and Rice, *Germany*, 234–238; Teltschik, *329*, 175–176.

other poorer countries, as we have seen, sought "cohesion" funding. Italy aimed to establish joint control of permanent French and British seats on the UN Security Council. Britain alone sought nothing new, except for better enforcement of existing laws.[141]

To an even greater extent than the monetary negotiations, the talks were managed successively by the Italian, the Luxembourgeois, and the Dutch presidencies. Assisted by a small team (fewer than ten officials) in the Council Secretariat, the Luxembourg presidency circulated questionnaires to national delegations in advance of the IGC to ascertain national positions. It placed an initial text on the table in early 1991. This text reflected what appeared to be majority positions, with alternative wording where there was fundamental disagreement. In April 1991 a draft treaty was offered, which contained around 80 percent of the provisions that would appear eight months later in the final treaty. The procedure worked so smoothly that many felt a final treaty could have been drawn up in June, had Kohl and others not sought to grant John Major a delay.[142]

Only the Commission, opposed altogether to negotiations on political union, failed to submit timely proposals. Yet Delors vehemently attacked the Luxembourg government's efforts. The Commission's position was largely defensive, focused on maintaining its own prerogatives. Delors criticized the absence of formal Commission powers in foreign policy and internal affairs, a "three pillar" arrangement proposed by France, which the Luxembourg presidency, rightly in retrospect, saw as a necessary condition for approval by the major governments. The Commission's alternative proposals, relatively few in number—including, for example, proposals for subsuming the WEU under the EC—were ignored until much later.[143]

Parliamentary agenda-setting was similarly futile. Well before serious negotiations started, parliamentarians were already disenchanted by exclusion and general dismissal of their proposals—including some concerning fundamental freedoms, EC resources, codecision and initiative for the Parliament, strengthened regional autonomy, and a genuine federal union. The Parliament had no formal power of ratification but tried to exploit its informal position to influence the negotiations. Its Institutional Committee voted 17–10 to protest the convening of the IGC. Numerous Italian, German, and Dutch national parliamentarians announced that their ratification rested in part on the Parliament's judgment.[144]

They were disappointed. On the first day of the Maastricht summit, the Parliament's president called for a unitary treaty, communitarization of CFSP, no opt-out clauses for EMU, Parliament codecision for all issues, and further democratization, none of which were taken seriously. Shortly before the final summit, the

[141] Middlemas, *Organising*, 191; Buchan, *Europe*, 32–34.
[142] Joseph Weyland, "Strategies and Perspectives of the Luxembourg Presidency," in Emil J. Kirchner and Anastassia Tsagkari, eds., *The EC Council Presidency: The Dutch and Luxembourg Presidencies* (Colchester, 1993), 17; interview with member-state ambassador. The Dutch and Italian governments drafted much of their own text; the Luxembourgeois relied more upon the Council Secretariat.
[143] Buchan, *Europe*, 32–34; interview with ambassador, 1994.
[144] Ludlow, "Reshaping," 433–434. The vote was later reversed.

president complained that the trend in the negotiations demonstrated "the supremacy of national administrations over policy." The Parliament's Socialist faction announced that it would evaluate the meeting according to whether it expanded Council majority voting, widespread codecision, strong social policy, a general opt-out for common defense, democratic control over monetary policy, and the rejection of two-track solutions. Though almost none was achieved, the Parliament quickly backed down; given its general support for integration, it was widely viewed as having little real choice. One observer noted that debate after the final agreement "hardly reads like the same parliament."[145]

Reaching a Bargain: The Triumph of a "Crippling" Compromise

With agreement on the basis of the Luxembourg proposals at hand, the Dutch presidency entered office during the second half of 1991 and suddenly pressed for a more federalist solution. Its canvas of member governments had reached the erroneous conclusion that eight of the twelve would support a stronger draft treaty. An entirely new draft was submitted in September, including many Commission proposals, including renunciation of the three-pillar structure and more QMV in CFSP and social policy. Unwilling to back federalist rhetoric with action, all governments except Belgium and the Netherlands rejected the text outright. This embarrassing episode, termed "Black Monday," forced a return to the Luxembourg draft. Delors's protest that the old draft was "crippling" and "inapplicable" were ignored. Final compromises were ironed out at meetings among senior ministers, supported by Council officials. A few issues, most notably the last-minute provision of a British opt-out on social policy, remained for the Council summit at Maastricht on 10–11 December 1991. The summit closed with a reminder from the Danish government, unheeded at the time, that ratification might be difficult because the treaty was too opaque to explain to domestic publics.[146]

The outcomes included rhetorical strengthening of foreign and security policy, an agreement without Britain on modest, nonfiscal social policy, a very modest expansion of qualified majority voting, a small transfer of power from the Commission to the Parliament through the codecision procedure, and, a few years later, a doubling of structural funding for poorer countries. In general, the outcome of these political union negotiations moved the EC very modestly in the federal direction favored by Germany. Yet the overall structure favored the status quo. This three-pillar structure, a metaphor proposed by the French representative Pierre de Boissieu, was designed to restrict definitively, through

[145] Martyn Bond, "The European Parliament's View of the Two Presidencies," Kirchner and Tsagkari, eds., *EC Council*, 37; *European Voice*, 9 May 1996, 10; *AE*, 6 December 1991, 9–10 December 1991, and 12/13 November 1991. A visit to each of the chief executives by Enrique Barón Crespe, EP president, was reported to have paved the way for acceptance of minor EP demands, a five-year term of Commissioners, to coincide with the EP term, and a rule that the entire Commission had to be formally endorsed by the EP.

[146] Interviews with two member-state ambassadors, Council Secretariat official, prime minister, and national representative, 1994–1996; Cloos et al., *Traité*, 8off; Corbett, *Treaty*, 293ff; Wester, "European." 212; Charles R. van Beuge, "Strategies and Perspectives of the Dutch Presidency," in Kirchner and Tsagkari, eds., *EC Council*, 28–29; Grant, *Delors*, 195; Ross, *Jacques*, 171–172.

qualitative institutional breaks, the Commission and Parliament's prerogatives in foreign and interior policy.[147] Let us consider the specific issues.

Common Foreign and Security Policy:
Majority Voting to "distribute non-smoking seats"

Proposals to deepen the EC's common foreign and security policies (CFSP) had appeared regularly on the EC agenda since the early 1980s. As negotiations neared, Italy, the Netherlands, Britain, Belgium, France, and Germany presented detailed proposals, followed in 1991 by Commission, Franco-German, and Anglo-Italian schemes.

All governments favored flexible cooperation but disagreed over whether to employ QMV and strengthen the role of the Commission and Court—policies favored only by Germany and a few others. A Franco-German proposal, which gained support from Spain, Greece, Belgium, and the Commission, called for unanimous decisions to take action but implementation by QMV. Britain, Denmark, Ireland, and others resolutely rejected QMV even on implementation. The final agreement was closest to the British position, restricting QMV to cases in which governments had voted unanimously to approve its use. Delors ridiculed the procedure, citing an imaginary meeting of ministers:

First we would have to decide, unanimously, whether the meeting was to be in Warsaw, Budapest or Prague. Then we would have to agree whether we were going by plane. Lunch? We would need an opt-out for vegetarians. No doubt we could use majority voting to decide where the smoking and non-smoking sections would be.[148]

Commission efforts to establish a formal role for supranational institutions in foreign and defense policy-making proved futile. More federalist governments, including Germany, Italy, Belgium, the Netherlands, Greece, and Ireland, backed by the Commission, sought to extend the traditional EC structure with Commission initiative and Court oversight into matters of foreign policy—a proposal naturally supported by supranational institutions. France, backed by Britain and Denmark, countered with a three-pillar design in which foreign policy, as well as interior affairs, would be conducted outside the traditional EC structure and centered on the European Council, the only institution involved in all three pillars. It would constrain the administrative, initiatory, adjudicative, and legislative roles of Court, Parliament, and Commission to their current domains. In this regard, the proposal was similar to certain elements of de Gaulle's old Fouchet Plan. Well before the IGC began, the three-pillar design had triumphed; a last-minute campaign by Delors to reestablish a single structure or

---

[147] Interview with members of Council Secretariat and permanent representative, 1994–1996.

[148] Buchan, *Europe*, 46. Also Ludlow, "Reshaping," 444; Cloos et al., *Traité*, 60; Lippert, *German*, 118–120. The substantive areas of cooperation mentioned in early Franco-German proposals were much cut back.

establish more than an advisory role for the Commission in foreign policy-making was ignored.[149]

On defense policy, the discussion focused on the role of the WEU; governments divided into three groups. Britain, backed by pro-NATO countries such as the Netherlands and Portugal with tacit support from independent Denmark and neutral Ireland, headed the first. All favored only a symbolic or advisory link between the EC and the WEU. An Anglo-Italian compromise in October 1991 explicitly recognized no more than a symbolic link between the WEU and the EC.

Germany headed a second group, including Italy, Spain, Greece, and Luxembourg, which sought a commitment to an eventual WEU role as the EC's defense arm. Even this group, however, saw EC activities as limited and not overlapping those of NATO. Coordination of UN peacekeeping was mentioned, suggesting that European cooperation would remain subordinate to other multilateral commitments. Smaller countries in this group favored Commission involvement as a safeguard against large-state dominance.

France, supported by the Commission and perhaps Belgium, favored a more direct alternative to NATO, including establishment of a European attack force and rapid integration of WEU into the EC—though how seriously Paris entertained this ambitious goal remains unclear. Even the French government avoided any direct challenge to NATO, preferring instead to work closely with Germany; the resulting Franco-German compromise would have placed the WEU under the loose supervision of the European Council.[150]

Symbolism aside, the concrete obligations in both foreign and defense policy contained in the Maastricht Treaty most closely realized British preferences. The EC was authorized to forward only nonbinding requests for action to the WEU. An exhortative provision noted that existing provisions "might in time lead to a common defense." Further discussion was postponed. John Major voiced satisfaction; other heads of government criticized it as "unimportant and without much substance"; the Commission dismissed it as "minimalist." This outcome reflected the manifest lack of consensus over questions like the EC's relationship to NATO, with France ostensibly alone in favor of a break, or the proper institutionalization of foreign policy, with France opposed to a stronger Commission or Court. As George Ross concludes: "The real problem was that Europe was not convinced about the need for a new defense identity." Moreover, there was never any credible threat of exclusion aimed at Britain. With its seat on the UN Security Council, nuclear arsenal, effective military, and effective foreign ministry, Britain was widely viewed as indispensable to any credible European foreign or defense policy arrangement.[151]

---

[149] Ross, *Jacques*, 143–148; Corbett, *Treaty*, 35–38; Lippert, 115–120; interview with Council Official.

[150] It is difficult to assess how strong such preferences were, however, since no such initiatives were taken. France sought instead to influence the process primarily through Franco-German schemes, which remained close to German preferences. Ross, *Jacques*, 143–144, 146–147, 181–182; Grant, *Delors*, 150, 186–188; van Wijnbergen, "Germany," 57–58.

[151] Ross, *Jacques*, 147, also 137–144. Interview with head of government (1995) and national chief negotiator (1994); Corbett, *Treaty*, 44–48; *L'Expres*, 20 December 1991, 16.

Justice and Home Affairs: Relegation to the Third Pillar

Proposals for cooperation in justice and home affairs, with particular attention to issues of asylum, migration, and police cooperation through EUROPOL, were advanced most actively by Germany. At the Luxembourg summit in June 1991, Kohl surprised even the Commission by proposing that immigration, asylum, and police cooperation be moved out of the intergovernmental "third pillar," where the Luxembourg draft had placed it, and back into the main EC structure—though he was prepared from the start to accommodate Britain with opt-out clauses on asylum and visa policy. The Commission and Parliament strongly supported the German proposal for "communitarizing" these policies, which would have greatly expanded their influence. Other countries viewed the proposals with considerable skepticism: Britain saw no substantive need for the policy, France was more positively inclined toward the substantive ends but remained skeptical of supranational means.[152]

The final agreement acknowledged pervasive skepticism by postponing the issue. The three-pillar design limited the role of Court, Commission, and Parliament in migration policy while strengthening that of the European Council. The only substantive change was agreement to decide common third-country visa regulations by unanimous vote and after 1996 by qualified majority, with the Commission enjoying a nonexclusive right of proposal. This change extended neither to asylum nor to immigration policy.

Social Policy: Eleven Governments Opt In

Both before and after Maastricht, the EC had only a minimal social policy. With the exception of clauses on gender equality and labor practices negotiated by France in the early years, which occasioned some important ECJ decisions, provisions for social policy were absent from the original Treaty of Rome. The SEA authorized QMV on the harmonization of health and safety regulations, an authority that the Commission interpreted as broadly as possible, but all other social policy measures, notably those regulating collective bargaining and financial provisions, continued to require an unreachable unanimity. In 1988 Delors had proposed a nonbinding European social charter, which all members except Britain had approved, but it generated little legislative activity.[153]

Participants in the Maastricht negotiations examined social policy proposals provided by at least eight national governments as well as the Commission. Disagreement quickly reduced to two issues: the scope of QMV and a provision providing for binding European-level, labor-management negotiations under threat of EC legislation (the "negotiate or we'll legislate" clause). QMV received strong support from relatively wealthy countries, including France, Belgium, Luxembourg, Italy, Denmark, and the Commission; Germany was also supportive but swiftly adopted a compromise position in favor of "reinforced QMV" and perhaps unanimity. Lower-income countries, led by Britain and Spain and qui-

---

[152] *Economist*, 30 November 1991, 48, and 7 December, 1991, 54; Ross, *Jacques*; Cloos, *Traité*, 68–69; Ludlow, "Reshaping," 444; interview with Council official.

[153] Corbett, *Treaty*, 49–50.

etly backed by Ireland, Portugal, and Greece, resolutely opposed a strong social policy. John Major went furthest, publicly stating early on that a veto or an opt-out was preferable to participation; Hurd later maintained that the Commons, dominated by Conservatives, would have rejected any treaty not containing a British opt-out.[154]

European business, represented by UNICE, opposed any regulation of "quantitative" issues (wages, vacation, social security) and collective bargaining. Little was left other than gender discrimination and worker safety, already subject to EC regulation. UNICE reluctantly supported, however, the Commission's "negotiate or we'll legislate" proposal for these areas, probably because it appeared easy to block proposals under it. By the end of October 1991 the member governments had reached a compromise: a few nonquantitative areas were included under QMV (e.g., information/consultation of workers in multinational firms), some quantitative areas were mentioned but remained unanimous (e.g., social security, employment contracts, collective defense of workers), and core issues of wage bargaining were specifically excluded from EC competence (e.g., remuneration, right to strike, trade union rights). In some areas, the "negotiate or we'll legislate" procedure was adopted.[155]

This social policy promised little beyond symbolism, yet Major remained intransigent. So the issue of British participation was left to the chief executives at Maastricht. Major proposed subjecting all social policy to unanimity, which Kohl rejected. At 1:00 A.M. on the last night of the summit, in face-to-face negotiations, Major and Kohl agreed that the eleven would move ahead without Britain outside EC institutions—an arrangement discussed with Mitterrand in advance and brokered by the Dutch presidency. Delors, employing materials prepared earlier by the Commission legal service, convinced all member governments to permit the eleven to act *within* the EC structure to adopt measures not applicable to Britain—a solution apparently developed secretly in the Commission, though some later claimed it also bore the imprint of the Council Secretariat. Major accepted the proposal over the objections of his advisers. The sudden British willingness to opt out surprised several other governments, including Mediterranean countries, Ireland, and the Netherlands, which had professed support for the social policy proposal all the while expecting Britain to water it down to insignificance. When Britain opted out, the others were faced with a stronger policy than expected and pressure to conclude the summit negotiations rapidly. Delors won over southern countries with promises of more substantial structural funding and, in the case of Spain, apparently with an appeal to Socialist solidarity.[156]

---

[154] Letter to the *Economist*, 15 June 1996; Ross, *Jacques*, 145–153; Corbett, *Treaty*, 49–51; *Economist*, 7 December 1991, 52; Peter Lange, "Maastricht and the Social Protocol: Why Did They Do It?" *Politics and Society* 21:1 (March 1993), 5–37.

[155] George Ross, "Assessing the Delors Era and Social Policy," in Paul Pierson and Stephan Leibfried, eds., *European Social Policy: Between Fragmentation and Integration* (Washington, D.C., 1995), 379ff.

[156] I was unable to corroborate persistent rumors, apparently emanating from the British Foreign Office, of a purported linkage to Yugoslavia. Cf. Susan Woodward, *Balkan Tragedy: Chaos and Dissolution after the Cold War* (Washington, D.C., 1995), 184–185; interview with German Staatssekretär, 1996; interview with prime minister, 1996.

The precise form of the social protocol is often said to exemplify the importance of unintended consequences and supranational entrepreneurship in European integration. The outcome, it is said, was less attractive to the British than keeping the social provisions out of the treaty altogether, and in particular upset the calculations of Britain's Mediterranean allies, such as Spain, as well as of some conservative governments in richer countries, whose rhetoric did not reflect real commitment but who were caught out by the last-minute British concession. Yet we should not make too much of this claim. With the election of the Blair government in 1997, the British government joined the arrangement anyway. In the interim it was essentially ignored, leading to the passage of only two, relatively minor provisions. Nonetheless, it is fair to say that Delors's intervention moved the resulting policy slightly in the direction of a more active social policy.[157]

The Expansion of Competences and QMV

National governments submitted dozens of detailed proposals to establish new policies or to extend QMV to new areas, including trans-European infrastructure, public health, tourism, transport safety, education and vocational training, culture, energy, consumer protection, industrial policy, civil protection, and youth. Southern governments tended to advocate new competences from which they might gain greater EC subsidies, such as tourism and public health provisions. Northern countries took the lead to legitimate existing high standards or forms of intervention which they practiced. As we have seen, governments entered into the negotiations with particular areas of interest and particular areas of opposition; there were few opportunities for agreement.

Hence nearly all of these efforts failed, and most were never treated as more than symbolic. There was little room for the expansion of competences, for no government supported a move to QMV without exceptions. France and Germany favored extension of QMV "in principle" to all "nonconstitutional" economic issues, it is true, but exceptions for Germany included some of the most important areas of economic activity not yet under majority voting, such as visa policies, mutual recognition of professionals, and indirect taxation. Britain, Spain, Ireland, Greece, and Portugal generally opposed even this much. Germany and Britain blocked French, Italian, and Commission proposals for a common industrial policy. Self-sufficient in energy, Britain and France rejected proposals, some decades old, for an EC energy policy. German, Dutch, and Danish efforts to promote environmental and consumer protection generated strong opposition from Britain and southern countries. German and Luxembourgeois advocacy of greater transport safety regulations came to nothing, as did Franco-Italian support for an EC cultural policy. Efforts to impose QMV on research programs were blocked by Britain in an 11–1 vote, though Kohl openly congratulated Major afterward. A symbolic "European citizenship" was created, but

---

[157] Interviews with prime minister, Delors, permanent representative, and commission official. For a critical assessment, see Wolfgang Streeck, "From Market-making to State-building: Reflections on the Political Economy of European Social Policy," in Pierson and Leibfried, eds., *European*, 389–431.

the only substantive policy related to it was a Spanish proposal to permit EC citizens to vote in local elections wherever they reside. Britain failed to block a provision for trans-European networks, strongly favored by business and other member-states, which would be decided by QMV—but this was an area in which governments participated on an ad hoc *juste retour* basis. Many other provisions in the Maastricht Treaty, such as the inclusion of consumer protection, education, and public health under Article 130, for the most part altered the legal basis of policies already being conducted by QMV under Article 100. The consequence was not always to expand EC competences: such changes tended to *restrict* influence previously enjoyed by Court and Commission. Delors failed to block the inclusion of consumer protection in the treaty, as well as new clauses on education and culture that explicitly limited efforts to coordinate national policies. Few issues went the Commission's way, and those that did were minor. Despite complaints by Spain about Commission meddling in environmental affairs, and demands from southern countries to retain unanimity, richer countries succeeded in extending QMV to some environmental issues, but fiscal measures and those having to do with land use, water, and energy were exempted. Here, too, much involved the reclassification of activities already conducted by QMV under Article 100.[158]

A final dimension of the negotiation over competences concerned "subsidiarity"—the general principle that policies should be promulgated at the lowest level (local, regional, state, or EC) possible. The treaty included a general subsidiarity clause, the legal meaning of which remained unclear. Different governments supported the clause for different reasons: in Britain it was seen as limiting integration; in France as limiting supranational bodies; in Germany as supporting regional governments. The same sort of pressure led to creation of a symbolically important but substantially impotent Committee of the Regions.[159]

The European Commission and Parliament: From Cooperation to Codecision

As in the SEA negotiations, Germany strongly supported an expansion of parliamentary powers. Backed by Italy, Belgium, and the Netherlands, Germany advanced two proposals. First, the Parliament should be granted power of initiative; it should be permitted to request that the Commission make proposals to the Council and, if the request were refused, to make its own proposals. Second, the cooperation procedure should be replaced by a codecision procedure whereby a "committee of conciliation" consisting of 12 MEPs and 12 ministers would vote on proposed parliamentary amendments. Five governments,

---

[158] *AE*, 14 November 1991, 3, and 12 December 1991; interviews with council official, Delors, commission member of cabinet, permanent representative, 1991–1996; Grant, *Delors*, 154–155; Ross, *Jacques*; *Economist*, 7 December 1991, 52–53. Consumer rights had previously been by QMV under Article 100a; since 1983 there had been Council meetings devoted to the issue—hence Delors's opposition to transferring it to a new article.

[159] Certain educational and training policies were moved under QMV when Germany supported southern countries. Fountain, "German." Some have argued that this reflected an effort by the federal government to increase its influence in areas traditionally run by the Länder.

including France, the United Kingdom, and Denmark, opposed these proposals. France favored instead increased power for the Council of Ministers and national parliaments, while the United Kingdom and Denmark opposed any expansion of European institutions.[160]

No government appears to have supported a large *net* increase in supranational power; even the German proposals would have increased Parliament's powers largely at the Commission's expense. In particular, Germany and others proposed that the Council be permitted to revise a proposal by qualified majority rather than unanimity vote, thereby reducing the influence of the Commission's unique power of proposal. In language reportedly drafted by Jean-Claude Piris of the Council Legal Service, seconded from the French Conseil d'Etat, a provision was considered that would have eliminated the Commission's right to withdraw legislation during the conciliation procedure. Delors denounced such schemes as an "enterprise to demolish the Commission, put the Commission on the sidelines."[161]

The Commission was placed on the defensive, but Delors's battle to avoid large reductions in Commission power was, in the end, modestly successful. At some lower-level meetings a majority of government representatives supported Franco-German efforts to restrict the Commission's existing powers of initiative—a level of hostility one Commission insider explains as a reaction to perceived Commission "arrogance." This effort was avoided at the last minute, after intensive intervention by Delors. The Commission did lose some rights to amend or veto parliamentary proposals in the second reading of the codecision procedure, but it maintained the right to rescind alterations during the Council-Parliament conciliation meetings. Delors also helped block efforts (sponsored by the British!) to promote greater parliamentary involvement in lieu of the Commission in policy implementation and greater parliamentary control over the Commission through rights of inquiry, petition, and a court of auditors. An Italian proposal that the Parliament vet each incoming Commissioner individually was rejected in favor of one general vote on the entire Commission—nearly equivalent to the Parliament's prior power to dismiss the Commission and in practice extremely hard to employ. Delors failed utterly to strengthen the existing cooperation procedure by permitting laws to come into force automatically if the Council did not act in three months rather than require Council QMV—a Commission proposal that would have increased net supranational influence and strengthened Commission power at the expense of the Council and probably also the Parliament.[162]

By mid-1991, with little support outside Germany for true Parliamentary initiative, debate shifted to codecision. Kohl persuaded Mitterrand to support

---

[160] This paragraph and the next are based on Ross, *Jacques*; Martial, "France," 121–122; interviews with German Chancellory official and Delors. Germany proposed extending the cooperation procedure to all EC issues, not just single market issues. Spain sought to water down codecision.

[161] Ross, *Jacques*, 149; interview with Council Secretariat official.

[162] Ross, *Jacques*, 148–149, 192–193; Ludlow, "Reshaping," 442; interviews with council official, Delors, commission official, permanent representative, 1991–1997; Grant, *Delors*, 154–155; *Economist*, 7 December 1991, 52–53.

codecision and QMV on many traditional economic topics. Yet the German government also accepted a compromise: if the conciliation committee failed, the proposal would be deemed not adopted, thereby splitting the blame, but the Council would be able to resume its common position in six weeks unless the Parliament explicitly rejected the entire law. Parliamentary power would thus be limited except where Parliament was willing to accept full public responsibility for failure, backed by an absolute majority vote—a difficult standard given that many MEPs rarely attend sessions. This sort of codecision was viewed as so minimal a reform, as compared to earlier proposals, that Parliament opposed it through most of the negotiation. Nonetheless Britain and Denmark opposed codecision except where Parliament was currently involved—the single market, environmental and R&D policy—and initially boycotted the discussions. The Netherlands sought to extend codecision to trans-European networks and consumer policy; France suggested industry, health, culture, and social policy. Genscher suggested a clause be added permitting future changes. In the end, the codecision procedure was extended to areas in which the cooperation procedure was already in place and to a few in which the EC had limited powers or decision-making was uncontroversial. In only one case, infrastructure policy, did the use of codecision generate an unambiguous increase in the net influence of supranational institutions, but this was an area in which governments generally participated on a voluntary *juste retour* basis.[163]

Overall changes in the powers of the Commission and Parliament lay close to the lowest common denominator among major governments, though this fact was carefully disguised. A very modest amount of influence was transferred from the Commission to the Parliament, while France and Britain—quietly supported, it seems, by Germany—blocked any significant *net* increase in the powers of supranational institutions. Hence even Britain and Denmark did not oppose changing a move from the cooperation procedure to the codecision procedure. If one believes that the Commission is more cohesive and effective than the Parliament in agenda-setting, as did Delors, the Maastricht Treaty may on balance have *constrained* supranational power. The major loser, as insider Émile Noël and Delors himself noted, was the Commission. Still Delors could count himself lucky that more radical Franco-German proposals for reductions in Commission powers failed—not least due to opposition from smaller governments.[164]

Explaining Interstate Bargaining and Institutional Choice

There is general agreement among participants that the negotiations were efficient. Few gains were "left on the table," and in distributing benefits linked to EMU at Maastricht, the Germans benefited the most. How is this observed

---

[163] Émile Noël, "A New Institutional Balance?" in Renaud Dehousse, ed., *Europe after Maastricht: An Ever Closer Union?* (Munich, 1994), 17; interview with Council official.

[164] Noël, "New," 16–25; interviews with council secretariat official, permanent representative; interview with Delors.

process and pattern of outcomes—efficient negotiations in which the concessions on the margin favor Germany because the core bargain favors others more—best explained?

Efficiency: The Negotiations are a "real nightmare" for Delors

Numerous analyses of bargaining at Maastricht stress supranational leadership. Wayne Sandholtz asserts flatly that "international leadership was necessary to define a pool of agreement."[165] Supranational bargaining theory predicts that we should observe a scarcity of necessary information and ideas (high transaction costs), resulting in interstate "bargaining failures"; a comparative advantage on the part of supranational actors in imagining innovative political solutions, inducing preference revelation, generating technical and legal solutions, advancing legitimate arguments, and assessing domestic political constraints; an apparent comparative advantage by supranational entrepreneurs in initiating, mediating, or mobilizing; and a resulting change in the outcomes. George Ross argues that Delors influenced "all the EMU levers which mattered" and played a decisive role by advocating and publicizing the advantages of EMU, particularly in the Delors Committee report.[166]

Closer inspection of the concrete predictions of supranational bargaining theory does not support these conclusions. The negotiations appear to have been Pareto-efficient and stable; long before the end of the negotiations, the probable results, with small exceptions, were obvious to all. Neither participants nor commentators have subsequently argued that potential gains were "left on the table." With one or two very minor exceptions, the Commission appears to have enjoyed no privileged access to information or expertise; to the contrary, its political information and judgment were overtly faulty, leading to interventions that were futile if not, in the word of a French minister at the time, "counterproductive."[167] Information and ideas were neither costly nor in short supply nor asymmetrically distributed in favor of supranational actors; governments appear to have been clearly aware of the alternatives and quickly ascertained the probable outcome. There was relatively little disagreement on the technical or legal fundamentals of monetary integration. To be sure, expert meetings and negotiations dragged on for three years, which might be taken as a sign of poor bargaining, yet this was not a Pareto-inefficient outcome; each postponement, we have seen, especially those of December 1989 and June 1991, came in response to specific German and British demands.

The Commission enjoyed no informational or ideational advantage over national governments. Initiatives were plentiful, as intergovernmental theory predicts, and nearly all governments and even subnational actors, such as the Bundesbank, circulated detailed proposals, even complete draft treaties, for both

---

[165] Sandholtz, "Choosing Union," 37. Like Lindberg and Haas, Sandholtz occasionally hints that leadership might also be provided by national actors, though the thrust of his argument stresses the need for supranational entrepreneurship.

[166] Ross, *Jacques*, 81–82. Also Grant, *Delors*; Schönfelder and Thiel, *Markt*, 42; Dyson and Featherstone, *Elusive*, 306–308.

[167] Interview with French minister.

monetary and political integration. On specific clauses there were often six or eight different views on the table. As the intergovernmental theory predicts, the strongest monetary initiatives came from the most interested country, France, which advanced some of the earliest concrete proposals and a draft treaty granting to the European Council greater powers than the Delors Report had recommended.[168] By contrast, Commission and Parliament submissions were slow to arrive, and "when Commission papers arrived in time to be read carefully they usually brought added value; but they had to share the table with the almost infinite number of similar papers from member states, so this was hardly enough to make them stand out."[169] Parliament reports did not expand the set of potential agreements. When they did arrive, the Commission and Parliament consistently misjudged the political situation, resulting in a series of spectacular failures reminiscent of Monnet and Hallstein's later initiatives. Commission management of information brought complaints from member-states that it was concealing information. Far from enjoying legitimacy, the Commission was viewed with suspicion. Some felt that the Commission's chief concern was to accumulate more power. Suspicion of proposals to increase Commission power—such as proposals for automatic passage of legislation if the Council failed to reach decision—was overt.[170]

Both monetary and political negotiations were in fact managed and mediated primarily by a few Council secretariat officials, the rotating national presidency, national government leaders, and in the monetary case officials from finance ministries and central bankers—suggesting that transaction costs were low relative to gains. In the political union negotiations, the Council presidency, backed by a team of fewer than a dozen Council officials, structured negotiations and drafted text, drawing on suggestions from national governments. There was stability in discussions and positions. In many cases the same proposals were raised repeatedly, even after decisions had been taken, from early 1988 through the end of 1991.

In the monetary negotiations, much credit has been given to Delors, particularly during the meetings of the Delors Committee. As a Commission official observed, "there was not a phrase in the final report that [Delors] did not author." Delors controlled "all the EMU levers which mattered," and the outcome, Ross concludes, was "a Delors designer product." As chair, others argue, Delors managed the meetings and moved the central bank governors "toward consensus on what the Commission President himself wanted," following up with an important role during the negotiations themselves.[171]

---

[168] After Spanish, French, and German submissions, the Luxembourg representative complained that every country seemed to be submitting a complete draft treaty. Interview with national representative; Heisenberg, *Mark*, 178–179; Ross, *Jacques*; Gaddum, *Deutsche*, 356–366.

[169] Ross, *Jacques*, 90, 89–92. One Commission official described the process: "Everyone tosses everything that runs through their mind onto the table . . . then . . . the differences that really count will come clear . . . eventually, towards the last few sessions, they'll split the differences and we'll have our text." Joly Dixon, quoted in Ross, *Jacques*, 85. Ludlow, "Reshaping," 426.

[170] Interview with Council secretariat official.

[171] Ross, *Jacques*, 81–82; Dyson and Featherstone, *Elusive*, 306–308; Schönfelder and Thiel, *Markt*, 42; Dyson and Featherstone. Endo, who has researched the question most closely of all, comes to the

Such conclusions, we have seen, are misleading. It is true that Delors drafted much of the wording; he nonetheless had little influence. He acted essentially in a technical secretariat function, as coordinator, rapporteur, and drafter; he drafted some compromise texts, as Ross states, but he did not influence their content; two members of the Delors Committee, we have seen, remember him neither proposing nor vetoing any important proposal. Ross's own source, on closer inspection, speaks of Delors "correcting" the texts, not drafting them. Delors refused to press the central bankers, shying away, for example, from proposing a timetable for the transition to monetary union, in part because of the celebrated failure of the member governments to meet the 1980 date suggested in the Werner Report. With the exception of the unwillingness to set a date and the greater deference to Germany's anti-inflationary preferences—both elements Delors himself opposed—the Delors Committee report bears a striking resemblance to that produced by the Werner Committee two decades earlier. If Delors's presence lent some prestige to the negotiations, it was only because Kohl and Mitterrand named him to the position precisely for that purpose.[172]

The outcome of the political union negotiations was efficient despite the Commission's apparent decision to take itself out of the game early. Delors boycotted the proceedings and traveled to national capitals to mobilize support against the Luxembourg draft, hoping the negotiations would collapse and the Commission could advance a wholly new proposal. Yet by June 1991 the member governments were clearly headed for agreement; they continued talking, with only modest results, for another six months, in large part to give the British more time to manage domestic politics. The Commission's last-ditch response, namely to back the Dutch draft, led only to the embarrassing debacle on "Black Monday" in September 1991. This suggests not only that the Commission lacked accurate political intelligence, but that the negotiations were relatively efficient in the sense that even a more activist position by agenda-setters could not have promoted deeper agreement. Similarly, Delors's proposal for CFSP, whereby any six countries could initiate action and the Commission would retain important powers of initiative and implementation, was immediately rejected by France, Britain, and the Council Secretariat. Such proposals were at least futile and may also have added to the cost and trouble of negotiation.[173] In the end Delors criticized the overall result of the political union negotiations, calling it "organized schizophrenia." The entire process was, he recalled, "a real nightmare."[174]

Three exceptions to Delors's general ineffectiveness deserve mention. First, during the year following the fall of the Berlin Wall, Delors efficiently managed

---

paradoxical conclusion that Delors was an effective entrepreneur because he did *not* wield influence directly, instead accepting Pöhl's demands. Endo, *Political*, chaps. 7–9.

[172] Interviews with two Delors Committee members, 1991, 1994. Pöhl argues that "the substance of the report came from the governors." Gros and Thygesen, *European*, 320.

[173] Ross, *Jacques*, 145–148; Grant, *Delors*, 189–198; interviews with Delors, member of Council secretariat. Endo, who in general thinks that leadership matters, concludes that this was a straight "failure" of leadership. Endo, *Political*, 8:98.

[174] Endo, *Political*, 8:103; Grant, *Delors*, 181.

the integration of former East Germany into the EC—a difficult issue including agricultural and financial issues that might have led to much conflict among EC members and perhaps also derailed the negotiations. Second, the Commission president fought a successful rearguard action to defend the Commission's unique right of proposal, which a majority of governments had favored revoking in early subministerial meetings, as well as the Commission's right to withdraw proposals from consideration. Third, Delors's last-minute intervention crafted a two-track social policy within the EC. This change probably expanded cooperation a bit beyond what governments themselves would have favored.[175]

The European Parliament fared even worse. Each of its five reports was either redundant or futile. Of its distinctive demands, it achieved only weak codecision procedures, a modest expansion of QMV and social policy, and limitations on EMU opt-outs—all of which can better be explained by the longstanding backing of major member-states. (The first two had been proposed in the SEA negotiation.) Direct influence appears to have been limited to small matters, such as changes in the length of the term, promoted by the Parliament president in a last-minute trip to national capitals. Even this, like codecision, reflected intergovernmental relations; the Parliament did not, in the words of one analyst, "swim against the tide" but took advantage of Germany's demand for a symbolic concession, which the Parliament was permitted to help fill.[176] By contrast, proposals for which the MEPs were most enthusiastic—many of which were contained in the Dutch draft—were rejected before the Parliament could offer its view. As we saw, the Parliament, favoring any integration decision over none, had little choice but to abandon its previous threats and vote in support of the treaty, as it had done five years earlier with the SEA.

Finally, there was no opportunity for mobilization of social groups, as had occurred with multinational business in the SEA negotiations. To be sure, the Commission helped publicize the advantages of EMU through various reports, including the Padoa-Schioppa study of 1987 and the report *One Market, One Money* in 1990—actions one commentary considers so important that it calls the entire intergovernmentalist account of bargaining into question. Yet no evidence has been presented to suggest that governments or social groups were swayed by this technocratic volume. French and Commission support for EMU, like British opposition to it and German insistence on "economist" preconditions, remained constant from 1984 onward, and the subsequent debates over Maastricht suggest the contrary: publicity served only to call EMU into question.[177]

Distribution: "Germany is in a position to impose conditions"

The central focus of the negotiations was not initiatives and efficiency but a round of distributional bargaining as intense as any in EC history. There was widespread agreement on movement to EMU with a single currency, but not

---

[175] Interview with Delors, 1996. See pp. 453–456 above.
[176] Ludlow, "Reshaping," 402, also 401–402, 416–417.
[177] Dyson and Featherstone, *Elusive*, 307–308.

on the eight distributional issues analyzed above. As in the EMS, the primary cleavage over these issues divided strong- from weak-currency countries, the core source of conflict being divergent preferences concerning the level of anti-inflationary credibility that governments desired. Britain opposed the entire arrangements, but others were prepared to move ahead—hence the day-to-day bargaining boiled down to a conflict between Germany and France. The outcomes strongly favored Germany.

Before moving to consider competing explanations, we should note that my description of the distributive outcomes as favoring Germany challenges the views of most political scientists, who have concluded that Germany did poorly in the negotiations.[178] (Nearly all participants see the outcome as a situation of perceived joint gains, but one in which marginal concessions favored Germany.) Such analyses rest, however, on two overt errors of inference.

First, they tend to assume that the Bundesbank position was the German national position. For Joseph Grieco and Geoffrey Garrett, for example, any compromise of extreme anti-inflationary probity marks a German concession. We have seen, however, that the German government's position had long reflected a compromise between the Bundesbank, on the one hand, and government and industry, on the other; traditionally, the coalition for monetary cooperation was more willing to accept some relaxation of discipline to stabilize exchange rates. As a whole, Germany favored strong anti-inflationary safeguards but not—whether for ideological or for economic reasons—the extreme position of the Bundesbank.

Second, most analyses that conclude that Germany did badly at Maastricht examine an unrepresentative sample of outcomes. Michael Baun focuses primarily on political integration, which leads him to term Kohl and the German government "major losers at Maastricht" even though the net outcome was—even in political union negotiations themselves—modestly in the direction favored by Germany and monetary negotiations were resolved almost entirely on German terms. Wayne Sandholtz deliberately limits his otherwise insightful analysis to three areas selected because "the Germans did not get their way." Any negotiation analysis that seeks to discount the bargaining power of one actor based on such a criterion assumes what it sets out to prove. Without an understanding of context, such analyses can be misleading. Sandholtz, for example, treats the agreement to accept 1994 as the starting date for the second stage as a major German concession yet ignores the quid pro quo, namely the reduction of the EMI to a symbolic organization and the imposition of convergence criteria for stage three. Participants, we saw above, uniformly believed that these quid pro quos rendered any German concession on the starting date meaningless. Grieco's theoretical analysis, like that of Sandholtz, is initially limited to those elements in which the Bundesbank did not get its way, which of course appear to confirm the neo-Realist hypothesis that "weaker . . . partners will seek to en-

---

[178] Baun, *Imperfect*, 97; Grieco, "Maastricht," 34–38; Garrett, "Politics," 105–124; Dyson and Featherstone, *Elusive*; Sandholtz, "Monetary," 126, 134–137; also Heisenberg, *Mark*, 177.

sure that the rules . . . provide sufficient opportunities for them to voice their concerns and interests." Grieco is quite correct to stress asymmetry and their ability to lock in a new arrangement through EMU, yet his Realist "relative gains-seeking" interpretation is at pains to explain German acceptance of the agreement. Leaving aside conjectures about alliance formation against Japan and the possible German belief that EMU would never actually happen (for neither of which is there evidence), Grieco speculates that perhaps Germany's acceptance reflected its "negotiating success in ensuring that EMU would have price stability as its principal goal." Yet this concedes that the overall negotiated outcome must have been advantageous to Germany—thus suggesting that joint gains as well as distributional conflict underlay the Maastricht treaty.

The approach taken in this chapter, namely to focus on the pattern of concessions across the context of the entire agreement, clearly reveals a pattern of outcomes favorable to Germany. To explain the distribution of concessions, outside of the core move to EMU, in favor of Germany, three theoretical explanations merit consideration: the influence of supranational officials, led by Jacques Delors; the transnational activities of an "epistemic community" of central bankers centered on the Delors Committee and other EC forums; and the intergovernmental model, based on Nash bargaining theory, that stresses the constraints imposed on the German win-set by the Bundesbank and the resulting need for a quid pro quo for the German concessions on EMU and a single currency. The preponderance of evidence supports the intergovernmental account over the supranational and transnational ones.

The role of Commission and Parliament need not detain us long. We have already seen that there is no reason to believe that supranational actors, or particular governments, benefited from asymmetrical access to technical, legal, and political ideas. Delors's intervention in the Committee that bore his name was ineffective; his support for the ill-fated "Dutch draft" was counterproductive. He was no more effective in subsequent distributive negotiations. Moreover, his fundamental but futile aims throughout were to soften the German position on EMU and to scrap the political union discussions. Delors was particularly hostile toward the core German demand: strict economic conditionality for membership and, therefore, a "two-speed" EMU. He criticized European finance ministers, who supported the demand, by noting: "I am no longer sure Britain is the biggest menace." Leaving aside their ineffectiveness, these efforts can hardly be invoked to explain the *opposite* outcome. Commission policy, though under Delors's direct control most of the time, failed to budge Kohl. The ineffectiveness of Delors's efforts is doubly odd, since by the opening of the negotiations, all governments quietly accepted the German position. Delors later recalled that among the things he had least expected about the IGC was the total victory of the German position—suggesting that his misreading of the political situation ran deep.[179]

---

[179] Ludlow, "Reshaping," 424, also 423–425; Heisenberg, *Mark,* 177; "Intergovernmental Conferences: Contributions by the Commission," *Bulletin of the EC* (Supplement 2/91). Interview with Delors.

A transnational explanation attributes German success to tactical alliances among the various central bankers on the Delors Committee. The central conclusion of David Cameron's lengthy analysis of the negotiations is the importance of institutionalized "transnational actors, at some moments *more* influential than *either* governmental or supranational actors"—though who influenced whom in this account sometimes remains unclear.[180] Dyson and Featherstone assert that "the creation of the Delors Committee weakened the ability of national governments to act as gatekeepers and control the content of early EMU proposals."[181] Claims do not fit neatly into the two bargaining theories tested here, but they are related to the claims of supranational bargaining theory about the importance of political entrepreneurs and the process of negotiation rather than the underlying structure of power. Yet the speculative nature of analyses of the Delors Committee as "transnational politics" is suggested by the incompatibility of the assertions (in addition to the assertion that Delors himself steered the process) that have been made about who influenced whom and why. None withstands close scrutiny.

One claim is that the transnational structure of the committee created a conduit through which one or more cross-national coalitions or "epistemic communities" of central bankers cooperated. Roland Vaubel and others have asserted that all central bankers acted as an epistemic community, colluding against governments and publics to assure that the final structure would serve their anti-inflationary interests—a view occasionally heard from disgruntled French and Italian policy-makers. Similarly, W. R. Smyser claims that Bundesbank president Pöhl organized a transnational coalition of other central bankers, whom he persuaded to accept the German vision of central bank autonomy. In this view, the Delors Committee multiplied the power of certain central bankers, resulting in a more autonomous, anti-inflationary ("German") ECB than would have emerged through traditional diplomatic procedures.[182]

The historical record does not confirm this view. Transnational tactics were secondary: Pöhl made no effort to persuade, because the outcome was structurally determined. He was openly contemptuous of Delors and made little effort to reach out. (Even if Pöhl had persuaded others, the resulting alliances would have made little difference, since other central bankers lacked the Bundesbank's domestic independence.) Accordingly, no member of the committee appears to have altered his views or exchanged concessions in the course of the discussions. To be sure, Leigh-Pemberton refused to issue a public dissent, as Thatcher and

---

[180] David Cameron, "Transnational Relations and the Development of European Economic and Monetary Union," in Thomas Risse-Kappen, ed., *Bringing Transnational Relations Back In: Non-State Actors, Domestic Structures and International Institutions* (Cambridge, 1995), 73–74.

[181] Dyson and Featherstone, *Elusive*, 308.

[182] Roland Vaubel, "A Public Choice View of the Delors Report," in Vaubel and Thomas Willett, eds., *The Political Economy of International Organizations: A Public Choice Approach* (Boulder, Colo., 1991), 306–310; Amy Verdun, *EMU—The Product of Policy Learning and Consensus among Monetary Experts,* Essex, European Policy Process Occasional Paper Series no. 7 (Colchester, 1996); Smyser, *German,* 273. On epistemic communities more generally, see Peter M. Haas, "Do Regimes Matter? Epistemic Communities and Mediterranean Pollution Control," *International Organization* 43:3 (Summer 1989), 377–404.

Lamont urged him to do, but this was because his advisers told him that this would neither dissuade others nor soften German demands, only diminish British influence; even virulent critics of EMU do not deny this evaluation.[183] Each participant understood that Germany would reject outright any proposal that did not grant the Eurofed substantial autonomy and an anti-inflationary mandate—Germany's position for over two decades. Pöhl, himself under pressure from the Bundesbank Committee, was generally recognized as the decisive member, because he held important domestic veto power in a country that itself held critical international veto power.

The outcome was—even Pöhl understood—predetermined, since it reflected the domestic power of the Bundesbank and the international power of Germany. French officials criticized the Delors Committee (and subsequent negotiators) for ignoring proposals for immediate EMS reform but accepted the outcome, understanding that the Bundesbank could impose preconditions for any deeper cooperation. A source close to French finance minister Bérégovoy recalled: "It was power politics. If the institutions were not created to the liking of the Bundesbank, there would be no European Central Bank. This was made explicit to Bérégovoy."[184]

Other analysts maintain the opposite view, namely that the Delors Committee empowered a transnational alliance of *non*-German central bankers, who persuaded or pressured Pöhl to accept EMU. Here there is more truth, but the analysis again overlooks the structural determinants of the outcome. It is misleading to see here an exercise of power by autonomous central bankers over Pöhl. Insofar as the committee constrained Pöhl, it was from the beginning as an instrument deliberately designed by Kohl and Mitterrand as part of a two-level strategy to bolster the power of the German government *vis-à-vis* the Bundesbank—a fact Pöhl himself acknowledged from the beginning. Kohl and Mitterrand called the committee into being, deliberately gave it salience by naming Delors head, and charged it with developing *means* to reach monetary integration rather than evaluating the *end*. This, along with a fundamental clash of economic goals, explains Pöhl's rejection of an anti-EMU alliance with Leigh-Pemberton. The mandate was the key decision, as Pöhl himself immediately recognized—hence his reluctance to serve. Yet even his acceptance was structurally constrained: his Bundesbank advisers saw little choice, because if Pöhl boycotted the proceedings, his advisers told him, he would have been fatally weakened in domestic debates and so would have wielded even less influence over the outcome. This outcome was not the result of transnational tactics or direct pressure from other central banks; it reflected the domestic balance of power within Germany. From beginning to end, the real dynamic was between Kohl and the Bundesbank. In short, David Cameron's assertion is quite true that "German and Dutch central bank officials, exercising their constitutional independence and autonomy, were

[183] Connally, *Rotten*, 78–79.
[184] Walsh, *Global*, 153; Heisenberg, *Mark*, 160. Also interviews with two members of the Delors Committee and a French minister; Gros and Thygesen, *European*, 320; Connolly, *Rotten*, 79; Howe, *Conflict*, 576–577; Lawson, *View*, 907ff; Thatcher, *Downing*, 708.

transnational actors and not simply agents of their governments," but there is no evidence that this fact influenced the outcome of the negotiations.[185]

To explain the outcome we need to turn from *persuasion*, stressed by supranational and transnational explanations, to *intergovernmental bargaining power*. Nearly all the major participants attested that the distribution of benefits reflected the German government's structural power, which in turn resulted from its possession of a relatively attractive alternative to agreement. The German government was tightly constrained, such that the asymmetrical EMS (or perhaps even floating rates) was an acceptable alternative. As in the case of the EMS, the constraints on the German win-set stemmed not from the unattractiveness of EMU per se, from which German business benefited, but from the credible veto threat issued by the Bundesbank, backed by public opinion—a "kinked winset," in the language of two-level games. The stability of the EMS was a concern, but even business supporters and the CDU demonstrated a very limited willingness to relax "economist" preconditions. The result was an advantageous bargaining position for Germany.

Other governments based their policies on the same assumption that the transnational form of the negotiations was epiphenomenal, while underlying structures of domestic influence and intergovernmental power would dictate the outcome. The head of the Dutch central bank recalled: "Precisely because Germany must make concessions in order to create a single currency, it is in a position to impose conditions. In my view, it is in the interest of Germany as well as Europe that the conditions be chosen so as to assure a stability-oriented policy in the future EMU."[186] The French, correctly perceiving the constraint to lie in German domestic politics, sought to weaken Bundesbank opposition through concessions within EMU; the British, to bolster the Bundesbank opposition by proposing alternatives to EMU. The French did better than the British, because of the decisive intervention of the German government, but substantial concessions to Germany were nonetheless required. The institutions in the final treaty, a national representative from a major country recalled, were carefully crafted to meet German demands over a four-year period. The outcome was reached "not by accident, but by design."[187]

Threats of exit and exclusion also played an important role in the negotiations, as intergovernmental theory predicts. Variations in the credibility of the threat and the costs it might impose on excluded parties explain the extent to which such threats influenced the result. The intergovernmental theory predicts that such threats must be credible and costly to the target. The target was Britain, by far the most recalcitrant government, having entered both monetary and political negotiations with an entirely negative brief and few positive initiatives. Where no threats of exclusion were made, Britain enjoyed considerable influence over the outcome; many observers noted that the other eleven gov-

---

[185] Cameron, "Transnational," 77.
[186] Rahmsdorf, "Währungspolitik," 126. Also interview with two members of the Delors Committee and a member-state ambassador.
[187] Interview with permanent representative, December 1996.

ernments continually weakened their initial position in a vain attempt to satisfy the twelfth. This observation helps to explain the modest results of the political union negotiations.[188]

The effectiveness of British obstruction was constrained, however, by the credibility and costs of exclusion, just as intergovernmental theory predicts. Consider three examples: social, monetary, and foreign policy. The British government was very skeptical of cooperation on social policy; Major credibly claimed that Tory MPs might reject the treaty on this ground alone. Hence Britain was granted an opt-out, which not only satisfied partisan concerns but permitted British business to maintain lower social standards than most EU countries. In the EMU negotiations, by contrast, the British government was just as skeptical but believed that it would be costly for the financial services industry in the City if it went forward without Britain. Aware that France and Germany were quite willing to exclude Britain, Major did not seek to block agreement but instead sought an opt-out with an option to join later. In CFSP, finally, many Continental governments believed that a European foreign or defense policy without Britain was not credible (and perhaps not desirable); hence British opposition to any important diminution of national sovereignty was successful.[189]

Linkages, also as intergovernmental theory predicted, remained almost entirely within, rather than across, issues. Most important, Germany proved unable to translate its power in the monetary negotiations into more than modest, mostly symbolic movement toward political union—though it gained a remarkable amount on EMU. To be sure, Germany achieved a minor expansion of competences and QMV in some areas of economic regulation, most of which were already handled under other treaty provisions. On other issues, ambitious and uniquely German initiatives failed. A proposal for Parliament initiative and strong codecision were watered down to a much more limited form of codecision, still largely at the Commission's expense. France and Britain blocked ambitious German proposals for closer foreign and interior policies. The result was the three-pillar structure, in which these policies remained intergovernmental, rather than the "single" EC structure favored by Germany. In defense policy, Britain blocked all but rhetorical reform, though it was unclear whether German and French proposals were either serious or compatible with one another. All other German gains reflected consensus among the three governments. All agreed to limit the EC role in education, to reject Commission proposals to expand control over taxation, to strengthen Court enforcement, and to block reforms to loosen oversight over the Commission ("comitology").

Institutional Delegation and Pooling: Explaining "organized chaos"

Maastricht involved major decisions to pool and delegate sovereignty. Among the most prominent were the creation of an independent European central bank, the three-pillar design restricting the formal reach of the Court and Com-

---

[188] *AE*, 12/13 November 1991, and 4 December 1991; Ludlow, "Reshaping."
[189] Interview with permanent representative, prime minister.

mission largely to economic issues, the extension of qualified majority voting to new areas, and the modest expansion of parliamentary codecision. This pattern of delegation and pooling is best explained as the result not of ideological or technocratic imperatives but of the desire for more credible commitments in areas where governments had significant conflicts of interest and future failure to implement or comply was possible.

We do not see support for the predictions of the technocratic explanation—namely, that delegation was required to economize on the production of expert information. Technical complexity does not seem to have been linked to delegation. Monetary policy was not so extraordinarily complex as to warrant an unprecedented, autonomous, supranational institution. Indirect taxation, environmental regulation, and other regulatory internal market issues were also complex, requiring great expertise, yet these remained more decentralized. It is true that domestic experts in some countries favored delegation to an independent central bank, but this was not universally the case; moreover, they favored the bank not in order to economize on information but to lock in a particular policy outcome. The key dispute was not whether experts or nonexperts would handle monetary policy but whether autonomous central bankers or more political finance ministries, both technically competent, would do so. There is no evidence that the argument that delegation of autonomy to supranational actors was required for competent management played a prominent role. The central cleavage concerned the level of political control over the institution, not its expertise.

There is somewhat stronger support for the predictions of an ideological explanation for delegation and pooling. We observe substantial variation across countries. Germany generally favored the largest amount of delegation and pooling in foreign policy and interior policy, whereas the British government favored the least—though these positions are also consistent with the substantive preferences of the governments. Ideology seems most clearly decisive in explaining positions on Parliamentary codecision and the relative power of the branches of EC governance—highly symbolic issues closely connected with democratic ideology, in which the substantive consequences of delegation were uncertain. As had traditionally been the case, France favored a stronger Council, Germany a stronger Parliament, and Britain no increase in supranational prerogatives. We observe, moreover, cooperation between France and Germany to strengthen both the Parliament and the Council at the expense of the Commission. During the Maastricht ratification debates in France and Denmark, overt criticism of delegation and pooling seemed to covary with Euroskepticism.

Yet neither technocratic information nor ideology seems to account for variation across issues and countries in the level of delegation and pooling. In particular, they offer little explanation of the most important cases of delegation and pooling, namely the creation of an autonomous ECB and the selective expansion of QMV to certain new areas respectively. Here the evidence strongly supports the predictions of the credible commitments explanation. Debates over the central bank were concerned almost entirely with the credibility of its anti-inflationary commitment; if anything, more federalist German politicians in the CDU favored a modest weakening of that autonomy. Germany, while supportive of expanded Parliamentary prerogatives and general democratic control in other areas, rejected them in the all-important monetary area, where they threatened to undermine the anti-inflationary mandate of the central bank. The description of debates leaves little doubt that in monetary policy the triple institutional guarantee—an autonomous ECB with an anti-inflationary mandate comprised of representatives of newly autonomous national central banks—was designed to satisfy the Bundesbank and others in Germany concerned about inflation. The unprecedented autonomy of the ECB among supranational institutions is consistent with the extremely high concern about defection from its mandate—just as is the case with domestic central banks. Domestic and international divisions over monetary institutions reflected efforts to lock in longstanding substantive preferences. The clear focus of the negotiations was on the establishment of a credible commitment sufficient to satisfy German skeptics. Strongly federalist governments split along substantive lines: Italy, Belgium, and Spain favored greater Commission and Council oversight, the Netherlands and Germany opposed it. Antifederalist Britain, though opposing EMU itself, favored the creation of a strong, autonomous central bank.

Splits over majority voting also tracked substantive commitments, as the credible commitments view predicts. Germany, for example, favored majority voting in areas such as foreign and environmental policy, where it would favor German aims, but also offered a long list of exceptions in other areas. Governments supporting QMV in environmental and social policy represented richer societies with higher environmental regulations; they were careful not to dilute the ability of such governments to provide higher domestic protection than the EC norm. Those that opposed them—Britain, Spain, and Portugal among them—tended to be poorer, lower-standard countries. As predicted by the credible commitment explanation, a central issue concerning the delegation of power, beside the credibility of the commitment, was the extent of democratic control and the scope of agency slack. The proper role of "unelected" central bankers became a major concern of decision-makers, publics, and analysts.

In contrast to the conventional wisdom, which stresses German unification, Commission entrepreneurship, and federalist sympathies, this explanation of the varied outcomes at Maastricht focuses primarily on slowly evolving economic interests, intergovernmental bargaining and relative power, and the need to institutionalize more credible commitments. The latter two steps of this causal chain are particularly unproblematic. If a legitimate debate was possible about the secondary significance of the Commission and Parliament in the emergence of the Single European Act, the Maastricht Treaty represented a return to the purely intergovernmental norm of EC decision-making. Similarly the logic of pooling and delegation, clearly one of creating credible commitments, was a return to type. The creation of the European Central Bank, the major act of delegation in the negotiation, was unambiguously aimed at enhancing the credibility of commitments in circumstances where the costs of defection to others could be very high.

The process of preference formation at Maastricht is more problematic and, in this respect, stands out in comparison to the other four major decisions in EC history. To be sure, German, French, and British national preferences were stable and reflected positions held by all three major governments for over a decade. Yet the precise balance of economic and geopolitical influences (in particular, ideology) remains more difficult to disentangle than in other cases. There certainly were strong economic impulses: the interest of the French government in offsetting asymmetries, thereby reducing domestic interest rates; the interest of the German government in assuring export competitiveness and increasing fiscal slack; and above all the high level of nominal convergence in macroeconomic policy. Still, it is unclear whether the economic benefits truly outweighed the costs for any single country, or whether the expectations of various governments were fully compatible. If the EMU turns out in fact to impose tight monetary discipline, it is unclear that it constitutes an improvement for weaker-currency countries. If it turns out in fact to loosen constraints imposed by the asymmetrical EMS, as both France and Germany appear to have hoped, it is unclear that it will greatly improve the economic performance of Germany, though it may encourage economic changes supported by export industry and a fiscally ambitious government. The nature of these real effects depends, moreover, on the adaptation of wages, prices, and government spending in each country to these new constraints. In short, even if governments acted on the basis of a set of apparently compatible economic interests, there was considerable economic risk involved in choosing EMU.

Where governments left key elements of the bargain open at Maastricht, we expect conflict to continue. And this is precisely what we observe. Kohl and Genscher pushed German domestic economic interests to the limit in the interest of a clear commitment to EMU, and they were forced to seek further concessions after the treaty was signed on issues such as the name of the currency, the location of the central bank, and the nature of budgetary controls. Over the next two years, the French government pursued a single-minded policy of defending the franc. The German government pressured the Bundesbank to support the franc, which it did by intervening at an unprecedented scale and in an unprecedented way, namely through public and intramarginal means. The result was unmanageable pressure on the pound, lire, and escudo. The German government was unwilling to take responsibility for the complete collapse of the EMS or to permit the DM to revalue upward alone through a unilateral float, as France proposed, while the Bundesbank was unwilling to let the system threaten German domestic economic stability. The result was an institutional arrangement—15 percent bands—that no longer greatly constrained governments.

The inconclusive outcome of the political union negotiations left unsatisfied those governments which had favored more intensive cooperation. This outcome was no mistake and did not reflect the absence of Commission involvement; instead, it resulted from the lack of intense support for deeper cooperation in any country, combined with disagreements about the direction to take. The fundamental lack of support was underscored by the outcome of the Intergovernmental Conference of 1996–97, where all conceivable issues of political union were reconsidered. Despite years of careful preparation, the reforms in the Treaty of Amsterdam were minimal—a modest increase in Parliamentary powers and greater institutional integration of the third pillar, though without much change in decision-making processes.

Perhaps the most enduring legacy of Maastricht was the growing realization that progress toward greater integration was not possible among all twelve governments without greater concessions to national particularities than had previously been the case. Even before the unexpectedly heated debates surrounding Maastricht ratification, the Treaty legitimated "two-track" and "flexible" solutions, in which some governments moved forward or participated, others did not. In 1988 only Margaret Thatcher was calling openly for greater flexibility, which would permit opt-outs and EC policies with less than all members as full participants. Five years later, flexibility, redubbed "enhanced cooperation," had become a legitimate policy option. The period in which reflexive rhetorical support for European federal union among supporters of integration could be taken for granted was at an end. Not only was such a goal now widely viewed as unattainable; it was increasingly viewed as undesirable. This is not to say the EC had become "Thatcherite." To the contrary, as the EC took steps toward flexibility, it was also constructing unprecedentedly autonomous centralized institutions, such as the ECB. The unresolved tension between these two visions of Europe remains a legacy of the Maastricht Treaty.

CHAPTER SEVEN

European Integration in Retrospect

> There will never be a United States of Europe . . . I refuse to identify myself
> with those who promote the disappearance of the nation-state . . . I seek instead
> a federation among strong nation-states.
>
> —Jacques Delors, former president of the Commission, 1996

With this statement the most distinguished EC visionary of the 1980s comes
full circle, returning to the view of his predecessor, Robert Schuman, whose statement began this book. Delors's sentiment recognizes that European integration
has been not a preordained movement toward federal union but a series of
pragmatic bargains among national governments based on concrete national
interests, relative power, and carefully calculated transfers of sovereignty. The
persistence of national power was the bitter lesson Delors drew from his difficult
experience in the Maastricht negotiation.[1]

This conclusion remains unchanged if we exchange the perspective of the
statesman for that of the scholar. The central argument of this book—the "liberal intergovernmentalist" argument—holds that European integration was a
series of rational adaptations by national leaders to constraints and opportunities stemming from the evolution of an interdependent world economy, the
relative power of states in the international system, and the potential for international institutions to bolster the credibility of interstate commitments. The
historical record of the five most salient negotiations in EC history—those surrounding the Treaty of Rome, Common Agricultural Policy, European Monetary
System, Single European Act, and Maastricht Treaty on European Union—
strongly supports this conclusion. This final chapter begins by summarizing the
empirical findings on the sources of national preferences, interstate bargaining outcomes, and institutional choices in the process of European integration;
briefly considers the (mostly negative) implications for "historical institutionalist" explanations of integration; then moves to implications for the comparative
study of regional integration and, finally, for general theories of international
conflict and cooperation.

---

[1] Interview with member of Jacques Delors's cabinet, October 1996.

472

What Drives Regional Integration?

The tripartite rationalist framework employed in this book implies that the collective decisions of national governments can be analyzed by assuming that each first formulates national preferences, then engages in interstate bargaining, and finally decides whether to delegate or pool sovereignty in international institutions. Within each stage, I have advanced a narrower theoretical claim about, respectively, the predominance of economic incentives stemming from rising trade and capital flows, the relative bargaining power created by asymmetrical policy interdependence, and the need for credible commitments against defection from particular agreements. The five case studies strongly and consistently support these explanations. The most widely cited alternative causes—geopolitical threats, European federalist ideas, technocratic imperatives to delegate, and intervention by supranational political entrepreneurs—played a decidedly secondary role. Each chapter has presented the details. Here aggregate patterns in the historical record are briefly sketched. Our confidence in the results reported in each individual chapter is strengthened by their consistency over all five cases.

Before I summarize the data, one important caveat deserves mention. The primary documentary record is far less extensive for the Maastricht Treaty and, though the problem is less acute, the Single European Act, than for the first three cases. Judgments about national preference formation may therefore be subject to revision in light of new documents and personal revelations. We must attach a higher degree of uncertainty to findings concerning these negotiations than to those drawn from the first two and a half decades of EC history.

National Preferences: The Preeminence of Economic Motivations

The bulk of the existing literature claims that the EC was founded primarily to address real and perceived geopolitical threats or to realize federalist ideas. Yet each of the five cases confirms that the most persistent and powerful source of varying national preferences concerning integration over the past four decades has been economic, in particular commercial, interest. This evidence supports not only the general importance of economic incentives but the particular theories of economic preference formation over trade and monetary issues advanced in chapter 1, which locates the source of European integration in the explosion of world trade after World War II. In response to these constraints and opportunities, governments tended to be heavily influenced by the commercial interests of domestic producer groups, interests that reflected respective positions in the global market. These circumstances created, according to the theory, strong incentives to liberalize but also differences about how far and in what areas to do so. We expect, moreover, that purely commercial motivations would be combined, particularly in the cases of regulatory harmonization and monetary policy, with economic motivations involving the provision of domestic public goods, notably regulatory protection and macroeconomic stability.

For each major issue facing each country in each negotiation, I employed internal documents, interviews, reliable memoirs, and, where necessary, the judgments of analysts to test hypotheses drawn from political economy and geopolitical theories. These hypotheses concerned five categories of observable implications: the cross-issue and cross-national distribution of preferences, the timing of preference shifts, policy consistency, the pattern of domestic cleavages, and the content of domestic discourse. (They are summarized in Table 1.2).

If we limit ourselves to German, French, and British preferences concerning the most important policy involved in each agreement—fifteen positions in all—we find that in *every* case the preponderance of evidence confirms the importance of political economic motivations over geopolitical interest or ideology. In seven of fifteen cases, *no* hard evidence suggests that geopolitical ideas or interests served as more than *ex post* public justifications for national positions. In the remaining eight cases—Germany and France in the Treaty of Rome and the 1960s, France during discussions of the SEA, and all three countries in the Maastricht negotiations—the historical record suggests that geopolitical ideology may have played a secondary or parallel role. In only four of those eight cases, however (Germany in the Treaty of Rome and the 1960s, France and Germany in the Maastricht negotiations), is there evidence that geopolitical considerations significantly altered final agreements on economic matters. And in only two, perhaps three, of these (Germany in the Treaty of Rome, the 1960s, and perhaps the Maastricht negotiations) does the preponderance of evidence suggest that geopolitical motivations actually altered the national position. To summarize, in twelve (or thirteen) out of fifteen core national positions, political economic concerns appear sufficient to explain national motivations; in all fifteen the predominant influence on national preferences was economic interest.

Preferences generally varied across issues and countries, as political economic theory predicts, rather than simply across countries, as geopolitical theory leads us to expect. Whether we examine the customs union and monetary cooperation or secondary, often stillborn, policies in areas such as transport, atomic energy, external tariff policy, industrial and R&D policy, or social policy, cross-issue variation in national positions consistently mirrors competitiveness in global markets, macroeconomic preferences, and regulatory commitments. The strongest support for tariff liberalization, for example, comes consistently from business in relatively competitive countries: Germany and Britain sought industrial liberalization but were cautious about liberalizing agriculture, the French position was the reverse. Even in the SEA, regulatory competitiveness remained the decisive concern: France placed special emphasis on a reduction in regulatory barriers on food products, Britain pressed for service deregulation, and Germany sought general reduction in industrial trade barriers.

The timing of shifts in preferences and positions offers further support for the political economic theory. Important changes in the priorities, policies, and preferences of national governments appear to have reflected shifts in the domestic and international economic environment. Examples include the clear impact of French devaluation in 1958 on business demands, the rapid British response to economic exclusion from the EC, and the response to global trends toward liberalization of service provision in the 1980s. Sustainable monetary initiatives emerged in times of macroeconomic convergence and dollar depreciation—as was the case just prior to each oil crisis and again in the late 1980s—but the effects of the two were difficult to separate. By contrast, important geopolitical events—the Suez Crisis of 1956, the founding of the French Fifth Republic in 1958, the collapse of the Fouchet Plan negotiations in 1962, the Anglo-American agreement at Nassau in 1963, the abandonment of the U.S. proposal for a multilateral force shortly thereafter, the launching of Ostpolitik in the late 1960s, the rise and fall of détente with the Soviet Union in the 1970s, and German unification in the 1980s—do not seem to have led to expected shifts in national preferences concerning the EC.

EC policies were, by contrast, consistent with positions in other international economic forums. French, British, and German policies on trade, agriculture, money, and regulation within the EC were in most cases consistent with their unilateral, bilateral, and global multilateral policies with regard to these same issues. Hence the Single European Act came into being only after considerable unilateral liberalization, bilateral Franco-German discussions, the regional Schengen Agreement, and negotiations in the GATT Tokyo Round on nontariff barriers. Germany launched a monetary initiative in the G-7 simultaneously with advocating EMS; France did the same when launching EMU. Only one important exception exists: Germany's aggressive liberalism in GATT tariff negotiations of the 1950s and 1960s and its protectionism concerning agriculture were not mirrored precisely in its position toward the EC customs union, though in the end Germany managed to achieve similar goals in both organizations.

National negotiating tactics—the major demands and counterdemands— tended to be economic in nature. Monetary negotiations focused consistently on whether government policies had already converged macroeconomically and the extent to which creditor and debtor governments would be obliged to converge further. Geopolitical concerns were consistently sacrificed to economic interests, as, for example, when Britain and Gaullist France repeatedly accepted federal institutions to achieve their economic objectives. By contrast, there were fewer attempts to make economic concessions in order to achieve explicit geopolitical objectives. It is particularly striking that neither de Gaulle nor Adenauer proposed anything of the kind. Where economic and geopolitical factors came directly into conflict—as in Adenauer's priority on atomic energy cooperation, de Gaulle's desire for intergovernmental institutions, Willy Brandt's proposal in the early 1970s for a monetary fund, and some symbolic initiatives by Georges Pompidou—economic imperatives tended to win out. British prime ministers repeatedly threatened geopolitically self-destructive actions, usually involving the British commitment to NATO, in an effort to extract economic concessions from their Continental counterparts.

Patterns of domestic cleavages and salient concerns in domestic deliberations provide further support for the economic theory. Cleavages formed consistently along economic lines, and salient arguments tended to be economic, particularly in confidential discussions. On not a single major issue did governments take a position openly opposed by a major peak industrial, financial, or agricultural interest group.[2] Business consistently split according to the relative competitiveness of sectors and firms. By the time of the Treaty of Rome negotiations and consistently thereafter, by contrast, debates over controversial political-military issues such as the European Defense Community, German NATO membership, the repatriation of the Saar, rapid German reunification, and the French nuclear program were resolved; many argued that European integration no longer had decisive geopolitical implications. This belief unblocked ideological opposition to integration that had formerly united French Gaullists, German Social Democrats, and British Conservatives. Economic considerations—the promotion of industrial modernization in France, export success in Germany, and the inevitable shift from Commonwealth to Continental trade in Britain—continued to be the most important determinant of the positions of key domestic groups on integration through the 1960s. In monetary negotiations from the EMS to EMU, domestic coalitions similarly formed around economic considerations: the economic demands of business groups, the concerns of central banks, and the macroeconomic priorities of governing political parties.

In exceptional cases geopolitical motivations appear to have played an important role: Adenauer's particular tendency to favor France, de Gaulle's views on supranational institutions, Thatcher's opposition to British participation in the EMS. Yet even here the concerns of economic interest groups placed tight constraints on national policy. Repeatedly we see leaders privileging economic over geopolitical concerns: de Gaulle considered "agricultural modernization" his most important European goal; Macmillan overcame Foreign Office objections with the argument that Britain "lives and dies by exports"; Adenauer was unable to impose Euratom on the recalcitrant German nuclear industry. In the 1970s, little evidence suggests that Schmidt or Giscard was thinking in geopolitical terms when he proposed monetary integration, nor that European leaders were primarily concerned with geopolitics during the reforms of the 1980s. The record does not support the notion that the move to EMU, which was decisively under way by late 1988, was bolstered in any important way by German unification.

The relative power of producer groups *vis-à-vis* more general economic concerns varied across policies with the preference intensity and power of producer groups. EC policy was, in this regard, a continuation of domestic politics by different means. Where producers were particularly strong and governments had traditionally been forced to provide subsidies, governments were forced to provide even for weak producers. Where producers were weaker, governments could force more economic adjustment upon them. The strongest were consistently farmers, whose postwar dominance is evident in their success, even before the EC, in extracting unilateral domestic subsidies in every country. Even relatively uncompetitive producers were well served. Producer views were slightly less domi-

---

[2] One case is particularly difficult to interpret, namely that of Germany during the 1960s. Farm groups opposed the lowering of German wheat prices, yet the side-payment—including higher prices on dairy products, direct subsidies, export opportunities, and Monetary Compensation Accounts a few years later—more than offset this disadvantage. Surely this cannot be seen as a defeat for German farmers.

nant in industrial tariff liberalization, where governments played more and less competitive producers off against one another. When regulatory and nontariff barriers came onto the agenda, significant regulatory concerns balanced producer influence. We observe relatively wealthy countries defending high standards through harmonization and safeguards, whereas poorer countries, and in this regard Britain was typical, sought more unconditional liberalization. Finally, in monetary negotiations over the EMS and the EMU, producer groups were balanced by strong national macroeconomic ideas and institutions. Hence the relative positions of strong- and weak-currency countries, which incorporated both commercial concerns and the views of governments and central banks, proved critical in shaping national preferences.

Yet we should not neglect geopolitical interests and ideas altogether. Over the past forty years their impact on European integration, though clearly secondary, has nonetheless been significant. If the fifty-year postwar boom in trade and investment among industrialized nations rendered a measure of trade liberalization, regulatory harmonization, and monetary stabilization inevitable, it is nonetheless likely that the EC would have evolved differently in the absence of a parallel set of geopolitical preferences for and against European integration. The likely outcome absent the impact of geopolitical concerns would have been a trade arrangement closer to the free trade area repeatedly proposed by Britain, backed by a series of bilateral and global agreements on multilateral trade and investment. Such an arrangement would likely have enticed Britain to participate and, as a result, would have permitted—as the French always feared— only ad hoc bilateral arrangements for agriculture. This alternative was favored by German business groups and by Ludwig Erhard, first as economics minister and then as chancellor. An FTA would likely have evolved toward consideration of NTBs, as did the GATT and various European standards bodies during the 1970s and 1980s; toward reduction of customs formalities, as did the ad hoc Schengen arrangement before the SEA; and toward service liberalization, as reflected in the unilateral policies of nearly all European governments, whether inside or outside the EC. Yet such policies—conducted on a bilateral, unilateral, or "flexible" basis, as occurred among non-EC European countries—would likely have remained uneven, uncoordinated, and decentralized. Similarly, although monetary cooperation along the lines of the EMS would have been a likely response to the collapse of Bretton Woods and policy convergence after the two oil shocks, it is difficult to imagine a more ad hoc arrangement evolving in the direction of EMU or arranging the sort of financial side-payments required to integrate countries such as Spain, Portugal, and Greece into Europe.

We can learn more about the role of geopolitical concerns by examining the pattern of national preferences across five cases. First, as the political economic theory itself predicts, geopolitical factors consistently tended to matter most where the costs and benefits of cooperation were uncertain, balanced, or weak. Adenauer exploited for geopolitical purposes the support of German business for *both* a free trade area and a customs union, whereas he was unable to overcome the outright opposition of business to atomic energy cooperation. De Gaulle pursued his geopolitical goals within the constraints set by the economic

477

demands of producer groups, but where the two clashed—as in the "empty chair" crisis, the creation of supranational institutions for agriculture, and the Fouchet Plan—economic concerns dominated.[3] Kohl was able to achieve EMU, in large part a geopolitical goal, only by working within constraints set by the compromise between business and the Bundesbank. General uncertainty about the consequences of EMU may also have assisted him, like Mitterrand, in maneuvering toward Maastricht. Geopolitical considerations tended to be important where issues had no immediate economic impact, as in foreign policy coordination and in purely institutional concerns, such as the role of the European Parliament. In such cases both theories rightly predict the predominance of concerns about security and sovereignty.

Second, it appears that significant geopolitical factors were more ideational than objective and often connected with prestigious national leaders. The historical record more strongly supports the "liberal constructivist" variant of geopolitical theory (the fourth presented in chapter 1) than those grounded in more objective, Realist power-balancing or in collective security. To be sure, threats from the Soviet Union and Germany lurked in the background, particularly in early EC history. They did not, however, generate overwhelming pressure for integration. Strong geopolitical support or opposition to European integration tended to reflect instead—as Stanley Hoffmann and others have long maintained—distinctive ideological interpretations of objective circumstances emanating from a domestic minority. Adenauer's pro-French conception of German alliance policy, de Gaulle's vision of an autonomous Europe, Thatcher's "root and branch" opposition to European federalism, and Kohl and Mitterrand's equally extreme support for this goal were all rather idiosyncratic minority positions. In each case there were numerous possible responses to objective threats, and of those responses European integration was neither the most obvious nor, often, the most popular.

Third, and perhaps most striking, Germany accounts for all three cases in which geopolitical factors appear to have actually influenced core national preferences: German preference formation in the Treaty of Rome, the 1960s, and the Maastricht negotiation. This observation, combined with the finding that geopolitical considerations tend to be mediated by ideology, suggests that postwar Germany's "semisovereign" status, in particular the postwar commitment of the German public and political elite to multilateralism, played a significant if secondary role in shaping the EC we know today.[4]

On balance, however, economic interests clearly remained dominant. Looking back over forty years, one is struck by the incremental nature of shifts in the relative positions of different states, despite the entry and exit of governments with radically different ideologies. Against a background of slowly deepening commitment to integration, the relative positions of Britain, France, and Ger-

---

[3] For a more detailed argument, see Andrew Moravcsik, "Prudence, Audacity, Seduction: De Gaulle and Europe Reconsidered," *Harvard Center for European Studies Working Paper* (Cambridge, Mass., 1998).

[4] For a defense of this position, see Peter Katzenstein, "United Germany in an Integrating Europe," in Katzenstein, ed., *Tamed Power: Germany in Europe* (Ithaca, N.Y., 1997), 1–48.

many on issues such as agricultural liberalization, safeguards on internal tariff reductions, GATT negotiations, and the application of competition policy have remained relatively constant—a point I shall return to. The steady deepening of economic interdependence among European governments seems to offer a ready explanation, whereas objective geopolitical motivations would lead us to expect some long-term decline in support for integration as colonial concerns, the German menace, the internal communist challenge, and lastly the Soviet threat receded.[5]

Interstate Bargaining: Interdependence and Power

The second stage in the rationalist model of international cooperation is interstate bargaining. Here the central question is: When European governments with diverse national preferences bargain over treaty-amending reforms, what determines the efficiency and distributional consequences of the agreements they reach? This book has tested intergovernmental and supranational bargaining theories. The first treats information and ideas as plentiful and predicts efficient negotiations with distributional bargaining shaped by asymmetrical interdependence. The second assumes that supranational political entrepreneurs enjoy privileged access to scarce information and ideas, which they exploit to set agendas, mediate, and mobilize supporters, thereby improving efficiency and altering the distributional outcome of negotiations. The theories were tested by examining three types of observable implications—the distribution of information, the performance of entrepreneurial tasks, and patterns in the efficiency and distributional outcomes of negotiations. (These are summarized in Table 1.3.)

The historical record consistently confirms intergovernmental theory. Information appears to have been plentiful, with governments better informed than supranational actors. Supranational actors appear to have lacked all the comparative advantages that might make for successful supranational entrepreneurship: more technical expertise, a reputation for neutrality, superior political skill and vision, greater legitimacy, consistently accurate political intelligence. Though they consistently acted as policy initiators, mediators, and mobilizers, Commission officials and Parliamentarians increased the efficiency of only one agreement, the Single European Act; they had no impact on the distribution of gains. Efficiency was assured by active *governmental* entrepreneurship. Distributional outcomes, far from favoring the Commission and Parliament, tended to reflect asymmetrical interdependence: those governments that most strongly favored the core of each agreement tended to make concessions to recalcitrant governments on the margin in order to achieve it.

Information and ideas, as intergovernmental bargaining theory predicts, were generally plentiful. They were widely available and symmetrically distrib-

---

[5] Only in the case of traditional neutrals may geopolitical factors have played an important role, but even here the evidence is at best ambiguous. Sieglinde Gstöhl, "Reluctant Europeans: Sweden, Norway, and Switzerland in the Process of European Integration (1950–1995), PhD. thesis, University of Geneva (1998).

uted among states. Supranational officials did not, in general, possess superior information or ideas. Often representatives of the most interested national governments were better informed. Technically, we saw that the Commission remained reliant on national officials, particularly in complex areas such as the CAP and monetary policy; sometimes the Commission simply could not (or was not permitted to) follow technical negotiations. The political information and judgment of Commission and Parliament officials were even less reliable. Supranational officials tended to ignore political constraints and render overoptimistic judgments about the political feasibility of their preferred options. This was true from the start. Ernst Haas sees 1956 as the year when "Monnet's doctrine of a strong, united Europe . . . resting on a large common market came into its own."[6] The truth was precisely the opposite: Monnet sought to persuade Konrad Adenauer and others to reject the customs union in favor of the creation of Euratom. It would be the same over the coming years. Hallstein sought to pressure de Gaulle to accept greater centralization of Commission control, and Delors sought to secure a more pro-French and federalist result in the Maastricht negotiations. Both efforts were futile and demonstrated a remarkable lack of political judgment.

Interested member governments or private individuals, not supranational officials, initiated and mediated major EC negotiations. Governments and private groups typically submitted dozens, sometimes hundreds, of proposals. When existing initiatives were unsatisfactory to a government, it typically offered alternatives, in some cases submitting entire draft treaties. The bias, if any, in the supply of proposals considered by governments was in favor of political viability, as intergovernmental theory predicts, not in favor of the vision of supranational actors. Proposals that appear to have been proposed by international actors were actually managed behind the scenes by major governments through classical diplomatic means, as in the case of the Spaak Report, the design of the CAP, Schmidt and Giscard's EMS proposal, and the Delors Report on EMU. More typical are situations in which too many proposals must be whittled down to one.

Lest one conclude that this whittling down itself required a third-party mediator, the Maastricht negotiations over political union provide a particularly satisfying test. The Commission stayed out of the negotiations, turning over entrepreneurial functions entirely to the rotating national presidency—held then by tiny Luxembourg, which was backed by fewer than a dozen officials drawn from the more intergovernmental EC Council secretariat. The Luxembourgeois swiftly sorted through hundreds of available national proposals and managed the negotiations using a single negotiating text. In this negotiation, as well as others, critical bargains were reached by chief executives (and, less often, ministers and diplomatic representatives), unmediated by third parties. The exceptions are few and scattered. Where mediators were employed, they tended to be third governments, as in the case of Maastricht. This finding, consistent with at least one recent comparative study of multilateral negotiations, suggests that transaction

---

[6] Ernst B. Haas, *The Uniting of Europe: Political, Social and Economic Forces, 1950–1957* (Stanford, Calif., 1958), 299, 317.

costs are low relative to the stakes for and capabilities of even the smallest EC member-state.[7]

Cross-case comparison casts an unfavorable light on certain widespread *ex post* claims concerning the powerful impact of entrepreneurs. Jacques Delors, for example, is often credited with decisively expediting the single market project by setting a clear deadline for its completion ("Europe 1992")—even though he was not the only one to propose a deadline. The importance of this tactic, much heralded by journalists at the time, seems plausible until we compare the 1992 initiative with the Commissioner's many earlier EC proposals that were ineffective despite the use of dates. Two earlier Commission schedules for the removal of nontariff barriers were ignored. The Werner Plan for EMU by 1980 failed entirely. Other outcomes were achieved more quickly than expected. The customs union, initially scheduled for 1970, was completed in 1968, though the Commission had proposed even earlier dates in the interim. Hence the lesson that deadlines are productive was far from obvious, even to other EC entrepreneurs. None other than Monnet believed the opposite: "Everything takes longer than one expects—which is why one must never set time-limits for succeeding."[8] Similarly, the reputation of Monnet, Hallstein, and Delors as visionary political entrepreneurs is tarnished by the fact that each was associated with early success, then failure and disappointment—Monnet with the EDC and EC, Hallstein in the "empty chair" crisis, and Delors at Maastricht. Successful outcomes create a reputation for great entrepreneurship as much as the reverse, and even supranational bargaining theorists are led to wonder whether Commissioners have an "asymmetrical incentive" to overreach.[9]

The efficiency of ad hoc mediation reflects in part the fact that governments only rarely can disguise the intensity of their preferences and the value of alternatives to agreement. Negotiated agreements appear to be efficient, whether or not supranational actors intervened, because preferences were transparent. True, there were some cases in which *neither* domestic nor foreign leaders were sure about the nature of domestic constraints in a particular country. But only de Gaulle's France was a case where there appears to have been significant divergence between domestic and foreign perceptions. Given de Gaulle's extraordinary personality and the extremely centralized decision-making appa-

---

[7] Fen Osler Hampson, assisted by Michael Hart, *Multilateral Negotiations: Lessons from Arms Control, Trade and the Environment* (Baltimore, Md., 1995). More generally, Donald Chisholm argues that within "multiorganizational systems"—of which the EC is surely a prime interstate example—"where formal organizational arrangements are absent, insufficient or inappropriate for providing the requisite coordination, informal adaptations develop [which] may be quite stable and effective, more so perhaps than formal hierarchical arrangements. Furthermore, because informal organization permits the continued existence of formally autonomous organizations in the face of mutual interdependence, it can achieve other values, such as reliability, flexibility and representativeness, that would otherwise be precluded or substantially diminished under formal arrangements." See Chisholm, *Coordination without Hierarchy: Informal Structures in Multiorganizational Systems* (Berkeley, 1989), 17–18.

[8] Martin Holland, "Jean Monnet and the Federal Functionalist Approach to European Union," in Philomena Murray and Paul B. Rich, eds., *Visions of European Unity* (Boulder, Colo., 1994), 93.

[9] George Ross, *Jacques Delors and European Integration* (Oxford, 1995), 13–14; Ken Endo, "Political Leadership in the European Community: The Role of the Commission Presidency under Jacques Delors, 1985–1995," mimeo (St. Anthony's College, Oxford University, 1995).

ratus of the early Fifth Republic, we might think of this as an exception that proves the rule. Far from being viewed as neutral, Commission and Parliament officials were treated as interested parties. Other governments were preferred as mediators in part because they were seen as less biased (or, if biased, perhaps more reliably so).

Negotiations tended, therefore, to be Pareto-efficient, at least at the interstate level. Although many outcomes disappointed federalists, I can identify not even one single case in EC history in which the interstate bargaining outcome was, given the preferences across outcomes actually held by national governments, Pareto-suboptimal. (I measured efficiency both by examining *ex post* criticisms and by reconstructing possible agreements, given data about the preferences of governments.) Similarly, in no major cases did national preferences appear to converge toward an agreement for which no appropriate initiative or compromise existed. No gains appear to have been "left on the table."

Informational or ideational asymmetries being absent, it is unsurprising that, with a few minor exceptions, supranational actors generally failed to influence the distribution of gains. Where Commission proposals were unique and innovative—examples include Sicco Mansholt's proposals for agriculture and Walter Hallstein's proposals for institutional changes in the 1960s, Roy Jenkins's proposals for financial redistribution in connection with the EMS, and Delors's proposals at Maastricht for political control of monetary policy and a more federalist political union—they were politely ignored. Generally only redundant proposals enjoyed success. The Parliament's involvement in such negotiations, particularly on its own behalf, was uniformly unsuccessful except in very minor matters. The intermittent advantages it gained were the result of pressure from federalist governments.

Distributional outcomes mirrored the relative bargaining power of governments, understood as the pattern of issue-specific asymmetrical interdependence. Governments were consistently constrained by credible threats to veto, which reflected the domestic ratifiability of agreements. This was the primary concern particularly of less forthcoming governments, such as those of Britain and France in the 1950s; Britain and Germany in the 1970s and in the 1990s; even, to some extent, de Gaulle's France in the 1960s. Within these constraints, governments that perceived themselves as benefiting most (in domestic political terms) from any core agreement—as Germany benefited from industrial tariff reductions in the 1950s, France from agricultural liberalization in the 1960s, Britain from the SEA in the 1980s, and France from the EMS and EMU agreements—proved most willing to compromise in order to achieve it. Analysis was complicated slightly in the EMS and EMU cases by the "kinked" shape of the German win-set, but there is compelling evidence that participants perceived the German win-set as the binding constraint on bargaining.

Governments also employed explicit threats of exit and exclusion, which altered the negotiated outcome to the extent those threats were credible and costly. Britain's structural vulnerability to exclusion offers one consistent example. Harold Macmillan in the initial accession negotiations, James Callaghan in the EMS negotiations, Margaret Thatcher in the SEA negotiations, and John

Major in the Maastricht negotiations were all explicitly threatened with exclusion. All four prime ministers respond by seeking to block agreement among the others, often by linking the negotiations to security threats—withdrawal of troops from Europe, or an Anglo-French nuclear alliance. When this tactic failed, they compromised. The compromises they reached reflected, as intergovernmental theory predicts, the perceived relative costs and benefits of exclusion. In an area such as the Maastricht social protocol, the British government perceived advantages from nonparticipation and welcomed exclusion. In areas such as tariff and monetary policy, it perceived disadvantages in exclusion and sought to compromise.

Explicit tactical linkages ("package deals") were used sparingly, mostly to balance out benefits rather than to impose losses—just as intergovernmental theory predicts. Efforts to link issues involving significant domestic concerns either failed outright (e.g., French efforts to link the EMS to agriculture or German efforts to link EMU to political union) or, if initially accepted, tended to be renegotiated (e.g., French efforts to impose the CAP on Germany, which was possible only with high prices initially opposed by France). Linkages involving major losses for a major country appear to have been possible only within particular sectors of the economy (e.g., among industrialists) because major net losers were unorganized or unrepresented—as in the case of the costs for the CAP born by third-country producers, consumers, and taxpayers.

There exists one major, if only partial, exception to the dismal record of supranational entrepreneurs.[10] The White Paper drafted by Arthur Cockfield, working with Delors, in preparation for the SEA is the only case I found of a successful major supranational initiative that was not first proposed in a similar form by a member-state. In addition, between 1979 and 1985, Parliament and Commission officials encouraged the mobilization of multinational firms into a coherent political force; those firms became strong supporters of the SEA. Initiation and mobilization by supranational officials may well have increased the efficiency of the SEA agreement by opening up the possibility of realizing common interests in NTB liberalization, though they did not alter distributional outcomes. Delors's own account clearly recognizes member-state opposition to any other proposals; he shelved his preferred proposals for monetary and institutional reform and became a late convert to trade liberalization. Parliamentary demands for fundamental institutional reform were never taken seriously, but its demands for internal market reform were.

The bulk of the recent literature on EC negotiations focuses on the SEA alone and asks why the Commission and Parliament were so powerful. A comparative

---

[10] There are also some minor exceptions. Examples include the development of high-technology programs in the early 1980s, though these programs, due to their unique adherence to *juste retour* principles, did not move far beyond reconfiguring existing national funds, and the eleven country "opt-in" on social policy at Maastricht, which may have slightly increased the strength of social policy over what otherwise the Mediterranean countries and, perhaps in the future, Britain would have accepted. On these see Wayne Sandholtz, *High-Tech Europe: The Politics of International Cooperation* (Berkeley, 1992); Paul Pierson, "The Path to European Union: An Historical Institutionalist Account," *Comparative Political Studies* 29:2 (April 1996), 123–164.

perspective reverses the question: Why is the SEA the *only* major example in EC history in which this is the case? This formulation permits us to propose a more precise reason for exceptional entrepreneurial influence.[11] Recall that Commissioners, Parliamentarians, and judges must enjoy privileged access to information and ideas critical for efficient negotiation, which in turn permits them to act as informal initiators, mediators, or mobilizers. As we have seen, none of the conventional reasons cited in the literature on integration, negotiation analysis, international law, and international regimes explain why supranational officials may possess such privileged access. Commissioners, Parliamentarians, and judges were not particularly neutral and trustworthy mediators of distributive conflict, more legitimate representatives of the popular will, more creative politicians, or more expert technocrats. None of these commonly cited reasons explains the SEA exception.

There is, however, good reason to believe that supranational entrepreneurs may enjoy a comparative advantage in redressing weaknesses in *domestic* bargaining, where the number and size of actors, the transparency of their preferences, the risk each bears, and nature of property rights suggests that bargaining failures should be more likely. Theories of comparative public policy suggest three conditions under which such entrepreneurship is likely to be effective: where potentially powerful domestic interests remain unorganized and therefore "latent," where organized groups lack access to domestic officials willing and able to represent their interests, and where the aggregation of interests within domestic political systems (domestic bureaucracies, parties, or parliaments) fails to bring viable proposals to the attention of national decision-makers. A centralized, autonomous, and coherent supranational bureaucracy dedicated to the single purpose of promoting integration might be able to overcome such difficulties by virtue of its independence from special interests, its ability to coordinate disparate policy areas, and its continuous access to interest groups from more than one country.[12]

This account may explain the singular influence of Commission and Parliament in the SEA negotiations. Alone among major EC bargains, the SEA linked a large number of issues with no substantive or bureaucratic connection among them, each of which was relatively novel and appealed primarily to an unorganized transnational constituency. EC member governments had long negotiated

[11] It also casts some light on the underlying reasons why the results reported here conflict with nearly all previous work on supranational influence in the EC. Previous studies tend disproportionately to investigate those cases in which supranational entrepreneurs were active and the outcomes were positive, then simply examine strategies that supranational entrepreneurs used, assuming their efficacy. There are few studies of overt failure. For every examination of the failure of the series of Mansholt Plans for CAP reform, there are dozens on Delors and Cockfield's initiative in the SEA negotiations. Moreover, studies tend to be uncontrolled for the simultaneous activities of other actors, notably national governments. Hence they assume a causal relation when supranational officials proposed initiatives and compromises and agreement was reached. As we have seen, the redundancy, futility, and flexibility of supranational entrepreneurs means that this cannot be assumed. For a more detailed argument based on these cases, see Andrew Moravcsik, "Informal Influence: European Integration and Political Entrepreneurship," *Weatherhead Center for International Affairs Working Paper* (Harvard University, 1998).

[12] See also Robert O. Keohane, *After Hegemony: Cooperation and Discord in the World Political Economy* (Princeton, 1984); Oliver E. Williamson, *The Economic Institutions of Capitalism* (New York, 1985).

tariff removal, agricultural policy, and exchange-rate stabilization, and each topic was firmly in the hands of one or a few lead ministries, but no single ministry was competent to judge financial and transport service liberalization, phylo-sanitary regulations, industrial standardization, the removal of customs controls, and environmental regulation—to name only the major areas covered by the SEA. Such a package deal was beyond the scope of any national bureaucracy. Moreover, the major social group that might have advocated liberalization, multinational business, was neither nationally nor internationally organized until Commission officials and parliamentarians encouraged its organization around common programs for research, high technology, and market liberalization. This "two-level" explanation views supranational entrepreneurs as important by virtue of their superior ability to influence the domestic level as "managers" of domestic and transnational "social networks," rather than by virtue of any unique ability to intervene at the international level as policy initiators and mediators. The suggestion that the true impediments to efficient interstate bargaining are domestic rather than international—and, therefore, that the decisive actions of supranational entrepreneurs involve *domestic* intervention—deserves further examination.

On balance, however, intergovernmental bargaining theory is decisively confirmed. Supranational entrepreneurs have only a rare and secondary impact on the efficiency of negotiations. The fact that we find some modest support for the supranational bargaining hypotheses is consistent with the view that they are correct in theory but of marginal importance in practice. Hence the EC has not banished power politics from Western Europe. Although the interests of member governments are too closely intertwined to render the use of military force or punitive sanctions cost-effective, asymmetrical patterns of interdependence remain the fundamental basis of international influence.

Institutional Delegation: The Centrality of Credibility

Why have European governments repeatedly chosen to pool and delegate sovereignty in common institutions? This book has tested three theories that seek to explain patterns of institutional choice. Those who stress federalist ideology hypothesize that federalist countries will support delegation and pooling, particularly on highly symbolic issues, and that supranational officials will be seen as federalist visionaries. Domestic cleavages and discourse follow the same pattern, with particular attention paid to democratic and ideological legitimacy. It is no surprise that this was the view held for decades in the European Parliament by leading federalists such as Altiero Spinelli. A second, technocratic explanation hypothesizes that delegation will take place where issues are complex but apolitical, expert information is of decisive importance, and centralized officials have a comparative advantage in its provision. We expect modest cross-national effects but a strong domestic role for experts.

Those who stress credible commitments hypothesize that supranational institutions resolve incomplete contracting problems. States opt for pooling and delegation when they seek to commit other governments—perhaps also their own future governments—to particular future policies, the details of which are uncertain. Where future policies are predictable, rules are employed instead. Preferences concerning institutions therefore vary across both countries and issues, following the substantive position of the government on particular issues. Those governments that favor deeper policy coordination at a median European level are most likely to support delegation; positive and, even more strongly, negative preference outliers will be more skeptical. Delegation is likely to be kept within limits, such as matters of enforcement or the implementation of common goals; even pooling is unlikely to be extended to entirely open-ended mandates, such as the creation of new policies.

Hypotheses were evaluated concerning three types of observable implications: cross-national and cross-issue variation in support, domestic cleavages and discourse, and the institutional form of the delegation. (These are summarized in Table 1.4.) All five case studies reveal strong support for an explanation resting on the need to bolster the credibility of interstate commitments, with a secondary yet significant role—one limited to situations in which the substantive risks and substantive consequences of decisions are modest—for ideology. The impact of technocratic imperatives for delegation and pooling seems, by contrast, to have been minimal.

National positions in Britain, France, and Germany concerning institutional delegation varied across both countries and issues, with national positions tracking substantive goals—as predicted by the credible commitments view. They did not vary primarily by country, as the ideological view predicts, or solely by issue, as the technocratic view predicts. Governments often opted, when it served their interests, for supranational institutions, regardless of ideology. Those governments that strongly supported a likely common policy—those, in other words, close to the European median position—tended to favor majority voting and delegation. Governments with outlying views, particularly recalcitrant ones, tended to be more cautious.

This pattern recurs. In the Treaty of Rome negotiations, France sought strong institutions in atomic energy and agriculture yet opposed binding commitments and procedures for trade liberalization. Germany took the opposite position, seeking to bind France with strict rules and decision-making procedures in industrial trade yet opposing them in agriculture and atomic energy. Indeed, Germany protected its veto on agriculture by demanding a very restrictive institutional arrangement—the Special Committee on Agriculture—and extending unanimity voting. During the first two decades of the EC, de Gaulle and Pompidou strongly opposed supranationalism in principle yet nonetheless advocated delegation and pooling in agricultural policy. Germany, federalist in principle, supported delegation and pooling in areas such as EC policies toward the GATT and competition (antitrust) matters but opposed French institutional proposals in agriculture, seeking to delay introduction of majority voting and then common prices by demanding introduction of monetary compensation accounts (MCAs). Similarly, when France sought to establish more binding supranational monetary institutions, Germany consistently resisted them, demanding strict enforcement of prior economic convergence. Similar concerns, albeit with both parties more willing to compromise, underlay the Maastricht negotiations over EMU. In the SEA negotiations, skeptics tended to be those governments, such as the Thatcher government in Britain, that feared expansion of regulation to areas favored by a majority of other governments. Equally revealing, if less widely acknowledged, is the point that majority voting was also explicitly limited by the caution of governments, such as those of Germany and Denmark, that sought to protect extensive systems of regulation. Hence Germany entered the negotiations insisting on a long list of specific exceptions to QMV and at the last minute demanded a special clause (Article 100A4) permitting countries with particularly high regulatory standards to opt out of certain decisions.

Technocratic motivations, by contrast, explain little. No correlation emerges between the technical or legal complexity of an issue and the level of cooperation. External tariff liberalization within the GATT, which was delegated to some extent, was not clearly more complex than internal tariff removal, which was governed entirely by rules. Competition policy concerning mergers, in which the Commission enjoyed considerable autonomy, was not inherently more complex than competition policy in which it did not, such as policing industrial subsidies. Regional subsidies and agricultural policy, with moderately high levels of delegation, were not clearly more complex than monetary policy under the EMS, with modest delegation and pooling. Monetary policy itself was unstable, with no delegation and minimal pooling in the 1980s and a commitment to extremely high monetary delegation in the 1990s. This view offers little explanation for the elimination of internal tariffs, which was handled almost entirely with explicit rules. The use of QMV was not limited to circumstances in which distributive consequences were insignificant (consistent with the technocratic and perhaps also ideological theories). To the contrary, agriculture, foreign trade, and, above all, monetary policy involve massive redistributive consequences.

Domestic cleavages and discourse further underscore the importance of credible commitments. Domestic debates were—except in the case of highly symbolic institutions with uncertain impact on policy, such as the European Parliament—dominated by instrumental considerations. This dominance of instrumental concerns is particularly clear in determining support for pooling sovereignty through QMV, due to the predictability of the outcomes. From the French government's careful calculation of safeguards and veto rights in the Treaty of Rome to the Thatcher government's careful calculation of the likely voting outcomes of all 279 proposals in the single market White Paper, governments have carefully calculated the consequences of delegation and pooling for their substantive interests. Majority voting and delegation of unique agenda power to the Commission were deliberately designed to increase the efficiency of decision-making and to reduce the potential for log-rolling. This institutional innovation responded to a demand by smaller countries, which sought to overcome the tendency of larger governments to strike separate bargains, though it was also supported by some in Germany and even France, who felt it would render decision-making more efficient. The Commission's right of proposal was limited, though never frontally attacked, by the French government. The primary justification for the SEA, which extended QMV and the "new approach," was that it would permit more efficient decision-making by allowing governments to outvote their opponents. To be sure, the Thatcher government was reluctant, in part for ideological reasons, to accept majority voting under Article 100. Yet Britain did in the end concede in order to achieve its economic objectives, and British policy reflected a realistic concern about the expansion of legislative activity to include regulations supported by most EC member governments but opposed by the neoliberal Thatcher government.

The importance of credible commitments was also reflected in the form that delegation and pooling have taken. Supranational actors were never viewed entirely as trusted, neutral experts; their powers have been carefully controlled. The creation of the Special Committee on Agriculture, the expansion of the system of oversight committees ("comitology"), the establishment of the EMS outside the normal EC institutions, the creation of the European Council, and the Luxembourg Compromise were all explicitly designed to *narrow* rather than broaden the scope for autonomous action by supranational actors. Though many wrongly blame the maintenance of de facto unanimity voting in the EC on the French alone, we find strong evidence that Germany and the Benelux countries quietly opposed the use of QMV, particularly in agriculture, until the 1980s. No serious effort was made to expand QMV for almost three decades.

Delegation and pooling appear to have been employed primarily to implement or enforce prior agreements by precommitting governments to greater compromise and thus more efficient decision-making. QMV tended to be used, as predicted, for smaller, nested decisions within broadly accepted constraints. Major constitutive decisions, by contrast, including those within the Treaty establishing the CAP and commercial policy, remained subject to unanimity. Delegation to the Commission of a unique power to propose legislation to the Council of Ministers, which member governments could revise only by unanimity, similarly "locked in" a particular pattern of future decision-making. This power permits the Commission to select among those proposals preferred to the status quo by all governments or, in the case of majority voting, a qualified majority of governments. The arrangement was deliberately constructed with the intention of rendering decision-making more efficient.

Again, we should not exclude ideological considerations entirely. Although the credible commitments view best explains the delegation and pooling of *specific* and *precise* powers, it leaves unexplained patterns of support for more *general* institutional commitments. The quasi-constitutional form of the EC—with Council, Parliament, Court, and Commission—was borrowed from the ECSC, which in turn reflected the views of many European federalists. The Anglo-French tradition of general opposition to increased supranational delegation and pooling, as well as the German support for them, appears to reflect public and parliamentary ideology. To be sure, such ideological concerns were often trumped by economic interest—as in Britain's bids for membership—but some residual support remained. De Gaulle's opposition to Commission power, for example, though limited by his overriding concern with agriculture and the electoral constraints imposed by farmers, clearly reflected his personal ideology. The concurrent unwillingness and occasional inability of Adenauer's successors, Ludwig Erhard and Gerhard Schröder, to voice publicly or act on their skepticism about autonomous supranational institutions, is difficult to explain in purely instrumental terms.

In the 1980s and 1990s patterns of support for general institutional provisions continued to reflect federalist ideology. This claim is clearest in support for the European Parliament, an institution supported by Germany and viewed with considerable skepticism in Britain and France, which favored the centralization of powers in the Council. To be sure, German support for Parliamentary co-decision is not inconsistent with its strong interest in the sort of environmental and social regulations favored by the Parliament, and it is important to remember that Parliamentary powers are generally increased at the expense more of the Commission than of the member-states. Still, domestic rhetoric and cleavages suggest the existence of strong ideological motivations. Such concerns were not absent from Thatcher's opposition to majority voting in the SEA and participation in the EMS and EMU.

European Integration and the Historical Institutionalist Challenge

The explanation of European integration I have presented is controversial not simply because some continue to assert the importance of geopolitical, ideological, technocratic, or supranational determinants of state behavior. In recent years the neofunctionalist search for a theory of integration as a self-reinforcing process of spillover has been revived. It is now termed "historical institutionalism" (HI). The research on which this book rests was not designed to test HI claims rigorously, but the evidence tends to disconfirm them.

The HI perspective develops the "path-dependent" view that shifting national preferences are an unintended consequence of prior integration. Preferences and power are endogenous to integration rather than exogenous structures. Economic integration and institutional development become self-reinforcing through continuous feedback, generally termed "spillover," which can proceed in two ways.[13] Previous decisions can induce changes in national preferences, which promote further integration. This "social spillover" argument is generally applied to economic adjustment, but some also stress ideological or ideational changes. Alternatively, international institutions may alter the terms under which governments negotiate new bargains—a process I shall term "political spillover."

Most advocates of HI, like their neofunctionalist predecessors, do not explicitly claim that it displaces a structural rationalist view entirely. Most concede that the most fundamental task is to explain individual decisions, even if the inputs are the result of previous decisions. Without a theory of individual decisions, we would not know what sort of feedback mattered. Yet many HI theorists nonetheless maintain that feedback and spillover effects are so massive as to swamp any consistent effort to develop consistent theories of national preferences or strategies.[14] The force of this argument lies in the claim that the consequences

[13] Stephen George, *Politics and Policy in the European Community* (Oxford, 1985).
[14] Two leading theorists make this explicit. Pierson, "Path," specifies conditions under which we should expect to observe such effects. See also Wayne Sandholtz, "Choosing Union: Monetary Politics and Maastricht," *International Organization* 47:1 (Winter 1993), 1–40.

of these decisions are often unforeseen, unintended, or undesired. As Perry Anderson puts it in a critique of recent EC scholarship, "If all historical undertakings are subject to the fatality of unintended consequences, the more deliberate they are the more pronounced the gap may become. The 'construction of Europe' . . . was bound to lead to . . . a persistent pattern of consequences that disconcerted and foiled the intentions of its architects."[15] In other words, if governments are constantly forced to react to unintended consequences of previous decisions, HI theorists ask, what sense does it make to speak, as I have done in this book, of discrete "choices for Europe"?

What light do the findings in this book shine on HI claims? Let us begin with social spillover. Structural economic trends underlying national preferences— trade liberalization, agricultural subsidization, capital mobility, regulatory harmonization, macroeconomic convergence—do *not* appear to have been induced primarily by prior decisions. These trends emerged nearly a decade *before* the EC. The swiftest period of export expansion in postwar Europe was the 1950s and early 1960s, before the EC could have had a decisive impact. British exports, for example, had completed the bulk of their shift from the Commonwealth to the Continent, with decisive consequences for Britain's EC policy, well before Britain joined the EC. Consistent with this finding are existing econometric models of trade flows, which suggest that only a modest percentage of the postwar increase in European trade can be attributed to policy changes; nearly all the increase, at least until the 1980s, reflects structural factors such as geographical proximity and per capita income. (The effect on agricultural trade is, as would be expected, much higher.)[16] The same can be said of decisive economic trends such as rising capital mobility, disinflation, financial liberalization, and disenchantment with industrial policy. Throughout the period all West European countries were greatly influenced by these structural trends, whether or not they were EC members.[17]

This is not to say that prior economic integration has had no impact on subsequent national preferences. It is clearly true that with rapid structural adjustment and rationalization, more competitive producers adapted to trade liberalization by expanding exports and investment whereas less competitive producers were eliminated or consolidated. On balance this dynamic created new constituencies for further liberalization and undermined its opponents. There is little doubt that structural adjustment and other economic feedback effects helped to "lock in" integration in Europe—a phenomenon that deserves more attention in studies of international regimes more generally. Sometimes feedback was ideological, as when the apparent success of Adenauer's initially controversial strategy of Franco-German cooperation rendered impossible a policy reversal perhaps desired by his successor, Ludwig Erhard. On this point there is agreement between HI theory and the interpretation advanced in this book.

---

[15] Perry Anderson, "Under the Sign of the Interim," *London Review of Books*, 4 January 1996, 17.

[16] Jeffrey A. Frankel, *Regional Trading Blocks in the World Economic System* (Washington, D.C., 1997), 83–86.

[17] David Andrews and Thomas D. Willett, "Financial Interdependence and the State: International Monetary Relations at Century's End," *International Organization* 51:3 (Summer 1997), 479–511.

Yet I suggest that these consequences were neither unforeseen nor unin-tended, as HI theory claims. To the contrary, it was the *deliberate triumphs* of European integration, not its *unintended side-effects*, that appear to have in-creased support for further integration. This is the key point of divergence between HI theory and the tripartite "liberal intergovernmentalist" interpreta-tion advanced here. For most governments, inducing economic moderniza-tion—even with unpleasant side-effects—was the major purpose of European integration.

The historical record reveals that the consequences of major decisions were in fact foreseen and desired by national governments to a much greater extent than most analysts have been aware. In some cases, among them the EMS and EMU, governments employed the EC explicitly as a scapegoat. Even where this was not the case, my analysis reveals, nearly all governments were generally well aware of the likely short- and long-term policy consequences of integration, good and bad. Sometimes, as with the SEA, they underestimated the success of a policy, but they almost never misperceived the direction of future change. Major national governments foresaw and accepted—indeed, often sought to in-duce—outcomes such as the rationalization of European industry in response to the customs union, the emergence of large CAP surpluses, the asymmetrical operation of the EMS, the reduction in governmental discretion after reducing nontariff barriers, and the possibility that majority voting on NTBs would per-mit governments to be outvoted on a range of important issues.

HI theorists overlook the foresight of governments because their analyses are rarely based on a detailed, primary-source analysis of national preference formation. Instead, they make do with public justifications by governments or with secondary sources.[18] Yet since governments often have an incentive to deny or simply ignore their responsibility for certain outcomes—CAP surpluses, monetary discipline, and downward pressure on social spending, for example—accounts based on secondary sources and their public justifications tend to generate inadequate, even misleading, support for claims about "unintended" consequences.

Some HI theorists focus instead on "political spillover." They argue that the feedback from prior policies to current ones is mediated not by economic adap-tation but by the deepening of supranational institutions. Some stress the entre-preneurial activities of supranational actors. It is often argued that European in-stitutions, such as majority voting or the powers of implementation in the hands of the Commission, have imposed unwanted policies on certain governments—an argument often advanced in studies of British policy. Others point to the ex-istence of "joint decision traps," where governments are locked into undesirable policies by the need to muster unanimous support for any new legislation or treaty amendment. This explanation is commonly cited for CAP surpluses or the absence of a fully developed EC social dimension.[19]

---

[18] For a partial exception, see Paul Pierson and Stephan Leibfried, eds., *European Social Policy* (Washington, D.C., 1995).

[19] Fritz Scharpf, "The Joint-Decision Trap: Lessons from German Federalism and European Inte-gration," *Public Administration* 66 (Autumn 1988), 239–278; Fritz Scharpf, "Politische Optionen in

Three findings of this book call this institutional variant of HI into question, though a definitive conclusion must await more focused research. We have seen that supranational entrepreneurs wielded relatively little influence, direct or indirect, on interstate negotiations. Neither their long-term efforts to structure the agenda, nor their efforts to mediate among governments, nor even their efforts at social mobilization had a consistent impact on negotiated agreements—the SEA being a significant but at most only a partial exception. In broader historical perspective, cases often cited by HI theorists as examples of feedback tend to be marginal and often transient deviations from historical trends, such as, for example, British policy with regard to the Maastricht social charter. If an HI argument is to be viable, it must rest on feedback loops that run through everyday decision-making.

Yet everyday decision-making highlights a second empirical finding that undermines HI claims. The study of major bargains reveals that the construction of an international regime in which legislation is voted over the opposition of minorities and rules are enforced against the obstruction of the recalcitrant—in short, the transfer of sovereignty and autonomy to supranational institutions—was not an unintended consequence of major EC decisions; *it was their primary purpose.* Most institutional constraints that HI theorists treat as unintended or unforeseen consequences of prior integration—for example, qualified majority voting and a certain autonomy for the Commission and Parliament—were in fact constructed deliberately to enhance the credibility of commitments. In the world assumed in this book, where governments with varied preferences negotiate and construct institutions in order to commit one another to linked sets of bargains, the inability of each state always to achieve its ideal outcome on every issue is hardly surprising. The working out of such bargains has been the central activity of the EC; had they been easy to reach without uncomfortable adjustment by any member-state, little bargaining and no institutions would have been necessary.

Governments were hardly unaware that they were assuming risks of being outvoted or overruled; to the contrary, we have seen that they repeatedly calculated the consequences in great (and, for the most part, accurate) detail. This is true even for policy outcomes—such as high agricultural surpluses—often mentioned as unintended consequences. As we saw in chapters 2 through 4, European governments were quite aware of the likely consequences of constructing the CAP as they did. If they failed to reverse policy, it was not because unanimous voting arrangements prevented them from doing so. (Never did a simple majority favor major CAP reform, and reductions in prices imposed by majority vote would have likely triggered unilateral noncompliance by Germany through means such as MCAs, as occurred early in the 1960s.) [20] Such provisions

---

vollendeten Binnenmarkt," in Markus Jachtenfuchs and Beate Kohler-Koch, eds., *Europäische Integration* (Opladen, 1996), 109–140; Pierson, "Path." The studies on Britain are too numerous to cite. For an overview of Commission activities, see Laura Cram, *Policy-Making in the EU: Conceptual Lenses and the Integration Process* (London, 1997).

[20] For a critique of Fritz Scharpf's claims about CAP, see Elmar Rieger, "Agrarpolitik: Integration durch Gemeinschaftspolitik?" in Jachtenfuchs and Kohler-Koch, eds., *Europäische*, 401–428. It is fair to note that Scharpf himself calls into question whether the CAP would have been different with re-

did hit certain governments—those, predictably, with extreme preferences—particularly hard. No surprise, therefore, that we encounter many case studies of Thatcher's Britain.[21] In sum, the existence of states dissatisfied by particular aspects of a political arrangement, far from disconfirming the ("liberal intergovernmentalist") theoretical account presented in this book, is a necessary implication of it—as it is of any regime-theoretical treatment of international cooperation.[22]

One last finding casts overall doubt on the HI interpretation of European integration. HI claims rest, in the final analysis, on the assumption that national preferences and interests are unstable and unpredictable. Only where this assumption holds is a substantive policy commitment or institutional arrangement accepted by a particular government at a particular point in time likely to be perceived by successor governments as an unpleasant and unexpected constraint. In short, the instability of preferences leads short-term and long-term national interests to diverge.

If we take all five major EC decisions as a whole, however, it is *the stability and continuity of preferences, not their instability, that stands out.* Although there has been a slow, linear deepening of support for various types of economic integration—mostly as a result of exogenous trends of which governments have been aware, just as the explanation of integration advanced in this book predicts—the relative positions of major governments on core issues such as CAP reform, tariff liberalization, GATT negotiations, monetary integration, foreign and defense policy, and the powers of the Council and Parliament have hardly changed in forty years. Germany has consistently sought high farm prices, low agricultural export subsidies, a liberal GATT policy, monetary cooperation on German "economist" terms, a common European foreign and defense policy consistent with NATO, and stronger powers for the Parliament. France has sought moderate farm prices, high export subsidies, a more protectionist GATT policy, monetary integration on "monetarist" terms, a more independent common foreign and defense policy, and stronger powers for the Council. Britain has sought a minimal CAP, a liberal GATT policy, minimal monetary cooperation, a modest foreign and defense policy, and weak supranational institutions. Time and time again, observers are struck by these continuities. Of the Maastricht negotiations, for example, one analyst observes: "[Hans] Tietmeyer and [Helmut] Schlesinger were also following, with remarkable consistency, the line the Bundesbank had taken thirty years previously when EMU and a European central bank had first been mooted."[23] With preferences so stable, HI theory itself predicts that we should rarely see EC bargains become unacceptable one or two decades later.

---

formed EC institutions. If there was a salient unforeseen consequence in the CAP, it was the *success* of the policy in stimulating European agricultural trade, which led to the formation of a set of vested interests in the system. This aspect of the customs union appears to have had a much greater impact on economic behavior than on industrial trade liberalization. Frankel, *Regional*, 85.

[21] Similarly, Germany has been an outlier in agricultural policy and a number of regulatory issues.

[22] Such analysts wrongly assume that Liberal Intergovernmentalist theory treats maximum discretion—protecting sovereignty—as the preeminent state preference. This is clearly incorrect. LI theory assumes that states seek the substantive goals of major domestic interests. Cf. Pierson, "Path."

[23] David Marsh, *The Bundesbank: The Bank That Rules Europe* (London, 1992), 212.

On balance, the empirical findings in this book suggest that HI theorists are correct to note that integration has politically significant consequences, notably shifts in the preferences and institutional environment in which future decisions are made, but that only in exceptional cases are these consequences unintended or undesired. Only a few of the conditions prescribed in HI theory for the emergence of a path-dependent process of unintended consequences are generally fulfilled. More appropriate to actual state behavior in the EC is a weaker version of HI—one that stresses intended rather than unintended "lock in" effects as a secondary force behind regional integration. This version should be viewed not as an alternative to the structural, rationalist explanation of integration advanced in this book but as an extension of it. Insofar as future shifts in preferences were foreseen, intended, even desired, HI provides an account of the consequences of integration consistent with the (more static) treatment of individual decisions presented here. Rather than contrast two ideal types of historical and structural analysis, we might profitably direct more attention toward the possibilities for synthesis.[24]

Generalizing the European Experience

Throughout this book I have focused on the benefits of applying general theories of comparative and international political economy to European integration. In closing, I reverse the focus and examine implications of the findings for international politics. It is striking that mainstream theories of international political economy have all but ignored the most successful of postwar international regimes. A first step toward generalization is to reconsider the EC in the context of attempts at regional integration elsewhere in the world; a second is to examine the implications for general theories of international cooperation and conflict.

Regional Integration: The European and Universal Process

From the European Free Trade Association to economic cooperation on distant continents, the past half-century has witnessed dozens of regional schemes for economic integration. In only a few areas, among them the Middle East and parts of Asia, are such efforts conspicuous by their absence. A comprehensive comparative study of all such efforts would take us well beyond the scope of this book, but a preliminary comparison between East Asia, North America, and Europe is possible. The results confirm the primary of economic incentives for which I have argued in this book.

Let us begin with the political economy theory introduced in chapter 1. Two factors closely associated with pressures for trade liberalization are export dependence and levels of intra-industry trade. If the economic theory is correct, we should see much higher levels in Europe than in North America or East Asia.

---

[24] For a more general argument relating international regime stability to societal "lock-in" effects, see Andrew Moravcsik, "Taking Preferences Seriously: A Liberal Theory of International Politics," *International Organization* 51:4 (Autumn 1997), 537.

Table 7.1. Regional trade dependence of Germany, United States, and Japan as a proportion of GNP, 1958 and 1990

	Intra-regional Trade/GNP (1960)	Intra-regional Trade/GNP (1990)	Intra-Industry Trade/ Regional Trade (1980s)
Germany (vis-à-vis EC6 then EC12)	6%	21%	66%
United States (vis-à-vis Canada & Mexico)	1%	2%	60%
Japan (vis-à-vis Northeast Asia, ASEAN & India)	2%	3%	25%

SOURCES: IMF, *Direction of Trade,* various reports; Marc Busch and Helen Milner, "The Future of the International Trading System," in Richard Stubbs and Geoffrey Underhill, eds., *Political Economy and the Changing Global Order* (New York, 1994), 272.

This is precisely what we find. Of countries in these three regions, EC members are by far the most export-dependent (as a percentage of GNP), as well as the most dependent on intraregional as compared to intercontinental trade. This relationship was visible early in the postwar period, well before regional trade liberalization could have had a decisive impact, and it has grown stronger over time.

Consider Germany, the United States, and Japan as examples. In 1960 Germany was between three and six times more dependent on its EC partners than the United States and Japan were on their regional partners; thirty years later the differential had grown—with the expansion of the EC as well as rising intra-industry trade—to a ratio of between seven and ten. The qualitative nature of trade within the three blocks also differs. Intra-industry trade (trade between similar sectors of the economy) is, we saw in chapter 1, particularly conducive to trade liberalization, because it tends to reduce the number of firms and sectors that find themselves net losers. Marc Busch and Helen Milner have observed that such firms tend also to be international traders and multinational investors with a strong vested interest in free trade, which supports their existing market advantages and furthers the realization of optimal economies of scale. The German level of intra-industry trade, though lower than the level in neighbors such as France, is nonetheless somewhat higher than that of the United States and several times higher than that of Japan.[25]

Bringing together these simple indicators—summarized in Table 7.1—the political economy theory predicts very strong pressures for trade liberalization in Europe, more moderate pressures in North America, and very little pressure in East Asia. This is indeed what we observe. By contrast, geopolitical theories have difficulty explaining this outcome. The United States and Canada are allies; Mexico is a friendly state. Japan, Northeast Asia, ASEAN, and India face a common Chinese threat. Japan, like Germany, was defeated in World War II, has a strong alliance relationship with the United States, and has consistently faced

[25] Marc Busch and Helen Milner, "The Future of the International Trading System: International Firms, Regionalism, and Domestic Politics," in Richard Stubbs and Geoffrey Underhill, eds., *Political Economy and the Changing Global Order* (New York, 1994), 269–272.

pressures to reassure neighboring governments. At best a geopolitical argument would be an ad hoc explanation after the fact.

These data are more suggestive than conclusive, but they do suggest that the primacy of political economy observed in postwar Europe is not just a contingent fact about Europe but a generalization about postwar industrial nations.[26] These data also cast some doubt on the claim, advanced by historians and political scientists alike, that regional integration was the result of a peculiarly European development of the social welfare state. On this basis, Alan Milward calls for development of a "European" theory of integration—as opposed to an "American" theory—because European integration was "something made in Europe springing from the evolution of the European nation-state."[27] Yet if the domestic developments that gave rise to European economic integration were found uniquely in postwar Europe, it is not because the European continent was subject to unique social processes but because the *intensity* of common influences—in this case, underlying trade flows—was higher. Surely, then, the comparative political economy of regionalism deserves more intensive study, beginning with the assumption that Europe and other regions face similar challenges and opportunities.

European Integration and Theories of International Cooperation

If the EC can be compared to other regional integration schemes, why should it not have potentially important implications for general theories of international cooperation?

Some of the general theoretical implications follow from the more specific findings reported above and are directed at specific debates. The findings strongly support, for example, endogenous tariff theories of international trade policy. The analysis of national preferences concerning the EMS and EMU points to the importance of relative inflation rates in shaping exchange-rate policy, suggesting a revision of interest-group theories of international monetary coordination.[28] By uncovering the general assumptions that underlie claims concerning the conditions under which political entrepreneurship by international officials is likely to be successful, this analysis moves beyond the anecdotal studies that currently dominate the literatures on international regimes, international negotiations, international law, and European integration.[29] The revisionist interpretation of Charles de Gaulle's European policy advanced here suggests that democratic politics imposes strict limits on the construction of "visionary" foreign policy, when such policies touch the interests of powerful groups, such as

---

[26] Although we can reject objective geopolitical circumstances as the source of preferences, we cannot entirely dismiss the role of ideas. Yet until ideas are clearly measured and more precisely theorized, claims for the importance of ideology and ideas cannot be more than speculative.

[27] Alan S. Milward, Francis M. B. Lynch, Ruggiero Ranieri, Frederico Romero, and Vibeke Sfrensen, *The Frontier of National Sovereignty: History and Theory, 1945–1992* (London, 1993), 4–5, 198.

[28] This avoids the need to call the entire political economy approach into question. Cf. Kathleen McNamara, *The Currency of Ideas* (Ithaca, 1998); Alberto Giovannini, "Economic and Monetary Union: What Happened? Exploring the Political Dimension of Optimum Currency Areas," in Centre for Economic Policy Research, *The Monetary Future of Europe* (London, 1993).

[29] For a more extensive argument and a literature review, see Moravcsik, "Informal Influence."

farmers, foreign policy becomes subject to electoral and interest group constraints. It becomes "low politics" regardless of whether concerns about national identity are at stake.[30] The analysis of the conditions under which European governments chose to transfer sovereignty to particular institutional forms suggests a link between the evolution of the EC and the emerging literature on the design of international regimes.[31]

At a broader level, the findings in this book tend to support Liberal theories of international relations against existing Realist alternatives. The central claim of Liberal international relations theory is that the pattern of underlying national preferences, not the distribution of power resources or institutionalized information, is the most fundamental determinant of state behavior in world politics.[32] Liberal theory focuses on state-society relations; specific variants stress variation in economic interdependence, domestic regime type, and national identities. Theories that stress variations in national preferences are, Liberals argue, more powerful empirically, more fundamental analytically, and often more parsimonious conceptually than are theories that stress variation in relative capabilities or participation in international institutions. Variation in state preferences is more fundamental, as we saw in chapter 1, not simply because it shapes the Pareto-frontier of potential agreements over which states engage in Realist bargaining but also because it helps determine the outcomes of that bargaining. In the Liberal view, asymmetrical interdependence—the relative intensity of preferences—offers a distinctive understanding of power in world politics, one even more fundamental than military capabilities. Though universally applicable, asymmetrical interdependence is particularly likely to explain outcomes among democratic states, where the use of military force is an unlikely eventuality—Robert Keohane and Joseph Nye's world of "complex interdependence."[33]

The consistent finding in EC history that economic interests and even ideology take precedence over objective geopolitical threats casts doubt on specific variants of Realism, including theories that stress "security externalities" and "relative gains-seeking." Both assume a hierarchy of national preferences with security concerns at the top and the expectation that military conflict is likely. Both argue that governments pursue economic cooperation when it supports their military alliances or undermines their security through dependence.[34] In the EC, we saw, there is little evidence of a stable Realist issue hierarchy. National

[30] See Moravcsik, "Prudence."

[31] The traditional categories used to categorize regimes (strength, form, scope) are only a starting point, as is the distinction between delegation and pooling, and unanimity voting employed here. Cf. Stephan Haggard and Beth Simmons, "Theories of International Regimes," *International Organization* 41:3 (Summer 1987), 491–517.

[32] Moravcsik, "Taking." See also Michael W. Doyle, "Kant, Liberal Legacies, and Foreign Affairs," *Philosophy and Public Affairs* 12:3–4 (Summer–Fall 1983), 205–235; 325–353.

[33] Robert O. Keohane and Joseph S. Nye, *Power and Interdependence: World Politics in Transition*, 2d ed. (Boston, 1989).

[34] Theories of "security externalities" have been applied primarily to postwar U.S. international economic arrangements. It is argued that security externalities matter more in a bipolar context. If we think of Europe in bipolar terms, due to the overriding threat from the USSR, the argument clearly holds. Whether this particular theory should be applied to concern over Germany is less clear. Cf. Joanne Gowa, *Allies, Adversaries and International Trade* (Princeton, 1994).

preferences tend instead to vary predictably across issues and countries in accordance with issue-specific, largely economic concerns. Balancing against the USSR was consistently among the weakest of the various motivations; checking German power was hardly more significant. The only salient examples of an explicit "relative gains" security concern were British arguments *against* EC membership under the Macmillan and Thatcher governments. In neither case was the argument decisive; policy-makers soon reversed course.

In addition to challenging Realist arguments about relative-gains seeking and security externalities, the EC challenges Realist theories of hegemonic stability. It is a clear challenge to those who would generalize from the postwar U.S. case to the conclusion that the existence of a single preeminent state is a necessary though not sufficient condition for the formation of international regimes. Such theories are so obviously misplaced in the EC context that they receive little serious consideration here or elsewhere. When compared to the postwar United States and Japan in the Far East, Germany in Europe is small *vis-à-vis* its neighbors. As a relatively influential state with moderately pro-European preferences and a large domestic market, Germany made concessions, ideologically motivated in part, that contributed to European integration, yet there is little evidence that Germany's size or concessions were decisive.[35] It might plausibly be argued that Germany, as the swing state between Britain and France, played a critical role; its decisions were particularly decisive for the future of Europe, yet this has little to do with hegemonic power. Perhaps the failure of contemporary international relations scholarship to take the EC seriously has biased the contemporary mix of leading theories in favor of factors consistent with the rise and stagnation of the U.S.-led Bretton Woods system—preeminent among them hegemonic stability.[36]

Finally, the historical record suggests that bargaining outcomes within the EC—or at least among three large states—consistently reflect issue-specific patterns of asymmetrical interdependence. This finding implies that studies of bargaining over the formation of international regimes might do well to set aside the "relative capability" models traditionally employed by Realists, as well as the excessive focus of hegemonic stability theory on the role of a single actor, in favor of the more general Nash bargaining model customarily employed by negotiation analysts. Such a model of bargaining along the Pareto-frontier, Stephen Krasner has argued, parsimoniously captures both the positive-sum and the zero-sum elements of bargaining in a single model, thus transcending the much criticized distinction between absolute and relative gains.[37] As David Baldwin has long argued, such a model would be more consistent than the capability-based view with basic social-scientific theories of power.[38]

[35] Busch and Milner, "Future," 263–265; McNamara, *Currency*, chap. 2; Dorothée Heisenberg, *The Mark of the Bundesbank: Germany's Role in European Monetary Cooperation* (Boulder, Colo., forthcoming); Andrei Markovits and Simon Reich, *The German Predicament: Memory and Power in the New Europe* (Ithaca, 1997).

[36] Robert Gilpin, *War and Change in International Politics* (New York, 1981).

[37] Stephen D. Krasner, "Global Communications and National Power: Life on the Pareto Frontier," *World Politics* 43:3 (April 1991), 336–366; Moravcsik, "Taking," 538–539, 543–544.

[38] David Baldwin, *Paradoxes of Power* (New York, 1989).

The primacy of national preferences over capabilities is most clearly reflected in the tripartite rationalist framework that structures each of the case studies. The five case studies confirm the appropriateness and the utility of the distinctions among preference formation, bargaining, and institutional choice. Internal documents, interviews, domestic cleavages, and national negotiating positions confirm that Germany, France, and Britain consistently made policy on the basis of stable, relatively transparent preferences across outcomes. Underlying shifts in bargaining positions and tactical maneuvers were relatively stable, weighted objectives. This assumption holds even when a superficial inspection might tempt one to draw the opposite conclusion—as when domestic preference formation was controversial, when more than one actor represented a government transnationally and transgovernmentally, or when each government targeted threats and concessions at particular domestic groups in foreign polities. The calculations of the German government in the Maastricht negotiations over Economic and Monetary Union are a striking example. Despite overt conflict, the institutions of German policy-making induced a relatively consistent bargaining position based on a compromise among business, government, and the Bundesbank. Subjective evidence confirms the conclusion: across the case studies, governmental and supranational actors consistently described their own and one another's policies in terms consistent with the rational, unitary actor assumption. Governments also treated transfers of sovereignty to international institutions as separate from—and generally subordinate to—substantive agreements. Similarly, international institutions were generally viewed as means to implement substantive bargains or realize ideological preferences—an instrumental view consistent with rational unitary action.

The tripartite rationalist framework is usefully generalizable to many international negotiations, for it offers a means of combining theories with a minimum sacrifice of structure.[39] It offers a superior alternative to the pervasive tendency among Realists (as well as Institutionalists) to combine different theories by privileging those explanations that treat state preferences as fixed and limiting the application of theories of state preferences to anomalies left by "systemic" theories. This approach, as I have argued elsewhere, is overtly and arbitrarily biased. The specific tripartite sequence proposed here is in fact the only ordering consistent with the rationalist assumptions that underlie most major theories of international relations.[40] The case studies in this book confirm that no assumption of fixed conflictual or convergent preferences would capture the subtly varied preferences of governments concerning trade, agriculture, money, and other issue-areas. Although it is useful for the limited purpose of exploring particular theories of strategic interaction, the a priori assumption that preferences are fixed has proved an unsatisfactory starting point for exploring most cases of state behavior—as we saw in chapter 1, it has weakened many existing research programs. It is striking that historians studying the same question reach precisely the same conclusion: explanations of EC decisions, Alan Milward and his

[39] Andrew M. Moravcsik, "Disciplining Trade Finance: The OECD Export Credit Arrangement," *International Organization* 43:1 (Winter 1989), 173–176.

[40] Moravcsik, "Taking," 542–544.

associates argue, have "no predictive power" in the absence of a convincing account of domestic politics.[41]

A common objection to the grounding of explanations of state behavior in more detailed investigations of national preference formation—voiced even by those who accept the theoretical and methodological case for doing so—is that such investigations are not only theoretically intractable but pose overwhelming empirical research challenges better left to historians. Such an admission of defeat is unnecessary.

Work from studies of the democratic peace to endogenous tariff policy demonstrate that explanations of variation in national preferences can be parsimonious and powerful. There is, however, an important methodological caution here. An accurate assessment of the nature and intensity of state preferences, as historians regularly remind us, must rest on more than the perusal of government statements and secondary or journalistic accounts. Such "soft" sources are so numerous and varied as to provide considerable support for almost any plausible conjecture about European integration.[42] This book confirms that there is no substitute for reliance on "hard" primary sources such as internal documents, interviews, reliable memoirs, and a close examination of policy; studies based entirely on secondary sources—even where there is historical consensus—may well be misleading.

Such general theoretical and methodological conclusions are of more than abstract interest. By subsuming European integration wherever possible under general theories, rather than treating it as *sui generis*, we invite outsiders to treat its lessons as relevant to their own political experience. Far from being unique, the history of European integration has much to teach those concerned with the World Trade Organization, the North Atlantic Free Trade Area, and other international institutions. The EC is a laboratory in which to investigate a series of common political phenomena developed further in Europe than elsewhere on the globe. I have explored some of these phenomena in this book—the conduct of international trade, monetary, and regulatory policy under extremely high levels of trade and capital mobility, interstate bargaining dynamics under complex interdependence, and the motivations for delegation and pooling of national sovereignty. Others deserve more intensive study, among them the operation of binding interstate legislative procedures and the dynamics of legal dispute resolution. In all these things, Europe is a global harbinger.

Yet we can draw reliable practical and theoretical lessons from Europe's extraordinary experience only if we employ general theories, shared concepts, and reliable methodologies. Only such instruments permit us to distinguish rigorously between general and contingent phenomena, and so to make accurate

---

[41] Milward et al., *Frontier*, 196.

[42] Even where a consensus exists, it can be biased or misleading, as we saw in examining the existing literature on the European policies of Harold Macmillan, Charles de Gaulle, and Helmut Kohl. Even accurate secondary accounts characteristically fail to investigate in theoretical terms those aspects of negotiations critically important for the reconstruction of interstate bargaining, including preference intensity, the boundaries of national win-sets, and the information available to each actor.

comparisons and transfer appropriate lessons from case to case. For this reason above all, the reintegration of Europe into the mainstream study of international and comparative politics should remain a priority for those who seek to understand the most successful international institution of modern times.

Critics will continue to contend that European integration has been in fact a contingent outcome: a response to geopolitical fears of a bygone era, the dreams of visionary European federalists, or pressures from technocratic believers in central planning. Some go even further, asserting that integration was unintended, a consequence unleashed by governments unaware of future consequences and incapable of conducting consistent policy. Such analyses naturally lead to deep concern and skepticism about the future of European integration. If the EC is based on no more than fears, dreams, schemes, or mistakes, what confidence can we have in its future?

The structural perspective advanced in this book suggests a different and more optimistic view. European integration was no accident. It continues to advance even as democratization pacifies western Europe, European federal union triggers popular backlash, and technocratic planning falls out of fashion. The EC has been, for the most part, the deliberate creation of statesmen and citizens seeking to realize economic interests through traditional diplomatic means. Over forty years European politicians and peoples have repeatedly widened and deepened the EC while remaining largely aware of its past, present, and future consequences. This transfer of sovereign prerogatives has, moreover, occurred entirely without bloodshed—a unique achievement in world history. The result has been an institution so firmly grounded in the core interests of national governments that it occupies a permanent position at the heart of the European political landscape. Therein lies the political achievement and the ongoing social-scientific puzzle.

Index

Abs, Hermann, 97
Action Committee for the United States of Europe, 56, 103, 107, 138, 151–152, 233, 245, 291; Euratom and nuclear weapons, 120, 145, 148–149
Adenauer, Konrad, 27–33, 90–91, 94–96, 99–100, 107, 119, 131–133, 136–137, 144–152, 157, 160, 165, 174, 182, 188, 191, 198–200, 213, 219, 231, 234, 301, 327, 480; agriculture and CAP, 101–102, 201, 204; and customs union, 91, 197, 201, 205–207, 477; and DBV, 200; and Euratom, 91, 97, 101–102, 135, 475–476; and EDC, 91; and European federalism, 91; and European political union, 91; and Fouchet Plan, 198, 227; and France, 91, 94–95, 102, 197–198, 202, 225–226, 476, 478; FTA and EFTA, 164, 170, 197, 201, 220, 477, 490; and German unification, 94; and Great Britain, 94, 220, 223; and institutional delegation, 102; and MLF, 227; and NATO, 202, 226; and the Saar, 102; and US, 94, 198
Agriculture. *See* Common Agricultural Policy (CAP)
Algeria, 107, 114–116, 179–180, 183
Amato, Giuliano, 433
Anderson, Perry, 68, 70, 490
Andreotti, Giulio, 290, 295–297, 363
Andrews, David, 411
Antitrust policy. *See* Competition policy
Apel, Hans, 251
Armand, Louis, 139
Association for Monetary Union in Europe, 393, 434, 440
Atomic energy. *See* Euratom and nuclear weapons.
Asylum policies. *See* Immigration and asylum policies
Attali, Jacques, 271, 351, 356, 414, 436
Austria, 288, 313

Baldwin, David, 498
Ball, George, 223
Balladur, Edouard, 265, 432–434

Bangemann, Martin, 397
Bank of England, 276–280, 283–285, 323, 421
Bank of France, 264–266, 271, 297, 305, 338
Barre, Raymond, 245, 261–263, 266–269, 287, 292, 295, 302, 305–306, 338–341
Basle Agreement (1972). *See* Snake.
Baun, Michael, 462
Beaverbrook, Lord, 171
Bech, Leo, 140
Becker, Gary, 36
Belgium, 410; and CAP, 209, 213, 224, 350, 488; competition policy, 219; customs union and Euratom, 142; and ECB, 444, 469; and European federalism, 309, 376, 429; and EP, 311, 366, 376, 455; and foreign policy cooperation, 226, 450–451; and German unification, 389; immigration and asylum policies, 447; and institutional delegation, 153–156, 219, 309–311, 350, 363, 366, 376, 488; justice and interior affairs, 447; and Maastricht Treaty, 449; and SEA, 318, 344, 348, 359–360, 363, 376; Snake, EMS and EMU, 241, 287, 294, 297–299, 416, 439, 443–445; and social policy, 452
Bénard, André, 356
Bérégovoy, Pierre, 271, 340, 414–415, 442, 445, 465
Berg, Fritz, 96–97, 199–200, 248
Berlin, 29, 34, 91, 94, 178, 197–198, 244
Beyen, Willem, 139, 140–141, 154
Blair, Tony, 425–427; 454
Blessing, Karl, 247
Blum, Leon, 121
Bourgès-Maunoury, Maurice, 103, 106, 114, 152
Brandt, Willy, 27–29, 95, 245, 251, 301; agriculture and CAP, 258, 304, 249–250, 258, 291–292, 305–306, 475; and EC budget, 258; and European Council, 259; European policy and *Ostpolitik*, 238, 244, 250; and foreign policy cooperation, 256; and France, 198, 227, 259; and regional policy, 258; and Snake, 244
Bretherton, Russell, 129, 133, 142–143, 172

507

Index